T0327334

BIDDERS AND TARGETS

This book is dedicated to

MAYER, BROWN & PLATT

where we have both learned so much over the years

Bidders and Targets

Mergers and Acquisitions
in the U.S.

Leo Herzel and Richard W. Shepro

Basil Blackwell

First published 1990

Basil Blackwell, Inc.
3 Cambridge Center
Cambridge, Massachusetts 02142, USA

Basil Blackwell Ltd
108 Cowley Road, Oxford, OX4 1JF, UK

Library of Congress Cataloging in Publication Data

Herzel, Leo
Bidders and targets: Mergers and acquisitions in the U.S.
Leo Herzel and Richard W. Shepro.
p.   cm.
Includes bibliographical references (p. 000)
ISBN 1–55786–096–3
1. Consolidation and merger of corporations–United States.
2. Tender offers (Securities)–United States.
I. Shepro, Richard W.   II. Title
KF1477.H48   1990
346.73′06626–dc20   90–442
[347.3066626]   CIP

British Library Cataloguing in Publication Data

A CIP catalogue record for this book is available from
the British Library.

Typeset in 10 on 12pt Monophoto Times by Butler & Tanner Ltd
Printed in Great Britain by
Butler & Tanner Ltd, Frome and London

Summary

Contents

PART III   CASE STUDY: THE TIME–WARNER
AGREEMENTS

Acknowledgments

W E are very grateful to our law firm, Mayer, Brown & Platt, for its support, manifested in countless ways, of our writing this book. We would also like to thank Oliver Hart of MIT, Leo Katz of the University of Michigan Law School and David Webb of the London School of Economics, who read the manuscript and made valuable suggestions. We have had many helpful discussions with Richard Brealey of the London Business School, who was an enthusiastic supporter of the project from the beginning. However, we bear the sole responsibility for the judgments and opinions in the book.

LEO HERZEL
RICHARD W. SHEPRO

I

Introduction

THIS book is an introduction to takeovers in the United States. It is intended for anyone who is interested in takeovers. We hope that it will be useful to beginners and experts alike, foreign readers and Americans, and business executives, lawyers and economists.

The book is divided into three parts. Part I is descriptive and analytic. It is intended to give the reader an understanding of the main legal and economic issues in takeovers in America. Part II approaches the same legal and economic subjects from the standpoint of bidders and targets. The emphasis in Part II is strategic and advisory.

From economic, strategic and legal standpoints, the combination of Time and Warner in 1989 was one of the most interesting and important mergers in recent years. Part III is organized around our annotation of the legal agreements used in that transaction. We also discuss this transaction in Chapter 3 and use it as an example throughout the book.

We have tried to avoid using technical terms extensively, but some are necessary. We have provided an extensive Glossary which both explains terms and connects important technical terms with the discussion in the book. A reader interested only in the book's main ideas should be able to skim highly technical discussions and still get the gist of the points being made. An Appendix contains the annotated texts of essential Federal and state statutes and rules and (as an illustration of the very important judicial role in U.S. corporation law) the opinion of the Delaware Supreme Court explaining the decision it made that doomed Paramount's attempt to stop Time's acquisition of Warner.

The outcomes of many takeover battles have been decisively influenced by takeover law, which is a mixture of Federal and state statutes and regulations and court decisions. Even more important, many takeovers probably are never attempted because of Federal and state takeover law. When there appears to be a conflict among Federal and state laws, the courts have to provide a solution for a choice using statutory construction and constitutional law principles. Occasionally the U.S. Supreme Court decides a takeover case and makes policy statements on this subject that lower courts must try to use as a guide.

Recently, most important takeover law has been created by state legislatures and courts. There are two main reasons for this. First, the consensus in the U.S. in favor of takeovers has dissolved in the last few years. Congress and the Bush Administration have been unable to agree on a takeover policy. The subject is now seen as controversial, complicated and politically dangerous and political prizes are not obvious yet. Second, the Reagan judicial appointees have begun to dominate the Federal courts, making them more conservative. In the U.S., at this time, being judicially conservative means being liberal in an historical sense, that is, giving the states as much legal room to determine their own fates as appears constitutionally possible.

Foreign readers and non-lawyers, especially, may be puzzled by several peculiarities of the U.S. legal system. The most obvious of these is the enormous importance of private litigation in resolving public policy issues as well as private controversies. In this process, the courts themselves create important law. The Delaware Supreme Court opinion in the litigation between Paramount and Time is a good illustration. Everything important in the opinion is court-created, including the precedents on which the court relied. Moreover, the opinion not only determined the outcome of a momentous takeover controversy, it will have a significant effect on takeover strategy generally, along with other court opinions. For these reasons, we discuss the nuances of court opinions more than foreign readers may be accustomed to.

Another peculiarity of the U.S. legal system is the importance of professional plaintiffs' lawyers who represent nominal clients in shareholder class actions or derivative suits on behalf of corporations. These plaintiffs' lawyers are in reality volunteer venturers who are compensated by court-awarded fees for their contributions in litigation.[1] They file lawsuits early in almost every important takeover. In litigation they are highly motivated to raise issues that the main litigants would prefer to leave alone. Generally, the more troublesome issues they raise, the higher their court-awarded fees are likely to be.

For example, in the Time–Paramount litigation, none of the principal parties had anything to gain from pressing a common argument against takeover defense, that the Time board of directors had a legal obligation to auction off the company. Neither Paramount nor Time desired an auction. Paramount's proposed takeover of Time would have been made even more uncertain and costly. And Time was opposed to any takeover. Nonetheless, the issue was raised by lawyers for shareholders. In this instance, in addition to several suits filed by plaintiffs' lawyers as soon as the original Time–Warner merger agreement was announced, there were also separate suits filed later by very large institutional and speculator shareholders who were paying their own lawyers.

For reasons that we explain later, Delaware is the most important state for corporation law in the U.S. Many large companies are incorporated there

---

[1] See 'shareholder litigation,' 'derivative suit' and 'class action' in the Glossary.

even though they have little other connection to the state. When we discuss corporate law or what courts do without specifying a state or court, we mean Delaware law and the Delaware courts. Where there are important differences among the states, we try to be specific as to whether we are talking about a Delaware statute or court or another state's statute or court.

Hostile takeovers and highly leveraged transactions have become enormously controversial. In this book, we acknowledge the validity of some of the arguments in support of them but are skeptical of others. The most compelling argument in favor of hostile takeovers is that they are an important discipline on the managements of likely target companies. While this appears to be true, it is a tremendously expensive and imprecise solution. The examples of Japan and Germany, where hostile takeovers are almost impossible to accomplish, make it clear that there are other solutions, although there is no way of knowing whether these are better or worse than the U.S. approach.

Moreover, viewing takeovers as a discipline on management is a one-sided view of a many-sided subject. It largely ignores bidders, who also have fallible managements and advisers. Legal rules provide almost no control over bidders and the takeover market has been at best a very sluggish and imperfect force in containing their imperfections. Furthermore, preoccupation with hostile takeovers may encourage managements to have an excessively short-term outlook.

In our judgment, the U.S. is already moving away from the 1980s' dominance of hostile takeovers. This change is noticeable in new state antitakeover statutes and court opinions. Just as important, respectable economics opinion is no longer uniformly so favorable to hostile takeovers. Among other things, concern is being expressed about tax subsidies for highly leveraged takeovers through interest deductions and about the replacement of equity by debt in U.S. corporations. Takeovers may create more tax revenues than the amount of the subsidies. For example, when target shareholders sell to a bidder at a premium price they may incur large tax liabilities. Nonetheless, the tax subsidies may create an undesirable incentive to replace equity with debt.

Questions are also being raised about whether hostile takeovers are one of the causes of a short-term management outlook in the U.S. and whether that contributes to the relatively poor performance by U.S. companies in international competition for the sale of highly sophisticated manufactured goods. Considerations such as these make it unlikely that the Administration and Congress could be induced to undertake a pro-takeover legislative program to reverse state laws and court decisions.

If we are correct on this point, the 1990s will bring new opportunities for mergers and other negotiated acquisitions similar to those accomplished by Time–Warner, Beecham–SmithKline and Bristol Myers–Squibb in 1989. Concern over increasing the exposure to a hostile takeover of one or both of the potential participants has been a tremendously important influence in dampening the market for negotiated acquisitions in the U.S.

However, we are not starry-eyed about negotiated acquisitions either. Nor do we ignore the good effects on managements caused by fear of takeovers. In the 1960s and 1970s, negotiated acquisitions by conglomerates were not, on the average, an economic success. Moreover, invulnerably entrenched managements like those described by Berle and Means in their famous book are not an attractive alternative.[2] But many things have changed since the 1960s and 1970s and, even more so, since Berle and Means wrote about the separation of ownership and control in 1933. There have been enormous increases in competitiveness in the international product market since the 1960s and changes in social attitudes away from the frozen 1930s, when the heads of corporations and their bankers were part of a sheltered social elite with a very conservative outlook.

Some lawyers and economists think that institutional investors may be the key to a solution.[3] So far, however, they have been much more prominent as participants in the frenzied hunt for quick gains from takeovers. Before institutions could provide an alternative solution, they would have to accept that as a group, many of their short-term gains from takeovers are illusory. What they gain as shareholders of targets they may lose as shareholders of bidders and creditors of targets. Some recent lawsuits by institutional bondholders attacking leveraged buyouts that have reduced the value of their bonds are a sign in that direction.[4] Moreover, if hostile takeovers are a cause of a short-term management outlook which reduces the effectiveness of U.S. industry, institutional investors (who hold highly diversified portfolios) lose, both as shareholders and as important participants in the U.S. economy.

Ideally, if institutional investors should have such a change of heart, they might be able to provide important members for boards of directors. Instead of the takeover market's monitoring management performance, directors who represent large shareholders might be able to accomplish the same thing more simply and less expensively. Incompetent managers would then fear being fired by boards, instead of being replaced in takeovers.

But this wouldn't be an easy adjustment for anyone. It may not be possible or, considering the difficulties, desirable. Institutional investors have become accustomed to competing through short-term performance while at the same time issuing pronouncements on non-economic goals to boards of companies in which they hold stock. Many of the top executives of institutions do not

[2] Adolph Berle and Gardiner Means, *The Modern Corporation and Private Property* (1933).

[3] See, for example, Louis Lowenstein, *What's Wrong With Wall Street: Short-Term Gain and the Absentee Shareholder* (1988); Arnold W. Sametz and James L. Bicksler (eds), *The Battle for Corporate Control: Shareholder Rights, Stakeholder Interests and Managerial Responsibilities* (1990).

[4] See Chapter 6 Section 9.

have skills or attitudes suitable for directors of large companies. Boards and managements, on the other hand, usually do not like to deal with board members who represent large shareholdings.

Most important, how could we control the performance of institutions if we give up short-term performance as the standard? It is usually impossible to make judgments about long-term performance until it is too late. In the end, we may have to find more modest solutions such as encouraging directors and managers to own more stock in their companies.

PART I

The Framework

2

If Only Directors Were Perfect

THE paradox of the takeover market is that shareholders sorely need boards of directors to negotiate for them, yet the directors cannot always be trusted to act in the shareholders' best interests. Under the laws that authorize the creation of corporations, the board of directors is charged with running the corporation. The directors do not own the business. They are agents and they have the legal responsibility to act in the best interests of shareholders and others.[1] This uneasy relationship is at the heart of almost all the controversial issues in takeovers.

It is impractical for shareholders to run a public corporation themselves. Letting agents do so is a wonderful solution. Without it large enterprises financed by the public could not exist. But giving agents a free rein has its problems too. Agents may not be sufficiently motivated to do a really good job or they may betray their masters. Courts try to deal with these problems by imposing on directors duties of care and loyalty to shareholders.

In recent years, the threat of takeovers, pressures from the financial community and foreign competition have improved the quality of boards of directors enormously. If boards often appear to be passive in non-crisis, non-takeover situations, it usually is because deferring to managements they respect is likely to give the best results, not because they are ignorant about the company's business.

However, there are still occasional examples of what appears to be startling directors' indolence. Betrayals by directors in takeover situations may be subtle and unintentional or they may be imaginary. It is not easy for courts and lawmakers to design legal rules to deal successfully with these issues.

A shareholder can sue the directors for acting carelessly or out of self-interest. However, a court will not ordinarily substitute its judgment for the business judgment of the board of directors. This is the famous business judgment rule in corporation law. It is well founded in experience. Courts

---

[1] Who those others are is a rapidly changing, highly controversial subject. New statutes are changing the rules rapidly. Economists who have favored an exclusive emphasis on shareholders are beginning to show signs of changing their minds. See, for example, Jay W. Lorsch with Elizabeth MacIver, *Pawns or Potentates: The Reality of America's Corporate Boards* (1989). Judges are also showing signs of change, even without new statutes, as the Paramount–Time case shows. *Paramount Communications Inc.* v. *Time Inc.*, 571 A.2d 1140 (Delaware Supreme Court 1990). The text of this opinion is reproduced as Appendix A.12. See Chapter 6 Section 7.

are not experts in business as, in most cases, they will readily agree. Under the business judgment rule courts give directors wide latitude to manage the day-to-day business of the corporation, so long as they have no conflict of interest and are adequately informed.[2]

Usually, for example, a dissident shareholder is not permitted to challenge a decision of the board to reinvest earnings instead of declaring a dividend. Nor, for example, can a shareholder in General Motors ask a court to stop the company from introducing a new model of automobile. However, when the directors have a conflict of interest, the duty of loyalty comes into play and the courts are much more willing to take a closer look at what the directors are doing.

Takeovers abound with situations where the directors can have, or appear to have, a conflict of interest with the shareholders. Faced with a hostile bid, directors usually take defensive steps to block the takeover, which can keep shareholders from receiving a premium price for their shares. Personal motives of the directors could be foremost. So could a desire to save the company from being sold at a bargain basement price or concern about other interests such as employees or communities. In a leveraged buyout, directors could agree to sell the company to their management friends on the cheap at the expense of the shareholders.

However, in practice the personal motives of the directors are not so easy to discern. It is true that directors who also hold management jobs may at times be concerned too much about their jobs and too little for shareholders. But by now most directors of public companies in the United States are not officers or employees of the company. The bulk of the income and prestige of these outside directors comes from other sources. The average cash compensation of outside directors of public companies is less than $25,000.[3] Directors also receive some fringe benefits such as health and life insurance and retirement benefits. Recently some companies have begun granting stock or stock options. Very large companies typically pay about $10,000 more in cash compensation. In takeovers, directors' motivation may be complex and their decisions may not please their shareholders, but usually they are not just stooges for the chief executive officer.

Directors can have many reasons to oppose a takeover. They do not like to be replaced. Their pride may be hurt by a bidder who explicitly or implicitly is saying that he will run the company better. Or they may sympathize with management and employees who will be replaced or communities that may lose out. Some directors oppose hostile takeovers for emotional or philo-

---

[2] The Delaware Supreme Court has referred to the business judgment rule as 'a presumption that in making a business decision the directors ... acted on an informed basis, in good faith and in the honest belief that the action taken was in the best interests of the company.' *Aronson* v. *Lewis*, 473 A.2d 805, 812 (Delaware Supreme Court 1984).

[3] Lorsch with MacIver, *Pawns or Potentates*, pp. 29, 17–31.

sophical reasons. Right or wrong, they may not have the same high opinion of takeovers as do most institutional investors and stock market professionals.

There are also reasons for chief executive officers and directors to welcome takeovers. Directors and managers have been smart enough to adapt to the era of sudden takeovers. Sometimes they own large amounts of company stock and options and will profit handsomely from a buyout at a high premium. And most chief executive officers and other top managers have lucrative severance arrangements from which they will receive large rewards if the company is sold.

Nonetheless, there is no getting around the fact that there is a possible conflict of interest in every takeover. Directors are close to the chief executive officer. They are paid by the target, and if they are replaced the payments stop. They also have pride in their work. Most of their conflicts would not be easy to eliminate. Directors will not work if they are not paid. And making sure that directors own stock, so that their financial interests are the same as the shareholders', does not completely eliminate identification with the chief executive officer or solve the pride problem. The legal rules we describe later in this chapter are intended to mitigate these irreducible conflicts of interest. Moreover, courts do not hesitate to invalidate board actions where there is a real conflict of interest or obvious carelessness.

2.1 THE PRISONER'S DILEMMA

Bidders are no different than other negotiators. Even when a bidder offers to buy a company at a large premium over recent stock exchange prices, it generally has more money in reserve if the target can extract it.[4] On October 19, 1988, for example, RJR Nabisco's management suggested a buyout of the company for $75 per share. On November 30, when final bids were due in the auction that followed, management offered a package of cash and securities it valued at $112 per share – an increase of well over $8 billion.[5]

Shareholders of public companies have no independent organization and cannot negotiate for themselves. Usually, there is nobody but the board of directors who can negotiate on their behalf. But for the reasons mentioned directors cannot always be trusted.

Consider an extreme case: a two-step hostile tender offer in which a bidder offers to buy two-thirds of the shares of a company right away, for 150% of their market price, with a vague promise (or threat) that the remaining

---

[4] Our analysis in this section is based on classical theories of bargaining. Two good introductions to bargaining theories are Thomas C. Schelling, *The Strategy of Conflict* (1960) and Howard Raiffa, *The Art and Science of Negotiation* (1985).

[5] *In re RJR Nabisco, Inc. Shareholders Litigation*, Fed. Sec. L. Rep. (CCH) ¶94,194 (Delaware Chancery Court 1989).

shareholders will be forced to exchange their shares some time in the future for securities worth much less. This sort of front-end loaded coercive offer used to be very common. An example is the famous attempt by T. Boone Pickens to buy Unocal in 1985, which we discuss later in this chapter. Front-end loaded offers have disappeared – mainly because directors can block them using takeover defenses such as poison pills and state antitakeover laws.

Target shareholders faced with a premium cash bid for all shares might like to hold out for more. Individually, they cannot do it. But if they could act in concert, they might be able to bargain for a much higher price. In other words, the shareholders are caught up in a prisoner's dilemma, a more general problem about cooperation that mathematicians and economists began to analyze in the early 1950s.

The prisoner's dilemma is the exemplar for situations in which members of a group are unable or unwilling to cooperate yet they would all benefit if they did. The following is one illustration of the classic situation. Two partners in crime are arrested and put in separate cells. If convicted of the most serious charge they would face 20 years of imprisonment. But the only way the prosecutor can hope to convict them of more than a comparatively minor offense carrying a one-year sentence is for one or both of them to confess. If only one confesses and testifies against the other, he goes free and the other prisoner receives a 20-year sentence. But if both confess they each receive a ten-year sentence in exchange for their cooperation with the prosecutor. What should each prisoner do?

Each is likely to reason: In case my partner confesses, I am better off confessing myself so I can avoid a life sentence. If my partner sits tight, I am still better off confessing, because then I will go free.

If both prisoners reason this way they will each get a ten-year sentence. But if the prisoners had cooperated with each other and neither had confessed, they would have received the elusive reward for cooperation – only one year each. In short, if each prisoner acts alone in his own self-interest, both will wind up worse off than if they had found a way to cooperate.[6]

In takeovers directors provide the only practical way for shareholders to cooperate. Target directors do the bargaining for the shareholders. Under present circumstances, the principal method of bargaining is takeover defense. When there is no defense directors have very little bargaining power since the bidder can ignore the board by making its bid directly to the shareholders. Ideally, the goal of defense is to prevent bidders from circumventing the board to exploit disorganized target shareholders. The crux of the takeover defense problem for courts and society is that it is hard to distinguish between hard bargaining and intransigence.

Boards of directors have the legal power to adopt the most potent defense,

---

[6] See 'prisoner's dilemma' in the Glossary for some additional explanation.

share purchase rights plans, without shareholder approval. These plans, usually called poison pills, put a preclusive penalty in the way of an unwanted bidder by giving other target shareholders the right to buy shares at half-price.[7]

Although it is becoming less common because of organized resistance from institutional shareholders, shareholders may themselves approve putting anti-takeover provisions in the company's charter. The most common of these provisions sets a formula floor on the price that can be paid for shares in a merger or similar transaction imposed by a large shareholder, or requires a special high shareholder vote to approve these transactions or does both. Friendly transactions are not affected by these charter provisions or poison pills since obtaining board approval in advance of becoming a large share-holder eliminates the defenses.

This prisoner's dilemma analysis is at odds with the free-rider paradox, another theoretical economics dilemma, that was put forth a decade ago.[8] Indirectly, through lawyers, this analysis has had an important influence on courts and regulators. According to this theory, there is a quite different shareholder cooperation problem – free riding. Instead of shareholders being forced to tender against their own interests (the prisoner's dilemma), they would have a tendency not to tender, so that many desirable bids would fail. They would not want to sell their shares because they would expect that, as minority shareholders, they would enjoy a free ride to the future higher value the bidder must anticipate. The paradox is that, if many shareholders decide to free ride, a tender offer that would benefit all shareholders would go unaccepted.

If this free-rider paradox were an accurate description of reality, a tender offer would be a very delicate thing. Even the most meager of takeover defenses could derail the shareholders' chance to benefit from a premium bid. But shareholders do not behave the way that the free-rider paradox predicts.

The reasons are quite clear. Under state corporation law minority share-holders have little power. They have no voice in management. They cannot require the payment of dividends and cannot force a successful bidder to buy them out. If the majority shareholder chooses to force the minority out,

---

[7] We discuss poison pills in detail in Chapter 8.

[8] The competing theories have been debated for over a decade. A 1979 article by Leo Herzel, John Schmidt and Scott Davis presented the prisoner's dilemma analysis as a reason why resistance to takeovers can benefit shareholders. Leo Herzel, John Schmidt and Scott Davis, 'Why Corporate Directors Have a Right to Resist Tender Offers,' 61 *Chicago Bar Record* 152 (1979). Sanford Grossman and Oliver Hart introduced the free-rider theory of takeovers the following year. Sanford Grossman and Oliver Hart, 'Takeover Bids, the Free-Rider Problem, and the Theory of the Corporation,' *Bell Journal of Economics* 42 (Spring 1980). See also Ronald Gilson, 'A Structural Approach to Corporations: The Case Against Defensive Tactics in Tender Offers,' 33 *Stanford Law Review* 819 (1981), and Frank H. Easterbrook and Daniel R. Fischel, 'The Proper Role of a Target's Management in Responding to a Tender Offer,' 94 *Harvard Law Review* 1161 (1981), both of which disagreed with the prisoner's dilemma analysis.

they have the right to ask for appraisal of their shares at a fair price in a court proceeding. However, in electing appraisal it is very difficult for shareholders to act collectively. The election procedure is highly technical and the court hearing and preliminaries, such as discovery and obtaining experts to testify, can be time-consuming and expensive.

Most shareholders, particularly professionals such as institutions and arbitragers, just want their money right away. Even when the target company's charter contains fair price protection for shareholders in squeeze-out transactions, minority shareholders show little inclination to hold out for a higher price. Arbitragers in particular appear to discount deferred payments at a fantastically high rate.

The empirical evidence confirms that takeover defense has in fact been a way out of the prisoner's dilemma for shareholders. Premiums paid are demonstrably higher for companies whose boards of directors have put up a fight.[9] Of course there is no way to know how many hostile bids are considered but never made because of the likelihood of a vigorous defense. And even when bids are made, hard bargaining through takeover defense reduces the likelihood of a deal being accomplished.[10] These bargaining problems, however, are not unique to directors or to takeovers.

Some studies have shown that companies' stock prices tend to decline slightly immediately after the adoption of defensive devices, especially in the case of poison pills adopted during a takeover battle. These stock price studies are hard to interpret. Short-term price changes of takeover targets tend to be heavily influenced by arbitragers and other professional takeover specialists. The price declines may simply mean that these professionals think the prospects for very quick takeover profits have been slightly diminished.[11]

Some state antitakeover laws increase the bargaining power of target boards of directors by imposing special, costly burdens on bidders who do not come to terms with the board.[12] There are rules in other countries that attempt to give greater bargaining power in takeover bids directly to target shareholders. For example, in Britain, a takeover bid for 30% or more of the shares of the company can only go forward if the same offer is made to all shareholders.[13] The British solution gives some protection against the

---

[9] A large number of economic studies are analyzed in Gregg A. Jarrell, James A. Brickley and Jeffry M. Netter, 'The Market for Corporate Control: The Empirical Evidence Since 1980,' 2 *Journal of Economic Perspectives* (Winter 1988) at 58–66.

[10] If there is no deal the stock price then typically goes down, but generally not quite to pre-bid levels. Id. at 55. However, in most cases there finally is a deal with the original bidder or someone else.

[11] Some of the limitations of poison pill price studies are discussed in a report by the Investor Responsibility Research Center Inc., an organization that is generally skeptical of takeover defense. See Peg O'Hara, Corporate Governance Service, *Poison Pills*, 1989 Background Report G, Investor Responsibility Research Center Inc.

[12] See Chapter 6.

[13] Mervyn King and Ailsa Roell, 'The Regulation of Takeovers and the Stock Markets,' *National Westminster Bank Review* 2 (February 1988).

prisoner's dilemma, but it is far from perfect. Some of the pressure on individual shareholders to tender is reduced. They are protected against being left behind if they do not tender, but they are still a disorganized group with no one to bargain for them.[14]

The benefits of takeover defense for target shareholders show why it is rash to assert generally that a board of directors is betraying the interests of its shareholders when it does not welcome a hostile bid with open arms. (If other interests such as employees and communities may be considered by directors there is even less ground.) No matter what the board's motives are, the shareholders need takeover defense by their board to help them out of their prisoner's dilemma. Similarly, when shareholders approve antitakeover charter amendments or otherwise acquiesce in actions that expand the bargaining power of the board of directors, they are not necessarily falling prey to a management ruse. They may quite reasonably see these devices as a substitute for cooperation which they cannot achieve by themselves.

But takeover defense replaces one problem with another. The board may be subtly disloyal to the shareholders. It may be looking out for management or other interests as well as those of shareholders. Or the board quite honestly may not share the view that it is always better to sell out at a premium.

There are limits to directors' discretion in these matters. These limits are constantly shifting as the result of changes in political and economic points of view and new legislation and court decisions. Usually, takeover defenses have made it possible for target directors to auction off targets at high prices. But so far, takeover defenses have rarely kept companies independent. Bidders, with the help of courts, have made sure of that.[15]

2.2 JUDGING BUSINESS JUDGMENT

It could once be safely said that, from a legal standpoint, directors had little to lose however bad their conduct. In 1906, some ruthless speculators in England founded the Brazilian Rubber Plantations and Estates, Limited. They chose as directors a singularly ill-suited group: Sir Arthur Aylmer, whom the court described as: 'absolutely ignorant of business. He only consented to act because he was told the office would give him a little pleasant employment without his incurring any responsibility'; H. W. Tugwell, 'seventy-five years of age and very deaf'; Edward Barber, 'a rubber broker,' who joined because he 'was told that all he would have to do would be to

[14] See *City Capital Associates Ltd. Partnership* v. *Interco Inc.,* 551 A.2d 787, 797–8 (Delaware Chancery Court 1988). See also Ronald Gilson and Reinier Kraakman, 'Delaware's Intermediate Standard for Defensive Tactics: Proportionality Review,' 44 *Business Lawyer* 247 (1989).

[15] The situation may be changing, however, because of recent antitakeover laws enacted in many states. See Chapter 6.

give an opinion as to the value of rubber when it arrived in England'; and E. H. Hancock, who joined only because Tugwell and Barber had joined.[16]

Having assembled this lackluster board of directors, the speculators proceeded to bamboozle it by selling the corporation some worthless Brazilian rubber plantations. To directors who were slightly more eager, alert, or experienced, the fraud would have been transparent, but not to this group. When the truth finally came out, the directors were sued by their shareholders – but without success. A director, the English Court of Chancery held, 'may undertake the management of a rubber company in complete ignorance of everything connected with rubber, without incurring responsibility for the mistakes which may result from such ignorance.'[17] The court was giving here an especially spacious interpretation to the business judgment rule.

Although courts were once quite doting on directors, the pendulum has moved a long way since then. Nowadays directors have to be very concerned about the possibility of liability, or at the least embarrassment, particularly when they are dealing with takeovers. It is no longer uncommon for business decisions made by directors to be blocked or undone by the courts when they find that the directors violated their duty to the shareholders. As a result, almost every move boards make is informed by legal and other expert advice.

The directors of Macmillan, Inc., the U.S. publishing giant, found the decisions they made in 1988 about selling the company overturned by the Delaware Supreme Court. In its opinion, the court excoriated the company's chairman and president for 'extraordinary' misconduct and for deceiving the board. It sharply criticized some of the company's advisers. The other directors were made to share the blame. The court found they had made 'the unprincipled conduct' of the management team possible by looking 'with a blind eye.'[18]

Although it is still very rare for directors to be ordered to pay damages to shareholders because of carelessness or ignorance, there is one important recent negligence case in which the directors were held personally liable for money damages.[19] The result in the case still dumbfounds lawyers and scares directors and insurance companies who insure directors. In 1980, the directors of Trans Union Corporation, a lessor of railroad cars, authorized a sale of the company to Chicago's Pritzker family which controls Hyatt hotels and a number of other important businesses.

---

[16] *In re Brazilian Rubber Plantations and Estates, Ltd.*, [1911] 1 Ch. 425, 427.

[17] Id. at 437.

[18] *Mills Acquisition Co.* v. *Macmillan, Inc.*, 559 A.2d 1261, 1280 and nn. 30 and 33 (Delaware Supreme Court 1989). We discuss the *Macmillan* case in more detail later in this chapter, and in Chapters 7 and 10.

[19] *Smith* v. *Van Gorkom*, 488 A.2d 858 (Delaware Supreme Court 1985) (usually called the Trans Union case).

The transaction unquestionably conferred major benefits on Trans Union shareholders. For years Trans Union had been struggling to find a way to use its investment tax credits. Finally, the sale let it cash in on them. Every Trans Union shareholder was paid in cash approximately 50% over the market price before the acquisition. Nevertheless, shareholders who thought the share price could have been still higher sued the directors in a class action.

Surprisingly, the Delaware Supreme Court agreed with them, although the Chancery Court had not. No conflict of interest was apparent but the court found the directors liable because of 'grossly negligent' procedures. The casualness of the approval and execution of the merger agreement disturbed the court.

The principal actor in the matter was the chairman and chief executive officer, Jerome Van Gorkom. The court was suspicious because Van Gorkom had put the deal together single-handedly, presented it to the board almost as a fait accompli and obtained the board's go-ahead in just two hours. After only a cursory reading, Van Gorkom signed the merger documents in his study during a break from a party he was giving to benefit the Chicago Lyric Opera. Apparently this struck the court as too insouciant. On top of all that, Trans Union's board committed what appeared to be, in the court's eyes, the unpardonable sin of not hiring an investment banking firm to give its opinion that the bid was fair.[20]

The court's decision was more than a little strange. Considering the large premium paid to the shareholders, the facts in the case did not quite add up to gross negligence by the directors. It is particularly odd that the only time target directors have been found personally liable for damages in a takeover case was when they were trying to get out of office by selling the business to an unrelated buyer.

It is possible that the court suspected a conflict of interest. But if it did it kept the thought to itself. Van Gorkom was not just a hired manager. He owned a large number of shares, so his interests appear to have been closely allied with those of the other shareholders. A good bargain for them was good for him as well.

For years statements of the business judgment rule have contained a qualification that no one thought about very much – the directors' decision has to be an 'informed' one. The court's emphasis in the Trans Union case on the procedure of becoming informed brings this abstract phrase to life.

Legal scholars and takeover lawyers have been poring over the Trans Union decision ever since it was handed down. Some look for hidden meanings. Here is one conjecture: By emphasizing slow-moving board procedures

---

[20] There was much jocular comment at the time that the court was trying to do investment banks a favor by ensuring them lots of work. But after the criticism of investment bankers in the *Macmillan* case, 559 A.2d 1261 (Delaware Supreme Court 1989), there was little to joke about.

the court made it easier for target boards to stall during a takeover attempt.[21]

Another possibility – more about this later[22] – is that the Delaware Supreme Court for political and personal reasons has a penchant for the high moral ground in its decisions and opinions. Trans Union's illustrious board was a good target for the court. These directors made a dramatic example that other directors are unlikely to forget. Moreover, it has not been hard for boards to avoid the problem with a little more attention to procedure.

One thing is certain. The Trans Union and *Macmillan* cases have generated apprehensiveness in boardrooms and among insurers. Directors have more to worry about than the paucity of actual damage awards would suggest. Even when a complaint about their conduct is dismissed they may incur very large legal bills. Most directors are protected by corporate by-laws authorizing indemnity or by special indemnity contracts and by directors' liability insurance purchased by the company. But there are practical and legal limits to indemnity. After a hostile change in control, the corporation may not gladly live up to its indemnity obligations to the old board. Insurance companies often will not pay without putting up an aggressive legal defense of their own to avoid or, more likely, reduce their responsibility.[23]

There are now so many effective takeover defenses available that suits by bidders and shareholders against targets and their directors have nearly replaced defensive litigation by targets. It is bidders who now must rely on a helping hand from the courts. Procedural mistakes by target boards, under severe pressure in a bidding war, can sometimes be as crucial to the outcome as the substance of a board's decision.[24] Concern about liability, or expensive litigation after a change in control, can cause a target board to back down.

2.3   THE STANDARDS FOR DEFENSE

When directors approve a transaction but have a financial interest contrary to the interests of the shareholders, the directors are not given the protection of the business judgment rule at all.[25] Instead, the courts require the directors

---

[21] See Jonathan R. Macey and Geoffrey P. Miller, 'Trans Union Reconsidered,' 98 *Yale Law Journal* 127 (1988).

[22] See Chapter 5 Sections 4 through 7.

[23] For more on director liability issues and indemnification see Leo Herzel, Richard W. Shepro and Leo Katz, 'Next-to-last Word on Endangered Directors,' 65 *Harvard Business Review* 38 (1987).

[24] See, once again, *Mills Acquisition Co.* v. *Macmillan, Inc.*, 559 A.2d 1261 (Delaware Supreme Court 1989).

[25] *Grobow* v. *Perot*, 539 A.2d 180 (Delaware Supreme Court 1988); *Aronson* v. *Lewis*, 473 A.2d 805 (Delaware Supreme Court 1984).

to establish the entire fairness of the transaction.[26] This is an exacting standard. It is rarely used but is typically fatal.[27]

Outside of takeover defense and takeover-related transactions, directors usually do not have to worry much that this rigorous scrutiny will be applied. There are plenty of innocent reasons why a director might have an interest contrary to the shareholders, and there are conventional ways to deal with them. Abstaining is an easy solution. A company, for example, might decide to sell some property to another company of which one of its directors is the chief executive officer. That director should leave the decision to the other directors.

However, in takeover defense cases, a general suspicion of conflict of interest hangs over all of the target's directors, even when there is no specific reason why. As a result, unless a definite conflict of interest can be shown, courts use a special, intermediate form of the business judgment rule in deciding takeover cases. Under that standard, courts approve a takeover defense if it is 'reasonable in relation to the threat posed' by the hostile bidder. Unfortunately, what is reasonable may not be clear in advance of a decision by the courts.

The standard was first used, quite casually, by the Delaware Supreme Court in *Unocal Corp.* v. *Mesa Petroleum Co.* in 1985.[28] The opinion did not say that an important new standard for takeover cases was being introduced. Only later decisions in the lower courts made that clear.[29]

Like many other good and bad innovations in takeover law, the new standard was a response to an aggressive and ingenious takeover defense. In the spring of 1985, T. Boone Pickens' Mesa made a cash tender offer for 64 million common shares of Unocal (approximately 37% of the total out-standing shares) at $54 per share. With the shares Mesa already owned, successful completion of the tender offer would have given it a majority of the outstanding Unocal common shares.

Unocal responded with a self-tender for 49% of its outstanding shares, at $72 per share, that excluded Mesa, Unocal's largest shareholder. Since Mesa already owned 14% of the outstanding Unocal shares the extraordinary purpose and effect of Unocal's offer was to exact an involuntary subsidy from Mesa for the benefit of other Unocal shareholders.

Mesa tried to obtain a preliminary injunction in the Federal district court

---

[26] *Weinberger* v. *UOP, Inc.*, 457 A.2d 701 (Delaware Supreme Court 1983).

[27] *Shamrock Holdings, Inc.* v. *Polaroid Corp.*, 559 A.2d 257 (Delaware Chancery Court 1989), is an interesting exception. See the discussion of the case at the end of this chapter and in Chapter 6 Section 8 and in Chapter 15 Section 3.

[28] *Unocal Corp.* v. *Mesa Petroleum Co.*, 493 A.2d 946, 955 (Delaware Supreme Court 1985). The case is also the main legal basis in Delaware for the discriminatory flip-in poison pill. See Chapter 8.

[29] See, for example, *AC Acquisitions Corp.* v. *Anderson, Clayton and Co.*, 519 A.2d 103 (Delaware Chancery Court 1986).

in California to block Unocal's defense, on the ground that the Federal tender offer law prohibited discriminatory tender offers. After examining the history of Federal tender offer law, the court refused to enjoin the self-tender.[30] (The Securities and Exchange Commission has since changed its rules and now does prohibit discriminatory tender offers.)[31] Following the decision of the Federal court, the Delaware Chancery Court held a hearing and confirmed its prior temporary restraining order by issuing a preliminary injunction against the self-tender.[32] The Chancery Court's main reason for its decision appeared self-evident at the time: directors have a fiduciary duty to treat all common shareholders equally and fairly and the self-tender discriminated against Mesa unfairly.

However, to the astonishment of most corporation lawyers, the Delaware Supreme Court reversed the Chancery Court in an emergency appeal by Unocal. The main point in the Supreme Court's reasoning was that the business judgment rule protects decisions of boards of directors when they resist takeovers if their decisions (1) are made in good faith, after reasonable investigation, and (2) are reasonable in the light of the threat posed.[33] On the facts of this particular dispute, the court found that the board of directors of Unocal met the new standard. The second element, reasonableness in relation to the threat posed, has turned out to be quite an important legal innovation in takeover cases. Under the traditional business judgment rule, if the board made its decision in good faith, after reasonable investigation, that would end the matter.

The court sympathized with the board's objective to protect Unocal shareholders from what Unocal had labeled a grossly inadequate and coercive two-tier, front-end loaded tender offer.[34] The court also agreed with another argument made by the Unocal directors: Mesa and Pickens may not really have been trying to acquire Unocal but may have had greenmail as their real goal.[35]

Although it described the matter in a different way, the court was acknowledging that action by the Unocal board was the only way to resolve the shareholders' prisoner's dilemma. But the court also understood that direc-

---

[30] *Unocal Corp.* v. *Pickens,* 608 F. Supp. 1081 (CD Cal. 1985).

[31] The text of the rule, Rule 14d-10, is contained in the Appendix, A.2.4.

[32] *Unocal Corp.* v. *Mesa Petroleum Co.,* Delaware Chancery Court No. 7977 (May 13, 1985).

[33] For a surprising endorsement of the court's casual establishment of a new standard, from a source usually highly critical of takeover defense, see Ronald J. Gilson and Reinier Kraakman, 'Delaware's Intermediate Standard for Defensive Tactics: Proportionality Review,' 44 *Business Lawyer* 247 (1989).

[34] Unocal meant that the tender offer price was much higher than the price would be in any future merger to eliminate the remaining public shareholders. The purpose of the two different prices was to coerce shareholders to tender. A typical prisoner's dilemma situation.

[35] In other words, in the court's view, Mesa's and Boone Pickens' prior activities justified a reasonable inference by the board that the principal objective of Mesa and Pickens was to be paid off by selling their stock back to Unocal at a premium over the market price.

tors were only fallible agents for the shareholders. The suspicion that falls on target directors during takeovers is the reason for the special inquiry into 'reasonableness' that is the main feature of the *Unocal* test. In this case the suspicion had a very special cause – the directors had approved a dramatic discrimination against Unocal's largest shareholder to prevent a change in control of the company. Under these highly unusual circumstances it is not surprising that the court wanted to delve more deeply into the motivation of the directors than it could have under the traditional business judgment rule.

It is likely that the courts have embraced the *Unocal* variation on the business judgment rule with so much enthusiasm because it appears to allow a reasonable compromise. Abandoning the business judgment rule in takeover cases would have the undesirable effect of leaving judges as the economic arbiters of the takeover business.[36] On the other hand, as the facts in the *Unocal* case illustrate, under the present balance of power between shareholders and directors some control by the courts over takeover defenses appears to be essential.

A recent example shows how this compromise has been working. Faced with a hostile $60 per share bid from Britain's Grand Metropolitan in 1988, Pillsbury tried to avoid being taken over by using a flip-in poison pill defense – if Grand Met had completed its acquisition, the pill would have allowed all shareholders other than Grand Met to buy additional shares in Pillsbury for half price.[37] Grand Met's $60 bid would have given Pillsbury shareholders a premium over recent market prices of nearly 100%.

For weeks there was a stalemate. Close to 90% of the shares of Pillsbury were tendered to Grand Metropolitan by the Pillsbury shareholders. Grand Met legally could have bought these shares if it had been willing to pay the penalty on the remaining shares imposed by the poison pill; practically, however, the price would have been too high.

The poison pill gave Pillsbury more time to explore other options. But after a while it became plain to the court that Pillsbury had no reasonable short-term alternative to offer. The prospects for its long-term plans did not impress the court either. When Grand Met raised its price to $63, the court ordered the pill redeemed on the ground that the defense was unreasonable in relation to the minimal threat posed by the all-cash offer. The pill had already given the board ample time to negotiate on behalf of the disorganized shareholders. An immediate peace with Pillsbury was still worth another three dollars per share to Grand Met, which quickly came to terms with the Pillsbury board at $66 per share.[38] In short, under the *Unocal* rule as applied

[36] See *City Capital Associates Ltd. Partnership* v. *Interco Inc.*, 551 A.2d 787, 796 (Delaware Chancery Court 1988).

[37] For more about poison pills, see Chapter 8.

[38] *Grand Metropolitan PLC* v. *Pillsbury Co.*, 558 A.2d 1049 (Delaware Chancery Court 1988). Probably, Pillsbury still had some bargaining power because of other takeover defenses it had

by this court the pill only assured more time for defense and more money for the shareholders, not independence.

However, the precise point at which the courts set the balance between offense and defense in takeovers is constantly shifting. In its decision in *Paramount Communications Inc. v. Time Inc.* the Delaware Supreme Court criticized an earlier case in which the Chancery Court had ordered a pill redeemed. Although the *Paramount–Time* opinion did not make it clear how far a target board can go with poison pills, a company in a predicament like Pillsbury's would appear to have somewhat more flexibility now than the *Pillsbury* decision suggested.[39]

2.4 THE STRICTER STANDARD

Despite the flexibility of the *Unocal* rule, courts do sometimes reject the business judgment standard and employ the more rigorous entire fairness analysis we mentioned at the beginning of the last section. There are two main reasons: conflict of interest or extremely flawed procedure.

How bad must these be? In the *Unocal* case, in a general discussion that reached far beyond the facts of the case, the Delaware Supreme Court said that any time a board of directors is faced with a hostile takeover there is a risk it may be acting primarily in its own interest. This persistent minimal conflict or suspicion of a conflict is not sufficient, however, to call into play the entire fairness standard. For this there must be a real conflict. Similarly, if the procedures of the board or management appear deceptive or manipulative or offend the court, it is more likely to employ the entire fairness standard.

The recent *Macmillan* case, which we have mentioned before, should help put the distinctions in perspective. Macmillan, a very large and diversified American publisher, was the subject of an intense series of takeover battles over a period of one and a half years. After the Robert Bass group made an unsolicited offer, Macmillan's board of directors approved a defensive restructuring that would have given senior management effective control of the company. The Bass group was able to obtain an injunction against the restructuring.[40]

---

used, mainly actions before state liquor commissions to block operation of Pillsbury's restaurant operations by Grand Met, which owned liquor distributorships.

[39] *Paramount Communications Inc. v. Time Inc.,* 571 A.2d 1140, 1153 (Delaware Supreme Court 1990), criticizing *City Capital Associates Ltd. Partnership* v. *Interco Inc.,* 551 A.2d 787 (Delaware Chancery Court 1988). We discuss the *Paramount–Time* decision extensively, beginning in Chapter 3.

[40] *Robert M. Bass Group, Inc. v. Evans,* 552 A.2d 1227 (Delaware Chancery Court 1988). The vice chancellor who heard the case employed the intermediate *Unocal* standard, perhaps out of politeness. Because the restructuring plan failed even the less rigorous test there was no need

In the next stage of the contest, Robert Maxwell, the British publishing tycoon, emerged as the new hostile bidder and Bass dropped out. Kohlberg Kravis Roberts and Co., the giant of the U.S. leveraged buyout industry, became the favored friendly bidder. Management was to have a 20% stake in the KKR buyout. At first, Macmillan's board of directors refused to deal with Maxwell at all. Then, after he began a hostile tender offer the board decided to conduct an auction. After several rounds of bidding KKR was declared the winner.

There was evidence, however, that the auction was rigged to favor KKR and the senior management of Macmillan. Macmillan's chairman leaked Maxwell's bid to KKR and then hid his action from the independent directors. In addition, Macmillan's financial advisers were said to have given groundless assurances to the board about the fairness of the auction. There were several other less important problems as well.

The Delaware Supreme Court chose to review the matter under the exacting standard of entire fairness. It did so, it said, because there were real conflicts of interest, not just a general suspicion. The court emphasized the deception involved and the 'illicit manipulation of a board's deliberative processes by self-interested fiduciaries.'[41] These lapses were too great to fall within the ambit of the *Unocal* rule.

Occasionally, flawed procedures alone are enough to lead to use of the entire fairness standard. The Delaware Chancery Court analyzed a Polaroid takeover defense using the entire fairness standard on the ground that the board of directors had not asked itself the *Unocal* questions – whether there was a threat and, if so, whether the response was reasonable. There were no specific conflicts of interest in the case. The *Polaroid* case was very unusual since the board's defensive actions were determined to be entirely fair. Although the *Unocal* standard might have been the more logical choice in this case, it is possible that the vice chancellor chose the more rigorous standard to increase the chances that her opinion would hold up on review by the Delaware Supreme Court.[42]

---

for the practical Chancery Court to seek to penalize management and the board any more by emphasizing the conflict of interest. The distinction might have become very important in litigation by Macmillan shareholders against the board.

[41] *Mills Acquisition Co.* v. *Macmillan, Inc.,* 559 A.2d 1261 (Delaware Supreme Court 1989).

[42] *Shamrock Holdings, Inc.* v. *Polaroid Corp.,* 559 A.2d 257 (Delaware Chancery Court 1989). See the discussion in Chapter 6 Section 8 and in Chapter 15 Section 3.

3

Shareholders Are Not Perfect Either

IN traditional corporation law and efficient market theory shareholders are the undisputed heroes in the shareholder versus director legal tug of war. However, this approach appears to encourage an excessive emphasis on the short term. From conventional legal and economic points of view shareholders are the intended and actual beneficiaries of takeover battles. Directors are there to protect them but they cannot always be relied on. Legal rules and the courts must make sure that directors do their jobs properly.

Shareholders respond to takeover bids, and occasionally vote in proxy contests, solely on the basis of their assessments of financial values; and usually these assessments turn out to be based upon very short-term considerations. In effect, shareholders are prepared to sell their shares at any time to the highest bidder. The arbitrage market fine-tunes the process in the marketplace. Target shareholders appear to be very big winners in the takeover boom. In contrast, acquirers and their shareholders, on average, do not do particularly well.[1]

Shareholders are not expected to exhibit qualities such as loyalty and commitment to the business they invest in or to the communities in which the business operates. They should not be faulted for this. But unless takeovers are a success for society as a whole there is a tremendous amount of waste going on. Transaction costs in the form of payments to investment bankers, lenders and lawyers, for example, are extremely high and there appear to be other costly side effects.

3.1 QUESTIONING TAKEOVER MANIA

It is difficult to get agreement on whether takeovers are good or bad on balance for society. One reason is that it is easy to find many individual cases and apparently valid arguments to support both sides of the dispute.

Efficient market economic theory is the intellectual backbone of the takeover market.[2] It provides takeover enthusiasts with forceful arguments. Unfortunately, efficient market theory does not appear to tell the whole story,

---

[1] See the discussion of this phenomenon in Chapter 11.
[2] See, for example, Michael C. Jensen (ed.), 'Symposium on the Market for Corporate Control: The Scientific Evidence,' 11 *Journal of Financial Economics* 5 (1983).

and some eminent economists have questioned its core assumption that markets behave rationally.[3] This is too bad – it is really easy and pleasant to think about the world in terms of this simple, elegant structure.

Undoubtedly, the knowledge that they may be replaced after a takeover bid makes directors and managers take their responsibilities to shareholders more seriously than they otherwise might. This is a key empirical insight of the efficient market approach to takeovers. Since it is obviously right, it has been used very effectively to support forceful arguments that takeovers should never be interfered with by managers, directors, courts or legislatures. However, even this insight is not perfect since it appears that many bidders overpay. That would make it difficult for even the most zealous managers and directors to devise a constructive, successful antitakeover strategy.

It also appears indisputable that takeovers have had a tremendously liberating effect on big business in America. Takeovers have helped to eliminate the complacent insularity that used to be such a discouraging characteristic of boards of directors and managements of big companies in America. But there also have been other reasons for this change and the fear of takeovers may no longer be so important. For example, foreign competition in the product market has had a powerful humbling effect on American business and large institutional shareholders have become more aggressive (short-term) monitors of their investments.

However, despite the persuasive empirical insights and theoretical arguments, there is no evidence that takeovers have improved the efficiency of U.S. industry. In addition, there is some evidence that takeovers on the average have not improved the efficiency of companies that have been taken over.[4] The possibility that there are serious drawbacks to a too active takeover market has been a growing concern. Takeovers and the threat of takeovers may be, on balance, a drain on the ability of U.S. companies to compete internationally.[5]

First, highly valuable human resources are used up in the takeover business. If takeovers do not promote efficiency, the tremendous amount of time and effort expended by top executives, investment bankers, commercial bankers and lawyers is squandered. Society would be much better served if these talented, ambitious people were producing better goods or other services.

[3] See, for example, James Tobin, 'On the Efficiency of the Financial System,' *Lloyds Bank Review* (July 1984). For a defense of the efficient market and a review of this sort of criticism see Robert Merton, 'On the State of the Efficient Market Hypothesis in Financial Economics,' in R. Dornbusch, S. Fisher and J. Bossons (eds), *Macroeconomics and Finance: Essays in Honor of Franco Modigliani* (1987).

[4] See the evidence we cite in Chapter 11.

[5] See, for example, Michael L. Dertouzos, Richard K. Lester and Robert M. Solow, *Made in America, Regaining the Productive Edge*, p. 144 (1989); Bruce R. Scott, 'Competitiveness: Self-Help for a Worsening Problem,' *Harvard Business Review* (July–August 1989).

(This is not the same as an argument that financial activity, or services in general, are less valuable than producing goods.)

Second, takeovers may contribute to an excessive, harmful focus by U.S. companies on the short run. If managers know that they are likely to lose their jobs if a hostile tender offer succeeds, they will try to manage their companies to move stock prices up immediately. To compound this effect, a significant portion of top management compensation is tied to stock prices or short-term profits through options and similar devices.

This is only a problem if stock prices are influenced excessively by short-term results – in other words, if the market does not sufficiently value long-term planning efforts such as research and development. For years, businessmen and lawyers have been saying that the market really is short-sighted. But economists and investment bankers have generally scoffed at these assertions, arguing that market forces keep stock prices in line with long-run considerations.[6] Their idea is simple and sounds quite convincing. Companies with successful research and development programs, for example, are often highly valued by the stock market. Nonetheless, research and development programs are extremely hard to evaluate accurately. To a large extent, the market is really placing its bets on history.

If information were perfect and we could predict the future, the long run would take care of itself. But these assumptions do not fit the real world very well.[7] For one thing companies cannot tell their version of the whole story to the market without competitors stealing their ideas. Even investment bankers become more modest in arguing that the market values long-term planning when they themselves are facing takeover.

The faith of the courts and legislators in the efficient market was shaken considerably by the October 1987 stock market crash when the market appeared to be astoundingly inefficient. Otherwise how could all of those smart professionals have decided at once, when nothing else unusual had happened, that their shares were overvalued? Revelations from the insider trading scandals that the arbitrage market gains some of its wisdom by cheating, not research and esoteric insights, did not help either.

Recently, the Massachusetts Institute of Technology Commission on Industrial Productivity espoused the view that 'the wave of hostile takeovers and leveraged buyouts encourages or enforces an excessive and dangerous overvaluation of short-term profitability.'[8] One of the three authors of the

---

[6] See, for example, Michael C. Jensen, 'The Takeover Controversy: Analysis and Evidence,' IV *Midland Corporate Finance Journal* 6, 11 (1986).

[7] For an economic analysis that emphasizes the distortions that can occur even in an efficient market because managers are too concerned about current stock prices, see Jeremy C. Stein, 'Efficient Capital Markets, Inefficient Firms: A Model of Myopic Corporate Behavior,' *Quarterly Journal of Economics* (November 1989), p. 655.

[8] Dertouzos, Lester and Solow, *Made in America*, p. 144. See also Scott, 'Competitiveness.'

Commission's report was Robert Solow, the 1987 Nobel laureate in economics. The Commission included a host of other distinguished economists, engineers and scientists associated with MIT.

The study found that Japanese and European executives differ from U.S. executives in two important ways. They are less preoccupied with earnings, dividends and stock prices and they show greater concern for their communities, employees, customers, suppliers and the continuing corporate enterprise itself.[9] The Japanese Government adopted this theme in trade talks late in 1989. Responding to claims that Japan competes unfairly, it argued that the costs of takeovers greatly diminishes the resources the U.S. needs to develop new products.[10] And in a controversial book describing Japan's economic advantages the chairman of Sony, Akio Morita, wrote, 'We are focusing on business years in advance, while you [U.S. businesses] seem to be concerned only with profits minutes from now. At that rate, you may well never be able to compete with us.'[11]

Even Michael Jensen, a Harvard Business School economist whose writings helped to provide a theoretical point of view for the takeover boom, has begun to distinguish between takeovers by cash-rich public companies (usually wasteful) and leveraged buyouts, which he argues promote efficiency through the discipline of leverage and realistically large incentives for management.[12] Still a pro-takeover position but a long way from the old consensus.

3.2   THE SHORT-RUN OUTLOOK OF INSTITUTIONAL SHAREHOLDERS

An incorrigible short-run outlook among shareholders, particularly institutional shareholders, appears to be the core of the problem. Although our main interest is the takeover boom of the past two decades, this problem is not unique to takeovers. John Maynard Keynes voiced the same concern in 1935, during the Great Depression. 'Investment based on genuine long-term expectation,' he wrote, 'is so difficult today as to be scarcely practicable.'[13]

[9] Dertouzos, Lester and Solow, *Made in America,* p. 62.
[10] Steven R. Weisman, 'Japan, Weary of Barbs on Trade, Tells Americans Why they Trail,' *New York Times* (Nov. 20, 1989), p. 1.
[11] Akio Morita, 'The Decline of an America Which can only See 10 Minutes Ahead,' in Akio Morita and Shintaro Ishihara, *The Japan that can Say 'No': The New U.S.–Japan Relations Card,* (typescript translation 1989), p. 9.
[12] See Michael C. Jensen, 'Eclipse of the Public Corporation,' 67 *Harvard Business Review* 61 (Sept.–Oct. 1989), and the remarkably large correspondence about this article published by the *Review* in the Nov.–Dec. 1989 issue.
[13] John Maynard Keynes, *The General Theory of Employment, Interest and Money* (1935), p. 157.

Keynes gave two reasons for the excessively short-run view of stock market investors. First, securities markets are very liquid, allowing the possibility of large short-run profits for individual investors. Second, because of the possibility of those profits institutional investment managers come under great pressure to produce them by investing for the short run only. Keynes was very cautious about suggesting a solution to this problem because he knew that liquidity was essential for private investment.

Since 1935 the situation has worsened. Markets have become much more liquid. And pressure for short-run results has intensified because of the enormous growth in institutional investment. The short-run success of money managers is closely monitored and encouraged by their clients. Even directors and managers who complain about this short-term outlook usually insist on it from the investment advisers for their companies' own pension funds.

The MIT study concludes on the same note as Keynes: 'Although some fund managers invest for the long term, most turn over their stock holdings rapidly in an effort to maximize the current value of their investment portfolio, since this is the main criterion against which their own performance is judged.'[14]

Unfortunately, there is no obvious alternative criterion. Put another way, if we abandon short-term performance as the main criterion, how could anyone monitor the institutional monitors? To summarize this situation as one in which shareholders have become too powerful would be too simple. They are too powerful and too weak, depending on the situation and on your point of view. We explained in Chapter 2 that the disorganization of shareholders puts them at a negotiating disadvantage when a company is being sold. In that situation they lack the ability to bargain and need boards of directors to bargain on their behalf. We analyzed that problem in terms of the prisoner's dilemma. At the same time, however, from the point of view of society, large institutional shareholders are in another cooperation dilemma. They appear to have too much power when a decision is being made about whether a company is going to be sold. Their short-run outlook virtually assures the success of takeover bids. Yet, because of their diversified portfolios they are often also shareholders of the bidder who may be over-paying. If institutions could cooperate, they might reject many of these bids. But there are enormous legal and practical barriers to this kind of cooperation.

[14] Dertouzos, Lester and Solow, *Made in America*, p. 63.

3.3   THE IMPOTENCE OF BIDDERS' SHAREHOLDERS

In our legal system, an imbalance exists between the rights of bidders' and targets' shareholders. Bidders' shareholders are far less powerful. This is illustrated by the lack of symmetry between the law's suspicious treatment of target directors' takeover decisions and the paucity of legal restrictions on bidders' directors. Bidders' shareholders generally need not be and are not consulted. They have no legal right to be involved in takeover decisions unless a bidder's stock is being issued in amounts that exceed stock exchange limits.

The combination of Time Incorporated with Warner Communications Inc. provides a dramatic illustration of the lack of symmetry in the legal treatment of bidders' and targets' shareholders.[15] In March 1989 the two companies had agreed that Warner would merge with a subsidiary of Time. Because this merger was structured as a stock-for-stock exchange, each company had to obtain the approval of its shareholders: Warner under Delaware law because it was merging with a Delaware subsidiary of Time, and Time under New York Stock Exchange rules because it was issuing a large number of its shares.

There was no way to avoid obtaining shareholder approval without resorting to a cash bid by one company for the other. But a cash bid was considered undesirable by the two companies since it would have radically changed the economics of the transaction. It would have required a premium price from the bidder and a large amount of debt to pay that price. In addition, under U.S. accounting rules, a cash bid would not have qualified for the pooling-of-interests accounting treatment both parties sought.[16]

Any likelihood that Time shareholders would approve the transaction disappeared after Paramount Communications intervened with a high-premium cash bid for Time in June 1989. At this crucial moment Time and Warner were able to make the legal requirement for a Time shareholder vote vanish. They restructured the transaction to make Time the cash bidder for Warner shares. This change drastically revised the economic bargain between Time and Warner shareholders, entailed a large amount of new debt for the surviving entity and lost the benefits of pooling-of-interests accounting. Legally, however, the success of Time's bid now depended only on acceptance by Warner shareholders. Time shareholders no longer had a role in the takeover, except in unsuccessful litigation attacking the bid.[17]

Yet, it is the bidders' shareholders who are frequently stuck with a bad

---

[15] We use this interesting transaction as an illustration of important issues many times in the book. See also Part III, which analyzes the principal legal agreements involved in the Time–Warner transaction.

[16] See 'pooling-of-interests accounting' in the Glossary.

[17] *Paramount Communications Inc.* v. *Time Inc.*, 571 A.2d 1140 (Delaware Supreme Court 1990). The text of this opinion is reproduced as Appendix A.12.

acquisition. Acquirers often do not do very well in acquisitions. There is even some evidence that companies that make a lot of acquisitions tend themselves to become more vulnerable to takeovers.[18]

3.4 POSSIBLE SOLUTIONS

The legal rights of bidders' shareholders could be increased quite easily. For example, stock exchange rules require bidders to obtain shareholder approval for large acquisitions only when the bidder is issuing stock in the acquisition. These rules could be expanded to include cash acquisitions.

Unfortunately, there appear to be no simple solutions to the problem of target shareholder myopia. It has been suggested that if institutional shareholders could become more involved in the companies that they invest in, they might develop a long-run outlook.[19] This would be possible only if institutions could cooperate. No institution acting alone could afford to forego short-term gains and take the risk of losing clients.

But if institutional shareholders could cooperate and give up their short-term outlook, it would become difficult or impossible for their clients to assess their performance. By looking at short-run performance of their investment managers, clients have an easy time monitoring their investments. The long run, on the other hand, is only a guess, an intuition, a hope.

If there were no objective way to assess their performance, institutional investor judgments could become petty and political. Many institutional investors tend to be either bureaucracies or quasi-political institutions. Occasionally, public pension funds and university endowments already act like politicians rather than investors on issues which arouse intense political feelings. On a large scale, bowing to pressure groups could lead to a politicized economy in which investment decisions would have less economic basis.

Some investors do have a long-term view. But even those who start with a long-term view may succumb to the promise of quick and easy money in the takeover market. An example is Warren Buffett, the chairman of Berkshire Hathaway, a diversified company similar to a closed-end investment company. Buffett has received enormous publicity for his long-term investment philosophy. His interests are firmly allied with his shareholders, because he is by far the largest shareholder and his pay is not determined by short-term incentives. But in recent years he has committed huge amounts of his

---

[18] Mark L. Mitchell and Kenneth Lehn, 'Do Bad Bidders Become Good Targets?', study by the Office of Economic Analysis, Securities and Exchange Commission (1988). See Chapter 11.

[19] See Louis Lowenstein, *What's Wrong with Wall Street: Short-Term Gain and the Absentee Shareholder* (1988), and Arnold W. Sametz and James L. Bicksler (eds), *The Battle for Corporate Control: Shareholder Rights, Stakeholder Interests and Managerial Responsibilities* (1990).

firm's capital to arbitrage, which in 1988 appeared to be his most profitable business.[20]

Keynes himself tried to adopt a long-term investment view after becoming disillusioned with speculation.[21] He admired the long-term investor as a market force promoting the public interest. But he also understood the short-run hardships that a long-run investor faces, particularly if he is investing money that belongs to someone else:

> For it is in the essence of his behaviour that he should be eccentric, unconventional and rash in the eyes of average opinion. If he is successful, that will only confirm the general belief in his rashness; and if in the short run he is unsuccessful, which is very likely, he will not receive much mercy. Worldly wisdom teaches that it is better for reputation to fail conventionally than to succeed unconventionally.[22]

Another possible solution is to reduce stock market liquidity by taxation or other means. A stiff tax on short-term capital gains with a gradual reduction as investments are held longer would serve this aim. But since many institutional investors are not required to pay taxes, their short-term capital gains would have to be made taxable. And to have a direct effect on arbitragers, short-term capital gains rates would have to be made much higher than the ordinary income tax rates which arbitragers now pay. In general, as Keynes understood, designing a framework to promote large reductions in liquidity would be difficult and probably dangerous. In any case, the Bush Administration has been pushing in a completely different direction. It wants to reduce capital gains taxes.[23]

So far, the most practical answer has been to increase the power of directors. In effect, that is what poison pills and state antitakeover laws do. This is not likely to be a stable solution, because of concern over director conflicts of interest.

The newest state antitakeover laws quite specifically shift the balance of power toward directors. They give directors who are responding to a takeover threat the legal right to consider the long-term interests of shareholders, the corporation and various other groups such as employees, customers, suppliers and communities. In effect these laws provide corporate boards with a simple basis for justifying actions to keep a target company independent.

---

[20] See Berkshire Hathaway, Inc., 1988 Annual Report to Shareholders, pp. 14–18 (commenting on arbitrage and on efficient market theory).

[21] See Nicholas Davenport, 'Keynes in the City,' in Milo Keynes (ed.), *Essays on John Maynard Keynes* (1975), pp. 225–9.

[22] Keynes, *The General Theory of Employment, Interest and Money*, pp. 157–8.

[23] A recent review of the short-term trading problem argued that an excise tax on securities transactions would be more effective than an increase in short-term capital gains rates. Lawrence H. Summers, 'The Case for a Securities Transactions Excise Tax,' paper presented at the Salomon Brothers/Rutgers Conference on the Fiduciary Responsibilities of Institutional Investors, June 14–15, 1990.

But these laws would be ineffectual without a poison pill made legal by statute or some other legal way for directors to restrict accumulations of stock by hostile bidders. For this reason it is usual for these new laws also to legalize use of flip-in poison pills by directors as an antitakeover device.[24]

Even so, directors are unlikely to have an entirely free hand. Courts probably will scrutinize the procedures that lead to directors' decisions, minutely examining whether directors have reasonable grounds for their decisions or are merely mouthing platitudes to invoke the protection of the new statutes. Moreover, directors are agents. How long can one expect them to resist when shareholders are clamoring for a sale?

State antitakeover laws are enacted piecemeal by legislators who are trying to satisfy many different interests. Poison pills and other defenses are developed and refined by lawyers and courts in the midst of takeover battles. This combination of antitakeover laws and defensive tactics is an improvised, rickety solution to a very important public policy issue that deserves better. But agreement on a better policy probably will not be possible for some time. Until we know more, flexible ad hoc solutions appear to be the best compromise.

---

[24] For poison pills see 'poison pill' in the Glossary and also Chapter 8, and for the new state laws see Chapter 6.

4

The Chief Executive Officer

So far we have focused mainly on boards of directors and shareholders and have said only a little about chief executive officers. There is an air of unreality about this. Usually it is the CEO, not the board of directors, who is in command. A reader unfamiliar with American company boards who walked into a board meeting after reading our discussion of directors might be surprised and disappointed. Under ordinary circumstances, what would be going on in the boardroom would correspond very little to the Delaware and other state law procedures we have described. The CEO would probably be the chairman of the meeting and completely in charge. Generally, he controls both the agenda and the flow of information to the directors. He dominates the meeting and the board plays a quite secondary role.

Shareholders and the market are far more interested in CEOs than directors. When we read about big businesses in the financial press, CEOs usually are the center of attention and directors are obscure. In fact, under normal circumstances very little attention is paid to directors by shareholders, the market or the press. Sometimes companies find it useful to include prominent people on the board (such as retired Presidents, astronauts or financial wise men) to assure the public of the venture's honesty or conscientiousness. But most of the time even analysts who specialize in a particular company are unlikely to know or care much about its directors. Only crisis brings boards up front. When, for example, the Campeau Corporation's department stores were clearly close to bankruptcy in early 1990, its directors suddenly became the subject of newspaper profiles. But while the acquisitions that got the company into trouble were being done Robert Campeau, the chairman, was riding high; he was treated by the press like a sole proprietor.

Yet the board, as we have seen, is supposed to be in charge. The key provision on directors in the Delaware corporation law says: 'The business and affairs of every corporation organized under this chapter shall be managed by or under the direction of a board of directors.'[1] However, except in times of acute crisis, no board of directors actually manages a large successful corporation. The additional phrase *under the direction of* is an attempt to make the Delaware statute correspond more closely to reality.

[1] Delaware General Corporation Law, §141(a), reproduced in the Appendix, A.4. The statute goes on to explain that corporations may limit the power of the board in the certificate of incorporation. However, public corporations never or rarely do so.

But, ordinarily, the business of a large corporation is under the board's direction only in a highly theoretical sense. It would be much more accurate to say that, until there is a crisis, the board is performing a watchdog function, usually with nothing earthshaking to watch out for.

A study of how boards of directors think and behave was recently completed by Professor Jay Lorsch of the Harvard Business School. Lorsch and his colleague, Elizabeth MacIver, conducted interviews with directors about their actual experiences in the boardroom. A comment from one director gives a revealing description of the division of labor between board and CEO. 'Directors don't run the company,' he said. 'Their job is to select the people who will run the company, and to ensure that those people are doing the best job possible. If they feel that management is not meeting expectations, then it's their job to remedy the situation.' Echoing a point of view common among directors, he went on to explain, 'They should not, however, be running the place; and if the CEO is calling all the time, then it's a pretty strong sign that perhaps he's not the right guy for the job.'[2]

Why do corporation statutes seem so different from reality? For one thing, what the statutes seem to require is not very practical. A board is not well suited for managing or even directing the management of a business. The main reasons are that running a successful business is not a part-time job nor is a committee usually the best way to do it. Responsibility and authority become too diffuse and lines of communication too complicated.[3] On the other hand, boards can be just right for oversight and for the management of crises. Fortunately, courts are much closer to reality on this subject than corporation statutes.

Moreover, practical considerations incline directors not to be very assertive under ordinary circumstances. Many of the most important, potentially aggressive directors are also CEOs of companies. They have too many demands on their time to prepare well enough to challenge another CEO on his home ground. More important, a CEO who knows that directors would not have the ability to run his company has good reason not to kick up an unessential fuss as a director at another CEO's meeting.

However, directors do have real power. They really have the ultimate authority. They can (and occasionally do) replace CEOs. Most of the time, however, the power is potential. As another director told Lorsch and MacIver, 'Directors are like firemen. They sit around doing very little until there's a fire alarm and then they spring into action.'[4] Although this metaphor captures

---

[2] Jay W. Lorsch with Elizabeth MacIver, *Pawns or Potentates: The Reality of America's Corporate Boards* (1989), p. 77.

[3] There is some interesting writing on this subject. See, for example, Kenneth Arrow, *The Limits of Organization* (1974); Oliver E. Williamson, *Markets and Hierarchies* (1975); Henry Mintzberg, *The Structuring of Organizations* (1979).

[4] Lorsch and MacIver, *Pawns or Potentates*, p. 97.

the essential point, it may exaggerate a little. Temperaments and personalities of CEOs differ. Some like to be challenged. They look to their boards for thoughtful commentary and the development of an informed consensus on difficult issues facing the company. Other CEOs, however, like to keep their board meetings as close to a legal formality as possible.

Lorsch and MacIver saw the same discrepancy between corporation statutes and reality and expressed it in the title of their book, *Pawns or Potentates: The Reality of America's Corporate Boards*. Their solution is to make the reality conform better to the statutes – for example, they recommend reversing normal practice in the United States by having an independent director instead of the CEO act as chairman of the board. However, even their ideal board would be limited to more aggressive oversight and the management of crisis.

Another way of looking at these problems may be helpful. Everyone keeps some commonsense model of the corporation in mind. The usual one used by economists and lawyers puts common shareholders at the top. As the real owners of the residual capital in the company they have certain ultimate powers in the company which they exercise by voting. They elect a board of directors to look after their interests. This model conforms reasonably well to corporation statutes, but less well to reality. As a practical matter, most shareholders are quite passive and transitory. Directors, as we have explained, usually are not a dominant force either.

Under most circumstances a model that emphasizes the CEO may be much closer to reality. Shareholders, bondholders and other lenders can be viewed as investors of capital in the CEO's business. Bondholders and other long-term lenders lend the CEO money under complex, formal contracts. On the other hand, since the shareholders provide the company's permanent capital, the bargain with them has to be indefinitely adjustable as conditions change over the long term. There is no way for the shareholders to take the money back if a covenant is breached. Selling the shares in the market does not get the money back. One shareholder can be substituted for another in the stock market, but the capital is still locked in the assets of the company. The market price of the stock reflects this fact. Corporation charters and corporation law establish the terms of this ingenious bargain. These terms are being renegotiated continuously in charters, legislatures and courts. In some situations, as we have seen, more is expected of directors, and in others less.

American academic lawyers have been debating a contract theory of corporation.[5] Proponents argue that there need not be any required terms in the corporate contract. In other words, shareholders and management should be free at the inception of the corporation (although some theorists argue the

---

[5] See the symposium, 'Contractual Freedom in Corporate Law,' 89 *Columbia Law Review* 1395–1774 (1989).

freedom should exist at any time) to agree, by contract, to eliminate any of the legal rules that would normally govern their relationship. Our concept of the corporation as a contract does not depend on whether we adopt this theory. From our standpoint, statutory and court-created legal rules governing the relationship between shareholders and management can be viewed as required terms of the corporate contract subject to continual renegotiation as part of the political, legal and corporate processes. Nonetheless, a contract.

A key element in the contract is that a board of directors acts as the intermediary between shareholders and CEO. Using a board keeps the bargain very flexible and makes a rigid agreement between the CEO and the shareholders unnecessary. The device provides continuous flexible oversight for the shareholders. These ideas do not fit the exact words of corporation statutes but they usually fit the facts quite well. Emphasizing the CEO also helps to clarify another important point. Shareholders are not the owners of a company in any ordinary sense of the word. For example, they have limited liability and their potential powers, although extensive, also have limits. Directors are not obliged to follow the wishes of the shareholders, as the Delaware Supreme Court emphasized at the end of its opinion in the *Paramount–Time* case:

Paramount argues that ... Time's response was unreasonable in precluding Time's shareholders from accepting the tender offer or receiving a control premium in the immediately foreseeable future. Once again, the contention stems, we believe, from a fundamental misunderstanding of where the power of corporate governance lies. Delaware law confers the management of the corporate enterprise to the stockholders' duly elected board of representatives.... The fiduciary duty to manage a corporate enterprise includes the selection of a time frame for achievement of corporate goals. That duty may not be delegated to the stockholders.... Directors are not obliged to abandon a deliberately conceived corporate plan for a short-term shareholder profit unless there is clearly no basis to sustain the corporate strategy.[6]

The model also provides a reasonably good picture of what happens in a takeover contest: two CEOs are bidding for the right to control the target's assets. In the process the identity of the providers of the capital and the types of capital usually change; for example, debt may be substituted for equity. In an unfriendly proposal for a leveraged buyout, the contest is between the target's CEO and the private providers of equity capital and credit for the buyout, who will put in their own CEO if they win. Some would argue that leveraged buyouts are more effective than other kinds of acquisitions because the providers of equity capital are real owners. On the other hand, proxy

---

[6] *Paramount Communications Inc.* v. *Time Inc.,* 571 A.2d 1140, 1154 (Delaware Supreme Court 1990), reproduced in the Appendix, A.12. See also the correspondence by Peter Rona and reply by Michael C. Jensen, 67 *Harvard Business Review* 187, 197–201 (Nov.–Dec. 1989).

contests are an example of a takeover contest where providers and types of capital do not change, at least not initially.

Takeovers are the ultimate crisis. Even then the CEO may continue to be dominant if he has no conflict of interest. Time's and Warner's CEOs were in charge of the Time–Warner combination from the start and maintained control throughout the struggle with Paramount. In fact, strong CEO leadership helped Time beat Paramount in court. By and large, Time's CEO and board members had a consistent story about how they viewed the combination with Warner. Most successful takeover defenses share these characteristics.

When the CEO has a clear conflict of interest in a takeover (more than the mere suspicion of conflict that arises simply because his job is on the line), the board is likely to take over. If the CEO is left in charge despite his conflict, the legal rules we have described impose an entire fairness standard of review for corporate decision making. Usually this is too high a price to pay, as the Macmillan cases[7] illustrate. When the board does take over in a crisis, the traditional director-oriented model of the corporation fits reality quite closely. However, the CEO model of the corporation is also reasonably consistent with this situation. Using an analogy from insolvency law, the CEO can be viewed as having been thrown into a receivership by the independent directors for the benefit of the shareholders, with the directors acting as receivers.

In a takeover crisis, if the board appoints a special committee of independent directors the committee acts as a substitute for the target's full board. Even more important, it is also a substitute for the CEO in managing the crisis.[8] The CEO is usually excluded from special committee meetings. If he appears, it is by invitation to provide information. Since committee members do not know a great deal about takeovers, even if they have been through one or two before, many very important decisions wind up being made by investment bankers and lawyers.

Unless the committee is a sham, its use will ultimately dictate the outcome in the takeover contest. However, the special committee members know far less about the company than the CEO does. By creating the committee, the target's board has turned away from its CEO and generally there is little left to do but sell out. The company no longer has a leader. Without a CEO the board is incapable of managing the company beyond the crisis.

CEOs and boards of bidders present a very different case. Acquisitions are rarely a crisis for the bidder. The main counterexamples are the very rare cases in which the target bids for the bidder, as a defensive maneuver. This happened in 1982 when target Martin Marietta bid for bidder Bendix, and

---

[7] *Robert M. Bass Group, Inc.* v. *Evans,* 552 A.2d 1227 (Delaware Chancery Court 1988); *Mills Acquisition Co.* v. *Macmillan, Inc.,* 559 A.2d 1261 (Delaware Supreme Court 1989). We discuss these cases in more detail in Chapters 2, 7 and 10.

[8] See our discussions of special committees in Chapters 5, 13 and 14.

again in 1988 when target American Brands successfully made a counter-bid for bidder E–II. There is very little judicial scrutiny of board decisions by acquirers. The special sensitivity target directors develop in a takeover is unusual on bidder boards. The danger is that a CEO with a history of apparently successful acquisitions will be treated like an emperor who can do no wrong, which may be one reason why, frequently, bidders' shareholders do not fare so well in takeovers.[9]

[9] See Chapter 11. For a striking description, see Leslie Wayne, 'How One Man's Ego Wrecked a Bank,' *New York Times* (March 4, 1990).

5

The Importance of State Corporation Law

U NDER the original acquisition agreement that Time Incorporated and Warner Communications Inc. signed in March of 1989, a newly created subsidiary of Time would have merged into Warner. At the conclusion of the merger, Warner would have become a subsidiary of Time. There would have been nothing unusual about this arrangement – except for its strategic audacity. The original design was a merger of equals. In the past this design has often exposed one or both companies to competing bids.[1] It was structured in a conventional way under Delaware law to take care of a number of problems, some of which arise in almost every acquisition. The structure was only possible because Delaware has been a leader in keeping its corporate laws flexible to allow such problems to be solved.

For example, the transaction was designed, in part, to keep Warner and its legal organization unchanged after the merger. As a result, most of the contracts, licenses, leases and other agreements in Warner's name could remain intact without the need to obtain large numbers of consents from the other parties. As we will see, there are also other benefits from this design that highlight the strategic importance of state law in the acquisitions world.

Sometimes companies take drastic action to become subject to the state law they want. In 1987, Singer Company, the famous maker of sewing machines that had also become a very large defense contractor, moved its headquarters from Stamford, Connecticut to Montvale, New Jersey. There was only one reason for the move. Singer management wanted to take advantage of a new antitakeover statute that had become part of New Jersey law. As it turned out, New Jersey's relative advantages were only temporary. Other states soon changed their laws. In addition, the statute's effectiveness was limited. Despite the move, Singer was taken over by a hostile bidder the following year. State antitakeover statutes have become very important and we have devoted an entire chapter to their effect on hostile acquisitions.[2]

---

[1] For a discussion of the reasons mergers of equals raise the possibility of a competing bid for one or both of the companies, see Chapter 12.
[2] Chapter 6.

5.1   THE SCOPE OF STATE LAW

A corporation is incorporated under a state law, not under Federal law.[3] Traditionally, the internal affairs of corporations have been governed by the law of the state of incorporation. Each state's corporation law establishes the legal framework for all corporations chartered in that state. The corporation law is the basic element in the contract among shareholders, directors and officers, and it governs many of the important relationships of the corporation with the rest of the world. The place a corporation is chartered may have nothing to do with its physical location or the operation of its business. A corporation with its headquarters in Indiana and its main manufacturing plants in Ohio might very well be chartered in Delaware.

State corporation law establishes limited liability for shareholders and governs the legal powers and duties of directors. It sets the procedures for important corporate transactions, such as mergers, and the boundaries for the ways a corporation can arrange shareholder voting rights, what kinds of decisions the directors must submit to the shareholders for a vote and what vote is required.

On many questions the state corporation statute establishes a minimum standard or allows a range of possible solutions. Within those limits, special rules may be embodied in the corporation's principal governing document, its charter.[4] The charter can be amended only with the consent of the shareholders. By-laws typically deal with internal structural and procedural matters and usually can be changed by either the directors or the shareholders. Quite often, very fine procedural considerations become crucial in takeover controversies.

The structure of an acquisition is partly a matter of state law and partly of Federal law, particularly SEC laws and regulations. There are two key acquisition forms. The simplest in theory is a merger, which must follow the precise procedures required by state law. After approval by the directors and shareholders of both companies, everything happens in one step. The two companies become one – the survivor of the merger. In many mergers, the bidder, for business or legal reasons, organizes a temporary subsidiary to merge with the target. Upon completion of the merger the target becomes a subsidiary of the bidder. However, for strategic reasons (mainly speed), simple one-step mergers are less common than two-step acquisitions, in which the bidder buys most of the target's shares in a cash tender offer, and then

---

[3] There are some exceptions: for example, national banks.
[4] Depending on the state, the charter may be officially called the Certificate of Incorporation (the name in Delaware), the Articles of Incorporation, the Articles of Association, or by some other name.

later acquires the remaining shares in a merger.[5] The tender offer rules are exclusively the subject of Federal (SEC) law.[6]

In a merger using a subsidiary, such as the one Time and Warner originally proposed, there are some special twists concerning shareholder approval. Normally, under Delaware law, approval by holders of a majority of the shares of both corporations would be necessary. Under the laws of some other states, such as New York, two-thirds approval is still necessary. However, by involving only a subsidiary and not Time itself in the merger, Time itself would not have merged, thus eliminating any state-law requirement for approval by Time's shareholders. Before 1967, this structure would not have been allowed even in Delaware. At that time, if a subsidiary of Time had been the party to the merger, only the subsidiary's stock could have been given to Warner shareholders, in which case no real merger would have taken place because the former Warner shareholders would still own interests in the Warner business, not in Time.

Despite Delaware's flexible merger statute, Time needed approval of its shareholders anyway because of a formalistic distinction made by the rules of the New York Stock Exchange, on which Time was listed. Under the NYSE rules, if Time had been paying cash, shareholder approval would not have been necessary, but Time's plan for the Warner shareholders to receive Time stock did require shareholder approval.

When Paramount made its hostile cash offer for Time, shareholder approval became Time's and Warner's biggest problem. Strategically, the only effective response that would save the deal was to find an alternative form for the transaction that could be accomplished under Delaware law and stock exchange rules without a shareholder vote. Under state law, Time had the right to complete the merger without shareholder approval and risk being delisted by the stock exchange. Although this was a potent rhetorical point in the lawsuit, Time's board does not appear ever to have considered it a practical possibility.

Court decisions in each jurisdiction supplement and refine state corporation statutes. For example, fiduciary obligations of directors and officers and among shareholders have mainly been created by court decisions. Legal rules change constantly under the pressure of private litigation, with the opinion of the court in each lawsuit becoming a precedent for the next situation. The huge stakes in takeovers make it economic for the participants to litigate lavishly any ambiguities in takeover law. When the corporation law of the state does not adequately address an issue, cases from other jurisdictions are usually invoked as persuasive authority. By far, the law of Delaware is the richest source.

---

[5] We discuss the structure of a transaction in more detail in Chapter 12.
[6] See Chapter 9.

5.2   THE PREEMINENCE OF DELAWARE

Delaware is, by a large margin, the most significant state for incorporations and for the development of corporation law. Delaware makes the most of the principle that corporations need not have operations or even conduct any business in the state in which they are incorporated.

It has with phenomenal success sought to become the state of choice for the incorporation of public companies. A majority of the very large corporations in the United States are incorporated in Delaware, although few have their headquarters or even modest operations in that state. Corporations and corporation law are one of the principal industries in the state.[7] They provide tax revenues and clients for another important Delaware business, corporation lawyers. Specialty businesses such as court reporters and hotels serve this industry and, in turn, help to sustain it. Other states, such as Nevada, have tried to compete, but so far they have not made a significant dent in Delaware's supremacy.[8]

The crucial Delaware competitive advantages are its corporation statute, court system and corporation lawyers. Committees of corporation lawyers continually make recommendations to the state legislature about revisions to the corporation statute that will make highly technical corporate transactions easier to accomplish. These proposals are generally accorded non-political treatment by the Delaware legislature and adopted without alteration. Corporate law issues are usually viewed as business transaction problems to be solved as closely as possible in accordance with the wishes of the parties involved, not as profound moral dramas or as causes for political blood-letting.

As a result of this process, the Delaware corporation statute has become a flexible form contract among shareholders, directors and management that is continually being renegotiated as problems arise. Moreover, this form contract usually provides plenty of room for variation by the parties in charters and by-laws to suit themselves.

A high volume of litigation helps preserve an efficient, expert and prosperous bar and court system. The case law interpreting the corporation statute is far more extensively developed than in any other state. Other states can copy the words of the Delaware statute, and even choose to follow the law in its case law precedents. Large states also could, if they had the political will, duplicate the court system. They already have the necessary lawyers in their big cities. But large states cannot provide legislatures and governors who are willing to keep corporation law out of normal politics.

---

[7] See generally Jonathan R. Macey and Geoffrey P. Miller, 'Toward an Interest-Group Theory of Delaware Corporate Law,' 65 *Texas Law Review* 469 (1987).

[8] For a more detailed analysis of this subject, see the foreword by Leo Herzel and Laura Richman to R. Franklin Balotti and Jesse A. Finkelstein, *The Delaware Law of Corporations and Business Organizations* (2d edn 1990).

Because the takeover market inspires constant innovation in offense and defense, frequent refinements in the laws that affect takeovers is necessary. However, in contrast to most other corporation law issues, this subject is so highly charged among Delaware's usually contented corporate clients and their large shareholders that agreed-upon legislative changes have been difficult to achieve. Most of the development in Delaware has been left to the courts and private litigation.

Takeover cases are heard by the Delaware Chancery Court, a specialized, separate trial court that usually resolves corporate litigation quickly without juries. It has no responsibility for criminal or most non-corporate civil cases. In other states (and in the Federal courts) these matters clog court calendars, making it much harder for judges to handle cases quickly and effectively or to develop expert knowledge of corporate and securities matters. The right to a jury trial is an additional problem in other courts. As a result, lawyers from the rest of the country, even plaintiffs' lawyers, usually prefer the Delaware courts as a place to fight their corporate battles. They trust Delaware judges, even though they do not always admire or agree with their decisions and opinions. Plaintiffs' lawyers have an additional incentive to litigate in Delaware. Unlike most other courts, the fees awarded to plaintiffs' lawyers in the Delaware Chancery Court are not based on the hours worked. They take into account other factors, particularly what the lawyers achieved in the case. Even defendants like this system better, because it makes it easier to settle cases early.

In important takeover cases where timing is critical, the Delaware Chancery Court can be counted on to accommodate the emergency needs of the litigants. It will hear argument without time limits and make decisions very quickly. In emergency appeals, the Delaware Supreme Court can also act with great speed, sometimes the same day. In some cases it issues a preliminary oral opinion to resolve an issue immediately, long before it delivers a written opinion that attempts to delineate the precedent for future cases. The *Revlon, Macmillan* and *Time* takeover contests were decided in this way.[9]

Occasionally, important new developments, particularly takeover legislation, are first seen in states other than Delaware. More often, however, the other states have a problem: too much irrelevant politics in the legislative process. Sometimes, there is plenty of politics in the Delaware legislative process, but it is much more closely related to the corporate law subject at

---

[9] *Revlon, Inc.* v. *MacAndrews and Forbes Holdings, Inc.*, 506 A.2d 173 (Delaware Supreme Court submitted Oct. 31, 1985, oral decision Nov. 1, 1985, written opinion March 13, 1986); *Mills Acquisition Co.* v. *Macmillan, Inc.*, 559 A.2d 1261 (Delaware Supreme Court submitted Nov. 2, 1988, oral decision Nov. 2, 1988, written opinion May 3, 1989); *Paramount Communications Inc.* v. *Time Inc.*, 571 A.2d 1140 (Delaware Supreme Court submitted July 24, 1989, oral decision July 24, 1989, written opinion February 25, 1990). We discuss these three cases throughout the book, and the *Paramount* opinion is reproduced as Appendix A.12.

hand. Particularly in large states, other concerns and special interests intrude. As a result, corporation law issues get mixed up with other issues. Tiny, relatively homogeneous Delaware, on the other hand, has only two main constituencies to satisfy: the state's own interest in keeping its largest industry (corporation law) healthy and the prosperity of Delaware corporation lawyers. Although the interests of shareholders and management can occasionally collide violently, making the state's own interest difficult to discern and protect, Delaware usually has managed to do a very good balancing job.

For example, in response to a crisis in the market for directors' liability insurance in 1986 (very high premiums and low availability), Delaware quickly passed a statute to help with the problem. It allows companies to amend their charters (which requires shareholder consent) to eliminate director liability for money damages for negligent conduct, a breach of the directors' duty of care to shareholders.[10] The duty of loyalty, so important to takeover cases, was not affected. The change was suggested by lawyers from outside the state but drafted, after debate, by the usual committees of Delaware lawyers. It turned out that large shareholders of Delaware corporations did not blink. Changes in corporate charters to take advantage of the new law were routinely approved without controversy. In Illinois, in striking contrast, attempts to adopt a similar law became involved in a highly charged controversy over doctors' malpractice liability and Illinois has still progressed no further with the matter.

In short, by and large Delaware has managed to reduce risks and costs for Delaware corporations. But on takeover law the right balance has not been so easy to find. As we will see in our discussion of state antitakeover statutes,[11] Delaware has been subject to intense conflicting pressures as a result of very tough new antitakeover laws passed by other states. A continuing high level of takeover activity promises high incomes for the Delaware law industry, but shareholder groups and managements have very different interests at stake. Delaware passed a compromise antitakeover statute in 1988.[12] But to maintain its preeminence it will have to work very hard at finding new compromises that will best suit the different interests it serves.

---

[10] See Leo Herzel, Richard W. Shepro and Leo Katz, 'Next-to-last Word on Endangered Directors,' 65 *Harvard Business Review* 38 (1987).

[11] See Chapter 6.

[12] Delaware General Corporation Law §203, which we discuss in Chapter 6 Section 2.

5.3   THE FEAR OF FEDERAL PREEMPTION

All publicly traded companies are subject to extensive regulation under the Federal securities laws. Under the U.S. Constitution, as interpreted by the U.S. Supreme Court, Federal laws can override state laws expressly or by implication. In addition, listed companies also are subject to the rules of the stock exchanges on which their stock is traded. Sometimes a company will have flexibility under its state corporation law that it cannot take advantage of because of a rule of a stock exchange or the Securities and Exchange Commission.[13] However, unless the United States were to move to a system of Federal incorporation – which today appears highly unlikely – Federal law will only impinge on state corporation laws, not replace them.

Nonetheless, the possibility of Federal intervention is very important to Delaware and serves as a check on what Delaware dares to do. A dramatic example is the Unocal self-tender we discussed in Chapter 2. Unocal defeated Boone Pickens' tender offer in 1985 with an offer to repurchase, at a substantial premium, a portion of the shares of each shareholder *other than Pickens*. When the Delaware Supreme Court allowed this discriminatory tender offer, there was a strong reaction in Congress and at the SEC. Within a year, the SEC amended the Federal tender offer rules to outlaw the very conduct that the Delaware court had approved.[14]

However, the new SEC rules could not bring a halt to further innovation in the takeover market. The change in the SEC's tender offer rules negated the Delaware Supreme Court's *Unocal* decision, but only with regard to discriminatory tender offers. The more general idea that discrimination against shareholders may be allowed under some circumstances has not been disturbed by Federal action. The *Unocal* case lives on as the basis for other takeover defenses in Delaware, most notably the very important discriminatory flip-in poison pill,[15] and has been followed in that regard by legislatures in a number of other states.

Federal intervention is far from inevitable, however, even when states take a strong antitakeover position. Congress has many members with many conflicting goals. In the next chapter we discuss state antitakeover laws, which are growing rapidly both in number and in potency. In May 1989, the Chairman of the SEC threatened Federal preemption, out of irritation over

---

[13] The SEC, in turn, has limits to its jurisdiction that are set by Congress and interpreted by Federal courts. For example, in 1988 the SEC adopted a controversial rule, Rule 19c–4, prohibiting use of non-voting stock by a public company in most instances. Delaware law had not interfered with this practice. In June 1990 a U.S. Court of Appeals overturned the rule, holding that the SEC had overstepped its authority. *The Business Roundtable* v. *SEC*, 905 F.2d 406 (D.C. Cir. 1990). See Chapter 9 Section 2.

[14] *Unocal Corp.* v. *Mesa Petroleum Co.*, 493 A.2d 946 (Delaware Supreme Court 1985).

[15] Poison pills are explained in some detail in Chapter 8 and in the Glossary.

some tough new Indiana antitakeover laws.[16] At the same time both the Senate and the House were holding hearings on how to discourage hostile takeovers by reducing tax incentives for leveraged buyouts and other debt-financed acquisitions.

Some congressmen now appear to be convinced that takeovers have had a bad effect in the United States. Few appear to believe any longer that takeovers are an unqualified good thing. If Congress acts in the near future, it appears much more likely to change tax and credit rules to discourage takeovers than to protect them from state regulation.

5.4   THE COURTS' PREOCCUPATION WITH PROCEDURE AND MORALITY

Through their takeover rulings the Delaware courts strongly influence some of the most important business decisions made in the United States today. The Delaware Supreme Court is at the pinnacle of this process. Like most courts of last resort, it is a political as well as a judicial institution. It has to satisfy many groups. How the court will rule in a close case may depend as much on the court's political goals as on precedents and technical legal arguments.

By far, the court's most important political consideration is the state of Delaware. In most of the court's highly controversial corporate cases, Delaware itself is the invisible third party. Managements and their lawyers have the power to decide whether a corporation will be incorporated in Delaware or some other state. Fewer incorporations would deal a blow to Delaware's most important industry. In the past the Delaware courts were frequently criticized for having a strong bias in favor of management. A once popular academic point of view was that Delaware was leading a competition among the states to see who could provide the most pro-management law to attract new incorporations.[17] Ironically, Delaware is now falling behind in the race for more pro-management antitakeover laws.

The Delaware Supreme Court is acutely aware that shareholder organizations and institutional investors have grown increasingly active and restless. Their voting power as shareholders can prevent managements from changing the place of incorporation to Delaware from another state. On the positive side (from Delaware's perspective), they can also prevent man-

---

[16] Remarks of David Ruder on leveraged buyouts before the American Banker-Bond Buyer Conference on Strategic Corporate Restructuring and Finance, New York City, May 22, 1989. We discuss the laws in Chapter 6.

[17] See, for example, William L. Cary, 'Federalism and Corporate Law: Reflections Upon Delaware,' 83 *Yale Law Journal* 663 (1974). For a contrary view, see Ralph K. Winter, 'The "Race for the Top" Revisited,' 89 *Columbia Law Review* 1526 (1989).

agements from moving out of Delaware to states with much more favorable antitakeover laws. But most important from the standpoint of Delaware, they could provide the pressure that would lead to the Federal Government's preempting state law with a new Federal law or, if the circumstances were right, to a Federal law of incorporation that would displace Delaware law entirely.

At one time the Delaware courts had points of view about many business matters. For example, they developed their own formula for valuing companies in squeeze-out merger cases that did not have much to do with the valuation methods used by businessmen and other experts who buy and sell companies. Now they are willing to listen to the testimony of experts. For a while, mergers were not allowed without a legitimate 'business purpose.' Now any purpose that is not dishonest, including consolidating the company under a single owner, is considered purpose enough.[18]

However, the Delaware Supreme Court has continued to show a predilection for procedure and morality. There are some quite good reasons for this. Courts are expert at procedure and, to some extent, business morality. If judges are to avoid winding up as the investment strategists for a state-run economy, focusing on procedure and morality is one answer. While a court is not a good judge of whether a company was sold for the best obtainable price, it can be a quite good judge of whether the board of directors was using an unbiased procedure in conducting the sale.

Moreover, a tough procedural stance has an appearance of neutrality that helps the court to satisfy its constituencies. If the court can find really objectionable behavior its job becomes even easier. Finding a villain makes it possible to avoid offending anyone other than the people involved.

Judges deciding takeover cases often focus on whether the board was acting in good faith. Many of the courts' technical formulations of legal standards include good faith as an element. As in common speech, good faith simply means that the directors believe in what they say and do and are not just faking with empty rhetoric. Proving or disproving good faith is not easy, however. Unless there is hard evidence of bad faith, when a court examines good faith, it usually returns to procedure.

But a procedural emphasis has its own dangers. It can easily appear ad hoc, confusing and unconvincing. Decisions become unpredictable and can appear capricious. The likely result is much less respect for the Delaware legal system. Delaware courts have also created a great deal of muddle by discovering the auction as a procedural concept in takeover cases. The issue arises mainly when a board of directors has made a decision to sell a company. From its beginnings in the *Revlon* case, where the Delaware Supreme Court

---

[18] The business purpose doctrine was overruled and the old valuation methods were pretty much abandoned in *Weinberger* v. *UOP, Inc.*, 457 A.2d 701 (Delaware Supreme Court 1983).

thought the board had a conflict of interest, the idea has been evolving slowly and confusingly.[19]

These good and bad aspects of an emphasis on procedure and morality are seen in three areas to which we now turn: disclosure, use of special committees and expert advice.

5.5 DISCLOSURE

There are now open-ended ad hoc disclosure obligations under Delaware law. Unlike Federal disclosure laws there are no statutes, rules or forms to use for guidance, only occasional court decisions.[20] The Delaware Supreme Court entered the disclosure business in 1977 in the case of *Lynch* v. *Vickers Energy Corp.*[21] Before that case disclosure was a matter of Federal law. With an offhand remark about the duty of complete candor owed by directors to shareholders the court added a completely new subject for Delaware courts to deal with.

On the other hand, the same case was a precursor of developments in later cases that have been good for Delaware because they have helped to counteract the idea that there is a pro-management bias in Delaware courts. These cases, like *Lynch* v. *Vickers*, involved the rights of minority share-holders who were being squeezed out by a majority shareholder in a merger. In examining squeeze-outs, the Delaware Supreme Court has emphasized the conflict of interest faced by the board of directors, which is controlled by the majority shareholder but owes a duty of fair treatment to the minority.

An important case decided by the Delaware Supreme Court in 1983 involved the squeeze-out of 49.5% of the shares of UOP, Inc. by its majority holder, the Signal Companies. In a very influential opinion the court divided the concept of fairness into two parts: fair dealing and fair price.[22] Fair dealing, according to the court, 'embraces questions of when the transaction was timed, how it was initiated, structured, negotiated, disclosed to the directors, and how the approvals of the directors and stockholders were obtained.'[23] As to price, the court emphasized the usefulness of obtaining an

---

[19] *Revlon, Inc.* v. *MacAndrews and Forbes Holdings, Inc.*, 506 A.2d 173 (Delaware Supreme Court 1986). The subject of auctions has been important and confusing enough that we devote substantial space to it later in the book. See our other discussions of the *Revlon* case in Chapters 7, 8, 10 and 11.

[20] For a more extensive treatment of this subject, see Leo Herzel and Richard W. Shepro, 'The New Delaware Law of Disclosure' in 'Setting the Boundaries for Disclosure,' 16 *Securities Regulation Law Journal* 179, 192–195 (1988).

[21] 383 A.2d 278 (Delaware Supreme Court 1977).

[22] *Weinberger* v. *UOP, Inc.*, 457 A.2d 701 (Delaware Supreme Court 1983). We discuss other issues related to squeeze-out mergers, including their mechanics, in Chapter 10.

[23] Id. at 711.

opinion from investment bankers that the squeeze-out price was fair. Signal had obtained a fairness opinion but the court thought it was based on cursory study and was drafted too quickly. One lesson of that case is that it may be better to omit a useful step – such as a fairness opinion – than to do it badly.

Several procedures from squeeze-out merger cases have become important in takeover defense cases. One is that many conflict of interest problems can be eliminated by using an independent committee of directors. Special committees are now widely used by target boards to evaluate takeover bids.

Involving shareholders in decisions always makes board actions easier to defend. In the *Weinberger* case the court said that if a merger is conditioned on approval by the minority shareholders then a shareholder who challenges the merger has the burden of proving unfairness. When approval by the minority is not a condition to the merger the burden of showing fairness falls on the majority. Approval does not have this cleansing action, however, if the minority is not treated with what the Delaware Supreme Court calls 'complete candor' and given all the information it might need to evaluate the merger.[24]

5.6 SPECIAL COMMITTEES

Because courts hearing takeover cases are so sensitive about conflicts of interest, one of the most important procedural steps a target board of directors can take is to turn over takeover decisions to a committee of directors who are independent of management – the special committee. Theoretically, this should eliminate all but the minimal suspicion of a conflict of interest that, as we explained in Chapter 2, appears always to be present in evaluating any takeover defense. In Delaware and most other states, a board of directors has the right to delegate most of its power to board committees. A special committee does not have the legal power actually to sell the company but if the full board adopts the committee's recommendations the result is the same from the standpoint of conflict of interest. The board is under great pressure to accept the committee's recommendations – rejection without a very good reason would usually be fatal in court. In addition, most crisis committees of this kind include a majority of the directors.

The effectiveness of this approach has been borne out by the actual behavior of special committees. Special committees, armed with independent legal and investment banking advisers, quickly develop their own strong – sometimes truculent – personalities. Members tend to take their special committee responsibilities very seriously, even if in the past they appeared to follow the chief executive officer without much independent questioning. They must do

---

[24] See *Lynch* v. *Vickers Energy Corp.*, 383 A.2d 278 (Delaware Supreme Court 1977).

so for legal reasons and to protect their reputations, but there are also important practical, psychological considerations pushing in the same direction. Committee members, like actors, frequently develop intense feelings about the roles to which they have been assigned. Moreover, a committee hires its own experts who tend to have a strong economic and professional bias toward independence from management and its experts.

Operating a special committee tends to bring out the abilities of board members, many of whom are CEOs of other companies. Committees usually function more effectively than boards as a whole because they are smaller. However, there is a practical limit on smallness – the risk of offending independent board members if they are not included in the special committee.

The runaway special committee is quite common when management is a bidder for the company. Up to the point when a special committee takes over, the CEO is still very much in charge. He can put a company in play by making a bid, as Chairman Ross Johnson of RJR Nabisco, Inc. did in 1988, whether the board likes it or not. Committees know that a competent chief executive officer usually knows much more about the company than any other bidder. Part of a special committee's job is to reduce the CEO's advantages as much as is practical by assuring that competing bidders have access to detailed information about the company and time to digest it.

In the case of RJR Nabisco, the special committee took charge very quickly. It did not favor or even attempt to please Ross Johnson. In fact, it appeared to be soliciting competing bidders with fervor. Because there was enormous publicity about the tremendous amount of money Johnson and other members of management would receive in the buyout, psychological factors, such as feelings of betrayal, moral disapproval and envy, probably contributed to the committee's aggressive independence.

Once a committee begins to insist on receiving competing bids, a management LBO or other favorite transaction of management will often lose out to higher bids from outsiders, as did Johnson's bid for RJR. In fact, that consideration is a very important factor in keeping down the number of management LBOs. Most managements do not want to put their jobs up for auction.

5.7 EXPERT ADVICE

An extreme example of the Delaware Supreme Court's emphasis on procedure and morality is its opinion in *Smith* v. *Van Gorkom*,[25] which we have mentioned before. (In this instance moralism might be a better choice of word than morality.) The directors of Trans Union Corporation had without much

[25] 488 A.2d 858 (Delaware Supreme Court 1985). See Chapter 2 Section 2.

deliberation approved a sale of the company to the entirely unrelated Pritzker family at a 50% premium. Although the Chancery Court approved the transaction, the Delaware Supreme Court reversed, finding the directors of Trans Union Corporation liable for gross negligence.

In the court's view, they had approved the sale without having adequate information about whether the price was fair. One of the procedural lapses that appeared to disturb the court the most was that the board had not hired an investment banker to advise it on the fairness of the price the Pritzkers were paying. Another was that they had not read the legal papers covering the transaction.

It is understandable and mainly laudable that courts encourage the use of investment bankers and other experts. This emphasis has some important drawbacks, however. The most important is that it can lead to useless, expensive legal formalism. In many instances encouraging reliance on outside financial experts by directors, who are themselves experts with extensive management and financial skills, may just lead to paying for a lot of expensive advice that is not really necessary. Reading legal papers instead of relying on summaries can also be a waste of directors' time and, worse, a distraction from the main issues. Bad decisions can be made while observing all the formalities. Good decisions can be reached without them. In short, special procedures, however sanctified, do not assure good decisions.

Legal advice can be as important a procedural consideration for a court as investment banking advice. When adopting an unusual antitakeover device the directors must rely on lawyers. On the other hand, insisting that directors understand the legal intricacies of what they are doing is another kind of legal formalism. For example, when poison pills were novel, directors' understanding of the legal and strategic details of the defense were often tested in lengthy out-of-court depositions and examinations in court.

5.8   THE LIMITS OF THE PROCEDURAL APPROACH

Emphasizing procedure forces courts into making fine distinctions between what is a business decision – to which it should defer – and what is a procedure – to which it should not give much respect. It becomes critical whether something is classified as part of the 'substance' or of the 'procedure,' a very elusive distinction. For example, why should the court have viewed Trans Union's failure to hire an investment banker[26] as part of the decision-making procedure in the merger rather than as a substantive decision about when to seek advice? Probably, because the court just did not like something about the deal and was looking for a procedural explanation. But this ad hoc

[26] Id.

finding was disorienting for everyone who must rely on Delaware corporation law.

The same can be said about some of the other procedural issues the court raised in the Trans Union case. Why should the failure to read the merger documents be viewed as part of the procedure rather than a decision about the best way for the board to deal with legal minutiae? For that matter, why should the failure of the board to deliberate more than two hours be viewed as part of the procedure rather than the substance of a decision about how long to meet under the circumstances?

Many perfectly sound legal distinctions become confusing in borderline cases. In the years since the Trans Union decision the courts have been forced by their own past decisions into making finer and finer procedural distinctions. For example, in a shareholder challenge to the RJR auction the Delaware Chancery Court reviewed a decision by the board of directors not to request an additional 'highest and best' bid from the two remaining competitors, who had made similar bids in the last round of the auction. The court concluded that this procedural decision by the board about how to run an auction was itself an important business decision and, on the facts of the case, it merited the protection of the business judgment rule.[27] But in a similar setting in the *Macmillan* case two months earlier when the Chancery Court had approved another abbreviated auction, it was reversed.[28] The reversal of Vice Chancellor Jacobs' opinion in that case is also a revealing example of an important difference between the Delaware Chancery Court (more practical) and the Supreme Court (more inclined to make moral statements).

It may be that the difference between the two cases can be better explained by differences as to how the board of directors handled conflicts of interest.[29] In the *RJR* case, the Chancery Court appears to have been convinced that the conflict had been resolved by the use of a special committee of obvious independence. But in the *Macmillan* case the special committee appointed was really under the control of the management bidders and the advisers management selected for them. On top of that, the management bidders were also closely involved with the auction and there were many clumsy procedural mistakes.

---

[27] *In re RJR Nabisco, Inc. Shareholders Litigation,* Fed. Sec. L. Rep. (CCH) ¶94,194 (Delaware Chancery Court 1989).
[28] *Mills Acquisition Co.* v. *Macmillan, Inc.,* Fed. Sec. L. Rep. (CCH) ¶94,071 (Delaware Chancery Court 1988), rev'd 559 A.2d 1261 (Delaware Supreme Court 1989).
[29] See our more detailed discussion of the *Macmillan* case in Chapter 7.

6

How State Antitakeover Laws Change
the Balance

THE fortunes of takeover offense and defense have been shifting back and forth for years. Federal tender offer rules and court decisions have long been key elements in the balance. Innovations such as junk bonds on the offensive side and poison pill rights on the defensive have been very important. Recently, however, without fanfare, the focus has shifted to state statutes.

Takeovers are generally unpopular at the local level for obvious commonsense reasons: concern about the loss of high-paying executive and manufacturing jobs and reduction in support for charitable and community projects. Beginning with the takeover boom in the 1960s, many states have tried to use their generally acknowledged power to regulate the internal affairs of corporations they have chartered in ways that restrict hostile takeovers. For state legislatures this has proven to be an uncertain process of trial and error to find the right combination of effectiveness and constitutionality.

The first state antitakeover laws were held unconstitutional on the ground that they interfered unreasonably with Federal tender offer regulation and with interstate commerce.[1] Then, in 1987, in *CTS Corp.* v. *Dynamics Corp. of America*,[2] the U.S. Supreme Court held that a state could restrict hostile takeovers through the use of its corporation laws. The subject of the case was an Indiana statute that prevented a hostile bidder from voting its shares before it won a special shareholder referendum.

The decision, somewhat of a surprise, appears to have been a turning point. It came immediately in the wake of the Wall Street insider trading scandals. Some of Wall Street's magic was gone. The efficient-market euphoria behind the takeover boom had begun to cool. The timing and outcome of the Supreme Court's decision were not entirely coincidental.

As a result of the decision, an Indiana-style antitakeover law would automatically have the Supreme Court's blessing, but not many states were interested in placing all of their antitakeover bets on that kind of statute. Instead, other states have been devising laws more to their liking, trying to find statutes that would be effective and constitutional.

---

[1] *Edgar* v. *MITE Corp.*, 457 U.S. 624 (1982).
[2] 481 U.S. 69 (1987).

States have taken a number of very different approaches.[3] One that is very important and now commonplace restricts mergers and similar transactions with an unwelcome large shareholder.[4] Even Delaware has enacted a mild version of that one. These laws have great strategic importance because they can prevent or seriously interfere with many types of bids.

The latest and potentially even more important type of state statute expands the powers of directors by allowing them to consider the long-term interests of the shareholders, the company and various other constituencies such as employees, customers, suppliers and local communities. The wording of these new 'constituency' laws usually makes it clear that they apply even when the board of a target company is facing a bid at a premium price. Combined with 'flip-in' poison pill rights the result in many situations could be conclusive – no takeover. We discuss these new laws extensively later in this chapter.

The principal constitutional arguments against antitakeover statutes are that they interfere unreasonably with Federal tender offer regulation and with interstate commerce. The New York statute restricting mergers played an important role in a number of takeover battles before its constitutionality was tested. In early 1989 a Federal trial court considered its constitutionality in an opinion that made what had appeared complex and controversial seem rather simple.[5] If the approach of this case is followed by other courts, any state antitakeover law would be held constitutional so long as it does not directly conflict with Federal regulations on takeovers or attempt to cover companies incorporated elsewhere.

Several months after the New York statute was upheld, an influential U.S. Court of Appeals held a similar Wisconsin statute constitutional.[6] This decision is important partly because the author of the opinion, Frank Easterbrook, is a scholarly and influential lawyer-economist. Judge Easterbrook came to the bench from the law faculty at the University of Chicago. He is an aggressive proponent of efficient market theory. His prolific academic writings forcefully argue that the threat of takeovers is crucial for economic efficiency because it keeps managers in constant fear for their jobs. Takeover defense, he argues, leaves shareholders and the economy decidedly worse off.[7]

Judge Easterbrook made it plain in his opinion on the Wisconsin statute

---

[3] An enumeration of state statutes is contained in the Appendix, together with some key examples from the laws of New York and New Jersey. Where we refer to a state statute without giving a citation the statute is included in the enumeration.

[4] See Section 1 later in the chapter.

[5] *Vernitron Corp.* v. *Kollmorgen Corp.*, 89 Civ. 241 (S.D.N.Y., Feb. 9, 1989) (unpublished transcript).

[6] *Amanda Acquisition Corp.* v. *Universal Foods Corp.*, 877 F.2d 496 (7th Cir. 1989).

[7] See, for example, Frank H. Easterbrook and Gregg A. Jarrell, 'Do Targets Gain From Defeating Tender Offers?' 59 *New York University Law Review* 277 (1984); Frank H. Easterbrook and Daniel R. Fischel, 'Corporate Control Transactions,' 91 *Yale Law Journal* 698 (1982).

that he has not altered any of these views. But for precedential and legal theoretical reasons he would not fight this battle on constitutional grounds. 'A law can be both economic folly and constitutional,' he wrote, quoting a concurring opinion by another conservative former University of Chicago law professor, Supreme Court Justice Antonin Scalia, in the *CTS* case.

In the light of these opinions, it is hard to see any constitutional limit on what antitakeover laws the states can adopt, so long as they observe two restrictions. First, they can only regulate activities of corporations incorporated in their state. Illinois, for example, cannot regulate all offers to shareholders who live in Illinois, as it once unsuccessfully tried to do, and New York cannot regulate takeovers of all companies listed on the New York Stock Exchange.[8] Second, the states cannot directly interfere with Federal tender offer law and the SEC rules that establish the mechanics of tender offers. Instead, they must design their state statutes in terms of traditional corporation law subjects.

There are good reasons to think this trend will continue. For one thing, beginning with the U.S. Supreme Court's 1987 pronouncement on the subject in the *CTS* case, courts have become less inclined than they had been to assume that takeovers are necessarily a good thing.[9] In general, in the U.S., ardor for hostile takeovers appears to be waning rapidly. There are signs everywhere that the old consensus supporting the takeover boom has broken up.[10] In the meantime, because of Reagan and Bush appointments, the Supreme Court and the Federal judiciary generally are rapidly becoming more conservative and, therefore, more reluctant to interfere with state legislation. The Court's controversial 1989 decision to allow states greater freedom to regulate abortions is another example of the same approach.[11]

6.1   LAWS THAT RESTRICT MERGERS

Laws that restrict mergers are among the most effective antitakeover statutes encountered today. Mergers are an important, often crucial, final step in takeovers. Some, but not many, bidders can afford to buy shares and live with minority shareholders indefinitely. In leveraged bids, a merger to eliminate minority shareholders following a successful tender offer is usually essential.

---

[8] See, for example, *TLX Acquisition Corp.* v. *The Telex Corp.*, 679 F. Supp. 1022 (W.D. Okla. 1987), which overturned an Oklahoma law purporting to regulate takeovers of companies with a significant Oklahoma presence that were incorporated under the laws of other states, such as Delaware.

[9] *CTS Corp.* v. *Dynamics Corp. of America*, 481 U.S. 69 (1987).

[10] See, for example, Leo Herzel and Richard W. Shepro, 'Bondholder Suits in the U.S.,' *Financial Times* (Dec. 21, 1989), p. 8.

[11] *Webster* v. *Reproductive Health Services*, 109 S.Ct. 3040 (1989).

A statute that rules out a merger makes it impossible or very hard for such a bidder to obtain financing.

The reason is that without 100% share ownership, control of the target is severely limited. It is likely to be illegal self-dealing under state law if the acquirer borrows money for its special benefit using the target's cash flow and assets as security. Similarly, selling off parts of the business mainly to meet the financing needs of the acquirer may create legal concerns. Lenders to highly leveraged borrowers do not like this kind of risk. With good reason: one example is the enormous LBO bankruptcy that came about at the end of 1989 because Hillsborough Holding Corporation could not sell assets to raise cash to pay interest charges. The hold on Hillsborough's assets was caused by a contingent liability (an asbestosis lawsuit), not the rights of minority shareholders, but the effect was similarly devastating.[12] And even unleveraged buyers usually are not keen to operate under legal restrictions, or with minority shareholders who may prove difficult to deal with.

At the same time, however, these statutes are by no means a universal takeover defense. By eliminating competition from leveraged bidders, these statutes may encourage acquisitions by patient, well-financed acquirers. After gaining control, these bidders can buy most of the minority stock in the market at a modest price. Faced with that kind of acquirer, minority shareholders have little incentive to hold on to their stock. They may not be receiving dividends, their legal leverage against such an acquirer is small, and they could not expect to receive cash in a merger for several years.[13] In most instances seeking appraisal is a cumbersome, expensive process. Large shareholders and arbitragers usually feel they have better things to do with their money than waiting for a merger and appraisal five or so years later. In these circumstances, their best alternative may be to sell their shares to the acquirer, either directly or by selling their shares in the stock market.

Sometimes even bidders with plenty of cash and borrowing power may find that statutes restricting mergers are very troublesome. A merger may be essential for integration with the bidder's other businesses. For example, one of the principal reasons the Bank of New York wanted to acquire Irving Trust[14] was potential cost savings from integration. Impediments to a merger in the New York statute troubled Bank of New York throughout the long takeover battle.

The New York statute was the first, and is still one of the strongest, laws restricting mergers with hostile bidders. Anyone who acquires 20% or more of

---

[12] See the discussion of Hillsborough's problems in Chapter 15 Section 2.

[13] See Chapter 10 Section 4 and the Glossary for discussions of squeeze-out mergers and of appraisal rights, which give minority shareholders the right to receive a cash amount determined in a court proceeding if they dissent from a merger.

[14] See the discussions of the Irving Trust takeover in Chapter 13 Section 4 and Chapter 15 Section 1.

the target's voting stock becomes an 'interested shareholder' and is prohibited from engaging in a business combination with the company for five years. 'Business combination' is defined very broadly to include squeeze-out mergers that eliminate the remaining minority shareholders, as well as every conceivable alternative transaction. There is an exemption if the target company's board has approved either the particular business combination being proposed or the stock purchase that put the interested shareholder over the 20% threshold.

The New York statute applies only to New York corporations that either have their principal offices in New York State or have at least 250 employees or 25% of all their employees located in New York State. Originally this limitation was even stricter, requiring the corporation to have its principal office in the state. Restrictions in addition to incorporation in the state were thought (incorrectly, it turns out) to be important in reducing the risk of constitutional attack. Probably a desire to encourage economic growth in New York was also important.

Trying to restrict mergers has a long history as an antitakeover device. Before state legislatures got involved, companies tried to do much the same thing, with shareholder approval, through charter provisions making use of the substantial flexibility that state corporation laws afford. These earlier devices are still in effect in many companies' charters. With shareholder approval, a company can include a provision in its charter restricting mergers with large shareholders. A typical such provision specifies that no large stockholder can merge with the company without paying a 'fair price' – generally defined through a complex, sometimes deliberately ambiguous, formula. There is usually an alternative or additional requirement: a high shareholder vote (for example, 80%) or a vote of those shareholders who are not affiliated with the large shareholder. Since the shares that the interested shareholder does not control are likely to be strategic or dedicated holdouts, acquiring more shares may make it harder, not easier, to meet the second test. These fair price provisions are designed to deter any bidder whose acquisition strategy or financing depends on being able to squeeze out the minority quickly at a low price.[15]

A great many corporations adopted fair price provisions during the 1970s and early 1980s. However, they were not very effective against the wealthy companies that comprised most of the bidders then. After institutional investors began to rebel at approving antitakeover charter amendments, a new

---

[15] The New York and similar statutes are also designed to have an effect even beyond the initial five years, after which a fair price provision takes over. The interested shareholder may then engage in a business combination only if the consideration paid by the interested shareholder satisfies statutory fair price criteria or if it obtains the approval of a majority of the unaffiliated shares.

technique that did not require shareholder approval was developed – the poison pill.

The first poison pills were based on the same theory. They were designed to deter mergers by making them prohibitively expensive. After a merger with a hostile bidder, the shareholders who had been squeezed out would have the right to buy stock in the surviving corporation for half price.[16] Refined poison pills were later developed to plug the strategic gap the original pill left for a bidder who did not propose a merger. For example, faced with this early pill when he was pursuing Crown Zellerbach, Sir James Goldsmith realized that the way around the pill was to buy more than 50% of the target's stock and then engage in a cat-and-mouse game with the minority shareholders. After accumulating his majority he devised a set of transactions to avoid the poison pill rights and settled lawsuits giving the holders of the rights less than a dollar a right.[17] State laws restricting mergers leave the same strategic gap.

6.2   THE DELAWARE VERSION OF THE NEW YORK STATUTE

As other states passed antitakeover laws in the late 1980s, Delaware came under increasing pressure from company managements and lawyers to do something. After lengthy debate, it adopted a much softened version of the New York law.[18] Because most Delaware corporations are based outside the state, it would not have been acceptable to limit the law's coverage, as New York and other states did, to companies with a strong economic tie to the state. Instead, the law applies to all Delaware corporations. As it turned out, this difference did not weaken the statute's legal position and its constitutionality has been repeatedly affirmed.[19]

In Delaware, it takes only 15% ownership to trigger the statute. But otherwise the statute is much less protective of targets than the New York law. The waiting period before a merger is three years, rather than five.[20] These compromises reflect the complicated corporate law politics in Delaware.

The statute does not apply if the interested shareholder acquires 85% of

---

[16] For more details about poison pills see Chapter 8 and the Glossary.

[17] *In re Crown Zellerbach*, No. 85 C 3286 (N.D. Ill. 1986). See also the discussion of the Crown Zellerbach pill and its defects in Chapter 8.

[18] Delaware General Corporation Law §203.

[19] *City Capital Associates Ltd. Partnership* v. *Interco Inc.*, 696 F. Supp. 1551 (D. Del. Sept. 23, 1988); *RP Acquisition Corp.* v. *Staley Continental, Inc.*, 686 F. Supp. 476 (D. Del. 1988); *BNS Inc.* v. *Koppers Co.*, 683 F. Supp. 458 (D. Del. 1988).

[20] However, in the Delaware statute there is no fair price restriction afterward although minority shareholders would still have the traditional appraisal remedy if they thought the squeeze-out merger price was too low. We discuss appraisal rights in Chapter 10 Section 4.

the target's stock not owned by directors, officers and certain employee stock plans, in the same transaction in which it becomes an interested shareholder. Generally, this means a tender offer must begin when the bidder owns less than 15% and must reach 85% in one step. A 15% block of stock in friendly hands can make this exemption unavailable.[21]

Like New York's statute, the Delaware statute is neutralized if the target board approves the stock purchase or business combination before the person becomes an interested shareholder. Moreover, it does not apply once a target has agreed to be sold to a third party. As a result, the Delaware statute cannot shield a friendly transaction from competition. (However, it is not clear that the courts would allow the New York statute to be used for that purpose.) This loophole presented a very technical problem in the Time–Warner–Paramount fight. Paramount went to the Delaware Chancery Court for a declaratory judgment and injunctions on the theory that Time's agreement with Warner neutralized the statute. In form, however, Warner was merging with a subsidiary of Time, not Time itself. The court denied the request for an injunction without ruling on the point. The statute probably will be amended to clear up this ambiguity.

The Delaware statute is also inapplicable if the business combination is approved (at any time) by the target's directors and by shareholders controlling two-thirds of the target's shares, excluding shares held by the interested shareholder. In addition to the political considerations, these loopholes were included to assure the constitutionality of the Delaware statute.[22] However, the judicial climate has changed enough that these loopholes appear not to be necessary anymore to assure constitutionality.

6.3   LAWS THAT RESTRICT VOTING

The Indiana statute that was held constitutional by the U.S. Supreme Court in the *CTS* case appears to be fading in importance. Indiana and many other states still have the statute, often along with several other antitakeover laws.

These statutes provide that a purchaser who crosses certain specified ownership thresholds (usually 20%, $33\frac{1}{3}$% and 50%) will not be permitted to vote any newly acquired shares unless the other shareholders (excluding the interested shareholders and directors) vote at a special meeting to give voting rights to the shares. In practice, no one would buy a large portion of a corporation's shares without knowing whether they could be voted. As a

---

[21] This was the issue in *Shamrock Holdings, Inc.* v. *Polaroid Corp.*, 559 A.2d 257 (Delaware Chancery Court 1989). See Chapter 2 Section 4 and Chapter 15 Section 3.

[22] *City Capital Associates Ltd. Partnership* v. *Interco Inc.*, 696 F. Supp. 1551 (D. Del. 1988); *RP Acquisition Corp.* v. *Staley Continental, Inc.*, 686 F. Supp. 476 (D. Del. 1988); *BNS Inc.* v. *Koppers Co.*, 683 F. Supp. 458 (D. Del. 1988).

result what the statute really means is that a bidder must secure prior shareholder approval before crossing any of the ownership thresholds. In addition, many of the statutes give minority shareholders a right to force the company to buy their shares in an appraisal proceeding if a bidder wins shareholder approval at a special meeting and acquires a majority of the shares.

The strategic effect of these statutes is obscure and untested. One reason Delaware did not adopt an Indiana-style statute was the concern of some lawyers that such a law might do more to attract raiders than to repel them. A bidder, for example, may be quite ready to take advantage of the statute by acquiring a foothold stake in the target that is not large enough to trigger a shareholder vote, and then making a tender offer that is contingent on shareholder approval. Considering the short-term outlook of U.S. shareholders, it appears quite likely that a majority would vote in favor of the bid if the premium were high enough. Thereafter, the directors would be hard pressed to resist the takeover, since they would then appear to be defying the shareholders' will.

The shareholder vote would, in effect, have put the company on the auction block. Since it would be clear that the shareholders want the company sold and what price is acceptable, the bidder could either buy the company or sell his shares at a profit to someone else. In short, the law does something shrewd negotiators always try to avoid: it invites your opponent to undermine the negotiator (the board of directors, in this case), by dealing directly with the principal (the shareholders) who may cave in at a point at which the negotiator could have held out for a much better deal. But, as we have frequently observed, shareholders do not trust boards completely in these matters.

6.4 HEIGHTENED DISCLOSURE STATUTES

At least 21 states have statutes that require bidders to make disclosures beyond those required by Federal law. Though rarely fatal, these laws pose one more burden for bidders, and give the target company grounds to complain in court about inadequate disclosures. However, state regulators and courts have a strong incentive to keep enforcement of these statutes reasonable. So long as the additional disclosures are minor and do not interfere with the time sequence provided for in Federal law, these laws are probably constitutional. But if the additional disclosures become burdensome, the Federal courts are likely to find them in conflict with the very extensive Federal regulation of disclosure in tender offers.

6.5 FAIR PRICE LAWS

At least 17 states have enacted fair price statutes, which are similar in purpose and effect to the fair price charter provisions we discussed before. These statutes do not deal directly with tender offers or other means of acquiring large blocks of shares. Instead, like the first poison pills and the New York and Delaware laws we have discussed, they try to make it difficult and expensive to eliminate minority shareholders by restricting mergers. For example, the Maryland statute requires that any business combination involving a Maryland corporation and a holder of 10% or more of the stock must be recommended by the board of directors and approved by 80% of the outstanding shares and two-thirds of all shares not held by an interested shareholder. An exception is created where the compensation received by minority shareholders satisfies the statute's fair price formula, which is defined as one that equals or exceeds the highest price paid by the interested shareholder during the previous two years for the corporation's stock, including the price paid in the first step of the transaction.

After the *CTS, Universal Foods* and *Vernitron* cases,[23] these statutes are almost certainly constitutional when limited to corporations incorporated in the same state.

6.6 SPECIAL APPRAISAL RIGHTS LAWS (PUT STATUTES)

Maine, Pennsylvania and Utah have adopted special appraisal rights statutes, which in effect give shareholders a put to any person who acquires more than a specified percentage of the target's stock (25 or 30%). The put price is fair value, which specifically includes a premium for the value of control of the corporation.

The constitutionality of these laws may be a somewhat close question since they directly regulate the large shareholder, rather than the target corporation and impose a tender offer requirement. In the *CTS* case the Supreme Court placed great emphasis on the traditional right of the states to regulate state-chartered corporations. Although state laws often protect dissenting shareholders in mergers by requiring the surviving corporation to pay fair value for their shares, state corporation statutes have not typically required shareholders to buy shares. It could also be argued (somewhat weakly) that forcing

[23] *CTS Corp.* v. *Dynamics Corp. of America,* 481 U.S. 69 (1987); *Amanda Acquisition Corp.* v. *Universal Foods Corp.,* 877 F.2d 496 (7th Cir. 1989); *Vernitron Corp.* v. *Kollmorgen Corp.,* 89 Civ. 241 (S.D.N.Y., Feb. 9, 1989) (unpublished transcript).

large shareholders to make tender offers conflicts with Federal regulation of tender offers and, therefore, with Federal supremacy.

6.7 A NEW WAVE OF STATE ANTITAKEOVER STATUTES

Far more radically, some states are adopting antitakeover laws that alter the traditional relationship between directors and shareholders. These new laws say specifically that they apply in takeover situations. They grant boards of directors the discretion to act in what they consider to be the long-term interests of the shareholders and the company and they may take into account various other constituencies such as employees, customers, suppliers and local communities. Some companies in other states have obtained shareholder approval to insert provisions of a more limited sort in their charters. In practical terms, state laws are better for the target than charter amendments. They do not require shareholder approval, which is becoming increasingly difficult to obtain for antitakeover measures, and their legality under state law is unassailable.

So far, a number of states, including Illinois, Indiana, Massachusetts, New York, New Jersey, Ohio and Pennsylvania, have adopted laws explicitly broadening the discretion of directors who are facing takeover bids. However, proposals for similar legislation are appearing across the country. Many of these statutes and bills also include provisions that legalize discriminatory flip-in poison pills. Unless directors can use this high-powered defense, their expanded discretion would be of no avail in the face of a tender offer made directly to shareholders. So far, Delaware is not among the states that have adopted these laws. However, Delaware courts sometimes talk as though directors have these rights, although as yet these remarks have not appeared in a case where the issue was very focused.[24]

The New York and Ohio statutes allow directors who are facing a takeover bid to consider both the long-term and the short-term interests 'of the corporation and its shareholders.' Ohio's version adds, 'including the possibility that these interests may be best served by the continued independence of the corporation.'[25]

Indiana has gone further. In the vanguard on takeover defense, it already had a statute giving directors the discretion to consider the effects of a hostile takeover on the community, employees, customers and suppliers, and anyone else they might consider relevant. A February 1989 amendment allows direc-

---

[24] *Unocal Corp.* v. *Mesa Petroleum Co.*, 493 A.2d 946 (Delaware Supreme Court 1985); *In re RJR Nabisco, Inc. Shareholders Litigation*, Fed. Sec. L. Rep. (CCH) ¶94,194 (Delaware Chancery Court 1989); *Paramount Communications Inc.* v. *Time Inc.*, 571 A.2d 1140 (Delaware Supreme Court 1990) (reproduced in Appendix A.12); *TW Services, Inc.* v. *SWT Acquisition Corp.*, Fed. Sec. L. Rep. (CCH) ¶94,334 (Delaware Chancery Court 1989).

[25] Ohio Rev. Code Ann. §1701.59; New York Business Corporation Law §717(b).

tors to consider the long run and says outright that their discretion is not constrained by any effect their action might have on a proposed takeover or on the possibility of shareholders receiving a premium bid. On top of that, the statute specifically endorses the right of directors not to redeem poison pill rights. In a curious aside, the statute also says that courts should not follow 'certain judicial decisions in Delaware and other jurisdictions' that require redemption of these rights.[26] The aside probably was intended to deal with a decision of a U.S. Court of Appeals applying Delaware law to an Indiana company to fill gaps in Indiana corporation law. The opinion was critical of a poison pill.[27]

The logical outcome of these statutes is that in many circumstances they could easily be the long-sought-after defense to unwelcome takeovers for target boards. Poison pill defenses against takeovers would become subject to the same business judgment rules as other board actions. Even when facing a premium bid, the directors would not have to redeem the pill. Since the duties of directors to shareholders have traditionally been governed by state law, it is highly unlikely, in the light of the U.S. Supreme Court's decision in the *CTS* case, that any of these statutes will be held unconstitutional.

However, whether these statutes will really stop takeovers will depend on more than technical state laws. Directors will not attempt to face down angry shareholders who own most of the company's shares unless they have strong moral support in influential governmental and community quarters. Even then, directors can be removed in proxy fights, although some poison pills are now being drafted to make it impossible for the new directors to eliminate the pill.

These constituency statutes raise old issues that economists and lawyers discussed for many years under traditional corporation statutes: should it be legal for boards of directors to consider other interests?[28] For example, should directors be allowed to give away shareholder money to charity or keep open an unprofitable plant to benefit the community? Outside of takeovers, the legal answer is that directors can do all these things, under the business

---

[26] Indiana Code §23.1.26, sections 1(d), (f) and (g). A Pennsylvania statute adopted in 1990 specifically instructs directors that they need not treat shareholders as any more important than their other constituencies:

The board of directors, committees of the board and individual directors shall not be required, in considering the best interests of the corporation or the effects of any action, to regard any corporate interest or the interests of any particular group affected by such action as a dominant or controlling interest or factor.

Pennsylvania Senate Bill No. 1310 (1989 Session). This controversial statute also includes a disgorgement provision under which a target company can recover the profits of a person or group that sells its stock within 18 months of seeking or obtaining control of the target. Ohio adopted a similar statute, also in 1990. These provisions are likely to deter bids by investors who are trying mainly to stir up takeover interest and attract other bidders. They should have less effect on dedicated, well financed acquirers.

[27] The opinion is *CTS Corp.* v. *Dynamics Corp. of America*, 794 F.2d 250 (7th Cir. 1986).

[28] See, for example, Oliver E. Williamson, *The Economics of Discretionary Behavior: Managerial Objectives in a Theory of the Firm* (1967); Milton Friedman, *Capitalism and Freedom* (1962); Adolph Berle and Gardiner Means, *The Modern Corporation and Private Property* (1933).

judgment rule, with very little likelihood of judicial interference except in extreme cases.[29] All the directors need to prevail is to assert the most rudimentary reasons for believing the activity will benefit the corporation. Probably the courts do not want to discourage corporate altruism, but they also have often recognized that altruism may pay off from a business standpoint by putting the company in a favorable light.

Cash bids for a company, however, are not part of its ordinary business. The shareholders are being offered cash to sell out. If they accept the offer they no longer have any concern about the future business of the company. As we will see in the next section, this is closely related to the reason the new statutes clearly authorizing board consideration of shareholder and company long-term interests in takeover situations are unlikely to be much help in protecting a friendly sale favored by management against another bid. By agreeing to a sale, the board appears to have conceded that there is no long-term interest to protect.

There is some irony in these new stockholder laws being adopted at the behest of large companies. Statutes requiring businesses to cater to interests other than their shareholders were being proposed long ago by labor unions, consumer groups and others who would like to broaden participation in corporations in the U.S. In other countries similar laws sometimes require important decisions to be approved by worker representatives or community groups. One very important difference is that these new laws, motivated by very different concerns, leave the questions of when and how to consider other groups exclusively to the directors.

6.8   THE NEXT RESPONSE FROM THE COURTS

The new state laws broadening directors' discretion are an attempt to alter the balance between takeover offense and defense in a decisive way. Target directors facing a high premium bid come under tremendous legal and psychological pressure from the bidder, the shareholders and the arbitrage market either to capitulate or find a better transaction. For target directors, the promise of the new state statutes is that for the first time independence may become a real possibility.

However, whether these new state laws will really provide the basis for staying independent remains to be seen. Their practical success will depend on the attitudes, determination and abilities of target directors and the reaction of the courts and society. So far, other highly potent defenses, like

---

[29] See, for example, *Steinway* v. *Steinway and Sons,* 40 N.Y.S. 718 (N.Y. Sup. Ct. 1896) which upheld the famous piano manufacturing corporation's construction of houses for employees and contributions to a neighborhood church, schools and library after a plant relocation.

poison pills, although very effective in obtaining higher prices for target shareholders, have turned out to be of little help in assuring independence once a bid is made.[30]

Judges may be uneasy with the new laws because they conflict with traditional corporation law concepts. They are used to putting shareholders' interests first and they have been told by economists that this is right. However, except for constitutional reasons, courts do not have the power to overrule or ignore an unambiguous statute. Within the constitutional limits set by the U.S. Supreme Court from time to time, state legislatures have the right to remake corporation law.

Nevertheless, the new statutes are unlikely to be interpreted so as to give target directors an entirely free hand. Once a decision has been made to sell the company, the directors, in practical terms, would have a hard time arguing that a lower-priced bid favored by management will be in the long-term interests of shareholders when compared to a higher-priced hostile bid. If the shareholders are being bought out for cash either way, there is no long run for them.[31] This economic fact is not changed by the statutes. On the other hand, in stock mergers, such as the Time–Warner merger, the shareholders continue and an argument about a long-run point of view is much more convincing.

The new statutes that allow directors to consider stakeholders other than shareholders are a different matter. Employees, for example, may fare quite differently under one buyer than another. In defending its combination with Warner, Time, for example, argued that its distinctive corporate culture could not be preserved under Paramount.[32] Still, it will not be enough for the directors simply to invoke generalities about long-term value and community interests. Directors' actions are likely to be examined very carefully by courts. Probably, courts once again will turn to the subject they know best, procedure, and will examine closely how the directors arrived at their decisions.[33]

Courts, for example, may overrule directors' defensive measures if they think they were so sloppy that they could not have been taken in good faith. The best way for a board to establish its good faith will be with careful procedures that connect the actions taken to the words in the statute. Bidders will try to attack target boards' theories by showing lack of preparation, inconsistencies and explanations concocted after the fact. Conflict of interest concerns may become even more important than they are now.

---

[30] See Chapter 8.

[31] The Delaware Chancellor, William Allen, made a similar observation analyzing the role of long-term interests in the absence of a special statute. *TW Services, Inc.* v. *SWT Acquisition Corp.*, Fed. Sec. L. Rep. (CCH) ¶94,334 (Delaware Chancery Court 1989).

[32] *Paramount Communications Inc.* v. *Time Inc.*, Fed. Sec. L. Rep. (CCH) ¶94,514 (Delaware Chancery Court, July 14, 1989), affirmed 571 A.2d 1140 (Delaware Supreme Court 1990).

[33] See Chapter 5 Sections 4 and 8.

These statutes often allow the directors to consider the long-run interests of the *corporation* in addition to those of the shareholders. Before they were enacted the legal system had not had to make this distinction and the exact nature of these corporate interests had usually been an abstract, unrewarding question. Now, pushed by practical considerations, boards and their lawyers probably will be very creative in trying to find separate interests of the corporation, although courts may resist. On the other hand, the interests of the corporation might be interpreted to include continuation of its business, products and services for the benefit of other groups, such as employees and communities. Since these other stakeholders are usually mentioned in the statutes, the point may not become important.

No matter how protective the statute, target boards and courts will still have to face the facts of economic life. Arbitragers are very cautious about tying up their money in takeover battles with an uncertain outcome. If they are persuaded that a defense based on these new laws will be successful they may not buy the stock. On the other hand, if arbitragers and institutional investors end up owning most of the stock, the target's board may face tremendous pressure.

Even if the statute protects directors from personal liability, the prospect of a running feud with a bitter, aggressive and probably increasingly unified group of shareholders would not be pleasant. From a practical personal standpoint, why would the directors want that? After all, directors are not soldiers sworn to protect society. Among other things, they have to worry about the uncertainties of indemnity and directors' and officers' insurance when there is a change in control. Yet, the *Time* case, which we have discussed, appears to provide a telling counterexample. For the most part the Time directors stayed together and did not lose their nerve, despite the reservations about the transaction that a few of them had. Advance education of directors about their legal rights and responsibilities and the way courts will judge their actions can make a big difference.

If the new laws prove potent, one pressure directors of targets will certainly face is the threat of proxy fights to remove them. Proxy fights could become the new principal avenue for hostile bidders.[34] In fact, the threat of a proxy fight could become the most effective way for shareholders to exert control over corporate managements.

However, proxy fights cannot become a satisfactory general solution for hostile bidders unless there is a change in attitude among shareholders and in the arbitrage market. It has been much more difficult for bidders to accomplish successful proxy fights than cash tender offers. In a proxy fight the bidder must persuade shareholders either that it can do a better job with the company than its present management or that it would very quickly buy

---

[34] See Chapter 13 Section 8.

out the shareholders at a premium. Compared to a cash tender offer, these are hardly sure things. Nor do proxy fights arouse enthusiastic buying in the arbitrage market, which reduces the effectiveness of proxy fights when compared to cash bids.

Employee stock ownership plans (ESOPs) are becoming much more important in takeover defense. Employees tend to vote with management because their jobs are usually more important to them than the price of their shares. The court approval of Polaroid's sale of 14% of the company to its employee stock ownership plan has encouraged many other companies to do the same thing.[35] An unsolved wrinkle, however, is whether there may be situations in which the trustees of these plans would have a fiduciary obligation to overrule the employees' decisions how to vote or whether to tender shares that are not yet allocated to any particular employee.[36]

None of this means that acquisitions will stop. A reduction in the risk of hostile bids would make friendly acquisitions safer and easier to accomplish. Until now, many deals did not get past the planning stage because of fears that a competing, hostile bid would gain the prize or that both companies would become takeover targets. However, in the past, friendly acquisitions have frequently not been an economic success.[37] In the future, the challenge for directors of bidders will be whether they can do better.

6.9 THE FUTURE IN DELAWARE

As more states adopt more powerful antitakeover statutes, Delaware will once again be under pressure to do something. The Delaware legislature has the power to put a potent damper on hostile takeovers. Will Delaware follow the lead of other states?

The answer depends on how a number of interests in Delaware will be balanced. Managements still have a big but reduced say in Delaware's corporate law politics, and will press for these changes. They probably will have significant opposition from shareholder groups who lobbied hard against the Delaware antitakeover statute restricting mergers. However, institutional shareholders appear to be developing some misgivings about takeovers. For example, insurance company bondholders recently brought lawsuits attacking the RJR Nabisco and Federated Department Stores leveraged buyouts.[38]

---

[35] *Shamrock Holdings, Inc.* v. *Polaroid Corp.*, 559 A.2d 257 (Delaware Chancery Court 1989).
[36] See Chapter 15 Section 3 on employee benefits.
[37] See Chapter 11.
[38] See Leo Herzel and Richard W. Shepro, 'Bondholder Suits in the U.S.,' *Financial Times* (Dec. 21, 1989), p. 8; *Hartford Fire Ins. Co.* v. *Federated Dep't Stores*, 723 F. Supp. 976 (S.D.N.Y. 1989); *Metropolitan Life Ins. Co.* v. *RJR Nabisco, Inc.*, 716 F. Supp. 1504 (S.D.N.Y. 1989); *Hartford Accident and Indem. Co.* v. *RJR Nabisco, Inc.*, 88 Civ. 8148 (S.D.N.Y., pending 1990).

And Delaware lawyers may have little motivation to support these new laws. They have grown enormously prosperous under the present legal rules because takeover controversies have been concentrated in the Delaware courts. As we have explained, in corporate legislative matters, the Delaware corporate bar has tremendous influence on the legislature. Its interests are almost as important as those of the state itself. How the state and the bar will evaluate the next step is still unknown. On the other hand there are strong signs in the Delaware Supreme Court's opinion in the *Paramount–Time* litigation that it understands the new signals.[39] If that court goes much further in expanding the powers of target directors there may be little incentive for new legislation in Delaware.

As we saw in the last chapter, the ultimate weapon for hostile bidders and target shareholders against state antitakeover laws is Federal preemption of the states' traditional role in governing corporations. This consideration clearly gets respectful attention in the Delaware legislature and courts. Yet, in this instance, the SEC probably would not attempt to overrule these laws without new legislation. But Congress and the Administration have become much less certain about whether takeovers are good or bad. In particular the ability to compete successfully in manufacturing with other countries is a growing concern in Congress and the Administration. Waning public ardor for hostile takeovers (low to begin with) is likely to reduce their desire to intervene.

[39] *Paramount Communications Inc.* v. *Time Inc.*, 571 A.2d 1140 (Delaware Supreme Court 1990).

7

Defending Friendly Acquisitions from Competition

I N recent years the standards imposed by courts have made it virtually impossible to protect a friendly acquisition from competition. Many techniques have been tried. The most likely to be held legal are those least likely to provide protection against higher bids. One of the most powerful of these devices, the lockup, has had the most trouble legally.

Time's ability to protect its acquisition of Warner Communications in the face of the high-premium hostile bid by Paramount is not quite a good counterexample to this statement, although it might at first appear to be. Paramount was asking the court's help to stop Time's acquisition of Warner. There was no lockup or poison pill at issue in the case. Paramount could not compete with the fast schedule of the Time tender offer unless the court stopped or slowed down Time.[1]

'No-shop' and 'best efforts' contractual clauses are a mild first line of protection against competition and are now commonplace. These are provisions in acquisition agreements in which the target board agrees not to attempt to sell the company to other bidders and to try its best to assure that the transaction takes place.

Typical no-shop provisions prohibit the target and its advisers from soliciting, discussing or encouraging an acquisition proposal with anyone else, and from providing anyone else with information about the company. No-shop clauses help by assuring that the target does not actually solicit competing bids. Best efforts clauses, although less specific than no-shop clauses, cover more ground. Shopping the company is probably incompatible with using best efforts to complete the transaction.

In theory, both clauses may give the acquirer a cause of action for damages against the target, its management and its board if they fail to honor them. However, in practice the target's board and management would insist that a successful competing bidder assume this liability in the acquisition agreement. As a result, some bidders will not want to get involved. Usually there is a settlement before the competing bidder goes ahead.

Competing bidders can avoid no-shop clauses by making a tender offer

---

[1] See our discussions of the Time–Warner transaction in Chapter 3 Section 3 and Chapter 10 Section 1.

directly to the target shareholders. Moreover, the elaborate disclosure requirements in the Williams Act and the proxy rules reduce the effectiveness of these clauses by providing competing bidders with large amounts of information. On top of that, courts are likely to be cautious about enforcing no-shop clauses in the face of a higher bid. (Despite Texaco's higher bid, however, a Texas jury found it liable for $10.53 billion for interfering with Pennzoil's agreement to buy Getty Oil.)[2]

There are a number of other protections friendly bidders can ask for. 'Break-up fees' are concessions extracted by friendly bidders, sometimes in exchange for a higher price agreed to at the last minute in a bidding contest. In essentials break-up fees are an agreement to make payments to the bidder in a negotiated acquisition if the acquisition fails because of a higher competing bid. 'Topping fees' are a variation on break-up fees, which entitle the bidder, if unsuccessful, to all or a share of any increment over the negotiated deal price. Break-up and topping fees enable the bidder to cover the costs of a losing bid and usually to gain something extra. To reduce the risk that these fees will be treated as a lockup by the courts, they cannot be so high that their main purpose appears to be to deter competition. In recent transactions, break-up fees of 1 to 3% of the purchase price have been common, except in extremely large transactions, where the percentage may be smaller.[3]

7.1   LOCKUPS: *REVLON* AND OTHER CASES

Lockups are a much more controversial device. They are agreements that give the acquirer the right to buy a significant division, subsidiary or other asset of the target at an agreed (and generally favorable) price when a competing bidder acquires a stated percentage of the target's shares. If enforceable, lockups may in some situations ensure that acquisition agreements cannot be circumvented by a tender offer to the target shareholders. What troubles courts about lockups is that they take the decision about whether (or to whom) to sell the company away from shareholders. Of course, the other side of this argument is that boards may be able to use lockups to negotiate deals that are more favorable to shareholders.

It is no overstatement to say that a competing bidder can usually get a court to set aside lockups on the ground that they are in breach of the fiduciary duty of the target's directors to their shareholders. There are special situations in which lockups may work legally but they are almost always risky.

---

[2] See the discussion of this apparent discrepancy in Chapter 12 Section 2.

[3] See the discussions of fees in *Cottle* v. *Storer Communication, Inc.*, 849 F.2d 570, 578–9 (11th Cir. 1988); *CRTF Corp.* v. *Federated Dep't Stores, Inc.*, 683 F. Supp. 422, 440 (S.D.N.Y. 1988); *Samjens Partners I* v. *Burlington Indus., Inc.*, 663 F. Supp. 614, 624–5 (S.D.N.Y. 1987).

The law surrounding lockups has been developing gradually. There have been three very important lockup cases in the last three years. Each of them illustrates important points that should be borne in mind. The cases arose in celebrated takeover battles: Ronald Perlman's takeover of Revlon,[4] Hanson Trust's purchase of SCM Acquisition[5] and the acquisition of the American publisher, Macmillan, Inc., by Robert Maxwell.[6]

One of these cases, *Revlon, Inc.* v. *MacAndrews and Forbes Holdings*, has been very influential (and confusing) for two reasons: the Delaware Supreme Court not only invalidated a lockup, it also made its notoriously cryptic comments about the requirement for an auction when a company is up for sale. However, in its opinion in the *Paramount–Time* case, the court tried very hard to reduce these mysteries. (We have mentioned the auction point before and will return to it again.) Ronald Perlman's company, Pantry Pride, the hostile bidder, made its first move with a cash tender offer. Initially, Revlon responded with purely defensive tactics, including an exchange offer in which about a third of Revlon's stock was exchanged for notes designed to make a takeover more difficult or impossible. When Pantry Pride responded with successively higher bids, Revlon's management began negotiating with two investment firms for a leveraged buyout. At first the management planned to participate in the buyout with the proceeds of their golden parachute severance contracts. And Revlon's board agreed to waive the 'poison pill' provisions in the notes in favor of the management buyout.

Revlon gave access to confidential financial data to the leveraged buyout bidders, but not to Pantry Pride. The favored bidders then increased their bid to match or exceed the Pantry Pride offer. (Differences in the timing of the payments in the two offers made exact comparison very difficult.) The leveraged buyout bidders bargained hard. In exchange for their higher bid, they extracted a no-shop provision, a large break-up fee, and other favorable terms, including bargain priced lockup options on Revlon's Vision Care and National Health Laboratories divisions.

To avoid conflict of interest problems, it was decided that management would not participate in the new leveraged buyout offer. But a new conflict of interest problem was introduced. The leveraged bidder agreed to support the price of the notes. This was an important consideration for the Revlon board. It was concerned about threatened suits by the noteholders since the price of the notes had dropped sharply when the company announced it would waive some protections for the noteholders in favor of the new leveraged buyout offer.

Pantry Pride raised its bid again, conditioned on the rescission of these

[4] *Revlon, Inc.* v. *MacAndrews and Forbes Holdings*, 506 A.2d 173 (Delaware Supreme Court 1986).

[5] *Hanson Trust PLC* v. *ML SCM Acquisition, Inc.*, 781 F.2d 264 (2d Cir. 1986).

[6] *Mills Acquisition Co.* v. *Macmillan, Inc.*, 559 A.2d 1261 (Delaware Supreme Court 1989).

concessions, and said it would match any increase in the friendly bid. The Delaware courts then enjoined enforcement of the lockups as inconsistent with the fiduciary duty of the Revlon board to act as 'auctioneers' to obtain the highest price for its shareholders.

It never was clear whether this duty would apply only in sale and conflict of interest situations like this one and the point caused much confusion among lawyers and in the Delaware Chancery Court. However, in its subsequent opinion in the *Time–Paramount* case, the Delaware Supreme Court rejected a duty to auction argument, putting total emphasis on whether the 'dissolution or breakup' of Time was inevitable: '[W]e premise our rejection of plaintiffs' *Revlon* claim on broader grounds, namely, the absence of any substantial evidence to conclude that Time's board, in negotiating with Warner, made the dissolution or breakup of the corporate entity inevitable, as was the case in *Revlon*.'[7] Reasonably clear as far as it goes. But it throws no light on lockups since none were involved in the case.

SCM, after spurning Hanson Trust's offer, found a white knight in a leveraged buyout put together by Merrill Lynch and SCM management. As the bidding spiraled upward, the buyout group topped Hanson with a final bid. As a condition of its last bid, the group extracted lockups at what Hanson alleged were fire-sale prices – the right to buy SCM's pigments business and Durkee Foods, if the group's bid were unsuccessful.[8]

On appeal, Hanson succeeded in invalidating the lockup. However, unlike the Delaware Supreme Court in the *Revlon* case, the Federal court of appeals appeared to be more concerned with what it considered negligent procedures employed by the directors in granting the lockup than with the conflict of interest issues. The court pointed out that the SCM board had made its decision after meeting for only three hours, had not asked the investment bankers the right questions, and had no clear idea of what the businesses that had been locked up were worth.

Three years after the *Revlon* decision, the Delaware Supreme Court had an opportunity to consider lockups again in a situation with some unusual facts. Macmillan, the diversified publishing and information services company, became the subject of a protracted takeover battle after Robert Bass made a hostile bid at $64 per share which Macmillan's management and board parried with a recapitalization proposal.[9] Macmillan's plan would have split Macmillan into two public companies. The company valued its plan at $64.15. Under the plan, Macmillan's senior management, who had previously not been large shareholders, would have wound up with 39% of

---

[7] *Paramount Communications Inc.* v. *Time Inc.*, 571 A.2d 1140, 1150 (Delaware Supreme Court 1990). This opinion is reproduced as Appendix A.12.

[8] *Hanson Trust PLC* v. *ML SCM Acquisition, Inc.*, 781 F.2d 264, 270–1 (2d Cir. 1986).

[9] *Mills Acquisition Co.* v. *Macmillan, Inc.*, 559 A.2d 1261 (Delaware Supreme Court 1989). For an analysis of the strategic role of recapitalizations, see Chapter 16.

one of the two companies (in effect a control position) as well as a large piece of the other company. Emphasizing the conflict of interest involved, the Bass group successfully challenged this defensive maneuver in the Delaware Chancery Court as a breach of fiduciary duty.[10]

Macmillan's directors then decided to auction off the company. Several rounds of bidding ensued. Maxwell Communications entered the competition with a bid of $80 and Bass dropped out. Macmillan's senior management then began arranging a leveraged buyout proposal with the buyout specialist firm, Kohlberg Kravis Roberts and Co., on terms that would have left management with 20% of the company.

After Maxwell had offered $86.80 per share in cash, topping a KKR bid that had a face value of $85, Macmillan and its investment bankers announced another round of bidding. Maxwell bid $89 cash. KKR made a more complicated bid using a combination of cash and securities with a face value of $89.50. However, it conditioned its offer on the grant of a lockup option to buy several of Macmillan's businesses. KKR said that its bid would expire if not accepted quickly or if Macmillan disclosed it to Maxwell (or any other bidder) or if a definitive agreement had not been signed by noon the next day.

KKR's bargaining stance was designed to put Macmillan's board under pressure. Delay or indiscretion could lose Macmillan a good price. However, KKR's position probably was a legal strategy as well as a bargaining strategy. A board's decision to agree to a lockup is likely to appear more reasonable to a court when the negotiations are very tough and rewarding for the target. This is clearest at the end of a long bidding contest when the target creates an incentive for the bidder to make one last increase in price.

Macmillan's board persuaded KKR to raise its bid to $90.05 per share, face amount, and also negotiated a more favorable lockup price covering fewer businesses than had been proposed by KKR. The next day Maxwell raised its cash offer yet again, to $90.25, and sued in the Delaware Chancery Court to invalidate the lockup and overturn the provisions for a break-up fee and reimbursement of KKR's expenses. The Chancery Court decided in favor of Macmillan on the ground that the lockups promoted the auction by helping to keep KKR bidding.[11]

However, Maxwell also alleged that the auction had been rigged for the benefit of KKR and senior management. The most damning fact was that Macmillan's chairman leaked Maxwell's bid to KKR, and then hid his action from the independent directors for some time. The auction procedure had other, less obvious, imperfections.

[10] *Robert M. Bass Group, Inc.* v. *Evans,* 552 A.2d 1227 (Delaware Chancery Court 1988).

[11] *Mills Acquisition Co.* v. *Macmillan, Inc.,* Fed. Sec. L. Rep. (CCH) ¶94,071 (Delaware Chancery Court 1988), rev'd, 559 A.2d 1261 (Delaware Supreme Court 1989).

In a clearly troubled but practical opinion, the vice chancellor criticized the auction procedure although he upheld the agreement with KKR. On balance, he said, he was not convinced that the imperfections had impeded the bidding. Not surprisingly,[12] the Delaware Supreme Court reversed, finding that the auction procedures were 'unsupportable,' given 'the divided loyalties that existed on the part of certain directors, and the absence of any serious oversight by the allegedly independent directors.'[13]

A lockup may also include an option to buy a block of target shares from the target that is large enough to make a competing bid more difficult or expensive to accomplish. However, exercises of stock options are subject to stock exchange requirements for shareholder approval. For example, the New York Stock Exchange Rule that requires shareholder approval for the issuance of stock increasing the outstanding shares by more than 20% also applies to the exercise of these options.[14]

An alternative is an exchange of shares by the two companies. There is an argument that a share exchange, such as the one Time and Warner agreed to when they signed their initial merger agreement, is a legitimate first step in a combination. It is a real business transaction, quite different from an option: if the main transaction fails the exchange is still there. When Paramount challenged the Time–Warner exchange, the Delaware chancellor declined to set it aside and the Delaware Supreme Court agreed.[15] The Supreme Court described the share exchange as a 'structural safety device' that 'does not trigger *Revlon*' but is 'properly subject to a *Unocal* analysis.'[16] Still, lockups must be viewed as economically ambiguous and legally precarious. In conflict of interest situations such as management leveraged buyouts, or other transactions in which the target management is a participant, they are unlikely to be upheld. In other situations, the courts appear to be ready to employ a *Unocal* test.

---

[12] See Chapter 5 Section 4.

[13] *Mills Acquisition Co.* v. *Macmillan, Inc.*, 559 A.2d 1261, 1264–5 (Delaware Supreme Court 1989).

[14] NYSE Listed Company Manual §312.00 at 3–10. In 1988, the NYSE proposed raising this threshold, retroactively, from 18.5 to 25%. 53 Fed. Reg. 28,930 (1988). When the SEC rejected the proposal the Exchange reduced the proposed threshold to 20% and the SEC approved the change. Securities Exchange Act Release No. 34-27035 (July 14, 1989).

[15] *Paramount Communications Inc.* v. *Time Inc.*, Fed. Sec. L. Rep. (CCH) ¶94,514 (Delaware Chancery Court, July 14, 1989), affirmed 571 A.2d 1140 (Delaware Supreme Court 1990).

[16] *Unocal Corp.* v. *Mesa Petroleum Co.*, 493 A.2d 946 (Delaware Supreme Court 1985), discussed in detail in Chapter 2 Section 3.

7.2 FIDUCIARY OUTS

The use of 'fiduciary outs' for target boards is a trend in the opposite direction from lockups. These provisions give target boards the right to withdraw their support of an acquisition or to terminate an agreement with a friendly bidder altogether in the face of a higher bid. The use of the fiduciary out is usually conditioned upon the target board's receipt of advice from its lawyers that it has an obligation to rely on it. Surprisingly, this concept appears to be spreading with little opposition by bidders.

Lawyers who are representing target boards frequently argue that fiduciary outs are the price the board must receive in exchange for provisions in the acquisition agreement that protect the bidders from the risks of competition. Often, they argue that a fiduciary out is a legal requirement. This argument is largely based on an unusual, highly controversial decision in which the Supreme Court of Nebraska, applying Delaware law, supplied its own non-contractual fiduciary out. Delaware courts have not picked up on this argument, although they have not been forced to rule on the issue. The Nebraska court held, over three strong dissents, that once a higher bid was received the target's directors had a fiduciary duty to withdraw their recommendation. Thus they were not liable when after receiving a higher bid they cancelled a shareholder meeting called to approve a merger agreement, even though they had agreed to use best efforts to complete the merger.[17] This is the opposite of the result in the Texas case in which Texaco was found liable for interfering with Pennzoil's contract to buy Getty Oil. Texaco's argument that there was an implied fiduciary out was rejected.[18]

In conflict of interest situations, such as the *Revlon* case, the legal argument in favor of a fiduciary out appears to be manifestly correct. The result is a complicated, unstable compromise. If there is a fiduciary out and no lockup, the best a bidder can ensure if it loses out to competition is that it would receive some payment through break-up fees. A lockup can make the fiduciary out useless, if it is economically potent enough and legal. But, as we have tried to show, this may be a very big 'if.'

---

[17] *Con Agra, Inc.* v. *Cargill, Inc.*, 222 Neb. 136, 382 N.W.2d 576 (Neb. 1986).
[18] *Texaco, Inc.* v. *Pennzoil Co.*, 729 S.W.2d 768 (Tex. App. 1987), *application for writ of error refused*, 748 S.W.2d 631 (Tex. 1988). See Chapter 12 Section 2.

8

Poison Pills and Other Defenses Against Takeovers

IN recent years, the significant developments in takeover law have dealt with two main issues: first, target company resistance to takeovers and, second, fair treatment of public shareholders in squeeze-out mergers, leveraged buyouts and similar situations. By a large margin resistance to takeovers has been the more difficult and controversial subject. Some takeover defenses, such as Unocal's discriminatory self-tender and Macmillan's defensive restructuring and leveraged buyout proposals, require the courts to face both issues at once.

Delaware law in these two areas has evolved primarily through frequent, intensive litigation and to a lesser extent through changes in legislation. As innovations in takeover defense are brought before the courts, the balance of power between bidders and targets often shifts quite abruptly. Financial innovations in the financing of bids (junk bonds, for example) have also affected this balance.

The most extraordinary defensive device yet approved by the courts is the poison pill, which is continually being refined. The flip-in version has become the standard first-line takeover defense. Most large public corporations in the United States have a flip-in poison pill. Those that do not can have one on short notice. A key and very controversial consideration in the popularity of these pills is that they can be adopted quickly by boards of directors without shareholder approval. In a nutshell, a flip-in poison pill is a stock purchase right issued as a dividend to shareholders. The right is designed to become suddenly valuable during a takeover attempt. When a bidder acquires a specified percentage of the target's outstanding shares without prior approval by the target's board, the rights flip in to allow all the other shareholders to buy additional shares from the company at half price. The triggering percentage is usually between 10 and 20.

Generally, the board of directors has the right to redeem the rights at a nominal price as long as no shareholder's ownership has reached the specified triggering percentage of the outstanding shares. However, a controversial version of the pill purports to prevent a new board (for example, after a successful proxy fight) from redeeming the pill.

The flip-in threat of bargain-price stock purchases is designed to serve as a preclusive economic deterrent to hostile acquisitions. The intended result is that no one dares to pass the flip-in triggering percentage, and bidders are forced to negotiate with target boards. However, many target boards really do not want to negotiate a takeover with anyone. They just want to say no. Can they do this legally under the protection of a poison pill? This is the key takeover issue facing state legislatures and courts today.

The unusual names probably can use a bit of historical explanation. The original poison pill rights, which we discussed briefly in Chapter 6, suddenly flipped over and became valuable only when a merger was imposed by a large shareholder. The improved pills retained this flip-over feature but also gave target shareholders the right to buy the target's stock at a discount at an earlier stage of an acquisition attempt (for example, if the amount payable on the exercise of the right is $100, it buys $200 worth of target stock). To distinguish it from the flip-over right, this feature became known as a flip-in.

A peculiarity of poison pills is that they are not designed to be used. This idea is a familiar one from nuclear defense strategy: deterrence through the threat of automatic retaliation. Nevertheless, even defenses that are not intended to be used must be designed to work in situations no one expects to arise. The complexity of the pill's provisions and the great difficulty in predicting likely outcomes if it were triggered add extra uncertainty to a hostile bidder's life.

In theory, it may not appear always unthinkable for a bidder to pay the cost of triggering a poison pill. Under some circumstances, a determined bidder with plenty of cash could decide to pay the price. The more shares the bidder buys in the tender offer that triggers the pill, the less the price would be . However, the penalties would usually still be extreme, depending on the exact terms of the pill and the numbers involved. The details of the specific pill and the actual arithmetic in each case are crucial. The important variables are:

1. the amount payable on exercise of a right;
2. the current price of the target's stock; and
3. the current price of the bidder's stock.

The general rule is that the lower the amount payable on the exercise of a right in relation to the current prices of the target's and bidder's shares, the more practical the idea of triggering the pill may be, because there will be less dilution of the bidder's position.[1] If the pill has been recently adopted the relationship with the target's share price would rarely be favorable to the hostile bidder. Moreover, the target board usually retains the power to redeem the rights and immediately issue a new pill at a higher exercise price.

---

[1] This may appear counterintuitive, but the right to pay $100 for stock at half price is twice as valuable as the right to pay $50.

One pill was actually taken on, intentionally, by a bidder. This was the flip-over prototype pill that was ruled on by the Delaware Supreme Court in 1985. It was used in 1984 by Crown Zellerbach to fend off Sir James Goldsmith. Under the terms of that pill, after Goldsmith acquired 20% of the company's shares without the consent of the target board, the poison pill rights became unredeemable and began to trade as separate securities. The pill also provided that when a large stockholder tried to accomplish a merger or similar transaction between itself and the target, the rights flipped over – the rights holders could purchase shares of stock in the surviving company at one-half of market price. Goldsmith bought over 50% of the company's shares on the market. He then squeezed out the remaining shareholders in a cash merger and settled the litigation with shareholders over whether the flip-over had been triggered for a relatively small amount.[2]

So far, poison pills have not kept companies independent once a bid has been made. Once bidders have decided to make a bid, they do not just capitulate. Instead, they rush into the courts where they argue that the rights should be redeemed because they are not being used in the shareholders' interests. Usually target shareholders bring their own suits as well. Directors who refuse to negotiate or find a better bid take the risk of infuriating shareholders and possibly incurring legal liability for blocking a favorable offer. If the bid is high a large portion of the shares end up in the hands of arbitragers; many of the remaining shares usually are held by institutions.

Court decisions in poison pill cases have severely restricted the way boards can use the pill. The most the target board can be sure of is that the poison pill will give its investment bankers enough time to find or put together competing proposals. Although the Federal tender offer rules assure at least a month's delay, additional time provided by a poison pill is a highly significant negotiating benefit for target boards. But after enough time has passed, if the bid premium is large enough and a board has not come up with an acceptable alternative the court is very likely to require redemption of the pill.[3] Nevertheless, there is some general language in the Delaware Supreme Court's opinion in the *Paramount–Time* litigation that suggests this might not necessarily always be the outcome.[4] Moreover, new developments in state statutes could alter these rules sharply, as we saw in Chapter 6.

When in November 1985 the Delaware Supreme Court first approved a simple flip-over poison pill, there was a very important qualification in its

---

[2] *In re Crown Zellerbach*, No. 85 C 3286 (N.D. Ill. 1986).

[3] See *Grand Metropolitan PLC* v. *Pillsbury Co.*, 558 A.2d 1049 (Delaware Chancery Court 1988).

[4] *Paramount Communications Inc.* v. *Time Inc.*, 571 A.2d 1140 (Delaware Supreme Court 1990). See also our discussion of *TW Services, Inc.* v. *SWT Acquisition Corp.*, Fed. Sec. L. Rep. (CCH) ¶94,334 (Delaware Chancery Court 1989) later in this chapter.

opinion.[5] The court only found the *adoption* of the pill to be a valid exercise of the directors' business judgment. It warned that this preliminary approval 'does not end the matter.' Since, at the time of adoption, the company was not in the middle of a takeover battle, the court said that the directors' 'use of the plan will be evaluated when and if the issue arises.'[6] In short, the legal rules for *using* the pill were left for the future.

8.1 DISCRIMINATION AND FLIP-IN PILLS

Astonishingly, the heart of poison pill flip-in rights rests on discrimination against the acquiring large shareholder after its actions trigger the flip-in. Since flip-in rights become void in the hands of the large shareholder who triggers them, the power of the other shareholders to buy shares from the company at half price is at the expense of that large shareholder. It is this twist that makes the flip-in device so effective. The only legal precedent in Delaware for excluding a large shareholder from benefits accorded to other shareholders is the discriminatory stock buy-back that Unocal used to defeat Boone Pickens' tender offer.[7] Flip-in pills quickly got into trouble in the courts applying New Jersey and New York law on the ground that the state corporation law does not allow discrimination among common shareholders.[8] However, in both states the flip-in pill was revived by legislation expressly permitting the discrimination.

Discrimination among common shareholders is a drastic departure from the usual corporate law rule of equal treatment. From the perspective of bidders and many large shareholders it is an outrageous innovation. From the point of view of the target management flip-in pills may have turned out to be a little too good to be true. Since they are potentially so potent, courts have placed limitations on their use.

In evaluating the flip-in, the courts have used the standard applied in the

---

[5] *Moran* v. *Household International, Inc.*, 500 A.2d 1346 (Delaware Supreme Court 1985). The pill adopted by Household International differed only in minor, technical details from the original pill issued by Crown Zellerbach, which we discuss at the end of Chapter 6 Section 1.

[6] 500 A.2d at 1357.

[7] See *Unocal Corp.* v. *Mesa Petroleum Co.*, 493 A.2d 946, 955 (Delaware Supreme Court 1985). We discussed this case and the legal standard the court applied in Chapter 2.

[8] *Bank of New York* v. *Irving Bank Corp.*, 536 N.Y.S.2d 923 (N.Y. Sup. 1988); *Amalgamated Sugar Co.* v. *NL Indus., Inc.*, 644 F. Supp. 1229 (S.D.N.Y. 1986). Flip-ins have also been overturned under Georgia and Virginia law. *West Point-Pepperell, Inc.* v. *Farley Inc.*, 711 F. Supp. 1088 (N.D. Ga. 1988); *Topper* v. *Emhart Corp.*, No. 89–00110–R (E.D. Va. March 23, 1989). Courts applying the laws of a number of other states have held the flip-in pills valid, applying analyses similar to that in the *Unocal* case. See *Georgia-Pacific Corporation*. v. *Great Northern Nekoosa Corp.*, 728 F. Supp. 807 (D. Maine 1990) (Maine law); *Gelco Corp.* v. *Coniston Partners*, 652 F. Supp. 829 (D. Minn. 1986); *Dynamics Corp.* v. *CTS Corp.*, 805 F.2d 705 (7th Cir. 1986) (Indiana law); *Harvard Industries, Inc.* v. *Tyson*, Fed. Sec. L. Rep. ¶93,064 (E.D. Mich. Nov. 25, 1986) (Michigan law).

Unocal case – (1) the board must believe, in good faith, with some reasonable basis for its belief, that the bid is a threat to the corporation or its shareholders and (2) the defensive response (the use of the discriminatory flip-in pill) must be reasonable in relation to the threat posed.

In practical terms, what all this has meant is that in the early stages of a takeover use of the flip-in pill is likely to be permitted as a bargaining or auctioning technique. For example, when Grand Met made its high-premium bid in autumn of 1988 for Pillsbury, Grand Met immediately filed suit in Delaware challenging Pillsbury's poison pill. The Delaware court did not interfere with the pill immediately. But when after several months Pillsbury failed to come up with a competitive alternative to the Grand Met bid, the court lost patience and ordered Pillsbury to redeem its pill.[9] Under the cases decided so far, the target's board of directors can continue to keep the pill in force only if it can make a reasonable case for being able to provide better value than the bid, usually through a restructuring or a sale to someone else. However, after the Delaware Supreme Court's opinion in the *Paramount– Time* litigation, the Delaware courts, applying the *Unocal* test, may be more tolerant of the use of poison pills by target boards to remain independent. In states with statutes that broaden the powers of target directors during takeovers, such an outcome is still more likely. Board procedures may be crucial in framing the issues for the courts to assure a favorable outcome.[10]

Naturally, low bids do not get much court sympathy. When, for example, the market price of the target's stock rises above the bid, it is not hard to convince the court not to interfere.[11] When the courts consider a bid coercive, they generally will say it is a threat that justifies using a poison pill. The classic example of a coercive bid is the one Boone Pickens used against Unocal – a cash tender offer at a high price for a slim majority of the shares. It is easy to argue that such bids are designed to stampede shareholders into tendering against their collective self-interests out of fear they would receive less valuable securities in the later merger to eliminate the minority.

Because coercive bids are easy to defend against and financing for all-cash offers became easier in the late 1980s with the advent of junk bonds, such bids largely disappeared. Sometimes other kinds of bids may appear coercive because of the timing, because of the way the price will be paid or because of other details.[12] Most recent offers have not been clearly coercive.

It would probably have appeared quite logical if courts had prohibited

[9] *Grand Metropolitan PLC* v. *Pillsbury Co.*, 558 A.2d 1049 (Delaware Chancery Court 1988).
[10] *Paramount Communications Inc.* v. *Time Inc.*, 571 A.2d 1140 (Delaware Supreme Court 1990).
[11] See, for example, *British Printing and Communication Corp. plc* v. *Harcourt Brace Jovanovich, Inc.*, 664 F. Supp. 1519 (S.D.N.Y. 1987).
[12] See, for example, *AC Acquisitions Corp.* v. *Anderson, Clayton and Co.*, 519 A.2d 103 (Delaware Chancery Court 1986).

takeover defenses against bids that are not clearly coercive and had restricted boards' defensive actions to arranging alternatives (within normal time limits under Federal tender offer law) and making arguments to shareholders about the value of the shares. However, courts have observed that an all-cash offer to all shareholders may be less than optimal for shareholders if the price can be improved through the hard bargaining the pill allows.[13] In other words, courts have recognized that every bid is coercive to some degree because it puts each shareholder in a prisoner's dilemma.

It is essential for the directors to negotiate vigorously if they are to be a solution to the shareholders' prisoner's dilemma. The board of directors provides what one Delaware Supreme Court justice called 'a substitute for the marketplace' whenever it takes over the responsibility of negotiating for the shareholders.[14] But the courts are concerned about the checks on directors. Although complete control of negotiation by boards can benefit shareholders, how can we be sure they can be trusted? When a board takes a tough stance in negotiations, there is no general formula for telling whether it is really looking out for shareholder interests or just being intransigent. If the board bargains too hard the buyer may walk away and there may be no transaction at any price. So when a poison pill appears likely to deprive the shareholders of the benefits of a very favorable transaction without a better alternative in sight, courts intervene.

A good illustration is the use of a flip-in pill by Federated Department Stores in early 1988. Federated was trying to fend off a hostile tender offer by Campeau Corporation. By its terms, the pill would have been triggered when a hostile bidder acquired 10% of Federated's stock. At that point all of Federated's shareholders, except the bidder, could exercise their special rights to buy Federated shares at half price. Campeau filed suit to challenge the pill. Meanwhile, Federated agreed to be purchased by a competing, favored bidder, Macy's.

The court did not actually strike down the pill, but allowed it to be used only to run a bidding contest between Campeau and Macy's. The court made the point that by preventing coercive tactics and large purchases on the open market[15] the pill could keep the auction orderly. But the court also made it plain that it would not tolerate selective waivers to favor Macy's. Campeau made the high bid and acquired control. By now this pattern has been repeated many times.[16] In the case of Campeau, the subsequent bankruptcy

---

[13] *City Capital Associates Ltd. Partnership* v. *Interco Inc.*, 551 A.2d 787 (Delaware Chancery Court 1988).

[14] Supreme Court Justice Walsh, writing for the Chancery Court, in *MacAndrews and Forbes Holdings, Inc.* v. *Revlon, Inc.*, 501 A.2d 1239, 1247 (Delaware Chancery Court 1985), aff'd 506 A.2d 173 (Delaware Supreme Court 1986). See our discussion of the *Revlon* case in Chapter 11.

[15] There are also other legal and practical limitations to buying on the open market. See Chapter 13 Section 9.

[16] *CRTF Corp.* v. *Federated Dep't Stores, Inc.*, 683 F. Supp. 422, 437–8 (S.D.N.Y. 1988). See

filing of the Federated Stores showed that bidders are not perfect either: the bid was too high. There are few legal constraints on corporate bidders, unlike targets. However, so far, neither the market nor the law has been able to deal successfully with this part of the takeover problem.

An unresolved problem is the role of the pill when the strategy is not to find or put together a competing transaction but to remain independent. So far the 'just say no' defense generally has failed because of court intervention. Two court decisions, however, have suggested that under some circumstances the poison pill may be used as a complete defense against an offer to which the target company has provided no alternative. In one case, a Federal court, applying Wisconsin law, allowed a target board to keep its poison pill in place, thus blocking a cash offer for all the company's shares. The directors thought the price was too low for shareholders and so highly leveraged that it was risky for the future of the corporation.[17]

The other case, *TW Services*, took a similar direction but in a milder way. As a Delaware case, it has more general significance.[18] In his opinion, the Delaware chancellor, William Allen, made some cryptic but potentially important remarks on the subject. He observed that in all the cases where pills have been ordered redeemed the board of directors has first proposed an alternative transaction. Startlingly, he went on to say that the Delaware courts have not yet decided when, if ever, a target board's duties require it to abandon concerns for long-term values and for constituencies other than shareholders. It would appear that when these concerns need not be abandoned the pill could be used to protect a 'just say no' defense. As we have pointed out before, the Delaware Supreme Court's opinion in the *Paramount–Time* case (which noted the *TW Services* opinion, apparently with approval) leaves this question open.[19]

There has been one interesting attempt to solve some of these problems through a variation of the poison pill. This pill has the typical flip-in and flip-over provisions but they are waived if the buyer wins a shareholder referendum. Usually the shareholder vote must be called before the acquirer accumulates 1% of the shares, and the target can wait 120 days before holding the referendum – an eternity in the takeover world. On the other hand, it may be quite easy for the bidder to get the vote.

By emphasizing shareholder approval the target hopes to mollify share-

---

also *Nomad Acquisition Corp.* v. *Damon Corp.*, Fed. Sec. L. Rep. (CCH) ¶94,040 (Delaware Chancery Court 1988); *Doskocil Cos.* v. *Griggy*, 1988 WL 105751 (Delaware Chancery Court, Oct. 7, 1988).

[17] *Amanda Acquisition Corp.* v. *Universal Foods Corp.*, 708 F. Supp. 984 (E.D. Wis. 1989).

[18] *TW Services, Inc.* v. *SWT Acquisition Corp.*, Fed. Sec. L. Rep. (CCH) ¶94,334 (Delaware Chancery Court 1989).

[19] *Paramount Communications Inc.* v. *Time Inc.*, 571 A.2d 1140 (Delaware Supreme Court 1990). New statutes in other states specifically permit directors to continue protecting these interests. See Chapter 6 Section 7.

holders and enhance the legal position of the pill in the courts even for a 'just say no' defense. If a shareholder vote is involved it may be much harder for a court to find that the pill usurps shareholder rights in favor of management. Courts have not ruled yet on these special provisions. In early 1990, Georgia-Pacific Corporation succeeded with a hostile bid for Great Northern Nekoosa despite this type of pill. Although it was unsuccessful in challenging the pill in court under Maine law, it was able to put pressure on the target's board by asking for a shareholder vote on the pill and at the same time waging a proxy fight for the open places on the target's staggered board.[20]

Whether on balance shareholders are helped or hurt by poison pills is hard to say. Clearly, the defense obtains much higher prices in many instances. On the other hand, it is impossible to measure the number of instances where a takeover proposal is not made because of the cost and uncertainty of fighting a poison pill. Even if we knew the number, it would be very hard to quantify the effect. We would have to be able to agree whether takeovers are good for shareholders of targets and bidders considered as a whole. But on this crucial point there is more disagreement than ever.[21]

SEC economists and other researchers have studied the short-term price effects of the announcement of poison pills. On the average, the stock prices of companies turn down slightly when they announce the adoption of a poison pill. The price effect is a little more pronounced when companies are already defending against a takeover.[22] But interpreting this information is no easy matter. The price reaction, after all, is only the market's very quick estimate on the target's side. And during a takeover, a large part of the market for the target's shares is arbitragers who have very intense short-term concerns.

8.2 PILLS AND STATE LAWS COMPARED

It is helpful to compare the effectiveness as a defensive maneuver of poison pills and state laws restricting mergers. Poison pills are adopted by boards of directors without shareholder consent. In Delaware pills have been held legal by the courts, but to make sure that these pills (particularly the potent flip-ins) are not being used to entrench incumbent directors and management the courts have imposed the restrictions we have described.

Probably courts will be less likely to interfere if the target directors have done nothing to impede the bidder except to rely on the protections afforded by a state antitakeover statute. Because the laws restricting mergers are

---

[20] *Georgia-Pacific Corp.* v. *Great Northern Nekoosa Corp.,* 728 F. Supp. 807 (D. Maine 1990).
[21] See Chapter 3.
[22] See summary of studies contained in Peg O'Hara, Corporate Governance Service, *Poison Pills,* 1989 Background Report G, Investor Responsibility Research Center Inc.

created by the state legislature, it may be harder for a court to characterize a board's refusal to waive a statutory right as a breach of fiduciary duty. But the point has barely been explored by the courts yet.

A good illustration is provided by the takeover of Federated Department Stores, which we mentioned in the preceding section. Federated agreed to a friendly deal with Macy's while trying to fend off a hostile tender offer by Campeau with a flip-in poison pill. Campeau filed suit to challenge Federated's defenses. Under the Delaware antitakeover statute the existence of an agreement for a friendly deal with Macy's opened one of the statute's loopholes, eliminating the three-year prohibition on a merger with Campeau if it were the successful bidder.[23] Since the court in effect restricted the use of the pill to running an auction, Campeau's high bid won.[24]

However, if Federated had been incorporated in New York and subject to its antitakeover law instead of Delaware's, the agreement with Macy's would not have automatically lifted the merger prohibition in the statute. It is less certain that a court would have intervened to help Campeau avoid the New York statute by forcing the Federated directors into an agreement with Campeau although the procedures followed by the board might have made a big difference.[25] Federated would also have had a better chance if it had been trying to stay independent rather than trying to protect an agreement with Macy's. But if Federated could have relied on the New York statute there might have been no need for an agreement with Macy's.

Furthermore, in a state like New York or New Jersey where by statute flip-in poison pills are expressly made legal and directors are given wider latitude than in Delaware, the position of the defense would be much stronger. Even in these states, however, in conflict of interest situations or where there is very poor board procedure it is highly likely the courts would still intervene.

8.3   OTHER DEFENSIVE DEVICES

The innovation that made poison pills so popular is that they could be adopted by boards of directors without shareholder approval. In the past, most antitakeover devices consisted of special provisions placed in the company's charter with shareholder approval. Fair price provisions in charters restrict mergers in the same way that New York's and Delaware's antitakeover laws do.[26] These provisions are still part of many charters. In fact,

---

[23] See the discussion of the Delaware statute in Chapter 6 Section 2.

[24] *CRTF Corp.* v. *Federated Dep't Stores, Inc.*, 683 F. Supp. 422 (S.D.N.Y. 1988).

[25] This is very similar to the procedures under the special referendum antitakeover statute we discussed in Chapter 6 Section 3.

[26] See Chapter 6.

there appears to be a minor resurgence in the use of these provisions. Some have been introduced as part of restructuring plans.[27]

Fair price provisions restrict mergers with shareholders having more than a specified percentage of the company's common stock (often 10%). The restriction is lifted if the shareholder pays a 'fair price,' which is usually defined based on a formula. Frequently the formula ensures that the merger price is at least as high as the price the shareholder paid in acquiring any of his shares in the last year or two. But it may be more elaborate. Some provisions require outside appraisals. For example, the price paid in the merger may have to be approved as fair by an independent investment banking firm selected by independent directors. In many cases more than one test is used, and the required fair price must at least match the highest of them. To ensure effectiveness, the provisions (like the statutes) typically cover every conceivable transaction that has an effect similar to a merger, and treat groups, affiliates and any other related parties as a single unit for calculating the threshold percentage ownership necessary to trigger the provision.

A less common charter provision requires a supermajority vote to approve a merger. Or sometimes, as in some of the antitakeover statutes (including Delaware's), there is a requirement for approval by shares not affiliated with the merger partner. For example, a merger with an affiliate of a holder of 10% or more might have to be approved by two-thirds of the shares the 10% holder did not own. The power of this kind of provision increases as a bidder obtains more shares. A small percentage in hands unfriendly to the bidder could easily become a blocking percentage. Sometimes a charter provision combines a fair price condition and a supermajority vote or makes them alternatives. Antitakeover charter provisions that require a supermajority vote are buttressed by provisions requiring the same supermajority vote to amend or eliminate them. Theoretically, these defenses create an opportunity to acquire a blocking percentage that could be a powerful bargaining tool for arbitragers or other speculators. Yet, as far as we know, they never appear to take advantage of these opportunities. Nonetheless, these provisions can worry some potential hostile bidders and, even more, their lenders.

Most states allow the members of the board of directors to be classified into groups of equal size or as nearly so as possible, with staggered terms.[28] Usually three groups are allowed, each elected in a different year for a three-year term. With this system, it could theoretically take two shareholder

---

[27] Investor Responsibility Research Center Inc., Corporate Governance Service, Update to 1989 Background Report C (July 19, 1989).

[28] In April 1990, Massachusetts adopted an antitakeover law that automatically classified the boards of all Massachusetts corporations. Beginning in 1992, Massachusetts corporations will have the option to restore a single board by a two-thirds vote of shareholders. The impetus for the proposal was a hostile tender offer and proxy fight for Norton, a Massachusetts manufacturer, by BTR, a British conglomerate. Massachusetts House Bill No. 5556.

meetings to gain control of the board of directors even for a majority shareholder. However, in practice the directors are very likely to resign after a hostile bidder acquires more than 50% of the shares. There is usually no reason for them to remain as unwelcome board members and there are risks. If there is (or will be) litigation the new owner may resist indemnifying the directors for their expenses. Directors' and officers' liability insurance is an uncertain safeguard, since insurers generally dispute claims. If the directors agree to resign, they can usually obtain an agreement from the new owner to indemnify them and provide insurance. Nonetheless, lenders cannot be sure when the directors will resign and this can make a big difference in some situations.

Staggered boards are more effective in proxy fights. Obtaining control of the board cannot be accomplished in a single proxy contest. Directors may be more willing to stay on since, unlike after a successful tender offer, there is no new majority shareholder.

Charter provisions allowing the directors to consider the long-term effects of a decision on shareholders and the *corporation*, as well as the short-term, or the effects of a decision on employees, suppliers, customers and communities, can give directors the additional room to maneuver that some new state laws are providing.[29] However, in states that do not expressly permit such a charter provision, it might be voided by the courts as inconsistent with the state's corporation statute or against public policy.

Other technical provisions are often included in company charters to assist defense. In Delaware, unless the charter states that shareholders may act only at a meeting, a bidder could take action without a meeting by obtaining written consents from a sufficient number of shareholders.[30] If a bidder has acquired a majority of the shares, he can act by consent immediately. When needed, consents from independent shares are obtained through solicitations similar to proxy contests. In some states such as New York, however, this procedure only applies to unanimous action by shareholders – obviously impractical for a public company.[31] Statutes and charters sometimes also provide that directors cannot be removed from office without cause such as dishonesty or fraud. Some statutes and charters make the right to call a meeting of shareholders the exclusive province of the board of directors.

Some of the provisions we have described are relatively mild. Nevertheless, a combination of a poison pill, many different types of charter defenses and state antitakeover laws can be extremely confusing for potential bidders and for their lenders. Bidders trying to plan a strategy (and being watched by their nervous lenders) may find that when they take a step around one defense they walk right into another.

[29] See Chapter 6 Section 7.
[30] Delaware General Corporation Law §228.
[31] See New York Business Corporation Law §615.

9

The Role of Federal Law

NOT so many years ago the primary legal battleground for takeovers was Federal law. Now questions of state law have become dominant. Those involving the relationships among management, directors and shareholders, as we have seen, can be quite complex and subtle. By contrast, Federal takeover rules appear to have become a field of hazards that can be maneuvered in a comparatively mechanical, although quite expensive, way. On the other hand, these rules can have enormous strategic importance in a contested takeover. Mistakes can be extremely costly and intentional violations disastrous.

Although there are still controversies over Federal law, almost no one disputes the need for the Federal Government to establish the procedural and disclosure rules for tender offers. Generally these rules have a tendency to increase competition among bidders and raise takeover prices because they impose delay. But there are plenty of other ways for targets to delay now, such as poison pills. The main controversies today are about such matters as the definition of insider trading,[1] the disclosure of pending merger plans and incursions on state corporation law by SEC rules.

9.1   THE SECURITIES LAWS

The Federal securities laws affecting takeovers stem mainly from two sources: the Securities Act of 1933 and the Securities Exchange Act of 1934. These laws were passed during the Great Depression, largely as a reaction to the sharp declines in stock market prices. Although the laws are almost always referred to by their original dates, they have been revised frequently over the years. Some proposals for changes are usually pending. Both acts allow the Securities and Exchange Commission to adopt legally binding rules. In theory, the SEC's authority to make rules helps to resolve ambiguities left by Congress and to keep the practical applications of the securities laws up to date. Occasionally, though, the SEC uses its rules more aggressively to expand the coverage of the securities laws, as it did when it adopted Rule 19c–4, the ill-fated, controversial one-share-one-vote rule we discuss later in this chapter.

---

[1] See the discussion of insider trading in Chapter 10.

The SEC's rulemaking reach has been quite extensive in connection with tender offers.[2]

The 1933 Act deals principally with registration procedures for securities offerings. It also imposes liabilities for failure to comply with these procedures and for misstatements and omissions in connection with sales of securities. The 1933 Act affects takeovers only when the bidder is offering shares or other securities to target shareholders instead of cash.

The 1934 Act covers many more subjects and is more important in takeovers. The part of the 1934 Act that governs tender offers, the Williams Act, was passed in 1968. SEC tender offer rules under that Act have tremendous strategic importance.[3] Despite the development of poison pills and state antitakeover laws, SEC rules that determine the timing, form and disclosures in tender offers can be critical. For example, a tender offer must be held open for at least 20 business days (about a month). Before the Williams Act a tender offer could be announced and completed on a first-come-first-served basis, creating tremendous time pressure, leaving shareholders and target directors no time to consider other options. Sometimes the time period was as little as 24 or 48 hours. Now, under the Williams Act, all shareholders are guaranteed equal treatment if they tender while the offer is open. In addition, during that time the bidder cannot purchase any shares either under the tender offer or in any other way. The Williams Act also forbids large secret accumulations of shares: ownership of 5% or more of a company's shares must be reported.[4]

The Williams Act and the SEC also provide special disclosure rules for tender offers by a company for its own stock and for going-private transactions, such as leveraged buyouts, in which management is involved. In creating special disclosure rules for these situations, where there is an unusual potential for conflict of interest, the SEC is to some extent invading traditional state law authority over the relationships among directors and shareholders.

Sometimes, as we have already seen, the SEC or Congress becomes so concerned by a particular practice that it acts to abolish it. The possibility that the Federal Government may intrude into the states' traditional authority over corporations serves as a check on what the state legislatures and courts, particularly Delaware, dare to allow corporations to do.[5]

Other than the threat of new Federal legislation, rulemaking is the SEC's most potent weapon to combat state law. We have noted, for example, that the SEC quickly outlawed discriminatory tender offers after the Delaware

---

[2] See SEC Regulations 14D and 14E, the texts of which are contained in the Appendix, A.2.4 and A.2.5.

[3] See Chapter 12.

[4] Securities Exchange Act of 1934, §13(d); Rule 13–d. The filing is made on Schedule 13D.

[5] See Chapter 5 Section 3.

Supreme Court approved them in the *Unocal* case.[6] The new rules require that every bidder making a tender offer, including an issuer making a defensive tender offer for its own shares, must extend the offer to all shareholders and pay to all tendering shareholders the highest price paid in the tender offer.[7]

Sometimes Federal statutes and SEC rules have been expanded still further by the Federal courts although this has stopped as Federal courts have become more conservative. SEC Rule 10b–5, which is the heart of U.S. insider trading law, was once referred to by the Supreme Court as a judicial oak that grew from a legislative acorn.[8] The broadly worded rule has been expanded through court decisions to cover a number of situations that would not be at all apparent from a reading of the rule, notably, insider trading.[9]

9.2   THE ONE-SHARE-ONE-VOTE CONTROVERSY

In recent years the one-share-one-vote controversy was the cause of one of the bitterest conflicts between state and Federal law. In the mid-1980s, some companies took advantage of flexible state corporation laws to reorganize themselves to give some shares of common stock a higher vote than others. Three large family-controlled newspaper businesses, for example, the parent companies of the *New York Times*, the *Washington Post* and the *Wall Street Journal*, all perfected dual common stock voting structures to assure continued family control. Other shareholders obtained stock with a lower vote and a slightly higher dividend. Hershey Foods, General Cinema and several other prominent companies joined in what became a controversial trend, prior approval from public shareholders for their recapitalizations, usually in exchange for a slightly higher dividend.

Egged on by institutional investors, the SEC, after long debate, acted in 1988 to stop this trend by adopting Rule 19c-4.[10] 'One common share, one vote,' a slogan taken from political democracy, had a magical appeal. However, the SEC's statutory authority to adopt the rule was questioned from the start, and two years later a Federal court of appeals struck down the rule. The court said the SEC had made a 'bad gamble' when it adopted the rule, overstepping its statutory authority by entering corporate governance – the territory of state law.[11] In general, the rule made it impossible for a public company to issue high-vote shares that dilute the voting rights of

---

[6] *Unocal Corp.* v. *Mesa Petroleum Co.*, 493 A.2d 946 (Delaware Supreme Court 1985).

[7] Rules 13e–4(f)(8)(i) and (ii) and 14d–10(a)(1) and (2).

[8] *Blue Chip Stamps* v. *Manor Drug Stores*, 421 U.S. 723, 737 (1975).

[9] The text of Rule 10b–5 is in the Appendix, A.1.2.

[10] The text of Rule 19c–4 is in the Appendix, A.3.

[11] *The Business Roundtable* v. *SEC*, 905 F.2d 406 (D.C. Cir. 1990). See Leo Herzel and Richard W. Shepro, 'U.S. Court of Appeals rules SEC overstepped its authority,' *Financial Times*, June 28, 1990, p. 8.

outstanding shares. The rule was a compromise. It did not attempt to interfere with companies that had already recapitalized before the effective date of the rule. Nor did it stop companies that were just going public from selling low-vote shares to the public if they could.

The action restricted the freedom of shareholders and managements to make their own contracts, reversing the Reagan Administration SEC's usual position of deference to the free market. Many ardent free market proponents, however, applauded these restrictions. One reason is that they like takeovers. Another is that they do not think shareholders can take care of themselves in their dealings with management. Ironically, this is the same argument about shareholder weakness that target boards make to justify defensive tactics in takeovers. There was testimony by economists before the SEC on this point when it was making its decision whether to adopt the rule. In addition, a widely discussed mathematical model developed by Sanford Grossman and Oliver Hart appears to show that, given a number of reasonable assumptions, when a company is being capitalized for the first time for public ownership, a one-share-one-vote structure should assure that the owners of the business receive the maximum price from their sale of shares to the public. However, Grossman and Hart agree that some owners may have quite good personal reasons for preferring control to a maximum share price.[12] In that case, why should anyone else care? To some extent Rule 19c-4 adopted this point of view by permitting companies going public for the first time to issue low-vote shares.

Although the court struck down Rule 19c-4 for lack of statutory authority, the SEC's policy behind the rule is not beyond question either. Companies that adopted new voting structures, with shareholder approval, may have been forging a harmonious bargain that benefited both shareholders and the control group. According to SEC studies, firms that recapitalized with high- and low-vote stock tended to be unusual companies. They had much higher insider holdings than other companies. They showed, on the average, statistically significant superior performance over market averages in the year before the recapitalizations, and their share prices increased after announcing their new voting plans.[13]

When large non-monetary benefits can be obtained from control, maximum share price may not be the owners' first concern. Owners of a family controlled newspaper, for example, may regard the paper as a means of furthering their

[12] Sanford Grossman and Oliver Hart, 'One Share/One Vote and the Market for Corporate Control,' 20 *Journal of Financial Economics* 175 (1988).

[13] The Effects of Dual-Class Recapitalizations on the Wealth of Shareholders, The Office of the Chief Economist, Securities and Exchange Commission (June 1, 1987) and Update Including Evidence from 1986 and 1987 (July 16, 1987). The price changes were measured from 20 days before the announcement date to 20 days after. There was little or no instant market reaction to the announcement.

political philosophy and desire for public service. The newspaper may also provide congenial employment for some family members and social prestige for others. When the newspaper becomes a public company, the family may, therefore, be willing to sacrifice some economic return to assure their continued control. The public shareholders are left with the bargain they made.

If the change in voting rights occurs later there still does not appear to be any ground for complaint. Modifying the voting structure as generations pass and the families grow larger allows the same family to stay in control while restive family members are allowed to cash out. The public shareholders knew about family control when they bought their stock. They may have bought the stock because they believed in the family's dedication and performance or they may have believed in family control of newspapers on principle.

Even with the SEC's rule out of the picture it is unlikely that there will be a rush by companies to two classes of common shares. The device is suitable only in very special circumstances, such as when there is already a majority, or very large, shareholder group in control. Moreover, stock exchanges and the NASD can adopt their own one-share-one-vote rules, although, as in pre-Rule 19c-4 days, competition for business among them may make it difficult to maintain a one-share-one-vote policy without some uniform legal compulsion from the outside.

9.3   ANTITRUST LAWS

Federal antitrust laws also affect the takeover market. Combinations that would illegally restrain trade are prohibited. The Sherman and Clayton Acts,[14] which establish what kind of conduct is prohibited, occasionally create opportunities for private litigation that can influence the outcome of a takeover bid. The Federal government is also charged with enforcement of these laws. It cannot be said that Federal enforcement of the antitrust laws was a priority of the Reagan Administration although the Bush Administration appears to be somewhat different. Courts, influenced by economists who believe that markets need minimal interference to remain competitive, have been cutting back on the right of private litigants to use the antitrust laws to stop takeovers. Furthermore, concern about foreign competition in the product market has made Congress, the Administration and courts much less enthusiastic about highly technical antitrust enforcement.

Nevertheless, the antitrust laws are a very important factor in the takeover process, even in acquisitions where the bidder and target are in completely

---

[14] Sherman Antitrust Act, 15 U.S.C. §§1–7; Clayton Antitrust Act, 15 U.S.C. §§12–27.

unrelated businesses. Preclearance procedures required by the Hart–Scott–Rodino provisions of the antitrust laws,[15] which we discuss in the next section, severely restrict secret accumulations of stock for a takeover. These very important strategic and timing considerations aside, however, most bids sail through this preclearance review. Following the review the transaction can be completed.

Compliance with antitrust filings does not guarantee that an antitrust problem will not come up later. The Federal Government could change its mind at any time about whether an antitrust issue exists. And, occasionally, this happens. For example, late in 1988 the Federal Trade Commission, one of the two Federal agencies that enforces the Federal antitrust laws, brought lawsuits under the Clayton Act against Hoechst Corporation for its acquisition of Celanese Corporation[16] and against an acquisition of assets of San Antonio Dr. Pepper Bottling Co. by Coca Cola Company of the Southwest.[17] In both cases the actions related to acquisitions that were more than a year old.

Other late challengers can also appear. When American Stores, an owner of retail grocery stores, made a bid to acquire Lucky Stores, another grocery chain, in 1988, it immediately submitted its antitrust filing to the Federal Trade Commission. After the FTC challenged the merger, American and the FTC reached a settlement allowing the companies to complete their merger if the two chains were held separate from each other until American sold some of its supermarkets. After American complied, the FTC approved the transaction and the companies merged.

However, the next day the State of California, which had been conducting its own antitrust investigation, sued under both Federal and state antitrust laws. A Federal judge in Los Angeles issued an injunction halting integration of the businesses. The U.S. Supreme Court decided that California had the right to sue under Federal antitrust laws to have the merger undone after it had been completed.[18]

Occasionally the Federal Government will take action against an acquisition that is exempt from the Hart–Scott–Rodino filing requirements. For example, Textron's 1989 acquisition of the British corporation, Ardel PLC, was exempt from HSR filing requirements because of low U.S. sales by Ardel. The purchase was accomplished through a tender offer made in England under English law. Nevertheless, Ardel's U.S. sales gave the FTC jurisdiction over the matter. The FTC was able to persuade a Federal court to order Textron to hold Ardel as a separate unit and to refrain from exercising any

---

[15] 15 U.S.C. §18a.
[16] *In re Hoechst Corporation,* FTC Docket No. 9216.
[17] *In re Coca Cola Co. of the Southwest,* FTC Docket No. 9215.
[18] *California* v. *American Stores Co.,* 110 S.Ct. 1853 (1990).

form of control until the antitrust case was decided on its merits.[19] This sort of hold-separate order is also sometimes used by buyers as a temporary solution for acquisitions that fail to gain approval in the preclearance review, especially if the antitrust problem is caused by a part of the business that the buyer would prefer to sell soon after completing the acquisition.

9.4 HOW ACQUISITIONS BECOME PUBLIC

As the insider trading scandals and their long-drawn-out aftermath have shown us, disclosure is an extremely sensitive issue for the takeover world. As the inverse of insider trading, disclosure is legally and practically a crucial issue. For arbitragers early information is the difference between huge profits and losses. A bidder (friendly or unfriendly) is concerned because disclosure of plans may invite resistance and competition. Furthermore, in friendly acquisitions disclosure can also impair delicate negotiations.

Friendly acquisitions have to contend with the ambiguous state of the law on when companies must disclose that they are engaged in merger negotiations. In its 1988 decision in *Basic, Inc.* v. *Levinson*, the U.S. Supreme Court made it clear that under some circumstances a target may be liable to its shareholders for lying about merger discussions.[20] The Court did not have to decide what would happen if, instead of lying, a target refused to comment. However, the New York Stock Exchange rules require 'a frank and explicit announcement' whenever 'rumors or unusual market activity indicate that information on impending developments has leaked out.'[21]

The Supreme Court rejected the rule, previously followed by several Federal courts of appeal, that merger discussions are not material information until the parties agree in principle on price and structure.[22] Instead, the Court imposed a reasonable investor test. A fact, it said, is material if there is a substantial likelihood that a reasonable investor would view it as significant. The decision probably makes negotiated acquisitions a little more difficult to accomplish. It increases the legal risk for a company that stalls with half truths when questioned by a stock exchange, NASDAQ or journalists about

---

[19] *Fed. Trade Comm'n* v. *Textron Inc.*, Civ. No. 89–0484 (D.D.C. March 2, 1989).

[20] 485 U.S. 224. The SEC has taken this position for some time and may bring its own enforcement actions. *See In re Carnation Co.*, Exchange Act Release No. 22214 (1985), which also suggests that, as a practical matter, a no-comment policy will only be effective if it applies to all merger negotiations.

[21] *NYSE Listed Company Manual* §202.03, at 3–10. The American Stock Exchange has a similar rule. [2 Constitution and Rules] *Am. Stock Ex. Guide* (CCH) ¶¶10,121–2. NASDAQ takes a similar position. See *NASD Manual* 1565–3 (By-Laws, pt II, sched. D, §1(c)(13)) (general disclosure requirements).

[22] See, e.g., *Flamm* v. *Eberstadt*, 814 F.2d 1169, 1174–9 (7th Cir. 1987); *Greenfield* v. *Heublein, Inc.*, 742 F.2d 751, 756–7 (3rd Cir. 1987); *Reiss* v. *Pan Am World Airways*, 711 F.2d 11, 14 (2d Cir. 1983).

unusual stock price or volume movements, which adds to the pressure for early disclosure of negotiations.

Basic, Inc. had been asked to comment on merger rumors by the New York Stock Exchange and denied them, knowing they were true. Although lying to the exchange as Basic did is a violation of an SEC antifraud rule, the legal consequences of violating the exchange rule by refusing to comment are still not entirely clear. But most boards of directors would not be very happy if the management got into a confrontation with a stock exchange over its rules. For one thing, if a company refuses to comment it may be delisted. The exchange could also force the company's hand by issuing a press release itself.

Sometimes acquirers try to reduce the risk from competition by secretly buying stock of the target in the market. The securities and antitrust laws substantially restrict market purchases of these foothold positions. Buyers of stock must disclose their identity, holdings and intentions to the Securities and Exchange Commission by filing a Schedule 13D within ten days after acquiring 5% or more of a company's publicly traded stock.[23] The ten-day grace period allows a bidder to keep on buying for ten days without disclosure. Some bidders have moved their footholds considerably beyond 5% before the filing deadline. In May 1985, for example, Carl Icahn filed an initial Schedule 13D showing that he had accumulated a foothold position of 20.5%. Accumulating such a large secret stake would be difficult or impossible to do in most large transactions today because of changes in the Hart–Scott–Rodino antitrust filing rules. The 13D filing is publicly available as soon as it is filed. Filings are very closely watched by potential targets and competing bidders and by arbitragers and other market professionals.

Prosecutors and the SEC are taking the disclosure requirements more seriously than ever before. Since the key concept in the ownership disclosure rules is beneficial ownership, it is illegal to conceal ownership by parking the stock with allies or controlling it with options or other side agreements. Some of the guilty pleas in the most dramatic of the insider trading scandals concerned disclosure violations. Boyd Jefferies, whose Los Angeles firm Jefferies and Company, Inc. had created a huge twenty-four-hours-a-day off-exchange market in securities, was convicted on criminal charges and nearly went to jail for parking stock for Ivan Boesky to hide beneficial ownership. He would have gone to jail had he not had useful information and trial testimony to contribute to the prosecution of others. Parking violations were an important element in Drexel Burnham Lambert's guilty plea on six felony violations of the securities laws and agreement to pay $650 million in fines. Paul Bilzerian, who became chairman of the Singer Company after a hostile

---

[23] Securities Exchange Act of 1934, §13(d) and SEC rules thereunder.

takeover, was convicted on criminal charges for concealing ownership by failing properly to disclose his financial backers.

Although Drexel's guilty pleas came on securities law charges mainly involving disclosure issues, the sledgehammer that stunned Drexel was the Racketeer Influenced and Corrupt Organizations Act (RICO) charges on these same issues.[24] RICO is an exceptionally broad statute originally designed to fight organized crime. It allows the government to seek treble damages and to ask the court to immobilize the defendant's assets before a trial. Once RICO charges are filed by the government, a securities firm may have little choice but to settle. Drexel had already seen a much smaller firm, Princeton/Newport Partners, forced into liquidation pending its trial on RICO charges.

Paradoxically, the disclosure requirement that currently has the greatest practical effect in large transactions is an antitrust law that was not intended to be a disclosure law at all. Believing that the antitrust laws would be stronger if government agencies had the opportunity to block mergers before they happened, Congress passed the Hart–Scott–Rodino Antitrust Improvements Act in 1976.[25] Since then, with few exceptions, the Department of Justice and the Federal Trade Commission have concentrated most of their merger activity on reviewing mergers at the time they are first announced through the Hart–Scott–Rodino filing process.

Under the Hart–Scott–Rodino rules, almost all acquisitions of the lesser of 15% or $15 million of the target's stock must be reported and precleared. Thus, in acquisitions of companies worth more than $300 million the antitrust filing requirement is reached sooner than the 5% filing requirement in the Williams Act.

While the bidder's Hart–Scott filing is not itself available to the public, the bidder must deliver a copy to the target. As a result, the filing tips off the target of a hostile bid. Since the filing is a material event to the target under SEC disclosure requirements it must be publicly announced by the target. The filing requires detailed economic information on both the target and the bidder. Unlike the 10-day grace period under the securities law disclosure requirement, the antitrust law does not allow the purchaser to pass the threshold amount until after the review.

There are a few exceptions to the antitrust filing rule, but for an established business trying to buy another they are unlikely to be of much assistance. If the stock is being acquired as an investment and not with a view toward an acquisition, the buyer need not make an antitrust filing until it reaches 10% of the outstanding stock. In that case there is no dollar limit. However, if the acquisition really is not for investment, or turns out not to be, the buyer can

---

[24] Racketeer Influenced and Corrupt Organizations Act, 18 U.S.C. §§1961–8.
[25] See 15 U.S.C. §18a and regulations promulgated thereunder.

find itself with serious problems under both the antitrust and securities laws.

Using a newly formed partnership with few assets used to be a way to take advantage of a large gap in the Hart–Scott–Rodino statute and rules. However, the Federal Trade Commission largely plugged this loophole in 1987. Now the owners of a new partnership must file unless no one corporation or individual controls more than half of the profits or assets of the partnership. Few established acquirers are willing to participate in a partnership with this kind of ownership.

However, LBO firms and other financial buyers are still able to circumvent the antitrust disclosure requirement. For example, no filing is required if the buyer is a partnership in which a corporation and its investment bankers are fifty–fifty partners. But the joint venture cannot be a sham or subject to options to purchase by one of the joint venturers. As a result, the exception is available to an ordinary business corporation only if it is willing to have a true 50% partner who could block its plans for the target. With the decline in the junk bond market and financial buyers, this loophole probably will be much less important.

These antitrust disclosure requirements have been criticized for having major effects on takeover strategy that are not required for antitrust enforcement. A proposal for a rule change has been made that would exempt from the filing requirements all accumulations of less than 10% of the outstanding stock, regardless of motive. In support it is argued that a 10% acquisition is unlikely to have anticompetitive effects and that the antitrust laws were not intended to generate securities disclosures.[26] However, this proposal has met with significant opposition and, since takeovers are no longer viewed by politicians with unallayed enthusiasm, may never be enacted.

9.5   FOREIGN BIDDERS

For years, a frequently debated issue in discussions of international trade and competition has been whether the United States should have special rules for acquisitions by foreigners. Some very tough measures were proposed but never received enough support. A bill introduced in Congress in 1980, for example, would have amended the securities laws to prohibit acquisitions of public companies by non-U.S. corporations unless the laws and regulations of the bidder's country would have allowed an acquisition of a similar company in the bidder's country by a U.S. corporation.[27]

In the past, some foreign buyers have aroused great animosity. Sir James

---

[26] 53 Fed. Reg. 36,831 (1988) (would be codified at 16 C.F.R. §§801–3) (proposed Sept. 22, 1988).
[27] H.R. 7750, 96th Cong., 2d Sess. (1980).

Goldsmith's 1986 attempt to buy Goodyear Tire and Rubber Company is one example. Another is Fujitsu Ltd, a Japanese company, that wanted to acquire Fairchild Semiconductor Corporation in 1987. Ironically, Fairchild was already owned by the French-controlled company, Schlumberger Ltd.

Fujitsu abandoned its bid in the midst of political controversy that was an important factor in the passage of the Exon–Florio Amendment. Until recently, however, the most that critics of foreign acquisitions could accomplish was a law to require cooperation with a minor information-gathering effort.[28] Foreign buyers have to fill out a few forms but the information is kept confidential and made public only in aggregate, statistical form. Another law that requires reporting was designed to prevent tax fraud by foreigners selling real estate.[29] Some Federal review processes make it difficult for foreigners to control some types of businesses, such as defense contracting, airlines and banking.[30]

Now, however, for the first time there is some potentially strong general legislation in place. The Exon–Florio Amendment to the Omnibus Trade and Competitiveness Act of 1988 gives the President or his designee extensive powers over foreign acquisitions if a threat to national security is found.[31] The law authorizes investigation of any acquisition, friendly or hostile, that could result in foreign control over a U.S. company. The Federal Government has 30 days *from the time it receives notice of the transaction* to decide whether to begin an investigation, 45 additional days to complete the investigation, and another 15 days to announce any decision to suspend or prohibit the transaction. If no notice is filed the time period does not begin running, so there is no deadline imposed on government efforts to stop the acquisition.

Under the statute, the Federal Government can stop an acquisition if it concludes that there is evidence that the foreign buyer might take action that could impair the national security of the United States. So far, this vague standard has not been refined much. However, under the law the major factors to be considered are the level of domestic production needed to support the national defense (including human resources, products, technology and materials) and the effects of foreign control on the ability of U.S. industry to meet these needs. Under proposed Exon–Florio regulations issued by the Treasury Department, the law would cover most types of acquisitions, including asset purchases where the assets constitute an ongoing, sustainable business. The final regulations may also cover proxy fights because they can

---

[28] International Investment and Trade in Services Survey Act of 1976, 22 U.S.C. §3103(b). Regulations are found at 15 C.F.R. §806.15 and 31 C.F.R. §129.
[29] Foreign Investment in Real Property Tax Act of 1980 ('FIRPTA'), 26 U.S.C. §§861, 871, 882, 897, 6039C, 6652. FIRPTA occasionally requires tax withholding.
[30] We discuss some of these restrictions in Chapter 15 Section 4.
[31] Omnibus Trade and Competitiveness Act of 1988, P.L. 100–418, §5021, amending Title VII of the Defense Production Act of 1950 (50 U.S.C. §2158).

create the possibility of control.[32] The decision of the President and his designees is not subject to review by the courts.

A high-level interagency governmental committee, the Committee on Foreign Investment in the United States, administers the statute. CFIUS was formed in 1975 to study foreign acquisitions but until the Exon–Florio Amendment was passed it did little of note. It is run by the Treasury Department and includes representatives from the Departments of Justice, State, Treasury, Defense and Commerce, the U.S. Trade Representative, the Council of Economic Advisers and the Office of Management and Budget. A request by any one of these groups is enough to trigger an investigation. Competitors and others can also request an investigation.

Even with the Exon–Florio Amendment, the United States is still a long way from the substantive preacquisition reviews that some other countries have imposed on foreign bidders,[33] to say nothing of the laws in some countries that in effect require foreign investors to bring in local partners. In India, for example, foreign businesses are normally subject to a requirement that they include significant local ownership. This is the reason Indians held a majority of the stock of the Union Carbide affiliate in Bhopal. The Coca-Cola Company and IBM withdrew from India rather than submit to partnership requirements. In Saudi Arabia, partnership requirements imposed through a mixture of tough registration requirements and requirements to license technology to locals are combined with high taxes on projects that do not include local ownership.[34]

The Exon–Florio Amendment can probably be viewed as one more indication that politicians in the United States are uneasy about takeovers in general. But U.S. legal rules could easily take a genuinely anti-foreigner turn. At this stage one should be very careful about predictions.

---

[32] 54 Fed. Reg. 29744–01 (1989). The proposed regulations are expected to become effective some time in 1990.

[33] See the Canadian statute, now repealed, Foreign Investment Review Act of 1973–4, Can. Rev. Stat. ch. 46 (1973) ('FIRA'); Australia also enacted a FIRA-type statute, the Foreign Takeovers Act of 1975.

[34] See Richard W. Shepro, 'Foreign Direct Investment in the United States: A Legal Analysis,' 4 *Wisconsin International Law Journal* 46 (1985).

10

Conflicts of Interest: Auctions, Squeeze-outs, Leveraged Buyouts and Insider Trading

THE backbone of a corporation is cooperation among shareholders, creditors, directors and management. Where cooperation is essential there is also a potential for conflict of interest. In some takeover situations, such as management-sponsored leveraged buyouts and restructurings, conflicts of interest are the key issue or at least very prominent. It is not surprising, therefore, that a central theme of this book is conflict of interest – how conflicts arise in takeovers and how legal rules, contracts and courts deal with the problem. In this chapter we look in more detail at the most important conflict issues.

10.1   WHEN ARE AUCTIONS REQUIRED?

Auctions became an important idea in takeover law a few years ago. In reviewing challenges to defensive measures, plaintiffs and courts frequently invoke the precedent of the *Revlon* case, where the Delaware Supreme Court first linked auctions with takeovers.[1] In the context of the Revlon transaction, the general idea of an auction made sense, especially when viewed as a judicial rhetorical flourish not intended to be understood as a literal rule. Taken out of context, though, the auction idea creates some murky, unnecessary complications. Recently, in its opinion in the *Paramount–Time* case, the Delaware Supreme Court tried to answer the most important question raised by the *Revlon* case: When must a target board conduct an auction of the company? Although it does not resolve all the issues, the court's answer is worth quoting in full:

Under Delaware law there are, generally speaking and without excluding other possibilities, two circumstances which may implicate *Revlon* duties. The first, and clearer one, is when a corporation initiates an active bidding process seeking to sell itself or to effect a business reorganization involving a clear break-up of the company.... However, *Revlon* duties may also be triggered where, in response to a bidder's offer, a target abandons its long-term strategy and seeks an alternative

---

[1] *Revlon, Inc.* v. *MacAndrews and Forbes Holdings, Inc.*, 506 A.2d 173, 182 (Delaware Supreme Court 1986). See Chapter 11.

transaction also involving the breakup of the company.... If, however, the board's reaction to a hostile tender offer is found to constitute only a defensive response and not an abandonment of the corporation's continued existence, *Revlon* duties are not triggered, though *Unocal* duties attach.[2]

Forearmed with this knowledge, can a board sell the company without an auction if it does not 'initiate an active bidding process'? Would it make any difference whether the buyer intended to break up the company? Clearly there is plenty of room here for new litigation. On the other hand, the opinion is an advance. We at least know that some sales, and some defensive reorganizations that do not involve a breakup of the company, may not require an auction. Nonetheless, the Delaware Supreme Court has still not revealed all of the *Revlon* case's mysteries.

In the *Revlon* case, Ronald Perlman's company, Pantry Pride, had made a hostile bid for Revlon in 1985. At first Revlon's board resisted, claiming the company was not for sale. Then it turned around and planned its own sale of the company in which the CEO and some other management directors would participate.

Later those directors dropped out of the transaction but the court still found an important conflict of interest in the boardroom. As the court explained the situation, the favored bidder had promised the directors to support the price of notes that had been issued to Revlon shareholders as a takeover defense. The notes, like a poison pill, were designed to become much more valuable if there were a hostile takeover. With the emergence of a friendly deal, Revlon's board had waived the poison pill provisions and the price of the notes had plummeted.

In the court's view, the favored bidder was helping the directors to avoid liability to unhappy holders of the notes. Requiring a fair auction ensured that the directors could not be swayed by this concern to ignore an offer that would bring more money to the shareholders. The chancery court opinion in the case had expressed puzzlement about the loyalties of Revlon's board: 'What motivated the Revlon directors to end the auction with so little objective improvement?'[3] The Supreme Court opinion sourly noted that Revlon's board could not show its good faith 'by preferring the noteholders and ignoring its duty of loyalty to the shareholders.'[4] As conflicts go, this one was at best highly ambiguous. It is not clear why a board faced with a takeover should not pay attention to a creditor grievance. It is hard to

---

[2] *Paramount Communications Inc.* v. *Time Inc.*, 571 A.2d 1140, 1150–51 (Delaware Supreme Court 1990), reproduced in the Appendix, A.12.

[3] *MacAndrews and Forbes Holdings, Inc.* v. *Revlon, Inc.*, 501 A.2d 1239, 1249 (Delaware Chancery Court 1985).

[4] *Revlon, Inc.* v. *MacAndrews and Forbes Holdings, Inc.*, 506 A.2d 173, 182 (Delaware Supreme Court 1986).

tell whether the court was really shocked or just looking for a conflict to emphasize.

Here is the language Delaware Supreme Court Justice Moore used to sum up the auction point:

> [W]hen Pantry Pride increased its offer to $50 per share, and then to $53, it became apparent to all that the break-up of the company was inevitable. The Revlon board's authorization permitting management to negotiate a merger or buyout with a third party was a recognition that the company was for sale. The duty of the board had thus changed from the preservation of Revlon as a corporate entity to the maximization of the company's value at a sale for the stockholders' benefit. This significantly altered the board's responsibilities under the *Unocal* standards. It no longer faced threats to corporate policy and effectiveness, or to the stockholders' interests, from a grossly inadequate bid. The whole question of defensive measures became moot. The directors' role changed from defenders of the corporate bastion to auctioneers charged with getting the best price for the stockholders at a sale of the company.[5]

The precise reason that the 'directors' role changed' is not evident from this passage, or from anything else in the opinion or any of the later opinions of the court before the *Paramount–Time* case. Was it the decision to sell the company, the lockup that protected the sale,[6] the failure to preserve Revlon as a corporate entity, the directors' conflict of interest or some combination of these? The *Paramount–Time* opinion appears to say that the decision to break up Revlon was an essential factor for the court. The special duty to act as an auctioneer was not caused simply by the increase in the unwelcome Pantry Pride offer.

In the *Time* case itself, the court said that the pivotal question was whether Time was put up for sale by the original merger agreement. The court's answer was 'no,' apparently because it believed that the board never abandoned its long-term strategy and that neither of the proposed Warner transactions made the breakup of Time inevitable.[7]

It appears that even in cases where a company is unquestionably being sold for cash, an auction may not be necessary if the 'corporate entity' is left intact. This is a very important point. If it were otherwise, a binding legal agreement for a friendly acquisition would be impossible, at least until the auction ended. Before the decision in the *Paramount–Time* case many lawyers thought that a target board negotiating a friendly acquisition had a legal obligation to try to ferret out other bidders. Furthermore, it now appears

---

[5] Id.

[6] We discussed the Revlon lockup in Chapter 7.

[7] See *Paramount Communications Inc.* v. *Time Inc.*, 571 A.2d 1140 (Delaware Supreme Court 1990). We discuss the structure of the transaction in more detail in Chapter 12 and the court's opinion is reproduced as Appendix A.12.

that defensive recapitalizations need not lead to an auction unless they split the company into parts.[8]

Nor does it appear that takeover defense alone would trigger the auction requirement. Where devices such as poison pills or lockups discourage the entry of other bidders, the standard probably is still the reasonableness of the defense under the *Unocal* case.[9] However, when there is a conflict of interest the *Revlon* auction requirement probably is still very much alive.

10.2 AUCTION PROCEDURE

As the auction concept has become more important the rules by which auctions must be conducted have also become important. Use of the term 'auctioneers' by the Delaware Supreme Court in its *Revlon* opinion was unfortunate. It appears to require a far more specific course of action than the court probably would have intended if it had given the subject more thought. The phrase describing the directors' duty that appears earlier in the same paragraph of the opinion seems more apt – 'maximization of the company's value.'[10]

The best way to obtain the highest price for a company is largely a matter of judgment. An auction is a procedure, not a goal. If there is an independent special committee in control of the procedure, a specific auction requirement probably adds more rigidity and room for accident than shareholder protection. When faced with an actual procedural issue, courts appear to recognize that there are many ways to sell a business. Clearly sales of large businesses cannot be treated like traditional auctions. In an auction at Sotheby's the procedure is simple. When the hammer goes down the bidding on that lot is over. By contrast, when investment bankers conduct auctions they usually try to force the bids up higher through informal discussions, bluff and negotiations with bidders.[11]

When the special committee procedure does not work, unfair auctions

[8] This may be consistent with the Chancery Court's injunction against the proposed recapitalization of Macmillan where the company would have been split into two parts. However, there was also a serious management conflict of interest in that case, which we discussed in Chapter 2. *Robert M. Bass Group, Inc.* v. *Evans*, 552 A.2d 1227 (Delaware Chancery Court 1988).

[9] In a 1987 case arising out of Ivanhoe Partners' attempt to acquire Newmont Mining, the Delaware Supreme Court pointed out explicitly that the *Revlon* case does not foreclose a takeover defense. *Ivanhoe Partners* v. *Newmont Mining Corp.*, 535 A.2d 1334, 1345 (Delaware Supreme Court 1987). The court reiterated the point in 1989 in its *Macmillan* decision, where it could have cleared up the auction controversy but did not. *Mills Acquisition Co.* v. *Macmillan, Inc.*. 559 A.2d 1261, 1285 n. 35 (Delaware Supreme Court 1989).

[10] 506 A.2d at 182. See also *Citron* v. *Fairchild Camera and Instrument Corp.*, 569 A.2d 53 (Delaware Supreme Court 1989).

[11] See our additional discussion about auctions in Chapter 16.

favoring management-sponsored buyouts can present problems. However, the danger of a lawsuit by an outraged bidder who is competing against a management bid is a potent pressure to assure fairness in auctions. The Delaware Supreme Court's decision in the *Macmillan* case presents the risk and the solution very clearly.[12] In the Macmillan auction, Robert Maxwell made a higher bid after Macmillan declared Kohlberg, Kravis, Roberts the winning bidder. Macmillan's investment bankers informed Maxwell that he was too late. Maxwell quickly returned to the Delaware courts where he already had a suit pending against Macmillan, and the Delaware Supreme Court invalidated the winning, management-sponsored KKR bid.

In doing so, the Supreme Court had to reverse the trial court's decision. In a rather sophisticated, pragmatic opinion the vice chancellor had reluctantly accepted the flawed auction procedure. In general the Delaware Chancery Court is more pragmatic and less likely to search for the moral high ground than the Supreme Court. The Supreme Court balked at several imperfections in the procedure. Probably the worst was that the top management of Macmillan had disclosed Maxwell's bid to KKR. It appears to have been very important to the Supreme Court that the case smelled of conflict of interest. Despite the obvious self-interest of management that had led the board to appoint a special committee of independent directors, management directors had been dominant in the making of all the important decisions.

There were also intense disputes in the RJR Nabisco auction over the fairness of the auction process. After the special board committee established a schedule, the initial bidding contest between Ross Johnson's management group and KKR was expanded to let in a third bidder. Then, after the last bids were due, the special committee accepted a late KKR bid. Some of the participants in the management bid complained bitterly but accepted the special committee's decision without going to court. Probably wisely. Delaware courts were unlikely to view favorably complaints about the committee's procedure from a management that had proposed an LBO at a low price that would have been enormously profitable for itself.[13] In general, accepting a higher later bid is more likely to be legal than cutting off bids prematurely to favor one bidder.

Bids also can take an unfair form although the courts have paid no attention to this issue so far. At one point, Maxwell, for example, offered to top any competing bid for Macmillan. Perlman did essentially the same thing, in the *Revlon* case. This form of bid can have an unfair, chilling effect on other bidders. It is similar to exacting a right of first refusal, which a target board ordinarily would not consider giving without payment. Besides, an

---

[12] *Mills Acquisition Co.* v. *Macmillan, Inc.,* 559 A.2d 1261 (Delaware Supreme Court 1989).
[13] There were also unsuccessful challenges to the auction procedure brought by plaintiffs' lawyers representing nominal plaintiffs. We discussed this action at the end of Chapter 5.

open-ended bid is unlikely to be completely serious or legally enforceable. But despite its usual procedural concerns, the Delaware Supreme Court seemed favorably impressed by this part of Maxwell's offer.

10.3   THE LEVEL PLAYING FIELD

The metaphorical bent of the courts has encouraged posturing by bidders. Turning to athletic competition for a neat phrase, bidders have argued that a target board must provide a level playing field for bidders.[14] The image has been used for a long time in discussions of government market regulation. In that context, it may provide an apt insight. But in acquisitions – unless there is a conflict of interest – it usually does not.

By and large, the Delaware Chancery Court has handled this issue deftly. Opinions in several cases have noted that the duty of loyalty runs to shareholders, not bidders. As a result, 'the board may tilt the playing field if it is in the shareholders' interest to do so.'[15] This might be the case, for example, when the board grants a break-up fee, topping fee or even a lockup[16] to secure a higher bid. Even without these devices there are many situations where a management bidder has a big advantage over someone making an unsolicited tender offer, simply because he knows the company from the inside.

However, when management is bidding the considerations are very different, and the level playing field metaphor sometimes makes more sense. A board 'may never appropriately favor one buyer over another for a selfish or inappropriate reason.'[17] In the *Macmillan* case, however, the Delaware Supreme Court appeared to be endorsing the level playing field simile generally when it reversed the trial court's judgment that the bidding imperfections had not mattered – even for cases where there is no conflict of interest. But this is probably only another instance of the court's fondness for the picturesque phrase and the moral high ground.[18] In short, the important insight is that boards have fiduciary obligations to shareholders, not to outsiders.[19]

---

[14] See, for example, *Mills Acquisition Co. v. Macmillan, Inc.*, 559 A.2d 1261 (Delaware Supreme Court 1989).

[15] *In re J.P. Stevens and Co.*, 542 A.2d 770, 782 (Delaware Chancery Court 1988).

[16] See Chapter 7.

[17] *In re Fort Howard Corp.*, 1988 WL 83147 at 14 (Delaware Chancery Court Aug. 8, 1988).

[18] *Mills Acquisition Co. v. Macmillan, Inc.*, 559 A.2d 1261 (Delaware Supreme Court 1989). See the preceding section and Chapter 5 Section 4.

[19] Another example of the same lesson was the Delaware Supreme Court's concern when the board of Revlon appeared to be favoring the interests of noteholders.

10.4 SQUEEZE-OUT MERGERS

Squeeze-outs of minority shareholders play a crucial role in takeovers from the standpoints of both bidders and target shareholders. Even a bidder who makes an uncontroversial high-premium cash tender offer for all the stock of a company knows that it will not succeed in getting every share. Inevitably some shareholders will not respond. A squeeze-out merger is the only way to gain complete control of the assets and cash flow of the company. Conversely, shareholders who do not tender their shares will know that they can be squeezed out. Fear of being squeezed out on less favorable terms strongly encourages shareholders to tender their shares. A number of the Federal tender offer rules are designed to help relieve this pressure. For example, the rules require that a tender offer be held open for 20 business days and that if more shares are tendered than the bidder has offered to purchase a pro-rata portion of each holder's shares must be accepted for payment.[20]

When a bidder buys enough stock of a target company to obtain voting control and then uses its power to squeeze out the minority shareholders we have a classic self-dealing situation. The bidder is acting in effect as both buyer and seller, because as the majority shareholder it has the power to decide on the terms of the bargain. State corporation fiduciary rules and appraisal laws protect minority shareholders by assuring them some level of fair treatment and by offering them the alternative of a judicially determined value of their shares.

How well the state laws protect minority shareholders has a strong practical effect on the takeover market. In the United States, particularly in Delaware, the rights of minorities are weak, although they are protected from being hurt very badly. There is no right to remain a shareholder.[21] Nor is there any right to receive dividends, no matter how profitable the enterprise, although if some shareholders receive dividends all must be treated equally. Except for rights of appraisal in mergers, minorities are only protected against fraud and breach of fiduciary duty. When rights of minority shareholders are weak the temptation to hang on (free ride) when not wanted by the majority shareholder is also weak, except in extraordinary situations.[22]

Recognizing minority shareholders' weakness, the SEC has established special rules on going-private transactions which require that the minority

---

[20] Rules 14e–1(a) and 14d–8, which are set forth in the Appendix, A.2.4 and A.2.5.

[21] This has not always been the case and is not necessarily the case in all jurisdictions. Delaware, for example, for a short time required a legitimate business purpose for squeezing out the minority, on the theory that a shareholder's desire to continue a particular investment should have some legal protection. See *Singer* v. *Magnavox*, 380 A.2d 969, 977–8 (Delaware Supreme Court 1977). The Delaware Supreme Court abandoned this view in 1983 in *Weinberger* v. *UOP, Inc.*, 457 A.2d 701.

[22] We discussed the theory of the free-rider problem in Chapter 2.

receive a large amount of information about the transaction, including a detailed explanation of their appraisal rights and of why the bidder believes the transaction is fair to them.[23]

Under Delaware court decisions, the duty to treat the minority shareholders fairly includes both paying a fair price in the merger and fair dealing (a procedural idea).[24] However, a minority shareholder is not entitled to bring a fiduciary suit if his *only* objection is the price.[25] Appraisal, the only alternative, is for most shareholders a clumsy, expensive remedy. It is the fiduciary duty standard, enforced in shareholder class litigation, that probably does the most to contain conflicts of interest in squeeze-outs of minorities. Although in a class action an individual shareholder may not have much control or receive much benefit from court-approved settlements, concern about this kind of litigation appears to impose a strong discipline on majorities. One statistical study seems to bear out this observation, concluding that squeeze-outs, on average, do not exploit minority shareholders.[26]

Squeeze-outs are accomplished through a merger. We have encountered the subject before in the context of the coercive, two-tier offer. One example was T. Boone Pickens' plan to buy Unocal. His corporation, Mesa, made a tender offer for approximately 37% of Unocal's common stock. Mesa already owned enough shares so that the tender offer, if successful, would have given it a bare majority. Under Delaware law, a majority vote is ordinarily all that is required to approve the terms of a merger. Mesa would have formed a subsidiary. After the acquisition of shares in the tender offer, this subsidiary would have been merged with Unocal. In the merger, the remaining public shareholders of Unocal would probably have received securities of the surviving company, although they might have been given any combination of cash and securities. Mesa would have ended up owning 100% of the outstanding common shares of Unocal.

Although Mesa would have been able to use its voting control to set the terms of the merger it would have had a fiduciary responsibility under Delaware law to treat the minority shareholders fairly. In addition, Unocal shareholders would have had the option of having the value of their shares appraised by the chancery court. To do this they would have had to follow the procedures prescribed in the appraisal statute, winding up with cash (probably several years later) after discovery, motions and a trial. When the court later determines the fair value of the shares it can add interest to cover

---

[23] The main provision is Rule 13e–3, but the proxy regulations, Regulations 14A and 14C, also contain some special disclosure provisions.

[24] *Weinberger* v. *UOP, Inc.*, 457 A.2d 701 (Delaware Supreme Court 1983). We discussed the development of this standard in Chapter 5 Section 5.

[25] Id.

[26] See Harry DeAngelo, Linda DeAngelo and Edward M. Rice, 'Going Private: Minority Freezeouts and Stockholder Wealth,' 27 *Journal of Law and Economics* 367 (1984).

the delay and an additional payment to cover the shareholders' expenses. However, under the Delaware appraisal statute, the court is not allowed to include any increase in the value of the shares 'from the accomplishment or expectation of the merger.'[27]

There are many discrepancies in the Delaware appraisal law (and in those of many other states). Minority shareholders, for example, have no appraisal rights if in the merger they receive only publicly traded stock of the surviving corporation or its publicly held parent. This is true even though they may not have had any say about how much stock they receive. This discrepancy figured in the initial merger agreement between Time and Warner that was structured as a merger. Holders of Warner's common stock would have received Time stock in the merger and would have had no appraisal rights. Warner's preferred shareholders, on the other hand, would have received a new security and would have had appraisal rights. However, in Delaware if there is some real unfairness in the determination of the exchange ratio, shareholders have the right to challenge a merger's fairness outside the statutory appraisal procedure as a breach of fiduciary duty. Appraisal rights are also unavailable, in Delaware and most other states, when a business is sold through a sale of assets instead of by merger.

Mesa's efforts to squeeze out the minority would have been thwarted for three years if the Delaware antitakeover law had been in effect.[28] A fair price provision[29] in Unocal's charter might have complicated or even prevented the merger. Either of these problems could have made financing the offer more difficult or impossible. A powerful flip-in poison pill could have prevented the tender offer and some of the original accumulation of shares. However, it was the Delaware Supreme Court's decision in the *Unocal* case that first made discriminatory flip-in pills possible.[30]

In a squeeze-out, except for the size of the merger price, the best way for the majority to prepare against the likely suit for breach of fiduciary duty is by close attention to procedure. An attempt by the majority shareholder of Sealy, Inc., a mattress manufacturer, to squeeze out the minority in 1987 is a good example of how procedure can go wrong.[31] The Delaware Chancery Court enjoined the merger in part because it was 'undisputed' that the directors of Sealy 'were completely uninformed' about the adequacy of the proposed merger price. They requested no documentation to support the decision on price and did not consider other possible transactions. The court

---

[27] Delaware General Corporation Law, §262. This provision of the Delaware Code is reproduced in the Appendix, A.6.

[28] Del. Code §203. We discussed this section in Chapter 6. Under the similar New York law Mesa could not have accomplished the merger for five years.

[29] See the discussion at the end of Chapter 8.

[30] See Chapter 8.

[31] *Sealy Mattress Co. of New Jersey, Inc.* v. *Sealy, Inc.*, 532 A.2d 1324 (Delaware Chancery Court 1987).

found that the information given to the minority had been highly misleading, giving the false impression that the price was based on arm's-length bargaining.[32] There were so many other procedural problems that the Delaware vice chancellor described the situation as 'a textbook study on how one might violate as many fiduciary precepts as possible in the course of a single merger transaction.'[33]

To get things right procedurally, the safest first step is to appoint a special committee of independent directors to negotiate on behalf of the minority. When properly furnished with its own independent lawyers and investment bankers the special committee's views are not likely to be successfully challenged on breach of fiduciary duty grounds.[34]

However, this solution brings new practical problems. The majority shareholder is likely to find the committee unpredictable and uncontrollable. In 1984, for example, Shell Oil Company set up a special committee to consider an offer by Royal Dutch Shell Group, its 70% parent, to acquire the remaining outstanding shares for $55 per share. The committee rejected the offer as inadequate and asked instead for $75 per share. The parent and the committee each had its own investment banker supporting its view of the value of the shares.

Royal Dutch Shell Group withdrew its offer and made a tender offer at $58 directly to the Shell shareholders. To increase the effectiveness of the bid, it announced that it would not propose either a merger or a tender offer at any higher price for at least 18 months. Lawyers for shareholders brought a class action in the Delaware Chancery Court. The court concluded that Shell had interfered with the evaluation by its own investment bankers by allowing them only publicly available information, when confidential information about reserves was the key to value. However, the special committee's bankers had obtained the data anyway. As a result, the court required Royal Dutch Shell to give the Shell shareholders more information and a right to rescind their acceptances of the offer.[35] Only a tiny percentage of shareholders rescinded. But the shareholder plaintiffs in the class action won a settlement of $2 more per share for all shareholders who waived their right to challenge the merger price. This payment amounted to about $200 million.[36] In addition,

---

[32] Id. at 1339.

[33] Id. at 1335.

[34] We discussed special committees in Chapter 5, and give advice about their use when facing hostile bids in Chapter 14.

[35] *Joseph* v. *Shell Oil Co.*, 9 Del. J. Corp. L. 191 (Delaware Chancery Court 1984).

[36] *Selfe* v. *Joseph*, 501 A.2d 409 (Delaware Supreme Court 1985). Plaintiffs' lawyers, who usually have the main economic interest in class actions, have their own conflicts of interest. The $2 per share, for example, is not likely to mean much to most shareholders but the $200 million settlement generated very large court-awarded fees for the plaintiffs' lawyers. The incentive to settle, therefore, may be quite different for the lawyers than for the members of the class. These settlements require court approval after notice to all shareholders and a hearing. This procedure provides some protection for shareholders. Moreover, the most important

several former shareholders who had refused to participate in the settlement sued to attack the short-form squeeze-out merger. After over five years of court proceedings, including a trial, the court found that Royal Dutch Shell had violated its fiduciary duty by failing to make several disclosures.[37]

As the Shell example indicates, squeeze-out mergers do not only occur as the second step after a change in control through a tender offer. Some companies have subsidiaries with long-established publicly traded minority interests. However, usually this is not a completely satisfactory situation for either the parent or the minority. The parent loses complete control over the assets and cash flow of the subsidiary and the minority is quite powerless. Shareholders of these subsidiaries have no right to remain shareholders. Although they can be squeezed out for cash by the parent company in short order, litigation is a big risk.

Moreover, fairness in a minority squeeze-out is more difficult to establish when there is a long time between the parent's initial purchase of control and the squeeze-out. A cash tender offer for a public company followed by a cash merger soon after at the same price is unlikely to arouse much controversy. If the price was not considered fair the tender offer probably would not have been successful. On the other hand, if the merger occurs after a long delay and the acquisition has been a success, the minority will expect to share in the success through a higher price.[38] In that case, whatever the price, it is likely to be challenged in shareholder suits.

10.5 LEVERAGED BUYOUTS AND RECAPITALIZATIONS

On first thought, leveraged acquisitions of public companies by top management would appear to have tremendous possibilities for abuse. The managers are the people who know the company best. They are selling the company to themselves, but they are supposed to be working for the shareholders. If they were not getting a real bargain why would they want to buy the company? Because of their special knowledge, this question remains even when, to lessen the conflict of interest, they are forced to negotiate with a completely independent special committee of directors.

One answer that is often given by economists and leveraged buyout professionals is that the business is worth more when it is run by owner–managers who have a direct incentive to make it more profitable. After the buyout, the organization and operations of the business become more efficient. However,

---

justification for this kind of litigation is the discouragement of wrongdoing, not the recovery of damages.

[37] *Smith* v. *Shell Petroleum, Inc.*, No. 8395 (Delaware Chancery Court, June 19, 1990).

[38] In other words, the minority shareholders will have had a free ride – unlike the shareholders in a typical takeover. See Chapter 2 Section 1.

the value created by switching to an organization run by principals instead of agents is shared by the public shareholders, who are paid a premium for their shares in the buyout.[39]

If that is all there is to it, then our system of public ownership of corporations is not working very well at all.[40] The failure is particularly evident in the cost-cutting argument. If managers are able to accomplish so much more after they own the business, why not before? One possible reason is that they are able to make unpleasant choices that improve productivity, using the pressure of the high debt burden as an excuse. There is a less positive way to make the same point. It is the argument that much of the profit in LBOs comes from redistribution of wealth away from employees, suppliers, customers and others whose explicit and implicit understandings with the company are broken by the new owners.[41]

In fact, the leveraged buyout phenomenon is more complicated than the simple model of managers selling a business to themselves. The huge LBOs of RJR Nabisco, Beatrice and other large public companies that receive so much publicity are not pure management buyouts. A better way to describe them is as takeovers by LBO promoters in which management participates.

Most leveraged buyouts, however, are private transactions in which public shareholders have no direct involvement. Many of these are sales of parts of large public companies – for example, the president of a subsidiary leads a group to buy the subsidiary from the parent company. But even these are rarely pure management buyouts. LBO promoters usually have a big role.[42] As a result, in most instances an LBO promoter will be management's new boss.

LBOs have some strong supporters among economists and investment bankers as a new form of business organization that is particularly well suited to producing gains in productivity.[43] We have already mentioned the main line of argument, that the pressure of heavy debt and the close supervision of managers by owners eliminate many of the conflict of interest problems that hamper public companies. For example, managers of public companies may have conflicts of interest when they bid for other companies instead of

[39] See Steven Kaplan, 'Sources of Value in Management Buyouts,' *Journal of Financial Economics* (forthcoming). Kaplan finds that the large subsidy caused by the deductibility of interest against taxable income accounts for most of the premium paid to shareholders in LBOs but not for the profit of the promoters.

[40] Exactly the position taken by Michael C. Jensen's controversial article, 'Eclipse of the Public Corporation,' 67 *Harvard Business Review* 61 (Sept.–Oct. 1989).

[41] See Andrei Shleifer and Lawrence Summers, 'Breach of Trust in Hostile Takeovers,' in Alan Auerbach (ed.), *Corporate Takeovers: Causes and Consequences* (1988).

[42] See Chapter 16.

[43] See, for example, Michael C. Jensen, 'Active Investors, LBOs, and the Privatization of Bankruptcy,' 2 *Journal of Applied Corporate Finance* 35 (Spring 1989).

paying the cash to their shareholders.[44] As one staunch advocate summed up the LBO philosophy, debt 'gets you out of bed in the morning; equity, on the other hand, lets you sleep late.'[45]

It has also been argued that because cash flow must be used to pay debt and to make distributions to investors an LBO company is not able to spend its cash flow on ill-advised acquisitions the way that public companies can.[46] Of course, the LBO sponsors also have to do something with their distributions and fees. With their skill in using leverage they can make their cash flow go a long way in acquiring new businesses. But from the standpoint of conflict of interest, the crucial difference is that some of the money is theirs, not someone else's.

However, conflicts of interest are not so easy to eliminate. They are protean and unpredictable. New ones tend to pop up when old ones are removed. In leveraged buyouts, the large fees paid are an important potential source of conflict of interest. For example, in the $25 billion RJR Nabisco buyout, Drexel Burnham Lambert received $225 million largely for placing the junk bonds used to finance the deal. There were enough banks, investment banks, law firms, accountants and other providers of services that the total fees have been estimated to have been $1.1 billion. (Even this figure does not include the commitment fees and other expenses of the losing buyout group.) These fees can be a tremendous source of conflict of interest because they are paid up front. Even if the transaction turns out to be an economic failure the fees are due. To make matters more complicated, some large fees must be paid even if there is no deal. In 1989, UAL Corp., the parent of United Airlines, wound up obligated to pay $58.7 million in fees on behalf of its senior management and pilots in a *failed* $6.8 billion bid.[47]

Furthermore, even if there are productivity gains, the new organizational structure is only a transitory phase. LBO buyers want to resell the business at a profit. They are not long-run owners. Typically, an LBO firm will not hold an investment for more than a few years unless its poor performance or market conditions make it difficult to sell. Many of the most successful LBOs have been reoffered directly to the public in a new public offering within a short time after the buyout. Some LBO companies are sold to public companies with the same organizational structure as the original seller. Colt Industries, Playtex and Dr. Pepper, for example, have been repeatedly sold.

[44] See Amar Bhide, 'The Causes and Consquences of Hostile Takeovers,' 2 *Journal of Applied Corporate Finance* 36 (Summer 1989); Mark L. Mitchell and Kenneth Lehn, 'Do Bad Bidders Become Good Targets?', study by the Office of Economic Analysis, Securities and Exchange Commission (1988).

[45] Letter to the *Financial Times* by Mark Gressle, Stern, Stewart and Co. (June 27, 1989).

[46] Michael C. Jensen, 'The Agency Costs of Free Cash Flow: Corporate Finance and Takeovers,' 76 *American Economic Review* (May 1986).

[47] Had the transaction been completed, investment banking, legal and bank commitment and other fees would have totaled at least $219 million.

In some of these transactions, the new private buyer releverages the company. Avis, the car rental firm, and Avis Europe have gone through a change in control every few years for two decades, with both private and public buyers. Following a public offering in 1973, Avis was acquired in 1977 by Norton Simon, which was acquired by Esmark in 1983. Esmark was bought in 1984 by Beatrice, which went private in a 1986 LBO. Wesray Capital bought Avis later the same year from KKR, the LBO sponsor, for $263 million. The following year Wesray sold it to an ESOP for $750 million and securities. Wesray, however, retained Avis Europe, which it took public. By the end of 1989, Cilva Holdings PLC, a Luxembourg holding company partially owned by Avis Inc., and General Motors, had acquired 84% of Avis Europe and had announced plans to take it completely private again.

Lawyers, economists and politicians probably have been focusing too much on management's conflicts of interest in leveraged buyouts and not enough on bidders to whom these businesses are resold. There is nothing special about buying from an LBO that should help the buyers do better than they have done in the past. If they do not do better some of the huge costs of LBOs are wasted from the standpoint of the economy.

Nor do LBOs appear likely to do much about the excessive concern for short-term profits in the U.S. Managers of an LBO company no longer feel the pressure of daily stock market results. But they have no greater incentive than managers of large public corporations to plan for the long term. The overwhelming goal of LBO managers is likely to be to sell the company as soon as possible at a profit and to move on to the next deal.

10.6   INSIDER TRADING

Illegal trading on insider information has a close relationship to takeover activity. We will probably never know how much of the takeover boom has been associated with illegal insider trading. Takeover arbitrage is a very important part of the takeover market. The financial stakes are huge and takeover arbitrage lives on information. It is no surprise that some arbitrage activity has crossed the line into illegal insider trading.[48]

Most of U.S. insider trading law can be derived from conflict of interest principles. Usually trading by insiders is perfectly legal. Insider trading rules contemplate that insiders own, buy and sell shares. Almost everyone agrees that promoting stock ownership by managers and directors helps to align their interests with shareholders. Furthermore, most trading on non-public information is legal, in keeping with the policy of encouraging securities research.

[48] See, for example, *SEC* v. *Boesky*, SEC Litigation Release No. 11288 (Nov. 14, 1986); *SEC* v. *Siegel*, SEC Litigation Release No. 11354 (Feb. 13, 1987); *U.S.* v. *Freeman*, No. 87–277 (S.D.N.Y. 1989).

However, there are some important legal restrictions on trading by insiders and others who have non-public information. Section 16(a) of the Securities Exchange Act of 1934 requires that directors and officers file public reports of their holdings and revise these reports when their holdings change. It also treats owners of 10% or more of a company's stock as insiders. Section 16(b) of the same statute discourages short-term profit-taking by insiders by requiring them to pay back to the corporation any gains made on stock held for less than six months. These rules help to discourage trading by insiders that involves obvious conflicts of interest.

These are the oldest Federal insider trading laws.[49] Moreover, they are the only general legal rules that punish trading by insiders rather than trading on insider or other non-public information. Between them these two sections are designed to discourage manipulation of corporate activities or news about corporate developments for the personal gain of insiders. Due to the disclosure requirements in §16(a), the short-swing trading provisions of §16(b) are enforced very effectively in private litigation by plaintiffs' lawyers who are awarded part of the recovery as fees.

Trading on insider and other non-public information is prohibited by other laws and rules. By far the most important of these is Rule 10b–5, a very general provision that prohibits fraud in securities transactions.[50] The SEC has a history of expanding the limits of what constitutes insider trading under Rule 10b–5 without warning. It is very hard just reading the rule to see how the SEC and the courts could have squeezed so much from that source. By now, however, court cases and SEC administrative proceedings and releases have made it clearer what conduct might be illegal, although there is still no general definition of insider trading in Rule 10b–5 or any statute or other rule.

Illegal insider trading can lead to both criminal charges and civil shareholder suits to recover damages. Criminal prosecutions also may be based on the Federal mail and wire fraud statutes.[51] There have been several important additions to Federal law in recent years. SEC Rule 14e–3 makes it illegal for anyone to trade in a security using non-public information if that person has reason to know that someone has taken substantial steps to begin a tender offer. It is not necessary to be an insider to violate the rule. Two Federal statutes provide damage remedies and civil and criminal penalties for insider trading (without defining it), govern liability of securities firms whose employees trade illegally and offer rewards to informers.[52]

---

[49] They were part of the original Securities Exchange Act of 1934.

[50] The text of the rule and of §10(b) of the Securities Exchange Act of 1934, the statute on which it is based, are contained in the Appendix, A.1.1 and A.1.2.

[51] *Carpenter* v. *United States*, 484 U.S. 19 (1987).

[52] Securities Exchange Act of 1934, §§21(d)(2) and 21A. In May 1990, when a U.S. Court of Appeals reversed a criminal conviction for insider trading, one of the two judges in the majority

It is clearly illegal for an insider to trade in securities based on material non-public information. The classic example of illegal insider trading is the director who buys company stock or options using information about a valuable company discovery before it has been disclosed to the public.[53] Some economists and lawyers have argued that permitting this conduct would increase the efficiency of securities markets by introducing information more quickly.[54] This is certainly true but it is not the whole story. The problem with this argument is revealed by considering a second argument made by proponents of legalized insider trading. They say that insider trading could be a useful way to compensate important executives.[55] But this would be like paying your employees by telling them to reach into the till and take out whatever they think they need or deserve. Not only would it be very costly, it would be ineffective because it would be unlikely that the compensation could be made to have any relationship to the usefulness of the employees.[56] Moreover, insiders would have a strong incentive to give away company secrets too soon by heavy trading in its stocks.

All of these restrictions can affect the positions investors take in a stock and whether they are willing to sit on a board of directors or get very involved in the company's business. A shareholder whose representative sits on the board or who owns 10% of the company's stock forfeits six-month in-and-out trading profits whether it has inside information or not. In general, shareholders are unable to do much trading in a stock if they frequently have or appear to have access to inside information. Ironically, this, among many other legal rules in the U.S., discourages large institutional investors from taking a more active role in companies or sitting on boards, which it is argued might over time lead to better monitoring of managements and to longer-term investment policies.

Insider trading prohibitions cover information that is stolen or obtained through a breach of fiduciary duty. This is where arbitrage and insider trading meet. The villains of the insider trading scandals of the 1980s were not officers and directors but arbitragers, investment bankers and other takeover professionals who were either cheating their employers or employers' customers or using others to do so.

On the other hand trading by arbitragers and other institutional investors, whether legal or not, keeps stock prices of takeover targets up to the minute based on the latest announcements, reasoned inferences and financial com-

---

said that the SEC had exceeded its statutory authority in issuing Rule 14e–3, which is reproduced in the Appendix, A.2.5. *U.S.* v. *Chestman*, Fed. Sec. L. Rep. (CCH) ¶95,214 (2d Cir. 1990).

[53] See *SEC* v. *Texas Gulf Sulphur Co.*, 401 F.2d 833 (2d Cir. 1968).

[54] Dennis W. Carleton and Daniel R. Fischel, 'The Regulation of Insider Trading,' 35 *Stanford Law Review* 857 (1983).

[55] Most prominently, Henry G. Manne, *Insider Trading and the Stock Market* (1966).

[56] See Leo Herzel and Leo Katz, 'Insider Trading: Who Loses?' 165 *Lloyds Bank Review*, 15–26 (July 1987).

munity rumors. This is a valuable form of securities research. It is generally agreed that legitimate securities research should not become illegal under laws that prohibit insider trading.

Often it is not hard to draw the line. Many of the insider trading cases that have been prosecuted involved blatant violations of fiduciary duties and stealing. For example, in 1984, quite likely for legitimate business reasons, Martin Siegel, a prominent young investment banker, urged his client Gordon Getty to put Getty Oil up for sale. However, once he knew Getty's planned course of action he sold the information to Ivan Boesky, who bought a large amount of Getty stock before the inevitable run-up in price. By the time Texaco bought Getty, Boesky had made many millions of dollars. Siegel was rewarded on this and other occasions with briefcases full of cash.[57]

Siegel's actions were corrupt by any standards. He knew he was stealing information that belonged to his employer and its customers. After being turned in by Boesky he pleaded guilty to criminal insider trading charges in 1987. This kind of stealing will probably never disappear as long as violating the law is so lucrative. Yet making insider trading legal would create tremendous incentives to show a company's hand too early by heavy trading in its stock as well as rewarding insiders on a haphazard basis.

An important insider trading policy question is whether enforcement should be by the Federal Government through the securities laws or by the states, who more typically are the ones to prosecute thefts of information and criminal breaches of trust. However, the Federal Government is probably the only practical enforcement agent. The transactions often involve several states and are often beyond the technical detection capabilities of state law enforcement agencies. Private lawsuits on the other hand generally reach only bidders, targets and shareholders and are unlikely to uncover wrongdoing by securities industry professionals. A related problem is what to do about transactions in U.S. securities that take place abroad. International trading is so easy to accomplish nowadays that cooperation of foreign governments has become essential to uncovering sophisticated insider trading schemes.[58]

---

[57] *SEC* v. *Siegel*, SEC Litigation Release No. 11354 (Feb. 13, 1987).

[58] For further information on this subject see Leo Herzel and Richard W. Shepro, 'Room for More U.S. Insider Trading Legislation,' *Financial Times* (Dec. 10, 1987) and Leo Herzel and Daniel Harris, 'Do We Need Insider Trading Laws?' 10 *Company Lawyer* 34 (1989).

PART II

Advice for Bidders and Targets

11

A Successful Bidder May Still Be a Loser

COMPETITION among bidders has become one of the dominant features of the U.S. takeover market. Once a bidder has identified a publicly held business for acquisition, its goal is to complete the acquisition quickly, before another bidder raises the stakes or makes off with the prize. Competition is usually a major concern whether the bid is a surprise hostile offer or a friendly, negotiated transaction. In a hostile bid, the minimum time required to complete a bid and the possibility of additional delay pit the original bidder against a host of potential competitors: the target's management, any friendly bidder the target can find and any other hostile bidder whose appetite may be piqued by the contest. Friendly transactions are subject to the same legal delays, but the bidder and the target usually share a common interest in getting the deal done before competing bidders can mobilize.

Because of Federal tender offer rules and other legal rules there will always be a delay of at least a month – often much more – between disclosure of the bid and its consummation. This delay is inevitable whether the bid is negotiated or hostile. Delay encourages competition: it gives competing bidders time, a free education and an excuse for entering the bidding.[1]

Moreover, there is legal pressure in favor of early disclosure. The Securities and Exchange Commission has been coming down very hard on bidders and speculators who accumulate secret stakes in violation of disclosure rules. Other legal and practical pressures for early disclosure make it difficult to get very far in a friendly transaction before tipping off potential competitors. In short, it is almost impossible for a bidder to avoid giving potential competing bidders plenty of time to consider a bid.[2]

Minimizing the effects of competition has therefore become the key strategic consideration in almost all acquisitions of publicly held companies. Some of the most important and controversial legal strategies that are being developed in the intensely innovative takeover market today are responses to competition.

Methods for dealing with competition depend on whether the transaction is hostile or negotiated. In a hostile acquisition, price and speed are the main techniques that a bidder can legally use to obtain an advantage over

---

[1] We discuss the Federal tender offer rules in Chapter 9. Strategic aspects of the timing rules are covered in Chapter 12.

[2] See Chapter 9 Section 4.

competitors. Conversely, delay is a potent target strategy for finding an alternative deal or obtaining a higher price from the original bidder. Anti-takeover statutes, poison pills and other defensive devices increase the target's bargaining power by making delay easy. However, in litigation brought by bidders and target shareholders, courts so far have been carefully scrutinizing and limiting private takeover defenses.[3]

In negotiated acquisitions the target usually is as much or more concerned with speeding up the transaction and forestalling competition as the acquirer. The target's management, for example, may prefer the alliance it has nego-tiated and dread a takeover by another company that is likely to bid. For this reason, targets have attempted to lock up the transaction for the favored bidder by granting options on stock or important parts of the target to make it uneconomic for competitors to bid. Here, again, courts have been active. Heavily influenced by economic concepts, courts are apt to study the effects and the motivation behind lockups to determine whether they facilitate or hinder the bargaining process.[4] How courts do this has been one of the central concerns of this book.

Target shareholders almost invariably receive extraordinary premiums in completed acquisitions. Fifty percent is an estimate of the average takeover and restructuring premium made by Harvard professor Michael Jensen.[5] A more common estimate is 30%.[6] However, this estimate is on the low side because it is based on statistical studies that do not attempt to pick up the usual anticipatory increase in the target's stock price before the announce-ment of a deal. The high premiums appear to be due in large measure to the competition for deals that is encouraged by legal rules.

I I.I   THE WINNER'S CURSE

For acquirers and their shareholders the news is less bright. Despite many strikingly successful acquisitions, statistical studies measuring short-term market price reactions to the announcements of acquisitions show, on the average, little or no gain in bidders' stock prices after announcement.[7] It is

---

[3] See particularly Chapters 2, 5 and 10.

[4] See Chapters 2, 5 and 7.

[5] 'Active Investors, LBOs, and the Privatization of Bankruptcy,' 2 *Journal of Applied Cor-porate Finance* 35 (1989).

[6] See, for example, Gregg A. Jarrell and Annette B. Poulsen, 'The Returns to Acquiring Firms in Tender Offers: Evidence from Three Decades,' study of the Office of Economic Analysis, Securities and Exchange Commission, working draft (June 1988).

[7] See Gregg A. Jarrell and Annette B. Poulsen, note 6 above; Michael C. Jensen and Richard S. Ruback, 'The Market for Corporate Control: The Scientific Evidence,' 11 *Journal of Financial Economics* 5 (1983).

possible that some of these gains were anticipated by the market.[8] However, for acquisitions in the 1980s, that seems a less likely explanation since these numbers appear to have been turning negative.[9] Even strong proponents of a highly competitive takeover market are conceding that, on balance, bidders other than financial buyers have not done well in acquisitions.[10]

It is true that short-term price changes are by no means the last word on whether an acquirer will make money. However, statistical studies using line of business accounting data paint an even bleaker picture. They suggest that, on the average, acquirers in the 1960s and 1970s were unable to improve the performance of the businesses they acquired at such high premiums.[11] If that is really so, then the high premiums paid by acquirers are wasted. Much more important, for society that would mean that the huge resources expended in takeover activities are wasted. But this issue is still not completely resolved. A more recent study of the 50 largest mergers between U.S. industrial companies during the period 1979 to 1983 showed significant improvements in pretax cash flow for the merged companies on an industry adjusted basis.[12] However, without an industry adjustment, pretax cash flow for the merged companies showed a decline.

It has been argued that business corporations that make acquisitions to expand into unrelated businesses have done the worst. Highly leveraged financial buyers, on the other hand, may do better. For one thing, they are often able to profit from the prior acquisition mistakes made by their targets.[13] Still, financial bidders play a high-risk game. They are not immune to competition and the winner's curse, nor to the risks of high leverage.

What is the explanation for the winner's curse? The most likely is that the intense competition in the takeover market fostered by legal rules forces acquirers to pay top dollar. The haste imposed by competition increases the risk of mistakes for acquirers. In short, takeover bargains appear to be hard to identify and they tend to disappear in the face of competition after they are identified.

---

[8] See Katherine Schipper and Rex Thompson, 'Evidence on the Capitalized Value of Merger Activity for Acquiring Firms,' 11 *Journal of Financial Economics* 85 (1983).

[9] See Gregg A. Jarrell and Annette B. Poulsen, note 6 above; Michael Bradley, Anand Desai and E. Han Kim, 'Synergistic Gains from Corporate Acquisitions and their Division between the Stockholders of Target and Acquiring Firms,' *Journal of Financial Economics* (forthcoming).

[10] See Michael C. Jensen, 'Eclipse of the Public Corporation,' 67 *Harvard Business Review* 61 (Sept.–Oct. 1989).

[11] See D. Ravenscraft and F. Scherer, *Mergers, Sell-offs and Economic Efficiency* (1987).

[12] Paul M. Healy, Krishna G. Palepu, and Richard S. Ruback, 'Does Corporate Performance Improve After Mergers?' (unpublished paper, April 1990).

[13] The evidence for this phenomenon is mounting. See Michael C. Jensen, 'Active Investors, LBOs, and the Privatization of Bankruptcy,' 2 *Journal of Applied Corporate Finance* 35 (1989). Mark L. Mitchell and Kenneth Lehn, 'Do Bad Bidders Become Good Targets?', study by the Office of Economic Analysis, Securities and Exchange Commission (1988). However, Healy, Palepu and Ruback, note 12 above, found no evidence that mergers of firms in related businesses were more successful.

Bids may be viewed as estimates of the value of the business. When there are many potential bidders their estimates are roughly distributed in a normal curve, with the majority of estimates bunched around the mean and fewer estimates at either extreme. We would expect the best estimate (assuming everyone has equal information) to be the arithmetic mean of the bids. Since the winning bid is the highest estimate, it is usually higher than the best estimate.[14] However, bidders are at least as clever as the rest of us. We would expect them to become familiar with the winner's curse and to discount their bids accordingly. But for a number of reasons it appears difficult for takeover bidders to make this adjustment successfully. They may not have the same information nor the same uses for targets and they usually do not have much repeated experience with takeover bids. Their investment banker advisers do, but they may have a bias toward over-optimism since they are usually paid much more when bids are successful. Even financial bidders, who usually do have extensive experience with takeover bidding, may have a bias toward over-optimism when they receive very large front-end fees for completing acquisitions.

Of course, paying a high price does not mean the purchase will be unprofitable. Many other considerations are involved in individual cases. Brilliance, or luck, may be factors. Financial bidders may be able to resell the acquired company in another auction, or in several auctions.

There is probably another important influence at work. It is very hard for shareholders or the market to monitor the decisions of bidders' managements. Under the legal rules we described in the first part of this book, bidders, unlike targets, are subject to only quite light legal restraints. Usually, for example, a corporate bidder does not need to obtain shareholder approval to make a very large bid or to borrow huge sums of money; and disclosure requirements are designed for targets' shareholders, not bidders'.

The Delaware Supreme Court's opinion in the *Revlon* case added a new difficulty for bidders and targets who are trying to put together friendly acquisitions. In that case the board of directors had a conflict of interest, but the court got carried away and said quite generally that when directors decide to sell a company it becomes their responsibility to act as 'auctioneers charged with getting the best price for the stockholders at a sale of the company.'[15] The precise meaning of this pronouncement in other situations has become a critical and controversial subject, which the court to some extent cleared up in its recent opinion in the *Time–Paramount* litigation.[16] One thing is

---

[14] See, for example, Bernard S. Black, 'Bidder Overpayment in Takeovers,' 41 *Stanford Law Review* 597 (1989).

[15] *Revlon, Inc.* v. *MacAndrews and Forbes Holdings, Inc.*, 506 A.2d 173 (Delaware Supreme Court 1986). See discussions in Chapters 7, 8 and 10.

[16] *Paramount Communications Inc.* v. *Time Inc.*, 571 A.2d 1140 (Delaware Supreme Court 1990), reproduced as Appendix A.12. See our discussion of the *Paramount–Time* and *Revlon* cases in Chapter 10.

certain, however – legal and economic pressures on target boards increase the number of auctions.[17]

[17] See also our discussions of special bargaining advantages for sellers (and disadvantages for bidders) when large businesses are sold at auction in Chapters 10 and 16.

12

Friendly Deals: What Good is a Contract?

SUCCESSFULLY completing a friendly acquisition involves several slippery strategic points that are closely related to the legal and economic issues we examined in Part I of this book. Foremost among these is when, if ever, does having a signed contract to buy a public company enable a bidder to thwart competition.

There are a number of reasons why friendly acquisitions are generally to be preferred. Hostile bids generate ill will and can be risky and costly. Negotiating an acquisition usually goes along with getting a much better look at a company and its potential problems. A hostile tender offer, in contrast, is based mainly on the publicly available information in the target's SEC filings.

For legal reasons, there are qualifications to this stark dichotomy. Takeover defense has developed to a point where most hostile bids must be completed, in form at least, as friendly deals. Without target cooperation, there may be too many separate hurdles for a purely hostile bid to succeed. Bidders may encounter poison pills, state antitakeover laws and required regulatory approvals all over the country. Moreover, courts often require targets protected by poison pill defenses to give the same information to hostile bidders as they give to a favored bidder, particularly if the favored bidder has a management connection.[1] Even so, a hostile bidder may miss important nuances. When the favored bidder is management it may be impossible for any other bidder to obtain information that would put it on an equal footing.

Mergers of equals are an extreme illustration of the perils created by competition. Almost by definition, in a merger of equals, there is little or no premium paid for the shares of either company. The share exchange ratio in the merger is closely related to the market values of the two companies in stock exchange trading. Control of the combined company's board is divided, usually equally, between the two companies. In terms of encouraging long-term strategies, minimizing debt and providing favorable accounting treatment, a well-thought-out merger of equals sounds like a very attractive proposition. But until the Time–Warner combination, mergers of equals had all but disappeared because of the risk that one or both companies would become a takeover target. The announcement of the merger puts a price on both companies, who become potential targets for anyone willing to pay

---

[1] See, for example, *Edelman* v. *Fruehauf Corp.*, 798 F.2d 882 (6th Cir. 1986).

more. For example, in 1985, American Hospital Supply Corporation and Hospital Corporation of America attempted a merger of equals. After the announcement had attracted a higher offer for American Hospital Supply from Baxter Travenol Laboratories the merger plan was abandoned.

Now, in the wake of the *Paramount–Time* case, some very large companies have been combining. Two giant pharmaceutical concerns, Britain's Beecham and the U.S. company Smith, Kline, Beckman, announced plans to combine a few months after Time and Warner did, and completed their merger soon after the final court decision in the *Paramount–Time* case.

The Delaware Supreme Court's decision in the *Paramount–Time* case was also followed (within days) by the announcement of a Bristol-Myers and Squibb merger and the friendly acquisition of Marion Laboratories by Dow Chemical. Bristol-Myers and Squibb completed a stock-for-stock merger identical in structure to the original Time–Warner deal, without incident, forming the world's second largest drug company.[2] After both the Time–Warner and Beecham–SmithKline merger announcements, the stock prices for the companies involved shot up quickly as if arbitragers expected competition to move in. However, the prices dropped once it became clear that potential competitors were being wary for business and legal reasons. The subsequent opinion of the Delaware Supreme Court in the *Paramount–Time* case is bound to lend encouragement to these developments.

12.1 THE STRUCTURE OF AN AGREED TRANSACTION

Legal forms of negotiated acquisitions are dictated mainly by strategic considerations. Sometimes tax, accounting, business and special legal considerations are also important. But the greatest risk is competing bids.

In theory, the simplest form of acquisition is a merger negotiated by the two companies and approved by the shareholders. This is what Time and Warner tried first. When the merger is complete the two companies become one. In practice, because of legal rules, this procedure is slow and therefore increases the danger of competition. As a result, the faster two-step procedure, in which a cash tender offer precedes a merger, is more common.

One-step Transactions

Mergers must follow the patterns allowed by state law. The merger procedure in a one-step transaction is the same as the second step in the two-step process, so we will consider the simpler one-step form first. In a one-step acquisition, the acquiring and target companies' boards approve a merger

---

[2] See Form 8–K filed with the SEC by Bristol-Myers Squibb Co., Oct. 4, 1989.

agreement, which is then submitted to the target's shareholders for their vote. The vote requirement varies from state to state and usually can be changed by charter. For example, the standard approval requirement under Delaware law is a majority vote. In New York it is two-thirds.[3]

One common structure is the one adopted by Time in its original plan for combining with Warner. As we have seen before, Time organized a wholly owned subsidiary corporation, which would have had only a transitory existence. On the effective date of the merger, Warner and the subsidiary of Time legally would have become one, with Warner surviving. Warner's old shares would have been automatically converted into the right to receive the consideration provided for in the merger agreement. All of the shares of the transitory corporation would have been owned by Time and after the merger they would have become the shares of the corporation that survived the merger. In effect both Time and Warner would have survived the merger intact, Warner as a subsidiary of Time. This would have avoided the difficult problem of transferring the many valuable licenses and contracts owned by Time and Warner.

The risk of competition increases as the time between the execution of the acquisition agreement and the actual change of control increases. In a one-step merger, control does not change until after the shareholders vote. Generally, the shareholders' meeting requires at least 20 calendar days' prior notice under state law.[4] Proxy materials are detailed and usually take at least several weeks to prepare. (The Time–Warner proxy statement, for example, contained 151 pages of principal text and 96 pages of appendices and exhibits.) Then these materials must be submitted to the Securities and Exchange Commission for review, which ordinarily takes from ten days to four weeks. Only after the review process is completed can they be mailed to shareholders. Accordingly, as a practical matter, obtaining shareholder approval takes at least 60 days from start to finish, and probably closer to 90 days, if there are no special problems. If stock or securities are part of the payment to target shareholders, registration under the Securities Act of 1933 may add more time to the process. The registration statement covering the shares and the proxy statement covering the vote on the merger can be done as a package, but then the SEC is likely to take more time with its examination.

Antitrust clearance is another timing consideration. Under the Hart–Scott–Rodino Antitrust Improvements Act of 1976,[5] acquirers of control cannot obtain more than the lesser of 15% or $15 million of the target's stock until information allowing analysis of the merger's effect on market dominance in the post-merger period has been submitted to the Federal Trade Commission

[3] Delaware General Corporation Law §251(c). New York Business Corporation Law §903(a)(2).

[4] See, e.g., Delaware General Corporation Law §251(c).

[5] 15 U.S.C. §18a. See Chapter 9.

and Department of Justice and the waiting period has expired. In one-step transactions, Hart–Scott–Rodino clearance time is 30 calendar days, although in simple cases the government may grant early termination of the waiting period.[6] If the government decides to request additional information, there is an additional waiting period that ends 20 days after the Government determines the request for additional information has been met.[7] Sometimes it may be possible to complete the transaction pending approval if the business is kept separate so that the transaction could be undone simply if approval is not obtained. Because of the delays caused by other legal rules, the Hart–Scott–Rodino filing requirements usually are not the cause of a delay in completing the transaction unless there is a real antitrust problem.

Regulated industries, such as banking and insurance, usually have special timing problems because of the need for state or Federal approvals and, sometimes, hearings. State antitakeover laws, other state laws and target company poison pills, charters and by-laws also may impose extensive delays and special vote requirements.[8] Even in friendly acquisitions, it is essential to examine any state laws that apply and the poison pill, charter and by-laws of a target before buying any target shares.

Two-step Transactions

In a two-step transaction, the acquiring company agrees to make a cash tender offer for the target's stock followed by a squeeze-out merger that eliminates the non-tendering shareholders at the same price. If the acquisition is for cash, the tender offer is generally for 100% of the shares. This format serves both sides. Ideally, it enables the acquiring company to acquire control of the target within 20 business days, letting the target's shareholders receive cash for their shares at an early date. This is close to the structure Time adopted after Paramount began its hostile tender offer for Time shares. Time then made a tender offer for approximately 57% of Warner's shares, and announced it would complete a merger with Warner some time in the future in which it would exchange a combination of cash and securities for the remaining Warner shares.

Under the Federal tender offer rules, a tender offer (whether friendly or hostile) must be kept open for at least 20 business days.[9] Tendering shareholders have a right to withdraw shares at any time while the offer remains open.[10] Professional shareholders usually do not tender until near the end of

---

[6] 16 C.F.R. §803.10(b).
[7] 16 C.F.R. §803.11(c).
[8] See examples in Chapters 6 and 14.
[9] The 20-business-day waiting period is prescribed by Rule 14e–1(a) under the Williams Act, the part of the Securities Exchange Act of 1934 that governs tender offers. See Appendix A.2.5.
[10] Rule 14d–7 issued under §14(d)(5) of the Securities Exchange Act of 1934.

the last day. They want to have their shares ready to hand so they can respond to higher competing offers.

Tender offers also require antitrust clearance under the Hart–Scott–Rodino law. The waiting period for a tender offer is 15 calendar days plus at least another 10 days if the government requests more information.[11] This period is only one-half the clearance time required in one-step transactions. If properly prepared forms are submitted promptly, antitrust clearance should not slow down a tender offer, unless there is a real antitrust issue. Since a conditional tender offer can begin during the Hart–Scott–Rodino waiting period, control can be obtained in a negotiated two-step cash transaction about one month after the offer is made.

Other Important Considerations

Paying the target shareholders in part or wholly in stock or other securities requires less cash outlay by the bidder. Under some circumstances, this may be an advantage for the bidder. In addition, if stock is used, there may be tax advantages for the bidder and the shareholders of the target who may be able to defer the recognition of gain or loss for tax purposes. But for many shareholders, deferral of tax may not be an important consideration. For example, they may not pay tax, they may have losses from other transactions or they may have a high tax basis in their stock. If the acquirer is a non-U.S. corporation, special rules applicable to exchanges of stock of non-U.S. corporations may prevent a tax-free exchange.

There may be other non-tax advantages for the bidder in using common stock. Time's original merger with Warner, for example, was structured to benefit from pooling-of-interests accounting treatment. A cash bid cannot qualify for pooling-of-interests accounting. Pooling-of-interests accounting combines the financial statements of both companies (essentially simple addition). This avoids the creation of good will on the books of the acquirer – the difference between purchase price and book value. Under U.S. accounting rules good will must be fully amortized by annual charges against reported earnings in 40 years or less. No deductions are allowed, however, for good will under U.S. income tax rules. Moreover, by offering stock, the bidder may be able to avoid paying a premium for control. (In the original Time–Warner plan – before the competitive bid from Paramount appeared – Time was paying about a 10% premium to Warner shareholders, which is tiny by takeover standards.)

Registration of the acquirer's securities may pose a problem by giving more time to competitors to make competing bids. This is particularly so if the

---

[11] 16 C.F.R. §803.10(b). The ten days begins running only when the government determines the request has been met.

new securities are speculative or for other reasons controversial or unfamiliar (a foreign issuer, for example). To compound the timing problem, securities of acquirers, especially newly formed acquisition companies or unknown foreign acquirers, may be less attractive to the shareholders of the target than cash. There is always uncertainty about how much the securities will be worth. This uncertainty can interfere with the deal itself. Even when there is a market for the securities, their value can fluctuate until the transaction is closed.

Offering securities in the first step squanders the timing benefits of a two-step deal. That is one reason that making a cash tender offer to the target's shareholders as the first step and issuing junk bonds to finance the offer was such a popular solution. The cash is attractive to the shareholders, especially arbitragers, and the controversy with shareholders over the value of securities is avoided. The junk bonds were sold to investors who wanted them, not forced on the target's shareholders. In hostile tender offers, using junk bonds in this way also preserved the strategic advantages of an all-cash bid, which is much harder for a target to defend against. Although the market for junk bonds has disappeared, the strategic benefits of a first step cash tender offer have not changed.

Foreign acquirers have the additional problem that issuing securities in the United States exposes them to U.S. securities regulations and the risk of liabilities under U.S. securities laws. If this is a new exposure, it augments the reasons for paying cash and financing the transaction by issuing securities in the foreign bidder's home market.

Acquisitions may appear cheaper when a public minority is left in place. But the bargain may be illusory for a number of reasons. Existence of a public minority imposes fiduciary duties upon the majority shareholder.[12] For example, transactions with the buyer have to be approved by independent directors to avoid scrutiny by courts under the strict entire fairness standard under state law. Approval by independent directors is also required by stock exchange rules. Concerns about the minority may give the board of directors and the management of the acquired company reasons for not doing what the majority shareholder wants. Important business economies and sales of unwanted parts of the business may be difficult or even impossible to achieve, although they may have been a main purpose of the acquisition.

Furthermore, the cost of buying out the minority later at a fair price and using a fair procedure may be much higher and more difficult, particularly if the acquisition is economically successful. In short, the minority may free ride on the bidder's success. In Chapter 2 we examined and disagreed with a theory of Grossman and Hart that target shareholders would have a tendency

---

[12] See, e.g., *Weinberger* v. *UOP, Inc.,* 457 A.2d 701 (Delaware Supreme Court 1983). See Chapter 5 Section 4.

to reject tender offers because of a desire to free ride. Nonetheless, leaving a public minority may create a free riding problem even though the target shareholders would not have chosen a free ride.

12.2   WHY IT IS HARD TO OBTAIN A LEGALLY BINDING AGREEMENT

To what extent is it possible to make a binding legal agreement for the acquisition of a public company? The practical implications of this question are very important. Friendly bidders (and targets) want to make deals that stick. Hostile bidders considering bids for targets that are under contract to be sold need to evaluate the legality of those contracts. And, in any case, they must prepare for the possibility that after the bid is made the target will attempt to negotiate an unassailable deal with a more favored buyer.

The question about the power to make a legally binding acquisition agreement may appear paradoxical. But it is a logical outcome of the structure of corporations imposed by state corporation laws. Contracts to acquire public companies are not like ordinary contracts. After the board of directors approves an acquisition and the contract is signed there may be a still higher authority – the shareholders.

Acquisition of control of a target company through a tender offer requires that the target's shareholders consent by tendering their shares for sale to the bidder. Forms of acquisition in which the target company itself is a party, such as mergers and purchases of assets, require first an acquisition agreement entered into by the directors and then shareholder assent in the form of a shareholder vote. If the vote is 'no' there is no sale despite the contract. The dominant role of competition in takeovers is directly related to this legal structure. Time Incorporated, for example, knew that its shareholders would vote down its merger with Warner Communications once Paramount had made a high premium cash offer for Time.

The most common reason why shareholders may not vote to approve an acquisition is that a competing bidder is offering more money. A competitor can offer the money either by making a proposal to the board of directors or by making a tender offer to buy shares directly from the shareholders. Shareholders are always free to sell their shares in a competing tender offer or in the market to arbitragers. Unless the target's board of directors can legally protect its decision to enter into an acquisition agreement with, for example, a poison pill or a lockup, it cannot provide the buyer with assurance that the purchase will be completed.[13]

It might appear possible for the friendly bidder to solve this problem by

---

[13] See the end of this chapter and Chapter 7.

quickly buying shares on the open market before the competition can get prepared. However, this approach is usually constrained by practical and legal considerations such as the Hart–Scott–Rodino waiting period and the SEC's detailed disclosure requirements at 5%. Moreover, a large number of shares may not be available until after the announcement of a tender offer or purchase program, when arbitragers begin to accumulate shares if the price looks right. Large market purchases, even if attainable, might create too much takeover speculation and drive the price up too high before the offer is announced, making the premium look puny.

From a legal standpoint there are two problems in addition to the Hart–Scott–Rodino statute and the SEC disclosure requirement at 5%. Open-market purchases have to be conducted carefully to avoid inadvertently engaging in an illegal tender offer. The securities laws do not define what a tender offer is. However, the term, 'creeping tender offer,' used for an illegal purchase program, suggests how fine the line can be.[14] Furthermore, once negotiations begin the bidder cannot trade without liability for insider trading.[15]

Many of these points are illustrated in General Electric's 1988 acquisition of Roper Corporation, a prominent stove manufacturer. On February 29, 1988, Whirlpool signed an agreement with Roper to buy the company for $37.50 per share in a tender offer followed by a cash merger. Five days later, GE stepped in with a better offer made directly to the shareholders as a tender offer at $45 a share. Both offers followed the two-step procedure described above. If the tender offer had been successful GE would have obtained control of the company and could have voted down the proposed sale, circumventing the agreement the Roper board had made with Whirlpool. Whirlpool then increased its offer to $50 but GE raised its tender offer to $54.

Roper's board decided it could not recommend an agreement that would give Roper shareholders a lower price. It withdrew its support for the Whirlpool bid and recommended that shareholders accept GE's offer. However, to make certain that Whirlpool would not claim that GE had illegally interfered with its contract, GE in effect settled with Whirlpool by negotiating the sale of several Roper divisions to Whirlpool before it accepted the tendered Roper shares.

General Electric probably was concerned about the calamitous example of Texaco's 1984 acquisition of Getty Oil. To acquire Getty Oil, Pennzoil had entered into agreements with the company and its two major shareholders, a Getty trust and the J. Paul Getty Museum. But Texaco intervened and acquired Getty by offering a higher price to the Getty board and the two

---

[14] See Chapter 13 Section 9.
[15] See Chapter 10 Section 6.

major shareholders. A year later Pennzoil was awarded $10.53 billion by a Texas state court jury on the ground that Texaco had interfered with Pennzoil's agreements. Texaco asserted unsuccessfully that Pennzoil's agreement with Getty Oil was unenforceable because the Getty directors had a legal duty to sell the company to Texaco at the higher price.[16] The Texas court of appeals disagreed. It said that, although there was some evidence that the Getty board had suspected it might have been able to get a better price from someone other than Pennzoil, other evidence indicated that the board made a reasonable decision 'to commit to a sure thing, rather than to speculate on whether other offers would materialize.' Now many acquisition agreements explicitly give the target directors the right to accept a higher offer (a fiduciary out) although they may not be given the right to look for one.

Texaco's mistake might appear to be a glaring contradiction of our statement that a binding agreement is difficult to achieve. But not so. If Texaco had been able to buy Getty Oil by making its offer directly to the Getty public shareholders, by means of a tender offer, there should have been no legal problem. Unlike the Getty trust and the museum, the Getty public shareholders had had no prior contract with Pennzoil.

However, Texaco was in a quite different position from GE. The Getty Trust and the Getty Museum together held a controlling block of over 52% of the stock of Getty Oil and they had agreed to sell their stock to Pennzoil. As a result, Texaco, unlike GE, could not have succeeded by making a bid for the publicly held shares. In more typical situations, not dominated by a few large shareholders who must be tied up in advance by contract, a competing bidder can avoid the Texaco problem without much trouble, as GE did in acquiring Roper.

Even when targets are prohibited from soliciting other offers, new bidders often appear without the target's encouragement. Competition in the takeover market cannot be escaped easily. More powerful devices designed to protect against competition, such as lockups, are generally not very effective because of legal problems, although the legal status of lockups may have been improved by the Delaware Supreme Court's opinion in the *Paramount–Time* case.[17] Our review of the subject in Chapter 7 showed a number of examples where lockups failed because they did not meet the standards imposed by the courts. If a device is truly capable of preventing competition, it is likely to be illegal for that very reason.

There are some limited exceptions to this general rule. A properly functioning special committee of independent directors has far more latitude than

---

[16] See *Texaco, Inc.* v. *Pennzoil Co.*, 729 S.W.2d 768, 807–8 (Tex. App. 1987), *application for writ of error refused*, 748 S.W.2d 631 (Tex. 1988); see also briefs in the Supreme Court of Texas, No. C–6432.

[17] *Paramount Communications Inc.* v. *Time Inc.*, 571 A.2d 1140 (Delaware Supreme Court 1990), reproduced as Appendix A.12.

a board with some interested members. Even more important, a lockup is more likely to be upheld if it can be shown to have had a crucial bargaining role in inducing a new higher bid at the end of an auction or other bidding contest. In litigation defending a lockup, it is important to have had the lockup come only after vigorous demands by the successful bidder and under bidding procedures that appear evenhanded. Even under the best of circumstances, however, lockups are likely to be risky legally.[18]

On the other hand, it is possible, and quite common in a friendly transaction, to protect the acquirer with some type of break-up fee. Then the acquirer is assured that it will not be a complete loser if a competing bidder appears and is successful. Break-up fees typically run from 1 to 3% of the purchase price of the friendly deal depending on the size of the deal and bargaining considerations. A related technique is for the target to grant a 'topping fee' giving the friendly bidder a specified percentage of the total increment in price provided by the higher bid.

Establishing a foothold position before the acquisition is worked out also provides some protection against losing out completely. Early purchases reduce the overall cost of an acquisition and may provide a strategic beachhead toward control. If a competing offer is successful, the foothold stock can be sold to the successful bidder at a profit. However, in the U.S. significant foothold positions are no longer common, for legal and practical reasons.[19]

---

[18] See our discussions of lockups in Chapter 7 and Chapter 14 Section 4.
[19] See Chapter 9 Section 4 and Chapter 13 Section 9.

13

Should I Make a Hostile Bid?

SUCCEEDING with a hostile takeover can be extremely expensive. Target directors, institutional shareholders and arbitragers agree on one point if nothing else. They want a high final price. But even a high price does not assure success for the bidder. Some competing bidder may be ready to pay more. A good illustration is Unilever's $60 per share bid for Richardson-Vicks, a 50% premium over market, in 1985. When Unilever's largest competitor, Procter and Gamble, emerged as a bidder willing to pay $69 Unilever backed off. Having spurred a competitor to expand, Unilever in the following year made an even larger deal by acquiring Chesebrough-Ponds as a white knight, topping American Brands' hostile bid.

Risk can be high in a hostile bid. The bidder is trying to buy a company without a good look inside and without the legal protection of a contract containing the assurances that a buyer typically receives in a negotiated transaction. Potential liabilities under environmental laws or for pensions are good examples.[1] The costs can be enormous. This is also a problem in some high-pressure auctions.[2] Furthermore, if there is a contest, it is easy for a bidder to get carried away with the excitement and overpay. To make matters worse, financial advisers may introduce an optimistic bias. They are usually paid much more when a bid is successful.

Losing can be very expensive too. Financing commitment fees and other costs must be paid, win or lose. Paramount's unsuccessful bid for Time was reported to have cost $50 million.

The law and practices of the takeover market strongly encourage very high prices. Takeover defenses, such as poison pills, are now powerful enough that they can only be defeated with the help of a court. But outcomes in the courts are influenced by what happens in the market. Judges will generally not intervene until they are quite sure the bidders' last dollar is on the table. When the British company Tate and Lyle asked the Delaware Chancery Court to order Staley Continental to recall its poison pill defense in 1988, the court refused. At the time the tender offer price was less than the market price and the court pointed out that the pill was 'obviously serving a useful

---

[1] See Chapter 15.
[2] See Chapter 16 Section 3.

purpose' since it allowed Staley's board 'to seek a more realistic offer.'[3] Now, after the Delaware Supreme Court's opinion in the *Paramount–Time* litigation, it would be an open question whether a target board in the same position could use its poison pill to 'just say no' to a hostile bid.

When the Canadian bidder, Campeau, sought the redemption of Federated Department Stores' poison pill, the case was heard by a Federal district court in New York, applying Delaware law. Noting that in takeover contests 'the initial tender offer is likely to be a mere opening bid regarded by the parties and the financial markets as a tentative feeler,'[4] the court left the defense in place to give the directors 'a shield to fend off coercive offers' and 'a gavel to run an auction.' Beazer's initial efforts to force Koppers to redeem its poison pill met a similar rebuff.[5] The court found that Koppers' directors had reason to believe the tender offer was too low compared to the company's long-term potential. Tate and Lyle, Campeau and Beazer eventually succeeded at higher prices. If a bid becomes high enough, the legal and shareholder supports of most takeover defenses usually give way. The bidder's dilemma is how to succeed without overpaying.

Recent trends favoring defense may make the bidder's job still harder. The success Time Incorporated had in protecting its combination with Warner Communications[6] and the additional discretion boards have under the new state antitakeover laws[7] introduce new difficult obstacles.

13.1 THE COMPETITION: WHY WERE THEY NOT BIDDING BEFORE?

Within a short time after a hostile bid is announced several competing bidders often appear. All of their bids are generally at a substantial premium over the previous market price. It is reasonable to ask, if the target is worth so much to so many people, where were all those bidders before? The bargain, if one exists, was probably there in the past.

One possible answer is that some very important information comes out in the offer itself. The bidder and the target are required to file large amounts of information with the SEC and mail it to the shareholders of the target. This information can include useful information or analyses not contained in the company's past SEC filings. The target's board must also release information when it issues its legally required recommendations to share-

---

[3] *Tate and Lyle PLC* v. *Staley Continental, Inc.,* Fed. Sec. L. Rep. (CCH) ¶93,764 (Delaware Chancery Court 1988).

[4] *CRTF Corp.* v. *Federated Dep't Stores, Inc.,* 683 F. Supp. 422 (S.D.N.Y. 1988).

[5] *BNS Inc.* v. *Koppers Co.,* 683 F. Supp. 458 (D. Del. 1988).

[6] See Section 8 of this chapter.

[7] See Chapter 6 Section 7.

holders with regard to the offer. If this information reveals a bargain, other bidders appear. Other important information may be revealed in litigation. Analysts' reports are prompted by a bid and add to the information. Investment bankers put together private studies to stir up new business from likely competing bidders once interest is piqued by a bid. Moreover, the information companies give out when they are looking for a friendly buyer as a takeover defense may be better. Usually when targets seek white knights they try to restrict where the information goes by making recipients sign confidentiality agreements, but probably this information leaks out anyway. It is also likely that sometimes there is important new information revealed by the mere facts that the bid is being made and by whom.

There is undoubtedly some truth in these answers, but it appears unlikely that the new information released is very often startling. Otherwise there must be something wrong with the quarterly and annual reports public companies must file and the other disclosure requirements that they are subject to in the ordinary course of business. Furthermore, what about the information provided by analysts' reports and financial journalists?

The psychology of the marketplace may be a better place to look for an answer. There is psychological safety in copying other people's plans. A board of directors, like any group, may be reluctant to try something new. An announcement of a fully financed bid lets other potential bidders (and their financing sources) know that the bid can be financed. The existence of other bids also tends to lend credibility to projections that add a high premium to the prior market price of the target. A similar psychology is sometimes seen in athletics. Once a milestone record – like the four-minute mile – is achieved many competitors find new abilities within themselves and are able to match the achievement. Maybe investment bankers just concentrate better when they know that the probability of a deal has increased enormously. Possibly these phenomena are responsible for much of the takeover market.[8]

Furthermore, despite the tremendous changes in business culture that have made hostile takeovers so much more acceptable, many potential bidders still do not want to start a hostile takeover. This hesitancy may show itself in several ways. Managers may not want to suggest initiating a hostile bid to their board of directors, possibly because they fear rebuff. Or they do not want their directors to feel at ease with hostile bids in case one should strike at home. Directors of potential bidders may be reluctant to start a hostile bid even if their management is not, especially directors who are themselves chief executive officers of companies that are likely targets.

Managements and directors of bidders who have never made hostile bids may be concerned about jeopardizing their reputations by making – especially by losing – a hostile bid. Paramount executives needed quite a thick skin in

---

[8] See the beginning of Section 8 of this chapter.

their battle with Time. Sir James Goldsmith has been repeatedly attacked in his attempts at U.S. acquisitions. Having launched a hostile bid to buy BAT Industries in 1989, he was reportedly astonished at the regulatory skepticism and political opposition in the U.S. (which caused the bid to fail the following year), even though he had been through rancorous hostile bids before. Some chief executives have never been the same after going through a bruising takeover battle in which they were personally attacked. Ernest Saunders, once the chairman of Guinness, is a good British takeover example. As the result of an intense struggle for Argyll Group in 1986, he was caught up in a major stock trading scandal, winding up a tragic figure.[9]

Some foreign bidders have received unwelcome publicity while making hostile bids because under their country's law they are essentially immune to takeover.[10] Many potential foreign bidders believe, with some justification, that their reputations are more fragile than those of U.S. companies. Fear of the unknown adds to this reluctance for anyone who has not been involved in a U.S.-style takeover. Litigation in a hostile takeover in the U.S. can be bruisingly intrusive. Facts can turn up that could be very harmful. In some instances foreign bidders may be risking trouble with their own governments. However, once someone else has started the process the reasons for cautious potential bidders to hold back may appear much less important. Furthermore, the process gives advisers a foothold for selling the idea of a competing bid.

13.2   SHOULD I TALK TO THE TARGET FIRST?

One of a bidder's first important decisions is whether to begin with a personal approach to the target's CEO or to let the tender offer or formal merger proposal to the board of directors be a surprise. Because of potent takeover defenses most bidders eventually have to negotiate with the target *after* the bid is irrevocably launched. However, in general, talking to the target before making a bid does more harm than good. Nevertheless, many bidders do decide to make a contact before committing themselves.

Many bidders optimistically overrate their own charm and persuasiveness and underestimate target management's animosity. Few target managements like a bidder any better just because it offers to talk first. At best targets may feign interest to buy time for defense. Moreover, a target may try to draw a bidder into making statements that are damaging later in litigation. Most bidders cannot afford to lose their precious time advantages. Perhaps the only bidder who has plenty of time is someone who does not want the target

---

[9] See Nick Kochan and Hugh Pym, *The Guinness Affair: Anatomy of a Scandal* (1987).
[10] See also the considerations we discuss in Chapter 15 Section 4.

very badly – an investor who mainly wants to stir up some takeover interest and attract other bidders.

In some instances there may be reasons to think the target is interested in a friendly deal. But since this appears to be a rare exception, there should be some solid evidence that the target might be genuinely interested. If not, going ahead with a tender offer (or a formal proposal to the target's board that it would have to make public) is probably necessary to introduce enough pressure to induce the target to bargain seriously. Even when there is a real chance for a friendly deal the bidder should not deceive itself into thinking that it will work miracles on the price. Competing bids are very hard to avoid.

On the other hand, tact is always in order. A polite last-minute call to the target's CEO informing him of the tender offer the night before the public announcement cannot hurt and may help later to keep tempers from getting out of hand. But the call should not carry with it the suggestion that the bidder will delay its plans. Otherwise there is a big risk of being considered a liar and making the situation worse.

13.3   PUBLIC RELATIONS

Statements to the press should not be unnecessarily critical of the target's board or management. (However, if the hostile bid also has to include a proxy fight, these problems cannot be avoided.)[11] Casual, inconsiderate statements can easily find their way into print or gossip. They can change an uncommitted board into a united dedicated enemy. Since most successful hostile bids must wind up as ostensibly friendly, unnecessary ill will only makes it harder to get to that place.

Sometimes, however, a provocative bidder can goad the target into ill-conceived responses that hurt its position in court. Intemperate actions and remarks by the target, for example, can be used effectively in court by the bidder's lawyers to suggest procedural flaws in the target board's decision making, lack of good faith or a tendency to prejudge issues. But the bidder should have a policy. If it is belligerent it should be so by design. And many bidders because of personal characteristics or organization are not suited for a successful belligerent strategy.

Appointing a single person at the outset to handle all press inquiries is the best way to maintain control over public relations. However, during takeover litigation it may be essential to allow lawyers to talk with the press. Otherwise, the target's lawyers can obtain exclusive access to the press in the courthouse. Because of the guarantees of free speech in the First Amendment, there are usually no prohibitions on lawyers in the U.S. discussing pending cases with

---

[11] See Section 8 of this chapter.

the press. Although takeover fights generally are not won in the press, how matters are reported in the press can be very important in keeping a board of directors and management united. Press coverage can also affect the arbitrage market.

13.4 WHY MOST SUCCESSFUL BIDS WIND UP 'FRIENDLY'

Hostile takeovers have changed completely from only a few years ago in one very important way. Now, it is generally very difficult to accomplish a hostile bid without the eventual cooperation of the target board. The bidder must maneuver the target board into formal acquiescence by a combination of market pressure and litigation. A few years ago targets went into court to try to block offers. It is now bidders who must resort to the courts to dismantle poison pills and other takeover defenses. The need for eventual board approval underscores the wisdom of avoiding personal slurs that may make future agreement more difficult.

Paramount's bid for Time is a good illustration of bidders' reliance on the courts. One of Paramount's biggest problems was that, because of Time's many broadcasting and cable television interests, Paramount needed to gain approvals from the FCC and from local cable television regulators across the country. Time was doing everything in its power to make this impossible. Paramount could not expect to obtain those approvals before the expiration of Time's tender offer, when Time could legally buy the tendered Warner shares. As a result, Paramount had to condition its bid on the success of its lawsuit in the Delaware courts attacking Time's takeover defenses. When Paramount lost in the Delaware courts it could not compete with Time's bid for Warner.[12]

Other takeover contests illustrate other reasons why target board cooperation may be essential for the bidder. KKR, for example, could never have purchased RJR Nabisco in a hostile bid. The sheer size of the transaction ($25 billion) meant that financing would have been impossible without target cooperation. Even as an agreed transaction it took months to put the financing together.

Sir James Goldsmith's unsuccessful attempt to take over BAT in 1989 and 1990 is an interesting illustration of how hard it is to combine a U.S. and foreign takeover without target board cooperation. Another example is Minorco's inability to complete its hostile bid, under English law, for Consolidated Gold Fields in 1989 because of a pending private antitrust suit

---

[12] *Paramount Communications Inc.* v. *Time Inc.,* 571 A.2d 1140 (Delaware Supreme Court 1990).

brought by Gold Fields and its affiliate, Newmont Mining, against Minorco under U.S. law in the United States.[13]

However, even where eventual target cooperation is essential, going to the target first usually does not help. Unless there are special reasons to think cooperation is likely, the bidder is just wasting valuable time. Economic pressure combined with litigation is generally the only solution for the bidder. If the bidder is successful in litigation, the court will ensure cooperation.

Bank of New York's acquisition of Irving Trust shows the power of litigation. After a long struggle, Bank of New York received, over Irving's opposition, the regulatory approvals it needed for its hostile acquisition. However, Bank of New York still faced two other major problems, Irving's flip-in poison pill and the New York antitakeover statute restricting mergers. The poison pill was effectively preventing Bank of New York from completing its hostile tender offer. But even if its tender offer had succeeded, the New York merger statute would have prevented a merger for five years, frustrating the introduction of important operating economies from combining the two banks. After the flip-in pill defense was held illegal by the New York courts because it was discriminatory,[14] Irving finally agreed to negotiate. Bank of New York had made it clear that it was ready to live with the inconvenience of the New York statute for five years. A less rich bidder probably would have been unable to obtain financing until it had complete control over the target's assets and cash flow.

Appointment of a special committee by the target board is not necessarily good news for a bidder.[15] Usually a special committee does get the decision making out of the hands of target management.[16] But, on the other hand, a special committee means that the company will probably be sold in an auction, with the committee's investment bankers aggressively soliciting competing bids. A top price is the likely result. Generally there is no reason for a bidder to slow down to negotiate when a special committee is appointed. The best strategy remains the same – maximum pressure through a pending tender offer and litigation. It puts pressure on the defense not to slow down the auction process to the hostile bidder's detriment. Campeau accomplished this effectively in its bid for Federated Department Stores in 1988. Federated had its preclusive flip-in poison pill in place but Campeau forced a fast court-

---

[13] *Consolidated Gold Fields PLC* v. *Minorco, S.A.*, 871 F.2d 252 (2d Cir. 1989).

[14] *Bank of New York* v. *Irving Bank Corp.*, 536 N.Y.S.2d 923 (N.Y. Sup. 1988). We discuss the regulatory aspects of the Bank of New York/Irving Trust battle in Chapter 15.

[15] See Chapter 14 Section 1.

[16] Special committees usually act independently, although the Macmillan cases, *Robert M. Bass Group, Inc.* v. *Evans*, 552 A.2d 1227 (Delaware Chancery Court 1988) and *Mills Acquisition Co.* v. *Macmillan, Inc.*, 559 A.2d 1261 (Delaware Supreme Court 1989), which we have discussed frequently, are counterexamples. See also *In re Trans World Airlines, Inc. Shareholders Litigation*, 1988 WL 111271 (Delaware Chancery Court Oct. 21, 1988).

supervised auction that it won.[17] However, it is possible that since then the Delaware Supreme Court's opinion in the *Paramount–Time* case may have made Delaware legal rules more favorable to targets in this kind of situation.[18]

13.5 COMPETING FRIENDLY BIDS

When a target company brings in a friendly bidder to compete with a hostile bid, procedural requirements imposed by the courts are likely to prevent the target from favoring the friendly bidder. A great deal of information about the company, including projections prepared by management, is likely to be furnished to a friendly bidder. Once the information is provided to the friendly bidder courts will generally insist that it also be provided to the hostile bidder.[19]

A hostile bidder has a decided litigating advantage when the target has an obvious conflict of interest. Attempts by the target to favor one bidder usually backfire in court, especially if that bidder is closely connected with management. This has been true in a number of the cases we have discussed in detail.[20] Even when a special committee is established to counteract a conflict of interest a bidder who believes it is disfavored may be able to seize on procedural irregularities to persuade a court that the conflict of interest has not been cured.

13.6 FAMILY HOLDINGS

Extended families with large holdings in a company formed by an ancestor several generations earlier are often not as invulnerable to takeover as they may appear. These loosely organized family shareholders are likely to succumb to the temptation of high prices combined with litigation pressure. At first, large family shareholders may appear to support management unwaveringly. There are important social advantages in being a member of a family that controls an important company, and there are family pressures and inertia. But usually there is a point (or a price) at which this support begins to falter, particularly if the target board of directors is not united in opposition to a takeover. Losing a court case and bad publicity, for example,

---

[17] *CRTF Corp.* v. *Federated Dep't Stores, Inc.*, 683 F. Supp. 422 (S.D.N.Y. 1988).

[18] *Paramount Communications Inc.* v. *Time Inc.*, 571 A.2d 1140 (Delaware Supreme Court 1990). See our discussion of auctions in Chapter 10.

[19] See, for example, *Edelman* v. *Fruehauf Corp.*, 798 F.2d 882 (6th Cir. 1986).

[20] For example, *Revlon, Inc.* v. *MacAndrews and Forbes Holdings, Inc.*, 506 A.2d 173 (Delaware Supreme Court 1986) and, especially, *Mills Acquisition Co.* v. *Macmillan, Inc.*, 559 A.2d 1261 (Delaware Supreme Court 1989).

may undermine family confidence in the management. Quaker Oats' 1986 acquisition of Anderson, Clayton and Co. is an excellent example.[21]

However, a family that can install a capital structure with two classes of common shares, with high and low voting power, is in a much better position to retain control. If the company or family members would like to sell shares they generally can do so without diluting the control of family members who continue to hold their shares.[22]

13.7 MARGIN REGULATIONS

Leveraged bidders also must comply with the Federal Reserve Board's margin regulations.[23] These rules regulate loans for the purchase of stock, where a pledge of the stock secures the loan. The general rule is that the loan against the margin stock must be no more than 50% of the stock's market value. If more money is being borrowed additional collateral must be supplied or the loan must be unsecured.

In 1986 the Federal Reserve Board began interpreting these rules so that they would apply to many acquisitions financed largely by borrowing. Now when a bidder sets up a new corporation to make an acquisition the Board presumes that its bank loans or other borrowings are secured by the stock of the target it hopes to acquire. This interpretation introduces the 50% borrowing limit, which can be fatal to bidders hoping to borrow 80 or 90% of the acquisition price.

However, the Board left some explicit exceptions that bidders try to fit into when they want to make a highly leveraged bid using a new corporation. When there is any ambiguity about whether the exceptions apply, targets of unfriendly bids can be expected to challenge the financing in court. For example, one exception covers situations where the borrowing is guaranteed by an entity with 'substantial' assets (other than margin stock) or cash flow. A healthy parent company is an uncontroversial example, but in other cases whether the assets are substantial could be hotly litigated.[24] The regulations only apply to debt financings, not to issuances of preferred stock. But whether

---

[21] *AC Acquisitions Corp.* v. *Anderson, Clayton and Co.*, 519 A.2d 103 (Delaware Chancery Court 1986). See Chapter 16 Section 2. See also *Unilever Acquisition Corp.* v. *Richardson-Vicks, Inc.*, 618 F. Supp. 407 (S.D.N.Y. 1985).

[22] See our discussion of different classes of voting stock and the SEC's response in Chapter 9 Section 2.

[23] The rules are contained in Regulations G, U and X established by the Federal Reserve Board under authority granted it by §7 of the Securities Exchange Act of 1934.

[24] See *MAI Basic Four, Inc.* v. *Prime Computer*, No. 88-2512-MA (D. Mass. Dec. 29, 1988), in which the court ordered the bidder to expand its disclosure of the risk that it would have to restructure the transaction to meet the margin requirements.

a security carrying the name preferred stock is really stock or only debt under another name can also be litigated.[25]

The margin rules are much easier to deal with in a friendly transaction. They contain exceptions for transactions where there is a signed merger agreement with the target's board of directors or when enough shares are acquired (usually at least 90%) to make it possible to accomplish a short-form merger.[26] The rules also indirectly benefit foreign acquirers, because they do not apply to credit obtained outside the United States by a borrower that is not controlled by U.S. persons or acting on their behalf.

13.8 PROXY FIGHTS

Before hostile tender offers became so common, the principal means of replacing management was a solicitation of shareholders' proxies to replace the incumbent board of directors with a dissident slate. Generally, this was not very successful. Before the takeover boom that began in the U.S. in the 1960s, there were no takeover booms based on proxy fights. In the early days of American big business there probably were many takeovers through the equivalent of market sweeps. Why did that end? Our best guess is that once CEOs of large corporations became part of the social elite, the banks and investment banks would not support a raider. There are psychological factors at work here that are similar to those seen in the decision of a particular board whether to make a hostile bid. On the other hand, the 1960s were a period of widespread social change, a continuation of the social upheaval caused by World War II.

When takeover defense became more effective because of poison pills and powerful new state antitakeover laws, proxy fights became much more important.[27] A good example is the two simultaneous shareholder solicitations that were pursued in early 1990 by Georgia-Pacific Corporation in support of its successful hostile tender offer for another paper manufacturer, Great Northern Nekoosa. One was a standard proxy fight to unseat the board. The other was a special shareholder referendum to eliminate the poison pill. This referendum was allowed under the terms of Great Northern's pill. The referendum provision appears to have been included in the pill as part of a compromise to appease institutional shareholders who had been promoting annual shareholder resolutions asking the board to redeem the pill.

Proxy fights are very thoroughly regulated by the SEC's proxy rules. The

---

[25] See *City Capital Associates Ltd. Partnership* v. *Interco Inc.*, 696 F. Supp. 1551 (D. Del. 1988).

[26] See the Glossary entries for 'short-form merger' and 'highly leveraged transaction'.

[27] See our analysis of the potential role of proxy fights in Chapter 6 Section 8.

SEC staff monitors compliance closely. During a proxy fight everything designed to influence the outcome of a shareholder vote is considered proxy material and must be submitted in advance to SEC examiners. This includes mailings to shareholders, newspaper advertisements and often even press releases. The SEC often insists on substantial rewording or additional disclosures.

When a proxy fight is not associated with a tender offer or some other proposal to get money to the target shareholders, it is a war of ideas. The choices are not as simple as they are when a buyout offer is on the table. An insurgent is trying to replace the board with its own nominees, who may have a program but cannot promise a specific price at a specific time. Instead, they are proposing a different management style, a new approach to the business or even a long-term business plan. Management can counter with arguments and plans of its own about the prospects for the future, management style, integrity and experience.

From the perspective of bidders, proxy fights are slow and their outcomes uncertain. Target shareholders want money, not talk. When it comes to talk, they usually prefer the management. More precisely, shareholders are reluctant to give up the chance of a high takeover premium in exchange for words. U.S. shareholders are even less likely to vote for a foreign insurgent about whom they probably know little or nothing.

Proxy contests can become extremely nasty and personal. These wars of ideas have a tendency to hit bottom in vicious attacks on individuals. Generally reputations can be hurt more in proxy fights than in tender offers.[28] GAF's current chairman, Samuel Heyman, reached his position only after a bitter proxy fight that got bogged down in disagreeable questions about how he and his mother handled his eccentric sister's financial affairs.[29] Many bidders have been the subject of strong attacks in newspaper ads. In its 1985 fight against Australian financier Robert Holmes à Court, Asarco Inc. placed a 19-page advertisement in the *Wall Street Journal* titled 'What You Should Know About Holmes à Court.'

However, when a cash bid is combined with a proxy fight, the promises made by the bidder and its insurgent slate can be quite specific. The main proxy fight issue can be made very simple: should my cash offer be accepted? Even then target shareholders, particularly arbitragers, show a strong preference for money in hand. Bank of New York combined a proxy fight, which it narrowly lost, with its tender offer for Irving Trust as a way to help it circumvent a myriad of takeover defenses. At the same time it kept up its litigation pressure against Irving's defenses so it only suffered a temporary setback when it lost its proxy fight.

[28] See our analysis of the effects of a hostile bid on reputations in Section 1 of this chapter.
[29] See *GAF Corp.* v. *Heyman*, 724 F.2d 727 (2d Cir. 1983).

Takeover defenses aimed particularly at proxy contests are in use, although courts are quite negative about attempts to limit the power of shareholders to decide elections unless these limitations are specifically authorized by state law.[30] In the *Paramount–Time* case, the Chancery Court was greatly troubled because Time switched strategies (from merging with Warner to buying Warner stock in a tender offer) to avoid a shareholder vote it knew it would lose, although the Delaware Supreme Court seemed less concerned about the issue.[31] Time, however, was merely switching from one typical method of doing an acquisition to another. Moreover, the vote was a requirement of the New York Stock Exchange, not Delaware law. The Delaware courts might not have held in Time's favor if it had been manipulating the Delaware electoral process.

Most states, however, allow a board of directors to be classified into three groups, each elected in a different year for a three-year term. When BTR attempted to acquire Norton Company in 1990, Massachusetts passed emergency legislation making staggered boards mandatory.[32] In theory, use of a staggered board of directors makes obtaining control in a single proxy contest impossible. Nevertheless, winning the available seats puts a great deal of pressure on the other directors to resign particularly when the insurgent owns a majority of the stock. Nonetheless, the possibility that the board would not resign can make nervous lenders much more nervous about financing a bid.

Staggered boards give targets an advantage in proxy fights. But they also create a disadvantage. Institutional investors are usually quite reluctant to give a raider control until they have seen his money. But with a staggered board, the institutional investors can have it both ways. They can help to elect some minority dissident directors to stir things up and show how displeased they are but at the same time be sure they are not turning over control to the dissidents.

In 1988, Carl Icahn tried to win five seats on Texaco's 14-member staggered board after he had, as a major shareholder, helped to work out the settlement of the lawsuit with Pennzoil. His slate of directors was committed to his ideas about how the company should reorganize itself coming out of bankruptcy and favored a sale of the company if the right price could be obtained. Before the vote Icahn also announced his own tender offer for the company.

Intensive efforts by Texaco management to win the votes of institutional investors were sufficiently persuasive to defeat Icahn's nominees by a vote of

---

[30] See, for example, *Frantz Mfg. Co.* v. *EAC Indus., Inc.*, 501 A.2d 401 (Delaware Supreme Court 1985); *Blasins Indus., Inc.* v. *Atlas Corp.*, Fed. Sec. L. Rep. (CCH) ¶93,965 (Delaware Chancery Court 1988); *Unilever Acquisition Corp.* v. *Richardson-Vicks, Inc.*, 618 F. Supp. 407 (S.D.N.Y. 1985).

[31] *Paramount Communications Inc.* v. *Time Inc.*, 571 A.2d 1140 (Delaware Supreme Court 1990).

[32] We discussed this defense near the end of Chapter 8.

58.6 to 41.4%. But the institutions bargained hard with management before giving their support. Texaco had to agree to their demands (supported by Icahn) for an institutional holders' seat on the board, a role for them (with management) in the nomination of future slates for the board and a watering down of a proposed poison pill. The compromise poison pill is especially interesting. It was designed to be inoperative against a fully financed offer held open for at least 45 days – hardly much of a defense these days.

This kind of negotiation by institutional investors could become much more common in the future. The Great Northern Nekoosa pill we mentioned earlier in this chapter is a similar example. But was the watered-down pill a clear victory for Texaco shareholders? The limitations on the poison pill should make it harder for the directors to obtain a high price for the company, because they will be less credible negotiators. On the other hand, the limitations on the pill give the shareholders more control over the board. In short, when shareholders can trust the board, this sort of compromise poison pill is probably a bad idea; but when they cannot, it is a good idea. Moreover, in this instance the shareholders were already quite well organized because of the bankruptcy and did not have to rely on the board completely for takeover defense. This result is a very practical illustration of the shareholder–director problems we discussed in detail in Part I.

13.9 STREET SWEEPS

Establishing a foothold position before the acquisition is worked out also provides some protection against a bidder's losing out completely. Early stock purchases reduce the overall cost of an acquisition and may provide a strategic beachhead toward control. If a competing offer is successful, the foothold stock can be sold to the successful bidder at a profit. However, in large acquisitions, because of the Hart–Scott–Rodino antitrust notification statute, the permitted advance purchases are very small as a percentage of a large transaction.[33] Moreover, as we have cautioned before, to avoid insider trading and other legal problems, a bidder must make its market purchases before discussions with the target begin.

One would expect the ferociously aggressive takeover market to devise some ingenious ways for bidders to work around the delays and purchase prohibitions prescribed by the Hart–Scott–Rodino statute, the Williams Act and SEC rules. They have done so, but with limited success. Hart–Scott–Rodino rules have been tightened to forestall the most obvious avoidance schemes. Violations of SEC rules have been enforced more aggressively, to the accompaniment of great publicity. Arrangements between Ivan Boesky

---

[33] See Chapter 9 Section 4.

and the prominent West Coast broker Boyd Jefferies to park stock to hide beneficial ownership helped Boesky make very large secret accumulations, but led to several criminal convictions. More recently, Paul Bilzerian, who became chairman of the Singer Company in 1988 after a successful hostile takeover, was convicted on criminal charges for failing properly to disclose his financial backers.[34] Many of the charges against Drexel Burnham Lambert and Michael Milken related to similar violations.[35]

The only legal technique is to make large private purchases. If they are large enough they must be conditional on Hart–Scott–Rodino clearance and disclosed under SEC rules. But these negotiated purchases usually involve tough sellers (arbitragers or other stock market professionals) who will not give up much on price. And state antitakeover laws and poison pills may make block purchases imprudent by foreclosing later options.[36]

Closely related is the street sweep which, though it can provide a crucial edge, can be used only in very special situations. In a street sweep, large purchases of securities are made, sometimes in a matter of hours, in the market and in privately negotiated transactions. When a tender offer is outstanding, it sometimes can be terminated and a market sweep substituted. But withdrawing an offer is legally and strategically very tricky. In two important takeover cases courts have found that market sweeps, under the circumstances, were not illegal tender offers.[37] Similar purchases, under different circumstances, were found in an older case not to have been 'privately negotiated' and thus to have been subject to the requirements for tender offers.[38] One reason for the confusion is that there is no statutory definition of tender offer. So far the SEC has failed to provide a definition by rule.

Furthermore, effective market sweeps are not always practical. They depend on large accumulations of target stock in the hands of arbitragers and other speculators having taken place. Even that is not always enough. Arbitragers will not sell their blocks of shares unless they believe that the sweep price is close to the top price of the deal. Neither of these conditions is likely to be fulfilled without a prolonged takeover fight during which speculators acquire target stock and have plenty of time to make estimates about the likely top deal price. In short, market sweeps are probably more accurately described as a result of delay rather than as a solution to delay.

---

[34] *SEC* v. *Bilzerian,* SEC Litigation Release No. 12144 (June 29, 1989).
[35] *SEC* v. *Drexel Burnham Lambert,* SEC Litigation Releases Nos. 12061, 12062 and 12171 (1989).
[36] See Chapter 6.
[37] *Hanson Trust PLC* v. *SCM Corp.,* 774 F.2d 47 (2d Cir. 1985) and *SEC* v. *Carter Hawley Hale Stores, Inc.,* 760 F.2d 945 (9th Cir. 1985).
[38] *Wellman* v. *Dickinson,* 475 F. Supp. 783 (S.D.N.Y. 1979).

14

How Should We Defend Against
a Hostile Bid?

> Valor has its limits like the other virtues, and these limits once
> transgressed, we find ourselves on the path of vice; so that we
> may pass through valor to temerity, obstinacy, and madness,
> unless we know its limits well – and they are truly hard to
> discern near the borderlines.[1]

One way or another takeover defense has an important connection with
everything in this book. It is one of the most difficult problems in the takeover
world. Bidders sometimes make lots of money by a combination of action
and luck and they sometimes lose a lot for the same reasons. For targets, on
the other hand, blundering into a successful defense against a high premium
cash offer is quite rare.

Some general defenses such as fair price charter provisions and staggered
boards must be in place long before there is a bid since they require shareholder approval. Once a bid is in sight shareholder approval for takeover
defenses (now difficult under any circumstances) is usually impossible to
obtain. Other defenses like employee stock ownership plans require time to
put in place. However, poison pills, the most potent defenses, do not require
shareholder approval. The main advantage of having a poison pill in place
in advance of any bid is that it may be a warning to potential bidders that
fierce resistance is inevitable and the takeover price is likely to be high. It
used to be said that having a pill in place in advance would increase the
likelihood that courts would hold that it is legal. That is no longer true, if it
ever was. On the other hand, having a pill in advance may provoke embarrassing institutional shareholder insistence that it should be redeemed.[2]

Once a bid appears inevitable, deciding on the goal for defense is crucial.
In many cases it may be the most important decision. One reason Pillsbury's

---

[1] Montaigne, 'One Is Punished for Defending a Place Obstinately Without Reason,' *The
Complete Essays of Montaigne* 47 (Frame transl. 1965) (first published in 1572–4).

[2] See, for example, *Georgia-Pacific Corp.,* v. *Great Northern Nekoosa Corp.*, 728 F. Supp. 807
(D. Me. 1990). Although its pill withstood legal attack, Great Northern Nekoosa was taken
over after defending itself with a poison pill, allowing shareholders to vote to redeem the pill at
a special referendum. It appears that the pill was a compromise offered to resistant institutional
shareholders.

defenses against Grand Metropolitan's cash bid in 1988 were so ineffectual appears to have been the lack of a convincing, coherent goal.[3] Making and communicating the decision quickly to shareholders and the market is also very important.

Usually, there are four main goals that can reasonably be considered:

1. Staying independent.
2. Combining with another company.
3. Selling the company to a favored buyer.
4. Selling the company at the highest possible price.

Since success can never be assured, some of these goals may be pursued as fallback positions. But the subordination of secondary goals must be clearly understood by the board, management and their advisers to avoid confusion. For example, it may be consistent (although very difficult) to try to stay independent while also looking for likely friendly buyers. But a mere yearning for independence contributes nothing positive and interferes with the search for a white knight.

Using publicity immediately to educate the investment community is important, particularly if the primary goal is to remain independent. When arbitragers are confused about a target's goals or do not understand the strengths of its takeover defenses, they may buy shares on mistaken assumptions. As the facts become clearer they feel betrayed. As a result the target is left with a group of extremely aggressive hostile shareholders. A bad outcome for both sides.

An important practical point for directors facing a hostile bid to keep in mind is that courts have a tendency to dwell on procedure.[4] Board procedures probably will be closely scrutinized in litigation. The slightest impropriety or mistake may become an embarrassing subject in litigation and may even determine the outcome. However, procedure should not be confused with formalistic legalism. Each procedural step should have a commonsense significance. Directors should understand the procedures and reasons for them so well that they can explain and defend them later when they are witnesses in litigation. A five-minute board meeting by conference telephone with a sharply defined point of view may be far more successful legally than a ceremonial two-day meeting on the wrong subjects.

Each of the four main goals raises special issues that are related to topics we examined in detail in Part I. We will look at each in turn but first we will discuss an extremely important procedural device, special board committees.

---

[3] See *Grand Metropolitan PLC* v. *Pillsbury Co.,* 558 A.2d 1049 (Delaware Chancery Court 1988), which we discuss in Chapter 8.

[4] We explained how and why this happens in Chapter 5.

14.1   SHOULD WE APPOINT A SPECIAL COMMITTEE?

As soon as possible the board of directors must decide who will be in charge of the response to the takeover bid. The only choices are the full board of directors or a special committee of independent directors. Special committees are such a simple, effective solution to the difficult problem of director conflict of interest, it might appear that target boards should always appoint them. However, there are some significant drawbacks. The main one is that special board committees are very divisive. They not only replace the board, they are also in effect an alternative management. Two groups are running the same company.

Creating a special committee to deal with a takeover almost always means eventually selling the company. There are tremendous legal pressures on the special committee to assert its independence from management. The safest and simplest way to do this is by running an auction. Trying to keep the company independent is the riskiest. Moreover, the committee's advisers usually have a strong incentive in favor of an auction where they can make more money and dominate the process professionally. In short, like court decisions that emphasize procedure, special committees may look like mere legal formalism but they turn out to have crucial substantive effects. But appointment of a special committee is not necessarily good news for a bidder, either. The almost inevitable auction will only drive up the price.[5]

Independent legal and investment banking advice is a very important procedural (and substantive) consideration for a special committee. If the advice is not independent, a court is less likely to view the committee as truly independent. Having independent lawyers and investment bankers present during special committee deliberations assures a different view of the situation and places pressure on committee members to take their independence seriously.

Even when a special committee hires its own lawyer, past connections between the law firm and management could raise an issue about how independent the advice is. On the other hand the independence of investment bankers can usually be judged by the incentives in their fee agreement. If the fee goes up sharply if there is a sale and with increases in the purchase price, there is much less reason to question their independence.

In the Time–Warner–Paramount takeover struggle a special committee had been created to oversee the merger but it never met or retained separate lawyers or investment bankers. An aggressive special committee would not have served the strategic interests of either Time or Paramount. Once the Time directors decided they were committed to the combination with Warner an aggressive special committee would have been a divisive force. The special

---

[5] See the last paragraph of Chapter 13 Section 4.

committee (and its advisers) might have had a strong temptation in the face of the Paramount bid to abandon the combination with Warner and hold an auction. Without such a committee the board remained united with management and committed to the Warner combination.

On the other hand, an aggressive special committee could have hurt Paramount's already troubled bid for Time. There may have been strong potential bidders for Time who were not willing to appear as hostile bidders. A special committee soliciting bids and offering information might have been able to interest some formidable new competitors.

14.2 STAYING INDEPENDENT

In general, independence has been extremely difficult to achieve in the face of a high-premium cash hostile bid. The companies that have stayed independent have done so by changing dramatically in a way that has made completion of the bid either economically impossible or unattractive.

In the late 1970s and early 1980s, before poison pills appeared, there were several rare exceptions. These were generally accomplished by completing a transaction that made business sense for the target company but would not work for the bidder. In 1978, Marshall Field and Co., the Chicago-based department store company, defended itself against a hostile bid by Carter Hawley Hale Stores, the California-based department store chain, by buying another chain of stores. In the climate of rigorous antitrust law enforcement then prevalent, this maneuver created enough of an obstacle for Carter Hawley Hale to cause it to withdraw its bid.

There was violent disagreement over whether Marshall Field's action really was a reasonable business decision. The price of Field's stock went down sharply when the defense succeeded and stayed down.[6] Field's and its directors were sued, unsuccessfully, by shareholders for their defensive actions.[7] Moreover, the defense only worked against that particular bidder. To avoid a bid by Carl Icahn a few years later Field's wound up being taken over by the British diversified tobacco giant, BAT, which later was itself threatened by a 'bust-up' takeover bid in London.[8] The theme of the bid for BAT, typical of the late 1980s, is that from the standpoint of shareholders, diversification is an ugly idea.[9] BAT defeated the bid by a combination of busting itself up

---

[6] See Frank H. Easterbrook and Daniel R. Fischel, 'The Proper Role of a Target's Management in Responding to a Tender Offer,' 94 *Harvard Law Review* 1161 (1981).

[7] The claims were based in part on Federal law. This case took place before the principal subject of tender offer litigation switched from Federal to state law. *Panter* v. *Marshall Field and Co.*, 646 F.2d 271 (7th Cir. 1981).

[8] The bid, led by Sir James Goldsmith, was abandoned in mid-1990.

[9] For a favorable commentary on this type of bid, see Michael C. Jensen, 'Eclipse of the Public Corporation,' 67 *Harvard Business Review* 61 (Sept.–Oct. 1989).

and legal maneuvers in the U.S., where it owned a large life insurance company.

Another successful pre-poison pill defense was achieved by Brunswick Corporation in 1982. Faced with a surprise tender offer by Whittaker Corporation, Brunswick negotiated an agreement with American Home Products for the sale of its Sherwood Medical division. American Home Products bought 64% of Brunswick's stock in a cash tender offer and immediately exchanged the Brunswick stock for all of Brunswick's Sherwood stock. Mainly, Sherwood was what Whittaker wanted. It dropped its offer after unsuccessfully challenging the legality of the agreement with American Home Products as purely defensive and not in the shareholders' best interests.[10] Since the Brunswick shareholders ended up with cash and Brunswick stock which immediately was worth more than Whittaker's offer, Whittaker was, in effect, outbid.

Although equally controversial, Brunswick's defense had a more successful ending than Marshall Field's. Even ardent opponents of takeover defense began to cite Brunswick's sale of Sherwood as an example of drastic defense tactics that clearly made money for the shareholders.[11] The strategy also paid off for the Brunswick shareholders in the long run. Brunswick found that the crisis atmosphere created by the takeover bid and its drastic, albeit successful, response allowed it to make highly beneficial organizational changes and reductions in operating expenses that it might not otherwise have been able to achieve. The success of the company in the years that followed may have been in large measure a result of these changes.[12] This defense was a precursor of the restructuring defenses that became so important in the late 1980s.

Recent restructurings usually have been based on dramatically increasing the company's debt burden and paying a large cash dividend to shareholders or buying back large amounts of stock at a premium price. Newmont Mining and Harcourt Brace Jovanovich were successful with this strategy in 1987.[13] In some of these restructurings the shareholders' interest in the company is reduced, while management and employee stock ownership plans (ESOPs) receive stock.[14] Polaroid, for example, mounted an effective defense in 1988 through the combined effects of the Delaware antitakeover law and sales of large blocks of stock to a leveraged ESOP and a friendly shareholder. The

---

[10] *Whittaker Corp.* v. *Edgar*, 535 F. Supp. 933 (N.D. Ill.), affirmed No. 82–1305 (7th Cir. March 5, 1982).

[11] Michael C. Jensen, 'Takeovers: Folklore and Science,' 62 *Harvard Business Review* 109, 119 (Nov.–Dec. 1984).

[12] See Leo Herzel and John R. Schmidt, 'Shareholders can Benefit from Sale of 'Crown Jewels,' " VI *Legal Times* 21 (1983).

[13] *British Printing and Communication Corp. plc* v. *Harcourt Brace Jovanovich, Inc.*, 664 F. Supp. 1519 (S.D.N.Y. 1987); *Ivanhoe Partners* v. *Newmont Mining Corp.*, 535 A.2d 1334 (Delaware Supreme Court 1987).

[14] *Shamrock Holdings, Inc.* v. *Polaroid Corp.*, 559 A.2d 257 (Delaware Chancery Court 1989).

large blocks of stock made it impossible for Shamrock, the bidder, to take advantage of an (intended) loophole in the Delaware antitakeover law restricting mergers. In turn this probably made it difficult or impossible for the bidder to obtain financing.[15]

Restructurings are a close relative of the leveraged buyout. Although debt is increased sharply, as in a leveraged buyout, the public shareholders continue to have a large interest in the company. Both can be quite risky because of the large amount of debt created.[16]

We have mentioned before several important examples of failed restructuring defenses. In one of these, court intervention blocked the publisher Macmillan from completing its recapitalization in the face of Robert Bass's bid. The court balked at the lack of clear advantage for the shareholders and the degree to which management would have boosted its interest in the company.[17]

Short of implementing a dramatic financial restructuring plan or altering the company in some other fundamental way, is there anything that target directors can do to maintain their independence? Recent Delaware cases suggest the possibility that there may be. In 1989, Time, as we have seen, was able to block Paramount's hostile bid by completing its acquisition of Warner. The Delaware courts upheld the right of a board to oppose a tender offer that is inconsistent with the board's long-term plans.[18]

That does not mean that, under Delaware law, boards of directors can use poison pills or any other defense they choose to block takeover bids that they believe are not in the long-term interests of shareholders. For Time, buying Warner only had a defensive effect because Paramount had made its tender offer contingent on Time's not acquiring or merging with Warner. In other words, Time had a perfectly legitimate corporate transaction under way that Paramount did not like. Nothing was standing in Paramount's way except its inability to complete its bid before Time combined with Warner. Time did have a poison pill but it was not an issue in the case since it was irrelevant to Paramount's inability to complete its offer. Furthermore, the courts pointed out that Time's acquisition of Warner would not preclude a hostile bid, although this was somewhat disingenuous since Time became a very large, different company after the acquisition.

Even after the *Paramount–Time* case, the receptiveness of the Delaware courts to arguments about long-term plans is likely to be less when a bid is

---

[15] We discuss this example in Chapter 6 Sections 1 and 2.
[16] We discuss recapitalizations in more detail in Chapter 16 Section 2.
[17] *Robert M. Bass Group, Inc.* v. *Evans*, 552 A.2d 1227 (Delaware Chancery Court 1988). Robert Maxwell eventually acquired Macmillan. We discuss this controversy in Chapters 2, 7 and 10.
[18] *Paramount Communications Inc.* v. *Time Inc.*, 571 A.2d 1140 (Delaware Supreme Court 1990) (reproduced as Appendix A.12).

being precluded by a defense. A flip-in poison pill, for example, in effect can usually prevent all takeovers attempted without target board approval unless the courts intervene. It is conceivable that under special circumstances a determined bidder with plenty of cash could at great cost override a poison pill defense. So far only Sir James Goldsmith has come close to taking this risk (in his pursuit of Crown Zellerbach), and that was against a much less potent flip-over pill.

We have seen that, so far, courts applying Delaware law have allowed these pills to be used only when they are fulfilling a bargaining role, not as a tool for maintaining complete independence.[19] But after the Delaware Supreme Court's opinion in the *Paramount–Time* case, this may have become an open issue again. There are some comments along this line by the Delaware chancellor, William Allen, in one 1989 case noting that the Delaware courts have ordered pills redeemed only when the pills favor a transaction proposed by management. The Delaware courts, he said, had not been called on to rule in a case where directors have decided a bid is too low to be in the shareholders' long-term interests and are using the pill as a means to prevent the low bid.[20] The Delaware Supreme Court appeared to refer favorably to this opinion in its *Paramount–Time* opinion.[21]

The idea that in a takeover situation directors may look out for the interests of constituencies other than shareholders received the blessing of the Delaware Supreme Court in the *Unocal* case and again in the *Paramount–Time* case,[22] but the limits of this discretion have never been specified.[23] In the *Revlon* case the court criticized the target board of directors for considering another constituency – the noteholders.[24] Normally, however, directors can always consider other interests who, if neglected, could assert a claim against the company or adversely affect it. The court probably viewed the noteholder action differently because it suspected conflict of interest in the board's motives.

Probably, the reason an independence theory has not been tested under Delaware law yet is that lawyers are not convinced that the strategy would work. In defending against the hostile bid from Grand Metropolitan, Pillsbury came close, but it combined 'just saying no' with a feeble plan to restructure its Burger King unit. Furthermore, Pillsbury was unable to persuade either the court or shareholders that shareholders might be better off

---

[19] We discuss the factors that would need to be considered in Chapter 8.

[20] *TW Services, Inc.* v. *SWT Acquisition Corp.*, Fed. Sec. L. Rep. (CCH) ¶94, 334 (Delaware Chancery Court 1989).

[21] *Paramount Communications Inc.* v. *Time Inc.*, 571 A.2d 1140, 1153 (Delaware Supreme Court 1990).

[22] Id.; *Unocal Corp.* v. *Mesa Petroleum Co.*, 493 A.2d 946 (Delaware Supreme Court 1985).

[23] See also Chapter 8.

[24] *Revlon, Inc.* v. *MacAndrews and Forbes Holdings, Inc.*, 506 A.2d 173 (Delaware Supreme Court 1986). See Chapter 10 Section 1.

sticking with the management's long-term plans instead of taking the large amount of money Grand Metropolitan was offering.[25] Maybe even after the Delaware Supreme Court's opinion in the *Paramount–Time* case that will remain a sticking point under Delaware law – unless the long-term plan is quite inspired.

However, in the future, companies incorporated in some other states might have more success. New York, for example, now has a statute specifically allowing directors of a target corporation to consider the long-term effect of a takeover on shareholders and the company. Other states have statutes that give target directors powers to consider in addition the effects on employees, suppliers, customers and communities. A recent Pennsylvania statute even gives these other interests an equal status with shareholders. These constituency statutes specifically apply to takeover situations and they also authorize boards of directors to use flip-in poison pills.[26]

Under these statutes the close questions about takeover defense that Delaware courts examine under the *Unocal* reasonableness rule[27] might be avoidable. Instead, a defense might be possible under the traditional business judgment rule, with courts deferring to boards of directors unless they are disloyal or reckless.

This prospect may suggest that apprehensive managements of likely targets incorporated in Delaware will try to reincorporate in states with these new statutes. However, institutional investor opposition to moving companies from one state to another to further antitakeover aims is running high. Since shareholder approval is required for these moves, few companies are likely to try. Furthermore, for the moment, some of these laws, such as the New York statute authorizing flip-in poison pills, apply only to companies that are incorporated in New York *and* also have some operations there. Although the defensive benefits of these statutes are likely to be confined to companies that are already incorporated in those states, more states will probably adopt similar laws. However, it is not clear whether Delaware will. For Delaware the calculation would be quite complicated.

Whatever the state of incorporation, the attitude of each member of the board of directors is crucial to the success or failure of any attempt to remain independent. As a hostile bid progresses the directors will feel more and more market and legal pressures. Any initial lack of enthusiasm for independence can become dissent as the process continues. Usually, if there is not well-informed unanimity on the board for staying independent, it may be better to choose another goal. Furthermore, when independence has been achieved over the strong opposition of shareholders, the board may still have to face

---

[25] See *Grand Metropolitan PLC* v. *Pillsbury Co.*, 558 A.2d 1049 (Delaware Chancery Court 1988), which we discuss in Chapter 8.
[26] We discuss these statutes in Chapter 6 Sections 7 and 8.
[27] See our discussion of the standards for director conduct in Chapter 2.

new takeover attempts or proxy fights organized by dissident shareholders. As we have noted before, it is very important to teach the market quickly, before large numbers of shares change hands, that there is determination and ability to stay independent.

Worth noting again, a key to independence is to avoid turning these decisions over to a special committee. Legal, practical and psychological considerations make it highly unlikely that a special committee will choose independence as a goal. The right and safe course for special committees usually is to sell the company for the best price possible.[28]

14.3 COMBINING WITH ANOTHER COMPANY

The *Paramount–Time* case may also have given new life to a strategy (sometimes a defense, sometimes not) that is not quite independence and not quite a sale to a white knight. A combination of equals between the target and another company will probably so alter the business that it will complicate the bidder's reasons for making the acquisition. However, as the courts stressed in the *Paramount–Time* case, it will not necessarily prevent or deter a bid from another bidder with different goals. With money, time and determination a bidder can take the combination apart.

Considering the reasoning in the opinions in the *Paramount–Time* case, it seems likely that one of the central legal issues affecting this defense will be timing. If the combination is thought up after the hostile bid is made, it may be difficult to convince the courts that the directors were pursuing a long-term goal. In other words, the story the directors tell in litigation will not appear credible if the transaction seems to be a defensive maneuver. However, even last-minute defensive decisions will probably stand up better in court if they have evolved from a strategy the board has been considering favorably before. This was a strong factor in the Delaware Chancery Court's decision not to enjoin Polaroid's sale of a large block of stock to an ESOP.[29]

Selling the strategy to shareholders and the market through a public relations campaign is important. Although the target is not likely to be able to whip up much enthusiasm among arbitragers for a long-term strategy that will not produce cash quickly, it may keep them from buying stock in the two companies. When arbitragers buy heavily, the combination has a highly motivated, aggressive enemy.

Timing of the combination may be less important in states with anti-takeover laws that give target boards the right to consider the long-term

---

[28] See Section 1 of this chapter, and Chapter 5 Section 6.

[29] *Shamrock Holdings, Inc.* v. *Polaroid Corp.*, 559 A.2d 257 (Delaware Chancery Court 1989). See Chapter 2 Section 4.

interests of shareholders and other constituencies. Although these laws may have changed some of the fundamental principles for director conduct, we cannot be sure until we have seen how they fare in the courts.

Another in-between strategy is selling a block of common or, more often, specially designed preferred stock to a friendly party – a grey knight – as Polaroid also did. But blocking a transaction in this way carries with it its own risk that the friendly party will try to exercise more control than the target will like. It is a compromise solution, not independence.[30]

14.4 SELLING THE COMPANY TO A FAVORED BUYER

Managements and boards of directors often find it more appealing to sell out to or combine with a company of their own choosing than to succumb to a hostile bid. But the mere fact that the management has chosen the other buyer highlights the possibility of an improper motive.

Nevertheless, picking a favorite is by no means always legally improper. In fact, if there are no takeover defenses other than the attempted sale to the white knight – no poison pill, no lockup – the hostile bidder should not have any legal or commonsense grounds for complaint. Under recent antitakeover laws such as those in Indiana, Illinois, New Jersey, New York and Pennsylvania,[31] the board of directors may even have the legal right under some circumstances to assist the transaction with a poison pill defense. Probably, the outcome will depend on how well the board can connect the interests protected by these statutes with the favored transaction. Under Delaware law, a poison pill may be helpful to gain the time needed for putting a sale to a white knight together. However, even after the *Paramount–Time* case, whether a pill can be used to protect a transaction from competing bids is still doubtful, although an unsolved issue.

Plaintiffs' lawyers in a shareholders' suit might argue that an auction would serve shareholders' interests better. But an auction will not necessarily bring the highest price. In the market for old art, where auctions have been very successful, there are still plenty of private sales. We have mentioned before the possibility stemming from the *Revlon* case that there might be a legal requirement for some type of auction procedure when a company is for sale. This ambiguity in the law, which the Delaware Supreme Court's opinion in the *Paramount–Time* case partly clears up, probably adds more rigidity than shareholder protection to the sales process.[32] The courts seem slowly to be endorsing this view, at least where the motives of the board of directors are

---

[30] See 'blocking preferred stock' and 'grey knight' in the Glossary.

[31] See Chapter 6.

[32] *Paramount Communications Inc.* v. *Time Inc.*, 571 A.2d 1140 (Delaware Supreme Court 1990) (reproduced as Appendix A.12). See Chapter 10 Section 1.

not suspect. However, as we have explained, special committees and their advisers may favor an auction anyway. If an auction with fair procedures is held, it should add some legal protection for the committee in litigation even if it was not legally required.

The reasons auctions may not always be appropriate are also reasons a sale to a chosen buyer often may be in the shareholders' best interest. Some suitable buyers may be willing to pay a high price in an agreed deal but averse to getting involved in an auction. Even without an auction, delaying to search informally for other bidders may sour a highly advantageous deal.

A lockup might appear to be an ideal solution to the risks of competition and auctions. However, as we have seen, the legality of lockups is uncertain. Although the law on the subject is a long way from clear, it is possible to offer some tentative practical guidelines on when lockups are most likely to be legal. They should be entered into with care and a procedural show of care. Only independent directors and advisers should be involved. A special committee of independent directors is probably best in this situation although these committees can create new problems since their actions are hard to control or predict.[33]

Above all the lockup price should be fair. Unfortunately, if the lockup price is really fair, the lockup may not be very useful. In fact, some competing highly leveraged bidders might welcome the cash they would receive immediately if they were the successful bidder. Another important point we have mentioned in other contexts is that the lockup should have a crucial bargaining role. If the lockup were essential to induce the purchaser to enter into a clearly advantageous acquisition agreement, courts are more likely to uphold it. For a merger of equals the *Paramount–Time* case may have introduced another idea. If the merger has a rational business purpose, it may be enough if the lockups keep the companies from being put in play.[34]

But, even when their legality is uncertain, lockups sometimes serve a useful purpose for an acquirer. They may deter some competing bids by creating additional obstacles. A competing bid will have to be conditioned (as, for example, was Maxwell's last bid for Macmillan) upon a court striking down the lockup, which may not happen. Just as important, lockups can provide bidders with bargaining power in settling up with the winner of the bidding. For example, a losing bidder protected by a lockup may be allowed to buy a desired division, as was the case when Macy's lost out in the bidding for Federated Department Stores.[35]

Defenses against hostile bids are not the only reason companies may seek out friendly buyers or partners for combinations. Another occasion when it

---

[33] See Section 1 of this chapter.

[34] For additional discussions of lockups, see Chapter 7 and the end of Chapter 12.

[35] See the discussion of the Federated matter in Chapter 8 and also 'Canadian Bidder Beats Macy in Fight for Federated Stores,' *New York Times* (Apr. 2, 1988), §1, p. 1.

may be considered sensible for a target board to pick out a friendly buyer is after defending successfully against a hostile bid. Even a weak bid may point up the exposed position of the target and lead its board to consider a quick alliance. CBS followed this approach. After it had successfully countered Ted Turner's bid in 1985 with a tender offer for some of its own shares, it brought in Loews Corporation as a large investor. However, as CBS learned, the new alliance may be the beginning of the end of independence. In defense, it is difficult to devise successful half-way measures.[36]

In many respects, Turner's CBS bid was similar to the unsuccessful bid by Sir James Goldsmith for BAT in 1989/90. In both instances the bidder wanted to obtain control of the target not by using the bidder's cash or securities but by recapitalizing the target. A nervy gambit. Because Goldsmith's bid was made under English law, which is designed to make defense difficult, BAT did not have the options CBS had to ward off Turner. However, BAT took full advantage of the defense possibilities in the U.S. raised by its ownership of a U.S. insurance subsidiary. Goldsmith's defeat before state insurance commissions led him to abandon the bid.

The procedures used in making board decisions – always important – are critical if the company is being sold to a favored bidder. Taking the safest course and using a special committee of independent directors would probably end up in an auction, for the reasons explained before. However, when management has a conflict of interest that is more substantial than mere skepticism of its motives, there may be no other choice. Unless the favored bidding group is making a bid that is unambiguously more valuable to shareholders than anyone else's, there is little chance that it would survive in the courts unless there were a special committee. Sometimes a board in which directors who are unaffiliated with management predominate may be sufficient to erase the taint of management's conflict without a special committee. This appears to be what happened in the Time–Warner transaction. However, it may not be clear in advance whether this will be so.

Target board members of a public company face the riskiest legal situation when they try to sell the business to a management group. However, as a practical matter, a sale to management is probably the hardest of all defenses to accomplish when it is competing against an all-cash bid by a bidder who can finance the bid without looking to the target's cash flow or assets. It usually takes too much time to put together a management buyout to compete with that kind of bidder. Finding financing is the most difficult part. New financing techniques such as large managed pools of buyout money and the junk bond market were beginning to make things easier but that appears to have ended.

---

[36] See 'blocking preferred stock' and 'grey knight' in the Glossary.

14.5 AIMING FOR THE HIGHEST PRICE

If the board or special committee has no particular concerns over who will gain control, a carefully organized fair auction procedure suitable to the business of the company may be a quite good alternative from a legal standpoint. For one thing, an auction is assurance against the sort of legal attack made on the Trans Union directors.[37] Even if a higher price or a more suitable buyer might be obtainable some other way, the additional legal risk may not be considered worthwhile by a board or committee in that frame of mind.

If there is no management conflict of interest there is probably no reason to appoint a special committee. Courts have shown great tolerance for poison pills when there is a fair auction and the board or committee running the auction has no conflict of interest. In this situation the poison pill's only function is to prevent bidders from circumventing the board during the auction process by making a tender offer to the shareholders or buying shares in the market. In other words, the pill becomes a legal device for solving the shareholders' prisoner's dilemma. The *Federated Department Stores* case is an example of how some courts have taken control of the poison pill to assure an effective auction in response to a hostile bid.[38]

---

[37] *Smith* v. *Van Gorkom*, 488 A.2d 858 (Delaware Supreme Court 1985). See Chapter 2 Section 2.

[38] *CRTF Corp.* v. *Federated Dep't Stores, Inc.*, 683 F. Supp. 422 (S.D.N.Y. 1988). See the Glossary and Chapter 2 for a discussion of the prisoner's dilemma. See Chapter 8 for additional discussion of the *Federated Department Stores* case.

15

Traps and Opportunities for Bidders

MOST of our discussion of takeover strategy has been concerned with the legal and strategic mechanics of the takeover market. We have not emphasized characteristics of individual target companies.[1] There are, however, a number of areas where the assessment of risks in individual companies becomes very important. An obvious example of a potential trouble spot is taxes. Any acquisition carries with it the risk of hidden tax liabilities. When tax returns that were filed by the target in the past are audited by the Internal Revenue Service, tax liabilities may be altered dramatically. Some companies are in businesses that depend on the continued availability of particular kinds of tax benefits, which brings with it the risk that tax laws will change and the company's main business can no longer be successful. Understanding a target's tax situation may require getting deeply into the target's business, prior tax returns and the likely direction of IRS tax policy and tax legislation.

Later in this chapter we discuss three important examples of other risks in detail: regulated industries, environmental risks and employee plans. Each is a complicated subject full of its own twists and turns. In any proposed acquisition these and similar concerns should be looked at carefully by specialists.

As we have said before, an important advantage of a negotiated acquisition is that legal protections may be obtained in the acquisition agreement. By contrast, a hostile tender offer is a blind bid (except for public information) where the buyer necessarily has to do without many of these legal protections and an investigation of the target's business. The heart of these protections are the seller's representations and warranties about the condition of the business. For example, a seller generally represents that there are no undisclosed contingent liabilities, that inventory is in good order and that the business has been conducted lawfully.

In a private sale the seller is usually obligated to pay damages if important problems are later discovered. How long this obligation continues is very often a matter for heated negotiation. It may survive for only a few months or for years.

However, when a public company is sold, there is usually no one to sue after the closing of the purchase. Shareholders are numerous and dispersed

[1] Some appear in our commentary on the Time–Warner agreements in Part III.

and probably cannot be reached. Officers and directors of the seller who approved the acquisition usually are protected by indemnities unless there is fraud. As a result it is rare for the buyer of a public company to have any recourse if the purchase turns out badly. Representations and warranties are still extensive but their main function is that if they are not true the buyer has the option of refusing to close the purchase.

There are several exceptions that are occasionally important. Someone who controls a very large block of shares of a public company might be persuaded to make promises that would survive the closing. But such a shareholder probably would not agree unless convinced that the price was extraordinarily advantageous and that the sale could not be made in any other way. Another is an escrow of part of the purchase price, a common practice in private acquisitions to satisfy future claims against the seller under the sale contract. After a period of time the residue of the escrow is paid over to the seller's shareholders. It need hardly be said that shareholders of a public company would not be pleased with this prospect. As a result escrowing funds is generally not a practical idea except in highly unusual circumstances – if, for example, the seller were faced with a very large environmental liability. Another possible compromise in this kind of situation is the buyer's agreeing to make an additional payment later if the problem turned out not to be as bad as anticipated.

A buyer can try to limit its exposure to the seller's liabilities. One way is to purchase the assets of the company rather than its stock. Ordinarily the liabilities will stay with the corporation. (There are important exceptions, for example, environmental laws discussed later in this chapter.) But the seller may be unwilling to sell what the buyer wants and keep the rest. One practical problem is that the seller would have to delay distribution to its shareholders of part of the sale price to meet the contingent liabilities. In a hostile takeover, protection against the target's liabilities is not a practical possibility.

A strategic problem in any negotiated transaction is how to avoid giving the buyer, in effect, a free option to purchase the business. If a purchase agreement is highly conditional or contains representations that make it likely some material inaccuracies inevitably will be discovered, there may be nothing that really binds the purchaser. Yet the purchaser may not be willing to pay anything for this option directly or indirectly.

15.1 REGULATED INDUSTRIES

Banking, communications, energy, insurance, transportation and defense businesses are all closely regulated in the United States. Usually changes in control must be approved in advance by a regulator. Many other businesses have to comply with tight government regulation of their operations but are not necessarily subject to change in control restrictions – drug manufacturers are an example.

When approval has to be obtained in advance, the main strategic issue is delay. If there is opposition, public hearings may be necessary before approval will be granted. Competing bidders, members of the public and the target may be permitted to oppose the transfer at these hearings. Even when only a quite small subsidiary or division of the target is subject to the regulation approval for a change in control may be required.

Bank regulation is one important example. A large number of state and Federal legal rules interact. Depending on the type of bank, acquiring control of any bank in the U.S. requires the approval of the Comptroller of the Currency, the Board of Governors of the Federal Reserve System or the Federal Deposit Insurance Corporation. Acquisition of control of state chartered banks also requires the approval of state regulatory agencies. Ownership of 25%, or sometimes considerably less, is considered control of a bank and is subject to prior approval.[2]

The Bank Holding Company Act sets strict limits on the activities of U.S.-controlled bank holding companies. They can only own bank-related assets. General Electric, for example, can own both General Electric Capital Corporation (which lends like a bank but is not a bank because it does not accept deposits) and Kidder Peabody (an investment bank) but it cannot own a bank. There are less strict rules about foreign-controlled bank holding companies' activities outside the U.S., and for U.S. bank operations abroad. Interstate banking is still usually prohibited, although this is changing. When permitted, the concession depends on a combination of state and Federal banking law.[3]

The long, ultimately successful struggle by Bank of New York to take over Irving Trust illustrates some of the most important issues. In September 1987 the holding company for Bank of New York made an unsolicited tender offer for the shares of the holding company for Irving Trust. It was the first takeover fight for a very large money center bank in memory. Bank of New York did not win control until over a year later. The struggle sapped the energies of both companies' managements and was estimated to have cost them $40 million in takeover related expenses.

Irving Trust was a New York state chartered bank and its holding company was organized under New York law. As a result, both the Federal Reserve Board and the New York banking regulators had authority over the bank and the holding company. The holding company was also subject to New York corporate law. Bank of New York had the same legal organization.

[2] 12 U.S.C. §§1842(a), 1841(a)(2); 12 C.F.R. §225.41.
[3] See 12 U.S.C. §1842(d). Two interesting examples of state laws are the Illinois national reciprocity law effective December 1, 1990, Ill. Ann. Stat. ch. 17 ¶2510.01 and the New York law, N.Y. Bank Law §413 (McKinney 1989).

The Federal Reserve Bank of New York gave Bank of New York a very hard time. It found the first application for approval to be 'seriously deficient' and demanded extremely detailed plans about how Irving's operations would be conducted. This lengthened the time required to obtain regulatory approval substantially. The Federal Reserve Bank also rejected requests to keep sensitive parts of the application from the public.

There was a New York state regulatory battle as well. The main issue for both regulators was the financial condition of the combined, highly leveraged holding company. In a bank acquisition a bidder cannot wage a proxy fight until it has regulatory approval, although it can begin a tender offer conditional on obtaining regulatory approval. Bank of New York began its tender offer immediately and a proxy fight as soon as it was legally able to.

Irving had its regulatory problems too. The Federal Reserve Bank refused to give it permission to pay a large dividend as a defensive measure during the proxy fight. However, Irving's flip-in poison pill gained it plenty of time in which to arrange a deal with Banco Commerciale Italiana, its white knight. Eventually the pill was struck down by the New York state courts on the ground that the discrimination among shareholders violated New York's corporation statute.[4]

Irving Trust's white knight never obtained Federal Reserve Board approval because it is controlled by Istituto per la Riconstruzione Industriale, the industrial holding company owned by the Italian Government. The Federal Reserve Board decided to classify IRI as a bank holding company, which meant at a minimum that it would have to provide financial data on its holdings in more than one hundred companies. The Federal Reserve Board also wanted IRI to apply for regulatory clearance and possibly to divest itself of its industrial holdings. Not surprisingly, these demands were unacceptable to IRI and the Italian bank, and the bank dropped its bid.

There are similar problems in other regulated industries. For example, the Federal Communications Commission has to approve all transfers of control of companies with FCC broadcast licenses, that is, all broadcast licenses for television, radio and microwave communications. The FCC is charged with protecting the broad public interest as well as evaluating the impact of the acquisition on the particular communities affected. Cable television has separate local regulation and these numerous licenses were one of Paramount's biggest headaches in its attempt to buy Time.

In recent years the FCC has not been very vigorous in monitoring individual changes in control. Instead it has concentrated on enacting and enforcing several general rules. A single owner, for example, cannot own more than twelve television stations, twelve FM stations and twelve AM stations; cannot

---

[4] *Bank of New York* v. *Irving Bank Corp.*, 536 N.Y.S.2d 923 (N.Y. Sup. 1988). A statute subsequently reinstated poison pills in New York. See Chapter 8 Section 1.

serve more than 25% of the nation's households with its television stations; and cannot own certain media combinations in a single geographic area. Rupert Murdoch, for example, had to sell the *Chicago Sun-Times* in 1986 because of television acquisitions. There is also a general rule against foreign ownership,[5] that may be waived only if the FCC finds the particular ownership to be in the public interest after public hearings. (Rupert Murdoch became a U.S. citizen.)

Other Federally regulated businesses include public utility holding companies, shipping, coastal fishing and operations on Federal lands. State and local regulations typically cover such matters as insurance and utilities providing telecommunications, gas, electricity or water services. Ownership of farm land by foreigners is regulated by many states although some of these laws may be vulnerable to constitutional challenge. Arkansas, for example, requires special registration.[6] South Dakota prohibits alien non-resident ownership of more than 160 acres of agricultural land, subject to foreign treaties.[7] Some other states, such as Nebraska, regulate or prohibit ownership of farm land by corporations that are not family owned regardless of domestic or foreign ownership.[8] Transfers of water rights are regulated in some western states and Hawaii.

Insurance is a particularly quirky and unpredictable state regulatory area. The rules are not uniform among the states and procedures are often relatively informal. A great many companies not in the insurance business may be subject to insurance regulations because they own captive insurance subsidiaries to handle their own losses.

15.2 DEALING WITH THE ENVIRONMENT

Since the early 1970s the importance of environmental laws has increased tremendously for most large industrial corporations. Potential liabilities can be vast and are difficult to assess in advance.

Even in a friendly acquisition environmental risk is very hard to investigate. Agreements can be made conditional on the satisfactory outcome of an investigation of environmental problems but at the time set for the closing much of the risk may still be inchoate. The buyer's decision whether to make the purchase and accept the risk may have to be based on little more than a hunch.

Environmental laws affect much more than such obvious industries as

---

[5] 47 C.F.R. §21.3.
[6] Arkansas Code of 1987 §2-3-108.
[7] South Dakota Codified Laws §43-2A-2.
[8] Nebraska Constitution, Art. XII §8.

mining and chemicals. Any business may own buildings with asbestos insulation or pipe wrapping, underground oil or gas storage tanks, or land that has been treated with pesticides or herbicides. An audit by an environmental consulting firm is now a standard practice for many buyers. Lenders in acquisitions routinely require environmental audits for certain types of transactions. But there are limits to how accurately these experts can foresee events. A buyer, for example, can become responsible for environmentally harmful activities conducted before the acquisition that were not illegal or even considered imprudent at that time or at the time of the acquisition. Environmental liability could also crop up relating to land the company had sold or stopped operating on years ago or land it had sent hazardous waste to no matter who owned the land.

Before the 1970s, waste disposal practices in the U.S. as in most other countries were casual. Companies used their vacant land freely as formal and informal disposal sites. There were leaks from underground tanks and pipelines, areas of frequent spills (such as loading and unloading sites and railroad rights of way) and waste piles and surface impoundments. What happened gradually over time can create enormous liabilities for the present owners.

One Federal statute enacted in the 1980s, the Comprehensive Environmental Response, Compensation and Liability Act (often called Superfund), illustrates some of the surprising ways the environmental laws can work. Superfund was designed to remedy waste disposal problems. It imposes liability for the costs of investigating and cleaning up contaminants and authorizes the U.S. Environmental Protection Agency to select the remedy to repair environmental damage. When the EPA requires a clean-up, its choice of a remedy can be challenged only in a few circumstances. If an owner or operator does not take the action recommended by the EPA, the agency can do the work and charge the owner or operator. The EPA also has the power to impose treble damages. There is no limit on clean-up costs. They can exceed the cost of the acquired business.

The Superfund law often makes several persons jointly liable (i.e., any one of them can be sued for the full amount). For example, hazardous wastes shipped to a dump are the responsibility of the owner of the land, the people who disposed of the waste and everyone whose hazardous waste went to the dump. The person who produced the waste is liable even if someone else agreed to take care of it. Furthermore, the sold company or the buyer may be liable even if the sale contract says all liability for past actions is retained by the seller. Ordinarily, to try to preclude liability for past actions, a buyer can buy assets used to conduct a business and assume only specific liabilities but not buy the corporation. Under the Superfund law, however, the buyer may still be liable if it is found to be conducting the same business. Under some circumstances, directors, officers and shareholders (usually a parent company) can also be found liable under Superfund.[9] Even lenders can be liable if they take over a business after a default or control its day-to-day operations.[10]

Other Federal laws can also impose liability for air and water pollution and treatment of hazardous wastes. Examples are the Clean Air Act of 1970, the Clean Water Act of 1972 and the Resource Conservation and Recovery Act. States have weighed in with their own cleanup and air and water pollution statutes. New Jersey was in the vanguard with a statute requiring that plant owners or operators notify state environmental authorities about any plans to sell or transfer a New Jersey plant, providing proof that there are no hazardous substances or wastes on site or a plan to clean them up if there are any. If the company does not comply with the law, the sale of the site can be voided either by the buyer or by the state. The buyer also can sue the seller for damages, if the seller still exists. However, as we explained earlier in this chapter, when a public company is acquired, there is usually no one left to sue after the closing. In reviewing declarations and cleanup plans under this law, the New Jersey environmental department has significantly delayed many business transactions. Some of these properties may never be sold. Other industrial states have enacted similar but less drastic laws, usually only requiring notice.

Several states impose superliens to pay for cleanup costs. Superliens supersede all other claims or interests. In Massachusetts, New Hampshire and New Jersey, state officials can clean up contaminated property and then put a superlien on any property owned by the person responsible for the contamination. Typically, superlien laws do not distinguish between property that must be cleaned up and other property owned by the same person.

In acquisitions, it is very difficult to allocate these risks. Sellers of private companies and public companies who sell subsidiaries or divisions do not want to assume environmental liabilities that might dwarf the price they were paid for the business. However, there may be some environmental liabilities that the seller cannot avoid even if the buyer agrees to assume all liabilities, for example, if the buyer should become insolvent.

In the acquisition of a public company it is not easy to protect the buyer. An arrangement could be made for a deferred payment if environmental liabilities are less than feared. However, this is unlikely to be an attractive idea for the seller's shareholders. Moreover, the time available for bringing environmental claims is usually so long that this would rarely be a practical arrangement.

When Kerr-McGee acquired American Potash in 1967, it anticipated some

---

[9] Compare *U.S.* v. *Kayser-Roth Corp.*, 724 F. Supp. 15 (D.R.I. Oct. 11, 1989), in which parent liability was found, with *Joslyn Mfg. Co.* v. *T. L. James & Co.*, 893 F.2d 80 (5th Cir. 1990), in which it was not.

[10] *U.S.* v. *Fleet Factors Corp.*, 1990 U.S. App. LEXIS 8266 (11th Cir. 1990).

environmental expenses. However, it later discovered that cleanup costs imposed by Federal, state and local agencies could reach $100 million. One old plant near Chicago had to be shut down because it had long ago been thoroughly impregnated with radioactive debris. The previous plant owner had produced metallic compounds from thorium, a naturally occurring radioactive ore, beginning in 1931, well before the dangers of low-level radiation were recognized. Ironically, much of the thorium was produced for the Federal Government. Fifteen years after the plant was shut down, Kerr-McGee is still cleaning up, having spent over $20 million without having solved the issue of permanent disposal. Probably, the worst expenses are yet to come.

Occasionally contingent environmental liabilities become the reason for bold bidders to try to make an acquisition. Union Carbide became a takeover target not long after the Bhopal disaster. In these cases the bidder is betting that the market is too pessimistic about the liabilities. Environmental liabilities are not the only liabilities that can create such opportunities for bidders. Texaco became a target after the huge judgment awarded to Pennzoil. Bidders were betting that they could settle the Pennzoil claim better than the market thought Texaco's management could.

These bids can also backfire. In 1988 the Jim Walter Corporation, a building materials conglomerate, was taken private in a $2.4 billion LBO sponsored by Kohlberg, Kravis, Roberts. The pricing of the acquisition was determined, in part, by KKR's belief that the stock market had undervalued Jim Walter's stock out of an excessive concern over asbestos-related lawsuits facing one of its subsidiaries. KKR sold the problem subsidiary in early 1990, retaining Jim Walter's other assets in a new company, Hillsborough Holdings. Nevertheless, Hillsborough and KKR itself became entangled in a $3 billion asbestosis lawsuit in a Texas state court. Because of the lawsuit (and Texas law) Hillsborough was legally unable to sell assets to meet debt payments and in the last days of 1989 it was forced into bankruptcy.

15.3 EMPLOYEE BENEFITS

Unfunded pension and medical benefits are also a difficult, dangerous source of exposure for acquirers but they are generally assessable through legal and statistical analysis. To begin with, the sums involved are often huge, and they have only recently begun to be reflected on companies' financial statements. Pension assets and liabilities were not required to be reflected in financial statements until December 1, 1988, when a new accounting rule established by the Financial Accounting Standards Board took effect. Possible future liabilities, such as disability payments, severance pay and other welfare benefits must also be considered, but may not be reflected in financial statements or in pension plan financial reports. However, there is a pending accounting rule that would require companies to include liabilities for retiree medical and life insurance benefits on financial statements.

General Motors, at the end of 1988, had assets worth $39.9 billion in its pension funds at a time when the book value of its plants, equipment and real estate was $32.8 billion. This was more than enough, according to calculations by GM's actuaries, to cover its pension liabilities, but only a few years earlier, at the end of 1982 (before the large increases in stock market prices of the 1980s), GM's pension funding had been short $1.9 billion. And there was nothing unusual about this situation. Firestone Tire and Rubber had $383 million in its pension fund at the end of 1986 and an unfunded liability of $159 million. The huge sums involved are a key to why managers of pension money play such important roles in the takeover market and the securities markets generally.

To encourage pension and welfare plans, the Federal income tax code gives employers substantial tax benefits, but only if the plans conform to very specific rules in the Employee Retirement Income Security Act of 1974 and regulations of the Department of Labor. These tax laws and ERISA are quite complex even by U.S. standards. It is not an easy matter to determine whether a business is in compliance or what changes would have to be made to stay in compliance after the two companies are combined.

Assets of a plan may exceed liabilities at the time an acquisition occurs, but changes in operations made by the buyer could reverse the situation. Shutting down part of a company's operations to reduce costs, for example, could trigger special early-retirement or plant-shutdown benefits for each employee whose job is eliminated. These benefits might easily exhaust a large amount of plan assets.

Tax rules may require treating businesses under common ownership as one. Or the acquisition may affect the tax status of benefit plans for other U.S. companies the buyer owns. Tax rules, for example, impose coverage tests that could have disastrous tax consequences to the employer unless a broad cross section of high-paid and low-salaried employees are covered. As a result, it may be prohibitively expensive for a buyer to make the target's employee benefit arrangements compatible with its own plans. Union-sponsored multiemployer plans may create special issues. There may be parachute payments due to employees and accelerations of employee benefits that are triggered by a change in control, even one that is friendly; and there may be special change-in-control provisions in employment agreements.

On the other hand, when a plan is overfunded a buyer may be able to terminate the plan, set up a new plan to cover the employees' benefits and take out the excess for its own use, for example, to pay off acquisition debt. Whether this can be done successfully under ERISA and the tax laws usually requires very careful study. Tax costs can be high. There is an ordinary income tax and an additional 15% excise tax on the amount that reverts to the employer.

There is also an important strategic business component to employee benefits. Shareholdings and stock options can make top employees rich after an acquisition. Rich employees are not easy for a new employer to handle and they usually do not stay with the company for long. Parachute payments increase the temptation to leave. If the acquirer is counting on these employees to run the business it is likely to be disappointed. On the other hand, when the buyer does not need the services of current management, severance payments may make it expensive to ask them to leave.

Employee stock ownership plans (ESOPs) can be a deciding factor in whether a hostile bid is practical. In keeping with U.S. policy to encourage employee ownership, ESOPs are highly favored by the tax laws. Typically, a leveraged ESOP borrows money to buy stock in the employer. The employer guarantees the loan and periodically makes tax deductible contributions to the ESOP on behalf of its employees. As the ESOP receives contributions it uses them to repay the loan. The stock is gradually allocated to the accounts of the employees.

Dividends paid on stock held by the ESOP are also deductible, so long as they are paid out currently to participating employees or are used to repay the ESOP's loan. Normally, in the United States, dividends are not deductible and do not qualify for tax credits. If an ESOP owns a majority of the company's stock it can borrow money at a below-market rate because qualified lenders to ESOPs are then allowed to exclude half of the interest they receive from taxable income. (In the past ESOPs could qualify for this special treatment regardless of their level of ownership; the old rule still applies to many existing ESOPs.)

Who controls voting and tendering of unallocated ESOP shares during a takeover fight is a controversial takeover issue. In the past, trustees or investment advisers of the ESOPs ordinarily had the power to decide whether to tender and how to vote shares that have not been allocated to specific employee accounts during a takeover battle. Both are considered fiduciaries under ERISA law and are required to act exclusively for the benefit of plan participants. However, recently adopted and amended plans pass this decision on to participants by requiring the fiduciary to tender and vote unallocated shares (most of the shares, in a new leveraged ESOP) in the same proportion that the participants voted their allocated shares. Since participants are also employees who generally value their jobs much more than their ESOP shares, they can be expected to oppose most takeovers.

As a result, having a substantial proportion of a company's stock held by an ESOP can be an effective takeover defense. Polaroid, as we have mentioned before, sold 14% of its stock to a newly formed ESOP during its 1988–9 takeover fight. Combined with a twist in Delaware's antitakeover law[11] this maneuver made the company essentially invulnerable to a highly leveraged bid.[12] Moreover, in a proxy challenge 14% of the shares would be a large head start for the management slate.

This ESOP strategy is controversial for two reasons. The Department of Labor, which administers ERISA, appears to see its role as a protector of shareholders as well as employees. It has issued a release saying there may be times when the trustee or investment adviser has a fiduciary obligation to tender unallocated shares on the economic merits, not in accordance with the wishes of the participants.[13] The Department may take the same position on voting shares in proxy contests, and at least one court has done so.[14]

Furthermore, if the directors of a company establish an ESOP as a takeover defense there is some risk even after the *Polaroid* case that a court would hold that by blocking favorable offers they are violating their duty to the shareholders under the *Unocal* case.[15] However, it is unlikely that a court would enjoin a plan unless there were an advantageous offer pending when the ESOP was created. Even with an offer pending the strategy has worked in two important cases. A Harcourt Brace Jovanovich plan was found justified as a help in increasing employee motivation during an austerity program brought on by its defensive recapitalization.[16] And Polaroid's sale was justified in part because the company, which had a history of providing employees generous work incentives, had been considering an ESOP for a long time.

Parachute payments are also controversial, legally and economically. Do golden parachutes for top executives protect the employer by giving its managers some financial security before, during and after a takeover? Or are they an unlawful waste of corporate assets? During a prolonged takeover controversy, the most able employees might leave. Moreover, generous protections for management when a takeover occurs might reduce incentives to resist advantageous takeovers, lessening conflict of interest concerns we have discussed. On the other hand, as we have noted, making employees rich makes it less likely they will stay on for long after a takeover.

Courts have usually refused to enjoin even generous parachute benefits.

---

[11] See Chapter 6 Section 2.

[12] *Shamrock Holdings, Inc.* v. *Polaroid Corp.*, 559 A.2d 257 (Delaware Chancery Court 1989). See Chapter 2 Section 4 and Chapter 14 Section 3.

[13] Labor Department Opinion Letter on Tender Offers, Feb. 23, 1989, 16 *BNA Pension Reporter* 390 (March 6, 1989).

[14] *The Central Trust Co., N.A.* v. *American Avents Corp.* (S.D. Ohio, filed May 26, 1989).

[15] See our discussion of *Unocal* in Chapter 2 Section 3. Several sales of shares to ESOPs have been enjoined. See *Buckhorn, Inc.* v. *Ropak Corp.*, 656 F. Supp. 209 (S.D. Ohio 1987); *Frantz Mfg. Co.* v. *EAC Indus., Inc.*, 501 A.2d 401 (Delaware Supreme Court 1985); *Norlin Corp.* v. *Rooney Pace, Inc.*, 744 F.2d 255 (2d Cir. 1984).

[16] *British Printing and Communication Corp. plc* v. *Harcourt Brace Jovanovich, Inc.*, 664 F. Supp. 1519 (S.D.N.Y. 1987). *Shamrock Holdings, Inc.* v. *Polaroid Corp.*, 559 A.2d 257 (Delaware Chancery Court 1989). See Chapter 2 Section 4 and Chapter 6 Section 8.

Although the amounts involved are often quite large they are rarely large enough to be decisive in a takeover battle. A bidder is usually glad to drop its objections if the target is willing to negotiate. On the other hand, governments have become involved in parachute payments. The Federal Government taxes them heavily if they exceed three times annual earnings, and recently several states have enacted statutes requiring parachute payments for all employees.

15.4 SPECIAL OPPORTUNITIES AND RISKS FOR FOREIGN BIDDERS

From the standpoint of U.S. law, most legal issues are no different for foreign than for U.S. bidders. However, this is not always the case. In earlier chapters we discussed some of the special concerns foreign bidders may have that discourage them from becoming hostile bidders.[17] We will return to these issues later in this section.

On the other hand, there are some situations in which foreign bidders may have a strategic advantage. For companies resisting hostile bids, for example, foreign buyers sometimes appear to be ideal white knights. There are several reasons why this may be so. Target company managers may feel less insecure about their jobs with a foreign acquirer since it may be less able to do without them than an American company. Where the American bidder is a financial group, target managers often do not like the prospect of aggressive, highly leveraged owners breathing down their necks.

There may occasionally be legal advantages for a late entrant to the fray. As we have seen,[18] lockup agreements designed to prevent competing bids may stand a better chance of getting by in the courts if they can be presented as an attempt to increase the bidding one last time. Foreign buyers may be ideally situated to take advantage of these last-minute opportunities. However, because of the need to act quickly, there are special business risks in being a white knight. In this situation, a white knight usually has to conduct its purchase investigations, negotiate and document the transaction and make its competing bid in a matter of several days. Signs of hesitation or other weakness may make a target reluctant to continue or signal to the hostile bidder that it would be worthwhile to persevere because the white knight may disappear under pressure.

American-style litigation is another deterrent to foreign bidders considering entering a takeover battle. If its bid is hostile, the foreign bidder must reconcile itself to being a plaintiff or failing. Target takeover defenses have become so

---

[17] See Chapter 13, and Chapter 9 Section 5.
[18] See the discussion of lockup agreements in Chapter 7.

effective, they generally cannot be overcome without the aid of a court. And if the bid is friendly, the foreign bidder may become a defendant.[19]

Once the litigation begins it has a bang-away style that may be discomforting for a foreign bidder, although some foreign companies are used to the U.S. legal system by now. Directors and officers may have to spend large amounts of time in hearings, depositions, preparation and in discussing litigation strategy. The extensive discovery system is very intrusive. Damaging or embarrassing information can easily emerge. The astonishing findings of British investigatory authorities that led to the Guinness takeover scandal would likely have been turned up much earlier in litigation between the parties if the same situation had occurred in the United States.[20]

Sometimes foreign bidders are especially susceptible to political attacks. Sir James Goldsmith's 1986 attempt to buy Goodyear Tire and Rubber Company created a firestorm of disapproval in Congress and in the state legislature of Ohio, where Goodyear is based. The reasons are obscure. Goodyear was a politically well-connected firm, but so are many other companies that have been sought by foreign bidders. Goldsmith has a flamboyant style but no more so than some other bidders who have been better received.

In 1989, soon after Goldsmith announced another controversial transaction, his $21 billion bid to buy the British conglomerate BAT Industries, 200 members of Congress signed a letter urging the U.S. State Department to convey their concern to the British Government that Goldsmith intended to 'purchase and then destroy a company that is important to hundreds of [U.S.] communities.'

Because of BAT's ownership of Farmers Group Inc., a large insurance business, he faced major regulatory approval hurdles in many U.S. states. Insurance, regulated mainly by state regulators, has been a problem in many acquisitions. BAT's biggest problem in its own hostile bid to acquire Farmers in 1988 had been state departments of insurance. Several ruled that the acquisition could not go through. But when a friendly deal was struck the opposition disappeared.

Goldsmith had learned from his prior experience. He counterattacked by pledging to have Farmers Group operated by an independent voting trust. The proposed trustees were three well-known U.S. citizens of impeccable credentials – a former governor and senator, a former Federal judge and cabinet member and the chairman of the New York Insurance Exchange. The offer probably cost him little since he was planning to sell Farmers Group immediately, but it did not satisfy the regulators either. Goldsmith eventually

---

[19] See Chapter 9 Section 5.
[20] See Leo Herzel and Richard W. Shepro, 'An American Look at the Guinness Affair,' *Financial Times* (Feb. 12, 1987).

obtained a firm purchase commitment from a large French insurance company. However, after nevertheless being turned down by the California department of insurance, he abandoned his bid. In the end, BAT's U.S. defenses, including the struggles before state insurance departments, had given it plenty of time to sell off large parts of the company, accomplishing most of what Goldsmith could have done if he had been successful.

Some foreign bidders may be susceptible to a different kind of political attack because they are themselves takeover proof. In the U.S., this protected status goes against the level playing field grain. State-owned businesses have a special problem today because by making a hostile bid they may unwittingly further the agenda of U.S. politicians who have important constituents brooding about unfair foreign competition. This is also true of companies that are takeover proof because of local law or customs (for example, because they restrict foreign ownership of their voting shares).

When a foreign bidder is involved, no takeover lawyer working for the target or for a competing bidder is likely to ignore the Exon–Florio law[21] if the target has a business that can be plausibly related in any way to national security. National security under the law is by no means limited to the defense business. Although there is limited experience with the statute, target companies are already preparing arguments and memoranda trying to define their connection with national security.

Under Exon–Florio, the President or his designee, the Committee on Foreign Investment in the United States, can block foreign acquisitions that could impair national security. CFIUS, which coordinates administration of the law, is an interagency committee chaired by the Treasury Department and made up of representatives from many parts of the executive branch. Both the target and unaffiliated third parties can try to use the law to thwart an acquisition by a foreign bidder. Like the antitrust preclearance procedures, Exon–Florio has potential effects on takeover activity that go far beyond its apparent original purpose.

When a hostile bid is made by a foreign bidder, the target will immediately press its position with CFIUS. The advantage of an Exon–Florio argument is that if it is successful it can completely prevent an acquisition. Appeal to the courts appears to be prohibited. There are very few perfect defenses but when it is applicable Exon–Florio may be one.

The investigation alone causes delay. The Federal Government has 30 days *from the time it receives notice of the transaction* to decide whether to begin an investigation and 45 additional days to complete it. The President must announce any decision to suspend or prohibit the transaction no later than 15 days after the investigation is finished. However, CFIUS may be able to delay further by threatening to make an adverse recommendation.

[21] See our discussion of Exon–Florio in Chapter 9 Section 5.

Unless the bidder gives notice itself, it can never be sure the time has run out. This has been a subject of controversy. It means that a prudent bidder will make an Exon–Florio filing even if the connection of the target business to the defense industry is tenuous.

Although much of the investigation will be about the target, the bidder's plans can be a key subject for inquiry. It is likely that some investigations will involve intensive inquiries into the foreign bidder's affairs. The bidder's behavior in prior acquisitions probably would be considered key information.

In the short time of its existence, Exon–Florio review has already become important. Only a few months after the law took effect, CFIUS blocked the acquisition of General Ceramics by a Japanese company, the Tokuyama Soda Company Ltd. In this case the national security connection was quite direct. General Ceramics made detonators for hydrogen bombs. The acquisition was allowed to proceed only after General Ceramics sold the production facility that makes the detonators.

Delay has turned out to be a common result of the Exon–Florio process. Consolidated Gold Fields' appeals to the panel delayed the hostile bid by Minorco, the Luxembourg-based South African mining giant, while a full-scale investigation was conducted. Although the Federal Government ultimately decided not to block the transaction, the delay was an important part of a successful takeover defense strategy that also included challenges under U.S. antitrust law and both British and U.S. takeover law.[22]

A foreign buyer must be prepared for the possibility that the Government will use the bargaining power the law gives it to insist on unusual arrangements. The 1989 friendly acquisition of Monsanto Electronic Materials Company by the West German company Heuls AG is a case in point. Monsanto was said to be the last major U.S.-owned manufacturer of silicon wafers for use in advanced semiconductors. CFIUS withheld its approval until Heuls agreed not to shut down the U.S. plant, not to shift its research and development activities outside of the United States and not to transfer its silicon wafer technology for at least five years.

In another case, the President decided not to block a proposed joint venture to distribute high-voltage electrical transformers between Westinghouse Electric Corporation and Asea Brown Boveri, a Swiss electrical engineering firm, only after CFIUS had received assurances that the transformers would continue to be designed and manufactured in the United States. It is noteworthy that this transaction did not directly involve what would normally be considered the defense industry.

CFIUS is a very high-level bureaucratic organization. On the basis of the evidence so far, it does not appear likely to intervene in matters where the connection to national security is remote. But it also appears likely to take

---

[22] See *Consolidated Gold Fields PLC* v. *Minorco, S.A.*, 871 F.2d 252 (2d Cir. 1989).

its responsibilities very seriously. There was some political fallout from the failure of any of the agencies that make up CFIUS to support investigating Saudi Arabian Oil Co.'s plan to buy 50% of Texaco's refining and marketing assets. In the future, as a result, when a reasonable case can be made that an acquisition might have national security implications there is likely to be an investigation and a significant delay.

Even if Exon–Florio clearance is obtained there may be other special hurdles for a foreign bidder. Defense contracting is a very special problem. Continuation of the business would be at risk after an acquisition if the work is classified. The Department of Defense is authorized to cancel contracts for classified work and can withdraw security clearances if the contractor is under foreign ownership, control or influence. However, there are some steps a foreign buyer may be able to take to eliminate this problem; for example, by transferring control to U.S. voting trustees or proxy holders (which of course may be impractical for a very long period of time). A defense contractor acquired by a foreign company could be barred from granting its parent access to the technology used in fulfilling contracts for classified work. Moreover, many sensitive manufactured products cannot be exported without an export license, which may be withheld in the interests of national security.[23]

The unsuccessful bid in 1990 by the British company, BTR, for Norton, a defense contractor, and the ultimate acquisition of Norton by a French white knight, Compagnie de Saint-Gobain, is a good illustration of most of the points that we make in this section. Although BTR was not launching a highly leveraged bid and pledged it had no plans to sell off parts of the company, close plants or move Norton's headquarters from Massachusetts, BTR received blasts of hostile publicity in the U.S. The legislature of Massachusetts (where Norton is incorporated) passed a special antitakeover law for Norton in an emergency session.[24] President Bush was presented with a letter signed by 120 Congressmen warning that a foreign acquisition of Norton would jeopardize national security. When BTR's chairman visited Massachusetts to try to explain his intentions, Norton employees held a demonstration where they burned the Union Jack. It was ironic but not completely surprising that in the end Norton found a foreign white knight, which paid a much higher price.

---

[23] See also the discussion of restrictions on foreign ownership of regulated industries in Section 1 of this chapter.

[24] See Chapter 8 Section 3.

16

Practical Thoughts on Leveraged Buyouts and Recapitalizations

I N politics timely change may sometimes forestall revolution. But change can also be the destabilizing force that makes revolution easier. Corporate managers of public companies face a similar paradox. Most often the reason managements have instigated leveraged buyouts or recapitalizations of public companies is as a response to a takeover bid or to forestall negative shareholder and market evaluations that could lead to takeover.

However, sometimes managements are clearly the aggressors. They are not defending or forestalling, they are trying to create the business opportunity of a lifetime for themselves. The failed proposal for a management buyout of RJR Nabisco is an example. In either case managers face one huge risk that cannot be avoided. The announcement of a leveraged buyout or recapitalization invites competing bids and can lead to managers losing control and to events taking on a life of their own. In short, from a management standpoint, to revolution.

16.1 LEVERAGED BUYOUTS AND THEIR STRATEGIC PROBLEMS

No matter who is the winner, public shareholders of the target receive a premium price for their shares. Premiums over market price in leveraged buyouts are not significantly different from other types of takeovers.[1] Equity in the new company is shared among the managers and their financial partners – usually an LBO specialist firm and its stable of institutional investors. Despite management's interest, control of the company generally is firmly in the hands of the financial partners.

Courts are highly aware of managements' intrinsic conflicts of interest in leveraged buyouts and recapitalizations of public companies in which management has a financial interest.[2] The legal rules on conflict of interest we have examined make defenses against competing bids unlikely to succeed

---

[1] See Steven Kaplan, 'Sources of Value in Management Buyouts,' *Journal of Financial Economics* (forthcoming); Harry DeAngelo, Linda DeAngelo and Edward Rice, 'Going Private: Minority Freezeouts and Stockholder Wealth,' 27 *Journal of Law and Economics* 367–401 (1984).

[2] See the discussion of leveraged buyouts in Chapter 10 Section 5.

and very risky legally. Appointment of a special committee of independent directors to conduct the sale is almost inevitable.[3] In short, legal rules assure that a proposal for an insider LBO of a public company puts the company on the auction block.

Another problem for many professional managers is that they prefer managing a public company. They do not like the prospect of close super-vision by their new financial partners in the leveraged buyout, who almost always end up with a majority of the equity. Furthermore, high leverage and thin equity put important practical restraints on what managers can do with the new company. High leverage and low equity can also cause legal problems for target directors, investors and lenders. For example, occasionally courts have treated leveraged buyout financings as fraudulent transfers, invalidating lenders' liens or subordinating their claims to claims of other creditors.[4]

What all this means is difficulty for investment bankers in selling the idea of LBOs to target managements, lenders and investors. The most obvious management candidates are chief executive officers of companies who are already facing a bid. These managers may feel they have little to lose. Occasionally a chief executive needs no prompting from investment bankers. This rare breed has the proclivity and ability to win even when it loses. For example, although Ross Johnson's LBO bid for RJR Nabisco was a loser and a disappointment to him, he still obtained many millions of dollars in severance benefits and other payments from RJR.[5]

Recently there has been much more difficulty in selling leveraged buyouts and recapitalizations to lenders. Bank regulators and to some extent prudence have forced banks to pull back. Similar considerations plus the abrupt disappearance of Drexel Burnham have badly damaged the market for new junk bond issues.

16.2   HOW RECAPITALIZATIONS ATTEMPT TO SOLVE SOME OF THE PROBLEMS OF LBOS

Specialist investment bankers who design and sell leveraged buyouts to managements have a very strong economic incentive to find solutions to these LBO problems. Recapitalizations are one attempt to produce a better investment banking product for target managements, although they do not always solve LBO credit problems. Like leveraged buyouts, recapitalizations make it possible for managers to compete in the takeover market by paying public shareholders high premiums. Moreover, they appear to solve a number

---

[3] See Chapter 14 Section 1.
[4] *U.S.* v. *Tabor Court Realty Corp.*, 803 F.2d 1288 (3d Cir. 1986).
[5] See our discussion of the RJR Nabisco buyout in Chapter 5 Section 6.

of strategic, economic and legal problems associated with leveraged buyouts.

Although the details of a recapitalization can be very complex, the key elements are simple. In recapitalizations, public shareholders usually receive a large amount of cash compared to the prior market value of their stock. But, unlike leveraged buyouts, they also keep a significant equity position in the recapitalized company. Sometimes control of the company remains with the public shareholders. Sometimes management and its financial partners obtain control although the public shareholders are left with a large equity interest. Occasionally an ESOP or other type of employee benefit plan winds up with a large chunk of shares. Usually, it is crucial for the competitive success of both LBOs and recapitalizations that control of the target can be obtained without the slow process of a shareholder vote. This eliminates complicated recapitalization plans that require shareholder approval of new classes of shares and other charter amendments.

The experiences of FMC Corporation and Anderson, Clayton and Co. show two sides of what can happen when a recapitalization is proposed. In 1986 FMC proposed a recapitalization that would have in effect given public shareholders $70 cash and one share in the recapitalized company for each old share. Before the recapitalization was announced, the old shares had been trading at $66. When shareholders sued, claiming inadequate consideration, FMC increased the cash payment to $80.

The most vocal shareholder in claiming the original price was inadequate had been Ivan Boesky. As an offshoot of the Boesky insider trading scandal, FMC later sued him and several investment bankers to recover the $10 per share increase in price, claiming that their misuse of insider information ran up the price of FMC stock before the recapitalization plan was announced. Reversing a trial court ruling dismissing the case, the U.S. Court of Appeals for the Seventh Circuit held that a recapitalized corporation can sue someone who causes its shareholders to receive more money in the recapitalization by using the corporation's confidential business information for insider trading.[6] Not an obvious result from either an economics or ethics standpoint but not easy to improve on either.

In the FMC recapitalization, management and two employee benefit plans exchanged each of their shares for almost six new shares (but no cash) and a third employee plan received cash and shares. In the aggregate, management and the employee plans boosted their share of FMC stock from about 19% to approximately 36% – not enough for complete control but probably enough to discourage consideration of a takeover by most bidders.

---

[6] The case was sent back to the trial court for further proceedings. *FMC Corp.* v. *Boesky,* 852 F.2d 981 (7th Cir. 1988).

Anderson, Clayton, a public company under family control, had a very different experience. It announced a plan similar to FMC's in 1986 under which it would become highly leveraged, with all shareholders receiving $37 in cash and new common stock valued at $6 to $10. New shares representing 25% of the company were to be issued to an employee stock ownership plan, giving management, employee plans and the founding family, combined, a majority interest in the company. The day before the announcement the old stock closed at $53¾ but dropped to around $50 over the next two months as the company worked out the details of the plan.

As in the case of FMC, the recapitalization plan was attacked in share-holder suits. But, far more important, a hostile $54 bid emerged a few days before the shareholders were to vote on the plan. (Apparently, Anderson, Clayton thought that because it was under family control it could afford the extra time required for a plan that had to be approved by a vote, but it was wrong.) The Delaware Chancery Court enjoined the recapitalization because the company had failed to disclose to shareholders that its board of directors was not seriously considering the hostile bid.[7] There was no special committee. After a hard-fought five-month takeover battle involving several bidders, a revised company plan and two court injunctions, Anderson, Clayton was finally acquired in a quickly negotiated transaction by The Quaker Oats Company for $66 cash per share.

In response to attempted takeovers, Phillips Petroleum, CBS and Union Carbide achieved results somewhat similar to FMC's through debt-financed stock repurchases.[8] Some recapitalization plans fail because the court thinks that the managers are trying to cut too good a deal for themselves. For example, the recapitalization plan attempted by Macmillan's management, without a special committee and in the face of a bid by the Robert Bass group, was structured so that management boosted a small stake into a control position. The plan was enjoined by the Delaware Chancery Court. Ultimately, with a helping hand from the Delaware Supreme Court, this led to a sale of the company at a much higher price to Robert Maxwell in an auction.[9]

The continuing role of public shareholders in a recapitalization usually makes more equity available than in an LBO, which means there is less need for management to bring in financial backers who might want to exercise control. And since there is more equity, there is also less chance that a court would find a fraudulent transfer. Nonetheless, from an accounting standpoint

---

[7] *In re Anderson, Clayton Shareholders Litigation,* 519 A.2d 669 (Delaware Chancery Court 1986). See the discussion in Chapter 13 Section 6.

[8] See also *In re Diamond Shamrock Corp.,* 1988 WL 94752 (Delaware Chancery Court Sept. 14, 1988).

[9] *Robert M. Bass Group, Inc.* v. *Evans,* 552 A.2d 1227 (Delaware Chancery Court 1988). See our discussions in Chapter 2 Section 4 and Chapter 7.

FMC and many other recapitalized companies have wound up with a negative net worth because they have had valuable assets on their books at a low value. Although this is only an accounting consideration, it can affect the attitudes of regulators, banks and other creditors. On the other hand, LBOs avoid this problem by writing up assets to market value and creating good will.

In recapitalizations, as in LBOs, management is likely to have a conflict of interest. In that case, if a better offer should come along, the board cannot allow management to blindly resist. This much was made clear in the litigation over the proposed Macmillan and Anderson, Clayton recapitalizations.[10] Nor is it likely that recapitalizations can hide behind poison pills, at least not when control is shifting to management.[11] When there is no change in control in a recapitalization or other management conflict of interest we are back with the unresolved issue of a 'just say no' defense.[12]

In some recapitalizations, giving stock to an employee stock ownership plan can be helpful strategically and economically. Employees are far more likely to support management than public shareholders if they have to vote in a proxy fight or to decide whether to tender their shares to a competing bidder.[13] There also are some important tax advantages in this arrangement. Stock is sold to the plan and gradually transferred to the accounts of individual employees as they earn their participation. The plan pays for stock by borrowing from a bank with a guarantee from the company and the loan is paid off from tax-deductible company contributions to the plan.

By the terms of some plans, the trustees may have the power to vote, and to decide whether to tender, shares that have not yet been allocated to individual employee accounts. Trustees often have a close relationship with management. Frequently, however, because of strict fiduciary rules, these alliances break down under the pressure of high premium offers. Recently, many plans have tried to give these powers to the employees who are the plan beneficiaries, but the Department of Labor has expressed doubts whether this is always legal under ERISA.[14]

---

[10] *Robert M. Bass Group, Inc.* v. *Evans*, 552 A.2d 1227 (Delaware Chancery Court 1988); *In re Anderson, Clayton Shareholders Litigation*, 519 A.2d 669 (Delaware Chancery Court 1986); *AC Acquisitions Corp.* v. *Anderson, Clayton & Co.*, 519 A.2d 103 (Delaware Chancery Court 1986).

[11] See Chapter 8.

[12] See Chapters 6 and 8 and Chapter 14 Section 2.

[13] We discuss employee benefits and their role in defense in Chapter 15 Section 3.

[14] Labor Department Opinion on Tender Offers, Feb. 23, 1989. 16 *BNA Pension Reporter* 390 (March 6, 1989). See Chapter 15 Section 3.

16.3   PRIVATE ACQUISITIONS AND AUCTIONS

Leveraged buyouts of public companies garner most of the legal problems
and publicity, but LBOs of private companies and pieces of public companies
are much more numerous. The breakup of companies acquired in leveraged
public acquisitions are important sources for these private sales.

These private sales of business raise strategic and legal questions that are
closely related to but different from the main subjects of this book. However,
these issues are important to every buyer of a public company who intends
to sell off some of the parts and to every potential buyer of the parts.

One of the important differences between sales of divisions or subsidiaries
and sales of entire public companies is that unless the division or subsidiary
represents a quite large percentage of the selling company's assets, the
approval of its public shareholders is not involved. Their votes are not legally
required and a competing tender offer would not be possible except for the
whole company.[15] Therefore, unless there is a conflict of interest, it is possible
to obtain a legally binding agreement, free of the threat of competition.[16]

In a private sale buyers also have more opportunity to complete a thorough
purchase investigation (often called 'due diligence') and to obtain contractual
protection from the seller against unforeseen or undisclosed problems in the
business. As in sales of public companies, these protections come in the form
of specific representations and warranties about the condition of the business.
But in sales of divisions and subsidiaries and other private sales these representations and warranties generally are backed up by indemnities, escrows
or deferred payment of some of the purchase price. In sales of public companies, on the other hand, representations and warranties usually expire at the
closing. However, private sales by auction, a recent development that we
discuss below, are often designed to avoid giving these protections.

In a private sale, there is usually no need to comply with Federal tender
offer or proxy rules. If, however, a public company is selling an important
division or subsidiary, the seller will have disclosure obligations to its shareholders even when their vote is not required.[17] Furthermore, the U.S. Supreme
Court held in 1985 that the very general SEC antifraud laws and regulations
apply to sales of the shares of privately held businesses.[18] These antifraud
protections are superimposed on any contractual representations, warranties
and indemnities. They can be an important additional protection for an
acquirer who buys shares but do not apply to a purchase of assets. A merger
is likely to be considered a purchase of shares. Hart–Scott–Rodino antitrust

---

[15] Del. Code Ann. tit. 8, §271 (1983 and Supp. 1986). See *Katz* v. *Bregman*, 431 A.2d 1274
(Delaware Chancery Court 1981).
[16] See Chapter 12.
[17] See *Basic, Inc.* v. *Levinson*, 108 S.Ct. 978 (1988) and Chapter 9 Section 4.
[18] *Landreth Timber Co.* v. *Landreth*, 471 U.S. 681 (1985).

clearance is necessary even for a private acquisition if the businesses involved are sufficiently large.[19]

In the sale of a division or subsidiary, the seller's board has fiduciary duties to its shareholders with regard to the disposition. However, unless the sale is a response to a challenge to control of the seller, the courts are not likely to be suspicious of the target board's motives and are more inclined to allow the board's decision to stand under the business judgment rule.

When the business that is being sought is controlled by a small group, some strategies more typical of hostile bids for public companies may help. An effective strategy, for example, may be to try to buy a controlling block directly from some of the shareholders. Family-held businesses that have passed into a second or third generation often have shareholders who feel locked in. They may be eager to strike their own deal with acquirers or at least to threaten to do so to break a family deadlock over the future of the company.

Problems with dissenting shareholders may be more acute in a sale of a closely held business than in a public transaction because the large percentage holdings of some shareholders may give them more bargaining power. For example, a single uncooperative relative could, by dissenting, spoil the chance for a tax-free deal or pooling-of-interests accounting.

A trend over the last five years or so for sellers to dispose of private companies and subsidiaries and divisions of public companies by auction has caused an exception to the rule that buyers in private sales have more opportunity for due diligence and indemnities. This use of auction procedure is an attempt to introduce into private transactions the pressures of competition from the world of public transactions. One goal of holding an auction is to keep buyers from insisting on potentially onerous representations, warranties, indemnities and escrows that could cost the seller a lot of money later. The auction form has been especially common when the sellers are aggressive, risk-taking financial professionals who bought the business in an LBO.

Many of the procedures in these auctions are similar to those used in auctions of public companies. But there may be an important difference in motive. Generally, public companies are sold by auction because of the real or apparent pressure of legal rules. In private transactions the auction form is used for economic reasons: sellers like the pressure auctions put on bidders.

The auction process usually involves establishing and enforcing a tight timetable. Investment bankers for the seller set up data rooms where information on the company may be inspected under close supervision. Frequently the seller's lawyers prepare form sale contracts that are distributed to bidders, appropriating a drafting role that was formerly considered a buyer's pre-

---

[19] See Chapter 9 Section 3 and Chapter 12 Section 1.

rogative. Only limited legal protections for the buyer are provided in the form. Rules for bidding are set forth concerning timing, financing requirements and other matters. Generally, sealed bids must be based on the form contract, with exact descriptions and explanations of any changes in it that the bidder proposes.

As in auctions of public companies, the sellers and their investment bankers tend to be vague about details of their auction procedures because they think that will help them to boost the price. A combination of cajoling and bluff is used. Information on bids is often leaked by the seller's investment bankers to increase the pressure on bidders. An especially well publicized example, from the sale of a public company by a special committee, occurred at the tail end of the RJR Nabisco auction where there was confusion about when bids were due and what opportunities there would be to rebid or to match a higher offer.[20]

The process, however, is not completely uncontrolled, largely because of practical constraints on the seller's investment bankers and lawyers. Although they have good reason to be hard bargainers, they also have reason not to be considered outrageously unfair. Since their business is transactions, today's dupe could be faced again tomorrow as a wiser competitor or as a potential client.

Auctions in private transactions make these acquisitions more expensive and riskier for all concerned, as they do in the sale of public companies. They are more risky for the buyer because its opportunities for investigation are quite limited. Despite SEC disclosure requirements, public information about divisions and subsidiaries rarely includes as much detail as bidders would like. Legal protection for the bidder in the sales contract is also limited. Furthermore, the pressure of the process may itself lead bidders to make mistakes. On the other hand, there are risks for sellers, too. These negative characteristics of auctions for bidders may cause them to drop out or to discount their bids sharply.

[20] *In re RJR Nabisco, Inc. Shareholders Litigation*, Fed. Sec. L. Rep. (CCH) ¶94,194 (Delaware Chancery Court 1989).

PART III

Case Study: The Time–Warner Agreements

Introduction

The next two chapters are commentaries on two actual acquisition agreements – the March 1989 merger agreement between Time Incorporated and Warner Communications Inc. and the revised agreement signed some two months later after the acquisition was restructured because of the hostile bid for Time made by Paramount Communications Inc.

We have described and analyzed this transaction in several places in the preceding chapters. The original plan called for a merger of equals and required approval by vote at meetings of both Time's and Warner's shareholders. The revised agreement called for Time to make a cash tender offer to purchase enough shares of Warner to gain control. That crucial step did not require the vote of either company's shareholders. Paramount challenged the tender offer in court, arguing that it was an unreasonable defensive measure. The Delaware Chancery Court did not agree and the Delaware Supreme Court, acting on an emergency appeal by Paramount, confirmed the ruling in Time's favor. The Delaware Supreme Court's opinion is reproduced as Appendix A.12.

We have chosen the Time–Warner transaction to comment on because of its importance to takeover law. Since we did not represent either party to the transaction we can comment freely on the agreements without the risks of bias or giving away any client confidences. (We did, however, represent some shareholders and banks who had an interest in the transaction.)

17

Commentary on the Original Time–Warner Merger Agreement

Our commentary in this chapter covers the merger agreement Time and Warner signed when they initially agreed to combine. In form, Time and Warner were not themselves going to merge. Instead, a newly formed subsidiary of Time with no assets would have merged into Warner, making Warner the surviving corporation, a wholly owned subsidiary of Time. This arrangement had legal advantages which we explain in our commentary on the agreement (see, for example, the comment to Section 3.1(k)).

The original form for the transaction was abandoned by Time and Warner in the face of Paramount's offer. At that time the agreement reproduced in Chapter 18 was substituted.

AGREEMENT AND PLAN OF MERGER

as Amended and Restated

among

TIME INCORPORATED

TW SUB INC.

and

WARNER COMMUNICATIONS INC.

The signed version of this agreement was typed on a word-processing system. The version reproduced here was printed professionally. In accordance with SEC rules, it was included as an exhibit to the proxy statement, a printed document mailed to all Time and Warner shareholders in connection with the solicitation of their proxies to vote for the merger.

Most acquisition agreements follow a standard organization. Here, **Articles I and II** describe what is going to happen in the merger. **Article III,** Representations and Warranties, contains the promises each side makes to the other about (1) its legal right to enter into and carry out the agreement and (2) the condition of its business. There is a rough parallelism between Warner's and Time's representations, which would be expected in a merger of equals.

TABLE OF CONTENTS

Article IV contains promises by both companies about how they will run their businesses and what actions they will (or will not) take between the times they sign the agreement and when the merger is completed. Statements in the Representations and Warranties section are, as is customary, promises that certain things are true, while the Covenants are promises about what will happen in the future.

Article V, the Additional Agreements section, covers a number of miscellaneous promises. In a complicated agreement it may make the organization a little bit clearer to separate these special promises from the section concerning conduct of the business, as the parties have done here.

Article VI is very important. It contains the conditions to each party's obligation to complete the transaction. In effect, it explains under what circumstances the agreement can be legally broken. These are in addition to the formal provisions for termination and amendment such as those that appear in Article VII.

ARTICLE V
ADDITIONAL AGREEMENTS

ARTICLE VI
CONDITIONS PRECEDENT

Article VII. The last article of most acquisition agreements contains miscellaneous provisions that do not fit anywhere else. These vary from standard provisions of little importance to extremely important, heavily negotiated provisions.

Exhibits. The exhibit numbers are keyed to the section of the provision in the agreement that calls for the information provided in the exhibit. This is a practical way to organize a complicated agreement. The disclosure schedules that are discussed in the text usually, as here, are not considered exhibits, are not listed in the table and, by custom, are not included in the version of the agreement that is made public.

ARTICLE VII
TERMINATION AND AMENDMENT

ARTICLE VIII
GENERAL PROVISIONS

Having a thorough index of defined terms can be very useful in an agreement of this complexity. The actual definitions appear where the terms are first used, so that someone reading the entire agreement will not have to keep flipping to a definitions section. On the other hand, having the definitions in both places would be even more convenient.

Index of Defined Terms

TW Sub Inc., one of the parties to the agreement, is a corporation that Time set up solely for the merger. It is a subsidiary of Time with nominal capitalization that is intended to have a transitory existence. In the merger, it would disappear after merging into Warner. All the corporations involved are incorporated in Delaware.

1st 'whereas' clause. Sub and Warner are the entities that will merge. The approval of their boards of directors is a condition under Delaware law to submitting the merger proposal to the shareholders of each corporation for a vote. Time's board has also approved the transaction because Time is a party to this agreement. It was essential for Warner that Time itself, where the economic substance was, should be a party bound by the agreement.

2nd 'whereas' clause. Sub's only shareholder is Time. Time, acting as Sub's shareholder, has approved the merger.

4th 'whereas' clause. The agreement was amended before the proxy statement was sent to shareholders because SEC comments revealed some problems. In the meantime, Warner has redeemed one series of convertible preferred stock and called another for redemption.

5th and 6th 'whereas' clauses. For clarity, the parties have restated the agreement in full instead of merely tacking on an amendment. But because the agreement contains many statements about what is true as of 'the date hereof,' restating the agreement creates a technical problem that is solved by the final 'whereas' clause.

Section 1.1. Repeats the provisions of Delaware law concerning when a merger becomes effective.

AGREEMENT AND PLAN OF MERGER dated as of March 3, 1989, as amended and restated as of May 19, 1989, among TIME INCORPORATED, a Delaware corporation ("Time"), TW SUB INC., a Delaware corporation and a wholly owned subsidiary of Time ("Sub"), and WARNER COMMUNICATIONS INC., a Delaware corporation ("WCI").

WHEREAS the respective Boards of Directors of Time, Sub and WCI have approved the merger of WCI and Sub;

WHEREAS, to effect such transaction, the respective Boards of Directors of Time, Sub and WCI, and Time acting as the sole stockholder of Sub, have approved the merger of WCI and Sub (the "Merger"), pursuant and subject to the terms and conditions of this Agreement, whereby each issued and outstanding share of Common Stock, par value $1 per share, of WCI ("WCI Common Stock") not owned directly or through a wholly-owned Subsidiary by Time or directly by WCI will be converted into the right to receive Common Stock, par value $1.00 per share, of Time ("Time Common Stock") and each issued and outstanding share of Preferred Stock, par value $1 per share, of WCI ("WCI Preferred Stock") not owned directly or through a wholly-owned Subsidiary by Time or WCI will be converted into the right to receive Preferred Stock, par value $1.00 per share, of Time, all as provided herein;

WHEREAS Time, Sub and WCI desire to make certain representations, warranties and agreements in connection with the Merger and also to prescribe various conditions to the Merger;

WHEREAS subsequent to the execution and delivery of the Agreement and Plan of Merger dated as of March 3, 1989 (the "March Agreement"), (i) WCI has redeemed its $3.625 Series A Convertible Exchangeable Preferred Stock, par value $1 per share (the "WCI Series A Preferred"), (ii) WCI has called for redemption its Series C Cumulative Convertible Preferred Stock, par value $1 per share (the "WCI Series C Preferred"), (iii) Time and WCI have entered into Amendment No. 1 to the Share Exchange Agreement, dated April 12, 1989, (iv) Time, Sub and WCI have entered into Amendment No. 1 to the March Agreement dated as of May 5, 1989 ("Amendment No. 1"), and (v) Time, Sub and WCI have agreed to make certain other changes to the March Agreement;

WHEREAS Time, Sub and WCI desire to amend and restate the March Agreement to reflect the redemptions and other amendments and changes referred to above; and

WHEREAS Time, Sub and WCI do not intend by this amendment and restatement to reaffirm as of any date subsequent to March 3, 1989, the representations and warranties previously made herein, unless the context otherwise requires, and accordingly they agree that all references to "the date of this Agreement", "the date hereof", and terms of similar import shall refer to March 3, 1989, the original date of execution and delivery of the March Agreement;

NOW, THEREFORE, pursuant to Section 7.3 of the March Agreement and in consideration of the premises and the representations, warranties and agreements herein contained, the March Agreement, as amended by Amendment No. 1, is hereby amended and restated in its entirety to read as follows:

ARTICLE I

THE MERGER

1.1. *Effective Time of the Merger.* Subject to the provisions of this Agreement, a certificate of merger (the "Certificate of Merger") shall be duly prepared, executed and acknowledged by the Surviving Corporation (as defined in Section 1.3) and thereafter delivered to the Secretary of State of the State of Delaware, for filing, as provided in the Delaware General Corporation Law (the "DGCL"), as soon as practicable on or after the Closing Date (as defined in Section 1.2). The Merger shall become effective upon the filing of the Certificate of Merger with the Secretary of State of the State of Delaware or at such time thereafter as is provided in the Certificate of Merger (the "Effective Time").

Section 1.2. The flurry of parenthetical phrases about what conditions need to be satisfied before the closing occurs shows how confusing this matter can become. One point to keep in mind is that it is undesirable for a transaction to be dependent on a condition that the other side controls. That in effect would give them an option.

Section 1.3(a). The par value of $1 and the reduction in number of shares of Warner after the merger will minimize the franchise tax Time has to pay the state of Delaware for the privilege of keeping its subsidiary incorporated. In general a low par value is more convenient for financial management. A high par value adds nothing to the value of the shares.

Section 1.3(b). The paragraph reciting the rights and obligations of the surviving corporation after the merger simply copies the language of the Delaware merger statute (with a few minor differences). Legally, the paragraph is not necessary. Under the statute the surviving company winds up in the same position. Delaware General Corporation Act §259(a). However, there is some benefit to having all the effects of the merger laid out in the agreement.

Section 2.1. 'without any action.' Delaware law does not require the formality of surrendering stock certificates in a stock-for-stock merger.

Section 2.1(a). 'fully paid and nonassessable share.' For obvious reasons, assessable shares, which may require the owner to contribute additional capital, do not exist in the public market.

Section 2.1(b). 'Cancelation of ... Time-Owned Stock.' Shares of Warner already owned by Time are canceled, not converted. This is for simplicity. It does not affect the arithmetic of the transaction. In fact, Time did not own a large number of Warner shares.

'Subsidiary.' The definition of subsidiary may appear long-winded but it is very important when there are partially owned subsidiaries that the company does not control or may not understand as well as its wholly owned subsidiaries.

1.2. *Closing.* The closing of the Merger (the "Closing") will take place at 10:00 a.m. on a date to be specified by the parties, which shall be no later than the second business day after satisfaction of the latest to occur of the conditions set forth in Sections 6.1, 6.2(b) (other than the delivery of the officers' certificate referred to therein), 6.2(e), 6.3(b) (other than the delivery of the officers' certificate referred to therein) and 6.3(d) (provided that the other closing conditions set forth in Article VI have been met or waived as provided in Article VI at or prior to the Closing) (the "Closing Date"), at the offices of Cravath, Swaine & Moore, One Chase Manhattan Plaza, New York, N.Y. 10005, unless another date or place is agreed to in writing by the parties hereto.

1.3. *Effects of the Merger.* (a) At the Effective Time, (i) the separate existence of Sub shall cease and Sub shall be merged with and into WCI (Sub and WCI are sometimes referred to herein as the "Constituent Corporations" and WCI is sometimes referred to herein as the "Surviving Corporation"), (ii) the Certificate of Incorporation of WCI shall be amended so that Article FOURTH of such Certificate of Incorporation reads in its entirety as follows: "The total number of shares of all classes of stock which the Corporation shall have authority to issue is 1,000, all of which shall consist of Common Stock, par value $1 per share.", and, as so amended, such Certificate shall be the Certificate of Incorporation of the Surviving Corporation and (iii) the By-laws of WCI as in effect immediately prior to the Effective Time shall be the By-laws of the Surviving Corporation.

(b) At and after the Effective Time, the Surviving Corporation shall possess all the rights, privileges, powers and franchises of a public as well as of a private nature, and be subject to all the restrictions, disabilities and duties of each of the Constituent Corporations; and all and singular rights, privileges, powers and franchises of each of the Constituent Corporations, and all property, real, personal and mixed, and all debts due to either of the Constituent Corporations on whatever account, as well as for stock subscriptions and all other things in action or belonging to each of the Constituent Corporations, shall be vested in the Surviving Corporation; and all property, rights, privileges, powers and franchises, and all and every other interest shall be thereafter as effectually the property of the Surviving Corporation as they were of the Constituent Corporations, and the title to any real estate vested by deed or otherwise, in either of the Constituent Corporations, shall not revert or be in any way impaired; but all rights of creditors and all liens upon any property of either of the Constituent Corporations shall be preserved unimpaired, and all debts, liabilities and duties of the Constituent Corporations shall thenceforth attach to the Surviving Corporation, and may be enforced against it to the same extent as if said debts and liabilities had been incurred by it.

ARTICLE II

EFFECT OF THE MERGER ON THE CAPITAL STOCK OF THE CONSTITUENT CORPORATIONS; EXCHANGE OF CERTIFICATES

2.1. *Effect on Capital Stock.* As of the Effective Time, by virtue of the Merger and without any action on the part of the holder of any shares of WCI Common Stock, WCI Preferred Stock or capital stock of Sub:

(a) *Capital Stock of Sub.* Each issued and outstanding share of the capital stock of Sub shall be converted into and become one fully paid and nonassessable share of Common Stock, par value $1 per share, of the Surviving Corporation.

(b) *Cancelation of Treasury Stock and Time-Owned Stock.* All shares of WCI Common Stock and WCI Preferred Stock that are owned by WCI as treasury stock and any shares of WCI Common Stock or WCI Preferred Stock owned by Time, Sub or any other wholly-owned Subsidiary of Time shall be canceled and retired and shall cease to exist and no stock of Time or other consideration shall be delivered in exchange therefor. All shares of Time Common Stock owned by WCI shall remain unaffected by the Merger. As used in this Agreement, the word "Subsidiary" means any corporation or other organization, whether incorporated or unincorporated, of which such party or any other Subsidiary of such party is a general partner (excluding partnerships, the general partnership interests of which held by such party or any Subsidiary of such party do not have a majority of the voting interest in such partnership) or at least a majority of the securities or other interests having by their terms ordinary voting

Section 2.1(c). The Exchange Ratio is the heart of the deal. In the merger, each share of Warner stock would become 0.465 shares of Time Warner Inc., the parent of the surviving company. On March 3, 1989, the last trading day before the agreement was announced, Time's stock had closed at $109\frac{1}{8}$ per share and Warner's at $45\frac{7}{8}$, a ratio of 0.420. Viewed from this perspective, Warner shareholders were receiving a slight premium for their shares in the merger (0.465/0.420, just under 11%). However, it is unlikely that this was really considered a premium by all the negotiators. The Warner negotiators may have been able to convince the Time negotiators that Time was over-valued in the market compared to Warner – possibly because of takeover rumors about Time. Some merger agreements use a floating exchange ratio that depends on future prices and some contain protective bands limiting how far a large fluctuation can change the ratio.

The poison pill rights issued by Time are considered to be represented by the stock certificates and do not trade separately until there is a Distribution Date caused by someone accumulating 15% or more of Time's stock or making a tender offer for 20% or more. In the merger, Warner shareholders get their proportionate number of poison pill rights. Poison pill rights have to be examined very carefully. They may have to be redeemed before the merger or even before the agreement is signed to avoid traps.

Section 2.1(e). Under Delaware law, holders of Warner common shares have no right to dissent from the merger because their shares are listed on a national securities exchange and they are receiving listed shares in the sur-viving corporation, that is, they are not being squeezed out for cash. In a cash merger they would have the right to dissent. The theory behind this legal distinction is not entirely logical. Even if they were receiving cash, they could buy Time shares. On the other hand if they were receiving unmarketable shares, it would make sense to give them a cash alternative. The Series B Preferred shareholder does have a right to dissent because its preferred stock is not publicly traded.

Where dissenters' rights are important, many agreements are conditioned on there being no more than a particular percentage of dissenting shares. There are many reasons why merging companies might be concerned about the issue. Dissenting shareholders are paid in cash, a drain on the surviving company's equity. Sometimes the cash payment can affect the accounting or tax treatment, eliminating the possibility of pooling-of-interests accounting treatment or affecting the continuity of interest required for a tax-free merger.

Section 2.1(f). The exchange ratio is based on the relative value of the two companies. If a dividend is paid out to shareholders of one of the companies, its shareholders should receive fewer shares of the survivor. Detailed anti-dilution provisions can become overly complex. Using the shorthand phrase, 'appropriate adjustment,' avoids having to provide a method in advance for dealing with unlikely events. It also avoids the risk of overlooking them.

power to elect a majority of the Board of Directors or others performing similar functions with respect to such corporation or other organization is directly or indirectly owned or controlled by such party or by any one or more of its Subsidiaries, or by such party and one or more of its Subsidiaries.

(c) *Exchange Ratio for WCI Common Stock.* Subject to Section 2.2(e), each issued and outstanding share of WCI Common Stock (other than shares to be canceled in accordance with Section 2.1(b)) shall be converted into the right to receive .465, subject to adjustment in accordance with Section 2.1(f) (the "Conversion Number"), of a fully paid and nonassessable share of Time Common Stock, including the corresponding percentage of a right (the "Right") to purchase shares of Series A Participating Preferred Stock of Time (the "Time Series A Preferred") pursuant to the Rights Agreement dated as of April 29, 1986, between Time and Morgan Shareholder Services Trust Company of New York, as Rights Agent, as amended by Amendment No. 1 dated as of January 19, 1989, and Amendment No.2 dated as of May 19, 1989 (the "Rights Agreement"). Prior to the Distribution Date (as defined in the Rights Agreement) all references in this Agreement to the Time Common Stock to be received pursuant to the Merger shall be deemed to include the Rights. All such shares of WCI Common Stock shall no longer be outstanding and shall automatically be canceled and retired and shall cease to exist, and each holder of a certificate representing any such shares shall cease to have any rights with respect thereto, except the right to receive the shares of Time Common Stock to be issued in consideration therefor upon the surrender of such certificate in accordance with Section 2.2, without interest.

(d) *Exchange of Preferred Stock.* Each share of Series B Variable Rate Cumulative Convertible Preferred Stock, par value $1 per share (the "WCI Series B Preferred"), of WCI outstanding immediately prior to the Effective Time (except shares of WCI Series B Preferred held by persons who object to the Merger and comply with all provisions of the DGCL concerning the right of such holders to dissent from the Merger and demand appraisal of their shares ("Dissenting Holders")) shall be converted into the right to receive one share of Series BB Variable Rate Cumulative Convertible Preferred Stock of Time, par value $1.00 per share ("Time Series BB Preferred"), such Time Series BB Preferred to have the terms set forth on Exhibit 2.1(d). All such shares of WCI Series B Preferred, other than shares held by Dissenting Holders, shall no longer be outstanding and shall automatically be canceled and retired and shall cease to exist, and each holder of a certificate representing any such shares of WCI Series B Preferred shall cease to have any rights with respect thereto, except the right to receive the shares of Time Series BB Preferred to be issued in consideration therefor upon the surrender of such certificate in accordance with Section 2.2, without interest.

(e) *Shares of Dissenting Holders.* Any issued and outstanding shares of WCI Series B Preferred held by a Dissenting Holder shall not be converted as described in Section 2.1(d) but shall from and after the Effective Time represent only the right to receive such consideration as may be determined to be due to such Dissenting Holder pursuant to the DGCL; *provided, however,* that shares of WCI Series B Preferred outstanding immediately prior to the Effective Time and held by a Dissenting Holder who shall, after the Effective Time, withdraw his demand for appraisal or lose his right of appraisal, in either case pursuant to the DGCL, shall be deemed to be converted, as of the Effective Time, into the right to receive the shares of Time Series BB Preferred specified in Section 2.1(d), without interest.

(f) *Adjustment to Conversion Number.* In the event of a Distribution (as defined below) the Conversion Number shall be adjusted to equal (i) .465 less (ii) an amount equal to the product of (A) 0.026 and (B) a fraction (1) the numerator of which is the number of shares of common stock of BHC, Inc., a Delaware corporation ("BHC"), to be distributed pursuant to such Distribution, and (2) the denominator of which is 425,000 (such amount being the number of shares of common stock of BHC into which the shares of Cumulative Convertible Preferred Stock, par value $.10 per share, of BHC currently owned by WCI are convertible); *provided that* the numbers in clauses (1) and (2) are subject to appropriate adjustment to reflect any recapitalization, reclassification, stock split, combination of shares or the like of BHC. For purposes of this Agreement, the term "Distribution" shall mean a pro rata dividend or other distribution by WCI (regardless of whether paid prior to or on or after the Effective Time) of any or all of its shares of capital stock of BHC to holders of record (as of any time on and after the date hereof and prior to the Effective Time) of shares of WCI Common Stock and WCI Series B

Section 2.1(f), cont'd.

A simpler way to deal with the problem is to prohibit dividends. In fact, this is done in Section 4.1(b), but there are two exceptions. One is the possible distribution of Warner's interest in BHC, a joint venture managed by Chris-Craft. The distribution plan came about as the settlement of a lawsuit between Warner and Chris-Craft. Time and Warner also are permitted to pay dividends at the usual annual rate for the period between the last dividend payment and the closing of the merger. (See Section 5.16.) However, only the BHC distribution would cause a change in the exchange ratio.

Section 2.2(c). Although it is not necessary under Delaware law for Warner shareholders to turn in their old stock certificates to become shareholders in Time Warner (the surviving corporation, after the merger and a name change), surrendering the stock certificate is required for the payment of dividends on the new stock. When a certificate is turned in late the dividends would be paid, but without interest. However, the provision says it is subject to applicable laws in case it turns out that it is illegal not to pay interest.

Preferred (treating such shares of WCI Series B Preferred as if they had been converted into shares of WCI Common Stock immediately prior to such record date pursuant to their terms).

2.2. *Exchange of Certificates.* (a) *Exchange Agent.* As of the Effective Time, Time shall deposit with Manufacturers Hanover Trust Company or such other bank or trust company designated by Time (and reasonably acceptable to WCI) (the "Exchange Agent"), for the benefit of the holders of shares of WCI Common Stock and WCI Series B Preferred, for exchange in accordance with this Article II, through the Exchange Agent, certificates representing the shares of Time Common Stock and Time Series BB Preferred (such shares of Time Common Stock and Time Series BB Preferred, together with any dividends or distributions with respect thereto, being hereinafter referred to as the "Exchange Fund") issuable pursuant to Section 2.1 in exchange for outstanding shares of WCI Common Stock and WCI Series B Preferred. To the extent Time owns shares of Time Common Stock as treasury stock, such shares shall be deposited into the Exchange Fund.

(b) *Exchange Procedures.* As soon as reasonably practicable after the Effective Time, the Exchange Agent shall mail to each holder of record of a certificate or certificates which immediately prior to the Effective Time represented outstanding shares of WCI Common Stock or WCI Series B Preferred (the "Certificates") whose shares were converted into the right to receive shares of Time Common Stock or Time Series BB Preferred pursuant to Section 2.1, (i) a letter of transmittal (which shall specify that delivery shall be effected, and risk of loss and title to the Certificates shall pass, only upon delivery of the Certificates to the Exchange Agent and shall be in such form and have such other provisions as Time and WCI may reasonably specify) and (ii) instructions for use in effecting the surrender of the Certificates in exchange for certificates representing shares of Time Common Stock and Time Series BB Preferred. Upon surrender of a Certificate for cancelation to the Exchange Agent or to such other agent or agents as may be appointed by Time and Sub, together with such letter of transmittal, duly executed, the holder of such Certificate shall be entitled to receive in exchange therefor a certificate representing that number of whole shares of Time Common Stock or Time Series BB Preferred which such holder has the right to receive pursuant to the provisions of this Article II, and the Certificate so surrendered shall forthwith be canceled. In the event of a transfer of ownership of WCI Common Stock or WCI Series B Preferred which is not registered in the transfer records of WCI, a certificate representing the proper number of shares of Time Common Stock or Time Series BB Preferred may be issued to a transferee if the Certificate representing such WCI Common Stock or WCI Series B Preferred is presented to the Exchange Agent, accompanied by all documents required to evidence and effect such transfer and by evidence that any applicable stock transfer taxes have been paid. Until surrendered as contemplated by this Section 2.2, each Certificate shall be deemed at any time after the Effective Time to represent only the right to receive upon such surrender the certificate representing shares of Time Common Stock or Time Series BB Preferred and cash in lieu of any fractional shares of Time Common Stock as contemplated by this Section 2.2.

(c) *Distributions with Respect to Unexchanged Shares.* No dividends or other distributions declared or made after the Effective Time with respect to Time Common Stock or Time Series BB Preferred with a record date after the Effective Time shall be paid to the holder of any unsurrendered Certificate with respect to the shares of Time Common Stock or Time Series BB Preferred represented thereby and no cash payment in lieu of fractional shares shall be paid to any such holder pursuant to Section 2.2(e) until the holder of record of such Certificate shall surrender such Certificate. Subject to the effect of applicable laws, following surrender of any such Certificate, there shall be paid to the record holder of the certificates representing whole shares of Time Common Stock or Time Series BB Preferred issued in exchange therefor, without interest, (i) at the time of such surrender, the amount of any cash payable in lieu of a fractional share of Time Common Stock to which such holder is entitled pursuant to Section 2.2(e) and the amount of dividends or other distributions with a record date after the Effective Time theretofore paid with respect to such whole shares of Time Common Stock or Time Series BB Preferred, and (ii) at the appropriate payment date, the amount of dividends or other distributions with a record date after the Effective Time but prior to surrender and a payment date subsequent to surrender payable with respect to such whole shares of Time Common Stock or Time Series BB Preferred.

Section 2.2(e). Fractional shares that result from applying the exchange ratio to Warner shareholders are converted into cash. However, the company does not simply determine the value of the shares and come up with the cash. Instead, the fractional shares are aggregated into round lots and sold in the market.

Section 2.2(g) asserts that the company will not be liable if it sends shares or pays money to a government body administering an abandoned property act, instead of tracking down the person who abandoned the property. This is the kind of obscure detail that accumulates over the years in forms for agreements.

(d) *No Further Ownership Rights in WCI Common Stock or WCI Series B Preferred.* All shares of Time Common Stock or Time Series BB Preferred issued upon the surrender for exchange of shares of WCI Common Stock or WCI Series B Preferred in accordance with the terms hereof (including any cash paid pursuant to Section 2.2(c) or 2.2(e)) shall be deemed to have been issued in full satisfaction of all rights pertaining to such shares of WCI Common Stock or WCI Series B Preferred, *subject, however,* to the Surviving Corporation's obligation to pay any dividends or make any other distributions with a record date prior to the Effective Time which may have been declared or made by WCI on such shares of WCI Common Stock or WCI Series B Preferred in accordance with the terms of this Agreement or prior to the date hereof and which remain unpaid at the Effective Time, and there shall be no further registration of transfers on the stock transfer books of the Surviving Corporation of the shares of WCI Common Stock or WCI Series B Preferred which were outstanding immediately prior to the Effective Time. If, after the Effective Time, Certificates are presented to the Surviving Corporation for any reason, they shall be canceled and exchanged as provided in this Article II.

(e) *No Fractional Shares.* (i) No certificates or scrip representing fractional shares of Time Common Stock shall be issued upon the surrender for exchange of Certificates, and such fractional share interests will not entitle the owner thereof to vote or to any rights of a stockholder of Time.

(ii) As promptly as practicable following the Effective Time, the Exchange Agent shall determine the excess of (x) the number of full shares of Time Common Stock delivered to the Exchange Agent by Time pursuant to Section 2.2(a) over (y) the aggregate number of full shares of Time Common Stock to be distributed to holders of WCI Common Stock pursuant to Section 2.2(b) (such excess being herein called the "Excess Shares"). As soon after the Effective Time as practicable, the Exchange Agent, as agent for the holders of WCI Common Stock, shall sell the Excess Shares at then prevailing prices on the NYSE, all in the manner provided in paragraph (iii) of this Section.

(iii) The sale of the Excess Shares by the Exchange Agent shall be executed on the New York Stock Exchange, Inc. (the "NYSE") through one or more member firms of the NYSE and shall be executed in round lots to the extent practicable. Until the net proceeds of such sale or sales have been distributed to the holders of WCI Common Stock, the Exchange Agent will hold such proceeds in trust for the holders of WCI Common Stock (the "Common Shares Trust"). Time shall pay all commissions, transfer taxes and other out-of-pocket transaction costs, including the expenses and compensation, of the Exchange Agent incurred in connection with such sale of the Excess Shares. The Exchange Agent shall determine the portion of the Common Shares Trust to which each holder of WCI Common Stock shall be entitled, if any, by multiplying the amount of the aggregate net proceeds comprising the Common Shares Trust by a fraction the numerator of which is the amount of the fractional share interest to which such holder of WCI Common Stock is entitled and the denominator of which is the aggregate amount of fractional share interests to which all holders of WCI Common Stock are entitled.

(iv) As soon as practicable after the determination of the amount of cash, if any, to be paid to holders of WCI Common Stock in lieu of any fractional share interests, the Exchange Agent shall make available such amounts to such holders of WCI Common Stock.

(f) *Termination of Exchange Fund.* Any portion of the Exchange Fund and Common Shares Trust which remains undistributed to the stockholders of WCI for six months after the Effective Time shall be delivered to Time, upon demand, and any stockholders of WCI who have not theretofore complied with this Article II shall thereafter look only to Time for payment of their claim for Time Common Stock or Time Series BB Preferred, as the case may be, any cash in lieu of fractional shares of Time Common Stock and any dividends or distributions with respect to Time Common Stock or Time Series BB Preferred.

(g) *No Liability.* Neither Time nor WCI shall be liable to any holder of shares of WCI Common Stock, WCI Series B Preferred, Time Common Stock or Time Series BB Preferred, as the case may be, for such shares (or dividends or distributions with respect thereto) or cash from the Common Shares Trust delivered to a public official pursuant to any applicable abandoned property, escheat or similar law.

Section 3.1 covers Warner's representations and warranties (promises that things are as described) to Time. Note that in many instances these promises may be qualified by schedules. Making the qualifications in schedules instead of in the agreement itself has some advantages: comparative confidentiality, convenience (avoidance of bulk and preservation of readability) and some schedules can be furnished after the agreement is signed (see Section 3.1(i)).

Section 3.1(a). Concepts such as due organization, good standing and authority are important to establish that an abstract entity like a corporation really exists and can do what it promises. To some degree, however, they preserve archaic distinctions that are not very useful. For example, it is not very meaningful to talk about a corporation that is in good standing yet does not exist and was not duly organized. Good standing is determined by the secretary of state of the state of incorporation and is the key concept.

Materiality is a slippery concept, although it is an important one in most agreements. The clarification at the end of paragraph (a) saves space every time the term is used. However it does not really try to define the term. This open-endedness may be in both parties' interests. Sometimes agreements try to define materiality in terms of a dollar amount, but that kind of definition is unlikely to work in all contexts.

Section 3.1(b). To understand exactly what is happening in the transaction, it is important to set out the capital structure with precision. This merger was commonly described as an exchange of shares, but that description only covers the common stock of the two parents. There were many other securities to deal with, and it is also necessary to have the promise of the other side that no other securities or rights of any kind exist.

ARTICLE III

REPRESENTATIONS AND WARRANTIES

3.1. *Representations and Warranties of WCI.* WCI represents and warrants to Time and Sub as follows:

(a) *Organization, Standing and Power.* Each of WCI and its Significant Subsidiaries is a corporation or partnership duly organized, validly existing and in good standing under the laws of its state of incorporation or organization, has all requisite power and authority to own, lease and operate its properties and to carry on its business as now being conducted, and is duly qualified and in good standing to do business in each jurisdiction in which the nature of its business or the ownership or leasing of its properties makes such qualification necessary other than in such jurisdictions where the failure so to qualify would not have a material adverse effect on WCI and its Subsidiaries taken as a whole. As used in this Agreement, (i) a "Significant Subsidiary" means any Subsidiary of WCI or Time, as the case may be, that would constitute a Significant Subsidiary of such party within the meaning of Rule 1-02 of Regulation S-X of the Securities and Exchange Commission (the "SEC"), and (ii) any reference to any event, change or effect being material with respect to any entity means an event, change or effect related to the condition (financial or otherwise), properties, assets, liabilities, businesses or operations of such entity.

(b) *Capital Structure.* As of the date hereof, the authorized capital stock of WCI consists of 500,000,000 shares of WCI Common Stock and 50,000,000 shares of WCI Preferred Stock. At the close of business on February 17, 1989, (i) 143,750,284 shares of WCI Common Stock were outstanding, 59,510,737 shares of WCI Common Stock were reserved for issuance upon the exercise of outstanding stock options or pursuant to WCI's Equity Unit Purchase Plan (such stock options and the Equity Unit Purchase Plan, collectively, the "WCI Stock Plans"), upon conversion of WCI Preferred Stock and upon conversion of $100,000,000 principal amount of 6% Convertible Senior Subordinated Debentures due August 17, 2001 (the "Lorimar Debentures"), of Lorimar Telepictures Corporation ("Lorimar"), (ii) 1,499,692 shares of WCI Common Stock were held by WCI in its treasury or by its wholly-owned Subsidiaries, (iii) 33,537,633 shares of WCI Series B Preferred, consisting of 11,152,552 shares of WCI Series A Preferred, 15,200,000 shares of WCI Series B Preferred and 7,185,081 shares of WCI Series C Preferred, were outstanding and, except for 15,836 shares of WCI Series A Preferred, none were held by WCI or any Subsidiary in its treasury, (iv) except for the Lorimar Debentures, no bonds, debentures, notes or other indebtedness having the right to vote (or convertible into securities having the right to vote) on any matters on which stockholders may vote ("Voting Debt"), were issued or outstanding and (v) WCI had contractual obligations with employees of or consultants to Lorimar to issue (the "Lorimar Stock Grants") (w) WCI Common Stock valued in the aggregate at not in excess of $50,000 on the date of issuance, (x) stock options with respect to WCI Common Stock valued in the aggregate at not in excess of $200,000 on the date of grant, (y) 40,424 shares of WCI Common Stock upon the exercise of options and (z) an option with respect to 9,187 shares of WCI Common Stock. All outstanding shares of WCI capital stock are, and any shares of WCI Common Stock issued pursuant to the Share Exchange Agreement dated as of March 3, 1989, as amended, by and between Time and WCI (the "Share Exchange Agreement") will be, validly issued, fully paid and nonassessable and not subject to preemptive rights. As of the date of this Agreement, except for this Agreement, the Lorimar Stock Grants, WCI Stock Options (as defined in Section 5.10), stock options disclosed in clause (v) of this Section 3.1(b), WCI Preferred Stock, obligations under WCI's Equity Unit Purchase Plan, the Lorimar Debentures, the Share Exchange Agreement and not in excess of 700,000 stock options available for issuance pursuant to the WCI Stock Plans, there are no options, warrants, calls, rights, or agreements to which WCI or any Subsidiary of WCI is a party or by which it is bound obligating WCI or any Subsidiary of WCI to issue, deliver or sell, or cause to be issued, delivered or sold, additional shares of capital stock or any Voting Debt of WCI or of any Subsidiary of WCI or obligating WCI or any Subsidiary of WCI to grant, extend or enter into any such option, warrant, call, right or agreement, other than agreements to issue no more than an aggregate of 1,000,000 shares of WCI Common Stock. Assuming compliance by Time with Section 5.10 and with the first sentence of Section 5.17, after the Effective Time, there will be no option, warrant, call, right or agreement obligating WCI or any Subsidiary of WCI to issue, deliver or sell, or

Section 3.1(c). In private transactions, the promise of each corporation that it has the authority to execute the agreement and accomplish the transaction generally is backed up by an opinion letter from its law firm. In mergers of public companies this is becoming less common. See our commentary to Section 6.3(d).

The promises that the transaction will not violate laws or any of the companies' agreements are much more difficult to verify, hence the carefully drawn qualification of the promises to material events.

The list of approvals that must be obtained appears again in Article VI covering conditions to the transaction.

Section 3.1(d). A representation that the companies' SEC filings are accurate has tremendous benefit both in simplifying the agreement and vastly reducing the amount of time spent negotiating representations and warranties. On the one hand, the recipient of the representation gets a great deal of protection because SEC requirements are so broad. On the other, the company making the representation cannot easily argue (except in highly unusual circumstances) that it is not sure enough about its SEC filings to stand behind them. Nevertheless there are some subtleties. The provision in this agreement promises that the filings comply with laws and rules. It goes on to add the well known antifraud language from Rule 10b–5. There has long been uncertainty whether Rule 10b–5 adds extra bite to the requirements of SEC forms or whether strict compliance with the applicable form protects a company from Rule 10b–5.

cause to be issued, delivered or sold, any shares of capital stock or any Voting Debt of WCI or any Significant Subsidiary of WCI, or obligating WCI or any Subsidiary of WCI to grant, extend or enter into any such option, warrant, call, right or agreement.

(c) *Authority*. WCI has all requisite corporate power and authority to enter into this Agreement and the Share Exchange Agreement and, subject to approval of this Agreement by the stockholders of WCI, to consummate the transactions contemplated hereby and thereby. The execution and delivery of this Agreement and the Share Exchange Agreement and the consummation of the transactions contemplated hereby and thereby have been duly authorized by all necessary corporate action on the part of WCI, subject to such approval of this Agreement by the stockholders of WCI. This Agreement and the Share Exchange Agreement have been duly executed and delivered by WCI and, subject to such approval of this Agreement by the stockholders of WCI, each constitutes a valid and binding obligation of WCI enforceable in accordance with its terms. The execution and delivery of this Agreement and the Share Exchange Agreement do not, and the consummation of the transactions contemplated hereby and thereby will not, conflict with, or result in any violation of, or default (with or without notice or lapse of time, or both) under, or give rise to a right of termination, cancelation or acceleration of any obligation or the loss of a material benefit under, or the creation of a lien, pledge, security interest or other encumbrance on assets (any such conflict, violation, default, right of termination, cancelation or acceleration, loss or creation, a "Violation"), pursuant to any provision of the Certificate of Incorporation or By-laws of WCI or any Subsidiary of WCI or, except (i) as set forth on Schedule 3.1(c) hereto or (ii) as contemplated by the next sentence hereof, result in any Violation of any loan or credit agreement, note, mortgage, indenture, lease, Benefit Plan (as defined in Section 3.1(j)) or other agreement, obligation, instrument, permit, concession, franchise, license, judgment, order, decree, statute, law, ordinance, rule or regulation applicable to WCI or any Subsidiary of WCI or their respective properties or assets which Violation would have a material adverse effect on WCI and its Subsidiaries taken as a whole. No consent, approval, order or authorization of, or registration, declaration or filing with, any court, administrative agency or commission or other governmental authority or instrumentality, domestic or foreign (a "Governmental Entity"), is required by or with respect to WCI or any of its Subsidiaries in connection with the execution and delivery of this Agreement and the Share Exchange Agreement by WCI or the consummation by WCI of the transactions contemplated hereby and thereby, the failure to obtain which would have a material adverse effect on WCI and its Subsidiaries, taken as a whole, except for (i) the filing of a premerger notification report by WCI under the Hart-Scott-Rodino Antitrust Improvements Act of 1976, as amended (the "HSR Act"), (ii) the filing with the SEC of (A) a joint proxy statement in definitive form relating to the meetings of WCI's and Time's stockholders to be held in connection with the Merger (the "Proxy Statement") and (B) such reports under Sections 13(a), 13(d) and 16(a) of the Securities Exchange Act of 1934, as amended (the "Exchange Act"), as may be required in connection with this Agreement, the Share Exchange Agreement and the transactions contemplated hereby and thereby, (iii) the filing of the Certificate of Merger with the Secretary of State of the State of Delaware and appropriate documents with the relevant authorities of other states in which WCI is qualified to do business, (iv) such filings, authorizations, orders and approvals (the "FCC Approvals") as may be required under the Communications Act of 1934, as amended (the "Communications Act"), and with and of state and local governmental authorities, including state and local authorities granting franchises to operate cable systems (the "Local Approvals") and pursuant to state takeover laws ("State Takeover Approvals"), (v) filings pursuant to Article 31-B of the New York Tax Law and (vi) such filings, authorizations, orders and approvals as may be required under foreign laws.

(d) *SEC Documents*. WCI has made available to Time a true and complete copy of each report, schedule, registration statement and definitive proxy statement filed by WCI with the SEC since January 1, 1986 (as such documents have since the time of their filing been amended, the "WCI SEC Documents") which are all the documents (other than preliminary material) that WCI was required to file with the SEC since such date. As of their respective dates, the WCI SEC Documents complied in all material respects with the requirements of the Securities Act of 1933, as amended (the "Securities Act"), or the Exchange Act, as the case may be, and the rules and regulations of the SEC thereunder

Section 3.1(d), cont'd.

The financial statements are warranted to comply as to form with accounting and SEC requirements and to have been prepared in accordance with generally accepted accounting principles applied on a consistent basis. Unaudited financial statements allow for 'normal, recurring audit adjustments.' There is a separate, much weaker standard (to the best of Warner's knowledge) for Lorimar, a television production company that Warner had acquired only a few months earlier and might not have been thoroughly familiar with.

Section 3.1(e). The Information Supplied section notes that Time and Warner are taking advantage of a slightly streamlined SEC filing procedure that allows the registration statement covering the shares issued in the merger to be combined with the proxy statement soliciting approval of the merger. The document becomes very long and bulky and contains a great deal of information. Some of it has not been developed yet. That is why the agreement momentarily lapses out of the present tense that is typical of the representations and warranties. The promise that information to be supplied will be accurate concerns future conduct which ordinarily is addressed by covenants. To avoid repeating a lot of language it is easier to cover it here.

Section 3.1(f). Warner and its subsidiaries probably hold so many permits that it would be impractical to review them all. Moreover, Warner's management may not be sure whether everything is as it should be. Consequently, Warner only promises that it has the permits that are 'material' to its entire business, 'taken as a whole.'

Section 3.1(g). The standards for the promise about litigation are a compromise. Warner only needs to disclose litigation that is reasonably likely to have a material effect on the entire business, and court and administrative agency orders that could have such an effect insofar as reasonably can be foreseen. Including arbitrators' orders in the list is a helpful up-to-date approach.

applicable to such WCI SEC Documents (other than, in the case of certain WCI Schedules 13D, with respect to the timely filing thereof) and none of the WCI SEC Documents contained any untrue statement of a material fact or omitted to state a material fact required to be stated therein or necessary to make the statements therein, in light of the circumstances under which they were made, not misleading. The financial statements of WCI included in the WCI SEC Documents comply as to form in all material respects with applicable accounting requirements and with the published rules and regulations of the SEC with respect thereto, have been prepared in accordance with generally accepted accounting principles applied on a consistent basis during the periods involved (except as may be indicated in the notes thereto or, in the case of the unaudited statements, as permitted by Form 10-Q of the SEC) and fairly present (subject, in the case of the unaudited statements, to normal, recurring audit adjustments) the consolidated financial position of WCI and its consolidated Subsidiaries (other than Lorimar) as at the dates thereof and the consolidated results of their operations and cash flows (or changes in financial position prior to the approval of Statement of Financial Accounting Standards Number 95 ("FASB 95")) for the periods then ended. To the best of WCI's knowledge, the inclusion of Lorimar in the financial statements referred to in the preceding sentence would not cause the representations contained in this Section 3.1(d) to be false.

(e) *Information Supplied.* None of the information supplied or to be supplied by WCI for inclusion or incorporation by reference in (i) the registration statement on Form S-4 to be filed with the SEC by Time in connection with the issuance of shares of Time Common Stock and Time Series BB Preferred in the Merger (the "S-4") will, at the time the S-4 is filed with the SEC and at the time it becomes effective under the Securities Act, contain any untrue statement of a material fact or omit to state any material fact required to be stated therein or necessary to make the statements therein not misleading, and (ii) the Proxy Statement will, at the date mailed to stockholders and at the times of the meetings of stockholders to be held in connection with the Merger, contain any untrue statement of a material fact or omit to state any material fact required to be stated therein or necessary in order to make the statements therein, in light of the circumstances under which they are made, not misleading. The Proxy Statement will comply as to form in all material respects with the provisions of the Exchange Act and the rules and regulations thereunder.

(f) *Compliance with Applicable Laws.* WCI and its Subsidiaries hold all permits, licenses, variances, exemptions, orders and approvals of all Governmental Entities which are material to the operation of the businesses of WCI and its Subsidiaries, taken as a whole (the "WCI Permits"). WCI and its Subsidiaries are in compliance with the terms of the WCI Permits, except where the failure so to comply would not have a material adverse effect on WCI and its Subsidiaries taken as a whole. Except as disclosed in the WCI SEC Documents filed prior to the date of this Agreement, the businesses of WCI and its Subsidiaries are not being conducted in violation of any law, ordinance or regulation of any Governmental Entity, except for possible violations which individually or in the aggregate do not, and, insofar as reasonably can be foreseen, in the future will not, have a material adverse effect on WCI and its Subsidiaries taken as a whole. Except as set forth in Schedule 3.1(f) hereto, as of the date of this Agreement, no investigation or review by any Governmental Entity with respect to WCI or any of its Subsidiaries is pending or, to the knowledge of WCI, threatened, nor has any Governmental Entity indicated an intention to conduct the same, other than, in each case, those the outcome of which, as far as reasonably can be foreseen, will not have a material adverse effect on WCI and its Subsidiaries taken as a whole.

(g) *Litigation.* As of the date of this Agreement, except as disclosed in the WCI SEC Documents filed prior to the date of this Agreement or in Schedule 3.1(g) hereto, there is no suit, action or proceeding pending, or, to the knowledge of WCI, threatened against or affecting WCI or any Subsidiary of WCI which is reasonably likely to have a material adverse effect on WCI and its Subsidiaries taken as a whole, nor is there any judgment, decree, injunction, rule or order of any Governmental Entity or arbitrator outstanding against WCI or any Subsidiary of WCI having, or which, insofar as reasonably can be foreseen, in the future could have, any such effect.

Section 3.1(h). Tax representations are tricky and can involve huge sums. Here the definition of tax is so broad that Warner is unlikely to have been able to verify the statement entirely. However, it gives general protection to Time anyway and does not present a great risk to Warner because many of the types of tax mentioned are not likely to be signficant.

The current audit of Warner's 1977–84 taxes should have given Time reason to pause. Time's lawyers and accountants probably spent a lot of time learning what issues have been raised in the audit so far.

Section 3.1(i). The provision covering important agreements shows the kind of problem that can arise when there is a need to complete an acquisition agreement in a great hurry (as there usually is). Speed is generally important to stay ahead of competing bidders and disgruntled shareholders and other naysayers who might try to stop the deal. Here the representations momentarily lapse into the future again. The exception for a schedule to be delivered is open-ended. Even though Time and Warner had been talking about the merger for years, by the time they were ready to sign Warner still did not have a list of all the important agreements covered by this provision. Time here is accepting a promise that could be undercut by a schedule delivered a month later that could (in theory) contain some real surprises. It is understandable that Warner did not want to make a promise it was not sure about. On the other hand, the broad SEC representation in 3.1(d) cuts down the risk a great deal. Time must have been relying heavily on these SEC filings and its own practical evaluation. It would have asked questions on subjects where surprises were likely.

(h) *Taxes.* To the best of WCI's knowledge, WCI and each of its Subsidiaries has filed all tax returns required to be filed by any of them and has paid (or WCI has paid on its behalf), or has set up an adequate reserve for the payment of, all taxes required to be paid as shown on such returns and the most recent financial statements contained in the WCI SEC Documents reflect an adequate reserve for all taxes payable by WCI and its Subsidiaries accrued through the date of such financial statements. No material deficiencies for any taxes aggregating in excess of $300,000,000 have been proposed, asserted or assessed against WCI or any of its Subsidiaries. Except with respect to claims for refund, the Federal income tax returns of WCI and each of its Subsidiaries consolidated in such returns have been examined by and settled with the United States Internal Revenue Service (the "IRS"), or the statute of limitations with respect to such years has expired, for all years through 1976. The Federal income tax returns of WCI and each of its Subsidiaries consolidated in such returns for the years 1977-84 are currently under examination by the IRS. For the purpose of this Agreement, the term "tax" (including, with correlative meaning, the terms "taxes" and "taxable") shall include all Federal, state, local and foreign income, profits, franchise, gross receipts, payroll, sales, employment, use, property, withholding, excise and other taxes, duties or assessments of any nature whatsoever, together with all interest, penalties and additions imposed with respect to such amounts.

(i) *Certain Agreements.* Except as disclosed in the WCI SEC Documents filed prior to the date of this Agreement, or in a schedule to be delivered to Time within thirty days of the date hereof, and except for this Agreement, as of the date of this Agreement, neither WCI nor any of its Subsidiaries is a party to any oral or written (i) consulting agreement not terminable on 60 days' or less notice involving the payment of more than $1,000,000 per annum or union, guild or collective bargaining agreement which agreement covers more than 1,000 employees, (ii) agreement with any executive officer or other key employee of WCI or any Significant Subsidiary of WCI the benefits of which are contingent, or the terms of which are materially altered, upon the occurrence of a transaction involving WCI of the nature contemplated by this Agreement or agreement with respect to any executive officer of WCI providing any term of employment or compensation guarantee extending for a period longer than three years and for the payment of in excess of $1,000,000 per annum, or (iii) agreement or plan, including any stock option plan, stock appreciation right plan, restricted stock plan or stock purchase plan, any of the benefits of which will be increased, or the vesting of the benefits of which will be accelerated, by the occurrence of any of the transactions contemplated by this Agreement or the value of any of the benefits of which will be calculated on the basis of any of the transactions contemplated by this Agreement.

(j) *Benefit Plans.* (i) With respect to each employee benefit plan (including, without limitation, any "employee benefit plan", as defined in Section 3(3) of the Employee Retirement Income Security Act of 1974, as amended ("ERISA")) (all the foregoing being herein called "Benefit Plans"), maintained or contributed to by WCI or any of its Subsidiaries, WCI has made available to Time a true and correct copy of (a) the most recent annual report (Form 5500) filed with the IRS, (b) such Benefit Plan, (c) each trust agreement and group annuity contract, if any, relating to such Benefit Plan and (d) the most recent actuarial report or valuation relating to a Benefit Plan subject to Title IV of ERISA.

(ii) With respect to the Benefit Plans, individually and in the aggregate, no event has occurred, and to the knowledge of WCI or any of its Subsidiaries, there exists no condition or set of circumstances in connection with which WCI or any of its Subsidiaries could be subject to any liability that is reasonably likely to have a material adverse effect on WCI and its Subsidiaries, taken as a whole (except liability for benefits claims and funding obligations payable in the ordinary course) under ERISA, the Internal Revenue Code of 1986, as amended (the "Code"), or any other applicable law.

(iii) Except as set forth in Schedule 3.1(j), with respect to the Benefit Plans, individually and in the aggregate, there are no funded benefit obligations for which contributions have not been made or properly accrued and there are no unfunded benefit obligations which have not been accounted for by reserves, or otherwise properly footnoted in accordance with generally accepted accounting principles, on the financial statements of WCI or any of its Subsidiaries, which obligations are reasonably likely to have a material adverse effect on WCI and its Subsidiaries, taken as a whole.

Section 3.1(k). Warner was not able to provide a list of all its cable television systems and FCC authorizations by the time the agreement was signed, but promises to do so within 30 days.

The complicated character of the cable network influenced the structure of the transaction. Because a subsidiary of Time would be merging into Warner, all of the cable agreements and licenses could stay in Warner's name and not have to be transferred, which is convenient and reduces expense and saves time. However, in many cases it would still have been necessary to obtain approval of a government body or a third party because of the change in control.

Section 3.1(n). Warner promises Time that it has received a fairness opinion from its investment bankers. Time wants this assurance because it wants to reduce the risk that the deal will founder over lawsuits by Warner's shareholders.

Section 3.1(o). Warner's certificate of incorporation contained an anti-takeover provision requiring a merger with a 10% shareholder to be approved by an 80% vote *and* by a majority of the shares not owned by the 10% holder, unless the board of directors approves the transaction. Provisions of this sort can be full of surprises. The same is true for the Delaware antitakeover statute, General Corporation Law §203 and, as we have mentioned before, for poison pills. The Share Exchange Agreement, reproduced below, adds to the concern. Time wants some assurance that Warner has carefully thought through the effect of these provisions on the merger and that there are no hidden surprises.

Section 3.1(p). It is important to be sure that there only needs to be one class vote, in which the common and the preferred shares are treated as a single unit. If the preferred shareholders were entitled to a separate vote as a class they would have a veto power over the transaction and they might have to be bought out. As it turned out, BHC, the holder of the Series B Preferred stock, thought it was entitled to a class vote. Time and Warner successfully filed suit in Delaware to obtain a court ruling that it did not.

(k) *Patents, Trademarks, etc.* WCI and its Subsidiaries have all patents, trademarks, trade names, service marks, trade secrets, copyrights and other proprietary intellectual property rights as are material in connection with the businesses of WCI and its Subsidiaries, taken as a whole.

(l) *CATV Systems, Franchises, Licenses, Permits, etc.* (i) WCI will provide Time, within thirty days of the date hereof, a complete list of the cable television systems ("CATV Systems") operated by WCI or any Subsidiary thereof as of the date hereof and the number of subscribers in each of such CATV Systems as of January 31, 1989.

(ii) WCI will provide Time, within thirty days of the date hereof, a list and brief description of all authorizations, approvals, certifications, licenses and permits issued by the FCC ("WCI FCC Authorizations") to WCI or any Subsidiary thereof as of the date hereof and all applications by WCI or any Subsidiary thereof for WCI FCC Authorizations which are pending on the date hereof.

(iii) WCI and its Subsidiaries (A) have all WCI FCC Authorizations and authorizations, approvals, franchises, licenses and permits of state or local governmental authorities ("Franchises") required for the operation of the CATV Systems being operated on the date hereof, (B) have duly and currently filed all reports and other information required to be filed by the FCC or any other governmental authority in connection with such WCI FCC Authorizations and Franchises and (C) are not in violation of any WCI FCC Authorization or Franchise, other than the lack of WCI FCC Authorizations or Franchises, delays in filing reports or violations which, insofar as can reasonably be foreseen, would not have a material adverse effect on the CATV business conducted by WCI and its Subsidiaries taken as a whole.

(m) *Absence of Certain Changes or Events.* Except as disclosed in the WCI SEC Documents filed prior to the date of this Agreement or in the audited consolidated balance sheet of WCI and its subsidiaries at December 31, 1988, and the related consolidated statements of operations, cash flows and changes in shareholders' equity (the "WCI 1988 Financials"), true and correct copies of which have been delivered to Time, or except as contemplated by this Agreement and the Share Exchange Agreement, since the date of the WCI 1988 Financials, WCI and its Subsidiaries have conducted their respective businesses only in the ordinary and usual course, and, as of the date of this Agreement, there has not been (i) any damage, destruction or loss, whether covered by insurance or not, which has, or insofar as reasonably can be foreseen in the future is reasonably likely to have, a material adverse effect on WCI and its Subsidiaries taken as a whole; (ii) any declaration, setting aside or payment of any dividend or other distribution (whether in cash, stock or property) with respect to any of WCI's capital stock, except for regular quarterly cash dividends of $.17 per share on WCI Common Stock and regular quarterly cash dividends on WCI Series B Preferred, in each case with usual record and payment dates for such dividends; or (iii) any transaction, commitment, dispute or other event or condition (financial or otherwise) of any character (whether or not in the ordinary course of business) individually or in the aggregate having or which, insofar as reasonably can be foreseen, in the future is reasonably likely to have, a material adverse effect on WCI and its Subsidiaries taken as a whole.

(n) *Opinion of Financial Advisor.* WCI has received the opinions of Lazard Freres & Co. dated the date hereof and May 19, 1989, to the effect that, as of such dates, the consideration to be received in the Merger by WCI's stockholders is fair to WCI's stockholders from a financial point of view, copies of which opinions have been delivered to Time.

(o) *Article SEVENTH of WCI Certificate of Incorporation and Section 203 of the DGCL Not Applicable.* Neither the provisions of Article SEVENTH of WCI's Certificate of Incorporation nor the provisions of Section 203 of the DGCL will, prior to the termination of this Agreement, assuming the accuracy of the representations contained in Sections 3.2(b) and 3.2(q) (without giving effect to the knowledge qualification thereof) apply to this Agreement, the Share Exchange Agreement, the Merger or to the transactions contemplated hereby and thereby.

(p) *Vote Required.* The affirmative vote of a majority of the votes that holders of the outstanding shares of WCI Common Stock and WCI Series B Preferred, voting together as a class, are entitled to cast is the only vote of the holders of any class or series of WCI capital stock necessary to approve this

Section 3.1(q). Pooling-of-interests accounting treatment (see Glossary entry) was thought to be important to the economics of the merger, although when it was restructured after Paramount's hostile bid the benefits of this accounting treatment were lost. Even if the stock market can see through differences in accounting presentations so that stock prices are not affected, pooling may have important advantages with, for example, administrative agencies and creditors. They also may be able to see through accounting differences but may be constrained by legal or political considerations.

Section 3.1(s). Warner is held to a lower standard concerning actions that its affiliates might have taken – it only says that 'to its best knowledge' it does not know of any. But what is the knowledge of a corporation? It is hard to tell whether there is someone somewhere in the organization who knows about something. Sometimes agreements define knowledge as something known by any of a number of specifically identified officers in specific positions. A court might interpret it to mean that the company giving the promise had made a reasonable inquiry into the subject. However, both parties know that Warner is saying something important and that a court would struggle to give the term a sensible meaning under the circumstances.

Section 3.2 covers the representations and warranties of Time. Most of them are parallel to those made by Warner. This is to be expected in a merger of equals. In a cash acquisition the buyer's representations usually are limited to assurances that it can pay and perform its other obligations as buyer.

For both sides, many of the representations are important because they play a discovery role, drawing out new facts as the negotiators talk about whether they can commit to a particular promise. The representation that Warner is not an interested stockholder or an acquiring person is a case in point. Warner knows the facts about its stock ownership. The representation forces it to think hard. On the other hand, Time should be able to interpret the provisions of its admittedly complex charter and poison pill better than Warner. Asking for the promise simply helps to gain information and helps to assure that there is no surprise hidden away.

Agreement and the transactions contemplated hereby (assuming the accuracy of the representations contained in Sections 3.2(b) and 3.2(q), without giving effect to the knowledge qualification thereof).

(q) *Accounting Matters.* Neither WCI nor, to its best knowledge, any of its affiliates, has through the date of this Agreement, taken or agreed to take any action that would prevent Time from accounting for the business combination to be effected by the Merger as a pooling of interests.

(r) *No Change in Capital Structure.* There has been no material change in the information set forth in the second sentence of Section 3.1(b) between the close of business on February 17, 1989, and the date hereof.

(s) *WCI Not an Interested Stockholder or an Acquiring Person.* As of the date hereof, neither WCI nor, to its best knowledge, any of its affiliates, is an "Interested Stockholder" as such term is defined in Article V of Time's Certificate of Incorporation or an "Acquiring Person" as such term is defined in the Rights Agreement.

3.2. *Representations and Warranties of Time and Sub.* Time and Sub represent and warrant to WCI as follows:

(a) *Organization; Standing and Power.* Each of Time and Sub and Time's Significant Subsidiaries is a corporation or partnership duly organized, validly existing and in good standing under the laws of its state of incorporation or organization and has all requisite power and authority to own, lease and operate its properties and to carry on its business as now being conducted, and is duly qualified and in good standing to do business in each jurisdiction in which the nature of its business or the ownership or leasing of its properties makes such qualification necessary other than in such jurisdictions where the failure so to qualify would not have a material adverse effect on Time and its Subsidiaries taken as a whole.

(b) *Capital Structure.* As of the date hereof, the authorized capital stock of Time consists of 200,000,000 shares of Time Common Stock and 25,000,000 shares of Preferred Stock, par value $1.00 per share, of Time ("Time Preferred Stock"). As of the close of business on February 17, 1989, 56,557,919 shares of Time Common Stock were outstanding, 7,688,615 shares of Time Common Stock were reserved for issuance pursuant to the Time stock option plans, the Time Employees' Stock Ownership Plan, the Time Stock Incentive Plan, the Time Employees' Savings Plan, the Time Dividend Reinvestment and Stock Purchase Plan, the American Television and Communications Corporation ("ATC") Employees Stock Savings Plan and Time restricted stock plans (collectively, "Time Stock Plans"), 6,809,915 shares of Time Common Stock were held by Time in its treasury, there were no shares of Time Preferred Stock or Voting Debt of Time issued or outstanding, and 750,000 shares of Time Series A Preferred were reserved for issuance upon exercise of the Rights. All outstanding shares of Time capital stock are, and the shares of Time Common Stock (x) to be issued pursuant to or as specifically contemplated by this Agreement, (y) to be issued pursuant to the Share Exchange Agreement and (z) when issued in accordance with this Agreement, upon exercise of the WCI Stock Options and Lorimar Stock Grants, in accordance with actions permitted by Section 4.1(c) and upon conversion of Time Series BB Preferred and the Lorimar Debentures, will be, validly issued, fully paid and nonassessable and not subject to preemptive rights. As of the date of this Agreement, except for this Agreement, Time Stock Plans, the Rights Agreement and pursuant to the Share Exchange Agreement, there are no options, warrants, calls, rights, commitments or agreements of any character to which Time or any Subsidiary of Time (other than ATC and its Subsidiaries, but only with respect to ATC or its Subsidiaries) is a party or by which it is bound obligating Time or any Subsidiary of Time (other than ATC and its Subsidiaries, but only with respect to ATC or its Subsidiaries) to issue, deliver or sell, or cause to be issued, delivered or sold, additional shares of capital stock or any Voting Debt securities of Time or of any Subsidiary of Time (other than ATC and its Subsidiaries, but only with respect to ATC or its Subsidiaries) or obligating Time or any Subsidiary of Time (other than ATC and its Subsidiaries, but only with respect to ATC or its Subsidiaries) to grant, extend or enter into any such option, warrant, call, right, commitment or agreement. As of the date hereof, the authorized capital stock of Sub consists of 100 shares of Common Stock, par value $1 per share, all of which are validly issued, fully paid and nonassessable and are owned by Time.

Section 3.2, cont'd.

The schedules to the exhibits also have a discovery role. The parties use the schedules to protect themselves. Once a potential problem is listed on a schedule it becomes the other side's responsibility to ask more questions if it wants more information.

(c) *Authority.* Time and Sub have all requisite corporate power and authority to enter into this Agreement and the Share Exchange Agreement and, subject to approval by the stockholders of Time of (i) this Agreement and the issuance of Time Common Stock and Time Series BB Preferred pursuant to the Merger, (ii) the amendments to Time's Certificate of Incorporation set forth on Exhibit 3.2(c)(ii) hereto ((i) and (ii), collectively, the "Time Vote Matter") and (iii) the Time Warner 1989 Stock Incentive Plan, which will be in substantially the form of Exhibit 3.2(c)(iii) hereto covering ten million shares of additional Time Common Stock (the "New Time Stock Plan"), to consummate the transactions contemplated hereby and thereby. The execution and delivery of this Agreement and the Share Exchange Agreement and the consummation of the transactions contemplated hereby and thereby have been duly authorized by all necessary corporate action on the part of Time and Sub, subject in the case of this Agreement to approval of the Time Vote Matter and the New Time Stock Plan by the stockholders of Time. This Agreement and the Share Exchange Agreement have been duly executed and delivered by Time and Sub and, subject in the case of this Agreement to such approval of the Time Vote Matter and the New Time Stock Plan by the stockholders of Time, each constitutes a valid and binding obligation of Time and Sub enforceable in accordance with its terms. The execution and delivery of this Agreement and the Share Exchange Agreement do not, and the consummation of the transactions contemplated hereby and thereby will not, result in any Violation pursuant to any provision of the Certificate of Incorporation or By-laws of Time or any of its Subsidiaries or, except as set forth on Schedule 3.2(c) hereto or as contemplated by the next sentence hereof, result in any Violation of any loan or credit agreement, note, mortgage, indenture, lease, Benefit Plan or other agreement, obligation, instrument, permit, concession, franchise, license, judgment, order, decree, statute, law, ordinance, rule or regulation applicable to Time or any of its Subsidiaries or their respective properties or assets which Violation would have a material adverse effect on Time and its Subsidiaries taken as a whole. No consent, approval, order or authorization of, or registration, declaration or filing with, any Governmental Entity is required by or with respect to Time or any of its Subsidiaries in connection with the execution and delivery of this Agreement and the Share Exchange Agreement by Time and Sub or the consummation by Time and Sub of the transactions contemplated hereby and thereby, the failure to obtain which would have a material adverse effect on Time and its Subsidiaries, taken as a whole, except for (i) the filing of a premerger notification report by Time under the HSR Act, (ii) the filing with the SEC of the Proxy Statement, the S-4 and such reports under Sections 13(a), 13(d) and 16(a) of the Exchange Act, as may be required in connection with this Agreement, the Share Exchange Agreement and the transactions contemplated hereby and thereby and the obtaining from the SEC of such orders as may be so required, (iii) the filing of such documents with, and the obtaining of such orders from, the various state authorities, including state securities authorities, that are required in connection with the transactions contemplated by this Agreement and the Share Exchange Agreement, (iv) the filing of the Certificate of Merger with the Secretary of State of the State of Delaware and appropriate documents with the relevant authorities of other states in which WCI is qualified to do business, (v) the FCC Approvals, Local Approval and State Takeover Approvals, (vi) filings pursuant to Article 31-B of the New York Tax Law and (vii) such filings, authorizing actions, orders and approvals as may be required under foreign laws.

(d) *SEC Documents.* Time has made available to WCI a true and complete copy of each report, schedule, registration statement and definitive proxy statement filed by Time or ATC with the SEC since January 1, 1986 (as such documents have since the time of their filing been amended, the "Time SEC Documents") which are all the documents (other than preliminary material) that Time or ATC was required to file with the SEC since such date. As of their respective dates, the Time SEC Documents complied in all material respects with the requirements of the Securities Act or the Exchange Act, as the case may be, and the rules and regulations of the SEC thereunder applicable to such Time SEC Documents, and none of the Time SEC Documents contained any untrue statement of a material fact or omitted to state a material fact required to be stated therein or necessary to make the statements therein, in light of the circumstances under which they were made, not misleading. The financial statements of Time and ATC included in the Time SEC Documents comply as to form in all material respects with applicable accounting requirements and with the published rules and regulations of the SEC with respect thereto, have been prepared in accordance with generally accepted accounting principles applied on a consistent basis during the periods involved (except as may be indicated in the notes thereto or, in the

case of the unaudited statements, as permitted by Form 10-Q of the SEC) and fairly present (subject, in the case of the unaudited statements, to normal, recurring audit adjustments) the consolidated financial position of Time and its consolidated Subsidiaries and ATC and its consolidated Subsidiaries as at the dates thereof and the consolidated results of their operations and cash flows (or changes in financial position prior to the approval of FASB 95) for the periods then ended.

(e) *Information Supplied.* None of the information supplied by Time or Sub for inclusion or incorporation by reference in (i) the S-4 will, at the time the S-4 is filed with the SEC and at the time it becomes effective under the Securities Act, contain any untrue statement of a material fact or omit to state any material fact required to be stated therein or necessary to make the statements therein not misleading and (ii) the Proxy Statement will, at the date mailed to stockholders and at the times of the meetings of stockholders to be held in connection with the Merger, contain any untrue statement of a material fact or omit to state any material fact required to be stated therein or necessary in order to make the statements therein, in light of the circumstances under which they are made, not misleading. The Proxy Statement will comply as to form in all material respects with the provisions of the Exchange Act and the rules and regulations thereunder, and the S-4 will comply as to form in all material respects with the provisions of the Securities Act and the rules and regulations thereunder.

(f) *Compliance with Applicable Laws.* Time and its Subsidiaries hold all permits, licenses, variances, exemptions, orders and approvals of all Governmental Entities which are material to the operation of the businesses of Time and its Subsidiaries, taken as a whole (the "Time Permits"). Time and its Subsidiaries are in compliance with the terms of the Time Permits, except where the failure so to comply would not have a material adverse effect on Time and its Subsidiaries taken as a whole. Except as disclosed in the Time SEC Documents filed prior to the date of this Agreement, the businesses of Time and its Subsidiaries are not being conducted in violation of any law, ordinance or regulation of any Governmental Entity, except for possible violations which individually or in the aggregate do not, and, insofar as reasonably can be foreseen, in the future will not, have a material adverse effect on Time and its Subsidiaries taken as a whole. Except as set forth on Schedule 3.2(f) hereto, as of the date of this Agreement, no investigation or review by any Governmental Entity with respect to Time or any of its Subsidiaries is pending or, to the knowledge of Time, threatened, nor has any Governmental Entity indicated an intention to conduct the same, other than, in each case, those the outcome of which, as far as reasonably can be foreseen, will not have a material adverse effect on Time and its Subsidiaries taken as a whole.

(g) *Litigation.* As of the date of this Agreement, except as disclosed in the Time SEC Documents filed prior to the date of this Agreement or on Schedule 3.2(g) hereto, there is no suit, action or proceeding pending, or, to the knowledge of Time, threatened against or affecting Time or any Subsidiary of Time which is reasonably likely to have a material adverse effect on Time and its Subsidiaries taken as a whole, nor is there any judgment, decree, injunction, rule or order of any Governmental Entity or arbitrator outstanding against Time or any Subsidiary of Time having, or which, insofar as reasonably can be foreseen, in the future could have, any such effect.

(h) *Taxes.* To the best of Time's knowledge, Time and each of its Subsidiaries has filed all tax returns required to be filed by any of them and has paid (or Time has paid on its behalf), or has set up an adequate reserve for the payment of, all taxes required to be paid as shown on such returns and the most recent financial statements contained in the Time SEC Documents reflect an adequate reserve for all taxes payable by Time and its Subsidiaries accrued through the date of such financial statements. No material deficiencies for any taxes aggregating in excess of $300,000,000 have been proposed, asserted or assessed against Time or any of its Subsidiaries. The Federal income tax returns of Time and each of its Subsidiaries consolidated in such returns have been examined by and settled with the IRS, or the statute of limitations with respect to such years has expired, for all years through 1978. The Federal income tax returns of Time and each of its Subsidiaries consolidated in such returns for the years 1979 through 1984 are currently under examination by the IRS.

(i) *Certain Agreements.* Except as disclosed in the Time SEC Documents filed prior to the date of this Agreement, or in a schedule to be delivered to WCI within thirty days of the date hereof, and except

for this Agreement, as of the date of this Agreement, neither Time nor any of its Subsidiaries is a party to any oral or written (i) consulting agreement not terminable on 60 days' or less notice involving the payment of more than $1,000,000 per annum or union, guild or collective bargaining agreement which agreement covers more than 1,000 employees, (ii) agreement with any executive officer or other key employee of Time or any Significant Subsidiary of Time the benefits of which are contingent, or the terms of which are materially altered, upon the occurrence of a transaction involving Time or any Subsidiary of Time of the nature contemplated by this Agreement or agreement with respect to any executive officer of Time providing any term of employment or compensation guarantee extending for a period longer than three years and for the payment of in excess of $1,000,000 per annum, or (iii) agreement or plan, including any stock option plan, stock appreciation rights plan, restricted stock plan or stock purchase plan, any of the benefits of which will be increased, or the vesting of the benefits of which will be accelerated, by the occurrence of any of the transactions contemplated by this Agreement or the value of any of the benefits of which will be calculated on the basis of any of the transactions contemplated by this Agreement.

(j) *Benefit Plans.* (i) With respect to each Benefit Plan maintained or contributed to by Time or any of its Subsidiaries, Time has made available to WCI a true and correct copy of (a) the most recent annual report (Form 5500) filed with the IRS, (b) such Benefit Plan, (c) each trust agreement and group annuity contract, if any, relating to such Benefit Plan and (d) the most recent actuarial report or valuation relating to a Benefit Plan subject to Title IV of ERISA.

(ii) With respect to the Benefit Plans, individually and in the aggregate, no event has occurred, and to the knowledge of Time or any of its Subsidiaries, there exists no condition or set of circumstances in connection with which Time or any of its Subsidiaries could be subject to any liability that is reasonably likely to have a material adverse effect upon Time and its Subsidiaries taken as a whole (except liability for benefits claims and funding obligations payable in the ordinary course) under ERISA the Code or any other applicable law.

(iii) Except as set forth in Schedule 3.2(j), with respect to the Benefit Plans, individually and in the aggregate, there are no funded benefit obligations for which contributions have not been made or properly accrued and there are no unfunded benefit obligations which have not been accounted for by reserves, or otherwise properly footnoted in accordance with generally accepted accounting principles, on the financial statements of Time or any of its Subsidiaries, which obligations are reasonably likely to have a material adverse effect on Time and its Subsidiaries taken as a whole.

(k) *Patents, Trademarks, etc.* Time and its Subsidiaries have all patents, trademarks, trade names, service marks, trade secrets, copyrights and other proprietary intellectual property rights as are material in connection with the businesses of Time and its Subsidiaries, taken as a whole.

(l) *CATV Systems, Franchises, Licenses, Permits, etc.* (i) Time will provide WCI, within thirty days of the date hereof, a complete list of the CATV Systems operated by Time or any Subsidiary thereof as of the date hereof and the number of subscribers in each of such CATV Systems as of January 31, 1989.

(ii) Time will provide WCI, within thirty days of the date hereof, a list and brief description of all authorizations, approvals, certifications, licenses and permits issued by the FCC ("Time FCC Authorizations") to Time or any Subsidiary thereof as of the date hereof and all applications by Time or any Subsidiary thereof for Time FCC Authorizations which are pending on the date hereof.

(iii) Time and its Subsidiaries (A) have all Time FCC Authorizations and Franchises required for the operation of the CATV Systems being operated on the date hereof, (B) have duly and currently filed all reports and other information required to be filed by the FCC or any other governmental authority in connection with such Time FCC Authorizations and Franchises, and (C) are not in violation of any Time FCC Authorization or Franchise other than the lack of Time FCC Authorizations, Franchises, delays in filing reports or violations which, insofar as can reasonably be foreseen, would not have a material adverse effect on the CATV business conducted by Time and its Subsidiaries taken as a whole.

Section 3.2(n). Why does Time promise fairness opinions from two investment banking firms? The reason is that it used two firms. The smaller one, Wasserstein Perella, is known mainly as a specialist in acquisitions. Time may have wanted its advice on merger strategy while assuring itself of the help from a much larger firm. But it may have had many other reasons: a desire to be fair to a firm that had provided advice free in the past; a wish to keep both firms on their mettle; or a feeling that the board would gain confidence in a difficult, controversial transaction from having two firms. What would Time have done if only one firm thought the merger was fair? Probably an unlikely outcome. However, possibly an insight into another reason for having two bankers: it reduces the bargaining power of each of them. On the other hand, having two investment bankers can cause confusion in formulating strategy and in negotiating with the other side and can reduce loyalty to the client.

Section 3.2(r). Time's promise that its poison pill will not cause a problem is designed to assure Warner that there are no hidden embarrassments here. As we have said before, there easily could be under the terms of many poison pills, even in a negotiated acquisition.

(m) *Absence of Certain Changes or Events.* Except as disclosed in the Time SEC Documents filed prior to the date of this Agreement or in the audited consolidated balance sheets of Time and its Subsidiaries and the related consolidated statements of income, shareholders' equity and cash flows as of and for the period ended December 31, 1988 (the "Time 1988 Financials"), true and correct copies of which have been delivered to WCI, or except as contemplated by this Agreement and the Share Exchange Agreement, since the date of the Time 1988 Financials, Time and its Subsidiaries have conducted their respective businesses only in the ordinary and usual course, and, as of the date of this Agreement, there has not been (i) any damage, destruction or loss, whether covered by insurance or not, which has, or insofar as reasonably can be foreseen in the future is reasonably likely to have, a material adverse effect on Time and its Subsidiaries taken as a whole; (ii) any declaration, setting aside or payment of any dividend or other distribution (whether in cash, stock or property) with respect to any of Time's capital stock, except for regular quarterly cash dividends of $.25 per share on Time Common Stock with usual record and payment dates for such dividends; or (iii) any transaction, commitment, dispute or other event or condition (financial or otherwise) of any character (whether or not in the ordinary course of business) individually or in the aggregate having or which, insofar as reasonably can be foreseen, in the future is reasonably likely to have, a material adverse effect on Time and its Subsidiaries taken as a whole.

(n) *Opinions of Financial Advisors.* Time has received the opinions of Shearson Lehman Hutton Inc. and Wasserstein Perella & Co., Inc., dated March 3, 1989, and May 16, 1989, and to the effect that, as of such dates, the financial terms of the Merger are fair to Time and its stockholders, from a financial point of view, copies of which opinions have been delivered to WCI.

(o) *Vote Required.* The affirmative vote of the holders of a majority of the outstanding shares of Time Common Stock is the only vote of the holders of any class or series of Time capital stock necessary to approve the Time Vote Matter and the transactions contemplated hereby (assuming the accuracy of the representations contained in Section 3.1(s)(without giving effect to the knowledge qualification thereof)).

(p) *Accounting Matters.* Neither Time nor, to its best knowledge, any of its affiliates, has through the date of this Agreement taken or agreed to take any action that would prevent Time from accounting for the business combination to be effected by the Merger as a pooling of interests.

(q) *Ownership of WCI Common Stock.* As of the date hereof, assuming consummation of the transactions contemplated by the Share Exchange Agreement neither Time nor, to its best knowledge, any of its affiliates or associates, (i) beneficially owns, directly or indirectly, or (ii) are parties to any agreement, arrangement or understanding for the purpose of acquiring, holding, voting or disposing of, in each case, shares of capital stock of WCI, which in the aggregate, represent 10% or more of the outstanding shares of capital stock of WCI entitled to vote generally in the election of directors.

(r) *Rights Agreement.* Assuming the accuracy of the representations contained in Section 3.1(s) (without giving effect to the knowledge qualification thereof) the consummation of the transactions contemplated by this Agreement and the Share Exchange Agreement will not result in an "Affiliate Merger", a "Triggering Event" or a "Business Combination", as such terms are defined in the Rights Agreement.

(s) *Article V of Time's Certificate of Incorporation and Section 203 of the DGCL Not Applicable.* Neither the provisions of Article V of Time's Certificate of Incorporation nor Section 203 of the DGCL will, prior to the termination of this Agreement, assuming the accuracy of the representations contained in Section 3.1(s) (without giving effect to the knowledge qualification thereof), apply to this Agreement, the Share Exchange Agreement, the Merger or the transactions contemplated hereby and thereby, including the purchase of shares of Time by WCI under the Share Exchange Agreement and the Board of Directors of Time, including a majority of the Disinterested Directors (as defined in the Time Certificate of Incorporation), have approved such transactions.

Article IV covers Time's and Warner's agreements on how they will run their businesses before the closing.

Section 4.1. The exception for employment and compensation arrangements is puzzling. There does not appear to be a limit. Yet the employment agreements for top management were a subject of intense negotiation. Maybe entertainment and publishing companies cannot afford to tie their hands on these issues even for a short time. However, the parties did commit themselves to some employment arrangements elsewhere in the agreement. See Section 5.14.

Section 4.1(a). The parties give the standard promise that they will operate the business in the ordinary course between the time the agreement is signed and when the merger takes place. They recognize that a business can change quickly and want to be sure that they are merging with the company with whom they struck their bargain. This is also the reason for most of the other promises in this article.

Section 4.1(b). See commentary to Section 2.1(f).

(t) *Interim Operations of Sub.* Sub was formed solely for the purpose of engaging in the transactions contemplated hereby, has engaged in no other business activities and has conducted its operations only as contemplated hereby.

(u) *No Change in Capital Structure.* There has been no material change in the information set forth in the second sentence of Section 3.2(b) between the close of business on February 17, 1989, and the date hereof.

ARTICLE IV

COVENANTS RELATING TO CONDUCT OF BUSINESS

4.1. *Covenants of WCI and Time.* During the period from the date of this Agreement and continuing until the Effective Time, WCI and Time each agree as to itself and its Subsidiaries that (except as expressly contemplated or permitted by this Agreement, the Share Exchange Agreement, or to the extent that the other party shall otherwise consent in writing and except with respect to employment and compensation arrangements entered into by WCI or Time):

(a) *Ordinary Course.* Each party and their respective Subsidiaries shall carry on their respective businesses in the usual, regular and ordinary course in substantially the same manner as heretofore conducted and use all reasonable efforts to preserve intact their present business organizations, keep available the services of their present officers and employees and preserve their relationships with customers, suppliers and others having business dealings with them to the end that their goodwill and ongoing businesses shall not be impaired in any material respect at the Effective Time.

(b) *Dividends; Changes in Stock.* No party shall, nor shall any party permit any of its Subsidiaries to, nor shall any party propose to, (i) declare or pay any dividends on or make other distributions in respect of any of its capital stock, except as provided in Section 5.16 and except that WCI may continue the declaration and payment of regular quarterly cash dividends (and any other dividend paid with respect to WCI Preferred Stock as a result of the declaration and payment of the dividend contemplated to be paid by WCI pursuant to Section 5.16 and in an amount appropriate to such dividend paid pursuant to Section 5.16) not in excess of $.17 per share of WCI Common Stock and regular quarterly cash dividends as provided by the terms of the WCI Preferred Stock in accordance with their present terms, and Time may continue the declaration and payment of regular quarterly cash dividends not in excess of $.25 per share of Time Common Stock in each case with usual record and payment dates for such dividends in accordance with such parties' past dividend practice, and except for dividends by a wholly-owned subsidiary of such party or such Subsidiary, and except that, whether pursuant to a court order or otherwise, WCI may declare and pay the Distribution and Time may declare and pay a pro rata dividend or other distribution of any or all of its shares of capital stock of BHC to holders of record (as of any time on or after the Effective Time) of shares of Time Common Stock and Time Series BB Preferred (treating such shares of Time Series BB Preferred as if they had been converted into shares of Time Common Stock immediately prior to such record date pursuant to their terms), (ii) split, combine or reclassify any of its capital stock or issue or authorize or propose the issuance of any other securities in respect of, in lieu of or in substitution for shares of its capital stock or (iii) repurchase or otherwise acquire, or permit any Subsidiary to purchase or otherwise acquire, any shares of its capital stock (other than, (x) in the case of WCI, repurchases of WCI Common Stock which WCI may be obligated to make under WCI's Equity Unit Purchase Plan, the Lorimar Restricted Stock Plan and redemptions of shares of WCI Series A Preferred and Series C Preferred pursuant to the terms thereof, (y) in the case of Time, redemption of the Rights as permitted by Section 4.1(k) and purchases of ATC shares pursuant to ATC's share repurchase program up to an aggregate of 3,000,000 ATC shares and (z) in the case of any party as required by stockholders agreements with minority investors in such party's Subsidiaries).

(c) *Issuance of Securities.* No party shall, nor shall any party permit any of its Subsidiaries to, issue, deliver or sell, or authorize or propose the issuance, delivery or sale of, any shares of its capital stock of

Section 4.1(e). This no-solicitation, or no-shop, clause appears at first to be very tightly drafted. It severely limits the ability of either side to enter into negotiations with other bidders. It covers all representatives of both companies; encouragement as well as solicitation; and actions that are not quite a competing bid but could be reasonably expected to lead to one. More important, it does not make an exception for discussions with someone who makes a superior offer. Such an exception (a fiduciary out) is often included. It allows the board of directors to deal with a competing bidder if it reasonably believes its legal duties to shareholders so require. Sometimes the board is required to get advice about its duties from its lawyers before it may begin discussions. Occasionally even solicitation of other bids is permitted. In general, the more permissive these provisions are, the more likely it is that break-up fees are part of the agreement.

Included in Section 4.1(l), which starts at the bottom of the next page, however, there is a fiduciary exception broad enough to cover this provision. The no-solicitation clause on this page does not mention the exception. This is a lesson in how an important provision can be misinterpreted if read out of context. See Section 7.1(c).

any class, any Voting Debt or any securities convertible into, or any rights, warrants or options to acquire, any such shares, Voting Debt or convertible securities, other than (i) the issuance of WCI Common Stock or Time Common Stock, as the case may be, upon the exercise of stock options or stock grants as disclosed in this Agreement, the conversion of convertible securities as disclosed in this Agreement, or pursuant to Time Stock Plans or WCI Stock Plans, in each case outstanding on the date of this Agreement (or as may be issued under such Plans) in each case in accordance with their present terms, or pursuant to the Share Exchange Agreement, (ii) the issuance of options pursuant to Time Stock Plans or WCI Stock Plans, in each case in accordance with their present terms, (iii) issuances of (a) common stock or (b) securities convertible into or exchangeable for, or rights or warrants or options to acquire, common stock, not in excess of an aggregate of 1,000,000 shares (with respect to WCI) or 1,000,000 shares (with respect to Time) of common stock of such party (*provided* such shares or securities shall be issued only to employees or consultants or in connection with acquisitions permitted by this Agreement), (iv) issuances by a wholly-owned Subsidiary of its capital stock to its parent, (v) in the case of Time, issuance of Time Series A Preferred upon exercise of the Rights and reservation for issuance of shares of Time Series A Preferred in addition to those presently reserved for issuance and (vi) Awards under (and as defined in) the New Time Stock Plan, such Awards to be made to employees or prospective employees of WCI, in respect of no more than an aggregate of 1,500,000 shares of Time Common Stock, and to be effective at the Effective Time. For purposes of this Section 4.1(c) only, Time Common Stock shall be deemed to include the Class A Common Stock, par value $.01 per share, of ATC and Time Stock Plans shall be deemed to include the 1986 Stock Option Plan for Key Employees of ATC and the Restricted Stock Plan of ATC.

(d) *Governing Documents.* No party shall amend or propose to amend its Certificate of Incorporation or By-laws nor shall Time amend the Rights Agreement in any way adverse to WCI, *provided, however,* that Time, at or prior to the Effective Time, shall amend its Certificate of Incorporation as set forth in Exhibit 3.2(c)(ii) hereto, shall amend its By-Laws and the Rights Agreement as provided in resolutions adopted by the Board of Directors of Time on March 3, 1989, as modified on April 20, 1989, and May 16, 1989, copies of which have been provided to WCI, shall file a Certificate of Designation substantially in the form of Exhibit 2.1(d) and may file a Certificate of Designation with respect to the Time Series A Preferred.

(e) *No Solicitations.* No party shall, nor shall any party permit any of its Subsidiaries to, nor shall it authorize or permit any of its officers, directors or employees or any investment banker, financial advisor (including the persons named in Sections 3.1(n) and 3.2(n)), attorney, accountant or other representative retained by it or any of its Subsidiaries to, solicit or encourage (including by way of furnishing information), or take any other action to facilitate, any inquiries or the making of any proposal which constitutes, or may reasonably be expected to lead to, any takeover proposal, or agree to or endorse any takeover proposal. Each party shall promptly advise the other orally and in writing of any such inquiries or proposals. As used in this Agreement, "takeover proposal" shall mean any tender or exchange offer, proposal for a merger, consolidation or other business combination involving a party hereto or any Significant Subsidiary of such party or any proposal or offer to acquire in any manner a substantial equity interest in, or a substantial portion of the assets of, such party or any of its Significant Subsidiaries other than the transactions contemplated by this Agreement and the Share Exchange Agreement and except with respect to acquisitions of the assets listed on Schedule 4.1(f) hereto.

(f) *No Acquisitions.* Other than (i) as permitted by Section 4.1(b), (ii) pursuant to the Share Exchange Agreement, (iii) acquisitions listed on Schedule 4.1(f) hereto or (iv) acquisitions in existing or related lines of business of the party making such acquisition not exceeding $100 million in the aggregate in the case of each party (and not exceeding an additional $500 million in the aggregate in the case of each party with respect to acquisitions relating to the cable television business of such party), no party shall, nor shall any party permit any of its Subsidiaries to, acquire or agree to acquire by merging or consolidating with, or by purchasing a substantial equity interest in or a substantial portion of the assets of, or by any other manner, any business or any corporation, partnership, association or other business organization or division thereof or otherwise acquire or agree to acquire any assets in each case which are material, individually or in the aggregate, to such party and its Subsidiaries taken as a whole.

Section 4.1(k). Warner is careful to retain the right to adopt a poison pill. However, the right is carefully circumscribed. The pill must not interfere with this agreement. Time also retains some flexibility to deal with its poison pill. However, whether a poison pill could have been used to protect this transaction is doubtful. The Delaware Supreme Court opinion in the litigation between Paramount and Time (reproduced in the Appendix, A.12) does not decide this issue.

Section 4.1(l). This provision elaborately sets out what each side can do if someone makes a tender offer for it or is positioning itself to make a bid by accumulating 10% of its stock (the trigger event). The provision appears to be a carefully thought-out compromise to fit the circumstances of this transaction. It balances the risk to the stability of the transaction with the need to give the directors of the Target Company enough discretion to protect it. Most of the creative effort in drafting a merger agreement goes into compromises like this one. They evolve based on past experience. The agreements become public documents when they are filed with the SEC and innovations spread very quickly. See the commentary on the preceding and following pages.

(g) *No Dispositions.* Other than (i) dispositions listed on Schedule 4.1(g), (ii) as may be required by law to consummate the transactions contemplated hereby or (iii) in the ordinary course of business consistent with prior practice, no party shall, nor shall any party permit any of its Subsidiaries to, sell, lease, encumber or otherwise dispose of, or agree to sell, lease, encumber or otherwise dispose of, any of its assets, which are material, individually or in the aggregate, to such party and its Subsidiaries taken as a whole.

(h) *Indebtedness.* No party shall, nor shall any party permit any of its Subsidiaries to, incur (which shall not be deemed to include entering into credit agreements, lines of credit or similar arrangements until borrowings are made under such arrangements) any indebtedness for borrowed money or guarantee any such indebtedness or issue or sell any debt securities or warrants or rights to acquire any debt securities of such party or any of its Subsidiaries or guarantee any debt securities of others other than (x) in each case in the ordinary course of business consistent with prior practice, (y) as may be necessary in connection with acquisitions permitted by Section 4.1(f) or (z) in the case of Time, incurrence of indebtedness, issuances of debt securities or guarantees not aggregating in excess of $500,000,000 in connection with a medium-term note program.

(i) *Other Actions.* Except as provided in Section 4.1(l), no party shall, nor shall any party permit any of its Subsidiaries to, take any action that would or is reasonably likely to result in any of its representations and warranties set forth in this Agreement being untrue as of the date made (to the extent so limited), or in any of the conditions to the Merger set forth in Article VI not being satisfied or in a violation of any provision of the Share Exchange Agreement.

(j) *Advice of Changes; SEC Filings.* Each party shall confer on a regular and frequent basis with the other, report on operational matters and promptly advise the other orally and in writing of any change or event having, or which, insofar as can reasonably be foreseen, could have, a material adverse effect on such party and its Subsidiaries taken as a whole. Each party shall promptly provide the other (or its counsel) copies of all filings made by such party with any state or Federal Governmental Entity in connection with this Agreement, the Share Exchange Agreement and the transactions contemplated hereby and thereby.

(k) *Investment Fund; Rights Plans.* Nothing contained herein shall be deemed to prohibit WCI from (i) investing up to $150,000,000 as equity in an investment fund, a limited partner of which will be WCI or an entity controlled by WCI, (ii) adopting a stockholder rights plan, *provided* that (x) no such plan shall prohibit, be "triggered" or otherwise have a material adverse effect on Time or on WCI and its Subsidiaries taken as a whole or materially change the number of outstanding equity securities of WCI as a result of the Merger or of any action of Time permitted under this Agreement or the Share Exchange Agreement, (y) none of Time, Sub or any affiliate of either shall, by virtue of its ownership of WCI Common Stock acquired pursuant to the Share Exchange Agreement, be defined as a person or entity similar to an "Acquiring Person" as such term is defined under the Rights Agreement, and (z) any such rights plan shall provide that any rights or other securities issued thereunder or pursuant thereto shall, at the Effective Time and without further action by WCI, Time or any affiliate of either, be canceled for no consideration and shall thereafter not be outstanding or (iii) selling all or a part of the shares of BHC owned by it to one or more third parties for fair value. Nothing herein shall be deemed to prohibit Time from (A) redeeming the Rights and (B) if the Rights are so redeemed, entering into a new rights agreement similar to the Rights Agreement which shall take effect immediately following the Effective Time.

(l) *Certain Actions.* In the event that (x) any person acquires securities representing 10% or more (other than a person who as of the date hereof is publicly disclosed in a filing with the SEC to own 10% or more), or commences a tender or exchange offer following the successful consummation of which the offeror and its affiliates would beneficially own securities representing 25% or more (any such acquisition or commencement being referred to herein as a"Trigger Event" and the date and time of such Trigger Event being referred to herein as the "Trigger Date"), of the voting power of Time or WCI, as the case may be (the issuer of such securities being referred to herein as the "Target Company"), and (y) at any time prior to the approval of this Agreement by the stockholders of the Target Company and

Once there is a trigger event, the board of directors of the Target Company is released from many of its promises if, with the advice of its lawyers and investment bankers and after consultation with the other side, it determines it is in the best interests of the shareholders to take action inconsistent with those promises. The agreement to operate in the ordinary course can be tossed aside and the target can recapitalize, pay a large dividend or do defensive acquisitions. Nor does the Target Company have to comply with the no-solicitation clause. However, the Target Company is not released from its basic promise to merge. For an additional caveat concerning the other side's right to terminate the agreement if this section is used, see the commentary to Section 7.1(c).

Article V covers additional agreements among the parties.

Section 5.3. The parties must use best efforts to obtain from their respective accountants customary comfort letters stating that they have not discovered errors in the company's financial statements and explaining the limitations on the scope of their review. This requirement is keyed in with the filing of the registration statement by Time for the stock being issued in the merger.

subsequent to the Trigger Date, the Board of Directors of the Target Company, acting with the advice of the Target Company's counsel and investment bankers, determines that it is in the best interest of the Target Company's stockholders to take, or seek to take, one or more actions in response to such Trigger Event, then no such action taken by the Board of Directors of the Target Company in response to such Trigger Event shall be deemed to be, or to result in, a breach of :

(i) any of the Target Company's representations and warranties contained in the fourth sentence of Section 3.1(c), Sections 3.1(f), 3.1(g), 3.1(j) and 3.1(p), the fourth sentence of Section 3.2(c) and Sections 3.2(f), 3.2(g), 3.2(j) and 3.2(o), nor shall any such representation or warranty be deemed to be untrue as a result of any such action;

(ii) any of the covenants or agreements of the Target Company contained in Section 4.1(a), Section 4.1(b), Section 4.1(c), Section 4.1(d), Section 4.1(f), Section 4.1(g), Section 4.1(h), Section 4.1(i) or Section 5.17; and

(iii) any of the covenants or agreements of the Target Company contained in Section 4.1(e);

provided, however, that the Board of Directors of the Target Company shall not take any such action until after reasonable notice to and consultation with the other party to this Agreement with respect to such action and that such Board of Directors shall continue to consult with such other party after taking such action and, in addition, in the case of clause (iii) above, (A) if the Target Company receives any takeover proposal (as defined in Section 4.1(e)) from any person other than the other party to this Agreement, then the Target Company shall promptly inform such other party of the terms and conditions of such proposal and the identity of the person making it and (B) the Target Company shall not take any action to solicit, encourage or otherwise facilitate any takeover proposal from any person other than such other party to this Agreement, except after reasonable consultation with such other party to this Agreement.

ARTICLE V

ADDITIONAL AGREEMENTS

5.1. *Preparation of S-4 and the Proxy Statement.* Time and WCI shall promptly prepare and file with the SEC the Proxy Statement and Time shall prepare and file with the SEC the S-4, in which the Proxy Statement will be included as a prospectus. Each of Time and WCI shall use its best efforts to have the S-4 declared effective under the Securities Act as promptly as practicable after such filing. Time shall also take any action (other than qualifying to do business in any jurisdiction in which it is now not so qualified) required to be taken under any applicable state securities laws in connection with the issuance of Time Common Stock and Time Series BB Preferred in the Merger and upon the exercise of WCI Stock Options (as defined in Section 5.10) and conversion of Time Series BB Preferred, and WCI shall furnish all information concerning WCI and the holders of WCI Common Stock and WCI Series B Preferred as may be reasonably requested in connection with any such action.

5.2. *Letter of WCI's Accountants.* WCI shall use its best efforts to cause to be delivered to Time a letter of Arthur Young & Company, WCI's independent auditors, dated a date within two business days before the date on which the S-4 shall become effective and addressed to Time, in form and substance reasonably satisfactory to Time and customary in scope and substance for letters delivered by independent public accountants in connection with registration statements similar to the S-4.

5.3. *Letter of Time's Accountants.* Time shall use its best efforts to cause to be delivered to WCI a letter of Ernst & Whinney, Time's independent auditors, dated a date within two business days before the date on which the S-4 shall become effective and addressed to WCI, in form and substance reasonably satisfactory to WCI and customary in scope and substance for letters delivered by independent public accountants in connection with registration statements similar to the S-4.

5.4. *Access to Information.* Upon reasonable notice, WCI and Time shall each (and shall cause each of their respective Subsidiaries to) afford to the officers, employees, accountants, counsel and other representatives of the other, access, during normal business hours during the period prior to the Effective

Section 5.5. Warner was required to obtain shareholder approval (a majority of the shares entitled to vote) by Delaware law since it was merging. Time was not merging with Warner (only its subsidiary was) and, therefore, Delaware law did not require approval by Time's shareholders (only of its subsidiary, the shareholder of which was Time itself). However, Time shareholder approval (a majority of those voting) was required by New York Stock Exchange rules. It is best to hold the shareholder meeting for both companies on the same day. Otherwise the shareholders of each company would be voting on different facts. For example, one company could have a windfall or suffer a catastrophe in the interim.

Section 5.6. The companies only agree to take 'reasonable actions' needed to satisfy legal requirements, while they use 'best efforts' for other promises. The concern is that best efforts in this instance might entail something unreasonable such as protracted litigation.

Section 5.7. The affiliate letter requirement helps to satisfy a technical securities law problem. Shareholders who are considered affiliates (directors and large shareholders) of Warner may be subject to restrictions on how and when they can sell their Warner stock outside of a public offering. After the merger these restrictions may apply to their Time Warner stock. Warner agrees to try to get these shareholders to sign an agreement acknowledging the restrictions and agreeing not to sell their shares without giving Time a legal opinion that the sale is legal. To alert brokers and buyers, their certificates would have borne legends noting that legal restrictions on resale might apply.

Time, to all its properties, books, contracts, commitments and records and, during such period, each of WCI and Time shall (and shall cause each of their respective Subsidiaries to) furnish promptly to the other (a) a copy of each report, schedule, registration statement and other document filed or received by it during such period pursuant to the requirements of Federal securities laws and (b) all other information concerning its business, properties and personnel as such other party may reasonably request. Unless otherwise required by law, the parties will hold any such information which is nonpublic in confidence until such time as such information otherwise becomes publicly available through no wrongful act of either party, and in the event of termination of this Agreement for any reason each party shall promptly return all nonpublic documents obtained from any other party, and any copies made of such documents, to such other party.

5.5. *Stockholder Meetings.* WCI and Time each shall call a meeting of its respective stockholders to be held as promptly as practicable for the purpose of voting upon this Agreement and related matters in the case of WCI and the Time Vote Matter and the New Time Stock Plan in the case of Time. WCI and Time will, through their respective Boards of Directors, recommend to their respective stockholders approval of such matters. WCI and Time shall coordinate and cooperate with respect to the timing of such meetings and shall use their best efforts to hold such meetings on the same day and as soon as practicable after the date hereof.

5.6. *Legal Conditions to Merger.* Each of WCI, Time and Sub will take all reasonable actions necessary to comply promptly with all legal requirements which may be imposed on itself with respect to the Merger or the Share Exchange Agreement (including furnishing all information required under the HSR Act, in connection with the FCC Approvals and the Local Approvals and in connection with approvals of or filings with any other Governmental Entity) and will promptly cooperate with and furnish information to each other in connection with any such requirements imposed upon any of them or any of their Subsidiaries in connection with the Merger. Each of WCI, Time and Sub will, and will cause its Subsidiaries to, take all reasonable actions necessary to obtain (and will cooperate with each other in obtaining) any consent, authorization, order or approval of, or any exemption by, any Governmental Entity or other public or private third party, required to be obtained or made by Time, WCI or any of their Subsidiaries in connection with the Merger or the taking of any action contemplated thereby or by this Agreement or the Share Exchange Agreement.

5.7. *Affiliates.* Prior to the Closing Date WCI shall deliver to Time a letter identifying all persons who are, at the time this Agreement is submitted for approval to the stockholders of WCI, "affiliates" of WCI for purposes of Rule 145 under the Securities Act. WCI shall use its best efforts to cause each such person to deliver to Time on or prior to the Closing Date a written agreement, substantially in the form attached as Exhibit 5.7 hereto.

5.8. *Stock Exchange Listing.* Each of Time and WCI shall use all reasonable efforts to cause shares of its common stock to be issued pursuant to the Share Exchange Agreement to be approved for listing on the NYSE and Pacific Stock Exchange upon official notice of issuance. Time shall use all reasonable efforts to cause the shares of Time Common Stock to be issued in the Merger and the shares of Time Common Stock to be reserved for issuance pursuant to the New Time Stock Plan, upon exercise of WCI Stock Options and Lorimar Stock Grants and upon conversion of the Lorimar Debentures and Time Series BB Preferred to be approved for listing on the NYSE and the Pacific Stock Exchange, subject to official notice of issuance, prior to the Closing Date.

5.9. *Employee Benefit Plans.* Time and WCI agree that the Benefit Plans of WCI and its Subsidiaries in effect at the date of this Agreement shall, to the extent practicable, remain in effect until otherwise determined after the Effective Time and, to the extent such Benefit Plans are not continued, it is the current intent of the parties that Benefit Plans which are no less favorable, in the aggregate, to the employees covered by such plans shall be provided. In the case of Benefit Plans under which the employees' interests are based upon WCI Common Stock, Time and WCI agree that such interests shall be based on Time Common Stock in an equitable manner (and in the case of any such interests existing at the Effective Time, on the basis of the Conversion Number).

Section 5.10. Treatment of stock options in a merger is a complicated subject involving corporate, securities and tax laws. Here the matter is even more complicated than usual because Time is assuming the options. In an acquisition for cash it is usual to pay cash to settle options. This is not ideal if an employee is expected to continue working for the acquirer and the option cash-out makes the employee rich. The prospects that a rich employee will continue to work for the successor for long are not very good. Employment agreements are often used to ease this problem during a transition period of two to three years. However, in a stock-for-stock merger of equals the shareholders are not receiving cash and it is difficult for management to ask for special treatment.

5.10. *Stock Options.* (a) At the Effective Time, each outstanding option to purchase shares of WCI Common Stock (a "WCI Stock Option") and each outstanding stock appreciation right (a "WCI SAR") or bonus unit (a "WCI Unit") issued pursuant to (A) the WCI 1986 Stock Option and Appreciation Rights Plan, the WCI 1982 Bonus Unit Plan and the WCI 1974 Common Stock Option Plan, and (B) the 1985 Employee Stock Option Plan, the 1983 Incentive Stock Option Plan, the 1980 (Incentive) Stock Option Plan, the 1981 Incentive Stock Option Plan, the 1985 Employee Stock Option Plan, the 1985 Non-Employee Stock Option Plan, the 1982 Non-Employee Stock Option Plan in each case of Lorimar or its predecessor (collectively, the "WCI Plans"), whether vested or unvested, shall be assumed by Time. Each WCI Stock Option shall be deemed to constitute an option to acquire, on the same terms and conditions as were applicable under such WCI Stock Option, the same number of shares of Time Common Stock as the holder of such WCI Stock Option would have been entitled to receive pursuant to the Merger had such holder exercised such option in full immediately prior to the Effective Time, at a price per share equal to (y) the aggregate exercise price for the shares of WCI Common Stock otherwise purchasable pursuant to such WCI Stock Option divided by (z) the number of full shares of Time Common Stock deemed purchasable pursuant to such WCI Stock Option; *provided, however,* that in the case of any option to which section 421 of the Code applies by reason of its qualification under any of sections 422-424 of the Code ("qualified stock options"), the option price, the number of shares purchasable pursuant to such option and the terms and conditions of exercise of such option shall be determined in order to comply with section 425(a) of the Code. Each holder of a WCI SAR or WCI Unit shall be entitled to that number of WCI SARs or WCI Units, as the case may be, and in either case as assumed by Time, determined by multiplying the number of WCI SARs or WCI Units held by such holder immediately prior to the Effective Time by the Conversion Number and the appreciation base or measuring price with respect to such WCI SARs or WCI Units, as the case may be, shall be adjusted by dividing such appreciation base or measuring price in effect immediately prior to the Effective Time by the Conversion Number.

(b) As soon as practicable after the Effective Time, Time shall deliver to the holders of WCI Stock Options, WCI SARs and WCI Units appropriate notices setting forth such holders' rights pursuant to the respective WCI Plans and the agreements evidencing the grants of such Options, SARs or Units, as the case may be, shall continue in effect on the same terms and conditions (subject to the adjustments required by this Section 5.10 after giving effect to the Merger). Time shall comply with the terms of the WCI Plans and ensure, to the extent required by, and subject to the provisions of, such Plans, that the WCI Stock Options which qualified as qualified stock options prior to the Effective Time continue to qualify as qualified stock options after the Effective Time. Time and WCI recognize that, pursuant to the terms of the WCI Plans and the agreements evidencing the grants of the WCI Stock Options, WCI SARs and WCI Units, appropriate adjustments may be necessary to give effect to any Distribution in order to preserve the anticipated benefits of such WCI Plans or agreements to the holders of such WCI Stock Options, WCI SARs and WCI Units.

(c) Time shall take all corporate action necessary to reserve for issuance a sufficient number of shares of Time Common Stock for delivery upon exercise of the WCI Stock Options assumed in accordance with this Section 5.10. As soon as practicable after the Effective Time, Time shall file a registration statement on Form S-3 or Form S-8, as the case may be (or any successor or other appropriate forms), or another appropriate form with respect to the shares of Time Common Stock subject to such options and shall use its best efforts to maintain the effectiveness of such registration statement or registration statements (and maintain the current status of the prospectus or prospectuses contained therein) for so long as such options remain outstanding. With respect to those individuals who subsequent to the Merger will be subject to the reporting requirements under Section 16(a) of the Exchange Act, where applicable, Time shall administer the WCI Plans assumed pursuant to this Section 5.10 in a manner that complies with Rule 16b-3 promulgated under the Exchange Act to the extent the applicable WCI Plan complied with such rule prior to the Merger.

(d) As contemplated by the 1982 WCI Equity Unit Purchase Plan, the committee administering such Plan may adjust the "Book Value Per Share" and the "Resale Price" of Units issued thereunder to equal, effective upon consummation of the Merger, the average of the closing sales prices of a share of Time Common Stock over the ten consecutive trading days commencing on the trading day immediately following the Effective Time and shall make such other changes as it deems appropriate to give effect to the Merger. These amounts are subject to further adjustments, as contemplated under such Plan, for changes in book

Section 5.11. Each party pays its own expenses. In some negotiated acquisitions the seller agrees to pay up to a specified amount of the buyer's expenses plus a break-up fee if the agreement is terminated because the seller's board exercises a fiduciary out. As we have explained, in this instance the fiduciary out has been made quite narrow. Moreover, break-up fees and expenses may have been considered a discordant concept in a merger of equals.

Section 5.13. Time's staggered board of directors is maintained and initially divided between Warner and Time representatives. Even the committee structure is worked out in advance. This provision supports the idea of a merger of equals. But it was also very important to reassure some of Time's directors and journalists who were concerned about interference in editorial matters.

Section 5.14. The employment agreements received a great deal of publicity. They were generous and for very long terms – up to ten years. The agreements even specified who would be chief executive or co-chief executive during the ten years. This bears out our point of view about the importance of successful CEOs in the bargain with shareholders and the relative unimportance of directors (Chapter 4).

Section 5.15(a). The indemnification provisions carefully follow Delaware law, and protect the directors to the full extent allowed by law. A very important point for the directors is that if they are sued the company will pay their expenses. If a director is found liable and a court determines in a final judgment that Delaware law does not allow him to be indemnified (for example, because of willful misconduct) he would have to pay the company back.

value per share of Time Common Stock occurring after the commencement of the first full fiscal quarter of Time following the Effective Time. Upon consummation of the Merger, Time will assume such Plan.

5.11. *Expenses.* Whether or not the Merger is consummated, all costs and expenses incurred in connection with this Agreement, the Share Exchange Agreement and the transactions contemplated hereby and thereby shall be paid by the party incurring such expense, and, in connection therewith, each of Time and WCI shall pay, with its own funds and not with funds provided by the other party, any and all property or transfer taxes imposed on such party or any real property tax imposed by New York State or New York City on any holder of shares in such party resulting from the Merger, except that expenses incurred in connection with printing and mailing the Proxy Statement and the S-4 shall be shared equally by Time and WCI.

5.12. *Brokers or Finders.* Each of Time and WCI represents, as to itself, its Subsidiaries and its affiliates, that no agent, broker, investment banker, financial advisor or other firm or person is or will be entitled to any broker's or finder's fee or any other commission or similar fee in connection with any of the transactions contemplated by this Agreement, except Lazard Freres & Co. and Alpine Capital Group, each of whose fees and expenses will be paid by WCI in accordance with WCI's agreement with such firm (copies of which have been delivered by WCI to Time prior to the date of this Agreement), and Shearson Lehman Hutton Inc. and Wasserstein Perella & Co., Inc., whose fees and expenses will be paid by Time in accordance with Time's agreements with such firms (copies of which have been delivered by Time to WCI prior to the date of this Agreement), and each of Time and WCI respectively agree to indemnify and hold the other harmless from and against any and all claims, liabilities or obligations with respect to any other fees, commissions or expenses asserted by any person on the basis of any act or statement alleged to have been made by such party or its affiliate.

5.13. *Time Board of Directors.* Time's Board of Directors will take action to cause the number of directors comprising the full Board of Directors of Time at the Effective Time to be 24 persons, 12 of whom shall be designated by Time prior to the Effective Time and 12 of whom shall be designated by WCI (and shall be elected by at least a two-thirds vote of the entire Board of Directors of Time) prior to the Effective Time. The initial allocation of such directors among the three classes of the Board of Directors of Time shall be agreed among the parties, the designees of each party to be divided equally among such classes; *provided, however,* that if, prior to the Effective Time, any of such designees shall decline or be unable to serve, the parties shall mutually designate another person to serve in such person's stead. Time's Board of Directors will also take action to cause the committees of the Board of Directors of Time at the Effective Time to be as set forth, and consisting of the designees from the parties set forth, on Exhibit 5.13.

5.14. *Employment Agreements.* WCI and Time shall, as of or prior to the Effective Time, enter into employment contracts with the persons set forth on Exhibit 5.14(x) on substantially the terms set forth in Exhibit 5.14(y) hereto.

5.15. *Indemnification; Directors' and Officers' Insurance.* (a) WCI shall, and from and after the Effective Time, Time and the Surviving Corporation shall, indemnify, defend and hold harmless each person who is now, or has been at any time prior to the date hereof or who becomes prior to the Effective Time, an officer, director or employee of WCI or any of its Subsidiaries (the "Indemnified Parties") against (i) all losses, claims, damages, costs, expenses, liabilities or judgments or amounts that are paid in settlement with the approval of the indemnifying party (which approval shall not be unreasonably withheld) of or in connection with any claim, action, suit, proceeding or investigation based in whole or in part on or arising in whole or in part out of the fact that such person is or was a director, officer or employee of WCI or any Subsidiary, whether pertaining to any matter existing or occurring at or prior to the Effective Time and whether asserted or claimed prior to, or at or after, the Effective Time ("Indemnified Liabilities") and (ii) all Indemnified Liabilities based in whole or in part on, or arising in whole or in part out of, or pertaining to this Agreement or the transactions contemplated hereby, in each case to the full extent a corporation is permitted under Delaware Law to indemnify its own directors, officers and employees, as the case may be (and Time and the Surviving Corporation, as the case may be, will pay expenses in advance of the final disposition of any such action or proceeding to each Indemnified Party to the full extent permitted by law upon receipt of any

Section 5.15(b). In addition to indemnification, the company agrees to maintain liability insurance for the past and present directors against judgments based on their actions as directors. This lasts six years, which is probably a guess at the maximum applicable statute of limitations.

Many companies take advantage of a provision of Delaware law that allows them to eliminate by charter amendment personal liability of directors in suits by shareholders for money damages for negligent (but not disloyal) breaches of their duties to the company or its shareholders. Many other states have passed similar, even stronger, statutes. (However, in Delaware this law does not allow the same limitations on the liability of officers. Delaware General Corporation Law §102(b)(7).)

Since directors' and officers' liability insurance does not generally cover intentional wrongdoing, as a practical matter the main benefits of insurance for directors of these companies are protection against liabilities where the courts may refuse to enforce indemnification, for example, under some of the Federal securities laws; insolvency of the company; and a falling out between the company and the director that might lead the company to try to avoid paying.

undertaking contemplated by Section 145(e) of the DGCL). Without limiting the foregoing, in the event any such claim, action, suit, proceeding or investigation is brought against any Indemnified Party (whether arising before or after the Effective Time), (i) the Indemnified Parties may retain counsel satisfactory to them and WCI (or them and Time and the Surviving Corporation after the Effective Time); (ii) WCI (or after the Effective Time, Time and the Surviving Corporation) shall pay all reasonable fees and expenses of such counsel for the Indemnified Parties promptly as statements therefor are received; and (iii) WCI (or after the Effective Time, Time and the Surviving Corporation) will use all reasonable efforts to assist in the vigorous defense of any such matter, provided that neither WCI, Time nor the Surviving Corporation shall be liable for any settlement of any claim effected without its written consent, which consent, however, shall not be unreasonably withheld. Any Indemnified Party wishing to claim indemnification under this Section 5.15, upon learning of any such claim, action, suit, proceeding or investigation, shall notify WCI, Time, or the Surviving Corporation (but the failure so to notify an indemnified party shall not relieve it from any liability which it may have under this Section 5.15 except to the extent such failure prejudices such party), and shall deliver to WCI (or after the Effective Time, Time and the Surviving Corporation) the undertaking contemplated by Section 145(e) of the DGCL. The Indemnified Parties as a group may retain only one law firm to represent them with respect to each such matter unless there is, under applicable standards of professional conduct, a conflict on any significant issue between the positions of any two or more Indemnified Parties.

(b) For a period of six years after the Effective Time, Time shall cause to be maintained in effect the current policies of directors' and officers' liability insurance maintained by WCI (provided that Time may substitute therefor policies of at least the same coverage and amounts containing terms and conditions which are no less advantageous) with respect to claims arising from facts or events which occurred before the Effective Time to the extent available on commercially reasonable terms.

(c) The provisions of this Section 5.15 are intended to be for the benefit of, and shall be enforceable by, each Indemnified Party, his heirs and his representatives.

5.16. *Dividend Adjustment.* Each of Time and WCI shall declare a dividend on each share of its Common Stock to holders of record of such shares as of the close of business on the business day next preceding the Effective Time in an amount equal to the product of (A) a fraction, (i) the numerator of which equals the number of days between the payment date with respect to the most recent regular dividend paid by Time or WCI, as the case may be, and the Effective Time and (ii) the denominator of which equals 91 and (B) the amount of the regular cash dividend most recently paid by Time or WCI, as the case may be.

5.17. *Additional Agreements; Reasonable Efforts.* Subject to the terms and conditions of this Agreement, each of the parties hereto agrees to use all reasonable efforts to take, or cause to be taken, all action and to do, or cause to be done, all things necessary, proper or advisable under applicable laws and regulations to consummate and make effective the transactions contemplated by this Agreement and the Share Exchange Agreement, subject to the appropriate vote of stockholders of Time and WCI described in Section 6.1(a), including cooperating fully with the other party, including by provision of information and making of all necessary filings in connection with, among other things, the FCC Approvals and the Local Approvals and under the HSR Act, and including assumption by Time of the obligation to issue shares of Time Common Stock pursuant to the Lorimar Stock Grants and upon conversion of Lorimar Debentures. In case at any time after the Effective Time any further action is necessary or desirable to carry out the purposes of this Agreement or to vest the Surviving Corporation with full title to all properties, assets, rights, approvals, immunities and franchises of either of the Constituent Corporations, the proper officers and directors of each party to this Agreement shall take all such necessary action.

Article VI covers the conditions to performance by the parties.

Section 6.1. The conditions to performance determine how firmly bound the parties are. When there is a financing condition, for example, the buyer has much more of a chance to back out. Its lenders are unlikely to provide financing in the face of a newly discovered problem in the deal. This contract, however, attempts to be as unconditional as possible.

The parties do not appear from the wording to be able to waive application of the conditions to both parties' obligations that are listed in Section 6.1. However, Sections 6.2 and 6.3 do allow waiver and Section 7.4 gives the directors of either company the right 'to the extent legally allowed' to waive compliance with any conditions. Some of the conditions in Section 6.1 clearly cannot be waived legally – for example, Warner's obligation under Delaware law to obtain shareholder approval for the merger.

On the other hand, approval of Time's shareholders was not required by Delaware law because Time's subsidiary, not Time itself, was merging with Warner. But shareholder approval was required by the New York Stock Exchange because of the large amount of Time stock that was being issued in the merger. In theory, Time's and Warner's boards could have waived approval by Time's shareholders and accepted delisting by the New York Stock Exchange. The test of the theory came later when it appeared highly unlikely that the Time shareholders would approve in the face of Paramount's cash tender offer for Time. Delisting was not considered a practical solution and the deal was transformed into a Time tender offer for Warner shares. The reasons for not delisting were probably legal and strategic. In the litigation, Paramount might have been able to make delisting look like a confession of wrongdoing. Although the over-the-counter market is now generally recognized as quite efficient, there are still reputational reasons for wanting to stay listed.

Section 6.1(c). There were so many cable television approvals to be obtained that the deal was structured to go ahead with only a percentage of the approvals that would theoretically be needed. There is a formula for determining the percentage.

Section 6.1(e). Lawsuits alone do not stop the deal, only a court order. This is somewhat unusual. Lawsuits by governmental agencies are often exceptions.

Section 6.2(a). If the representations and warranties of each side are not true at the closing the other side does not have to perform. In a merger between public companies, where these promises do not survive the closing, this is the main purpose of representations and warranties.

ARTICLE VI

CONDITIONS PRECEDENT

6.1. *Conditions to Each Party's Obligation To Effect the Merger.* The respective obligation of each party to effect the Merger shall be subject to the satisfaction prior to the Closing Date of the following conditions:

(a) *Stockholder Approval.* This Agreement shall have been approved and adopted by the affirmative vote of a majority of the votes that the holders of the outstanding shares of WCI Common Stock and WCI Series B Preferred, voting together as a class, are entitled to cast, and the Time Vote Matter shall have been approved by the affirmative vote of the holders of a majority of the outstanding shares of Time Common Stock.

(b) *NYSE Listing.* The shares of Time Common Stock issuable to WCI stockholders pursuant to this Agreement and such other shares required to be reserved for issuance in connection with the Merger shall have been authorized for listing on the NYSE upon official notice of issuance.

(c) *Other Approvals.* Other than the filing provided for by Section 1.1, any filing pursuant to Article 31-B of the New York Tax Law, Local Approvals and State Takeover Approvals, all authorizations, consents, orders or approvals of, or declarations or filings with, or expirations of waiting periods imposed by, any Governmental Entity the failure to obtain which would have a material adverse effect on Time or the Surviving Corporation, taken as a whole, shall have been filed, occurred or been obtained. Local Approvals representing CATV Systems of Time and WCI serving at least 50% of the combined number of subscribers to basic cable television service as of January 31, 1989, in CATV Systems as to which Local Approvals shall be required shall have been obtained (*provided*, that (x) as to those CATV systems the construction of which is not substantially completed, the number of subscribers to basic cable television service being served by Time and WCI shall be deemed to be the number of subscribers actually served plus 30% of the number of homes in the unbuilt franchise area to be served by such CATV Systems and (y) as to those CATV systems not wholly-owned by WCI or Time, as the case may be, only the percentage of subscribers in such CATV systems equal to the percentage ownership interest of WCI or Time, as the case may be, in such CATV System shall be counted in determining the number of subscribers to such CATV System). Time shall have received all state securities or "Blue Sky" permits and other authorizations necessary to issue the Time Common Stock and Time Series BB Preferred in exchange for the WCI Common Stock and WCI Series B Preferred and to consummate the Merger.

(d) *S-4.* The S-4 shall have become effective under the Securities Act and shall not be the subject of any stop order or proceedings seeking a stop order.

(e) *No Injunctions or Restraints.* No temporary restraining order, preliminary or permanent injunction or other order issued by any court of competent jurisdiction or other legal restraint or prohibition (an "Injunction") preventing the consummation of the Merger shall be in effect.

6.2. *Conditions of Obligations of Time and Sub.* The obligations of Time and Sub to effect the Merger are subject to the satisfaction of the following conditions unless waived by Time and Sub:

(a) *Representations and Warranties.* The representations and warranties of WCI set forth in this Agreement shall be true and correct in all material respects as of the date of this Agreement and (except to the extent such representations and warranties speak as of an earlier date) as of the Closing Date as though made on and as of the Closing Date, except as otherwise contemplated by this Agreement, and Time shall have received a certificate signed on behalf of WCI by the chief executive officer or a member of the Office of the President and by the chief financial officer of WCI to such effect.

(b) *Performance of Obligations of WCI.* WCI shall have performed in all material respects all obligations required to be performed by it under this Agreement and the Share Exchange Agreement at or prior to the Closing Date, and Time shall have received a certificate signed on behalf of WCI by the chief executive officer or a member of the Office of the President and by the chief financial officer of WCI to such effect.

Section 6.2(a), cont'd.

On its face an officer's certificate is a curious item. Why is not a promise from the company not good enough? Neither survives the closing (Section 8.1). Psychological considerations provide the answer. When an individual must sign a document on his own behalf he thinks about it more. Personalizing the representations helps flush out extra information that may be very important. That being said, not all closings of acquisitions of public companies require officers' certificates any more.

(c) *Letters from WCI Affiliates.* Time shall have received from each person named in the letter referred to in Section 5.7 an executed copy of an agreement substantially in the form of Exhibit 5.7 hereto.

(d) *Tax Opinion.* The opinion of Cravath, Swaine & Moore, counsel to Time, to the effect that the Merger will be treated for Federal income tax purposes as a reorganization within the meaning of Section 368(a) of the Code, and that Time, Sub and WCI will each be a party to that reorganization within the meaning of Section 368(b) of the Code, dated on or about the date that is two business days prior to the date the Proxy Statement is first mailed to stockholders of WCI and Time, shall not have been withdrawn or modified in any material respect.

(e) *Consents Under Agreements.* WCI shall have obtained the consent or approval of each person (other than the Governmental Entities referred to in Section 6.1(c)) whose consent or approval shall be required in order to permit the succession by the Surviving Corporation pursuant to the Merger to any obligation, right or interest of WCI or any Subsidiary of WCI under any loan or credit agreement, note, mortgage, indenture, lease or other agreement or instrument, except those for which failure to obtain such consents and approvals would not, in the reasonable opinion of Time, individually or in the aggregate, have a material adverse effect (x) on WCI and its Subsidiaries taken as a whole or (y) on the Surviving Corporation and its Subsidiaries taken as a whole upon the consummation of the transactions contemplated hereby.

(f) *Rights Agreement.* If WCI has adopted a stockholder rights plan as permitted by Section 4.1(k), no event similar to those described in Section 11(d)(i) or (ii)(A) or (B) of the Rights Agreement, or any other event thereunder shall have occurred that would, in the reasonable opinion of Time, have a material adverse effect on Time or on WCI and its subsidiaries taken as a whole, or that has or would materially change the number of outstanding equity securities of WCI, and the rights issued thereunder shall not have become nonredeemable.

(g) *No Amendments to Resolutions.* Neither the Board of Directors of WCI nor any committee thereof shall have amended, modified, rescinded or repealed the resolutions adopted by the Board of Directors on March 3, 1989, as supplemented by resolutions adopted by such Board of Directors on April 21, 1989, and May 19, 1989 (accurate and complete copies of which have been provided to Time) and shall not have adopted any other resolutions in connection with this Agreement and the transactions contemplated hereby inconsistent with such resolutions.

(h) *Redemption or Conversion of WCI Series C Preferred.* All shares of WCI Series C Preferred shall have been redeemed or converted into shares of WCI Common Stock, in accordance with the Certificate of Designation thereof.

6.3. *Conditions of Obligations of WCI.* The obligation of WCI to effect the Merger is subject to the satisfaction of the following conditions unless waived by WCI:

(a) *Representations and Warranties.* The representations and warranties of Time and Sub set forth in this Agreement shall be true and correct in all material respects as of the date of this Agreement and (except to the extent such representations speak as of an earlier date) as of the Closing Date as though made on and as of the Closing Date, except as otherwise contemplated by this Agreement, and WCI shall have received a certificate signed on behalf of Time by the Chief Executive Officer or the President or the Vice Chairman or by the chief financial officer of Time to such effect.

(b) *Performance of Obligations of Time and Sub.* Time and Sub shall have performed in all material respects all obligations required to be performed by them under this Agreement and the Share Exchange Agreement at or prior to the Closing Date, and WCI shall have received a certificate signed on behalf of Time by the Chief Executive Officer or the President or the Vice Chairman and by the chief financial officer of Time to such effect.

(c) *Tax Opinion.* The opinion of Paul, Weiss, Rifkind, Wharton & Garrison, counsel to WCI, to the effect that the Merger will be treated for Federal income tax purposes as a reorganization within the meaning of Section 368(a) of the Code, and that Time, Sub and WCI will each be a party to that

Section 6.3(c). The tax opinions in the combined proxy statement/registration statement are required by SEC rules. They also help gain shareholder support for the merger; sophisticated, large shareholders look at them carefully.

The traditional lawyer's opinions covering corporate law issues are dispensed with in this agreement, as is becoming more common in acquisitions of public companies. This is a striking development. One reason often given is that so much is known about the parties from SEC filings that it is not necessary to add another layer of paperwork. There is also the problem that, with representations and warranties not surviving the closing (Section 8.1), the lawyers could be left holding the bag. The amounts involved are big enough to swamp their liability insurance. Investment bankers do not give opinions without indemnities. Another reason why law firms may be refusing to give opinions in these big deals is because they do not know the companies well enough. Inside law departments are taking over the day-to-day legal business of large companies.

Section 7.1(c) in the termination section is an exception to the exception (Section 4.1(l)) to the no-solicitation clause (Section 4.1(e)). Here is how these complicated sections fit together. When Paramount made its hostile bid, Section 4.1(e) prevented Time from negotiating with Paramount. But under the exception in Section 4.1(l) it could do so if it consulted with Warner first. However, despite that exception, Section 7.1(c) would give Warner the right to terminate the agreement under Section 7.1(b) if Time did not stop negotiating within five days after Warner complained. It works out that way under Section 7.1(b) because, except for Sections 4.1(l) and 7.1(c), negotiating with Paramount would be a material breach of a covenant. However, Section 7.1(c) also says that Warner could not terminate without having its financial and legal advisers attempt, in good faith and for a reasonable time, to negotiate a new deal with Time.

Section 7.1(d). In takeover jargon, the drop dead date. The parties do not want to be tied down by the agreement beyond that date.

Section 7.2. The Effect of Termination provision tries to clear up in advance what would be left of the agreement after termination. The Share Exchange Agreement continues, along with the agreement to return shared information and keep it confidential, to pay their own expenses and not to be liable for brokers representing the other side. Either party can sue for damages if the other side willfully breaches the agreement unless the breach is under court order (See section 8.7).

reorganization within the meaning of Section 368(b) of the Code, dated on or about the date that is two business days prior to the date the Proxy Statement is first mailed to stockholders of WCI and Time, shall not have been withdrawn or modified in any material respect.

(d) *Consents Under Agreements.* Time shall have obtained the consent or approval of each person (other than the Governmental Entities referred to in Section 6.1(c)) whose consent or approval shall be required in connection with the transactions contemplated hereby under any loan or credit agreement, note, mortgage, indenture, lease or other agreement or instrument, except those for which failure to obtain such consents and approvals would not, in the reasonable opinion of WCI, individually or in the aggregate, have a material adverse effect on Time and its Subsidiaries, taken as a whole, or upon the consummation of the transactions contemplated hereby.

(e) *Rights Agreement.* None of the events described in Section 11(d)(i)or 11(d)(ii)(A) or (B) of the Rights Agreement shall have occurred, and the Rights shall not have become nonredeemable.

(f) *No Amendments to Resolutions.* Neither the Board of Directors of Time nor any committee thereof shall have amended, modified, rescinded or repealed the resolutions adopted by the Board of Directors at a meeting duly called and held on March 3, 1989, as supplemented by resolutions adopted by such Board of Directors on April 20, 1989, and May 16, 1989 (accurate and complete copies of which have been provided to WCI), and shall not have adopted any other resolutions in connection with this Agreement and the transactions contemplated hereby inconsistent with such resolutions.

ARTICLE VII

TERMINATION AND AMENDMENT

7.1. *Termination.* This Agreement may be terminated at any time prior to the Effective Time, whether before or after approval of the matters presented in connection with the Merger by the stockholders of WCI or Time:

(a) by mutual consent of Time and WCI;

(b) by either Time or WCI if there has been a material breach of any representation, warranty, covenant or agreement on the part of the other set forth in this Agreement or the Share Exchange Agreement which breach has not been cured within 5 business days following receipt by the breaching party of notice of such breach, or if any permanent injunction or other order of a court or other competent authority preventing the consummation of the Merger shall have become final and non-appealable;

(c) by either Time or WCI if, but for the provisions of Section 4.1(l), such party would have the right to terminate this Agreement pursuant to Section 7.1(b); *provided, however,* that prior to any such termination Time and WCI shall, and shall cause their respective financial and legal advisors to, negotiate in good faith and for a reasonable period of time to make such adjustments in the terms and conditions of the Merger as would enable the party seeking termination to proceed with the transaction;

(d) by either Time or WCI if the Merger shall not have been consummated before February 28, 1990; or

(e) by either party if any required approval of the stockholders of WCI or of Time (only in the case of the Time Vote Matter) shall not have been obtained by reason of the failure to obtain the required vote upon a vote held at a duly held meeting of stockholders or at any adjournment thereof.

7.2. *Effect of Termination.* In the event of termination of this Agreement by either WCI or Time as provided in Section 7.1, this Agreement shall forthwith become void and there shall be no liability or obligation on the part of Time, Sub or WCI or their respective officers or directors except (x) with respect to the last sentence of Section 5.4, and Sections 5.11 and 5.12, (y) with respect to the representations and warranties contained in Sections 3.1 and 3.2 insofar as such representations and warranties relate to the Share Exchange Agreement and (z) to the extent that such termination results from the willful breach by a party hereto of any of its representations, warranties, covenants or agreements set forth in this Agreement except as provided in Section 8.7.

Section 7.5. The Additional Termination provision covers a very interesting point. If the share exchange would change the accounting treatment from pooling of interests to purchase accounting, then if one party initiates the share exchange the other side can terminate the merger agreement. There is a qualification requiring negotiation in good faith and for a reasonable time. The share exchange, however, would still be accomplished.

Why do Time and Warner care so much about pooling accounting when most financial economists would tell them it does not matter because the stock market should see through accounting differences? In other places we have offered our speculation: essentially that legal and credit institutions are built around book accounting. Nonetheless, as we have pointed out, Time and Warner did have to sacrifice pooling when they changed the form of the deal to a cash tender by Time for Warner, followed by a merger.

Section 8.1. Because the representations do not survive the closing their main effect is that their continued accuracy is a condition to the merger.

7.3. *Amendment.* This Agreement may be amended by the parties hereto, by action taken or authorized by their respective Boards of Directors, at any time before or after approval of the matters presented in connection with the Merger by the stockholders of WCI or of Time, but, after any such approval, no amendment shall be made which by law requires further approval by such stockholders without such further approval. This Agreement may not be amended except by an instrument in writing signed on behalf of each of the parties hereto.

7.4. *Extension; Waiver.* At any time prior to the Effective Time, the parties hereto, by action taken or authorized by their respective Board of Directors, may, to the extent legally allowed, (i) extend the time for the performance of any of the obligations or other acts of the other parties hereto, (ii) waive any inaccuracies in the representations and warranties contained herein or in any document delivered pursuant hereto and (iii) waive compliance with any of the agreements or conditions contained herein. Any agreement on the part of a party hereto to any such extension or waiver shall be valid only if set forth in a written instrument signed on behalf of such party.

7.5. *Additional Termination.* If the issuances of the shares of Time Common Stock and WCI Common Stock at a closing held pursuant to clause (ii) of the first sentence of Section 3 of the Share Exchange Agreement would have resulted in a breach of the representations and warranties contained in Section 3.1(q) or 3.2(p) of this Agreement had such representations and warranties been made and spoken as of the time immediately after such issuances, then the party receiving the notice referred to in said clause (ii) shall have the right to terminate this Agreement; *provided, however,* that prior to any such termination the parties shall, and shall cause their financial and legal advisors to, negotiate in good faith and for a reasonable period of time to make such adjustments in the terms and conditions of the Merger as would enable the party seeking termination to proceed with the transaction.

ARTICLE VIII

GENERAL PROVISIONS

8.1. *Nonsurvival of Representations, Warranties and Agreements.* None of the representations, warranties and agreements in this Agreement or in any instrument delivered pursuant to this Agreement shall survive the Effective Time, except for the agreements contained in Sections 2.1, 2.2, 5.9 through 5.17, the last sentence of Section 7.3 and Article VIII, and the agreements of the "affiliates" of WCI delivered pursuant to Section 5.7.

8.2. *Notices.* All notices and other communications hereunder shall be in writing and shall be deemed given if delivered personally, telecopied (which is confirmed) or mailed by registered or certified mail (return receipt requested) to the parties at the following addresses (or at such other address for a party as shall be specified by like notice):

(a) if to Time or Sub, to

    Time Incorporated
    Time & Life Building
    Rockefeller Center
    New York, N.Y. 10020
    Telecopy No. (212) 522-1252

    Attention of Corporate Secretary;

with a copy to

Samuel C. Butler, Esq.
Cravath, Swaine & Moore
One Chase Manhattan Plaza
New York, N.Y. 10005
Telecopy No. (212) 428-3700

Section 8.3. The Interpretation provision combines some standard and some less standard language that is designed to make the agreement a little more readable with no loss of rigor. Without it, meticulous drafters might succeed in complicating the already complicated provisions so much that even lawyers would find the agreement difficult to get through.

Section 8.4. The Counterparts provision allows the agreement to be executed without having all signatories meet in one room. Often counterparts are exchanged by telecopy to demonstrate that all parties have signed.

Section 8.5. The integration clause makes it clear that it is not necessary to look to other documents to understand this one, except as specifically noted. It also prevents claims that the agreement has been orally modified. The Chris-Craft material was added to Section 8.5 when this agreement was amended and restated after the settlement of a lawsuit. It is a little odd to have it buried at the end of this paragraph.

Section 8.6. An alternative governing law could have been New York, where both companies are based. Delaware corporate law applies to these Delaware corporations anyway. The parties may have chosen Delaware law to increase the chance that they would have any disputes litigated in the Delaware Chancery Court which does not try cases with juries. It is also much quicker than and at least as accurate as other courts. In some respects this is like an agreement to arbitrate disputes.

and

(b) if to WCI, to

Warner Communications Inc.
75 Rockefeller Plaza
New York, N.Y. 10019
Telecopy No. (212) 333-3987

Attention of General Counsel

with a copy to

Arthur L. Liman, Esq.
Paul, Weiss, Rifkind, Wharton & Garrison
1285 Avenue of the Americas
New York, N.Y. 10019
Telecopy No. (212) 757-3990

8.3. *Interpretation.* When a reference is made in this Agreement to Sections, such reference shall be to a Section of this Agreement unless otherwise indicated. The table of contents and headings contained in this Agreement are for reference purposes only and shall not affect in any way the meaning or interpretation of this Agreement. Whenever the words "include", "includes" or "including" are used in this Agreement, they shall be deemed to be followed by the words "without limitation". The phrase "made available" in this Agreement shall mean that the information referred to has been made available if requested by the party to whom such information is to be made available. The phrases "the date of this Agreement", "the date hereof", and terms of similar import, unless the context otherwise requires, shall be deemed to refer to March 3, 1989.

8.4. *Counterparts.* This Agreement may be executed in two or more counterparts, all of which shall be considered one and the same agreement and shall become effective when two or more counterparts have been signed by each of the parties and delivered to the other parties, it being understood that all parties need not sign the same counterpart.

8.5. *Entire Agreement; No Third Party Beneficiaries; Rights of Ownership.* This Agreement (including the documents and the instruments referred to herein, including the Share Exchange Agreement) (a) constitutes the entire agreement and supersedes all prior agreements (including the Agreement between WCI and Time dated as of April 22, 1988) and understandings, both written and oral, among the parties with respect to the subject matter hereof, (b) except as provided in Section 5.15, is not intended to confer upon any person other than the parties hereto any rights or remedies hereunder. The parties hereby acknowledge that, except as otherwise specifically provided in the Share Exchange Agreement or as hereinafter agreed to in writing, no party shall have the right to acquire or shall be deemed to have acquired shares of common stock of the other party pursuant to the Merger until consummation thereof. Notwithstanding anything to the contrary contained in this Agreement, no representations or warranties shall be deemed to have been made by WCI with respect to the Shareholders Agreement, dated as of February 21, 1984, among WCI, Chris-Craft Industries, Inc. and BHC, as amended, including by an Agreement, dated as of February 7, 1986; *provided, however,* that nothing contained herein shall be construed to mean that a consent or waiver is required with respect thereto in connection with the execution, delivery and performance of this Agreement and the Share Exchange Agreement and the consummation of the transactions contemplated hereby and thereby.

8.6. *Governing Law.* This Agreement shall be governed and construed in accordance with the laws of the State of Delaware.

8.7. *No Remedy in Certain Circumstances.* Each party agrees that, should any court or other competent authority hold any provision of this Agreement or the Share Exchange Agreement or part hereof or thereof to be null, void or unenforceable, or order any party to take any action inconsistent herewith or not to take any action required herein, the other party shall not be entitled to specific performance of such provision or part hereof or thereof or to any other remedy, including but not limited to money damages, for breach hereof or thereof or of any other provision of this Agreement or the Share Exchange Agreement or part hereof or thereof as a result of such holding or order.

Section 8.9. Sub gets the right to assign to any affiliate because Time might want to restructure the deal for tax or other reasons and because, except from a technical, corporate law point of view, Sub is not very important anyway.

Signatures and Attestation. With the public announcements and SEC filings that will be made there is not really much reason to require having the signatures attested. It is still required in New York, however.

The names of people who signed the agreement often appear twice in the printed version or conformed copy of an agreement. The one on the signature line represents the signature.

8.8. *Publicity.* Except as otherwise required by law or the rules of the NYSE, so long as this Agreement is in effect, neither WCI nor Time shall, or shall permit any of its Subsidiaries to, issue or cause the publication of any press release or other public announcement with respect to the transactions contemplated by this Agreement without the consent of the other party, which consent shall not be unreasonably withheld.

8.9. *Assignment.* Neither this Agreement nor any of the rights, interests or obligations hereunder shall be assigned by any of the parties hereto (whether by operation of law or otherwise) without the prior written consent of the other parties, except that Sub may assign, in its sole discretion, any or all of its rights, interests and obligations hereunder to Time or to any direct or indirect wholly owned Subsidiary of Time. Subject to the preceding sentence, this Agreement will be binding upon, inure to the benefit of and be enforceable by the parties and their respective successors and assigns.

IN WITNESS WHEREOF, Time, Sub and WCI have caused this Agreement, as amended and restated, to be signed by their respective officers thereunto duly authorized, all as of May 19, 1989.

TIME INCORPORATED,

by J. R. Munro
    Name: J. R. Munro
    Title: Chairman and Chief
          Executive Officer

Attest:

    Thomas W. McEnerney
Name: Thomas W. McEnerney
Title: Assistant Secretary

TW SUB INC.,

by Philip R. Lochner, Jr.
    Name: Philip R. Lochner, Jr.
    Title: Vice President
          and Assistant Secretary

Attest:

    Thomas W. McEnerney
Name: Thomas W. McEnerney
Title: Assistant Secretary

WARNER COMMUNICATIONS INC.,

by Steven J. Ross
    Name: Steven J. Ross
    Title: Chairman of the Board and
          Chief Executive Officer

Attest:

    Eli T. Bruno
Name: Eli T. Bruno
Title: Assistant Secretary

The Share Exchange Agreement gives each party the right to call for an exchange of shares after a Trigger Date under the merger agreement. After the exchange Time and Warner would each own a large block of the other (approximately 10% of the outstanding shares). Several features in the agreement were designed to give it legal validity as a business transaction independent of its being a defense of the merger agreement against other potential bidders. It continues in effect, for example, even if the merger agreement is terminated, and neither party is allowed to vote its shares to affect the merger votes. However, they could vote their shares against someone else's takeover proposal. Time and Warner argued in the litigation with Paramount that the agreement was designed principally to give each party an investment in the other, regardless of whether the merger succeeded. It turned out that the agreement did not figure prominently in the outcome of the litigation. The chancellor assumed the worst case for Time – that its principal purpose was to discourage efforts to upset the transaction – but found that it had been adopted for a rational business purpose. The Delaware Supreme Court agreed.

The advantages for Time and Warner in this agreement are not clear-cut. Undoubtedly, it has some antitakeover effect for each of them. Consider, for example, the Paramount tender offer for Time. If the Paramount bid had been successful, the exchanged Warner shares would have been an unwanted, inherited asset for Paramount. Paramount could have sold the Warner shares, but only subject to the restrictions in this agreement. A premium for the shares would have been very difficult to count on. Yet these shares are one of the Time assets for which Paramount would have paid a high premium. Moreover, Warner could have voted its Time shares against a Paramount sponsored cash squeeze-out merger for Time, making it very difficult for Paramount to obtain complete control over Time's cash flow and assets. This, in turn, would have made it difficult for Paramount to finance its highly leveraged bid for Time.

On the other hand there were important disadvantages for Time and Warner in the agreement. If the merger agreement had been terminated, with neither party at fault, both would have been left with a large unwanted asset. Furthermore, Time shareholders would have been exposed to the risk that Warner would have a windfall profit from a negotiated acquisition of Time and *vice versa*. (See Section 7.1(c) of the merger agreement and Section 7(c) of this agreement.)

Section 1(a). Time would issue approximately 11.1% of its outstanding stock to Warner. Note the attention paid to the poison pill rights going along with the stock.

Section 1(b). Warner would issue approximately 9.4% of its outstanding stock to Time. The two blocks had approximately equal value, based on the average closing prices for the five trading days preceding the announcement

SHARE EXCHANGE AGREEMENT

SHARE EXCHANGE AGREEMENT, dated as of March 3, 1989, as amended as of April 12, 1989, by and between TIME INCORPORATED, a Delaware corporation ("Time"), and WARNER COMMUNICATIONS INC., a Delaware corporation ("WCI").

WHEREAS, concurrently with the execution and delivery of this Agreement, Time, WCI and TW Sub Inc., a Delaware corporation and a wholly-owned subsidiary of Time ("T-Sub"), are entering into an Agreement and Plan of Merger, dated as of the date hereof (the "Merger Agreement"), which provides that, among other things, upon the terms and subject to the conditions thereof, T-Sub will be merged with and into WCI (the "Merger"), with WCI continuing as the surviving corporation; and

WHEREAS, as a condition to their willingness to enter into the Merger Agreement, each of the parties hereto has requested that the other agree, and each has so agreed, to issue to the other its Exchange Shares (as hereinafter defined) on the terms and subject to the conditions set forth herein.

NOW, THEREFORE, in consideration of the foregoing and of the mutual covenants and agreements set forth herein and in the Merger Agreement and for other good and valuable consideration, the receipt and adequacy of which are hereby acknowledged, the parties hereto agree as follows:

1. *Issue and Transfer of Exchange Shares.*

(a) *Issuance of Time Exchange Shares.* In consideration of and subject to the issuance of the shares referred to in Section 1(b), at the Closing (as defined in Section 3), Time will issue and deliver to WCI 7,080,016 shares (the "Time Exchange Shares") of its Common Stock, par value $1.00 per share (the "Time Common Stock"), including the associated rights (the "Rights") to purchase shares of Series A Participating Preferred Stock of Time pursuant to the Rights Agreement, dated as of April 29, 1986, between Time and Morgan Shareholder Services Trust Company of New York, as amended by Amendment No. 1, dated as of January 19, 1989, and as further amended from time to time. All references in this Agreement to shares of Time Common Stock issued to WCI hereunder shall be deemed, prior to the Distribution Date (as defined in the Rights Agreement), to include the Rights.

(b) *Issuance of WCI Exchange Shares.* In consideration of and subject to the issuance of the shares referred to in Section 1(a), at the Closing, WCI will issue and deliver to Time 17,292,747 shares (the "WCI Exchange Shares") of its Common Stock, par value $1 per share (the "WCI Common Stock").

(c) *Defined Terms.* For purposes of this Agreement: (i) the term "Exchange Shares" shall mean the Time Exchange Shares and the WCI Exchange Shares, and reference to "its Exchange Shares" with respect to Time or WCI shall mean the Time Exchange Shares or the WCI Exchange Shares, as the case may be; (ii) the term "Purchaser" shall mean the recipient of Exchange Shares and its successors and assigns; (iii) the term "Subject Company" shall mean the issuer of Exchange Shares and its successors and assigns; (iv) the term "Common Stock" shall mean the Time Common Stock or the WCI Common Stock, as the case may be, and, in each case, shall include any other securities issued or exchanged with respect to such shares as a result of one or more recapitalizations, reclassifications, mergers, consolidations or the like; (v) the term "Securities Act" shall mean the Securities Act of 1933, as amended; (vi) the term "Exchange Act" shall mean the Securities Exchange Act of 1934, as amended; (vii) the terms "affiliate" and "associate" shall have the respective meanings ascribed to such terms in Rule 12b-2 promulgated under the Exchange Act; (viii) the term "business day" shall mean any day other than a Saturday or Sunday or other day on which banks are authorized to close in The City of New York; and (ix) the term "Person" shall mean any corporation, partnership, individual, trust, unincorporated association or other entity or Group (within the meaning of Section 13(d)(3) of the Exchange Act). References in this Agreement to a party shall mean such party and its successors and assigns.

2. *Conditions to Closing.* The obligation of each Subject Company to issue its Exchange Shares to a Purchaser hereunder is subject to the conditions, which (other than the conditions described in clauses (i) and (iii) below) may be waived by such Subject Company in its sole discretion, that (i) all waiting

Section 1(b), cont'd.

of the merger. This means that the share exchange ratio did not reflect the premium Time was paying for Warner shares under the merger agreement. (But see our comments, below, about Section 4.)

Section 2. There is nothing in the closing conditions that is unusual. It is noteworthy that the waiting period under the Hart–Scott–Rodino Act prevents an immediate exchange of these large blocks of shares. This impairs the usefulness of share exchanges as last minute antitakeover measures. We discuss the reason for requiring officers' certificates in the commentary to Section 6.2(a) of the original merger agreement.

Section 3. Paramount's hostile tender offer was the cause of a Trigger Date. After the Delaware Chancery Court denied Paramount's motion to invalidate the exchange agreement (because the court found it could provide Paramount adequate relief later), Warner gave the required notice and the closing took place. As originally signed on March 3, 1989, the exchange agreement did not have a 'Trigger Date' concept. In its original form, the agreement called for exchanging shares as soon as the conditions in Section 2 were met. Practically speaking, this would have meant a closing as soon as the Hart–Scott–Rodino waiting period had expired. These conditions were met well before Paramount made its offer. However, the SEC took the position that an actual exchange of shares would preclude pooling-of-interests accounting. (One would not expect the usually pro-shareholder SEC staff to be sympathetic to a share exchange agreement, which is a type of lockup.) The agreement was amended to include the Trigger Date requirement and to permit a closing only when a Trigger Date was caused.

Section 4. The share adjustment described would increase Warner's holdings so that the total shares exchanged would be in proportion to the exchange ratio in the merger. When the transaction was restructured in the merger agreement dated June 16, 1989 (Chapter 18) the exchange ratio concept was dropped in favor of Merger Consideration. See Sections 2.1(c) and 2.1(f) of the June 16 merger agreement. In Section 1.8 of that agreement Warner waived its right to receive any shares under this provision.

Section 5. One obvious purpose of the share exchange would have been to increase control over the vote in the merger. However, the voting rules in the agreement do not allow this. In votes on the merger and the stock incentive plan the parties' votes must be counted in the same proportion for and against as the other shareholder votes cast, so that the outcome of the vote would not be affected. However, on other matters, including proxy contests, the parties vote their shares as they see fit.

An exchange designed to affect the merger vote might have increased the risk that the exchange agreement would be declared illegal. As a practical matter, this concession on voting probably was not a big loss. It is unlikely, for example, that 11.1% of the Time shares held by Warner would periods, if any, under the Hart-Scott-Rodino Antitrust Improvements Act of 1976, as amended, and the rules and regulations promulgated thereunder ("HSR Act"), applicable to the issuances of the Exchange Shares hereunder shall have expired or have been terminated, and all consents, approvals, orders or authorizations of, or registrations, declarations or filings with, any federal administrative agency or commission or other federal governmental authority or instrumentality, if any, required in connection with the issuance of the Exchange Shares hereunder shall have been obtained or made, as the case may be; (ii) the Exchange Shares shall have been approved for listing on the New York Stock Exchange upon official notice of issuance; (iii) no preliminary or permanent injunction or other order by any court of competent jurisdiction prohibiting or otherwise restraining such issuance shall be in effect; (iv) the representations and warranties of such Purchaser contained in Section 3.2, in the case of Time, and Section 3.1, in the case of WCI, of the Merger Agreement shall be true and correct in all material respects as of the date of this Agreement and (except to the extent such representations and warranties speak as of an earlier date) as of the Closing Date (as defined in Section 3) as though made on and as of the Closing, except as otherwise contemplated by the Merger Agreement, and such Subject Company shall have received a certificate signed on behalf of such Purchaser by two of its senior officers to such effect and to the effect that such Purchaser is acquiring the Exchange Shares to be issued to it for its own account and not with a view to the distribution thereof and will not sell any of such shares except in compliance with the Securities Act; and (v) such Purchaser shall not then be in breach of the Merger Agreement, and such Subject Company shall have received a certificate signed on behalf of such Purchaser by two of its senior officers to such effect.

3. *Closing; Closing Date.* The issuance and exchange of the Time Exchange Shares and the WCI Exchange Shares provided for in this Agreement shall take place, subject to the satisfaction or waiver of the conditions referred to in Section 2 (other than the delivery of the officers' certificates referred to therein), at a closing (the "Closing") to be held at the offices of Paul, Weiss, Rifkind, Wharton & Garrison, 1285 Avenue of the Americas, New York, New York, 10019, at 10:00 a.m., local time, on the earlier to occur of (i) February 28, 1990 and (ii) the fifth business day following the giving of written notice subsequent to a Trigger Date (as such term is defined in the Merger Agreement) by either party to the other party of its election to cause the Closing to occur. Notwithstanding anything to the contrary contained herein, if the required approval of the Merger by the stockholders of Time or WCI shall not have been obtained by reason of the failure to obtain the required vote upon a vote held at a duly held meeting of stockholders or any adjournment thereof, and the Exchange Shares have not theretofore been issued and exchanged, then the Closing hereunder shall not occur and neither Subject Company shall issue its Exchange Shares to the other party pursuant to this Agreement. The time and date upon which the Closing occurs is herein called the "Closing Date." At the Closing, Time and WCI will each deliver to the other a single certificate in definitive form representing the appropriate number of Time Exchange Shares and WCI Exchange Shares, respectively, each such certificate to be registered in the name of the Purchaser thereof and to bear the legend set forth in Section 9.

4. *Share Adjustment.* Immediately prior to the consummation of the Merger, Time shall issue and transfer to WCI a number of shares of Time Common Stock equal to the excess of (i) the product of (A) the number of WCI Exchange Shares issued to Time pursuant to Section 1(b) and (B) the Conversion Number (as defined in Section 2(c) of the Merger Agreement), over (ii) the number of Time Exchange Shares issued to WCI pursuant to Section 1(a).

5. *Voting of Shares.* Subject to Section 10, until the termination of the Merger Agreement, each Purchaser shall vote the Exchange Shares issued to it with respect to all matters, other than Excepted Matters (as defined below), for and against such matters in the same proportion as the votes of the other stockholders of the issuer of such shares are voted (whether by proxy or otherwise) for and against such matters. Subject to Section 10, following the termination of the Merger Agreement and prior to the Expiration Date (as defined in Section 6(c)), each Purchaser shall vote the Exchange Shares issued to it and all other shares of captial stock of the issuer of such Exchange Shares beneficially owned (within the meaning of Rule 13d-3 promulgated under the Exchange Act) by such Purchaser (collectively, the "Restricted Shares") on each matter submitted to a vote of the stockholders of such issuer for and against such matter in the same proportion as the votes of all other stockholders of such issuer are voted (whether by proxy or otherwise) for and against such matter. For purposes of this Section 5, the term "Excepted Matters" shall mean all matters (other than any vote with respect to the

Section 5, cont'd.

have made much difference in the vote of Time shareholders on the original, abandoned Time–Warner merger after Paramount made its tender offer for Time shares. In tender offers the concentration of shares caused by the arbitrage market and large institutional shareholders generally makes a favorable or unfavorable outcome overwhelming.

Section 6 is a standstill agreement (see Glossary entry). While the merger agreement is in effect, neither Time nor Warner, acting alone or with someone else, may buy shares in the other or participate in takeover activities (very broadly defined in Section 6(b)) against the other. There is a highly technical exception for Warner if it has an opportunity to exercise its poison pill rights to buy cheap shares of Time. If the merger agreement is terminated a somewhat broader list of impermissible actions applies.

The standstill provisions last for ten years (about as long a period as one is likely to see in such provisions) unless a change of control occurs. Standstill agreements are commonly used in settlements of takeover contests and after defensive repurchases of shares from would-be acquirers of a company (greenmail). However, greenmail payments have declined sharply in the U.S. recently. Some company charters have been amended to prohibit them.

Merger, the Time Vote Matter and the Stock Incentive Plan (each, as defined in the Merger Agreement)) to be voted upon by the stockholders of such issuer pursuant to which solicitations of proxies or consents are being made by any Person other than such Purchaser, such Subject Company or any of their affiliates.

6. *Restriction on Certain Actions.*

(a) *Restrictions Prior to Termination of the Merger Agreement.* Following the date hereof and prior to the termination of the Merger Agreement, neither party shall, and neither party shall permit its affiliates, directly or indirectly, to (i) purchase or otherwise acquire or agree to acquire any equity interest in such other party, other than pursuant to this Agreement or, with respect to WCI, pursuant to the Rights, or, with respect to Time, pursuant to any similar rights that may be issued by WCI in accordance with Section 4.1(k) of the Merger Agreement (collectively, "Permitted Purchases"), or (ii) take any of the actions described in Section 6(b) in concert or in conjunction with or through any other Person or Group.

(b) *Restrictions following Termination of the Merger Agreement.* Subject to Section 10, following the termination of the Merger Agreement and prior to the Expiration Date without the prior written consent of the other party, neither party shall, and neither party shall permit its affiliates to, directly or indirectly, alone or in concert or conjunction with any other Person or Group (i) in any manner acquire, agree to acquire or make any proposal to acquire, any securities of, equity interest in, or any material property of, the other party or any of its subsidiaries (other than Permitted Purchases), (ii) except at the specific written request of the other party, propose to enter into any merger or business combination involving the other party or any of its subsidiaries or to purchase a material portion of the assets of the other party or any of its subsidiaries, (iii) make or in any way participate in any "solicitation" of "proxies" (as such terms are used in Regulation 14A promulgated under the Exchange Act) to vote, or seek to advise or influence any Person with respect to the voting of any voting securities of the other party or any of its subsidiaries, (iv) form, join or in any way participate in a Group with respect to any voting securities of the other party or any of its subsidiaries, (v) seek to control or influence the management, Board of Directors or policies of the other party, (vi) disclose any intention, plan or arrangement inconsistent with the foregoing, (vii) advise, assist or encourage any other Person in connection with the foregoing, or (viii) request the other party (or its directors, officers, employees or agents), to amend or waive any provision of this Section 6, or take any action which may require the other party to make a public announcement regarding the possibility of a business combination or merger with such party.

(c) *Expiration Date.* For purposes of this Agreement, the term "Expiration Date" with respect to any obligation or restriction imposed on a party shall mean the earlier to occur of (i) the tenth anniversary of the date hereof and (ii) such time as the other party shall have suffered a Change of Control. A "Change of Control" shall be deemed to have occurred:

(A) whenever a majority of the members of the Board of Directors of such other party elected at any meeting or by written consent shall have been so elected against the recommendation of the management of such other party or the Board of Directors of such other party in office immediately prior to such election;

(B) whenever any Person (other than such party or any employee benefit plan of such other party) or Persons acting in concert shall acquire (whether by merger, consolidation, sale, assignment, lease, transfer or otherwise, in one transaction or any related series of transactions) or otherwise beneficially own (I) a majority of the voting power of the outstanding securities of such other party generally entitled to vote for the election of directors, or (II) all or substantially all of the assets of such other party; or

(C) upon consummation of a consolidation or merger of such other party with another Person in which the holders of voting securities of such other party immediately prior to such consolidation or merger would not own securities representing at least 50% of the outstanding voting power of such Person or its ultimate parent upon consummation of such consolidation or merger.

Section 7. The transfer provisions are complex but the main ideas are simple. While the merger agreement is in effect transfers of the exchanged shares are not allowed.

If the merger agreement is terminated, either party may sell its shares but only after giving the other notice (24 hours or three, five, or ten business days, depending on the circumstances) to buy the shares at a formula price based on recent market prices. If the other party does not buy the shares they may be sold freely for 45 days but not at a below-market price. If not sold during that 45-day period, the shares become subject to the same restrictions again.

7. *Restrictions on Transfer; Right of First Refusal.*

(a) *Restrictions on Transfer.* Subject to Section 10, prior to the Expiration Date, neither party shall, directly or indirectly, by operation of law or otherwise, sell, assign, pledge or otherwise dispose of or transfer any Restricted Shares beneficially owned by such party, other than (i) pursuant to Section 4, (ii) pursuant to the Merger Agreement or (iii) in accordance with Section 7(b), 7(c) or 8.

(b) *Right of First Refusal.* If at any time following the termination of the Merger Agreement a party (the "Seller") shall propose to sell any Restricted Shares beneficially owned by it (other than as permitted by Section 7(c)), it shall, by written notice (an "Offer Notice") to the issuer of such shares (the "Issuer"), give the Issuer the opportunity to purchase such shares for cash at a price (the "Purchase Price") equal to the product of (i) the number of such shares proposed to be sold and (ii) the Fair Market Value (as defined below) of such shares. The Issuer (and/or any Person designated by the Issuer) shall have the right, exercisable by written notice (the "Purchase Notice") delivered to the Seller within ten business days (or, if a Relevant Offer (as defined below) is then outstanding, five business days; such ten or five business day period being referred to herein as the "Decision Period") after receipt of the Offer Notice, to agree irrevocably to purchase for cash all or any portion of the shares specified in the Offer Notice (the "Subject Shares"). If the Issuer and/or such designee exercises its right of first refusal pursuant to the preceding sentence (the "First Refusal Right"), the closing of the purchase of the Subject Shares shall occur at the principal executive offices of the Issuer or its counsel at any reasonable date and time designated by the Issuer and/or such designee in its Purchase Notice within 20 business days after delivery of the Purchase Notice and payment for such shares to be purchased shall be made by delivery at the time of such closing of the Purchase Price in immediately available funds, provided that if a tender or exchange offer for more than 50% of the outstanding Common Stock of such Issuer (a "Relevant Offer"), is outstanding at the time of delivery of the Purchase Notice, such closing shall take place following the exercise by the Issuer and/or its designee of its First Refusal Right on the earlier to occur of (A) the third business day following the delivery of the Purchase Notice or (B) 24 hours prior to the then scheduled expiration date of such Relevant Offer. If the Issuer or such designee has not exercised its First Refusal Right prior to the expiration of the Decision Period, the Seller shall have the right during the 45 days immediately following the expiration of the Decision Period to consummate the sale of the Subject Shares at a per share price at least equal to the lowest Closing Sale Price (as defined below) of shares of Common Stock of the Issuer during the period commencing with the delivery of the Offer Notice and ending on the date such sale is consummated; *provided,* that if such sale is not consummated within such 45-day period, the provisions of this Section 7(b) shall again be applicable to any such proposed sale. For purposes of this Section 7(b) and Section 8, the term "Fair Market Value" shall mean the average during the ten trading days immediately prior to the day on which (x) the Seller gives an Offer Notice (for purposes of this Section 7(b)), or (y) a Designated Holder (as defined below) gives a Registration Notice (for purposes of Section 8), of the daily closing sale price (regular way) of the shares of Common Stock of such Issuer as reported on the New York Stock Exchange—Composite Transaction Tape, or any successor thereto on which sales of such shares are reported, or, if such shares are no longer traded on the New York Stock Exchange, as reported on the principal national securities exchange on which such shares are listed or admitted to trading, or, if such shares are not listed or admitted to trading on any national securities exchange, as reported by the National Association of Securities Dealers, Inc. through NASDAQ or a similar organization if NASDAQ is no longer reporting such information (the "'Closing Sale Price"). Notwithstanding the foregoing, for purposes of this Section 7(b), if a Relevant Offer is outstanding, the Fair Market Value of the Subject Shares shall equal the higher of (I) the highest price per share being offered pursuant to such Relevant Offer as of the date the Purchase Notice is given or (II) the Fair Market Value of such shares determined in accordance with the preceding sentence. If at the time of the purchase of any Subject Shares by an Issuer pursuant to this Section 7(b) a Relevant Offer is outstanding, then the Issuer shall from time to time promptly pay to the Seller such additional amounts, if any, so that the consideration received by the Seller with respect to each Subject Share shall equal the highest price paid for a share of Common Stock of the Issuer pursuant to such Relevant Offer, or pursuant to any other tender or exchange offer outstanding at any time the Relevant Offer is outstanding, provided such other offer is for more than 50% of the outstanding Common Stock of such Issuer.

Section 7(c). Either party may sell its shares into a friendly tender offer, however, if the merger agreement is terminated. Friendly tender offer is carefully defined.

Section 8. This section is a limited exception to the restrictions in Section 7. The exchanged shares are unregistered when delivered at the closing and as a result could not be sold to the public immediately even if Section 7 did not restrict transfer. Subject to several restrictions, either party may request registration of its exchanged shares under the Securities Act of 1933 and then sell them to the public. If the merger agreement is terminated either party may request that the other register the shares. The underwriters for the offering must commit themselves to a wide distribution of the shares at a price at least 80% of the average recent market price. Alternatively, the issuer of the shares has the option to buy the shares or arrange for someone else to buy them at 100% of market. The issuer of the shares is given reasonable flexibility to delay the offering for business reasons.

(c) *Permitted Sales.* Following the termination of the Merger Agreement, a party shall be permitted to sell any Restricted Shares beneficially owned by it without complying with the restrictions contained in Section 7(b) if such sale is made pursuant to a tender or exchange offer that has been approved or recommended, or otherwise determined to be fair and in the best interests of such Issuer's stockholders, by a majority of the members of the Board of Directors of such Issuer (which majority shall include a majority of directors who were directors prior to the announcement of such tender or exchange offer).

8. *Registration Rights.* Following the termination of the Merger Agreement, each party hereto (a "Designated Holder") may by written notice (the "Registration Notice") to the other party (the "Registrant") request the Registrant to register under the Securities Act all or any part of the Restricted Shares beneficially owned by such Designated Holder (the "Registrable Securities") pursuant to a *bona fide* firm commitment underwritten public offering in which the Designated Holder and the underwriters shall effect as wide a distribution of such Registrable Securities as is reasonably practicable and shall use their best efforts to prevent any Person (including any Group) and its affiliates from purchasing through such offering Restricted Shares representing more than 1% of the outstanding shares of Common Stock of the Registrant on a fully diluted basis (a "Permitted Offering"). The Registration Notice shall include a certificate executed by the Designated Holder and its proposed managing underwriter, which underwriter shall be an investment banking firm of nationally recognized standing (the "Manager"), stating that (i) they have a good faith intention to commence promptly a Permitted Offering and (ii) the Manager in good faith believes that, based on the then prevailing market conditions, it will be able to sell the Registrable Securities at a per share price equal to at least 80% of the Fair Market Value of such shares. The Registrant (and/or any Person designated by the Registrant) shall thereupon have the option, exercisable by written notice delivered to the Designated Holder within 10 business days after receipt of the Registration Notice, irrevocably to agree to purchase all or any part of the Registrable Securities for cash at a price (the "Option Price") equal to the product of (i) the number of Registrable Securities and (ii) the Fair Market Value of such shares. Any such purchase of Registrable Securities by the Registrant hereunder shall take place at a closing to be held at the principal executive offices of the Registrant or its counsel at any reasonable date and time designated by the Registrant and/or such designee in such notice within 20 business days after delivery of such notice. Any payment for the shares to be purchased shall be made by delivery at the time of such closing of the Option Price in immediately available funds.

If the Registrant does not elect to exercise its option pursuant to this Section 8 with respect to all Registrable Securities, it shall use its best efforts to effect, as promptly as practicable, the registration under the Securities Act of the unpurchased Registrable Securities; *provided, however*, that (i) neither party shall be entitled to more than an aggregate of two effective registration statements hereunder and (ii) the Registrant will not be required to file any such registration statement during any period of time (not to exceed 40 days after such request in the case of clause (A) below or 90 days in the case of clauses (B) and (C) below) when (A) the Registrant is in possession of material non-public information which it reasonably believes would be detrimental to be disclosed at such time and, in the written opinion of counsel to such Registrant, such information would have to be disclosed if a registration statement were filed at that time; (B) such Registrant is required under the Securities Act to include audited financial statements for any period in such registration statement and such financial statements are not yet available for inclusion in such registration statement; or (C) such Registrant determines, in its reasonable judgment, that such registration would interfere with any financing, acquisition or other material transaction involving the Registrant or any of its affiliates. If consummation of the sale of any Registerable Securities pursuant to a registration hereunder does not occur within 120 days after the filing with the Securities and Exchange Commission of the initial registration statement, the provisions of this Section 8 shall again be applicable to any proposed registration; *provided, however*, that neither party shall be entitled to request more than two registrations pursuant to this Section 8. The Registrant shall use its reasonable best efforts to cause any Registrable Securities registered pursuant to this Section 8 to be qualified for sale under the securities or Blue-Sky laws of such jurisdictions as the Designated Holder may reasonably request and shall continue such registration or qualification in effect in such jurisdiction; *provided, however*, that the Registrant shall not be required to qualify to do business in, or consent to general service of process in, any jurisdiction by reason of this provision.

Section 8, cont'd.

The registration expenses of the offering are paid for by the issuer of the shares and the underwriting and related costs are paid by the seller. The agreements covering indemnification and the underwriting agreement are quite brief, considering the complexity of the usual indemnifications and underwriting agreements. Treating the subjects in one sentence works because there is general agreement in the securities industry about the main points that are found in these agreements. Moreover, there are limits on tolerance for detail even in negotiating agreements for huge transactions like this one.

Section 9. The restrictive legend alerts potential buyers under Section 7 and anyone who deals with them about resale problems.

Section 10. In this section Time and Warner make sure that the exchange agreement serves as an inducement not to breach the merger agreement. If there is a breach of the merger agreement, the other party is relieved from the major restrictions and obligations imposed by the exchange agreement.

Section 11. This paragraph fills out the story on transfer. The resale restrictions in the agreement only apply to Time and Warner, not to someone who buys in compliance with its provisions. However, if Time or Warner later reacquires the shares the restrictions come back into play. Otherwise transferring shares and then immediately buying them back could nullify the restrictions.

Section 12. Here Time and Warner do their best to assure that a court would order specific performance of the agreement if there is a violation. They are concerned that otherwise a court would award only money damages, which is not what Time and Warner are interested in.

The registration rights set forth in this Section 8 are subject to the condition that the Designated Holder shall provide the Registrant with such information with respect to such holder's Registrable Securities, the plans for the distribution thereof, and such other information with respect to such holder as, in the reasonable judgment of counsel for the Registrant, is necessary to enable the Registrant to include in such registration statement all material facts required to be disclosed with respect to a registration hereunder.

A registration effected under this Section 8 shall be effected at the Registrant's expense, except for underwriting discounts and commissions and the fees and the expenses of counsel to the Designated Holder, and the Registrant shall provide to the underwriters such documentation (including certificates, opinions of counsel and "comfort" letters from auditors) as are customary in connection with underwritten public offerings as such underwriters may reasonably require. In connection with any such registration, the parties agree (i) to indemnify each other and the underwriters in the customary manner and (ii) to enter into an underwriting agreement in form and substance customary to transactions of this type with the Manager and the other underwriters participating in such offering.

9. *Restrictive Legends.* Each certificate representing Exchange Shares issued to a Purchaser hereunder shall include a legend in substantially the following form:

THE SECURITIES REPRESENTED BY THIS CERTIFICATE HAVE NOT BEEN REGISTERED UNDER THE SECURITIES ACT OF 1933, AS AMENDED, AND MAY BE REOFFERED OR SOLD ONLY IF SO REGISTERED OR IF AN EXEMPTION FROM SUCH REGISTRATION IS AVAILABLE. SUCH SECURITIES ARE ALSO SUBJECT TO ADDITIONAL RESTRICTIONS ON TRANSFER AS SET FORTH IN THE SHARE EXCHANGE AGREEMENT, DATED AS OF MARCH 3, 1989, A COPY OF WHICH MAY BE OBTAINED FROM [SUBJECT COMPANY].

10. *Relief From Obligations Following Willful Breach.* Notwithstanding anything to the contrary contained in this Agreement, if the Merger Agreement is terminated as the result of a willful breach by a party (or, with respect to Time, by T-Sub) of any of its representations, warranties, covenants or agreements set forth in the Merger Agreement, the other party shall not be subject to the restrictions and obligations otherwise imposed upon it pursuant to Sections 5, 6 and 7 (other than in its capacity as an Issuer under Section 7(b)) of this Agreement.

11. *Binding Effect; No Assignment.* This Agreement shall be binding upon and inure to the benefit of the parties hereto and their respective successors, and permitted assigns. Except as expressly provided for in this Agreement, neither this Agreement nor the rights or the obligations of any party hereto are assignable, except by operation of law, or with the written consent of the other party. Nothing contained in this Agreement, express or implied, is intended to confer upon any person other than the parties hereto and their respective permitted assigns any rights or remedies of any nature whatsoever by reason of this Agreement. Any Restricted Shares sold by a party in compliance with the provisions of Section 7 or Section 8 shall, upon consummation of such sale, be free of the restrictions imposed with respect to such shares by this Agreement, unless and until such party shall repurchase or otherwise become the beneficial owner of such shares, and any transferee of such shares shall not be entitled to the rights of such party. Certificates representing shares sold in a registered public offering pursuant to Section 8 shall not be required to bear the legend set forth in Section 9.

12. *Specific Performance.* The parties recognize and agree that if for any reason the other fails to issue any Exchange Shares required to be issued hereunder or if any of the other provisions of this Agreement are not performed in accordance with their specific terms or are otherwise breached, immediate and irreparable harm or injury would be caused for which money damages would not be an adequate remedy. Accordingly, each party agrees that, in addition to other remedies, the parties shall be entitled to an injunction restraining any violation or threatened violation of the provisions of this Agreement or to specific performance or other equitable relief to enforce the provisions of this Agreement. In the event that any action should be brought in equity to enforce the provisions of this Agreement, no party will allege, and each party hereby waives the defense, that there is adequate remedy at law.

13. *Entire Agreement.* This Agreement and the Merger Agreement (including the exhibits and schedules thereto) constitute the entire agreement among the parties with respect to the subject matter hereof and supersede all other prior agreements (including the Agreement between WCI and Time dated as of April 22, 1988) and understandings, both written and oral, among the parties or any of them with respect to the subject matter hereof.

14. *Further Assurances.* Each party will execute and deliver all such further documents and instruments and take all such further action as may be necessary in order to consummate the transactions contemplated hereby.

15. *Validity.* The invalidity or unenforceability of any provision of this Agreement shall not affect the validity or enforceability of the other provisions of this Agreement, which shall remain in full force and effect. In the event any court or other competent authority holds any provision of this Agreement to be null, void or unenforceable, the parties hereto shall negotiate in good faith the execution and delivery of an amendment to this Agreement in order, as nearly as possible, to effectuate, to the extent permitted by law, the intent of the parties hereto with respect to such provision. Each party agrees that, should any court or other competent authority hold any provision of this Agreement or part hereof to be null, void or unenforceable, or order any party to take any action inconsistent herewith, or not to take any action required herein, the other party shall not be entitled to specific performance of such provision or part hereof or to any other remedy, including but not limited to money damages, for breach hereof or of any other provision of this Agreement or part hereof as the result of such holding or order.

16. *Notices.* Any notice or communication required or permitted hereunder shall be in writing and either delivered personally, telegraphed or telecopied or sent by certified or registered mail, postage prepaid, and shall be deemed to be given, dated and received when so delivered personally, telegraphed or telecopied or, if mailed, five business days after the date of mailing to the following address or telecopy number, or to such other address or addresses as such person may subsequently designate by notice given hereunder:

(a) if to Time, to:

> Time Incorporated
> Time and Life Building
> Rockefeller Center
> New York, New York 10020
> Telecopy No. (212) 522-1252
>
> Attention of Vice President and
> General Counsel

with a copy to

> Samuel C. Butler, Esq.
> Cravath, Swaine & Moore
> One Chase Manhattan Plaza
> New York, New York 10005
> Telecopy No. (212) 428-3700

and

(b) if to WCI, to

Warner Communications Inc.
75 Rockefeller Plaza
New York, New York 10019
Telecopy No. (212) 333-3987

Attention of General Counsel

with a copy to

Arthur L. Liman, Esq.
Paul, Weiss, Rifkind, Wharton & Garrison
1285 Avenue of the Americas
New York, New York 10019
Telecopy No. (212) 757-3990

17. *Governing Law.* This Agreement shall be governed by and construed in accordance with the laws of the State of Delaware applicable to agreements made and to be performed entirely within such State.

18. *Descriptive Headings.* The descriptive headings herein are inserted for convenience of reference only and are not intended to be part of or to affect the meaning or interpretation of this Agreement.

19. *Counterparts.* This Agreement may be executed in counterparts, each of which shall be deemed to be an original, but all of which, taken together, shall constitute one and the same instrument.

20. *Expenses.* Except as otherwise expressly provided herein, all costs and expenses incurred in connection with the transactions contemplated by this Agreement shall be paid by the party incurring such expenses.

21. *Amendments; Waiver.* This Agreement may be amended by the parties hereto and the terms and conditions hereof may be waived only by an instrument in writing signed on behalf of each of the parties hereto, or, in the case of a waiver, by an instrument signed on behalf of the party waiving compliance.

IN WITNESS WHEREOF, the parties hereto have caused this Agreement to be executed by their respective duly authorized officers, all as of the day and year first above written.

TIME INCORPORATED

By: .... /s/ J. RICHARD MUNRO ....
TITLE: *Chairman and Chief*
Executive Officer

WARNER COMMUNICATIONS INC.

By: .... /s/ STEVEN J. ROSS ....
TITLE: *Chairman of the Board*
and Chief Executive Officer

D-8

18

Commentary on the Revised Time–Warner Agreement

TIME and Warner restructured their agreement in response to the hostile bid for Time Incorporated made by Paramount Communications Inc. Under the new agreement, instead of using a single-step merger, Time would acquire Warner in two steps. First, it would buy a majority of the shares of Warner in a cash tender offer. Then, some time in the future, it would merge a wholly owned subsidiary into Warner, giving Warner's remaining shareholders a package of securities worth as much as the cash paid in the first step.

An essential characteristic of the new structure was that Time did not need the favorable vote of its shareholders to make the tender offer, which would give it control of Warner. With the Paramount offer available to them, approval by Time's shareholders was no longer a practical possibility. A major disadvantage of this restructuring was that the economics of the acquisition had been thoroughly changed. This was not a mere change in legal form. Warner shareholders were now receiving (and the Time shareholders paying) a large premium. In addition, the cash tender offer would cause the new company to be highly leveraged. Furthermore, Time would lose the benefits of pooling-of-interests accounting treatment (see Glossary entry), which are only available in acquisitions using common stock. This meant that Time's reported earnings would be sharply reduced because approximately $9 billion of good will would have to be amortized over 40 years using purchase accounting.

The new structure required substantial revision to the agreement. Some of the changes were simply a matter of form. But there were also important new issues for negotiation. In the litigation with Paramount, Time and Warner both presented a picture of Warner as a reluctant participant in the restructuring rather than an enthusiastic participant in a windfall. Clearly this was a good picture for the litigation. This departs sharply from common sense since the Warner shareholders were the chief beneficiaries of the new form. It is no answer to say Time shareholders would end up with most of the equity. There was nothing to stop the Warner shareholders from using their premiums to buy shares in Time Warner Inc after the acquisition. Nonetheless, the picture may also have been true. Warner's CEO, who was staying on in the combined company as co-CEO, may have had a strong preference for the original safer financial structure of the combined company. In short, the interests of Warner management and shareholders could have been quite different.

Many of our general comments on the earlier agreement also apply to this one, so we have not repeated them here. Where there is no commentary on a provision readers should look to the commentary on the corresponding provision in Chapter 17.

AGREEMENT AND PLAN OF MERGER

As Amended and Restated
as of May 19, 1989,
as Further Amended and Restated
as of June 16, 1989,

among

TIME INCORPORATED,

TW SUB INC.

and

WARNER COMMUNICATIONS INC.

Article I has been expanded and revised to cover the tender offer in addition to the merger.

TABLE OF CONTENTS

ARTICLE IV
COVENANTS RELATING TO CONDUCT OF BUSINESS

ARTICLE V
ADDITIONAL AGREEMENTS

This agreement had to be prepared under more time pressure than the earlier version. Time and Warner wanted to announce a response to Paramount's tender offer as soon as possible so they had to renegotiate quickly. The version of this revised agreement filed with the SEC contained a number of handwritten corrections that the lawyers working in haste made at the last minute. These corrections were incorporated in a corrected printed version of the agreement that was filed with the SEC as an amendment. We used the corrected version here. We comment on some of the more significant of these last-minute changes because of the light they throw on the negotiations.

ARTICLE VI
CONDITIONS PRECEDENT

ARTICLE VII
TERMINATION AND AMENDMENT

ARTICLE VIII
GENERAL PROVISIONS

Index of Defined Terms

TW Sub Inc. remains a party to the agreement because its merger into Warner is still contemplated, although at some unspecified time in the future.

1st 'whereas' clause. The merger referred to in the earlier agreement has evolved into the more complicated 'business combination.'

2nd 'whereas' clause. Buying the 100,000,000 shares would give Time majority control of Warner. The price is 'net to the seller in cash' because there are no brokerage commissions, transfer taxes or other items subtracted from what the shareholders would receive. The subsequent merger retains the structure described in the old agreement. Most important, Warner demanded and received a substantial premium for its shareholders in the restructured deal (53% based on Warner's trading price of $45\frac{7}{8}$ the day before the merger was announced).

Section 1.1. Under SEC rules, a cash tender offer must begin and the required tender offer papers (Schedule 14D–1) must be filed with the SEC within five business days of its announcement to the public. Time did not wait, which is not unusual. It filed its documents and mailed the offer to Warner shareholders on June 16, the day it announced the restructured transaction.

The conditions to the tender offer that are mentioned are a key part of the offer. Exhibit A has been included at the end of the agreement. The terms of the offer that Time can change without Warner's consent are also very important to both parties. Warner wants to keep as much control as possible over the tender offer. Time is allowed, with Warner's consent, to increase the tender offer price and to buy more than 100,000,000 shares if more are tendered. On the other hand, Time must extend the offer if necessary to obtain financing.

AGREEMENT AND PLAN OF MERGER dated as of March 3,1989, as amended and restated as of May 19, 1989, as further amended and restated as of June 16, 1989, among TIME INCORPO-RATED, a Delaware corporation ("Time"), TW SUB INC., a Delaware corporation and a wholly owned subsidiary of Time ("Sub"), and WARNER COMMUNICATIONS INC., a Delaware corporation ("WCI").

WHEREAS the respective Boards of Directors of Time, Sub and WCI have approved the business combination of Time and WCI;

WHEREAS to effect such transaction, the respective Boards of Time, Sub and WCI, and Time acting as the sole stockholder of Sub, have approved (i) a tender offer by Time for 100,000,000 shares of WCI's common stock, par value $1 per share ("WCI Common Stock"), at a price per share of $70, net to the seller in cash, pursuant and subject to the terms and conditions of this Agreement (the "Offer"), and (ii) the subsequent merger of WCI and Sub (the "Merger"), pursuant and subject to the terms and conditions of this Agreement, whereby each issued and outstanding share of WCI Common Stock not owned directly or through a wholly-owned Subsidiary (as defined in Section 2.1(b)) by Time or directly or through a wholly-owned Subsidiary by WCI will be converted into the right to receive the Merger Consideration (as defined below) and each issued and outstanding share of Preferred Stock, par value $1 per share, of WCI ("WCI Preferred Stock") not owned directly or through a wholly-owned Subsidiary by Time or WCI will be converted into the right to receive Preferred Stock, par value $1.00 per share, of Time, all as provided herein;

WHEREAS Time, Sub and WCI desire to make certain representations, warranties and agreements in connection with the Offer and the Merger and also to prescribe various conditions of the Offer and the Merger;

WHEREAS subsequent to the execution and delivery of the Agreement and Plan of Merger dated as of March 3, 1989 (as amended and restated on May 19, 1989, the "Original Agreement"), (i) WCI has redeemed its $3.625 Series A Convertible Exchangeable Preferred Stock, par value $1 per share (the "WCI Series A Preferred"), (ii) WCI has redeemed its Series C Cumulative Convertible Preferred Stock, par value $1 per share (the "WCI Series C Preferred") and (iii) Time and WCI have entered into Amendment No. 1 to the Share Exchange Agreement, dated April 12, 1989 (as amended, the "Share Exchange Agreement");

WHEREAS Time, Sub and WCI desire to amend and restate the Original Agreement to reflect the amendments and changes referred to above; and

WHEREAS Time, Sub and WCI do not intend by this amendment and restatement to reaffirm as of any date subsequent to March 3, 1989, the representations and warranties previously made herein, unless the context otherwise requires, and accordingly they agree that all references to "the date of this Agreement", "the date hereof", and terms of similar import shall refer to March 3, 1989, the original date of execution and delivery of the Original Agreement.

NOW, THEREFORE, pursuant to Section 7.3 of the Original Agreement and in consideration of the premises and the representations, warranties and agreements herein contained, the Original Agreement is hereby amended and restated in its entirety to read as follows:

ARTICLE I

THE OFFER AND THE MERGER

1.1. *The Offer.* (a) *General.* Subject to the provisions of this Agreement, as promptly as practicable, but in no event later than five business days after June 16, 1989, Time shall commence the Offer. The obligations of Time to commence the Offer and accept for payment, and pay for, any shares of WCI Common Stock tendered pursuant to the Offer shall be subject to the conditions set forth in Exhibit A, any of which may be waived by Time in its sole discretion (other than the Minimum Tender Condition (as defined in Exhibit A), which may be waived only with the consent of WCI). Time expressly reserves the right to modify the terms of the Offer, except that, without the consent of WCI, Time shall not (i) amend the Offer so that it is at a price less than $70 net per share in cash (adjusted as provided in Section 1.1(c)), (ii) amend the Offer so that it is for more or less than 100,000,000 shares of

Section 1.1(b). This provision is another compromise on how the risks of delay are shared. Time agrees that the price will go up at the 9% rate, but not during an injunction and not to the extent of the dividends accruing after a future date. See Section 5.15 on dividends. Probably, the treatment of the payment is in part driven by the interest that accrues after 60 days on the merger consideration. See Section 2.1(f).

Section 1.1(c). The adjustment in case Warner distributes its interest in the Chris-Craft joint venture is similar to the adjustment of the exchange ratio under Section 2.1(f) of the old agreement.

Section 1.1(d). Mainly, Time and Warner are agreeing to meet their obligations under the securities laws with respect to the tender offer. What is gained from this kind of provision is that it is made explicit that each of the parties has a right to terminate if the other does not fulfill the obligation.

WCI Common Stock, (iii) modify or add to the conditions set forth in Exhibit A, (iv) extend the Offer, (v) change the form of consideration payable in the Offer or (vi) make any other change in terms or conditions in the Offer that is otherwise materially adverse to the holders of shares of WCI Common Stock; *provided, however,* that Time may without the consent of WCI, (a) extend the Offer if at the scheduled expiration date of the Offer any of the conditions to Time's obligation to purchase shares of WCI Common Stock shall not be satisfied until such time as such terms or conditions are satisfied and, (b) extend the Offer for any reason for a period of not more than 60 days beyond July 17, 1989. Notwithstanding the failure to satisfy the Minimum Tender Condition, Time shall (unless permitted to terminate the Offer pursuant to paragraphs (b) or (d) of Exhibit A) extend the Offer (i) pursuant to clause (b) of the foregoing proviso to satisfy its obligation under Section 5.21 to arrange the funds necessary to consummate the Offer and the Merger and (ii) pursuant to clause (a) of the foregoing proviso during the pendency of any Injunction (as defined in Section 6.1(b)) to the extent it shall toll the period referred to in Section 7.1(e). Subject to the terms and conditions of the Offer and this Agreement, Time shall pay for the number of shares of WCI Common Stock sought pursuant to the Offer which are validly tendered and not withdrawn pursuant to the Offer as soon as practicable after termination of the Offer.

(b) *Additional Consideration; Per Share Price; Purchase Time.* If the Purchase Time (as defined below) shall occur after the 60th day following the day on which the Offer shall have commenced, Time shall pay additional consideration equal to interest on the amount otherwise required to be paid per share at the Purchase Time pursuant to the terms of the Offer at the rate of 9% per annum (calculated on the basis of the actual number of days in the period) from but excluding such 60th day to but including the day on which the Purchase Time occurs; *provided, however,* that any day during such 60 day period or thereafter during which the acceptance for payment of shares of WCI Common Stock is not possible because of an Injunction (as defined in Section 6.1(b)) shall not be included in the calculation of such 60 day period or the number of days in respect of which such additional consideration shall be so payable and *provided, further,* that the amount of any such additional consideration per share otherwise payable shall be reduced by the amount of any cash dividend per share paid by WCI after August 17, 1989.

As used in this Agreement, (i) the term "Per Share Price" shall mean the price per share of WCI Common Stock paid by Time pursuant to the Offer (which includes any amendments to the terms thereof pursuant hereto), excluding any additional consideration paid pursuant to this Section 1.1(b), and (ii) the term "Purchase Time" shall mean the time at which Time accepts for payment shares of WCI Common Stock in the Offer.

(c) *BHC Distribution.* In the event of a Distribution (as defined below) to holders of record of WCI Common Stock as of any time prior to the Purchase Time, the price to be paid in the Offer shall be reduced to an amount net per share in cash equal to $70 minus an amount equal to the sum of (x)(1) the BHC Per Share Offer Value times (2) the number of shares of Common Stock, par value $.10 per share ("BHC Common Stock"), of BHC, Inc., a Delaware corporation ("BHC"), distributed per share of WCI Common Stock in the Distribution plus (y) the amount of any cash in lieu of fractional shares distributed per share of WCI Common Stock in the Distribution. The term "BHC Per Share Offer Value" shall mean the average of the closing or last sale prices of the BHC Common Stock for the 20 trading days (or if 20 trading days shall not have elapsed, such fewer number of trading days, not less than five as shall have elapsed) immediately prior to the second trading day preceding the day on which the Purchase Time occurs on the principal trading market for the BHC Common Stock. The term "Distribution" shall mean a pro rata dividend or other distribution by WCI (regardless of whether paid prior to or on or after the Effective Time) of any or all of its shares of capital stock of BHC to holders of record of shares of WCI Common Stock and WCI Series B Preferred (as defined in Section 2.1(d)) (treating such shares of WCI Series B Preferred as if they had been converted into shares of WCI Common Stock immediately prior to such record date pursuant to their terms).

(d) *Offer Documents.* As promptly as reasonably practicable, Time shall file with the Securities and Exchange Commission (the "SEC") a Tender Offer Statement on Schedule 14D-1 with respect to the Offer, which shall contain an offer to purchase and a related letter of transmittal and summary advertisement (such Schedule 14D-1 and the documents therein pursuant to which the Offer will be

2

Section 1.1, cont'd.

The reference to comments from the SEC or its staff on the offer documents reflects a recent development. Under the statute and SEC rules, tender offer documents do not have to be filed and cleared with the SEC in advance, unlike materials used to sell securities or to solicit proxies. Tender offer documents must be filed no later than the day the offer begins. In the past the SEC did not comment on them on a routine basis. Now, however, the SEC routinely gives comments on tender offer filings. It is quite clear in the statute that the SEC cannot act as a censor in tender offers. In fact, the offer to purchase is usually well under way by the time the SEC begins its review. But its comments have to be taken seriously, which generally means an amended filing and a new mailing to shareholders. Lesson: even under free-market Republican administrations bureaucracies have a tendency to expand.

Section 1.2. A company that is the subject of a tender offer has the option, under SEC rules, to keep the names of its shareholders to itself and to do the mailing of the offer for the bidder at the bidder's expense or to give the list of shareholders to the bidder. Rule 14d–5. In negotiated acquisitions there is usually no reason for the target to limit cooperation.

Section 1.3. Under SEC rules a target company's board must take a position (for, against or neutral) on a tender offer within ten business days. In a friendly transaction the recommendation of the target company's board is included as a part of the bidder's tender offer mailing. Shareholders then understand right away that their board of directors favors the transaction. This procedure also avoids confusing shareholders with a second mailing.

Section 1.4. Many tender offers are made by a special-purpose subsidiary set up to make the offer (TW Sub, for example). Generally, as here, the parent company stands behind the offer. Time is reserving the right to make certain formal changes in the form of the acquisition. None of these changes should affect the economic or legal positions of the Warner shareholders.

made, together with any supplements or amendments thereto, the "Offer Documents"). The Offer Documents shall comply as to form in all material respects with the requirements of the Securities Exchange Act of 1934, as amended (the "Exchange Act"), and the rules and regulations promulgated thereunder and, on the date filed with the SEC and on the date first published, sent or given to the holders of shares of WCI Common Stock, shall not contain any untrue statement of a material fact or omit to state any material fact required to be stated therein or necessary in order to make the statements therein, in light of the circumstances under which they are made, not misleading, except that no representation is made by Time with respect to information supplied by WCI specifically for inclusion in the Offer Documents. Each of Time, Sub and WCI agrees promptly to correct any information supplied by it specifically for inclusion in the Offer Documents if and to the extent that such information shall have become false or misleading in any material respect, and Time further agrees to take all steps necessary to cause the Offer Documents as so corrected to be filed with the SEC and to be disseminated to holders of shares of WCI Common Stock, in each case as and to the extent required by applicable Federal securities laws. Time agrees to provide WCI and its counsel in writing with any comments Time or its counsel may receive from the SEC or its staff with respect to the Offer Documents promptly after the receipt of such comments.

1.2. *Stockholder Lists.* In connection with the Offer, WCI shall (a) cause its transfer agent to furnish Time with mailing labels containing the names and addresses of the record holders of WCI Common Stock as of a recent date and of those persons becoming record holders after such date, together with copies of all security position listings and computer files and all other information in WCI's possession or control regarding the beneficial owners of WCI Common Stock, and (b) furnish to Time such information and assistance as Time may reasonably request in communicating the Offer to WCI's stockholders. Subject to the requirements of law, and except for such steps as are necessary to disseminate the Offer and any other documents necessary to consummate the Merger, Time and Sub shall hold in confidence the information contained in any such labels and lists, will use such information only in connection with the Offer and the Merger and, if this Agreement is terminated, will, upon request, deliver to WCI all copies of, and any extracts or summaries from, such information then in their possession.

1.3. *WCI Action.* WCI hereby consents to the Offer. WCI shall, as soon as practicable on or after the date of commencement of the Offer, file with the SEC a Solicitation/Recommendation Statement on Schedule 14D-9 (as amended from time to time, the "Schedule 14D-9") which shall reflect the recommendations of WCI's Board of Directors described in Section 3.1(o); and copies of the Schedule 14D-9 (excluding exhibits) shall be enclosed with the Offer Documents to be mailed to stockholders of WCI in connection with the Offer. The Schedule 14D-9 shall comply as to form in all material respects with the requirements of the Exchange Act and the rules and regulations promulgated thereunder and, on the date filed with the SEC and on the date first published, sent or given to the holders of shares of WCI Common Stock, shall not contain any untrue statement of a material fact or omit to state any material fact required to be stated therein or necessary in order to make the statements therein, in light of the circumstances under which they are made, not misleading, except that no representation is made by WCI with respect to information supplied by Time or Sub specifically for inclusion in the Schedule 14D-9. Each of WCI, Time and Sub agrees promptly to correct any information supplied by it specifically for inclusion in the Schedule 14D-9 which shall have become false or misleading in any material respect and WCI agrees to take all steps necessary to cause the Schedule 14D-9 as so corrected to be filed with the SEC and disseminated to holders of shares of WCI Common Stock, in each case as and to the extent required by applicable Federal securities laws. WCI agrees to provide Time and its counsel in writing with any comments WCI or its counsel may receive from the SEC or its staff with respect to the Schedule 14D-9 promptly after the receipt of such comments.

1.4. *Time May Transfer Obligations.* Time shall have the right effective upon written notice to WCI to transfer or assign, in whole or from time to time in part, to Sub or to one or more other wholly-owned subsidiaries of Time, the right to purchase shares of WCI Common Stock tendered pursuant to the Offer, but any such transfer or assignment will not relieve Time of its obligations under the Offer and will in no way prejudice the rights of tendering stockholders to receive payment for their shares of WCI Common Stock validly tendered and accepted for payment pursuant to the Offer.

Sections 1.5–1.7. In the original agreement the closing was to be held at 10:00 a.m. on an unspecified date. Now the time is left open. After the Paramount offer created a crisis it probably made sense to have the flexibility to hold a closing in the middle of the night if necessary. Of course that could have been done anyway by amending the agreement. But that might have been awkward, particularly when faced with so much litigation. Otherwise, the mechanics of the merger are unchanged from the earlier agreement.

Section 1.8. The Share Exchange Agreement does not allow Time and Warner to vote the exchanged shares for the merger agreement, but they can vote any other shares they own. See the discussion of the Share Exchange Agreement in Chapter 17.

1.5. *Effective Time of the Merger.* Subject to the provisions of this Agreement, a certificate of merger (the "Certificate of Merger") shall be duly prepared, executed and acknowledged by the Surviving Corporation (as defined in Section 1.7) and thereafter delivered to the Secretary of State of the State of Delaware, for filing, as provided in the Delaware General Corporation Law (the "DGCL"), as soon as practicable on or after the Closing Date (as defined in Section 1.6). The Merger shall become effective upon the filing of the Certificate of Merger with the Secretary of State of the State of Delaware or at such time thereafter as is provided in the Certificate of Merger (the "Effective Time").

1.6. *Closing of the Merger.* The closing of the Merger (the "Closing") will take place at a time and on a date to be specified by the parties, which shall be no later than the second business day after satisfaction of the latest to occur of the conditions set forth in Article VI (the "Closing Date"), at the offices of Cravath, Swaine & Moore, One Chase Manhattan Plaza, New York, N.Y. 10005, unless another time, date or place is agreed to in writing by the parties hereto.

1.7. *Effects of the Merger.* (a) At the Effective Time, (i) the separate existence of Sub shall cease and Sub shall be merged with and into WCI (Sub and WCI are sometimes referred to herein as the "Constituent Corporations" and WCI is sometimes referred to herein as the "Surviving Corporation"), (ii) the Certificate of Incorporation of WCI shall be amended so that Article FOURTH of such Certificate of Incorporation reads in its entirety as follows: "The total number of shares of all classes of stock which the Corporation shall have authority to issue is 1,000, all of which shall consist of Common Stock, par value $1 per share.", and, as so amended, such Certificate shall be the Certificate of Incorporation of the Surviving Corporation and (iii) the By-laws of WCI as in effect immediately prior to the Effective Time shall be the By-laws of the Surviving Corporation.

(b) At and after the Effective Time, the Surviving Corporation shall possess all the rights, privileges, powers and franchises of a public as well as of a private nature, and be subject to all the restrictions, disabilities and duties of each of the Constituent Corporations; and all and singular rights, privileges, powers and franchises of each of the Constituent Corporations, and all property, real, personal and mixed, and all debts due to either of the Constituent Corporations on whatever account, as well as for stock subscriptions and all other things in action or belonging to each of the Constituent Corporations, shall be vested in the Surviving Corporation; and all property, rights, privileges, powers and franchises, and all and every other interest shall be thereafter as effectually the property of the Surviving Corporation as they were of the Constituent Corporations, and the title to any real estate vested by deed or otherwise, in either of the Constituent Corporations, shall not revert or be in any way impaired; but all rights of creditors and all liens upon any property of either of the Constituent Corporations shall be preserved unimpaired, and all debts, liabilities and duties of the Constituent Corporations shall thenceforth attach to the Surviving Corporation, and may be enforced against it to the same extent as if said debts and liabilities had been incurred by it.

1.8. *Share Exchange Agreement.* Neither the consummation of the Offer nor the consummation of the Merger shall be deemed to be prohibited by the Share Exchange Agreement and nothing in the Share Exchange Agreement shall be deemed to prohibit Time or Sub from voting any WCI Common Stock acquired by it other than pursuant to the Share Exchange Agreement in favor of the Merger. Time and WCI hereby waive any requirement for the issuance of shares of Time Common Stock pursuant to Section 4 of the Share Exchange Agreement. Except as set forth herein, no provision of the Share Exchange Agreement shall be deemed to be waived by virtue of this Agreement.

ARTICLE II

EFFECT OF THE MERGER ON THE CAPITAL STOCK OF THE CONSTITUENT CORPORATIONS; EXCHANGE OF CERTIFICATES

2.1. *Effect on Capital Stock.* As of the Effective Time, by virtue of the Merger and without any action on the part of the holder of any shares of WCI Common Stock, WCI Preferred Stock or capital stock of Sub:

4

Section 2.1(c). The description of the effects of the merger is also unchanged from the earlier agreement, except that the most important fact – what consideration the Warner shareholders will receive for their shares in the merger – is no longer specified. See commentary to Page 6.

(a) *Capital Stock of Sub.* Each issued and outstanding share of the capital stock of Sub shall be converted into and become one fully paid and nonassessable share of Common Stock, par value $1 per share, of the Surviving Corporation.

(b) *Cancelation of Treasury Stock and Time-Owned Stock.* All shares of WCI Common Stock and WCI Preferred Stock that are owned by WCI as treasury stock or by any Subsidiary of WCI, and any shares of WCI Common Stock or WCI Preferred Stock owned by Sub or any affiliate of Sub shall be canceled and retired and shall cease to exist and no stock of Time or other consideration shall be delivered in exchange therefor. All shares of common stock, par value $1.00 per share, of Time ("Time Common Stock") owned by WCI shall remain unaffected by the Merger. As used in this Agreement, the word "Subsidiary" means any corporation or other organization, whether incorporated or unincorporated, of which such party or any other Subsidiary of such party is a general partner (excluding partnerships, the general partnership interests of which held by such party or any Subsidiary of such party do not have a majority of the voting interest in such partnership) or at least a majority of the securities or other interests having by their terms ordinary voting power to elect a majority of the Board of Directors or others performing similar functions with respect to such corporation or other organization is directly or indirectly owned or controlled by such party or by any one or more of its Subsidiaries, or by such party and one or more of its Subsidiaries.

(c) *WCI Common Stock.* Each issued and outstanding share of WCI Common Stock (other than shares to be canceled in accordance with Section 2.1(b)) outstanding immediately prior to the Effective Time (except shares of WCI Common Stock held by persons who object to the Merger and comply with all provisions of the DGCL concerning the right of such holders to dissent from the Merger and demand appraisal of their shares ("Dissenting Common Holders"), unless such rights are not available to such holders under the DGCL) shall be converted into the right to receive the Merger Consideration (as defined below). All such shares of WCI Common Stock, other than shares held by Dissenting Common Holders, shall no longer be outstanding and shall automatically be canceled and retired and shall cease to exist, and each holder of a certificate representing any such shares shall cease to have any rights with respect thereto, except the right to receive the Merger Consideration in consideration therefor upon the surrender of such certificate in accordance with Section 2.2, without interest.

(d) *Exchange of Preferred Stock.* Each share of Series B Variable Rate Cumulative Convertible Preferred Stock, par value $1 per share (the "WCI Series B Preferred"), of WCI outstanding immediately prior to the Effective Time (except shares of WCI Series B Preferred held by persons who object to the Merger and comply with all provisions of the DGCL concerning the right of such holders to dissent from the Merger and demand appraisal of their shares ("Dissenting Preferred Holders" and together with Dissenting Common Holders "Dissenting Holders")) shall be converted into the right to receive one share of Series BB Variable Rate Cumulative Convertible Preferred Stock of Time, par value $1.00 per share ("Time Series BB Preferred"), such Time Series BB Preferred to have the terms set forth on Exhibit 2.1(d). All such shares of WCI Series B Preferred, other than shares held by Dissenting Preferred Holders, shall no longer be outstanding and shall automatically be canceled and retired and shall cease to exist, and each holder of a certificate representing any such shares of WCI Series B Preferred shall cease to have any rights with respect thereto, except the right to receive the shares of Time Series BB Preferred to be issued in consideration therefor upon the surrender of such certificate in accordance with Section 2.2, without interest.

(e) *Shares of Dissenting Holders.* Any issued and outstanding shares of WCI Common Stock or WCI Series B Preferred held by a Dissenting Holder shall not be converted as described in Sections 2.1(c) and (d) but shall from and after the Effective Time represent only the right to receive such consideration as may be determined to be due to such Dissenting Holder pursuant to the DGCL; *provided, however,* that shares of WCI Common Stock or WCI Series B Preferred outstanding immediately prior to the Effective Time and held by a Dissenting Holder who shall, after the Effective Time, withdraw his demand for appraisal or lose his right of appraisal, in either case pursuant to the DGCL, shall be deemed to be converted, as of the Effective Time, into the

Section 2.1 (f). Time and Warner did not have time to agree on what the Warner shareholders would receive in the merger. Moreover, in the light of the intense opposition they were facing, they may have thought it unwise to be too specific. This long paragraph gives the details that could be agreed upon, but omits those that shareholders would care most about.

What is given is a formula and a method for resolving disputes. Time agrees to pay some combination of cash and securities in the merger. The general principle is that this package must be worth what was paid in the tender offer. As originally filed with the SEC, three references in the printed text to 'an approximate value' that the merger securities would have were corrected by hand to 'value.' If the parties and their investment bankers could not agree on the package, a large amount of cash would be included, reducing the magnitude of the valuation problem. If they still could not agree, the bankers for the two sides would select a third firm to resolve the dispute.

The last paragraph ensures that the merger consideration increases at a 9% interest rate if the merger is delayed. Otherwise, a delay could make what shareholders receive in the merger worth less than the tender offer price. This possibility might have opened both Time and Warner to criticism by Warner shareholders for making the offer coercive to encourage tendering. Courts have been critical of 'front-end loaded' offers both as hostile bids and as defensive responses. See *Unocal Corp.* v. *Mesa Petroleum Co.*, 493 A.2d 946 (Delaware Supreme Court 1985); *AC Acquisitions Corp.* v. *Anderson, Clayton & Co.*, 519 A.2d 103 (Delaware Chancery Court 1986).

right to receive the Merger Consideration, as specified in section 2.1(c), or the shares of Time Series BB Preferred, specified in Section 2.1(d), in either case without interest.

(f) *Merger Consideration.* Subject to the immediately succeeding paragraph, the term "Merger Consideration" shall mean cash or debt or equity securities of Time, which may include, without limitation, Time Common Stock or preferred stock of Time or securities convertible into or exchangeable for Time Common Stock or preferred stock of Time (collectively the "Merger Securities"), or a combination thereof, as shall be agreed upon by Time and WCI, having a value (in the case of Merger Securities, on a fully distributed basis) per share of WCI Common Stock, equal, as nearly as practicable, in the opinion of two investment banking firms of national reputation as of the date of their opinion, one selected by Time and one selected by WCI, to the Merger Consideration Amount (as defined below); *provided, however,* that if within 30 days following the day on which the Purchase Time occurs (i) Time and WCI have been unable to agree on the combination of cash and/or securities constituting the Merger Consideration or (ii) either of such investment banking firms have been unable to provide the opinion referred to above, then the Merger Consideration shall consist of (x) equity securities of Time as shall be agreed upon by Time and WCI having a value (on a fully distributed basis) per share of WCI Common Stock (determined on the basis of two opinions of investment banking firms of national reputation as provided above as of the date of their opinion) equal, as nearly as practicable, to 40% (or at the option of Time 60%) of the Merger Consideration Amount, and (y) cash equal to 60% (or 40% if Time exercises such option) of the Merger Consideration Amount; and *provided, further,* that if within 15 days following the expiration of the 30 day period set forth above (i) Time and WCI have been unable to agree on the equity securities component of the Merger Consideration referred to in clause (x) of the foregoing proviso or (ii) either of such investment banking firms have been unable to provide the opinion referred to in such proviso, then the equity securities component of the Merger Consideration referred to in clause (x) of the foregoing proviso shall be determined as follows: (A) within seven days following the expiration of such 15-day period, two investment banking firms of national reputation, one selected by Time and one selected by WCI, shall each propose equity securities of Time which in the opinion of such investment banking firm have a value as of the date of their opinion (on a fully distributed basis) per share of WCI Common Stock equal, as nearly as practicable, to 40% (or 60% if Time exercises the option referred to above) of the Merger Consideration Amount, and (B) within seven days after the expiration of such initial seven-day period, a third investment banking firm of national reputation selected by the two firms referred to in the foregoing clause (A) shall select the proposal of one of such investment banking firms which in its opinion has a value equal, as nearly as practicable, to 40% (or 60% if Time exercises the option referred to above) of the Merger Consideration Amount but if in its opinion neither proposal is so equal then, in making its selection, such third investment banking firm shall be entitled to adjust the yield or change the amount (but not the type) of any equity securities included in the proposal selected by such firm so as to enable such firm to give its opinion; and the proposal so selected (as so adjusted) shall constitute the equity securities component of the Merger Consideration. The term "Merger Consideration Amount" shall mean the Per Share Price; *provided, however,* that in the event of a Distribution to holders of record of WCI Common Stock as of any time after the Purchase Time and prior to the Effective Time, the term Merger Consideration Amount shall mean the Per Share Price minus an amount equal to the sum of (x) (1) the BHC Per Share Merger Value times (2) the number of shares of BHC Common Stock, distributed per share of WCI Common Stock in the Distribution plus (y) the amount of any cash distributed in lieu of fractional shares per share of WCI Common Stock in the Distribution. The term "BHC Per Share Merger Value" shall mean the average of the closing or last sale prices of the BHC Common Stock for the 20 trading days (or if 20 trading days shall not have elapsed, such fewer number of trading days, not less than five as shall have elapsed) immediately prior to the day on which the Effective Time occurs on the principal trading market for the BHC Common Stock. Subject to the terms of this Agreement, Time and Sub shall consummate the Merger as soon as practicable following the determination of the Merger Consideration.

If the Effective Time shall occur after the 60th day following the day on which the Offer shall have commenced, Time shall pay additional consideration (which shall be deemed to form part of

6

Section 2.1(g). In this agreement the options are cashed out. In the earlier version they became options for Time stock. The change is consistent with the change in the form of the transaction. Warner is now being acquired. On the other hand, many of the hallmarks of a merger of equals still survive, such as an initial board chosen by the two sides and a sharing of top executive positions. Clearly this change is likely to be highly advantageous for Warner management. They are cashed out on their old options at a premium and no doubt will receive new options in Time stock. Yet, as we have pointed out, they appear to have had a clear preference for the original deal with a financially stronger surviving company.

A last-minute, handwritten marginal change in the version originally filed with the SEC took care of a detail that could be worth a significant amount of money to Warner optionholders. The words 'without giving effect to a Distribution' were added to the formulas in (i) and (ii). If BHC shares are distributed Warner as a company is less valuable and the value of the consideration paid in the merger goes down. The option value would not go down, however.

Stock appreciation rights are treated similarly.

the Merger Consideration) equal to interest on the Merger Consideration Amount at a rate of 9% per annum (calculated on the basis of the actual number of days in the period) from but excluding such 60th day to but including the day on which the Effective Time occurs; *provided, however,* that any day during such 60 day period or thereafter during which the acceptance for payment of shares of WCI Common Stock pursuant to the Offer or consummation of the Merger is not possible because of an Injunction (as defined below) shall not be included in the calculation of such 60 day period or the number of days in respect of which such additional consideration shall be so payable; and *provided, further,* that the amount of any such additional consideration per share otherwise payable shall be reduced by the amount of any cash dividend per share paid by WCI after August 17, 1989.

(g) *Stock Options, Bonus Units, etc.* (i) Immediately prior to the Effective Time, each stock option (a "WCI Stock Option") granted by WCI or Lorimar pursuant to (A) the WCI 1986 Stock Option and Appreciation Rights Plan (other than options held by persons who have agreed otherwise with WCI), and the WCI 1974 Common Stock Option Plan, and (B) the 1985 Employee Stock Option Plan, the 1983 Incentive Stock Option Plan, the 1980 (Incentive) Stock Option Plan, the 1981 Incentive Stock Option Plan, the 1985 Employee Stock Option Plan, the 1985 Non-Employee Stock Option Plan, the 1982 Non-Employee Stock Option Plan in each case of Lorimar or its predecessor which is then outstanding, whether or not then vested or exercisable in accordance with its terms, shall become exercisable in full and shall be canceled in exchange for an amount of cash which is equal to the product of (1) the amount by which the Per Share Price (plus any additional consideration paid pursuant to Section 2.1(f)) but without giving effect to a Distribution exceeds the exercise price per share of such option and (2) the number of shares of WCI Common Stock issuable pursuant to the unexercised portion of such option, subject to any required withholding of taxes.

(ii) Immediately prior to the Effective Time, each stock appreciation right ("SAR") (other than an SAR which is only exercisable in lieu of a stock option) granted by WCI pursuant to the WCI 1986 Stock Option and Appreciation Rights Plan and each bonus unit (a "Bonus Unit") granted by WCI pursuant to the WCI 1982 Bonus Unit Plan which is then outstanding, whether or not then vested or exercisable in accordance with its terms, shall become exercisable in full and shall be canceled in exchange for amount of cash which is equal to the product of (1) the amount by which the Per Share Price (plus any additional consideration paid pursuant to Section 2.1(f)) but without giving effect to a Distribution exceeds the appreciation base per share of WCI Common Stock for such SAR or measuring price per share of WCI Common Stock for such Bonus Unit, as the case may be and (2) the number of shares of WCI Common Stock covered by such SAR or Bonus Unit, as the case may be, subject to any required withholding of taxes.

(iii) WCI shall use its best efforts to obtain all necessary waivers, consents and amendments in order to implement the provisions of this Section 2.1(g). Such provisions will not apply, however, in any case where such waiver, consent or amendment has not been obtained.

2.2. *Exchange of Certificates.* (a) *Exchange Agent.* As of the Effective Time, Time shall deposit with Manufacturers Hanover Trust Company or such other bank or trust company designated by Time (and reasonably acceptable to WCI) (the "Exchange Agent"), for the benefit of the holders of shares of WCI Common Stock and WCI Series B Preferred, for exchange in accordance with this Article II, through the Exchange Agent, cash and/or securities representing the Merger Consideration and Time Series BB Preferred (such Merger Consideration and Time Series BB Preferred, together with any interest, dividends or distributions with respect thereto, being hereinafter referred to as the "Exchange Fund") to be paid pursuant to Section 2.1 in exchange for outstanding shares of WCI Common Stock and WCI Series B Preferred in the Merger.

(b) *Exchange Procedures.* As soon as reasonably practicable after the Effective Time, the Exchange Agent shall mail to each holder of record of a certificate or certificates which immediately prior to the Effective Time represented outstanding shares of WCI Common Stock or WCI Series B Preferred (the "Certificates") whose shares were converted into the right to receive Merger Consideration or shares of Time Series BB Preferred pursuant to Section 2.1, (i) a letter of transmittal (which shall specify that delivery shall be effected, and risk of loss and title to the Certificates shall pass,

Section 2.2. These merger details are essentially unchanged. The possibility that cash or securities other than common stock may be issued required some rewording.

only upon delivery of the Certificates to the Exchange Agent and shall be in such form and have such other provisions as Time and WCI may reasonably specify) and (ii) instructions for use in effecting the surrender of the Certificates in exchange for Merger Consideration or shares of Time Series BB Preferred. Upon surrender of a Certificate for cancelation to the Exchange Agent or to such other agent or agents as may be appointed by Time and Sub, together with such letter of transmittal, duly executed, the holder of such Certificate shall be entitled to receive in exchange therefor a check and/or one or more certificates representing that amount of cash and that number of whole denominations of Merger Securities or Time Series BB Preferred which such holder has the right to receive pursuant to the provisions of this Article II, and the Certificate so surrendered shall forthwith be canceled. In the event of a transfer of ownership of WCI Common Stock or WCI Series B Preferred which is not registered in the transfer records of WCI, a check and/or one or more certificates representing the proper amount of cash and proper number of whole denominations of Merger Securities or Time Series BB Preferred may be issued to a transferee if the Certificate representing such WCI Common Stock or WCI Series B Preferred is presented to the Exchange Agent, accompanied by all documents required to evidence and effect such transfer and by evidence that any applicable stock transfer taxes have been paid. Until surrendered as contemplated by this Section 2.2, each Certificate shall be deemed at any time after the Effective Time to represent only the right to receive upon such surrender the check and one or more certificates representing denominations of Merger Securities or Time Series BB Preferred and any cash in lieu of any fractional Merger Security as contemplated by this Section 2.2.

(c) *Distributions with Respect to Unexchanged Shares.* No interest paid or dividends or other distributions declared or made after the Effective Time with respect to Merger Securities or Time Series BB Preferred with a record date after the Effective Time shall be paid to the holder of any unsurrendered Certificate with respect to the Merger Securities or Time Series BB Preferred represented thereby and no cash payment in lieu of fractional Merger Securities shall be paid to any such holder pursuant to Section 2.2(e) until the holder of record of such Certificate shall surrender such Certificate. Subject to the effect of applicable laws, following surrender of any such Certificate, there shall be paid to the record holder of the certificates representing whole denominations of Merger Securities or Time Series BB Preferred issued in exchange therefor, without interest, (i) at the time of such surrender, the amount of any cash payable in lieu of a fractional Merger Security to which such holder is entitled pursuant to Section 2.2(e) and the amount of interest, dividends or other distributions with a record date after the Effective Time theretofore paid with respect to such Merger Securities or Time Series BB Preferred, and (ii) at the appropriate payment date, the amount of interest, dividends or other distributions with a record date after the Effective Time but prior to surrender and a payment date subsequent to surrender payable with respect to such Merger Securities or Time Series BB Preferred.

(d) *No Further Ownership Rights in WCI Common Stock or WCI Series B Preferred.* The Merger Consideration or Time Series BB Preferred paid or issued upon the surrender for exchange of shares of WCI Common Stock or WCI Series B Preferred in accordance with the terms hereof (including any cash paid pursuant to Section 2.2(c) or 2.2(e)) shall be deemed to have been issued in full satisfaction of all rights pertaining to such shares of WCI Common Stock or WCI Series B Preferred, *subject, however,* to the Surviving Corporation's obligation to pay any dividends or make any other distributions with a record date prior to the Effective Time which may have been declared or made by WCI on such shares of WCI Common Stock or WCI Series B Preferred in accordance with the terms of this Agreement or prior to the date hereof and which remain unpaid at the Effective Time, and there shall be no further registration of transfers on the stock transfer books of the Surviving Corporation of the shares of WCI Common Stock or WCI Series B Preferred which were outstanding immediately prior to the Effective Time. If, after the Effective Time, Certificates are presented to the Surviving Corporation for any reason, they shall be canceled and exchanged as provided in this Article II.

(e) *No Fractional Merger Securities.* (i) No certificates or scrip representing fractional denominations of Merger Securities shall be issued upon the surrender for exchange of Certificates, and such fractional interests will not entitle the owner thereof to vote or to any rights of a securityholder of Time.

8

Section 3.1. Most of the representations and warranties are repeated from the earlier agreement.

(ii) As promptly as practicable following the Effective Time, the Exchange Agent shall determine the excess of (x) the aggregate amount of each Merger Security delivered to the Exchange Agent by Time pursuant to Section 2.2(a) over (y) the aggregate amount of such Merger Security to be distributed to holders of WCI Common Stock pursuant to Section 2.2(b) (such excess being herein called the "Excess Securities"). As soon after the Effective Time as practicable, the Exchange Agent, as agent for the holders of WCI Common Stock, shall sell the Excess Securities of each Merger Security at then prevailing prices in the principal market for such Merger Security, all in the manner provided in paragraph (iii) of this Section.

(iii) The sale of the Excess Securities of any Merger Security by the Exchange Agent shall be executed through one or more firms of national standing which are participants in the relevant market for such Merger Security and shall be executed in round lots to the extent practicable. Until the net proceeds of such sale or sales have been distributed to the holders of WCI Common Stock, the Exchange Agent will hold such proceeds in trust for the holders of WCI Common Stock (the "Trust"). Time shall pay all commissions, transfer taxes and other out-of-pocket transaction costs, including the expenses and compensation, of the Exchange Agent incurred in connection with such sale of the Excess Securities. The Exchange Agent shall determine the portion of the Trust to which each holder of WCI Common Stock shall be entitled, if any, by multiplying the amount of the aggregate net proceeds comprising the Trust by a fraction the numerator of which is the amount of the fractional Merger Security interest to which such holder of WCI Common Stock is entitled and the denominator of which is the aggregate amount of fractional Merger Security interests to which all holders of WCI Common Stock are entitled.

(iv) As soon as practicable after the determination of the amount of cash, if any, to be paid to holders of WCI Common Stock in lieu of any fractional share interests, the Exchange Agent shall make available such amounts to such holders of WCI Common Stock.

(f) *Termination of Exchange Fund.* Any portion of the Exchange Fund and Trust which remains undistributed to the stockholders of WCI for six months after the Effective Time shall be delivered to Time, upon demand, and any stockholders of WCI who have not theretofore complied with this Article II shall thereafter look only to Time for payment of their claim for Merger Consideration, any cash in lieu of fractional Merger Security interests and any interest, dividends or distributions with respect to Merger Securities or Time Series BB Preferred.

(g) *No Liability.* Neither Time nor WCI shall be liable to any holder of shares of WCI Common Stock, WCI Series B Preferred, Merger Securities or Time Series BB Preferred, as the case may be, for such shares (or interest, dividends or distributions with respect thereto) or cash from the Trust delivered to a public official pursuant to any applicable abandoned property, escheat or similar law.

ARTICLE III
REPRESENTATIONS AND WARRANTIES

3.1 *Representations and Warranties of WCI.* WCI represents and warrants to Time and Sub as follows:

(a) *Organization, Standing and Power.* Each of WCI and its Significant Subsidiaries is a corporation or partnership duly organized, validly existing and in good standing under the laws of its state of incorporation or organization, has all requisite power and authority to own, lease and operate its properties and to carry on its business as now being conducted, and is duly qualified and in good standing to do business in each jurisdiction in which the nature of its business or the ownership or leasing of its properties makes such qualification necessary other than in such jurisdictions where the failure so to qualify would not have a material adverse effect on WCI and its Subsidiaries taken as a whole. As used in this Agreement, (i) a "Significant Subsidiary" means any Subsidiary of WCI or Time, as the case may be, that would constitute a Significant Subsidiary of such party within the meaning of Rule 1-02 of Regulation S-X of the SEC, and (ii) any reference to any event, change or effect being material with respect to any entity means an event, change or effect related to the condition (financial or otherwise), properties, assets, liabilities, businesses or operations of such entity.

(b) *Capital Structure.* As of the date hereof, the authorized capital stock of WCI consists of 500,000,000 shares of WCI Common Stock and 50,000,000 shares of WCI Preferred Stock. At the close of business on February 17, 1989, (i) 143,750,284 shares of WCI Common Stock were outstanding, 59,510,737 shares of WCI Common Stock were reserved for issuance upon the exercise of outstanding stock options or pursuant to WCI's Equity Unit Purchase Plan (such stock options and the Equity Unit Purchase Plan, collectively, the "WCI Stock Plans"), upon conversion of WCI Preferred Stock and upon conversion of $100,000,000 principal amount of 6% Convertible Senior Subordinated Debentures due August 17, 2001 (the "Lorimar Debentures"), of Lorimar Telepictures Corporation ("Lorimar"), (ii) 1,499,692 shares of WCI Common Stock were held by WCI in its treasury or by its wholly-owned Subsidiaries, (iii) 33,537,633 shares of WCI Preferred Stock, consisting of 11,152,552 shares of WCI Series A Preferred, 15,200,000 shares of WCI Series B Preferred and 7,185,081 shares of WCI Series C Preferred, were outstanding and, except for 15,836 shares of WCI Series A Preferred, none were held by WCI or any Subsidiary in its treasury, (iv) except for the Lorimar Debentures, no bonds, debentures, notes or other indebtedness having the right to vote (or convertible into securities having the right to vote) on any matters on which stockholders may vote ("Voting Debt"), were issued or outstanding and (v) WCI had contractual obligations with employees of or consultants to Lorimar to issue (the "Lorimar Stock Grants") (w) WCI Common Stock valued in the aggregate at not in excess of $50,000 on the date of issuance, (x) stock options with respect to WCI Common Stock valued in the aggregate at not in excess of $200,000 on the date of grant, (y) 40,424 shares of WCI Common Stock upon the exercise of options and (z) an option with respect to 9,187 shares of WCI Common Stock. All outstanding shares of WCI capital stock are, and any shares of WCI Common Stock issued pursuant to the Share Exchange Agreement will be, validly issued, fully paid and nonassessable and not subject to preemptive rights. As of the date of this Agreement, except for this Agreement, the Lorimar Stock Grants, WCI Stock Options, stock options disclosed in clause (v) of this Section 3.1(b), WCI Preferred Stock, obligations under WCI's Equity Unit Purchase Plan, the Lorimar Debentures, the Share Exchange Agreement and not in excess of 700,000 stock options available for issuance pursuant to the WCI Stock Plans, there are no options, warrants, calls, rights, or agreements to which WCI or any Subsidiary of WCI is a party or by which it is bound obligating WCI or any Subsidiary of WCI to issue, deliver or sell, or cause to be issued, delivered or sold, additional shares of capital stock or any Voting Debt of WCI or of any Subsidiary of WCI or obligating WCI or any Subsidary of WCI to grant, extend or enter into any such option, warrant, call, right or agreement, other than agreements to issue no more than an aggregate of 1,000,000 shares of WCI Common Stock. Assuming compliance by Time with Sections 2.1(g), and 5.20 and with the first sentence of Section 5.18, after the Effective Time, there will be no option, warrant, call, right or agreement obligating WCI or any Subsidiary of WCI to issue, deliver or sell, or cause to be issued, delivered or sold, any shares of capital stock or any Voting Debt of WCI or any Significant Subsidiary of WCI, or obligating WCI or any Subsidiary of WCI to grant, extend or enter into any such option, warrant, call, right or agreement.

(c) *Authority.* WCI has all requisite corporate power and authority to enter into this Agreement and the Share Exchange Agreement and, subject to approval of this Agreement by the stockholders of WCI, to consummate the transactions contemplated hereby and thereby. The execution and delivery of this Agreement and the Share Exchange Agreement and the consummation of the transactions contemplated hereby and thereby have been duly authorized by all necessary corporate action on the part of WCI, subject to such approval of this Agreement by the stockholders of WCI. This Agreement and the Share Exchange Agreement have been duly executed and delivered by WCI and, subject to such approval of this Agreement by the stockholders of WCI, each constitutes a valid and binding obligation of WCI enforceable in accordance with its terms. The execution and delivery of this Agreement and the Share Exchange Agreement do not, and the consummation of the transactions contemplated hereby and thereby will not, conflict with, or result in any violation of, or default (with or without notice or lapse of time, or both) under, or give rise to a right of termination, cancelation or acceleration of any obligation or the loss of a material benefit under, or the creation of a lien, pledge, security interest or other encumbrance on assets (any such conflict, violation, default, right of termination,

cancelation or acceleration, loss or creation, a "Violation"), pursuant to any provision of the Certificate of Incorporation or By-laws of WCI or any Subsidiary of WCI or, except (i) as set forth on Schedule 3.1(c) hereto or (ii) as contemplated by the next sentence hereof, result in any Violation of any loan or credit agreement, note, mortgage, indenture, lease, Benefit Plan (as defined in Section 3.1(j)) or other agreement, obligation, instrument, permit, concession, franchise, license, judgment, order, decree, statute, law, ordinance, rule or regulation applicable to WCI or any Subsidiary of WCI or their respective properties or assets which Violation would have a material adverse effect on WCI and its Subsidiaries taken as a whole. No consent, approval, order or authorization of, or registration, declaration or filing with, any court, administrative agency or commission or other governmental authority or instrumentality, domestic or foreign (a "Governmental Entity"), is required by or with respect to WCI or any of its Subsidiaries in connection with the execution and delivery of this Agreement and the Share Exchange Agreement by WCI or the consummation by WCI of the transactions contemplated hereby and thereby, the failure to obtain which would have a material adverse effect on WCI and its Subsidiaries, taken as a whole, except for (i) the filing of a premerger notification report by WCI under the Hart-Scott-Rodino Antitrust Improvements Act of 1976, as amended (the "HSR Act"), (ii) the filing with the SEC of (A) the Schedule 14D-9, (B) a proxy or information statement in definitive form relating to the meeting or action by written consent of WCI's stockholders to be held in connection with the Merger (the "Proxy Statement") and (C) such reports under Sections 13(a), 13(d) and 16(a) of the Securities Exchange Act of 1934, as amended (the "Exchange Act"), as may be required in connection with this Agreement, the Share Exchange Agreement and the transactions contemplated hereby and thereby, (iii) the filing of the Certificate of Merger with the Secretary of State of the State of Delaware and appropriate documents with the relevant authorities of other states in which WCI is qualified to do business, (iv) such filings, authorizations, orders and approvals (the "FCC Approvals") as may be required under the Communications Act of 1934, as amended (the "Communications Act"), and with and of state and local governmental authorities, including state and local authorities granting franchises to operate cable systems (the "Local Approvals") and pursuant to state takeover laws ("State Takeover Approvals"), (v) filings pursuant to Article 31-B of the New York Tax Law and (vi) such filings, authorizations, orders and approvals as may be required under foreign laws.

(d) *SEC Documents*. WCI has made available to Time a true and complete copy of each report, schedule, registration statement and definitive proxy statement filed by WCI with the SEC since January 1, 1986 (as such documents have since the time of their filing been amended, the "WCI SEC Documents") which are all the documents (other than preliminary material) that WCI was required to file with the SEC since such date. As of their respective dates, the WCI SEC Documents complied in all material respects with the requirements of the Securities Act of 1933, as amended (the "Securities Act"), or the Exchange Act, as the case may be, and the rules and regulations of the SEC thereunder applicable to such WCI SEC Documents (other than, in the case of certain WCI Schedules 13D, with respect to the timely filing thereof) and none of the WCI SEC Documents contained any untrue statement of a material fact or omitted to state a material fact required to be stated therein or necessary to make the statements therein, in light of the circumstances under which they were made, not misleading. The financial statements of WCI included in the WCI SEC Documents comply as to form in all material respects with applicable accounting requirements and with the published rules and regulations of the SEC with respect thereto, have been prepared in accordance with generally accepted accounting principles applied on a consistent basis during the periods involved (except as may be indicated in the notes thereto or, in the case of the unaudited statements, as permitted by Form 10-Q of the SEC) and fairly present (subject, in the case of the unaudited statements, to normal, recurring audit adjustments) the consolidated financial position of WCI and its consolidated Subsidiaries (other than Lorimar) as at the dates thereof and the consolidated results of the operations and cash flows (or changes in financial position prior to the approval of Statement of Financial Accounting Standards Number 95 ("FASB 95")) for the periods then ended. To the best of WCI's knowledge. the inclusion of Lorimar in the financial statements referred to in the preceding sentence would not cause the representations contained in this Section 3.1(d) to be false.

Section 3.1(e). The representation concerning information supplied by Warner has not been expanded to cover information it gives Time for use in the tender offer statement which is filed with the SEC (Schedule 14D–1). This is also true for Time's parallel representation to Warner. See Section 3.2(e). Probably, the information supplied is the same as the information supplied for the registration statement (Form S–4) and the proxy statement.

(e) *Information Supplied.* None of the information supplied or to be supplied by WCI for inclusion or incorporation by reference in (i) the registration statement on Form S-4 to be filed with the SEC by Time in connection with the issuance of any Merger Securities and Time Series BB Preferred in the Merger (the "S-4") will, at the time the S-4 is filed with the SEC and at the time it becomes effective under the Securities Act, contain any untrue statement of a material fact or omit to state any material fact required to be stated therein or necessary to make the statements therein not misleading, and (ii) the Proxy Statement will, at the date mailed to stockholders and at the time of the meetings of stockholders to be held in connection with the Merger, contain any untrue statement of a material fact or omit to state any material fact required to be stated therein or necessary in order to make the statements therein, in light of the circumstances under which they are made, not misleading. The Proxy Statement will comply as to form in all material respects with the provisions of the Exchange Act and the rules and regulations thereunder.

(f) *Compliance with Applicable Laws.* WCI and its Subsidiaries hold all permits, licenses, variances, exemptions, orders and approvals of all Governmental Entities which are material to the operation of the businesses of WCI and its Subsidiaries, taken as a whole (the "WCI Permits"). WCI and its Subsidiaries are in compliance with the terms of the WCI Permits, except where the failure so to comply would not have a material adverse effect on WCI and its Subsidiaries taken as a whole. Except as disclosed in the WCI SEC Documents filed prior to the date of this Agreement, the businesses of WCI and its Subsidiaries are not being conducted in violation of any law, ordinance or regulation of any Governmental Entity, except for possible violations which individually or in the aggregate do not, and, insofar as reasonably can be foreseen, in the future will not, have a material adverse effect on WCI and its Subsidiaries taken as a whole. Except as set forth in Schedule 3.1(f) hereto, as of the date of this Agreement, no investigation or review by any Governmental Entity with respect to WCI or any of its Subsidiaries is pending or, to the knowledge of WCI, threatened, nor has any Governmental Entity indicated an intention to conduct the same, other than, in each case, those the outcome of which, as far as reasonably can be foreseen, will not have a material adverse effect on WCI and its Subsidiaries taken as a whole.

(g) *Litigation.* As of the date of this Agreement, except as disclosed in the WCI SEC Documents filed prior to the date of this Agreement or in Schedule 3.1(g) hereto, there is no suit, action or proceeding pending, or, to the knowledge of WCI, threatened against or affecting WCI or any Subsidiary of WCI which is reasonably likely to have a material adverse effect on WCI and its Subsidiaries taken as a whole, nor is there any judgment, decree, injunction, rule or order of any Governmental Entity or arbitrator outstanding against WCI or any Subsidiary of WCI having, or which, insofar as reasonably can be foreseen, in the future could have, any such effect.

(h) *Taxes.* To the best of WCI's knowledge, WCI and each of its Subsidiaries has filed all tax returns required to be filed by any of them and has paid (or WCI has paid on its behalf), or has set up an adequate reserve for the payment of, all taxes required to be paid as shown on such returns and the most recent financial statements contained in the WCI SEC Documents reflect an adequate reserve for all taxes payable by WCI and its Subsidiaries accrued through the date of such financial statements. No material deficiencies for any taxes aggregating in excess of $300,000,000 have been proposed, asserted or assessed against WCI or any of its Subsidiaries. Except with respect to claims for refund, the Federal income tax returns of WCI and each of its Subsidiaries consolidated in such returns have been examined by and settled with the United States Internal Revenue Service (the "IRS"), or the statute of limitations with respect to such years has expired, for all years through 1976. The Federal income tax returns of WCI and each of its Subsidiaries consolidated in such returns for the years 1977-84 are currently under examination by the IRS. For the purpose of this Agreement, the term "tax" (including, with correlative meaning, the terms "taxes" and "taxable") shall include all Federal, state, local and foreign income, profits, franchise, gross receipts, payroll, sales, employment, use, property, withholding, excise and other taxes, duties or assessments of any nature whatsoever, together with all interest, penalties and additions imposed with respect to such amounts.

(i) *Certain Agreements.* Except as disclosed in the WCI SEC Documents filed prior to the date of this Agreement, or in a schedule to be delivered to Time within thirty days of the date hereof,

and except for this Agreement, as of the date of this Agreement, neither WCI nor any of its Subsidiaries is a party to any oral or written (i) consulting agreement not terminable on 60 days' or less notice involving the payment of more than $1,000,000 per annum or union, guild or collective bargaining agreement which agreement covers more than 1,000 employees, (ii) agreement with any executive officer or other key employee of WCI or any Significant Subsidiary of WCI the benefits of which are contingent, or the terms of which are materially altered, upon the occurrence of a transaction involving WCI of the nature contemplated by this Agreement or agreement with respect to any executive officer of WCI providing any term of employment or compensation guarantee extending for a period longer than three years and for the payment of in excess of $1,000,000 per annum, or (iii) agreement or plan, including any stock option plan, stock appreciation rights plan, restricted stock plan or stock purchase plan, any of the benefits of which will be increased, or the vesting of the benefits of which will be accelerated, by the occurrence of any of the transactions contemplated by this Agreement or the value of any of the benefits of which will be calculated on the basis of any of the transactions contemplated by this Agreement.

(j) *Benefit Plans.* (i) With respect to each employee benefit plan (including, without limitation, any "employee benefit plan", as defined in Section 3(3) of the Employee Retirement Income Security Act of 1974, as amended ("ERISA")) (All the foregoing being herein called "Benefit Plans"), maintained or contributed to by WCI or any of its Subsidiaries, WCI has made available to Time a true and correct copy of (a) the most recent annual report (Form 5500) filed with the IRS, (b) such Benefit Plan, (c) each trust agreement and group annuity contract, if any, relating to such Benefit Plan and (d) the most recent actuarial report or valuation relating to a Benefit Plan subject to Title IV of ERISA.

(ii) With respect to the Benefit Plans, individually and in the aggregate, no event has occurred, and to the knowledge of WCI or any of its Subsidiaries, there exists no condition or set of circumstances in connection with which WCI or any of its Subsidiaries could be subject to any liability that is reasonably likely to have a material adverse effect on WCI and its Subsidiaries, taken as a whole (except liability for benefits claims and funding obligations payable in the ordinary course) under ERISA, the Internal Revenue Code of 1986, as amended (the "Code"), or any other applicable law.

(iii) Except as set forth in Schedule 3.1(j), with respect to the Benefit Plans, individually and in the aggregate, there are no funded benefit obligations for which contributions have not been made or properly accrued and there are no unfunded benefit obligations which have not been accounted for by reserves, or otherwise properly footnoted in accordance with generally accepted accounting principles, on the financial statements of WCI or any of its Subsidiaries, which obligations are reasonably likely to have a material adverse effect on WCI and its Subsidiaries, taken as a whole.

(k) *Patents, Trademarks, etc.* WCI and its Subsidiaries have all patents, trademarks, trade names, service marks, trade secrets, copyrights and other proprietary intellectual property rights as are material in connection with the businesses of WCI and its Subsidiaries, taken as a whole.

(l) *CATV Systems, Franchises, Licenses, Permits, etc.* (i) WCI will provide Time, within thirty days of the date hereof, a complete list of the cable television systems ("CATV Systems") operated by WCI or any Subsidiary thereof as of the date hereof and the number of subscribers in each of such CATV Systems as of January 31, 1989.

(ii) WCI will provide Time, within thirty days of the date hereof, a list and brief description of all authorizations, approvals, certifications, licenses and permits issued by the FCC ("WCI FCC Authorizations") to WCI or any Subsidiary thereof as of the date hereof and all applications by WCI or any Subsidiary thereof for WCI FCC Authorizations which are pending on the date hereof.

(iii) WCI and its Subsidiaries (A) have all WCI FCC Authorizations and authorizations, approvals, franchises, licenses and permits of state or local governmental authorities ("Franchises") required for the operaton of the CATV Systems being operated on the date hereof, (B) have duly and currently filed all reports and other information required to be filed by the FCC or any other governmental authority in connection with such WCI FCC Authorizations and

Section 3.1(n). The investment banker's fairness opinion in the earlier agreement covered the fairness of 'the consideration to be received in the Merger.' The opinion was expanded for this agreement to cover the tender offer.

Section 3.1(o). This new section has been introduced because of the tender offer. The Warner board of directors promises it will recommend the offer to Warner shareholders. There were two last-minute changes here revealed by handwritten corrections on the first filing of this document. The first one made sure that Warner's directors were considering the fairness of the offer and merger together, giving Time some assurances in the face of possible arguments about coercion and timing risk. The second change was more interesting. A statement that the offer and merger are 'fair to and in the best interests of' Warner's shareholders was reduced to a statement that they are fair to them. Evidently the Warner board or its advisers saw an important distinction between fairness and best interests. Maybe they thought best interests involved too much speculation about the future. Warner's directors must have believed the distinction was tremendously important because they were willing to leave a roadmap emphasizing the omission for lawyers challenging the transaction.

The old section (q) concerning the desirability of pooling-of-interests accounting treatment has been eliminated. Now that Time was making a cash tender offer for more than one-half of the shares, pooling-of-interests accounting was no longer a possibility.

Franchises and (C) are not in violation of any WCI FCC Authorization or Franchise, other than the lack of WCI FCC Authorizations or Franchises, delays in filing reports or violations which, insofar as can reasonably be foreseen, would not have a material adverse effect on the CATV business conducted by WCI and its Subsidiaries taken as a whole.

(m) *Absence of Certain Changes or Events.* Except as disclosed in the WCI SEC Documents filed prior to the date of this Agreement or in the audited consolidated balance sheet of WCI and its Subsidiaries at December 31, 1988, and the related consolidated statements of operations, cash flows and changes in shareholders' equity (the "WCI 1988 Financials"), true and correct copies of which have been delivered to Time, or except as contemplated by this Agreement and the Share Exchange Agreement, since the date of the WCI 1988 Financials, WCI and its Subsidiaries have conducted their respective businesses only in the ordinary and usual course, and, as of the date of this Agreement, there has not been (i) any damage, destruction or loss, whether covered by insurance or not, which has, or insofar as reasonably can be foreseen in the future is reasonably likely to have, a material adverse effect on WCI and its Subsidiaries taken as a whole; (ii) any declaration, setting aside or payment of any dividend or other distribution (whether in cash, stock or property) with respect to any of WCI's capital stock, except for regular quarterly cash dividends of $.17 per share on WCI Common Stock and regular quarterly cash dividends on WCI Series B Preferred, in each case with usual record and payment dates for such dividends; or (iii) any transaction, commitment, dispute or other event or condition (financial or otherwise) of any character (whether or not in the ordinary course of business) individually or in the aggregate having or which, insofar as reasonably can be foreseen, in the future is reasonably likely to have, a material adverse effect on WCI and its Subsidiaries taken as a whole.

(n) *Opinion of Financial Advisor.* WCI has received the opinion of Lazard Freres & Co. dated June 16, 1989, to the effect that, as of such date, the consideration to be received by the stockholders of WCI in the Offer and the Merger, when taken together, is fair to WCI's stockholders from a financial point of view, a copy of which opinion has been delivered to Time.

(o) *Recommendation of WCI Board of Directors.* The Board of Directors of WCI by the unanimous vote of all directors present has approved each of the Offer and the Merger and determined that the Offer and the Merger are fair to and in the best interests of WCI's stockholders and has adopted resolutions recommending acceptance of the Offer and approval and adoption of the Merger Agreement and the Merger by the stockholders of WCI.

(p) *Article SEVENTH of WCI Certificate of Incorporation and Section 203 of the DGCL Not Applicable.* Neither the provisions of Article SEVENTH of WCI's Certificate of Incorporation nor the provisions of Section 203 of the DGCL will, prior to the termination of this Agreement, assuming the accuracy of the representations contained in Sections 3.2(b) and 3.2(p) (without giving effect to the knowledge qualification thereof) apply to this Agreement, the Share Exchange Agreement, the Offer, the Merger or to the transactions contemplated hereby and thereby.

(q) *Vote Required.* The affirmative vote of a majority of the votes that holders of the outstanding shares of WCI Common Stock and WCI Series B Preferred, voting together as a class, are entitled to cast is the only vote of the holders of any class or series of WCI capital stock necessary to approve this Agreement and the transactions contemplated hereby (assuming the accuracy of the representations contained in Sections 3.2(b) and 3.2(p), without giving effect to the knowledge qualification thereof).

(r) *No Change in Capital Structure.* There has been no material change in the information set forth in the second sentence of Section 3.1(b) between the close of business on February 17, 1989, and the date hereof.

(s) *WCI Not an Interested Stockholder or an Acquiring Person.* As of the date hereof, neither WCI nor, to its best knowledge, any of its affiliates, is an "Interested Stockholder" as such term is defined in Article V of Time's Certificate of Incorporation or an "Acquiring Person" as such term is defined in the Rights Agreement.

14

Section 3.2. On the Time side, the accounting representation dealing with pooling of interests has also been eliminated, as has the representation about the necessary shareholder vote. Pooling-of-interests accounting was no longer possible and the vote of Time shareholders was no longer necessary because of the change in the form of the transaction.

3.2. *Representations and Warranties of Time and Sub.* Time and Sub represent and warrant to WCI as follows:

(a) *Organization; Standing and Power.* Each of Time and Sub and Time's Significant Subsidiaries is a corporation or partnership duly organized, validly existing and in good standing under the laws of its state of incorporation or organization and has all requisite power and authority to own, lease and operate its properties and to carry on its business as now being conducted, and is duly qualified and in good standing to do business in each jurisdiction in which the nature of its business or the ownership or leasing of its properties makes such qualification necessary other than in such jurisdictions where the failure so to qualify would not have a material adverse effect on Time and its Subsidiaries taken as a whole.

(b) *Capital Structure.* As of the date hereof, the authorized capital stock of Time consists of 200,000,000 shares of Time Common Stock and 25,000,000 shares of Preferred Stock, par value $1.00 per share, of Time ("Time Preferred Stock"). As of the close of business on February 17, 1989, 56,557,919 shares of Time Common Stock were outstanding, 7,688,615 shares of Time Common Stock were reserved for issuance pursuant to the Time stock option plans, the Time Employees' Stock Ownership Plan, the Time Stock Incentive Plan, the Time Employees' Savings Plan, the Time Dividend Reinvestment and Stock Purchase Plan, the American Television and Communications Corporation ("ATC") Employees Stock Savings Plan and Time restricted stock plans (collectively, "Time Stock Plans"), 6,809,915 shares of Time Common Stock were held by Time in its treasury, there were no shares of Time Preferred Stock or Voting Debt of Time issued or outstanding, and 750,000 shares of Time Series A Preferred were reserved for issuance upon exercise of the Rights. All outstanding shares of Time capital stock are, and the shares of Time Common Stock (x) to be issued pursuant to or as specifically contemplated by this Agreement, (y) to be issued pursuant to the Share Exchange Agreement and (z) when issued in accordance with this Agreement, upon exercise of the WCI Stock Options and Lorimar Stock Grants, in accordance with actions permitted by Section 4.1(c) and upon conversion of Time Series BB Preferred and the Lorimar Debentures, will be, validly issued, fully paid and nonassessable and not subject to preemptive rights. As of the date of this Agreement, except for this Agreement, Time Stock Plans, the Rights Agreement and pursuant to the Share Exchange Agreement, there are no options, warrants, calls, rights, commitments or agreements of any character to which Time or any Subsidiary of Time (other than ATC and its Subsidiaries, but only with respect to ATC or its Subsidiaries) is a party or by which it is bound obligating Time or any Subsidiary of Time (other than ATC and its Subsidiaries, but only with respect to ATC or its Subsidiaries) to issue, deliver or sell, or cause to be issued, delivered or sold, additional shares of capital stock or any Voting Debt securities of Time or of any Subsidiary of Time (other than ATC and its Subsidiaries, but only with respect to ATC or its Subsidiaries) or obligating Time or any Subsidiary of Time (other than ATC and its Subsidiaries, but only with respect to ATC or its Subsidiaries) to grant, extend or enter into any such option, warrant, call, right, commitment or agreement. As of the date hereof, the authorized capital stock of Sub consists of 100 shares of Common Stock, par value $1 per share, all of which are validly issued, fully paid and nonassessable and are owned by Time.

(c) *Authority.* Time and Sub have all requisite corporate power and authority (x) to enter into this Agreement and the Share Exchange Agreement and (subject to any stockholder approval required in connection with the issuance of equity securities as part of the Merger Consideration) to consummate the transactions contemplated hereby and thereby. The execution and delivery of this Agreement and the Share Exchange Agreement and the consummation of the transactions contemplated hereby and thereby have been duly authorized by all necessary corporate action on the part of Time and Sub, subject in the case of Sub to the approval of this Agreement by Time as sole stockholder of Sub and subject to any stockholder approval required in connection with the issuance of equity securities as part of the Merger Consideration by the stockholders of Time. This Agreement and the Share Exchange Agreement have been duly executed and delivered by Time and Sub and, subject as aforesaid, each constitutes a valid and binding obligation of Time and Sub enforceable in accordance with its terms. The execution and delivery of this Agreement and the Share Exchange Agreement do not, and the consummation of the transactions contemplated hereby and thereby will not, result in any Violation pursuant to any provision of the Certificate of

Incorporation or By-laws of Time or any of its Subsidiaries or, except as set forth on Schedule 3.2(c) hereto or as contemplated by the next sentence hereof, result in any Violation of any loan or credit agreement, note, mortgage, indenture, lease, Benefit Plan or other agreement, obligation, instrument, permit, concession, franchise, license, judgment, order, decree, statute, law, ordinance, rule or regulation applicable to Time or any of its Subsidiaries or their respective properties or assets which Violation would have a material adverse effect on Time and its Subsidiaries taken as a whole. No consent, approval, order or authorization of, or registration, declaration or filing with, any Governmental Entity is required by or with respect to Time or any of its Subsidiaries in connection with the execution and delivery of this Agreement and the Share Exchange Agreement by Time and Sub or the consummation by Time and Sub of the transactions contemplated hereby and thereby, the failure to obtain which would have a material adverse effect on Time and its Subsidiaries, taken as a whole, except for (i) the filing of a premerger notification report by Time under the HSR Act, (ii) the filing with the SEC of the Offer Documents, the Proxy Statement, the S-4 and such reports under Sections 13(a), 13(d) and 16(a) of the Exchange Act, as may be required in connection with this Agreement, the Share Exchange Agreement and the transactions contemplated hereby and thereby and the obtaining from the SEC of such orders as may be so required, (iii) the filing of such documents with, and the obtaining of such orders from, the various state authorities, including state securities authorities, that are required in connection with the transactions contemplated by this Agreement and the Share Exchange Agreement, (iv) the filing of the Certificate of Merger with the Secretary of State of the State of Delaware and appropriate documents with the relevant authorities of other states in which WCI is qualified to do business, (v) the FCC Approvals, Local Approvals and State Takeover Approvals, (vi) filings pursuant to Article 31-B of the New York Tax Law and (vii) such filings, authorizing actions, orders and approvals as may be required under foreign laws.

(d) *SEC Documents.* Time has made available to WCI a true and complete copy of each report, schedule, registration statement and definitive proxy statement filed by Time or ATC with the SEC since January 1, 1986 (as such documents have since the time of their filing been amended, the "Time SEC Documents") which are all the documents (other than preliminary material) that Time or ATC was required to file with the SEC since such date. As of their respective dates, the Time SEC Documents complied in all material respects with the requirements of the Securities Act or the Exchange Act, as the case may be, and the rules and regulations of the SEC thereunder applicable to such Time SEC Documents, and none of the Time SEC Documents contained any untrue statement of a material fact or omitted to state a material fact required to be stated therein or necessary to make the statements therein, in light of the circumstances under which they were made, not misleading. The financial statements of Time and ATC included in the Time SEC Documents comply as to form in all material respects with applicable accounting requirements and with the published rules and regulations of the SEC with respect thereto, have been prepared in accordance with generally accepted accounting principles applied on a consistent basis during the periods involved (except as may be indicated in the notes thereto or, in the case of the unaudited statements, as permitted by Form 10-Q of the SEC) and fairly present (subject, in the case of the unaudited statements, to normal, recurring audit adjustments) the consolidated financial position of Time and its consolidated Subsidiaries and ATC and its consolidated Subsidiaries as at the dates thereof and the consolidated results of their operations and cash flows (or changes in financial position prior to the approval of FASB 95) for the periods then ended.

(e) *Information Supplied.* None of the information supplied by Time or Sub for inclusion or incorporation by reference in (i) the S-4 will, at the time the S-4 is filed with the SEC and at the time it becomes effective under the Securities Act, contain any untrue statement of a material fact or omit to state any material fact required to be stated therein or necessary to make the statements therein not misleading and (ii) the Proxy Statement will, at the date mailed to stockholders and at the times of the meetings of stockholders to be held in connection with the Merger, contain any untrue statement of a material fact or omit to state any material fact required to be stated therein or necessary in order to make the statements therein, in light of the circumstances under which they are made, not misleading. The Proxy Statement will comply as to form in all material respects with the provisions of the Exchange Act and the rules and regulations thereunder, and the S-4 will

comply as to form in all material respects with the provisions of the Securities Act and the rules and regulations thereunder.

(f) *Compliance with Applicable Laws.* Time and its Subsidiaries hold all permits, licenses, variances, exemptions, orders and approvals of all Governmental Entities which are material to the operation of the businesses of Time and its Subsidiaries, taken as a whole (the "Time Permits"). Time and its Subsidiaries are in compliance with the terms of the Time Permits, except where the failure so to comply would not have a material adverse effect on Time and its Subsidiaries taken as a whole. Except as disclosed in the Time SEC Documents filed prior to the date of this Agreement, the businesses of Time and its Subsidiaries are not being conducted in violation of any law, ordinance or regulation of any Governmental Entity, except for possible violations which individually or in the aggregate do not, and, insofar as reasonably can be foreseen, in the future will not, have a material adverse effect on Time and its Subsidiaries taken as a whole. Except as set forth on Schedule 3.2(f) hereto, as of the date of this Agreement, no investigation or review by any Governmental Entity with respect to Time or any of its Subsidiaries is pending or, to the knowledge of Time, threatened, nor has any Governmental Entity indicated an intention to conduct the same, other than, in each case, those the outcome of which, as far as reasonably can be foreseen, will not have a material adverse effect on Time and its Subsidiaries taken as a whole.

(g) *Litigation.* As of the date of this Agreement, except as disclosed in the Time SEC Documents filed prior to the date of this Agreement or on Schedule 3.2(g) hereto, there is no suit, action or proceeding pending, or, to the knowledge of Time, threatened against or affecting Time or any Subsidiary of Time which is reasonably likely to have a material adverse effect on Time and its Subsidiaries taken as a whole, nor is there any judgment, decree, injunction, rule or order of any Governmental Entity or arbitrator outstanding against Time or any Subsidiary of Time having, or which, insofar as reasonably can be foreseen, in the future could have, any such effect.

(h) *Taxes.* To the best of Time's knowledge, Time and each of its Subsidiaries has filed all tax returns required to be filed by any of them and has paid (or Time has paid on its behalf), or has set up an adequate reserve for the payment of, all taxes required to be paid as shown on such returns and the most recent financial statements contained in the Time SEC Documents reflect an adequate reserve for all taxes payable by Time and its Subsidiaries accrued through the date of such financial statements. No material deficiencies for any taxes aggregating in excess of $300,000,000 have been proposed, asserted or assessed against Time or any of its Subsidiaries. The Federal income tax returns of Time and each of its Subsidiaries consolidated in such returns have been examined by and settled with the IRS, or the statute of limitations with respect to such years has expired, for all years through 1978. The Federal income tax returns of Time and each of its Subsidiaries consolidated in such returns for the years 1979 through 1984 are currently under examination by the IRS.

(i) *Certain Agreements.* Except as disclosed in the Time SEC Documents filed prior to the date of this Agreement, or in a schedule to be delivered to WCI within thirty days of the date hereof, and except for this Agreement, as of the date of this Agreement, neither Time nor any of its Subsidiaries is a party to any oral or written (i) consulting agreement not terminable on 60 days' or less notice involving the payment of more than $1,000,000 per annum or union, guild or collective bargaining agreement which agreement covers more than 1,000 employees, (ii) agreement with any executive officer or other key employee of Time or any Significant Subsidiary of Time the benefits of which are contingent, or the terms of which are materially altered, upon the occurrence of a transaction involving Time or any Subsidiary of Time of the nature contemplated by this Agreement or agreement with respect to any executive officer of Time providing any term of employment or compensation guarantee extending for a period longer than three years and for the payment of in excess of $1,000,000 per annum, or (iii) agreement or plan, including any stock option plan, stock appreciation rights plan, restricted stock plan or stock purchase plan, any of the benefits of which will be increased, or the vesting of the benefits of which will be accelerated, by the occurrence of any of the transactions contemplated by this Agreement or the value of any of the benefits of which will be calculated on the basis of any of the transactions contemplated by this Agreement.

(j) *Benefit Plans.* (i) With respect to each Benefit Plan maintained or contributed to by Time or any of its Subsidiaries, Time has made available to WCI a true and correct copy of (a) the most recent annual report (Form 5500) filed with the IRS, (b) such Benefit Plan, (c) each trust agreement and group annuity contract, if any, relating to such Benefit Plan and (d) the most recent actuarial report or valuation relating to a Benefit Plan subject to Title IV of ERISA.

(ii) With respect to the Benefit Plans, individually and in the aggregate, no event has occurred, and to the knowledge of Time or any of its Subsidiaries, there exists no condition or set of circumstances in connection with which Time or any of its Subsidiaries could be subject to any liability that is reasonably likely to have a material adverse effect upon Time and its Subsidiaries taken as a whole (except liability for benefits claims and funding obligations payable in the ordinary course) under ERISA, the Code or any other applicable law.

(iii) Except as set forth in Schedule 3.2(j), with respect to the Benefit Plans, individually and in the aggregate, there are no funded benefit obligations for which contributions have not been made or properly accrued and there are no unfunded benefit obligations which have not been accounted for by reserves, or otherwise properly footnoted in accordance with generally accepted accounting principles, on the financial statements of Time or any of its Subsidiaries, which obligations are reasonably likely to have a material adverse effect on Time and its Subsidiaries taken as a whole.

(k) *Patents, Trademarks, etc.* Time and its Subsidiaries have all patents, trademarks, trade names, service marks, trade secrets, copyrights and other proprietary intellectual property rights as are material in connection with the businesses of Time and its Subsidiaries, taken as a whole.

(l) *CATV Systems, Franchises, Licenses, Permits, etc.* (i) Time will provide WCI, within thirty days of the date hereof, a complete list of the CATV Systems operated by Time or any Subsidiary thereof as of the date hereof and the number of subscribers in each of such CATV Systems as of January 31, 1989.

(ii) Time will provide WCI, within thirty days of the date hereof, a list and brief description of all authorizations, approvals, certifications, licenses and permits issued by the FCC ("Time FCC Authorizations") to Time or any Subsidiary thereof as of the date hereof and all applications by Time or any Subsidiary thereof for Time FCC Authorizations which are pending on the date hereof.

(iii) Time and its Subsidiaries (A) have all Time FCC Authorizations and Franchises required for the operation of the CATV Systems being operated on the date hereof, (B) have duly and currently filed all reports and other information required to be filed by the FCC or any other governmental authority in connection with such Time FCC Authorizations and Franchises, and (C) are not in violation of any Time FCC Authorization or Franchise other than the lack of Time FCC Authorizations, Franchises, delays in filing reports or violations which, insofar as can reasonably be foreseen, would not have a material adverse effect on the CATV business conducted by Time and its Subsidiaries taken as a whole.

(m) *Absence of Certain Changes or Events.* Except as disclosed in the Time SEC Documents filed prior to the date of this Agreement or in the audited consolidated balance sheets of Time and its Subsidiaries and the related consolidated statements of income, shareholders' equity and cash flows as of and for the period ended December 31, 1988 (the "Time 1988 Financials"), true and correct copies of which have been delivered to WCI, or except as contemplated by this Agreement and the Share Exchange Agreement, since the date of the Time 1988 Financials, Time and its Subsidiaries have conducted their respective businesses only in the ordinary and usual course, and, as of the date of this Agreement, there has not been (i) any damage, destruction or loss, whether covered by insurance or not, which has, or insofar as reasonably can be foreseen in the future is reasonably likely to have, a material adverse effect on Time and its Subsidiaries taken as a whole; (ii) any declaration, setting aside or payment of any dividend or other distribution (whether in cash, stock or property) with respect to any of Time's capital stock, except for regular quarterly cash dividends of $.25 per share on Time Common Stock with usual record and payment dates for such dividends; or (iii) any transaction, commitment, dispute or other event or condition (financial

Section 3.2(n). Time's investment bankers limit themselves to addressing the fairness of the 'financial terms' of the tender offer and the merger. In 3.1(n), the corresponding provision for the Warner investment bankers, this modifying phrase is omitted. However, since both opinions are 'from a financial point of view,' it is hard to see how this difference is very important.

Section 3.2(q). This provision reassures Warner that the revised form of the transaction does not trigger Time's poison pill. An unintended triggering of the pill could have had disastrous effects on Warner's shareholders. The poison pill had been amended the day before, as a result of Paramount's offer, so that after a hostile tender offer the rights are not distributed automatically but only if the board of directors takes special action. If the pill had not been amended, the rights would have separated from the common shares ten days after Paramount made its offer. Separate certificates would then have been issued by Time for the rights, which would have been listed on the New York Stock Exchange as a separate security.

Section 4.1. The conduct of business covenants now relate to the period from the signing of the agreement to the purchase of shares in the tender offer. At that point Time would own a majority of the shares of Warner and have half the seats on Warner's board of directors. And Warner would have half the seats on Time's board.

or otherwise) of any character (whether or not in the ordinary course of business) individually or in the aggregate having or which, insofar as reasonably can be foreseen, in the future is reasonably likely to have, a material adverse effect on Time and its Subsidiaries taken as a whole.

(n) *Opinions of Financial Advisors.* Time has received the opinions of Shearson Lehman Hutton Inc. and Wasserstein Perella & Co., Inc., dated June 16, 1989, and to the effect that, as of such date, the financial terms of the Offer and the Merger are fair to Time and its stockholders, from a financial point of view, copies of which opinions have been delivered to WCI.

(o) *No Change in Capital Structure.* There has been no material change in the information set forth in the second sentence of Section 3.2(b) between the close of business on February 17, 1989, and the date hereof.

(p) *Ownership of WCI Common Stock.* As of the date hereof, assuming consummation of the transactions contemplated by the Share Exchange Agreement, neither Time nor, to its best knowledge, any of its affiliates or associates, (i) beneficially owns, directly or indirectly, or (ii) are parties to any agreement, arrangement or understanding for the purpose of acquiring, holding, voting or disposing of, in each case, shares of capital stock of WCI, which in the aggregate, represent 10% or more of the outstanding shares of capital stock of WCI entitled to vote generally in the election of directors.

(q) *Rights Agreement.* Assuming the accuracy of the representations contained in Section 3.1(s) (without giving effect to the knowledge qualification thereof) the consummation of the transactions contemplated by this Agreement and the Share Exchange Agreement will not result in an "Affiliate Merger", a "Triggering Event" or a "Business Combination", as such terms are defined in the Rights Agreement, dated as of April 29, 1986, between Time and First Chicago Trust Company of New York, as Rights Agent, as amended by Amendment No. 1 dated as of January 19, 1989, Amendment No. 2 dated as of May 19, 1989, and Amendment No. 3 dated as of June 15, 1989 (the "Rights Agreement"), pursuant to which Time has issued rights (the "Rights") to purchase its Series A Participating Preferred Stock, par value $1.00 per share (the "Time Series A Preferred").

(r) *Article V of Time's Certificate of Incorporation and Section 203 of the DGCL Not Applicable.* Neither the provisions of Article V of Time's Certificate of Incorporation nor Section 203 of the DGCL will, prior to the termination of this Agreement, assuming the accuracy of the representations contained in Section 3.1(s) (without giving effect to the knowledge qualification thereof), apply to this Agreement, the Share Exchange Agreement, the Offer, the Merger or the transactions contemplated hereby and thereby, including the purchase of shares of Time by WCI under the Share Exchange Agreement and the Board of Directors of Time, including a majority of the Disinterested Directors (as defined in the Time Certificate of Incorporation), have approved such transactions.

(s) *Interim Operations of Sub.* Sub was formed solely for the purpose of engaging in the transactions contemplated hereby, has engaged in no other business activities and has conducted its operations only as contemplated hereby.

ARTICLE IV
COVENANTS RELATING TO CONDUCT OF BUSINESS

4.1. *Covenants of WCI and Time.* During the period from the date of this Agreement and continuing until the time Time's nominees are elected to the Board of Directors of WCI pursuant to Section 5.16 hereof and WCI's nominees are elected to the Board of Directors of Time pursuant to Section 5.12 hereof, WCI and Time each agree as to itself and its Subsidiaries that (except as expressly contemplated or permitted by this Agreement, the Share Exchange Agreement, or to the extent that the other party shall otherwise consent in writing and except with respect to employment and compensation arrangements entered into by WCI or Time):

(a) *Ordinary Course.* Each party and its Subsidiaries shall carry on their respective businesses in the usual, regular and ordinary course in substantially the same manner as heretofore conducted

Section 4.1(b). The list of exceptions to the prohibition on dividends and stock repurchases no longer includes Time's possible redemption of the poison pill rights. Under the Rights Agreement, however, the rights could still be redeemed after Paramount's offer was made if the redemption were approved by the independent directors of Time who were in office before Paramount made its bid. However, Time now seems bound not to redeem the pill by its agreement with Warner. Although a court could override the agreement, Time no longer has that option.

and use all reasonable efforts to preserve intact their present business organizations, keep available the services of their present officers and employees and preserve their relationships with customers, suppliers and others having business dealings with them to the end that their goodwill and ongoing businesses shall not be impared in any material respect at the Effective Time.

(b) *Dividends; Changes in Stock.* No party shall, nor shall any party permit any of its Subsidiaries to, nor shall any party propose to, (i) declare or pay any dividends on or make other distributions in respect of any of its capital stock, except as provided in Section 5.15 and except that WCI may continue the declaration and payment of regular quarterly cash dividends (and any other dividend paid with respect to WCI Preferred Stock as a result of the declaration and payment of the dividend contemplated to be paid by WCI pursuant to Section 5.15 and in an amount appropriate to such dividend paid pursuant to Section 5.15) not in excess of $.17 per share of WCI Common Stock and regular quarterly cash dividends as provided by the terms of the WCI Preferred Stock in accordance with their present terms, and Time may continue the declaration and payment of regular quarterly cash dividends not in excess of $.25 per share of Time Common Stock in each case with usual record and payment dates for such dividends in accordance with such parties' past dividend practice, and except for dividends by a wholly-owned subsidiary of such party or such Subsidiary, and except that, whether pursuant to a court order or otherwise, WCI may declare and pay the Distribution and Time may declare and pay a pro rata dividend or other distribution of any or all of its shares of capital stock of BHC to holders of record (as of any time on or after the Effective Time) of shares of Time Common Stock and Time Series BB Preferred (treating such shares of Time Series BB Preferred as if they had been converted into shares of Time Common Stock immediately prior to such record date pursuant to their terms), (ii) split, combine or reclassify any of its capital stock or issue or authorize or propose the issuance of any other securities in respect of, in lieu of or in substitution for shares of its capital stock or (iii) repurchase or otherwise acquire, or permit any Subsidiary to purchase or otherwise acquire, any shares of its capital stock (other than, (x) in the case of WCI, repurchases of WCI Common Stock which WCI may be obligated to make under WCI's Equity Unit Purchase Plan, the Lorimar Restricted Stock Plan and redemptions of shares of WCI Series A Preferred and Series C Preferred pursuant to the terms thereof, (y) in the case of Time, purchases of ATC shares pursuant to ATC's share repurchase program up to an aggregate of 3,000,000 ATC shares and (z) in the case of any party as required by stockholders agreements with minority investors in such party's Subsidiaries).

(c) *Issuance of Securities.* No party shall, nor shall any party permit any of its Subsidiaries to, issue, deliver or sell, or authorize or propose the issuance, delivery or sale of, any shares of its capital stock of any class, any Voting Debt or any securities convertible into, or any rights, warrants or options to acquire, any such shares, Voting Debt or convertible securities, other than (i) the issuance of WCI Common Stock or Time Common Stock, as the case may be, upon the exercise of stock options or stock grants as disclosed in this Agreement, the conversion of convertible securities as disclosed in this Agreement, or pursuant to Time Stock Plans or WCI Stock Plans, in each case outstanding on the date of this Agreement (or as may be issued under such Plans) in each case in accordance with their present terms, or pursuant to the Share Exchange Agreement, (ii) the issuance of options pursuant to Time Stock Plans or WCI Stock Plans, in each case in accordance with their present terms, (iii) issuances of (a) common stock or (b) securities convertible into or exchangeable for, or rights or warrants or options to acquire, common stock, not in excess of an aggregate of 1,000,000 shares (with respect to WCI) or 1,000,000 shares (with respect to Time) of common stock of such party (*provided* such shares or securities shall be issued only to employees or consultants or in connection with acquisitions permitted by this Agreement), (iv) issuance by a wholly-owned Subsidiary of its capital stock to its parent, (v) in the case of Time, issuance of Time Series A Preferred upon exercise of the Rights and reservation for issuance of shares of Time Series A Preferred in addition to those presently reserved for issuance and (vi) Awards under (and as defined in) the 1989 Incentive Plan (as defined in Section 5.20), such Awards to be made to employees or prospective employees of WCI, in respect of no more than an aggregate of 1,500,000 shares of Time Common Stock, subject to consummation of the Merger. For purposes of this Section 4.1(c) only, Time Common Stock shall be deemed to include the Class A Common Stock, par value $.01 per share, of ATC and Time Stock Plans shall be deemed to

Section 4.1(e). The long proviso to the first sentence is new. Warner now has an express fiduciary out to the no-solicitation provision, based on the standard that it must have a good faith belief based on its lawyers' advice that it has an obligation to its shareholders to entertain the proposal or to withdraw its support for the transaction. See also Section 4.1(l) and Article VII, 'Termination and Amendment.' This change was probably caused by a concern that, as a result of the change in the form of the deal, Warner was being sold to Time. In that event, the *Revlon* case might impose a duty on the Warner directors to auction the company off at the highest price. See our discussion of the auction requirement in Chapter 10 Section 1. Furthermore, the Warner directors might have a separate duty under corporate fiduciary and tender offer rules to revise their recommendation of the tender offer in the face of a higher offer. This provision is a compromise attempt to deal with these issues.

Section 4.1(h). This is a crucial modification to allow Time to take on the significant new indebtedness it would be incurring to carry out the tender offer.

include the 1986 Stock Option Plan for Key Employees of ATC and the Restricted Stock Plan of ATC.

(d) *Governing Documents.* No party shall amend or propose to amend its Certificate of Incorporation or By-laws nor shall Time amend the Rights Agreement in any way adverse to WCI, *provided, however,* that Time, at or prior to the Effective Time, shall amend its By-Laws and the Rights Agreement as provided in resolutions adopted by the Board of Directors of Time on March 3, 1989, as modified on April 20, 1989, and May 16, 1989, copies of which have been provided to WCI, shall file a Certificate of Designation substantially in the form of Exhibit 2.1(d) and may file a Certificate of Designation with respect to the Time Series A Preferred.

(e) *No Solicitations.* No party shall, nor shall any party permit any of its Subsidiaries to, nor shall it authorize or permit any of its officers, directors or employees or any investment banker, financial advisor (including the persons named in Sections 3.1(n) and 3.2(n)), attorney, accountant or other representative retained by it or any of its Subsidiaries to, solicit or encourage (including by way of furnishing information), or take any other action to facilitate, any inquires or the making of any proposal which constitutes, or may reasonably be expected to lead to, any takeover proposal, or agree to or endorse any takeover proposal; *provided, however,* that (i) WCI may furnish or cause to be furnished information concerning WCI and its businesses, properties or assets to a third party, (ii) WCI may engage in discussions or negotiations with a third party, (iii) following receipt of a takeover proposal WCI may take and disclose to its stockholders a position contemplated by Rule 14e-2(a) under the Exchange Act or otherwise make disclosure to WCI's stockholders and/or (iv) following receipt of a takeover proposal the Board of Directors of WCI may withdraw, modify or amend its recommendation referred to in Section 3.1(o), but in each case referred to in the foregoing clauses (i) through (iv) only to the extent that the WCI Board of Directors shall conclude in good faith on the basis of advice from outside counsel that such action is necessary or appropriate in order for the WCI Board of Directors to act in a manner which is consistent with its fiduciary obligations under applicable law. Each party shall promptly advise the other orally and in writing of any such inquiries or proposals. As used in this Agreement, "takeover proposal" shall mean any tender or exchange offer, proposal for a merger, consolidation or other business combination involving a party hereto or any Significant Subsidiary of such party or any proposal or offer to acquire in any manner a substantial equity interest in, or a substantial portion of the assets of, such party or any of its Significant Subsidiaries other than the transactions contemplated by this Agreement and the Share Exchange Agreement and except with respect to acquisitions of the assets listed on Schedule 4.1(f) hereto.

(f) *No Acquisitions.* Other than (i) as permitted by Section 4.1(b), (ii) pursuant to this Agreement and the Share Exchange Agreement, (iii) acquisitions listed on Schedule 4.1(f) hereto or (iv) acquisitions in existing or related lines of business of the party making such acquisition not exceeding $100 million in the aggregate in the case of each party (and not exceeding an additional $500 million in the aggregate in the case of each party with respect to acquisitions relating to the cable television business of such party), no party shall, nor shall any party permit any of its Subsidiaries to, acquire or agree to acquire by merging or consolidating with, or by purchasing a substantial equity interest in or a substantial portion of the assets of, or by any other manner, any business or any corporation, partnership, association or other business organization or division thereof or otherwise acquire or agree to acquire any assets in each case which are material, individually or in the aggregate, to such party and its Subsidiaries taken as a whole.

(g) *No Dispositions.* Other than (i) dispositions listed on Schedule 4.1(g), (ii) as may be required by law to consummate the transactions contemplated hereby or (iii) in the ordinary course of business consistent with prior practice, no party shall, nor shall any party permit any of its Subsidiaries to, sell, lease, encumber or otherwise dispose of, or agree to sell, lease, encumber or otherwise dispose of, any of its assets, which are material, individually or in the aggregate, to such party and its Subsidiaries taken as a whole.

(h) *Indebtedness.* No party shall, nor shall any party permit any of its Subsidiaries to, incur (which shall not be deemed to include entering into credit agreements, lines of credit or similar arrangements until borrowings are made under such arrangements) any indebtedness for borrowed

Section 4.1(k). Warner is still allowed to adopt a poison pill if it will not prevent the tender offer and merger from being accomplished.

Section 4.1(l). This elaborate provision combined with Section 4.1(e) gives the principal fiduciary outs. The terms of this section are similar to those in the earlier agreement. Once there is a trigger event, the board of directors of the Target Company is given the flexibility to deal with the situation without violating this agreement, if it determines it is acting in its shareholders' best interests. However, it must act with the advice of its investment bankers and lawyers. This flexibility does not extend to terminating the agreement, although the other side can terminate if one side uses this provision.

But now the parties are acknowledging even as they sign the agreement that Paramount's tender offer for Time shares has created a trigger event for Time. Warner's sole remedy if Time does take action under this provision is to terminate the agreement after consultation with Time. See Section 7.1(d).

Paramount argued in the Delaware litigation that this provision and Time's tender offer conditions should have been much broader. According to Paramount, Time's board should have negotiated the right to abandon the offer if Paramount or another bidder made a more favorable offer to Time's shareholders that was conditioned on Time backing out. The courts recognized, however, that Warner would not have accepted such a provision. The opinion of the Delaware Supreme Court is reproduced in the Appendix, A.12.

money or guarantee any such indebtedness or issue or sell any debt securities or warrants or rights to acquire any debt securities of such party or any of its Subsidiaries or guarantee any debt securities of others other than (x) in each case in the ordinary course of business consistent with prior practice, (y) as may be necessary in connection with acquisitions permitted by Section 4.1(f) or (z) in the case of Time, (A) incurrence of indebtedness, issuances of debt securities or guarantees not aggregating in excess of $500,000,000 in connection with a medium-term note program and (B) in connection with the Offer.

(i) *Other Actions.* Except as provided in Section 4.1(l), no party shall, nor shall any party permit any of its Subsidiaries to, take any action that would or is reasonably likely to result in any of its representations and warranties set forth in this Agreement being untrue as of the date made (to the extent so limited), or in any of the conditions to the Merger set forth in Article VI not being satisfied or in a violation of any provision of the Share Exchange Agreement.

(j) *Advice of Changes; SEC Filings.* Each party shall confer on a regular and frequent basis with the other, report on operational matters and promptly advise the other orally and in writing of any change or event having, or which, insofar as can reasonably be foreseen, could have, a material adverse effect on such party and its Subsidiaries taken as a whole. Each party shall promptly provide the other (or its counsel) copies of all filings made by such party with any state or Federal Governmental Entity in connection with this Agreement, the Share Exchange Agreement and the transactions contemplated hereby and thereby.

(k) *Investment Fund; Rights Plans.* Nothing contained herein shall be deemed to prohibit WCI from (i) investing up to $150,000,000 as equity in an investment fund, a limited partner of which will be WCI or an entity controlled by WCI, (ii) adopting a stockholder rights plan, *provided* that (x) no such plan shall prohibit, be "triggered" or otherwise have a material adverse effect on Time or on WCI and its Subsidiaries taken as a whole or materially change the number of outstanding equity securities of WCI as a result of the Offer, the Merger or of any action of Time permitted under this Agreement or the Share Exchange Agreement, (y) none of Time, Sub or any affiliate of either shall, by virtue of its ownership of WCI Common Stock acquired pursuant to the Offer or the Share Exchange Agreement, be defined as a person or entity similar to an "Acquiring Person" as such term is defined under the Rights Agreement, and (z) any such rights plan shall provide that any rights or other securities issued thereunder or pursuant thereto shall, at the Effective Time and without further action by WCI, Time or any affiliate of either, be canceled for no consideration and shall thereafter not be outstanding or (iii) selling all or a part of the shares of BHC owned by it to one or more third parties for fair value.

(l) *Certain Actions.* In the event that (x) any person acquires securities representing 10% or more (other than a person who as of the date hereof is publicly disclosed in a filing with the SEC to own 10% or more), or commences a tender or exchange offer following the successful consummation of which the offeror and its affiliates would beneficially own securities representing 25% or more (any such acquisition or commencement being referred to herein as a "Trigger Event," the date and time of such Trigger Event being referred to herein as the "Trigger Date" and it being acknowledged that a Trigger Event occurred on June 7, 1989, as a result of the offer to purchase all outstanding shares of Time Common Stock by KDS Acquisition Corp.), of the voting power of Time or WCI, as the case may be (the issuer of such securities being referred to herein as the "Target Company"), and (y) at any time prior to the approval of this Agreement by the stockholders of the Target Company and subsequent to the Trigger Date, the Board of Directors of the Target Company, acting with the advice of the Target Company's counsel and investment bankers, determines that it is in the best interest of the Target Company's stockholders to take, or seek to take, one or more actions in response to such Trigger Event, then no such action taken by the Board of Directors of the Target Company in response to such Trigger Event shall be deemed to be, or to result in, a breach of:

(i) any of the Target Company's representations and warranties contained in the fourth sentence of Section 3.1(c), Sections 3.1(f), 3.1(g), 3.1(j) and 3.1(q), the fourth sentence of Section 3.2(c) and Sections 3.2(f), 3.2(g) and 3.2(j), nor shall any such representation or warranty be deemed to be untrue as a result of any such action;

22

Section 5.5. The emphasis of the shareholder meeting provision has changed significantly. Time is no longer required to call a meeting. In fact, the need to avoid a shareholder vote was the only point of the change in the form of the acquisition. The Warner meeting is significant only for the merger that would follow a successful tender offer. By the time of the shareholder meeting, Time would be able to control the vote. Warner wants to be sure that this agreement sufficiently commits Time to complete the merger, which is why Time promises here and on the top of the next page to vote its Warner shares in favor of the merger.

(ii) any of the covenants or agreements of the Target Company contained in Section 4.1(a), Section 4.1(b), Section 4.1(c), Section 4.1(d), Section 4.1(f), Section 4.1(g), Section 4.1(h), Section 4.1(i) or Section 5.18; and

(iii) any of the covenants or agreements of the Target Company contained in Section 4.1(e);

provided, however, that the Board of Directors of the Target Company shall not take any such action until after reasonable notice to and consultation with the other party to this Agreement with respect to such action and that such Board of Directors shall continue to consult with such other party after taking such action and, in addition, in the case of clause (iii) above, (A) if the Target Company receives any takeover proposal (as defined in Section 4.1(e)) from any person other than the other party to this Agreement, then the Target Company shall promptly inform such other party of the terms and conditions of such proposal and the identity of the person making it and (B) the Target Company shall not take any action to solicit, encourage or otherwise facilitate any takeover proposal from any person other than such other party to this Agreement, except after reasonable consultation with such other party to this Agreement.

ARTICLE V
ADDITIONAL AGREEMENTS

5.1. *Preparation of S-4 and the Proxy Statement.* Time and WCI shall promptly prepare and file with the SEC the Proxy Statement and Time shall prepare and file with the SEC the S-4, in which the Proxy Statement will be included as a prospectus. Time shall use its best efforts to have the S-4 declared effective under the Securities Act as promptly as practicable after such filing. Time shall also take any action (other than qualifying to do business in any jurisdiction in which it is now not so qualified) required to be taken under any applicable state securities laws in connection with the issuance of Merger Securities and Time Series BB Preferred in the Merger and upon the exercise of WCI Stock Options and conversion of Time Series BB Preferred, and WCI shall furnish all information concerning WCI and the holders of WCI Common Stock and WCI Series B Preferred as may be reasonably requested in connection with any such action.

5.2. *Letter of WCI's Accountants.* WCI shall use its best efforts to cause to be delivered to Time a letter of Arthur Young & Company, WCI's independent auditors, dated a date within two business days before the date on which the S-4 shall become effective and addressed to Time, in form and substance reasonably satisfactory to Time and customary in scope and substance for letters delivered by independent public accountants in connection with registration statements similar to the S-4.

5.3. *Letter of Time's Accountants.* Time shall use its best efforts to cause to be delivered to WCI a letter of Ernst & Whinney, Time's independent auditors, dated a date within two business days before the date on which the S-4 shall become effective and addressed to WCI, in form and substance reasonably satisfactory to WCI and customary in scope and substance for letters delivered by independent public accountants in connection with registration statements similar to the S-4.

5.4. *Access to Information.* Upon reasonable notice, WCI and Time shall each (and shall cause each of their respective Subsidiaries to) afford to the officers, employees, accountants, counsel and other representatives of the other, access, during normal business hours during the period prior to the Effective Time, to all its properties, books, contracts, commitments and records and, during such period, each of WCI and Time shall (and shall cause each of their respective Subsidiaries to) furnish promptly to the other (a) a copy of each report, schedule, registration statement and other document filed or received by it during such period pursuant to the requirements of Federal securities laws and (b) all other information concerning its business, properties and personnel as such other party may reasonably request. Unless otherwise required by law, the parties will hold any such information which is nonpublic in confidence until such time as such information otherwise becomes publicly available through no wrongful act of either party, and in the event of termination of this Agreement for any reason each party shall promptly return all nonpublic documents obtained from any other party, and any copies made of such documents, to such other party.

5.5. *Stockholder Meeting.* WCI shall call a meeting of its stockholders to be held as promptly as practicable following the Purchase Time for the purpose of voting upon this Agreement and related

The Share Exchange Agreement does not allow Time to vote the Warner shares it obtained in the share exchange in favor of the merger. Instead, Time is required to vote them for or against the merger in the same percentage that other shareholders vote. With the change in form of the transaction, this does not really matter since after the tender offer is completed Time would have enough other shares to control the vote. See our commentary to the Share Exchange Agreement at the end of Chapter 17.

Section 5.8. The exchanged shares by now have been listed. Why should there be any uncertainty about whether Warner would want Time securities issued in the merger to be listed on the New York and Pacific exchanges? The likely answer is that at this time the securities that would be issued in the merger had not been agreed upon. If Time should issue 20% or more of its common stock in the merger, Time shareholder approval would be required under stock exchange rules. Approval of the Time shareholders is not required under Delaware law because TW Sub, not Time, is merging. NASDAQ does not have a shareholder approval requirement related to the issuance of shares.

Section 5.10. This section probably should have been revised to provide that each party pays its own expenses whether or not the Merger *or Offer* is consummated.

matters. Subject to Section 4.1(e), WCI will, through its Board of Directors, recommend to its stockholders approval of such matters. At the WCI stockholders meeting, Time shall vote, and shall cause its subsidiaries to vote, all shares owned by it or any of them in favor of approval of this Agreement and the Merger, subject, however, to the requirements of the Share Exchange Agreement.

5.6. *Legal Conditions to Merger.* Each of WCI, Time and Sub will take all reasonable actions necessary to comply promptly with all legal requirements which may be imposed on itself with respect to the Offer, the Merger or the Share Exchange Agreement (including furnishing all information required under the HSR Act, in connection with the FCC Approvals and the Local Approvals and in connection with approvals of or filings with any other Governmental Entity) and will promptly cooperate with and furnish information to each other in connection with any such requirements imposed upon any of them or any of their Subsidiaries in connection with the Offer or the Merger. Each of WCI, Time and Sub will, and will cause its Subsidiaries to, take all reasonable actions necessary to obtain (and will cooperate with each other in obtaining) any consent, authorization, order or approval of, or any exemption by, any Governmental Entity or other public or private third party, required to be obtained or made by Time, WCI or any of their Subsidiaries in connection with the Offer, the Merger or the taking of any action contemplated thereby or by this Agreement or the Share Exchange Agreement.

5.7. *Affiliates.* Prior to the Closing Date WCI shall deliver to Time a letter identifying all persons who are, at the time this Agreement is submitted for approval to the stockholders of WCI, "affiliates" of WCI for purposes of Rule 145 under the Securities Act. WCI shall use its best efforts to cause each such person to deliver to Time on or prior to the Closing Date a written agreement, substantially in the form attached as Exhibit 5.7 hereto.

5.8. *Stock Exchange Listing.* The shares of common stock of Time and WCI issued pursuant to the Share Exchange Agreement have been approved for listing on the New York Stock Exchange, Inc. ("NYSE") and Pacific Stock Exchange upon official notice of issuance. To the extent requested by WCI, Time shall use all reasonable efforts to cause any Merger Securities to be issued in the Merger as part of the Merger Consideration and the shares of Time Common Stock to be reserved for issuance pursuant to the 1989 Incentive Plan (as defined in Section 5.20), to be approved for listing on the NYSE and the Pacific Stock Exchange, subject to official notice of issuance, prior to the Closing Date.

5.9. *Employee Benefit Plans.* Time and WCI agree that the Benefit Plans of WCI and its Subsidiaries in effect at the date of this Agreement shall, to the extent practicable, remain in effect until otherwise determined after the Effective Time and, to the extent such Benefit Plans are not continued, it is the current intent of the parties that Benefit Plans which are no less favorable, in the aggregate, to the employees covered by such plans shall be provided.

In the case of Benefit Plans under which the employee's interests are based upon WCI Common Stock, Time and WCI agree that such interests shall be based on Time Common Stock in an equitable manner.

5.10. *Expenses.* Whether or not the Merger is consummated, all costs and expenses incurred in connection with this Agreement, the Share Exchange Agreement and the transactions contemplated hereby and thereby shall be paid by the party incurring such expense, and, in connection therewith, each of Time and WCI shall pay, with its own funds and not with funds provided by the other party, any and all property or transfer taxes imposed on such party or any real property tax imposed by New York State or New York City on any holder of shares in such party resulting from the Merger, except that expenses incurred in connection with printing and mailing the Proxy Statement and the S-4 shall be shared equally by Time and WCI.

5.11. *Brokers or Finders.* Each of Time and WCI represents, as to itself, its Subsidiaries and its affiliates, that no agent, broker, investment banker, financial advisor or other firm or person is or will be entitled to any broker's or finder's fee or any other commission or similar fee in connection with any of the transactions contemplated by this Agreement, except Lazard Freres & Co. and Alpine Capital Group, each of whose fees and expenses will be paid by WCI in accordance with WCI's agreement with such firm (copies of which have been delivered by WCI to Time prior to the date of this Agreement), and Shearson Lehman Hutton Inc. and Wasserstein Perella & Co., Inc., whose fees and expenses will

Section 5.12(a). Half of Time's board is still to be made up of Time's designees and half of Warner's. But now the change comes when Time gains control in the tender offer. Two-thirds of the Time directors are required to approve the Warner designees. And, if a designee is unable to serve, his successor is designated by the side that chose him, instead of by the full board. This approach appears to fit the spirit of the deal better than that of the prior agreement.

Section 5.12(b), an entirely new provision, takes care of a new problem in an unusual way. Under the new structure, Warner's representatives are to be brought onto the board while there are still many things to be resolved under the agreement. Warner would still exist, but as a majority-owned subsidiary of Time. Warner directors should not have a say in making Time's decisions under the merger agreement (such as deciding what Time would propose as payment in the merger for the remaining shares and whether to terminate). If there is a dispute about the payment the Warner directors should not be allowed to participate on Time's side in choosing the investment banker who would represent Time. Among other things, some of the Warner directors might have a personal stake in the issue because they own shares. This provision in effect leaves these and similar decisions exclusively to the continuing Time directors. See Section 5.16(b).

Section 5.13. The long-term employment agreements for some of Warner's top management were revised in connection with the negotiations over restructuring the transaction. Although they are to be signed when (or before) Time buys shares under the tender offer, they do not begin until the merger has been accomplished. The employment agreements were an issue in the litigation but the court did not appear to view the new arrangements as significantly more favorable to the Warner management than in the earlier version of the transaction.

be paid by Time in accordance with Time's agreements with such firms (copies of which have been delivered by Time to WCI), and each of Time and WCI respectively agree to indemnify and hold the other harmless from and against any and all claims, liabilities or obligations with respect to any other fees, commissions or expenses asserted by any person on the basis of any act or statement alleged to have been made by such party or its affiliate.

5.12. *Time Board of Directors.* (a) *Designation.* Time's Board of Directors will take action to cause the number of directors comprising the full Board of Directors of Time at the Purchase Time to be 24 persons, 12 of whom shall be designated by Time prior to the Purchase Time and 12 of whom shall be designated by WCI (and shall be elected by at least a two-thirds vote of the entire Board of Directors of Time) prior to the Purchase Time. The initial allocation of such directors among the three classes of the Board of Directors of Time shall be agreed among the parties, the designees of each party to be divided equally among such classes; *provided, however,* that if, prior to the Effective Time, any of such designees shall decline or be unable to serve, the party whose designee is unable to serve shall designate another person to serve in such person's stead. Time's Board of Directors will also take action to cause (i) the committees of the Board of Directors of Time at the Purchase Time to be as set forth, and consisting of the designees from the parties set forth, on Exhibit 5.12(a) and (ii) the persons indicated on Exhibit 5.12(b) to be elected to the offices specified in such Exhibit.

(b) *Certain Votes Thereafter.* Notwithstanding anything in this Agreement to the contrary, if WCI's designees are elected to the Board of Directors of Time, then on or after the Purchase Time and prior to the Effective Time, the affirmative vote of a majority of the Time directors then on the Board of Directors of Time who are directors of Time as of June 16, 1989 ("Present Time Directors", which term includes any successor director (other than a Present WCI Director) elected upon the recommendation of the remaining Time directors) shall be required to (i) amend or terminate this Agreement or the Share Exchange Agreement by Time, (ii) agree as to the components of Merger Consideration on behalf of Time, (iii) select investment banking firms on behalf of Time for purposes of the determination of the Merger Consideration, (iv) exercise or waive any of Time's rights or remedies under this Agreement or the Share Exchange Agreement or (v) extend the time for performance of any of WCI's obligations under this Agreement or the Share Exchange Agreement.

5.13. *Employment Agreements.* WCI and Time shall, as of or prior to the Purchase Time, enter into employment contracts with the persons set forth on such Exhibit on substantially the terms set forth in Exhibit 5.13(y) hereto. Such contracts shall be effective as of the Effective Time.

5.14. *Indemnification; Director's and Officers' Insurance.* (a) WCI shall, and from and after the Effective Time, Time and the Surviving Corporation shall, indemnify, defend and hold harmless each person who is now, or has been at any time prior to the date hereof or who becomes prior to the Effective Time, an officer, director or employee of WCI or any of its Subsidiaries (the "Indemnified Parties") against (i) all losses, claims, damages, costs, expenses, liabilities or judgments or amounts that are paid in settlement with the approval of the indemnifying party (which approval shall not be unreasonably withheld) of or in connection with any claim, action, suit, proceeding or investigation based in whole or in part on or arising in whole or in part out of the fact that such person is or was a director, officer or employee of WCI or any Subsidiary, whether pertaining to any matter existing or occurring at or prior to the Effective Time and whether asserted or claimed prior to, or at or after, the Effective Time ("Indemnified Liabilities") and (ii) all Indemnified Liabilities based in whole or in part on, or arising in whole or in part out of, or pertaining to this Agreement or the transactions contemplated hereby, in each case to the full extent a corporation is permitted under Delaware Law to indemnify its own directors, officers and employees, as the case may be (and Time and the Surviving Corporation, as the case may be, will pay expenses in advance of the final disposition of any such action or proceeding to each Indemnified Party to the full extent permitted by law upon receipt of any undertaking contemplated by Section 145(e) of the DGCL). Without limiting the foregoing, in the event any such claim, action, suit, proceeding or investigation is brought against any Indemnified Party (whether arising before or after the Effective Time), (i) the Indemnified Parties may retain counsel satisfactory to them and WCI (or them and Time and the Surviving Corporation after the Effective Time); (ii) WCI (or after the Effective Time, Time and the Surviving Corporation) shall pay all reasonable fees and expenses of such counsel for the Indemnified Parties promptly as statements

Section 5.16. Under this form of the agreement the Warner board of directors would have important functions until the merger. The new Warner board would have a responsibility to see that the public shareholders were not treated unfairly at the expense of Time. During that period it is treated like the Time board. Membership is split between the two companies, with the continuing Warner directors to decide issues related to this agreement. See Section 5.12.

Section 5.17. Time is now contractually committed to maintaining its poison pill rights as a defense against Paramount. This provision is not one that can be waived by Time's exercising its fiduciary out. See Section 4.1(l)(ii). Thus Time would have had an additional argument in support of its pill if its use had become an issue in the court struggle with Paramount. It did not because Paramount was in no position to complete its offer even without interference from a Time poison pill. However, there was plenty of other interference by Time and Warner, particularly in connection with Paramount's attempts to obtain regulatory approvals for a change in control of Time's television licenses.

therefor are received; and (iii) WCI (or after the Effective Time, Time and the Surviving Corporation) will use all reasonable efforts to assist in the vigorous defense or any such matter, provided that neither WCI, Time nor the Surviving Corporation shall be liable for any settlement of any claim effected without its written consent, which consent, however, shall not be unreasonably withheld. Any Indemnified Party wishing to claim indemnification under this Section 5.14, upon learning of any such claim, action, suit, proceeding or investigation, shall notify WCI, Time, or the Surviving Corporation (but the failure so to notify an Indemnified Party shall not relieve it from any liability which it may have under this Section 5.14 except to the extent such failure prejudices such party), and shall deliver to WCI (or after the Effective Time, Time and the Surviving Corporation) the undertaking contemplated by Section 145(e) of the DGCL. The Indemnified Parties as a group may retain only one law firm to represent them with respect to each such matter unless there is, under applicable standards of professional conduct, a conflict on any significant issue between the positions of any two or more Indemnified Parties.

(b) For a period of six years after the Effective Time, Time shall cause to be maintained in effect the current policies of directors' and officers' liability insurance maintained by WCI (provided that Time may substitute therefor policies of at least the same coverage and amounts containing terms and conditions which are no less advantageous) with respect to claims arising from facts or events which occurred before the Effective Time to the extent available on commercially reasonable terms.

(c) The provisions of this Section 5.14 are intended to be for the benefit of, and shall be enforceable by, each Indemnified Party, his heirs and his representatives.

5.15. *Dividend Adjustment.* In the event that the Merger Securities include Time Common Stock, each of Time and WCI shall declare a dividend on each share of its Common Stock to holders of record of such shares as of the close of business on the business day next preceding the Effective Time in an amount equal to the product of (A) a fraction, (i) the numerator of which equals the number of days between the payment date with respect to the most recent dividend paid by Time or WCI, as the case may be, and the Effective Time and (ii) the denominator of which equals 91 and (B) the amount of the regular cash dividend most recently paid by Time or WCI, as the case may be.

5.16. *WCI Board of Directors.* (a) *Designation.* WCI's Board of Directors will take action to cause the number of directors comprising the full Board of Directors of WCI at the Purchase Time to be 24 persons, 12 of whom shall be designated by WCI prior to the Purchase Time and 12 of whom shall be designated by Time prior to the Purchase Time. The initial allocation of such directors among the three classes of the Board of Directors of WCI shall be agreed among the parties, the designees of each party to be divided equally among such classes; *provided, however,* that if, prior to the Effective Time, any of such designees shall decline or be unable to serve, the party whose designee is unable to serve shall designate another person to serve in such person's stead. WCI's Board of Directors will also take action to cause (i) the committees of the Board of Directors of WCI at the Purchase Time to be as set forth, and consisting of the designees from the parties set forth, on Exhibit 5.16(a) and (ii) the persons indicated on Exhibit 5.16(b) to be elected to the offices specified in such Exhibit.

(b) *Certain Votes Thereafter.* Notwithstanding anything in this Agreement to the contrary, if Time's designees are elected to the Board of Directors of WCI, then on or after the Purchase Time and prior to the Effective Time, the affirmative vote of a majority of the WCI directors then on the Board of Directors of WCI who are directors of WCI as of June 16, 1989 ("Present WCI Directors", which term includes any successor (other than a Present Time Director) elected upon the recommendation of the remaining WCI directors), shall be required to (i) amend or terminate this Agreement or the Share Exchange Agreement by WCI, (ii) agree as to the components of Merger Consideration on behalf of WCI, (iii) select investment banking firms on behalf of WCI for purposes of the determination of the Merger Consideration, (iv) exercise or waive any of WCI's rights or remedies under this Agreement or the Share Exchange Agreement or (v) extend the time for performance of any of Time's or Sub's obligations under this Agreement or the Share Exchange Agreement.

5.17. *Time Rights Plan.* Time shall not redeem the Rights or amend or terminate the Rights Agreement prior to the Effective Time unless it shall be required to do so by order of a court of competent jurisdiction; *provided, however,* that Time shall be entitled to amend the Rights Agreement from time to time to delay the occurrence of a Distribution Date (as defined therein).

Section 5.18. A technical point has been added. Warner must take all steps necessary to help avoid problems with regulatory agencies and under state antitakeover laws. Problems with state securities ('blue sky') laws were unlikely under a merger where New York Stock Exchange listed common stock of Time would be issued. Under the new agreement, however, there was the possibility that specially created securities for this transaction might give state securities commissioners pause. There should have been no problem expected with Delaware's antitakeover law because of the exemption provided by the existence of this agreement. State antitakeover laws other than Delaware's probably would have been held unconstitutional insofar as they were applied to a company incorporated in another state, but Time's lawyers were taking no chances. The importance of this point is probably the reason the standard formulation, 'take all steps *reasonably* necessary,' is not used.

Section 5.19. Time and Warner are not going to wait for the merger to change Time's name.

Section 5.20. This is an entirely new provision. Warner management option-holders are getting their old options cashed out, and are also receiving commitments for stock options and equity units under new Time Warner plans.

Section 5.21. Time is committed to taking all steps necessary to obtain the funds to complete the merger. There is no financing out. However, if Time had taken all steps necessary and failed, it is unlikely that Warner would have had a legal remedy.

5.18. *Additional Agreements; Reasonable Efforts.* Subject to the terms and conditions of this Agreement, each of the parties hereto agrees to use all reasonable efforts to take, or cause to be taken, all action and to do, or cause to be done, all things necessary, proper or advisable under applicable laws and regulations to consummate and make effective the transactions contemplated by this Agreement and the Share Exchange Agreement, subject to the appropriate vote of stockholders of WCI described in Section 6.1(a), including cooperating fully with the other party, including by provision of information and making of all necessary filings in connection with, among other things, the FCC Approvals and the Local Approvals and under the HSR Act, and including, in the case of WCI, taking all steps necessary or requested by Time in order to cause the Offer, the Merger and the other transactions contemplated by this Agreement and the Share Exchange Agreement to be exempt and otherwise not subject to the provisions of, any blue sky, antitakeover or similar law of any jurisdiction. In case at any time after the Effective Time any further action is necessary or desirable to carry out the purposes of this Agreement or to vest the Surviving Corporation with full title to all properties, assets, rights, approvals, immunities and franchises of either of the Constituent Corporations, the proper officers and directors of each party to this Agreement shall take all such necessary action.

5.19. *Name Change.* Time shall cause its corporate name to be changed to Time Warner Inc. as soon as practicable on or after the Purchase Time.

5.20. *Certain Incentive Compensation Plans.* (a) *Stock Options.* Time shall, as promptly as practicable following the Effective Time, take all corporate action necessary and shall otherwise use its best efforts (i) to adopt and implement the Time Warner 1989 Stock Incentive Plan (the "1989 Incentive Plan"), in substantially the form of Exhibit 5.20 hereto, covering 10 million shares of Time Common Stock, (ii) obtain stockholder approval of the 1989 Incentive Plan within one year following the Effective Time, (iii) issue to persons (except to the extent they otherwise agree with WCI), who own, immediately prior to the Purchase Time, (x) options under the WCI Stock Plans, (y) SARs or (z) Bonus Units (other than Bonus Units so owned by Steven J. Ross, who will receive options pursuant to his employment contract with Time), options to purchase that number of shares of Time Common Stock under the 1989 Plan ("New Options") as is equal to the number of shares of WCI Common Stock covered by WCI options, SARs and Bonus Units so owned by such persons, multiplied by .465, each such New Option to have an exercise price equal to the greater of (A) $150 per share of Time Common Stock and (B) the average of the closing sales prices of a share of Time Common Stock over the ten consecutive trading day period commencing on the trading day immediately following the Effective Time, (iv) reserve for issuance a sufficient number of shares of Time Common Stock for delivery upon exercise of the foregoing options and (v) file a registration statement on Form S-3 or Form S-8, as the case may be (or any successor or other appropriate forms), or another form with respect to the shares of Time Common Stock subject to such New Options and maintain the effectiveness of such registration statement or registration statements (and maintain the current status of the prospectus or prospectuses contained therein) for so long as such New Options remain outstanding.

(b) *Equity Units.* As contemplated by the 1982 WCI Equity Unit Purchase Plan, the committee administering such Plan may adjust the "Book Value Per Share" and the "Resale Price" of units issued thereunder to equal, effective immediately prior to consummation of the Merger, the Merger Consideration Amount which shall include any additional consideration payable pursuant to Section 2.1(f) (based upon shares of WCI Common Stock included within such units) and shall make such other changes as it deems appropriate to give effect to the Merger. These amounts are subject to further adjustments, as contemplated under such Plan, for changes in book value per share of Time Common Stock occurring after the commencement of the first full fiscal quarter of Time following the Effective Time. Upon consummation of the Merger, Time will assume such Plan.

5.21. *Financing.* Time shall take all steps necessary to secure the funds necessary to consummate the Offer and the Merger.

Section 6.1. The conditions to the merger have been cut to a bare minimum. The Warner shareholder vote is required by law. A Time shareholder vote, which is not mentioned elsewhere in the agreement, could still be necessary under New York Stock Exchange rules if Time issued more than 20% of its outstanding stock in the merger. Otherwise, the only thing that could stop the merger would be a court order. '[U]ndertaking (with the mutual consent of the parties)' probably refers to an agreement in litigation suggested to the parties by a court to avoid the issuance of an injunction before the court can hold a hearing.

However, it is not possible to tell from this provision alone whether the agreement is quite as tight as it appears. There are separate conditions to the tender offer agreed upon in Section 1.1. In fact, however, those conditions, which we have reproduced at the end of the agreement (Exhibit A), do not give Time much room to maneuver. There are also some new termination provisions in Section 7.1.

Section 7.1(b) and (d). Note the modifying phrase, 'prior to the Purchase Time.' The agreement is now designed so that Time would have an almost impossible time getting out of the merger once it purchases control in the tender offer. This is a standard idea in two-step acquisitions. Even if after Time buys the shares in the tender offer Warner's business should change materially or Time should discover that Warner's representations and warranties were rife with mistakes, Time would still be committed.

Section 7.1(e) and (f). Time and Warner also have additional termination options if the tender offer has become stalled, giving Warner shareholders additional withdrawal rights under the Federal tender offer rules, or if Warner has exercised its fiduciary out options. These termination rights are a compromise. The parties would like certainty but the combination of business considerations and legal rules is too complicated for them to be able to achieve it.

ARTICLE VI
CONDITIONS PRECEDENT

6.1. *Conditions to Each Party's Obligation To Effect the Merger.* The respective obligation of each party to effect the Merger shall be subject to the satisfaction prior to the Closing Date of the following conditions:

(a) *Stockholder Approval.* If at the time required by applicable law, this Agreement shall have been approved and adopted by the affirmative vote of a majority of the votes that the holders of the outstanding shares of WCI Common Stock and WCI Series B Preferred, voting together as a class, are entitled to cast, and, if required by applicable law or NYSE rules, the issuance of equity securities as part of the Merger Consideration shall have been approved by the stockholders of Time; and

(b) *No Injunctions or Restraints.* No temporary restraining order, preliminary or permanent injunction or other order issued by any court of competent jurisdiction or other legal restraint, undertaking (with the mutual consent of the parties) or prohibition (an "Injunction") preventing the consummation of the Merger shall be in effect.

ARTICLE VII
TERMINATION AND AMENDMENT

7.1. *Termination.* This Agreement may be terminated at any time prior to the Effective Time, whether before or after approval of the matters presented in connection with the Merger by the stockholders of WCI:

(a) by mutual consent of Time and WCI;

(b) prior to the Purchase Time, by either Time or WCI if there has been a material breach of any covenant or agreement on the part of the other set forth in this Agreement or the Share Exchange Agreement which breach has not been cured within 5 business days following receipt by the breaching party of notice of such breach;

(c) by either Time or WCI if (i) any permanent injunction or other order of a court or other competent authority preventing the consummation of the Merger shall have become final and nonappealable or (ii) if the Offer shall have been terminated in accordance with its terms without Time having purchased any shares of WCI Common Stock thereunder;

(d) prior to the Purchase Time, by either Time or WCI if, but for the provisions of Section 4.1(1), such party would have the right to terminate this Agreement pursuant to Section 7.1(b); *provided, however,* that prior to any such termination Time and WCI shall, and shall cause their respective financial and legal advisors to, negotiate in good faith and for a reasonable period of time to make such adjustments in the terms and conditions of the Merger as would enable the party seeking termination to proceed with the transaction;

(e) by either Time or WCI if Time shall not have purchased any shares of WCI Common Stock pursuant to the Offer within 60 days following the commencement of the Offer (determined pursuant to Rule 14d-2 under the Exchange Act); *provided, however,* that the passage of the period referred to in this Section 7.1(e) shall be tolled for any part thereof (but not in excess of an additional 60 days) during which (i) any party hereto shall be subject to an Injunction prohibiting the purchase of shares of WCI Common Stock pursuant to the Offer, the consummation of the Merger or the transactions contemplated by the Share Exchange Agreement or (ii) the Offer shall have been extended pursuant to clause (b) of the first proviso to the third sentence of Section 1.1(a);

(f) by Time if (i) the Board of Directors of WCI shall have withdrawn or modified in any respect adverse to Time its approval or recommendation of the Offer, this Agreement or the Merger or if the Board of Directors of WCI shall have recommended that stockholders of WCI accept any takeover proposal of any other party, (ii) if WCI shall directly or through agents or representatives continue discussions with any third party concerning any takeover proposal for WCI for more than 15 business days after having first furnished information or commenced

28

The Additional Termination provision found at Section 7.5 of the prior agreement has been deleted. It related principally to accounting concerns and was no longer necessary.

discussions with that party (whichever shall be earlier) with respect thereto or (iii) if (x) WCI shall have received a takeover proposal which contains a proposal as to price (without regard to the specificity of such price proposal), (y) the fact that such proposal has been made shall have been publicly disclosed and (z) WCI shall not have rejected such proposal within the later of 10 business days of its receipt or the date its existence first becomes publicly disclosed; or

(g) by WCI if it shall exercise the right specified in clause (iv) of the proviso to Section 4.1(e).

7.2. *Effect of Termination.* In the event of termination of this Agreement by either WCI or Time as provided in Section 7.1, this Agreement shall forthwith become void and there shall be no liability or obligation on the part of Time, Sub or WCI or their respective officers or directors except (x) with respect to the last sentence of Section 5.4, and Sections 5.10, 5.11 and 5.21, (y) with respect to the representations and warranties contained in Sections 3.1 and 3.2 insofar as such representations and warranties related to the Share Exchange Agreement and (z) to the extent that such termination results from the wilful breach by a party hereto of any of its covenants or agreements set forth in this Agreement except as provided in Section 8.7.

7.3. *Amendment.* This Agreement may be amended by the parties hereto, by action taken or authorized by their respective Boards of Directors, at any time before or after approval of the matters presented in connection with the Merger by the stockholders of WCI, but, after any such approval, no amendment shall be made which by law requires further approval by such stockholders without such further approval. This Agreement may not be amended except by an instrument in writing signed on behalf of each of the parties hereto.

7.4. *Extension; Waiver.* At any time prior to the Effective Time, the parties hereto, by action taken or authorized by their respective Board of Directors, may, to the extent legally allowed, (i) extend the time for the performance of any of the obligations or other acts of the other parties hereto, (ii) waive any inaccuracies in the representations and warranties contained herein or in any document delivered pursuant hereto and (iii) waive compliance with any of the agreements or conditions contained herein. Any agreement on the part of a party hereto to any such extension or waiver shall be valid only if set forth in a written instrument signed on behalf of such party.

ARTICLE VIII
GENERAL PROVISIONS

8.1. *Nonsurvival of Representations, Warranties and Agreements.* None of the representations, warranties and agreements in this Agreement or in any instrument delivered pursuant to this Agreement shall survive the Effective Time, except for the agreements contained in Sections 2.1, 2.2, 5.9 through 5.21, the last sentence of Section 7.3 and Article VIII, and any agreements of the "affiliates" of WCI delivered pursuant to Section 5.7.

8.2. *Notices.* All notices and other communications hereunder shall be in writing and shall be deemed given if delivered personally, telecopied (which is confirmed) or mailed by registered or certified mail (return receipt requested) to the parties at the following addresses (or at such other address for a party as shall be specified by like notice):

(a) if to Time or Sub, to

Time Incorporated
Time & Life Building
Rockefeller Center
New York, N.Y. 10020
Telecopy No. (212) 522-1252

   Attention of Corporate Secretary;

with a copy to

Samuel C. Butler, Esq.
Cravath, Swaine & Moore
One Chase Manhattan Plaza

New York, N.Y. 10005
Telecopy No. (212) 428-3700

and

(b) if to WCI, to

Warner Communications Inc.
75 Rockefeller Plaza
New York, N.Y. 10019
Telecopy No. (212) 333-3987

Attention of General Counsel;

with a copy to

Arthur L. Liman, Esq.
Paul, Weiss, Rifkind, Wharton & Garrison
1285 Avenue of the Americas
New York, N.Y. 10019
Telecopy No. (212) 757-3990

8.3. *Interpretation.* When a reference is made in this Agreement to Sections, such reference shall be to a Section of this Agreement unless otherwise indicated. The table of contents and headings contained in this Agreement are for reference purposes only and shall not affect in any way the meaning or interpretation of this Agreement. Whenever the words "includes" or "including" are used in this Agreement they shall be deemed to be followed by the words "without limitation". The phrase "made available" in this Agreement shall mean that the information referred to has been made available if requested by the party to whom such information is to be made available. The phrases "the date of this Agreement", "the date hereof", and terms of similar import, unless the context otherwise requires, shall be deemed to refer to March 3, 1989.

8.4. *Counterparts.* This Agreement may be executed in two or more counterparts, all of which shall be considered one and the same agreement and shall become effective when two or more counterparts have been signed by each of the parties and delivered to the other parties, it being understood that all parties need not sign the same counterpart.

8.5. *Entire Agreement; No Third Party Beneficiaries; Rights of Ownership.* This Agreement (including the documents and the instruments referred to herein, including the Share Exchange Agreement) (a) constitutes the entire agreement and supersedes all prior agreements (including the Agreement between WCI and Time dated as of April 22, 1988) and understandings, both written and oral, among the parties with respect to the subject matter hereof and (b) except as provided in Section 5.14, is not intended to confer upon any person other than the parties hereto any rights or remedies hereunder. Notwithstanding anything to the contrary contained in this Agreement, no representations or warranties shall be deemed to have been made by WCI with respect to the Shareholders Agreement, dated as of February 21, 1984, among WCI, Chris-Craft Industries, Inc. and BHC, as amended, including by an Agreement, dated as of February 7, 1986; *provided, however,* that nothing contained herein shall be construed to mean that a consent or waiver is required with respect thereto in connection with the execution, delivery and performance of this Agreement and the Share Exchange Agreement and the consummation of the transactions contemplated hereby and thereby.

8.6. *Governing Law.* This Agreement shall be governed and construed in accordance with the laws of the State of Delaware.

8.7. *No Remedy in Certain Circumstances.* Each party agrees that, should any court or other competent authority hold any provision of this Agreement or the Share Exchange Agreement or part hereof or thereof to be null, void or unenforceable, or order for any party to take any action inconsistent herewith or not to take any action required herein, the other party shall not be entitled to specific performance of such provision or part hereof or thereof or to any other remedy, including but not limited to money damages, for breach hereof or thereof or of any other provision of this Agreement or the Share Exchange Agreement or part hereof or thereof as a result of such holding or order.

8.8. *Publicity.* Except as otherwise required by law or the rules of the NYSE, so long as this Agreement is in effect, neither WCI nor Time shall, or shall permit any of its Subsidiaries to, issue or cause the publication of any press release or other public announcement with respect to the transactions contemplated by this Agreement without the consent of the other party, which consent shall not be unreasonably withheld.

8.9. *Assignment.* Neither this Agreement nor any of the rights, interests or obligations hereunder shall be assigned by any of the parties hereto (whether by operation of law or otherwise) without the prior written consent of other parties, except that Sub may assign, in its sole discretion, any or all of its rights, interests and obligations hereunder to Time or to any direct wholly owned Subsidiary of Time. Subject to the preceding sentence, this Agreement will be binding upon, inure to the benefit of and be enforceable by the parties and their respective successors and assigns.

IN WITNESS WHEREOF, Time, Sub and WCI have caused this Agreement, as amended and restated, to be signed by their respective officers thereunto duly authorized, all as of June 16, 1989.

TIME INCORPORATED,

by   J. R. MUNRO
Name: J. R. Munro
Title: Chairman of the Board and Chief Executive Officer

Attest:

THOMAS W. MCENERNEY
Name: Thomas W. McEnerney
Title: Assistant Secretary

TW SUB INC.,

by   GERALD M. LEVIN
Name: Gerald M. Levin
Title: Vice Chairman of the Board

Attest:

THOMAS W. MCENERNEY
Name: Thomas W. McEnerney
Title: Assistant Secretary

WARNER COMMUNICATIONS INC.,

by   STEVEN J. ROSS
Name: Steven J. Ross
Title: Chairman of the Board and Chief Executive Officer

Attest:

ALLAN B. ECKER
NAME: Allan B. Ecker
Title: Secretary

32

Conditions of the Offer. The tender offer conditions are the heart of any tender offer. Arbitragers and other sophisticated shareholders scrutinize them to see how firm the offer really is. Courts are very concerned about them. Their analysis of the reasonableness of takeover defenses often focuses on the likelihood that the offer would actually be completed. As the testimony in the litigation between Time and Paramount showed, the Time directors' negative view of the value of the Paramount offer was based in part on the risk that the highly conditional Paramount tender offer would not be completed.

Time's offer had only a bare minimum of conditions, as is shown by the conditions reproduced on the opposite page. Warner officials testified in the Time–Paramount litigation that they negotiated a tight commitment because they were concerned, among other things, that the tender offer would expose them to other bids.

The minimum tender condition had to be met so that Time would be assured of control. Releasing Time if the merger agreement were terminated or if it terminated the offer with Warner's consent is easy to understand. Nor could Time buy the shares in the face of an injunction or if the purchase were illegal.

Paragraph (c) at the beginning looks like a rather broad condition which would allow Time not to buy shares if there is a calamity in financial markets or a war. But even these events turn out at the end of the paragraph to be relevant only if they would materially impair Time's ability to get financing on terms reasonably acceptable to it. If Time had or could obtain the financing it would have had to make the purchase even if, for example, a stock market crash cut the price of most stocks, including Warner's, by 50%, leaving Time with an extremely high tender offer price. Incidentally, clause (c)(ii) is a condition that only came into general use after the October 19, 1987 market crash during which trading was never suspended and therefore clause (c)(i) would not have been enough.

In contrast, Paramount's offer for Time understandably had a number of highly significant conditions. Without them, Paramount would have risked a disaster. Because of these conditions Time's management called the offer 'smoke and mirrors.' They included a requirement for termination of the Time–Warner agreement or amendment of it to include a shareholder vote that would be controlled by Paramount; Paramount's being satisfied in its sole discretion that it had obtained all approvals necessary to transfer Time's programming and cable television businesses on terms satisfactory to Paramount; and removal or invalidation of Time's takeover defenses.

CONDITIONS OF THE OFFER

Notwithstanding any other provision of the Offer, Time will not be required to accept for payment or, subject to any applicable rules and regulations of the Securities and Exchange Commission, including Rule 14e-1(c) (relating to Time's obligation to pay for or return tendered shares promptly after the termination or withdrawal of the Offer), to pay for, any shares not theretofore accepted for payment or paid for, and may terminate or amend the Offer as provided herein, if: (i) subject to Section 1.1(a) of the Merger Agreement, at the expiration date of the Offer the Minimum Tender Condition (as defined below) has not been satisfied or (ii) at the expiration date of the Offer, in the case of paragraphs (a) or (c) below, or at any time on or after June 16, 1989, and before the acceptance of such shares for payment or the payment therefor, in the case of the following paragraphs (b) or (d), any of the following conditions exist:

(a) an Injunction which prevents the acceptance for payment of, or payment for, any Shares shall have been issued and shall remain in effect (it being understood that Time is obligated pursuant to Section 1.1(a) of the Merger Agreement to extend the Offer subject to the right of termination provided in Section 7.1(e) during the pendency of any non-final Injunction);

(b) there shall be any action taken, or any statute, rule, regulation or order enacted, promulgated or issued or deemed applicable to the Offer or the Merger by any United States Federal or state government or governmental agency or instrumentality or court, which would make the acceptance for payment of, or payment for, any shares, of WCI Common Stock, or consummation of the Merger, illegal;

(c) there shall have occurred (i) any general suspension of trading in, or limitation on prices for, securities on any national securities exchange or in the over-the-counter market in the United States, (ii) any extraordinary or material adverse change in the financial markets or major stock exchange indices in the United States, (iii) any material adverse change in United States currency exchange rates or a suspension of, or limitation on, the markets therefor, (iv) a declaration of a banking moratorium or any suspension of payments in respect of banks in the United States, (v) any limitation (whether or not mandatory) by any government or governmental authority or agency, domestic or foreign on, or other event that, in the reasonable judgment of Time, might affect, the extension of credit by banks or other lending institutions or (vi) a commencement of a war or armed hostilities or other national or international calamity directly or indirectly involving the United States, which in the case of any of the matters described in (i) through (vi) materially adversely affects the ability of Time to obtain financing for the Offer on terms reasonably acceptable to Time; or

(d) the Merger Agreement shall have been terminated in accordance with its terms or the Offer shall have been terminated with the consent of WCI.

The foregoing conditions are for the sole benefit of Time and may be asserted by Time regardless of the circumstances giving rise to such condition or may be waived by Time in whole or in part at any time and from time to time in their sole discretion. The failure by Time at any time to exercise any of the foregoing rights shall not be deemed a waiver of any such right, the waiver of any such right with respect to particular facts and other circumstances shall not be deemed a waiver with respect to any other facts and circumstances, and each such right shall be deemed an ongoing right that may be asserted at any time and from time-to-time.

For purposes of the Offer, the Minimum Tender Condition shall mean at least 100,000,000 shares being validly tendered and not withdrawn prior to the expiration of the Offer.

APPENDIX

Some Important Statutes and Rules and the *Paramount–Time* Opinion

Contents

Introduction

In any legal system, general solutions ultimately must be tested by how they deal with details. The Appendix contains the text of some of the most important Federal and state takeover statutes and SEC rules. It is designed to help a reader to understand better how the U.S. legal system deals with the practical details of the takeover concepts we have discussed in the book. Every item in the Appendix has played an important role in the prior three sections and usually is referred to in the Glossary. We have also included the Delaware Supreme Court's opinion in the *Paramount–Time* case. Non-lawyers and foreign lawyers are encouraged to use the Appendix. They should find it very useful once they have read the discussions in Parts I and II.

A.1

General Antifraud Provisions in the Federal Securities Laws

> The Federal antifraud provisions include the highly general §10(b) of the Securities Exchange Act of 1934 and the corresponding SEC Rule 10b–5. These are the foundation for most of the insider trading law in the United States and are a favorite of plaintiffs' lawyers in shareholder suits alleging securities law violations. There are similar antifraud rules in the SEC proxy regulations and in other Federal securities laws.

A.1.1 SECURITIES EXCHANGE ACT OF 1934 §10

Section 10. Regulation of the Use of Manipulative and Deceptive Devices

It shall be unlawful for any person, directly or indirectly, by the use of any means or instrumentality of interstate commerce or of the mails, or of any facility of any national securities exchange –

(a) To effect a short sale, or to use or employ any stop-loss order in connection with the purchase or sale, of any security registered on a national securities exchange, in contravention of such rules and regulations as the Commission may prescribe as necessary or appropriate in the public interest or for the protection of investors.

(b) To use or employ, in connection with the purchase or sale of any security registered on a national securities exchange or any security not so registered, any manipulative or deceptive device or contrivance in contravention of such rules and regulations as the Commission may prescribe as necessary or appropriate in the public interest or for the protection of investors.

A.1.2 SECURITIES AND EXCHANGE COMMISSION RULE 10b–5

Rule 10b–5. Employment of Manipulative and Deceptive Devices

It shall be unlawful for any person, directly or indirectly, by the use of any means or instrumentality of interstate commerce, or of the mails, or of any facility of any national securities exchange,

(a) to employ any device, scheme, or artifice to defraud,

(b) to make any untrue statement of a material fact or to omit to state a material fact necessary in order to make the statements made, in the light of the circumstances under which they were made, not misleading, or

(c) to engage in any act, practice, or course of business which operates or would operate as a fraud or deceit upon any person, in connection with the purchase or sale of any security.

A.2

Federal Tender Offer Statute and Regulations

The Federal tender offer statute and regulations are the rulebook for tender offers. Tender offer strategies require a very close reading of these rules. The rules include two controversial provisions, Rules 14d–10 and 14e–3, that have been criticized as examples of the SEC's overstepping its authority. (Another controversial SEC rule, Rule 19c–4, was overturned by court action in 1990. See Appendix, A.3.)

With these excerpts we have also included §13(d) of the 1934 Act (and the corresponding SEC rules). These cover accumulations of shares and require reports by any person or group controlling 5% or more of the stock of a public company.

A.2.1 SECURITIES EXCHANGE ACT OF 1934 §13(D)

(1) Any person who, after acquiring directly or indirectly the beneficial ownership of any equity security of a class which is registered pursuant to section 12 of this title, or any equity security of an insurance company which would have been required to be so registered except for the exemption contained in section 12(g)(2)(G) of this title, or any equity security issued by a closed-end investment company registered under the Investment Company Act of 1940 or any equity security issued by a Native Corporation pursuant to section 37(d)(6) of the Alaska Native Claims Settlement Act, is directly or indirectly the beneficial owner of more than 5 per centum of such class shall, within ten days after such acquisition, send to the issuer of the security at its principal executive office, by registered or certified mail, send to each exchange where the security is traded, and file with the Commission, a statement containing such of the following information, and such additional information, as the Commission may by rules and regulations prescribe as necessary or appropriate in the public interest or for the protection of investors –

(A) The background, and identity, residence, and citizenship of, and the nature of such beneficial ownership by, such person and all other persons by whom or on whose behalf the purchases have been or are to be effected;

(B) the source and amount of the funds or other consideration used or to be used in making the purchases, and if any part of the purchase price or proposed purchase price is represented or is to be represented by funds or other consideration borrowed or otherwise obtained for the purpose of acquiring, holding, or trading such security, a description of the transaction and the names of the parties thereto, except that where a source of funds is a loan made in the ordinary course of business by a bank, as defined in section 3(a)(6) of this title, if the person filing such statement so requests, the name of the bank shall not be made available to the public;

(C) if the purpose of the purchases or prospective purchases is to acquire control of the business of the issuer of the securities, any plans or proposals which such persons may have to liquidate such issuer, to sell its assets to or merge it with any other persons, or to make any other major change in its business or corporate structure;

(D) the number of shares of such security which are beneficially owned, and the number of shares concerning which there is a right to acquire, directly or indirectly, by (i) such person, and (ii) by each associate of such person, giving the background, identity, residence and citizenship of each such associate; and

(E) information as to any contracts, arrangements, or understandings with any person with respect to any securities of the issuer, including but not limited to transfer of any of the securities, joint ventures, loan or option arrangements, puts or calls, guaranties of loans, guaranties against loss or guaranties of profits, division of losses or profits, or the giving or withholding of proxies, naming the persons with whom such contracts, arrangements, or understandings have been entered into, and giving the details thereof.

(2) If any material change occurs in the facts set forth in the statements to the issuer and the exchange, and in the statement filed with the Commission, an amendment shall be transmitted to the issuer and the exchange and shall be filed with the Commission, in accordance with such rules and regulations as the Commission may prescribe as necessary or appropriate in the public interest or for the protection of investors.

(3) When two or more persons act as a partnership, limited partnership, syndicate, or other group for the purpose of acquiring, holding, or disposing of securities of an issuer, such syndicate or group shall be deemed a 'person' for the purposes of this subsection.

(4) In determining, for purposes of this subsection, any percentage of a class

of any security, such class shall be deemed to consist of the amount of the outstanding securities of such class, exclusive of any securities of such class held by or for the account of the issuer or a subsidiary of the issuer.

(5) The Commission, by rule or regulation or by order, may permit any person to file in lieu of the statement required by paragraph (1) of this subsection or the rules and regulations thereunder, a notice stating the name of such person, the number of shares of any equity securities subject to paragraph (1) which are owned by him, the date of their acquisition and such other information as the Commission may specify, if it appears to the Commission that such securities were acquired by such person in the ordinary course of his business and were not acquired for the purpose of and do not have the effect of changing or influencing the control of the issuer nor in connection with or as a participant in any transaction having such purpose or effect.

(6) The provisions of this subsection shall not apply to –

(A) any acquisition or offer to acquire securities made or proposed to be made by means of a registration statement under the Securities Act of 1933;

(B) any acquisition of the beneficial ownership of a security which, together with all other acquisitions by the same person of securities of the same class during the preceding twelve months, does not exceed 2 per centum of that class;

(C) any acquisition of an equity security by the issuer of such security;

(D) any acquisition or proposed acquisition of a security which the Commission, by rules or regulations or by order, shall exempt from the provisions of this subsection as not entered into for the purpose of, and not having the effect of, changing or influencing the control of the issuer or otherwise as not comprehended within the purposes of this subsection.

A.2.2   SECURITIES EXCHANGE ACT OF 1934 §14

(a) It shall be unlawful for any person, by the use of the mails or by any means or instrumentality of interstate commerce or of any facility of a national securities exchange or otherwise, in contravention of such rules and regulations as the Commission may prescribe as necessary or appropriate in the public interest or for the protection of investors, to solicit or to permit the use of his name to solicit any proxy or consent or authorization in respect of any security (other than an exempted security) registered pursuant to section 12 of this title.

(b) (1) It shall be unlawful for any member of a national securities exchange, or any broker or dealer registered under this title, or any bank, association, or other entity that exercises fiduciary powers, in contravention of such rules and regulations as the Commission may prescribe as necessary or appropriate in the public interest or for the protection of investors, to give, or to refrain from giving a proxy, consent, or authorization in respect of any security registered pursuant to section 12 of this title and carried for the account of a customer.

(2) With respect to banks, the rules and regulations prescribed by the Commission under paragraph (1) shall not require the disclosure of the names of beneficial owners of securities in an account held by the bank on the date of enactment of this paragraph unless the beneficial owner consents to the disclosure. The provisions of this paragraph shall not apply in the case of a bank which the Commission finds has not made a good faith effort to obtain such consent from such beneficial owners.

(c) Unless proxies, consents, or authorizations in respect of a security registered pursuant to section 12 of this title are solicited by or on behalf of the management of the issuer from the holders of record of such security in accordance with the rules and regulations prescribed under subsection (a) of this section, prior to any annual or other meeting of the holders of such security, such issuer shall, in accordance with rules and regulations prescribed by the Commission, file with the Commission and transmit to all holders of record of such security information substantially equivalent to the information which would be required to be transmitted if a solicitation were made, but no information shall be required to be filed or transmitted pursuant to this subsection before July 1, 1964.

(d) (1) It shall be unlawful for any person, directly or indirectly, by use of the mails or by any means or instrumentality of interstate commerce or of any facility of a national securities exchange or otherwise, to make a tender offer for, or a request or invitation for tenders of, any class of any equity security which is registered pursuant to section 12 of this title, or any equity of an insurance company which would have been required to be so registered except for the exemption contained in section 12(g)(2)(G) of this title, or any equity security issued by a closed-end investment company registered under the Investment Company Act of 1940, if, after consummation thereof, such person would, directly or indirectly, be the beneficial owner of more than 5 per centum of such class, unless at the time copies of the offer or request or invitation are first published or sent or given to security holders such person has filed with the Commission a statement containing such of the information specified in section 13(d) of this title, and such additional information as the Commission may by rules and regulations prescribe as necessary or appropriate in the public interest or for the protection of investors. All requests or invitations for tenders or advertisements making a tender offer or requesting or inviting tenders of such a security shall be filed as a part of such statement and shall contain such of the information contained in such statement as the Commission may by rules and regulations prescribe. Copies of any additional material soliciting or requesting such tender offers subsequent to the initial solicitation or request shall contain such information as the Commission may by rules and regulations prescribe as necessary or appropriate in the public interest or for the protection of investors, and shall be filed with the Commission not later than the time copies of such material are first published or sent or given to security holders. Copies of all statements, in the form in which such material is furnished to security holders and the Commission, shall be sent to the issuer not later than the date such material is first published or sent or given to any security holders.

(2) When two or more persons act as a partnership, limited partnership, syndicate, or other group for the purpose of acquiring, holding, or disposing of securities of an issuer, such syndicate or group shall be deemed a 'person' for purposes of this subsection.

(3) In determining, for purposes of this subsection, any percentage of a class of any security, such class shall be deemed to consist of the amount of the outstanding securities of such class, exclusive of any securities of such class held by or for the account of the issuer or a subsidiary of the issuer.

(4) Any solicitation or recommendation to the holders of such a security to accept or reject a tender offer or request or invitation for tenders shall be made in accordance with such rules and regulations as the Commission may prescribe as necessary or appropriate in the public interest or for the protection of investors.

(5) Securities deposited pursuant to a tender offer or request or invitation for tenders may be withdrawn by or on behalf of the depositor at any time until the expiration of seven days after the time definitive copies of the offer or request or invitation are first published or sent or given to security holders, and at any time after sixty days from the date of the original tender offer or request or invitation, except as the Commission may otherwise prescribe by rules, regulations, or order as necessary or appropriate in the public interest or for the protection of investors.

(6) Where any person makes a tender offer, or request or invitation for tenders, for less than all the outstanding equity securities of a class, and

where a greater number of securities is deposited pursuant thereto within ten days after copies of the offer or request or invitation are first published or sent or given to security holders than such person is bound or willing to take up and pay for, the securities taken up shall be taken up as nearly as may be pro rata, disregarding fractions, according to the number of securities deposited by each depositor. The provisions of this subsection shall also apply to securities deposited within ten days after notice of an increase in the consideration offered to security holders, as described in paragraph (7), is first published or sent or given to security holders.

(7) Where any person varies the terms of a tender offer or request or invitation for tenders before the expiration thereof by increasing the consideration offered to holders of such securities, such person shall pay the increased consideration to each security holder whose securities are taken up and paid for pursuant to the tender offer or request or invitation for tenders whether or not such securities have been taken up by such person before the variation of the tender offer or request or invitation.

(8) The provisions of this subsection shall not apply to any offer for, or request or invitation for tenders of, any security –

(A) if the acquisition of such security, together with all other acquisitions by the same person of securities of the same class during the preceding twelve months, would not exceed 2 per centum of that class;

(B) by the issuer of such security; or

(C) which the Commission, by rules or regulations or by order, shall exempt from the provisions of this subsection as not entered into for the purpose of, and not having the effect of, changing or influencing the control of the issuer or otherwise as not comprehended within the purposes of this subsection.

(e) It shall be unlawful for any person to make any untrue statement of a material fact or omit to state any material fact necessary in order to make the statements made, in the light of the circumstances under which they are made, not misleading, or to engage in any fraudulent, deceptive, or manipulative acts or practices, in connection with any tender offer or request or invitation for tenders, or any solicitation of security holders in opposition to or in favor of any such offer, request, or invitation. The Commission shall, for the purposes of this subsection, by rules and regulations define, and prescribe means reasonably designed to prevent, such acts and practices as are fraudulent, deceptive, or manipulative.

A.2.3 SECURITIES AND EXCHANGE COMMISSION REGULATIONS 13D–G

Rule 13d–1. Filing of Schedules 13D and 13G

(a) Any person who, after acquiring directly or indirectly the beneficial ownership of any equity security of a class which is specified in paragraph (d), is directly or indirectly the beneficial owner of more than five percent of such class shall, within 10 days after such acquisition, send to the issuer of the security at its principal executive office, by registered or certified mail, and to each exchange where the security is traded, and file with the Commission, a statement containing the information required by Schedule 13D. Six copies of the statement, including all exhibits, shall be filed with the Commission.

(b)(1) A person who would otherwise be obligated under paragraph (a) to file a statement on Schedule 13D may, in lieu thereof, file with the Commission, within 45 days after the end of the calendar year in which such person became so obligated, six copies, including all exhibits, of a short form statement on Schedule 13G and send one copy each of such schedule to the issuer of the security at its principal executive office, by registered or certified mail, and to the principal national securities exchange where the security is traded: *Provided*, That it shall not be necessary to file a Schedule 13G unless the percentage of the class of equity security specified in paragraph (d) of this section beneficially owned as of the end of the calendar year is more than five percent: And *provided further*, That:

(i) Such person has acquired such securities in the ordinary course of his business and not with the purpose nor with the effect of changing or influencing the control of the issuer, nor in connection with or as a participant in any transaction having such purpose or effect, including any transaction subject to Rule 13d–3(b); and

(ii) Such person is:

(A) A broker or dealer registered under Section 15 of the Act;

(B) A bank as defined in Section 3(a)(6) of the Act;

(C) An insurance company as defined in Section 3(a)(19) of the Act;

(D) An investment company registered under Section 8 of the Investment Company Act of 1940;

(E) An investment adviser registered under Section 203 of the Investment Advisers Act of 1940;

(F) An employee benefit plan, or pension fund which is subject to the provisions of the Employee Retirement Income Security Act of 1974 ('ERISA') or an endowment fund;

(G) A parent holding company, provided the aggregate amount held directly by the parent, and directly and indirectly by its subsidiaries which are not persons specified in Rule 13d–1(b)(ii)(A) through (F), does not exceed one percent of the securities of the subject class;

(H) A group, provided that all the members are persons specified in Rule 13d–1(b)(1)(ii)(A) through (G); and

(iii) Such person has promptly notified any other person (or group within the meaning of Section 13(d)(3) of the Act) on whose behalf it holds, on a discretionary basis, securities exceeding five percent of the class, of any acquisition or transaction on behalf of such other person which might be reportable by that person under Section 13(d) of the Act. This paragraph only requires notice to the account owner of information which the filing person reasonably should be expected to know and which would advise the account owner of an obligation he may have to file a statement pursuant to Section 13(d) of the Act or an amendment thereto.

(2) Any person relying on Rules 13d–1(b)(1) and 13d–2(b) shall, in addition to filing any statements required thereunder, file a statement on Schedule 13G, within 10 days after the end of the first month in which such person's direct or indirect beneficial ownership exceeds 10 percent of a class of equity securities specified in Rule 13d–1(c) computed as of the last day of the month, and thereafter within 10 days after the end of any month in which such person's beneficial ownership of securities of such class, computed as of the last day of the month, increases or decreases by more than five percent of such class of equity securities. Six copies of such statement, including all exhibits, shall be filed with the Commission and one each sent, by registered or certified mail, to the issuer of the security at its principal executive office and to the principal national securities exchange where the security is traded. Once an amendment has been filed reflecting beneficial ownership of five percent or less of the class of securities, no additional filings are required by this paragraph (b)(2) unless the person thereafter becomes the beneficial owner of more than 10 percent of the class and is required to file pursuant to this provision.

(3)(i) Notwithstanding paragraphs (b)(1) and (2) and Rule 13d–2(b), a person shall immediately become subject to Rules 13d–1(a) and 13d–2(a) and shall promptly, but not more than 10 days later, file a statement on Schedule 13D if such person:

(A) Has reported that it is the beneficial owner of more than five percent of a class of equity securities in a statement on Schedule 13G pursuant to paragraph (b)(1) or (b)(2), or is required to report such acquisition but has not yet filed the schedule;

(B) Determines that it no longer has acquired or holds such securities in the ordinary course of business or not with the purpose nor with the effect of changing or influencing the control of the issuer, nor in connection with or as a participant in any transaction having such purpose or effect, including any transaction subject to Rule 13d–3(b); and

(C) Is at that time the beneficial owner of more than five percent of a class of equity securities described in Rule 13d–1(c).

(ii) For the 10-day period immediately following the date of the filing of a Schedule 13D pursuant to this paragraph (b)(3), such person shall not: (A) Vote or direct the voting of the securities described in paragraph (b)(3)(i)(A); nor, (B) Acquire an additional beneficial ownership interest in any equity securities of the issuer of such securities, nor of any person controlling such issuer.

(4) Any person who has reported an acquisition of securities in a statement on Schedule 13G pursuant to paragraph (b)(1) or (b)(2) and thereafter ceases to be a person specified in paragraph (b)(1)(ii) shall immediately become subject to Rules 13d–1(a) and 13d–2(a) and shall file, within 10 days thereafter, a statement on Schedule 13D, in the event such person is a beneficial owner at that time of more than five percent of the class of equity securities.

(c) Any person who, as of December 31, 1978 or as of the end of any calendar year thereafter, is directly or indirectly the beneficial owner of more than five percent of any equity security of a class specified in paragraph (d) and who is not required to file a statement under paragraph (a) by virtue of the exemption provided by Section 13(d)(6)(A) or (B) of the Act, or because such beneficial ownership was acquired prior to December 22, 1970 or because such person otherwise (except for the exemption provided by Section 13(d)(6)(C) of the Act) is not required to file such statement, shall, within 45 days after the end of the calendar year in which such person became obligated to report under this paragraph, send to the issuer of the security at its principal executive office, by registered or certified mail, and file with the Commission a statement containing the information required by Schedule 13G. Six copies of the statement, including all exhibits, shall be filed with the Commission.

(d) For the purpose of this regulation, the term 'equity security' means any equity security of a class which is registered pursuant to Section 12 of that Act, or any equity security of any insurance company which would have been required to be so registered except for the exemption contained in Section 12(g)(2)(G) of the Act, or any equity security issued by a closed-end investment company registered under the Investment Company Act of 1940; *provided*, such term shall not include securities of a class of non-voting securities.

(e) For the purposes of Sections 13(d) and 13(g), any person, in determining the amount of outstanding securities of a class of equity securities, may rely upon information set forth in the issuer's most recent quarterly or annual report, and any current report subsequent thereto, filed with the Commission pursuant to this Act, unless he knows or has reason to believe that the information contained therein is inaccurate.

(f)(1) Whenever two or more persons are required to file a statement containing the information required by Schedule 13D or Schedule 13G with respect to the same securities, only one statement need be filed, *provided* that:

(i) Each person on whose behalf the statement is filed is individually eligible to use the schedule on which the information is filed;

(ii) Each person on whose behalf the statement is filed is responsible for the timely filing of such statement and any amendments thereto, and for the completeness and accuracy of the information concerning such person contained therein; such person is not responsible for the completeness or accuracy of the information concerning the other persons making the filing, unless such person knows or has reason to believe that such information is inaccurate; and

(iii) Such statement identifies all such persons, contains the required information with regard to each such person, indicates that such statement is filed on behalf of all such persons, and includes, as an exhibit, their agreement in writing that such a statement is filed on behalf of each of them.

(2) A group's filing obligation may be satisfied either by a single joint filing or by each of the group's members making an individual filing. If the group's members elect to make their own filings, each such filing should identify all members of the group but the information provided concerning the other persons making the filing need only reflect information which the filing person knows or has reason to know.

Rule 13d-2. Filing of Amendments to Schedule 13D or 13G

(a) Schedule 13D – If any material change occurs in the facts set forth in the statement required by Rule 13d-1(a), including, but not limited to, any material increase or decrease in the percentage of the class beneficially owned, the person or persons who were required to file such statement shall promptly file or cause to be filed with the Commission and send or cause to be sent to the issuer at its principal executive office, by registered or certified mail, and to each exchange on which the security is traded an amendment disclosing such change. An acquisition or disposition of beneficial ownership of securities in an amount equal to one percent or more of the class of securities shall be deemed 'material' for purposes of this rule; acquisitions or dispositions of less than such amounts may be material, depending upon the facts and circumstances. Six copies of each such amendment shall be filed with the Commission.

(b) Schedule 13G – Notwithstanding paragraph (a) of this rule, and provided that the person or persons filing a statement pursuant to Rule 13d–1(b) continues to meet the requirements set forth therein, any person who has filed a short form statement on Schedule 13G shall amend such statement within 45 days after the end of each calendar year if, as of the end of such calendar year, there are any changes in the information reported in the previous filing on the schedule: *Provided, however*, that such amendment need not be filed with respect to a change in the percent of class outstanding previously reported if such change results solely from a change in the aggregate number of securities outstanding. Six copies of such amendment, including all exhibits, shall be filed with the Commission and one each sent, by registered or certified mail, to the issuer of the security at its principal executive office and to the principal national securities exchange where the security is traded. Once an amendment has been filed reflecting beneficial ownership of five percent or less of the class of securities, no additional filings are required unless the person thereafter becomes the beneficial owner of more than five percent of the class and is required to file pursuant to Rule 13d–1.

Note: For persons filing a short form statement pursuant to Rule 13d–1(b), see also Rule 13d–1(b)(2), (3) and (4).

Rule 13d–3. Determination of Beneficial Owner

(a) For the purposes of Sections 13(d) and 13(g) of the Act, a beneficial owner of a security includes any person who, directly or indirectly, through any contract, arrangement, understanding, relationship, or otherwise has or shares:

(1) Voting power which includes the power to vote, or to direct the voting of, such security; and/or

(2) Investment power which includes the power to dispose, or to direct the disposition of, such security.

(b) Any person who, directly or indirectly, creates or uses a trust, proxy, power of attorney, pooling arrangement or any other contract, arrangement, or device with the purpose or effect of divesting such person of beneficial ownership of a security or preventing the vesting of such beneficial ownership as part of a plan or scheme to evade the reporting requirements of Section 13(d) or 13(g) of the Act shall be deemed for purposes of such sections to be the beneficial owner of such security.

(c) All securities of the same class beneficially owned by a person, regardless of the form which such beneficial ownership takes, shall be aggregated in calculating the number of shares beneficially owned by such person.

(d) Notwithstanding the provisions of paragraphs (a) and (c) of this rule:

(1)(i) A person shall be deemed to be the beneficial owner of a security, subject to the provisions of paragraph (b) of this rule, if that person has the right to acquire beneficial ownership of such security, as defined in Rule 13d–4(a) within 60 days, including but not limited to any right to acquire: (A) through the exercise of any option, warrant or right; (B) through the conversion of a security; (C) pursuant to the power to revoke a trust, discretionary account, or similar arrangement; or (D) pursuant to the automatic termination of a trust, discretionary account or similar arrangement; provided, however, any person who acquires a security or power specified in paragraph (A), (B) or (C), above, with the purpose or effect of changing or influencing the control of the issuer, or in connection with or as a participant in any transaction having such purpose or effect, immediately upon such acquisition shall be deemed to be the beneficial owner of the securities which may be acquired through the exercise or conversion of such security or power. Any securities not outstanding which are subject to such options, warrants, rights or conversion privileges shall be deemed to be outstanding for the purpose of computing the percentage of outstanding securities of the class owned by such person but shall not be deemed to be outstanding for the purpose of computing the percentage of the class by any other person.

(ii) Paragraph (i) remains applicable for the purpose of determining the obligation to file with respect to the underlying security even though the option, warrant, right or convertible security is of a class of equity security, as defined in Rule 13d–1(c), and may therefore give rise to a separate obligation to file.

(2) A member of a national securities exchange shall not be deemed to be a beneficial owner of securities held directly or indirectly by it on behalf of another person solely because such member is the record holder of such securities and, pursuant to the rules of such exchange, may direct the vote of such securities, without instruction, on other than contested matters or

matters that may affect substantially the rights or privileges of the holders of the securities to be voted, but is otherwise precluded by the rules of such exchange from voting without instruction.

(3) A person who in the ordinary course of business is a pledgee of securities under a written pledge agreement shall not be deemed to be the beneficial owner of such pledged securities until the pledgee has taken all formal steps necessary which are required to declare a default and determines that the power to vote or to direct the vote or to dispose or to direct the disposition of such pledged securities will be exercised, provided that:

(i) The pledgee agreement is bona fide and was not entered into with the purpose nor with the effect of changing or influencing the control of the issuer, nor in connection with any transaction having such purpose or effect, including any transaction subject to Rule 13d–3(b);

(ii) The pledgee is a person specified in Rule 13d–1(b)(ii), including persons meeting the conditions set forth in paragraph (G) thereof; and

(iii) The pledgee agreement, prior to default, does not grant to the pledgee:

(A) The power to vote or to direct the vote of the pledged securities; or

(B) The power to dispose or direct the disposition of the pledged securities, other than the grant of such power(s) pursuant to a pledge agreement under which credit is extended subject to Regulation T and in which the pledgee is a broker or dealer registered under Section 15 of the Act.

(4) A person engaged in business as an underwriter of securities who acquires securities through his participation in good faith in a firm commitment underwriting registered under the Securities Act of 1933 shall not be deemed to be the beneficial owner of such securities until the expiration of 40 days after the date of such acquisition.

Rule 13d–4. Disclaimer of Beneficial Ownership

Any person may expressly declare in any statement filed that the filing of such statement shall not be construed as an admission that such person is, for the purposes of Section 13(d) or 13(g) of the Act, the beneficial owner of any securities covered by the statement.

Rule 13d–5. Acquisition of Securities

(a) A person who becomes a beneficial owner of securities shall be deemed to have acquired such securities for purposes of Section 13(d)(1) of the Act, whether such acquisition was through purchase or otherwise. However, executors or administrators of a decedent's estate generally will be presumed not to have acquired beneficial ownership of the securities in the decedent's estate until such time as such executors or administrators are qualified under local law to perform their duties.

(b)(1) When two or more persons agree to act together for the purpose of acquiring, holding, voting or disposing of equity securities of an issuer, the group formed thereby shall be deemed to have acquired beneficial ownership, for purposes of Sections 13(d) and 13(g) of the Act, as of the date of such agreement, of all equity securities of that issuer beneficially owned by any such persons.

(2) Notwithstanding the previous paragraph, a group shall be deemed not to have acquired any equity securities beneficially owned by the other members of the group solely by virtue of their concerted actions relating to the purchase of equity securities directly from an issuer in a transaction not involving a public offering; *provided* that:

(i) All the members of the group are persons specified in Rule 13d–1(b)(1)(ii);

(ii) The purchase is in the ordinary course of each member's business and not with the purpose nor with the effect of changing or influencing control of the issuer, nor in connection with or as a participant in any transaction having such purpose or effect, including any transaction subject to Rule 13d–3(b);

(iii) There is no agreement among or between any members of the group to act together with respect to the issuer or its securities except for the purpose of facilitating the specific purchase involved; and

(iv) The only actions among or between any members of the group with respect to the issuer or its securities subsequent to the closing date of the non-public offering are those which are necessary to conclude ministerial matters directly related to the completion of the offer or sale of the securities.

Rule 13d–6. Exemption of Certain Acquisitions

The acquisition of securities of an issuer by a person who, prior to such acquisition, was a beneficial owner of more than five percent of the outstanding securities of the same class as those acquired shall be exempt from Section 13(d) of the Act, provided that:

(a) The acquisition is made pursuant to preemptive subscription rights in an offering made to all holders of securities of the class to which the preemptive subscription rights pertain;

(b) Such person does not acquire additional securities except through the exercise of his pro rata share of the preemptive subscription rights; and

(c) The acquisition is duly reported, if required, pursuant to Section 16(a) of the Act and the rules and regulations thereunder.

Rule 13d–7. Fees for Filing Schedule 13D or 13G

The initial Schedule 13D or 13G filed by a person shall be accompanied by a fee of $100 payable to the Commission, no part of which shall be refunded. No fees shall be required with respect to the filing of any amended Schedule 13D or 13G: *Provided, however,* That once an amendment has been filed reflecting beneficial ownership of five percent or less of such class, an additional fee of $100 shall be paid with the next filing of that person which reflects ownership of more than five percent thereof.

A.2.4 SECURITIES AND EXCHANGE COMMISSION REGULATION 14D

Rule 14d–1. Scope of and Definitions Applicable to Regulations 14D and 14E

(a) *Scope.* Regulation 14D shall apply to any tender offer which is subject to Section 14(d)(1) of the Act, including, but not limited to, any tender offer for securities of a class described in that section which is made by an affiliate of the issuer of such class. Regulation 14E shall apply to any tender offer for securities (other than exempted securities) unless otherwise noted therein.

(b) *Definitions.* Unless the context otherwise requires, all terms used in Regulation 14D and Regulation 14E have the same meaning as in the Act and in Rule 12b–2 promulgated thereunder. In addition, for purposes of Sections 14(d) and 14(e) of the Act and Regulations 14D and 14E, the following definitions apply:

(1) The term 'bidder' means any person who makes a tender offer or on whose behalf a tender offer is made; *Provided, however,* That the term does not include an issuer which makes a tender offer for securities of any class of which it is the issuer;

(2) The term 'subject company' means any issuer of securities which are sought by a bidder pursuant to a tender offer;

(3) The term 'security holders' means holders of record and beneficial

owners of securities which are the subject of a tender offer;

(4) The term 'beneficial owner' shall have the same meaning as that set forth in Rule 13d–3: *Provided, however,* That, except with respect to Rule 14d–3, Rule 14d–9(d) and Item 6 of Schedule 14D–1, the term shall not include a person who does not have or share investment power or who is deemed to be a beneficial owner by virtue of Rule 13d–3(d)(1);

(5) The term 'tender offer material' means:

(i) The bidder's formal offer, including all the material terms and conditions of the tender offer and all amendments thereto;

(ii) The related transmittal letter (whereby securities of the subject company which are sought in the tender offer may be transmitted to the bidder or its depository) and all amendments thereto; and

(iii) Press releases, advertisements, letters and other documents published by the bidder or sent or given by the bidder to security holders which, directly or indirectly, solicit, invite or request tenders of the securities being sought in the tender offer;

(6) The term 'business day' means any day, other than Saturday, Sunday or a Federal holiday, and shall consist of the time period from 12:01 a.m. through 12:00 midnight Eastern time. In computing any time period under Section 14(d)(5) or Section 14(d)(6) of the Act or under Regulation 14D or Regulation 14E, the date of the event which begins the running of such time period shall be included *except that* if such event occurs on other than a business day such period shall begin to run on and shall include the first business day thereafter; and

(7) The term 'security position listing' means, with respect to securities of any issuer held by a registered clearing agency in the name of the clearing agency or its nominee, a list of those participants in the clearing agency on whose behalf the clearing agency holds the issuer's securities and of the participants' respective positions in such securities as of a specified date.

Rule 14d–2. Date of Commencement of a Tender Offer

(a) *Commencement.* A tender offer shall commence for the purposes of Section 14(d) of the Act and the rules promulgated thereunder at 12:01 a.m. on the date when the first of the following events occurs:

(1) The long form publication of the tender offer is first published by the bidder pursuant to Rule 14d–4(a)(1);

(2) The summary advertisement of the tender offer is first published by the bidder pursuant to Rule 14d–4(a)(2);

(3) The summary advertisement or the long form publication of the tender offer is first published by the bidder pursuant to Rule 14d–4(a)(3);

(4) Definitive copies of a tender offer, in which the consideration offered by the bidder consists of securities registered pursuant to the Securities Act of 1933, are first published or sent or given by the bidder to security holders; or

(5) The tender offer is first published or sent or given to security holders by the bidder by any means not otherwise referred to in paragraphs (a)(1) through (a)(4) of this section.

(b) *Public announcement*. A public announcement by a bidder through a press release, newspaper advertisement or public statement which includes the information in paragraph (c) of this section with respect to a tender offer in which the consideration consists solely of cash and/or securities exempt from registration under Section 3 of the Securities Act of 1933 shall be deemed to constitute the commencement of a tender offer under paragraph (a)(5) of this section *except that* such tender offer shall not be deemed to be first published or sent or given to security holders by the bidder under paragraph (a)(5) of this section on the date of such public announcement if within five business days of such public announcement, the bidder either:

(1) Makes a subsequent public announcement stating that the bidder has determined not to continue with such tender offer, in which event paragraph (a)(5) of this section shall not apply to the initial public announcement; or

(2) Complies with Rule 14d–3(a) and contemporaneously disseminates the disclosure required by Rule 14d–6 to security holders pursuant to Rule 14d–4 or otherwise in which event:

(i) The date of commencement of such tender offer under paragraph (a) of this section will be determined by the date the information required by Rule 14d–6 is first published or sent or given to security holders pursuant to Rule 14d–4 or otherwise; and

(ii) Notwithstanding paragraph (b)(2)(i) of this section, Section 14(d)(7) of the Act shall be deemed to apply to such tender offer from the date of such public announcement.

(c) *Information*. The information referred to in paragraph (b) of this section is as follows:

(1) The identity of the bidder;

(2) The identity of the subject company; and

(3) The amount and class of securities being sought and the price or range of prices being offered therefor.

(d) *Announcements not resulting in commencement.* A public announcement by a bidder through a press release, newspaper advertisement or public statement which only discloses the information in paragraphs (d)(1) through (d)(3) of this section concerning a tender offer in which the consideration consists solely of cash and/or securities exempt from registration under Section 3 of the Securities Act of 1933 shall not be deemed to constitute the commencement of a tender offer under paragraph (a)(5) of this section.

(1) The identity of the bidder;

(2) The identity of the subject company; and

(3) A statement that the bidder intends to make a tender offer in the future for a class of equity securities of the subject company which statement does not specify the amount of securities of such class to be sought or the consideration to be offered therefor.

(e) *Announcement made pursuant to Rule 135.* A public announcement by a bidder through a press release, newspaper advertisement or public statement which discloses only the information in Rule 135(a)(4) concerning a tender offer in which the consideration consists solely or in part of securities to be registered under the Securities Act of 1933 shall not be deemed to constitute the commencement of a tender offer under paragraph (a)(5) of this section; *Provided* That such bidder files a registration statement with respect to such securities promptly after such public announcement.

Rule 14d–3. Filing and Transmission of Tender Offer Statement

(a) *Filing and transmittal.* No bidder shall make a tender offer if, after consummation thereof, such bidder would be the beneficial owner of more than five percent of the class of the subject company's securities for which the tender offer is made, unless as soon as practicable on the date of the commencement of the tender offer such bidder:

(1) Files with the Commission 10 copies of a Tender Offer Statement on Schedule 14D–1, including all exhibits thereto;

(2) Hand delivers a copy of such Schedule 14D–1, including all exhibits thereto:

(i) To the subject company at its principal executive office; and

(ii) To any other bidder, which has filed a Schedule 14D–1 with the

Commission relating to a tender offer which has not yet terminated for the same class of securities of the subject company, at such bidder's principal executive office or at the address of the person authorized to receive notices and communications (which is disclosed on the cover sheet of such other bidder's Schedule 14D-1);

(3) Gives telephonic notice of the information required by Rule 14d-6(e)(2)(i) and (ii) and mails by means of first class mail a copy of Schedule 14D-1, including all exhibits thereto:

(i) To each national securities exchange where such class of the subject company's securities is registered and listed for trading (which may be based upon information contained in the subject company's most recent Annual Report on Form 10-K filed with the Commission unless the bidder has reason to believe that such information is not current) which telephonic notice shall be made when practicable prior to the opening of each such exchange; and

(ii) To the National Association of Securities Dealers, Inc. ('NASD') if such class of the subject company's securities is authorized for quotation in the NASDAQ inter-dealer quotation system.

(b) *Additional materials.* The bidder shall file with the Commission 10 copies of any additional tender offer materials as an exhibit to the Schedule 14D-1 required by this section, and if a material change occurs in the information set forth in such Schedule 14D-1, 10 copies of an amendment to Schedule 14D-1 (each of which shall include all exhibits other than those required by Item 11(a) of Schedule 14D-1) disclosing such change and shall send a copy of such additional tender offer material or such amendment to the subject company and to any exchange and/or the NASD, as required by paragraph (a) of this section, promptly but not later than the date such additional tender offer material or such change is first published, sent or given to security holders.

(c) *Certain announcements.* Notwithstanding the provisions of paragraph (b) of this section, if the additional tender offer material or an amendment to Schedule 14D-1 discloses only the number of shares deposited to date, and/or announces an extension of the time during which shares may be tendered, then the bidder may file such tender offer material or amendment and send a copy of such tender offer material or amendment to the subject company, any exchange and/or the NASD, as required by paragraph (a) of this section, promptly after the date such tender offer material is first published or sent or given to security holders.

Rule 14d–4. Dissemination of Certain Tender Offers

(a) *Materials deemed published or sent or given.* A tender offer in which the consideration consists solely of cash and/or securities exempt from registration under Section 3 of the Securities Act of 1933 shall be deemed 'published or sent or given to security holders' within the meaning of Section 14(d)(1) of the Act if the bidder complies with all of the requirements of any one of the following subparagraphs; *Provided, however,* That any such tender offers may be published or sent or given to security holders by other methods, but with respect to summary publication, and the use of stockholder lists and security position listings pursuant to Rule 14d–5, paragraphs (a)(2) and (a)(3) of this section are exclusive.

(1) *Long-form publication.* The bidder makes adequate publication in a newspaper or newspapers of long-form publication of the tender offer.

(2) *Summary publication.*

(i) If the tender offer is not subject to Rule 13e–3, the bidder makes adequate publication in a newspaper or newspapers of a summary advertisement of the tender offer; and

(ii) Mails by first class mail or otherwise furnishes with reasonable promptness the bidder's tender offer materials to any security holder who requests such tender offer materials pursuant to the summary advertisement or otherwise.

(3) *Use of stockholder lists and security position listings.* Any bidder using stockholder lists and security position listings pursuant to Rule 14d–5 shall comply with paragraph (a)(1) or (a)(2) of this section on or prior to the date of the bidder's request for such lists or listing pursuant to Rule 14d–5(a).

(b) *Adequate publication.* Depending on the facts and circumstances involved, adequate publication of a tender offer pursuant to this section may require publication in a newspaper with a national circulation or may only require publication in a newspaper with metropolitan or regional circulation or may require publication in a combination thereof; *Provided, however,* That publication in all editions of a daily newspaper with a national circulation shall be deemed to constitute adequate publication.

(c) *Publication of changes.* If a tender offer has been published or sent or given to security holders by one or more of the methods enumerated in paragraph (a) of this section, a material change in the information published, sent or given to security holders shall be promptly disseminated to security holders in a manner reasonably designed to inform security holders of such change; *Provided, however,* That if the bidder has elected pursuant to Rule

14d–5(f)(1) of this section to require the subject company to disseminate amendments disclosing material changes to the tender offer materials pursuant to Rule 14d–5, the bidder shall disseminate material changes in the information published or sent or given to security holders at least pursuant to Rule 14d–5.

Rule 14d–5. Dissemination of Certain Tender Offers by the Use of Stockholder Lists and Security Position Listings

(a) *Obligations of the subject company.* Upon receipt by a subject company at its principal executive offices of a bidder's written request, meeting the requirements of paragraph (e) of this section, the subject company shall comply with the following subparagraphs.

(1) The subject company shall notify promptly transfer agents and any other person who will assist the subject company in complying with the requirements of this section of the receipt by the subject company of a request by a bidder pursuant to this section.

(2) The subject company shall promptly ascertain whether the most recently prepared stockholder list, written or otherwise, within the access of the subject company was prepared as of a date earlier than 10 business days before the date of the bidder's request and, if so, the subject company shall promptly prepare or cause to be prepared a stockholder list as of the most recent practicable date which shall not be more than 10 business days before the date of the bidder's request.

(3) The subject company shall make an election to comply and shall comply with all of the provisions of either paragraph (b) or paragraph (c) of this section. The subject company's election once made shall not be modified or revoked during the bidder's tender offer and extensions thereof.

(4) No later than the second business day after the date of the bidder's request, the subject company shall orally notify the bidder, which notification shall be confirmed in writing, of the subject company's election made pursuant to paragraph (a)(3) of this section. Such notification shall indicate (i) the approximate number of security holders of the class of securities being sought by the bidder and, (ii) if the subject company elects to comply with paragraph (b) of this section, appropriate information concerning the location for delivery of the bidder's tender offer materials and the approximate direct costs incidental to the mailing to security holders of the bidder's tender offer materials computed in accordance with paragraph (g)(2) of this section.

(b) *Mailing of tender offer materials by the subject company.* A subject company which elects pursuant to paragraph (a)(3) of this section to comply with the provisions of this paragraph shall perform the acts prescribed by the following subparagraphs.

(1) The subject company shall promptly contact each participant named on the most recent security position listing of any clearing agency within the access of the subject company and make inquiry of each such participant as to the approximate number of beneficial owners of the subject company securities being sought in the tender offer held by each such participant.

(2) No later than the third business day after delivery of the bidder's tender offer materials pursuant to paragraph (g)(1) of this section, the subject company shall begin to mail or cause to be mailed by means of first class mail a copy of the bidder's tender offer materials to each person whose name appears as a record holder of the class of securities for which the offer is made on the most recent stockholder list referred to in paragraph (a)(2) of this section. The subject company shall use its best efforts to complete the mailing in a timely manner but in no event shall such mailing be completed in a substantially greater period of time than the subject company would complete a mailing to security holders of its own material relating to the tender offer.

(3) No later than the third business day after the delivery of the bidder's tender offer materials pursuant to paragraph (g)(1) of this section, the subject company shall begin to transmit or cause to be transmitted a sufficient number of sets of the bidder's tender offer materials to the participants named on the security position listings described in paragraph (b)(1) of this section. The subject company shall use its best efforts to complete the transmittal in a timely manner but in no event shall such transmittal be completed in a substantially greater period of time than the subject company would complete a transmittal to such participants pursuant to security position listings of clearing agencies of its own material relating to the tender offer.

(4) The subject company shall promptly give oral notification to the bidder, which notification shall be confirmed in writing, of the commencement of the mailing pursuant to paragraph (b)(2) of this section and of the transmittal pursuant to paragraph (b)(3) of this section.

(5) During the tender offer and any extension thereof the subject company shall use reasonable efforts to update the stockholder list and shall mail or cause to be mailed promptly following each update a copy of the bidder's tender offer materials (to the extent sufficient sets of such materials have been furnished by the bidder) to each person who has become a record holder since the later of (i) the date of preparation of the

most recent stockholder list referred to in paragraph (a)(2) of this section or (ii) the last preceding update.

(6) If the bidder has elected pursuant to paragraph (f)(1) of this section to require the subject company to disseminate amendments disclosing material changes to the tender offer materials pursuant to this section, the subject company, promptly following delivery of each such amendment, shall mail or cause to be mailed a copy of each such amendment to each record holder whose name appears on the shareholder list described in paragraphs (a)(2) and (b)(5) of this section and shall transmit or cause to be transmitted sufficient copies of such amendment to each participant named on security position listings who received sets of the bidder's tender offer materials pursuant to paragraph (b)(3) of this section.

(7) This subject company shall not include any communication other than the bidder's tender offer materials or amendments thereto in the envelopes or other containers furnished by the bidder.

(8) Promptly following the termination of the tender offer, the subject company shall reimburse the bidder the excess, if any, of the amounts advanced pursuant to paragraph (f)(3)(iii) over the direct costs incidental to compliance by the subject company and its agents in performing the acts required by this section computed in accordance with paragraph (g)(2) of this section.

(c) *Delivery of stockholder lists and security position listings.* A subject company which elects pursuant to paragraph (a)(3) of this section to comply with the provisions of this paragraph shall perform the acts prescribed by the following subparagraphs.

(1) No later than the third business day after the date of the bidder's request, the subject company shall furnish to the bidder at the subject company's principal executive office a copy of the names and addresses of the record holders on the most recent stockholder list referred to in paragraph (a)(2) of this section and a copy of the names and addresses of participants identified on the most recent security position listing of any clearing agency which is within the access of the subject company.

(2) If the bidder has elected pursuant to paragraph (f)(1) of this section to require the subject company to disseminate amendments disclosing material changes to the tender offer materials, the subject company shall update the stockholder list by furnishing the bidder with the name and address of each record holder named on the stockholder list, and not previously furnished to the bidder, promptly after such information becomes available to the subject company during the tender offer and any extensions thereof.

(d) *Liability of subject company and others.* Neither the subject company nor any affiliate or agent of the subject company nor any clearing agency shall be:

(1) Deemed to have made a solicitation or recommendation respecting the tender offer within the meaning of Section 14(d)(4) based solely upon the compliance or noncompliance by the subject company or any affiliate or agent of the subject company with one or more requirements of this section;

(2) Liable under any provision of the Federal securities laws to the bidder or to any security holder based solely upon the inaccuracy of the current names or addresses on the stockholder list or security position listing, unless such inaccuracy results from a lack of reasonable care on the part of the subject company or any affiliate or agent of the subject company;

(3) Deemed to be an 'underwriter' within the meaning of Section (2)(11) of the Securities Act of 1933 for any purpose of that Act or any rule or regulation promulgated thereunder based solely upon the compliance or noncompliance by the subject company or any affiliate or agent of the subject company with one or more of the requirements of this section;

(4) Liable under any provision of the Federal securities laws for the disclosure in the bidder's tender offer materials, including any amendment thereto, based solely upon the compliance or noncompliance by the subject company or any affiliate or agent of the subject company with one or more of the requirements of this section.

(e) *Content of the bidder's request.* The bidder's written request referred to in paragraph (a) of this section shall include the following:

(1) The identity of the bidder;

(2) The title of the class of securities which is the subject of the bidder's tender offer;

(3) A statement that the bidder is making a request to the subject company pursuant to paragraph (a) of this section for the use of the stockholder list and security position listings for the purpose of disseminating a tender offer to security holders;

(4) A statement that the bidder is aware of and will comply with the provisions of paragraph (f) of this section;

(5) A statement as to whether or not it has elected pursuant to paragraph (f)(1) of this section to disseminate amendments disclosing material changes to the tender offer materials pursuant to this section; and

(6) The name, address and telephone number of the person whom the subject company shall contact pursuant to paragraph (a)(4) of this section.

(f) *Obligations of the bidder*. Any bidder who requests that a subject company comply with the provisions of paragraph (a) of this section shall comply with the following subparagraphs.

(1) The bidder shall make an election whether or not to require the subject company to disseminate amendments disclosing material changes to the tender offer materials pursuant to this section, which election shall be included in the request referred to in paragraph (a) of this section and shall not be revocable by the bidder during the tender offer and extensions thereof.

(2) With respect to a tender offer subject to Section 14(d)(1) of the Act in which the consideration consists solely of cash and/or securities exempt from registration under Section 3 of the Securities Act of 1933, the bidder shall comply with the requirements of Rule 14d–4(a)(3).

(3) If the subject company elects to comply with paragraph (b) of this section:

(i) The bidder shall promptly deliver the tender offer materials after receipt of the notification from the subject company as provided in paragraph (a)(4) of this section;

(ii) The bidder shall promptly notify the subject company of any amendment to the bidder's tender offer materials requiring compliance by the subject company with paragraph (b)(6) of this section and shall promptly deliver such amendment to the subject company pursuant to paragraph (g)(1) of this section;

(iii) The bidder shall advance to the subject company an amount equal to the approximate cost of conducting mailings to security holders computed in accordance with paragraph (g)(2) of this section;

(iv) The bidder shall promptly reimburse the subject company for the direct costs incidental to compliance by the subject company and its agents in performing the acts required by this section computed in accordance with paragraph (g)(2) of this section which are in excess of the amount advanced pursuant to paragraph (f)(3)(iii) of this section; and

(v) The bidder shall mail by means of first class mail or otherwise furnish with reasonable promptness the tender offer materials to any security holder who requests such materials.

(4) If the subject company elects to comply with paragraph (c) of this section:

(i) The subject company shall use the stockholder list and security position listings furnished to the bidder pursuant to paragraph (c) of this section exclusively in the dissemination of tender offer materials to security holders in connection with the bidder's tender offer and extensions thereof;

(ii) The bidder shall return the stockholder lists and security position listings furnished to the bidder pursuant to paragraph (c) of this section promptly after the termination of the bidder's tender offer;

(iii) The bidder shall accept, handle and return the stockholder lists and security position listings furnished to the bidder pursuant to paragraph (c) of this section to the subject company on a confidential basis;

(iv) The bidder shall not retain any stockholder list or security position listing furnished by the subject company pursuant to paragraph (c) of this section, or any copy thereof, nor retain any information derived from any such list or listing or copy thereof after the termination of the bidder's tender offer;

(v) The bidder shall mail by means of first class mail, at its own expense, a copy of its tender offer materials to each person whose identity appears on the stockholder list as furnished and updated by the subject company pursuant to paragraphs (c)(1) and (c)(2) of this section;

(vi) The bidder shall contact the participants named on the security position listing of any clearing agency, make inquiry of each participant as to the approximate number of sets of tender offer materials required by each such participant, and furnish, at its own expense, sufficient sets of tender offer materials and any amendment thereto to each such participant for subsequent transmission to the beneficial owners of the securities being sought by the bidder;

(vii) The bidder shall mail by means of first class mail or otherwise furnish with reasonable promptness the tender offer materials to any security holder who requests such materials; and

(viii) The bidder shall promptly reimburse the subject company for direct costs incidental to compliance by the subject company and its agents in performing the acts required by this section computed in accordance with paragraph (g)(2) of this section.

(g) *Delivery of materials, computation of direct costs.*

(1) Whenever the bidder is required to deliver tender offer materials or

amendments to tender offer materials, the bidder shall deliver to the subject company at the location specified by the subject company in its notice given pursuant to paragraph (a)(4) of this section a number of sets of the materials or of the amendment, as the case may be, at least equal to the approximate number of security holders specified by the subject company in such notice, together with appropriate envelopes or other containers therefor; *Provided, however,* That such delivery shall be deemed not to have been made unless the bidder has complied with paragraph (f)(3)(iii) of this section at the time the materials or amendments, as the case may be, are delivered.

(2) The approximate direct cost of mailing the bidder's tender offer materials shall be computed by adding (i) the direct cost incidental to the mailing of the subject company's last annual report to shareholders (excluding employee time), less the cost of preparation and printing of the report, and postage, plus (ii) the amount of first class postage required to mail the bidder's tender offer materials. The approximate direct costs incidental to the mailing of the amendments to the bidder's tender offer materials shall be computed by adding (iii) the estimated direct costs of preparing mailing labels, of updating shareholder lists and of third party handling charges plus (iv) the amount of first class postage required to mail the bidder's amendment. Direct costs incidental to the mailing of the bidder's tender offer materials and amendments thereto when finally computed may include all reasonable charges paid by the subject company to third parties for supplies or services, including costs attendant to preparing shareholder lists, mailing labels, handling the bidder's materials, contacting participants named on security position listings and for postage, but shall exclude indirect costs, such as employee time which is devoted to either contesting or supporting the tender offer on behalf of the subject company. The final billing for direct costs shall be accompanied by an appropriate accounting in reasonable detail.

Rule 14d–6. Disclosure Requirements with Respect to Tender Offers

(a) *Information required on date of commencement.*

(1) *Long-form publication.* If a tender offer is published, sent or given to security holders on the date of commencement by means of long-form publication pursuant to Rule 14d–4(a)(1), such long-form publication shall include the information required by paragraph (e)(1) of this section.

(2) *Summary publication.* If a tender offer is published, sent or given to security holders on the date of commencement by means of summary publication pursuant to Rule 14d–4(a)(2):

(i) The summary advertisement shall contain, and shall be limited to, the information required by paragraph (e)(2) of this section; and

(ii) The tender offer materials furnished by the bidder upon the request of any security holder shall include the information required by paragraph (e)(1) of this section.

(3) *Use of stockholder lists and security position listings.* If a tender offer is published or sent or given to security holders on the date of commencement by the use of stockholder lists and security position listings pursuant to Rule 14d–4(a)(3):

(i) Either (A) the summary advertisement shall contain, and shall be limited to, the information required by paragraph (e)(2) of this section, or (B) if long-form publication of the tender offer is made, such long-form publication shall include the information required by paragraph (e)(1) of this section; and

(ii) The tender offer materials transmitted to security holders pursuant to such lists and security position listings and furnished by the bidder upon the request of any security holder shall include the information required by paragraph (e)(1) of this section.

(4) *Other tender offers.* If a tender offer is published or sent or given to security holders other than pursuant to Rule 14d–4(a), the tender offer materials which are published or sent or given to security holders on the date of commencement of such offer shall include the information required by paragraph (e)(1) of this section.

(b) *Information required in summary advertisement made after commencement.* A summary advertisement published subsequent to the date of commencement of the tender offer shall include at least the information specified in paragraphs (e)(1)(i)-(iv) and (e)(2)(iv) of this section.

(c) *Information required in other tender offer materials published after commencement.* Except for summary advertisements described in paragraph (b) of this section and tender offer materials described in paragraphs (a)(2)(ii) and (a)(3)(ii) of this section, additional tender offer materials published, sent or given to security holders subsequent to the date of commencement shall include the information required by paragraph (e)(1) and may omit any of the information required by paragraphs (e)(1)(v)–(viii) of this section which has been previously furnished by the bidder in connection with the tender offer.

(d) *Material changes.* A material change in the information published or sent or given to security holders shall be promptly disclosed to security holders in additional tender offer materials.

(e) *Information to be included.*

(1) *Long-form publication and tender offer materials.* The information required to be disclosed by paragraphs (a)(1), (a)(2)(ii), (a)(3)(i)(B) and (a)(4) of this section shall include the following:

(i) The identity of the bidder;

(ii) The identity of the subject company;

(iii) The amount of class of securities being sought and the type and amount of consideration being offered therefor;

(iv) The scheduled expiration date of the tender offer, whether the tender offer may be extended and, if so, the procedures for extension of the tender offer;

(v) The exact dates prior to which, and after which, security holders who deposit their securities will have the right to withdraw their securities pursuant to Section 14(d)(5) of the Act and Rule 14d–7 and the manner in which shares will be accepted for payment and in which withdrawal may be effected;

(vi) If the tender offer is for less than all the outstanding securities of a class of equity securities and the bidder is not obligated to purchase all of the securities tendered, the period or periods, and in the case of the period from the commencement of the offer, the date of the expiration of such period during which the securities will be taken up pro rata pursuant to Section 14(d)(6) of the Act or Rule 14d–8, and the present intention or plan of the bidder with respect to the tender offer in the event of an oversubscription by security holders;

(vii) The disclosure required by Items 1(c); 2 (with respect to persons other than the bidder, excluding sub-items (b) and (d)); 3; 4; 5; 6; 7; 8; and 10 of Schedule 14D–1 or a fair and adequate summary thereof; *Provided, however,* That negative responses to any such item or sub-item of Schedule 14D–1 need not be included; and

(viii) The disclosure required by Item 9 of Schedule 14D–1 or a fair and adequate summary thereof. (Under normal circumstances, the following summary financial information for the period covered by the financial information furnished in response to Item 9 will be a sufficient summary. If the information required by Item 9 is summarized, appropriate instructions shall be included stating how complete financial information can be obtained.)

Income Statement:

Net sales and operating revenues and other revenues

Income before extraordinary items

Net income

Balance sheet (at end of period):

Work capital

Total assets

Total assets less deferred research and development charges and excess cost of assets acquired over book value

Total indebtedness

Shareholders' equity

Per share[1]

Income per common share before extraordinary items

Extraordinary items

Net income per common share (and common share equivalents, if applicable)

Net income per share on a fully diluted basis

(ix) If the financial statements are prepared according to a comprehensive body of accounting principles other than those generally accepted in the United States, the summary financial information shall be accompanied by a reconciliation to generally accepted accounting principles of the United States.

(2) *Summary publication.* The information required to be disclosed by paragraphs (a)(2)(i) and (a)(3)(i)(A) of this section in a summary advertisement is as follows:

(i) The information required by paragraph (e)(1)(i) through (vi) of this section;

(3) *No transmittal letter.* Neither the initial summary advertisement nor any subsequent summary advertisement shall include a transmittal letter (whereby securities of the subject company which are sought in the tender offer may be transmitted to the bidder of its depository) or any amendment thereto.

---

[1] Average number of shares of common stock outstanding during each period was ... (as adjusted to give effect to stock dividends or stock splits).

Rule 14d–7. Additional Withdrawal Rights

(a) *Rights.* In addition to the provisions of section 14(d)(5) of the Act, any person who has deposited securities pursuant to a tender offer has the right to withdraw any such securities during the period such offer request or invitation remains open.

(b) *Notice of withdrawal.* Notice of withdrawal pursuant to this section shall be deemed to be timely upon the receipt by the bidder's depository of a written notice of withdrawal specifying the name(s) of the tendering stockholder(s), the number or amount of the securities to be withdrawn and the name(s) in which the certificate(s) is (are) registered, if different from that of the tendering security holder(s). A bidder may impose other reasonable requirements, including certificate numbers and a signed request for withdrawal accompanied by a signature guarantee, as conditions precedent to the physical release of withdrawn securities.

Rule 14d–8. Exemption from Statutory Pro Rata Requirements

Notwithstanding the pro rata provisions of Section 14(d)(6) of the Act, if any person makes a tender offer or request or invitation for tenders, for less than all of the outstanding equity securities of a class, and if a greater number of securities are deposited pursuant thereto than such person is bound or willing to take up and pay for, the securities taken up and paid for shall be taken up and paid for as nearly as may be pro rata, disregarding fractions, according to the tenders, for less than all of the outstanding equity securities of a class, and if a greater number of securities are deposited pursuant thereto than such person is bound or willing to take up and pay for, the securities taken up and paid for shall be taken up and paid for as nearly as may be pro rata, disregarding fractions, according to the number of securities deposited by each depositor during the period such offer, request or invitation remains open.

Rule 14d–9. Solicitation/Recommendation Statements with Respect to Certain Tender Offers

(a) *Filing and transmittal of recommendation statement.* No solicitation or recommendation to security holders shall be made by any person described in paragraph (d) of this section with respect to a tender offer for such securities unless as soon as practicable on the date such solicitation or recommendation is first published or sent or given to security holders such person complies with the following subparagraphs.

(1) Such person shall file with the Commission eight copies of a Tender

Offer Solicitation/Recommendation Statement on Schedule 14D–9, including all exhibits thereto; and

(2) If such person is either the subject company or an affiliate of the subject company:

(i) Such person shall hand-deliver a copy of the Schedule 14D–9 to the bidder at its principal office or at the address of the person authorized to receive notices and communications (which is set forth on the cover sheet of the bidder's Schedule 14D–1 filed with the Commission); and

(ii) Such person shall give telephonic notice (which notice to the extent possible shall be given prior to the opening of the market) of the information required by Items 2 and 4(a) of Schedule 14D–9 and shall mail a copy of the schedule to each national securities exchange where the class of securities is registered and listed for trading and, if the class is authorized for quotation in the NASDAQ interdealer quotation system, the National Association of Securities Dealers, Inc. ('NASD').

(3) If such person is neither the subject company nor an affiliate of the subject company:

(i) Such person shall mail a copy of the schedule to the bidder at its principal office or at the address of the person authorized to receive notices and communications (which is set forth on the cover sheet of the bidder's Schedule 14D–1 filed with the Commission); and

(ii) Such person shall mail a copy of the schedule to the subject company at its principal office.

(b) *Amendments.* If any material change occurs in the information set forth in the Schedule 14D–9 required by this section, the person who filed such Schedule 14D–9 shall:

(1) File with the Commission eight copies of an amendment on Schedule 14D–9 disclosing such change promptly, but not later than the date such material is first published, sent or given to security holders; and

(2) Promptly deliver copies and give notice of the amendment in the same manner as that specified in paragraph (a)(2) or paragraph (a)(3) of this section, whichever is applicable; and

(3) Promptly disclose and disseminate such change in a manner reasonably designed to inform security holders of such change.

(c) *Information required in solicitation or recommendation.* Any solicitation or recommendation to holders of a class of securities referred to in Section 14(d)(1) of the Act with respect to a tender offer for such securities shall include the name of the person making such solicitation or recommendation and the information required by Items 1, 2, 3(b), 4, 6, 7 and 8 of Schedule 14D–9 or a fair and adequate summary thereof; *provided, however*, that such solicitation or recommendation may omit any of such information previously furnished to security holders of such class of securities by such person with respect to such tender offer.

(d) *Applicability.*

(1) Except as is provided in paragraphs (d)(2) and (e) of this section, this section shall only apply to the following persons:

(i) The subject company, any director, officer, employee, affiliate or subsidiary of the subject company;

(ii) Any record holder or beneficial owner of any security issued by the subject company, by the bidder, or by any affiliate of either the subject company or the bidder; and

(iii) Any person who makes a solicitation or recommendation to security holders on behalf of any of the foregoing or on behalf of the bidder other than by means of a solicitation or recommendation to security holders which has been filed with the Commission pursuant to this section or Rule 14d–3.

(2) Notwithstanding paragraph (d)(1) of this section, this section shall not apply to the following persons:

(i) A bidder who has filed a Schedule 14D–1 pursuant to Rule 14d–3;

(ii) Attorneys, banks, brokers, fiduciaries or investment advisers who are not participating in a tender offer in more than a ministerial capacity and who furnish information and/or advice regarding such tender offer to their customers or clients on the unsolicited request of such customers or clients or solely pursuant to a contract or a relationship provided for advice to the customer or client to whom the information and/or advice is given.

(e) *Stop-look-and-listen communication.* This section shall not apply to the subject company with respect to a communication by the subject company to its security holders which only:

(1) Identifies the tender offer by the bidder;

(2) States that such tender offer is under consideration by the subject company's board of directors and/or management;

(3) States that on or before a specified date (which shall be no later than

10 business days from the date of commencement of such tender offer) the subject company will advise such security holders of (i) whether the subject company recommends acceptance or rejection of such tender offer; expresses no opinion and remains neutral toward such tender offer; or is unable to take a position with respect to such tender offer and (ii) the reason(s) for the position taken by the subject company with respect to the tender offer (including the inability to take a position); and

(4) Requests such security holders to defer making a determination whether to accept or reject such tender offer until they have been advised of the subject company's position with respect thereto pursuant to paragraph (e)(3) of this section.

(f) *Statement of management's position.* A statement by the subject company of its position with respect to a tender offer which is required to be published or sent or given to security holders pursuant to Rule 14e–2 shall be deemed to constitute a solicitation or recommendation within the meaning of this section and Section 14(d)(4) of the Act.

Rule 14d–10. Equal Treatment of Security Holders

(a) No bidder shall make a tender offer unless:

(1) The tender offer is open to all security holders of the class of securities subject to the tender offer; and

(2) The consideration paid to any security holder pursuant to the tender offer is the highest consideration paid to any other security holder during such tender offer.

(b) Paragraph (a)(1) of this section shall not:

(1) Affect dissemination under Rule 14d–4; or

(2) Prohibit a bidder from making a tender offer excluding all security holders in a State where the bidder is prohibited from making the tender offer by administrative or judicial action pursuant to a State statute after a good faith effort by the bidder to comply with such statute.

(c) Paragraph (a)(2) of this section shall not prohibit the offer of more than one type of consideration in a tender offer, provided that:

(1) Security holders are afforded equal right to elect among each of the types of consideration offered; and

(2) The highest consideration of each type paid to any security holder is paid to any other security holder receiving that type of consideration.

(d) If the offer and sale of securities constituting consideration offered in a tender offer is prohibited by the appropriate authority of a State after a good faith effort by the bidder to register or qualify the offer and sale of such securities in such State:

(1) The bidder may offer security holders in such State an alternative form of consideration; and

(2) Paragraph (c) of this section shall not operate to require the bidder to offer or pay the alternative form of consideration to security holders in any other State.

(e) This section shall not apply to any tender offer with respect to which the Commission, upon written request or upon its own motion, either unconditionally or on specified terms and conditions, determines that compliance with this section is not necessary or appropriate in the public interest or for the protection of investors.

A.2.5 SECURITIES AND EXCHANGE COMMISSION REGULATION 14E

Rule 14e–1. Unlawful Tender Offer Practices

As a means reasonably designed to prevent fraudulent, deceptive or manipulative acts or practices within the meaning of Section 14(e) of the Act, no person who makes a tender offer shall:

(a) Hold such tender offer open for less than 20 business days from the date such tender offer is first published or sent or given to security holders;

(b) *Increase or decrease* the percentage of the class of securities being sought or the consideration offered or the dealer's soliciting fee to be given in a tender offer unless such tender offer remains open for at least 10 business days from the date that notice of such increase or decrease is first published or sent or given to security holders; *Provided, however,* That, for purposes of this paragraph, the acceptance for payment by the bidder of an additional amount of securities not to exceed two percent of the class of securities that is the subject of the tender offer shall not be deemed to be an increase. For purposes of this paragraph, the percentage of a class of securities shall be calculated in accordance with Section 14(d)(3) of the Act.

(c) Fail to pay the consideration offered or return the securities deposited by or on behalf of security holders promptly after the termination or withdrawal of a tender offer;

(d) Extend the length of a tender offer without issuing a notice of such extension by press release or other public announcement, which notice shall include disclosure of the approximate number of securities deposited to date and shall be issued no later than the earlier of (i) 9:00 a.m. Eastern time, on the next business day after the scheduled expiration date of the offer or (ii) if the class of securities which is the subject of the tender offer is registered on one or more national securities exchanges, the first opening of any one of such exchanges on the next business day after the scheduled expiration date of the offer.

Rule 14e–2. Position of Subject Company with Respect to a Tender Offer

(a) *Position of subject company.* As a means reasonably designed to prevent fraudulent, deceptive or manipulative acts or practices within the meaning of Section 14(e) of the Act, the subject company, no later than 10 business days from the date the tender offer is first published or sent or given, shall publish, send or give to security holders a statement disclosing that the subject company:

(1) Recommends acceptance or rejection of the bidder's tender offer;

(2) Expresses no opinion and is remaining neutral toward the bidder's tender offer; or

(3) Is unable to take a position with respect to the bidder's tender offer.

Such statement shall also include the reason(s) for the position (including the inability to take a position) disclosed therein.

(b) *Material change.* If any material change occurs in the disclosure required by paragraph (a) of this section, the subject company shall promptly publish, send or give a statement disclosing such material change to security holders.

Rule 14e–3. Transactions in Securities on the Basis of Material, Non-public Information in the Context of Tender Offers

(a) If any person has taken a substantial step or steps to commence, or has commenced, a tender offer (the 'offering person'), it shall constitute a fraudulent, deceptive or manipulative act or practice within the meaning of Section 14(e) of the Act for any other person who is in possession of material information relating to such tender offer which information he knows or has reason to know is non-public and which he knows or has reason to know has been acquired directly or indirectly from (1) the offering person, (2) the issuer of the securities sought or to be sought by such tender offer, or (3) any officer, director, partner or employee or any other person acting on behalf of the offering person or such issuer, to purchase or sell or cause to be purchased or sold any of such securities or any securities convertible into or exchangeable for any such securities or any option or right to obtain or to dispose of any of the foregoing securities, unless within a reasonable time prior to any purchase or sale such information and its source are publicly disclosed by press release or otherwise.

(b) A person other than a natural person shall not violate paragraph (a) of this section if such person shows that:

(1) The individual(s) making the investment decision on behalf of such person to purchase or sell any security described in paragraph (a) or to cause any such security to be purchased or sold by or on behalf of others did not know the material, non-public information; and

(2) Such person had implemented one or a combination of policies and procedures, reasonable under the circumstances, taking into consideration the nature of the person's business, to ensure that individual(s) making investment decision(s) would not violate paragraph (a), which policies and procedures may include, but are not limited to, (i) those which restrict any purchase, sale and causing any purchase and sale of any such security or (ii) those which prevent such individual(s) from knowing such information.

(c) Notwithstanding anything in paragraph (a) to the contrary, the following transactions shall not be violations of paragraph (a) of this section:

(1) Purchase(s) of any security described in paragraph (a) by a broker or by another agent on behalf of an offering person; or

(2) Sale(s) by any person of any security described in paragraph (a) to the offering person.

(d)(1) As a means reasonably designed to prevent fraudulent, deceptive or manipulative acts or practices within the meaning of Section 14(e) of the Act, it shall be unlawful for any person described in paragraph (d)(2) of this section to communicate material, non-public information relating to a tender offer to any other person under circumstances in which it is reasonably foreseeable that such communication is likely to result in a violation of this section *except* that this paragraph shall not apply to a communication made in good faith:

(i) To the officers, directors, partners or employees of the offering person, to its advisers or to other persons, involved in the planning, financing, preparation or execution of such tender offer;

(ii) To the issuer whose securities are sought or to be sought by such tender offer, to its officers, directors, partners, employees or advisers or to other persons, involved in the planning, financing, preparation or execution of the activities of the issuer with respect to such tender offer; or

(iii) To any person pursuant to a requirement of any statute or rule or regulation promulgated thereunder.

(2) The persons referred to in paragraph (d)(1) of this section are:

(i) The offering person or its officers, directors, partners, employees or advisers;

(ii) The issuer of the securities sought or to be sought by such tender offer or its officers, directors, partners, employees or advisers;

(iii) Anyone acting on behalf of the persons in paragraph (d)(2)(i) or the issuer or persons in paragraph (d)(2)(ii); and

(iv) Any person in possession of material information relating to a tender offer which information he knows or has reason to know is non-public and which he knows or has reason to know has been acquired directly or indirectly from any of the above.

A.3

Securities and Exchange Commission's One-Share-One-Vote Rule

> Rule 19c–4 is the SEC's controversial one-share-one-vote rule. It is an unusual Federal interference with the regulation of shareholder voting. In June 1990 a U.S. Court of Appeals overturned the rule, holding that the SEC had overstepped its statutory authority by entering territory (corporate governance) that Congress had left for state law. See Chapter 9 Section 2.

Rule 19c–4. Governing Certain Listing or Authorization Determinations by National Securities Exchanges and Associations

(a) The rules of each exchange shall provide as follows: No rule, stated policy, practice, or interpretation of this exchange shall permit the listing, or the continuance of the listing, of any common stock or other equity security of a domestic issuer, if the issuer of such security issues any class of security, or takes other corporate action, with the effect of nullifying, restricting or disparately reducing the per share voting rights of holders of an outstanding class or classes of common stock of such issuer registered pursuant to Section 12 of the Act.

(b) The rules of each association shall provide as follows: No rule, stated policy, practice, or interpretation of this association shall permit the authorization for quotation and/or transaction reporting through an automated inter-dealer quotation system ('authorization'), or the continuance of authorization, of any common stock or other equity security of a domestic issuer, if the issuer of such security issues any class of security, or takes other corporate action, with the effect of nullifying, restricting, or disparately reducing the per share voting rights of holders of an outstanding class or classes of common stock of such issuer registered pursuant to Section 12 of the Act.

(c) For the purposes of paragraphs (a) and (b) of this section, the following shall be presumed to have the effect of nullifying, restricting, or disparately reducing the per share voting rights of an outstanding class or classes of common stock:

(1) corporate action to impose any restriction on the voting power of shares of the common stock of the issuer held by a beneficial or record holder based on the number of shares held by such beneficial or record holder;

(2) corporate action to impose any restriction on the voting power of shares of the common stock of the issuer held by a beneficial or record holder based on the length of time such shares have been held by such beneficial or record holder;

(3) any issuance of securities through an exchange offer by the issuer for shares of an outstanding class of the common stock of the issuer, in which the securities issued have voting rights greater than or less than the per share voting rights of any outstanding class of the common stock of the issuer.

(4) any issuance of securities pursuant to a stock dividend, or any other type of distribution of stock, in which the securities issued have voting rights greater than the per share voting rights of any outstanding class of the common stock of the issuer.

(d) For the purpose of paragraphs (a) and (b) of this section, the following, standing alone, shall be presumed not to have the effect of nullifying, restricting, or disparately reducing the per share voting rights of holders of an outstanding class or classes of common stock:

(1) the issuance of securities pursuant to an initial registered public offering;

(2) the issuance of any class of securities, through a registered public offering, with voting rights not greater than the per share voting rights of any outstanding class of the common stock of the issuer;

(3) the issuance of any class of securities to effect a bona fide merger or acquisition, with voting rights not greater than the per share voting rights of any outstanding class of the common stock of the issuer.

(4) corporate action taken pursuant to state law requiring a state's domestic corporation to condition the voting rights of a beneficial or record holder of a specified threshold percentage of the corporation's voting stock on the approval of the corporation's independent shareholders.

(e) *Definitions*

The following terms shall have the following meanings for purposes of this section, and the rules of each exchange and association shall include such definitions for the purposes of the prohibition in paragraphs (a) and (b), respectively, of this section:

(1) The term 'Act' shall mean the Securities Exchange Act of 1934, as amended.

(2) The term 'common stock' shall include any security of an issuer designated as common stock and any security of an issuer, however designated, which, by statute or by its terms, is a common stock (*e.g.*, a security which entitles the holders thereof to vote generally on matters submitted to the issuer's security holders for a vote).

(3) The term 'equity security' shall include any equity security defined as such pursuant to Rule 3a11–1 under the Act.

(4) The term 'domestic issuer' shall mean an issuer that is not a 'foreign private issuer' as defined in Rule 3b–4 under the Act.

(5) The term 'security' shall include any security defined as such pursuant to Section 3(a)(10) of the Act, but shall exclude any class of security having a preference or priority over the issuer's common stock as to dividends, interest payments, redemption or payments in liquidation, if the voting rights of such securities only become effective as a result of specified events, not relating to an acquisition of the common stock of the issuer, which reasonably can be expected to jeopardize the issuer's financial ability to meet its payment obligations to the holders of that class of securities.

(6) the term 'exchange' shall mean a national securities exchange, registered as such with the Securities and Exchange Commission pursuant to Section 6 of the Act, which makes transaction reports available pursuant to Rule 11Aa3–1 under the Act; and

(7) the term 'association' shall mean a national securities association registered as such with the Securities and Exchange Commission pursuant to Section 15A of the Act.

(f) An exchange or association may adopt a rule, stated policy, practice, or interpretation, subject to the procedures specified by Section 19(b) of the Act, specifying what types of securities issuances and other corporate actions are covered by, or excluded from, the prohibition in paragraphs (a) and (b) of this section, respectively, if such rule, stated policy, practice, or interpretation is consistent with the protection of investors and the public interest, and otherwise in furtherance of the purposes of the Act and this section.

A.4

Organization of Corporations under Delaware Law

DELAWARE CORPORATION LAW §141

> Section 141 of the Delaware Corporation Law contains many important provisions dealing with directors.

141. Board of directors; powers; number, qualifications, terms and quorum; committees; classes of directors; non-profit corporations; reliance upon books; action without meeting; removal

(a) The business and affairs of every corporation organized under this chapter shall be managed by or under the direction of a board of directors, except as maybe otherwise provided in this chapter or in its certificate of incorporation. If any such provision is made in the certificate of incorporation, the powers and duties conferred or imposed upon the board of directors by this chapter shall be exercised or performed to such extent and by such person or persons as shall be provided in the certificate of incorporation.

(b) The board of directors of a corporation shall consist of 1 or more members. The number of directors shall be fixed by, or in the manner provided in, the bylaws, unless the certificate of incorporation fixes the number of directors, in which case a change in the number of directors shall be made only by amendment of the certificate. Directors need not be stockholders unless so required by the certificate of incorporation or the bylaws. The certificate of incorporation or bylaws may prescribe other qualifications for directors. Each director shall hold office until his successor is elected and qualified or until his earlier resignation or removal. Any director may resign at any time upon written notice to the corporation. A majority of the total number of directors shall constitute a quorum for the transaction of business unless the certificate of incorporation or the bylaws require a greater number. Unless the certificate of incorporation provides otherwise, the bylaws may provide that a number less than a majority shall constitute a quorum which in no case shall be less than 1/3 of the total number of directors except that when a board of 1 director is authorized under the provisions of this section, then 1 director shall constitute a quorum. The vote of the majority of the directors present at a meeting at which a quorum is present shall be the act of the board of directors unless the certificate of incorporation or the bylaws shall require a vote of a greater number.

(c) The board of directors may, by resolution passed by a majority of the whole board, designate 1 or more committees, each committee to consist of 1 or more of the directors of the corporation. The board may designate one or more directors as alternate members of any committee, who may replace any absent or disqualified member at any meeting of the committee. The bylaws may provide that in the absence or disqualification of a member of a committee, the member or members present at any meeting and not disqualified from voting, whether or not he or they constitute a quorum, may unanimously appoint another member of the board of directors to act at the meeting in the place of any such absent or disqualified member. Any such committee, to the extent provided in the resolution of the board of directors, or in the bylaws of the corporation, shall have and may exercise all the powers and authority of the board of directors in the management of the business and affairs of the corporation, and may authorize the seal of the corporation to be affixed to all papers which may require it, but no such committee shall have the power or authority in reference to amending the certificate of incorporation (except that a committee may, to the extent authorized in the resolution or resolutions providing for the issuance of shares of stock adopted by the board of directors as provided in subsection (a) of §151 of this title, fix the designations and any of the preferences or rights of such shares relating to dividends, redemption, dissolution, any distribution of assets of the corporation or the conversion into, or the exchange of such shares for, shares of any other class or classes or any other series of the same or any other class or classes of stock of the corporation or fix the number of shares of any series of stock or authorize the increase or decrease of the shares of any series), adopting an agreement of merger or consolidation under §251 or 252 of this title, recommending to the stockholders the sale, lease or exchange of all or substantially all of the corporation's property and assets, recommending to the stockholders a dissolution of the corporation or a revocation of a dissolution, or amending the bylaws of the corporation; and, unless the resolution, bylaws, or certificate of incorporation expressly so provides, no such committee shall have the power or authority to declare a dividend, to authorize the issuance of stock or to adopt a certificate of ownership and merger pursuant to §253 of this title.

(d) The directors of any corporation organized under this chapter may, by the certificate of incorporation or by an initial bylaw, or by a bylaw adopted by a vote of the stockholders, be divided into 1, 2 or 3 classes; the term of office of those of the first class to expire at the annual meeting next ensuing; of the second class 1 year thereafter; of the third class 2 years thereafter; and at each annual election held after such classification and election, directors shall be chosen for a full term, as the case may be, to succeed those whose terms expire. The certificate of incorporation may confer upon holders of any class or series of stock the right to elect 1 or more directors who shall serve for such term, and have such voting powers as shall be stated in the certificate of incorporation. The terms of office and voting powers of the directors elected in the manner so provided in the certificate of incorporation may be greater than or less than those of any other director or class of directors. If the certificate of incorporation provides that directors elected by the holders of a class or series of stock shall have more or less than 1 vote per director on any matter, every reference in this chapter to a majority or other proportion of directors shall refer to a majority or other proportion of the votes of such directors.

(e) A member of the board of directors, or a member of any committee designated by the board of directors, shall, in the performance of his duties, be fully protected in relying in good faith upon the records of the corporation and upon such information, opinions, reports or statements presented to the corporation by any of the corporation's officers or employees, or committees of the board of directors, or by any other person as to matters the member reasonably believes are within such other person's professional or expert competence and who has been selected with reasonable care by or on behalf of the corporation.

(f) Unless otherwise restricted by the certificate of incorporation or bylaws, any action required or permitted to be taken at any meeting of the board of directors or of any committee thereof may be taken without a meeting if all members of the board or committee, as the case may be, consent thereto in writing, and the writing or writings are filed with the minutes of proceedings of the board or committee.

(g) Unless otherwise restricted by the certificate of incorporation or bylaws, the board of directors of any corporation organized under this chapter may hold its meetings, and have an office or offices, outside of this State.

(h) Unless otherwise restricted by the certificate of incorporation or bylaws, the board of directors shall have the authority to fix the compensation of directors.

(i) Unless otherwise restricted by the certificate of incorporation or bylaws, members of the board of directors of any corporation, or any committee designated by the board, may participate in a meeting of such board or committee by means of conference telephone or similar communications equipment by means of which all persons participating in the meeting can hear each other, and participation in a meeting pursuant to this subsection shall constitute presence in person at the meeting.

(j) The certificate of incorporation of any corporation organized under this chapter which is not authorized to issue capital stock may provide that less than 1/3 of the members of the governing body may constitute a quorum thereof and may otherwise provide that the business and affairs of the corporation shall be managed in a manner different from that provided in this section. Except as may be otherwise provided by the certificate of incorporation, this section shall apply to such a corporation, and when so applied, all references to the board of directors, to members thereof, and to stockholders shall be deemed to refer to the governing body of the corporation, the members thereof and the members of the corporation, respectively.

(k) Any director or the entire board of directors may be removed, with or without cause, by the holders of a majority of the shares then entitled to vote at an election of directors, except as follows:

(1) Unless the certificate of incorporation otherwise provides, in the case of a corporation whose board is classified as provided in subsection (d) of this section, shareholders may effect such removal only for cause; or

(2) In the case of a corporation having cumulative voting, if less than the entire board is to be removed, no director may be removed without cause if the votes cast against his removal would be sufficient to elect him if then cumulatively voted at an election of the entire board of directors, or, if there be classes of directors, at an election of the class of directors of which he is a part.

Whenever the holders of any class or series are entitled to elect 1 or more directors by the certificate of incorporation, this subsection shall apply, in respect to the removal without cause of a director or directors so elected, to the vote of the holders of the outstanding shares of that class or series and not to the vote of the outstanding shares as a whole.

A.5

Delaware Merger and Antitakeover Statutes

Section 251 is Delaware's principal merger statute. It establishes the procedures and effects of a merger between two Delaware corporations. Delaware law also includes related statutes covering mergers between a Delaware and non-Delaware corporation (§252) and a parent and its 90% or more subsidiary (§253).

The Delaware antitakeover statute (§203) restricts mergers initiated by hostile bidders. It is an elaborate compromise version of §912 of the New York corporation law that we reproduce below (Appendix A.8). This kind of compromise is part of the delicate balance Delaware needs to strike among managements, institutional shareholders and the Delaware bar. We discuss the statute at length in Chapter 6.

A list of state antitakeover statutes is provided at Appendix A.11.

A.5.1 DELAWARE MERGER STATUTE: DELAWARE CORPORATION LAW §251

251. Merger or consolidation of domestic corporations

(a) Any 2 or more corporations existing under the laws of this State may merge into a single corporation, which may be any 1 of the constituent corporations or may consolidate into a new corporation formed by the consolidation, pursuant to an agreement of merger or consolidation, as the case may be, complying and approved in accordance with this section.

(b) The board of directors of each corporation which desires to merge or consolidate shall adopt a resolution approving an agreement of merger or consolidation. The agreement shall state:

(1) the terms and conditions of the merger of consolidation;

(2) the mode of carrying the same into effect;

(3) in the case of a merger, such amendments or changes in the certificate of incorporation of the surviving corporation as are desired to be effected by the merger, or, if no such amendments or changes are desired, a

statement that the certificate of incorporation of the surviving corporation shall be its certificate of incorporation;

(4) in the case of a consolidation, that the certificate of incorporation of the resulting corporation shall be as is set forth in an attachment to the agreement;

(5) the manner of converting the shares of each of the constituent corporations into shares or other securities of the corporation surviving or resulting from the merger or consolidation, and, if any shares of any of the constituent corporations are not to be converted solely into shares or other securities of the surviving or resulting corporation, the cash, property, rights or securities of any other corporation which the holders of such shares are to receive in exchange for, or upon conversion of such shares and the surrender of any certificates evidencing them, which cash, property, rights or securities of any other corporation may be in addition to or in lieu of shares or other securities of the surviving or resulting corporation; and

(6) such other details or provisions as are deemed desirable, including, without limiting the generality of the foregoing, a provision for the payment of cash in lieu of the issuance or recognition of fractional shares, interests or rights, or for any other arrangement with respect thereto, consistent with the provisions of §155 of this title. The agreement so adopted shall be executed and acknowledged in accordance with §103 of this title. Any of the terms of the agreement of merger or consolidation may be made dependent upon facts ascertainable outside of such agreement, provided that the agreement is clearly and expressly set forth in the agreement of merger or consolidation.

(c) The agreement required by subsection (b) of this section shall be submitted to the stockholders of each constituent corporation at an annual or special meeting for the purpose of acting on the agreement. Due notice of the time, place and purpose of the meeting shall be mailed to each holder of stock, whether voting or nonvoting, of the corporation at his address as it appears on the records of the corporation, at least 20 days prior to the date of the meeting. The notice shall contain a copy of the agreement or a brief summary thereof, as the directors shall deem advisable. At the meeting, the agreement shall be considered and a vote taken for its adoption or rejection. If a majority of the outstanding stock of the corporation entitled to vote thereon shall be voted for the adoption of the agreement, that fact shall be certified on the agreement by the secretary or assistant secretary of the corporation. If the agreement shall be so adopted and certified by each constituent corporation, it shall then be filed and shall become effective, in accordance with §103 of this title. It shall be recorded in the office of the recorder of the county of this State in which the registered office of each such constituent corporation is located; or if any of the constituent corporations shall have been specially created by a public act of the General Assembly, then the agreement shall be recorded in the county where such corporation had its principal place of business in this State. In lieu of filing and recording the agreement of merger or consolidation required by this Section, the surviving or resulting corporation may file a certificate of merger or consolidation executed in accordance with §103 of this title, which states:

(1) The name and state of incorporation of each of the constituent corporations;

(2) That an agreement of merger or consolidation has been approved, adopted, certified, executed and acknowledged by each of the constituent corporations in accordance with this Section;

(3) The name of the surviving or resulting corporation;

(4) In the case of a merger, such amendments or changes in the certificate of incorporation of the surviving corporation as are desired to be effected by the merger, or, if no such amendments or changes are desired, a statement that the certificate of incorporation of the surviving corporation shall be its certificate of incorporation;

(5) In the case of a consolidation, that the certificate of incorporation of the resulting corporation shall be as is set forth in an attachment to the certificate;

(6) That the executed agreement of consolidation or merger is on file at the principal place of business of the surviving corporation, stating the address thereof; and

(7) That a copy of the agreement of consolidation or merger will be furnished by the surviving corporation, on request and without cost, to any stockholder of any constituent corporation.

(d) Any agreement of merger or consolidation may contain a provision that at any time prior to the filing of the agreement with the Secretary of State, the agreement may be terminated by the board of directors of any constituent corporation notwithstanding approval of the agreement by the stockholders of all or any of the constituent corporations. Any agreement of merger or consolidation may contain a provision that the boards of directors of the constituent corporations may amend the agreement at any time prior to the filing of the agreement (or a certificate in lieu thereof) with the Secretary of State, provided that an amendment made subsequent to the adoption of the agreement by the stockholders of any constituent corporation shall not (1) alter or change the amount or kind of shares, securities, cash, property and/or rights to be received in exchange for or on conversion of all or any of the shares of any class or series thereof of such constituent corporation, (2) alter or change any term of the certificate of incorporation of the surviving corporation to be effected by the merger or consolidation, or (3) alter or change any of the terms and conditions of the agreement if such alteration or change would adversely affect the holders of any class or series thereof of such constituent corporation.

(e) In the case of a merger, the certificate of incorporation of the surviving corporation shall automatically be amended to the extent, if any, that changes in the certificate of incorporation are set forth in the agreement of merger.

(f) Notwithstanding the requirements of subsection (c) of this section, unless required by its certificate of incorporation, no vote of stockholders of a constituent corporation surviving a merger shall be necessary to authorize a merger if (1) the agreement of merger does not amend in any respect the certificate of incorporation of such constituent corporation, (2) each share of stock of such constituent corporation outstanding immediately prior to the effective date of the merger is to be an identical outstanding or treasury share of the surviving corporation after the effective date of the merger, and (3) either no shares of common stock of the surviving corporation and no shares, securities or obligations convertible into such stock are to be issued or delivered under the plan of merger, or the authorized unissued shares of the treasury shares of common stock of the surviving corporation to be issued or delivered under the plan of merger plus those initially issuable upon conversion of any other shares, securities or obligations to be issued or delivered under such plan do not exceed 20% of the shares of common stock of such constituent corporation outstanding immediately prior to the effective date of the merger. No vote of stockholders of a constitutent corporation shall be necessary to authorize a merger or consolidation if no shares of the stock of such corporation shall have been issued prior to the adoption by the board of directors of the resolution approving the agreement of merger or consolidation. If an agreement of merger is adopted by the constituent corporation surviving the merger, by action of its board of directors and without any vote of its stockholders pursuant to this subsection, the secretary or assistant secretary of that corporation shall certify on the agreement that the agreement has been adopted pursuant to this subsection and that, as of the date of such certificate, the outstanding shares of the corporation were such as to render this subsection applicable. The agreement so adopted and certified shall then be filed and shall become effective, in accordance with §103 of this title. Such filing shall constitute a representation by the person who executes the agreement that the facts stated in the certificate remain true immediately prior to such filing.

A.5.2 DELAWARE ANTITAKEOVER STATUTE
DELAWARE CORPORATION LAW §203

203. Business combinations with interested stockholders

(a) Notwithstanding any other provisions of this chapter, a corporation shall not engage in any business combination with any interested stockholder for a period of 3 years following the date that such stockholder became an interested stockholder, unless (1) prior to such date the board of directors of the corporation approved either the business combination or the transaction which resulted in the stockholder becoming an interested stockholder, or (2) upon consummation of the transaction which resulted in the stockholder becoming an interested stockholder, the interested stockholder owned at least 85% of the voting stock of the corporation outstanding at the time the transaction commenced, excluding for purposes of determining the number of shares outstanding those shares owned (i) by persons who are directors and also officers and (ii) employee stock plans in which employee participants do not have the right to determine confidentially whether shares held subject to the plan will be tendered in a tender or exchange offer, or (3) on or subsequent to such date the business combination is approved by the board of directors and authorized at an annual or special meeting of stockholders, and not by written consent, by the affirmative vote of at least $66\frac{2}{3}\%$ of the outstanding voting stock which is not owned by the interested stockholder.

(b) The restrictions contained in this section shall not apply if:

(1) the corporation's original certificate of incorporation contains a provision expressly electing not to be governed by this section;

(2) the corporation, by action of its board of directors, adopts an amendment to its bylaws within 90 days of the effective date of this section, expressly electing not to be governed by this section, which amendment shall not be further amended by the board of directors;

(3) the corporation, by action of its stockholders, adopts an amendment to its certificate of incorporation or bylaws expressly electing not to be governed by this section, provided that, in addition to any other vote required by law, such amendment to the certificate of incorporation or bylaws must be approved by the affirmative vote of a majority of the shares entitled to vote. An amendment adopted pursuant to this paragraph shall not be effective until 12 months after the adoption of such amendment and shall not apply to any business combination between such corporation and any person who became an interested stockholder of such corporation on or prior to such adoption. A bylaw amendment adopted pursuant to this paragraph shall not be further amended by the board of directors;

(4) the corporation does not have a class of voting stock that is (i) listed on a national securities exchange, (ii) authorized for quotation on an inter dealer quotation system of a registered national securities association or (iii) held of record by more than 2,000 stockholders, unless any of the foregoing results from action taken, directly or indirectly, by an interested stockholder or from a transaction in which a person becomes an interested stockholder;

(5) a stockholder becomes an interested stockholder inadvertently and (i) as soon as practicable divests sufficient shares so that the stockholder ceases to be an interested stockholder and (ii) would not, at any time within the 3 year period immediately prior to a business combination between the corporation and such stockholder, have been an interested stockholder but for the inadvertent acquisition; or

(6) the business combination is proposed prior to the consummation or abandonment of and subsequent to the earlier of the public announcement or the notice required hereunder of a proposed transaction which (i) constitutes one of the transactions described in the second sentence of this paragraph; (ii) is with or by a person who either was not an interested stockholder during the previous 3 years or who became an interested stockholder with the approval of the corporation's board of directors; and (iii) is approved or not opposed by a majority of the members of the board of directors then in office (but not less than 1) who were directors prior to any person becoming an interested stockholder during the previous 3 years or were recommended for election or elected to succeed such directors by a majority of such directors. The proposed transactions referred to in the preceding sentence are limited to (x) a merger or consolidation of the corporation (except for a merger in respect of which, pursuant to section 251(f) of the chapter, no vote of the stockholders of the corporation is required); (y) a sale, lease, exchange, mortgage, pledge, transfer or other disposition (in one transaction or a series of transactions), whether as part of a dissolution or otherwise, of assets of the corporation or of any direct or indirect majority-owned subsidiary of the corporation (other than to any direct or indirect wholly-owned subsidiary or to the corporation) having an aggregate market value equal to 50% or more of either that aggregate market value of all of the assets of the corporation determined on a consolidated basis or the aggregate market value of all the outstanding stock of the corporation; or (z) a proposed tender or exchange offer for 50% or more of the outstanding voting stock of the corporation. The corporation shall give not less than 20 days' notice to all interested stockholders prior to the consummation of any of the transactions described in clauses (x) or (y) of the second sentence of this paragraph. Notwithstanding paragraphs (1), (2), (3) and (4) of this subsection, a corporation may elect

by a provision of its original certificate of incorporation or any amendment thereto to be governed by this section, provided that any such amendment to the certificate of incorporation shall not apply to restrict a business combination between the corporation and an interested stockholder of the corporation if the interested stockholder became such prior to the effective date of the amendment.

(c) As used in this section only, the term:

(1) 'affiliate' means a person that directly, or indirectly through one or more intermediaries, controls, or is controlled by, or is under common control with, another person.

(2) 'associate,' when used to indicate a relationship with any person, means (i) any corporation or organization of which such person is a director, officer or partner or is, directly or indirectly, the owner of 20% or more of any class of voting stock, (ii) any trust or other estate in which such person has at least a 20% beneficial interest or as to which such person serves as trustee or in a similar fiduciary capacity, and (iii) any relative or spouse of such person, or any relative of such spouse, who has the same residence as such person.

(3) 'business combination,' when used in reference to any corporation and any interested stockholder of such corporation, means:

(i) any merger or consolidation of the corporation or any direct or indirect majority-owned subsidiary of the corporation with (A) the interested stockholder, or (B) with any other corporation if the merger or consolidation is caused by the interested stockholder and as a result of such merger or consolidation subsection (a) of this section is not applicable to the surviving corporation;

(ii) any sale, lease, exchange, mortgage, pledge, transfer or other disposition (in one transaction or a series of transactions), except pro-portionately as a stockholder of such corporation, to or with the interested stockholder, whether as part of a dissolution or otherwise, of assets of the corporation or of any direct or indirect majority-owned subsidiary of the corporation which assets have an aggregate market value equal to 10% or more of either the aggregate market value of all the assets of the corporation determined on a consolidated basis or the aggregate market value of all the outstanding stock of the corporation;

(iii) any transaction which results in the issuance or transfer by the corporation or by any direct or indirect majority-owned subsidiary of the corporation of any stock of the corporation or of such subsidiary to the interested stockholder, except (A) pursuant to the exercise, exchange or conversion of securities exercisable for, exchangeable for or convertible into stock of such corporation or any such subsidiary which securities were outstanding prior to the time that the interested stockholder became such, (B) pursuant to a dividend or distribution paid or made, or the exercise, exchange or conversion of securities exercisable for, exchangeable for or convertible into stock of such corporation or any such subsidiary which security is distributed, pro rata to all holders of a class or series of stock of such corporation subsequent to the time the interested stockholder became such, (C) pursuant to an exchange offer by the corporation to purchase stock made on the same terms to all holders of said stock, or (D) any issuance or transfer of stock by the corporation, provided however, that in no case under (B)–(D) above shall there be an increase in the interested stockholder's proportionate share of the stock of any class or series of the corporation or of the voting stock of the corporation;

(iv) any transaction involving the corporation or any direct or indirect majority-owned subsidiary of the corporation which has the effect, directly or indirectly, of increasing the proportionate share of the stock of any class or series, or securities convertible into the stock of any class or series, of the corporation or of any such subsidiary which is owned by the interested stockholder, except as a result of immaterial changes due to fractional share adjustments or as a result of any purchase or redemption of any shares of stock not caused, directly or indirectly, by the interested stockholder; or

(v) any receipt by the interested stockholder of the benefit, directly or indirectly (except proportionately as a stockholder of such corporation) of any loans, advances, guarantees, pledges, or other financial benefits (other than those expressly permitted in subparagraphs (i)–(iv) above) provided by or through the corporation or any direct or indirect majority-owned subsidiary.

(4) 'control,' including the term 'controlling,' 'controlled by' and 'under common control with,' means the possession, directly or indirectly, of the power to direct or cause the direction of the management and policies of a person, whether through the ownership of voting stock, by contract, or otherwise. A person who is the owner of 20% or more of a corporation's outstanding voting stock shall be presumed to have control of such corporation, in the absence of proof by a preponderance of the evidence to the contrary. Notwithstanding the foregoing, a presumption of control shall not apply where such person holds voting stock, in good faith and not for the purpose of circumventing this section, as an agent, bank, broker, nominee, custodian or trustee for one or more owners who do not

individually or as a group have control of such corporation.

(5) 'interested stockholder' means any person (other than the corporation and any direct or indirect majority-owned subsidiary of the corporation) that (i) is the owner of 15% or more of the outstanding voting stock of the corporation, or (ii) is an affiliate or associate of the corporation and was the owner of 15% or more of the outstanding voting stock of the corporation at any time within the 3-year period immediately prior to the date on which it is sought to be determined whether such person is an interested stockholder; and the affiliates and associates of such person; provided, however, that the term 'interested stockholder' shall not include (x) any person who (A) owned shares in excess of the 15% limitation set forth herein as of, or acquired such shares pursuant to a tender offer commenced prior to, December 23, 1987, or pursuant to an exchange offer announced prior to the aforesaid date and commenced within 90 days thereafter and continued to own shares in excess of such 15% limitation or would have but for action by the corporation or (B) acquired said shares from a person described in (A) above by gift, inheritance or in a transaction in which no consideration was exchanged; or (y) any person whose ownership of shares in excess of the 15% limitation set forth herein is the result of action taken solely by the corporation provided that such person shall be an interested stockholder if thereafter he acquires additional shares of voting stock of the corporation, except as a result of further corporate action not caused, directly or indirectly, by such person. For the purpose of determining whether a person is an interested stockholder, the voting stock of the corporation deemed to be outstanding shall include stock deemed to be owned by the person through application of paragraph (8) of this subsection but shall not include any other unissued stock of such corporation which may be issuable pursuant to any agreement, arrangement or understanding, or upon exercise of conversion rights, warrants or options, or otherwise.

(6) 'person' means any individual, corporation, partnership, unincorporated association or other entity.

(7) 'voting stock' means stock of any class or series entitled to vote generally in the election of directors.

(8) 'owner' including the terms 'own' and 'owned' when used with respect to any stock means a person that individually or with or through any of its affiliates or associates:

(i) beneficially owns such stock, directly or indirectly; or

(ii) has (A) the right to acquire such stock (whether such right is exercisable immediately or only after the passage of time) pursuant to any agreement, arrangement or understanding, or upon the exercise of conversion rights, exchange rights, warrants or options, or otherwise; provided, however, that a person shall not be deemed the owner of stock tendered pursuant to a tender or exchange offer made by such person or any of such person's affiliates or associates until such tendered stock is accepted for purchase or exchange; or (B) the right to vote such stock pursuant to any agreement, arrangement or understanding; provided, however, that a person shall not be deemed the owner of any stock because of such person's right to vote such stock if the agreement, arrangement or understanding to vote such stock arises solely from a revocable proxy or consent given in response to a proxy or consent solicitation made to 10 or more persons; or

(iii) has any agreement, arrangement or understanding for the purpose of acquiring, holding, voting (except voting pursuant to a revocable proxy or consent as described in item (B) of clause (ii) of this paragraph), or disposing of such stock with any other person that beneficially owns, or whose affiliates or associates beneficially own, directly or indirectly, such stock.

(d) No provision of a certificate of incorporation or bylaw shall require, for any vote of stockholders required by this section a greater vote of stockholders than that specified in this section.

(e) The Court of Chancery is hereby vested with exclusive jurisdiction to hear and determine all matters with respect to this section.

A.6

Appraisal Rights under Delaware Law
Delaware Corporation Law §262

> The Delaware appraisal statute, §262 of the Delaware Corporation Law, provides the statutory remedy of a fair price for minority shareholders who are squeezed out in a merger. In theory it is enormously important, but in practice it is difficult and expensive for small shareholders to use.

262. Appraisal rights

(a) Any stockholder of a corporation of this State who holds shares of stock on the date of the making of a demand pursuant to subsection (d) of this section with respect to such shares, who continuously holds such shares through the effective date of the merger or consolidation, who has otherwise complied with subsection (d) of this section and who has neither voted in favor of the merger or consolidation nor consented thereto in writing pursuant to §228 of this title shall be entitled to an appraisal by the Court of Chancery of the fair value of his shares of stock under the circumstances described in subsections (b) and (c) of this section. As used in this section, the word 'stockholder' means a holder of record of stock in a stock corporation and also a member of record of a nonstock corporation; the words 'stock' and 'share' mean and include what is ordinarily meant by those words and also membership or membership interest of a member of a nonstock corporation.

(b) Appraisal rights shall be available for the shares of any class or series of stock of a constituent corporation in a merger or consolidation to be effected pursuant to §251, 252, 254, 257, 258 or 263 of this title:

(1) Provided, however, that no appraisal rights under this section shall be available for the shares of any class or series of stock which, at the record date fixed to determine the stockholders entitled to receive notice of and to vote at the meeting of stockholders to act upon the agreement of merger or consolidation, were either (i) listed on a national securities exchange or (ii) held of record by more than 2,000 stockholders; and further provided that no appraisal rights shall be available for any shares of stock of the constituent

corporation surviving a merger if the merger did not require for its approval the vote of the stockholders of the surviving corporation as provided in subsection (f) of §251 of this title.

(2) Notwithstanding paragraph (1) of this subsection, appraisal rights under this section shall be available for the shares of any class or series of stock of a constituent corporation if the holders thereof are required by the terms of an agreement of merger or consolidation pursuant to §§251, 252, 254, 257, 258 and 263 of this title to accept for such stock anything except:

a. Shares of stock of the corporation surviving or resulting from such merger or consolidation;

b. Shares of stock of any other corporation which at the effective date of the merger or consolidation will be either listed on a national securities exchange or held of record by more than 2,000 stockholders;

c. Cash in lieu of fractional shares of the corporations described in the foregoing subparagraphs a. and b. of this paragraph; or

d. Any combination of the shares of stock and cash in lieu of fractional shares described in the foregoing subparagraphs a., b. and c. of this paragraph.

(3) In the event all of the stock of a subsidiary Delaware corporation party to a merger effected under §253 of this title is not owned by the parent corporation immediately prior to the merger, appraisal rights shall be available for the shares of the subsidiary Delaware corporation.

(c) Any corporation may provide in its certificate of incorporation that appraisal rights under this section shall be available for the shares of any class or series of its stock as a result of an amendment to its certificate of incorporation, any merger or consolidation in which the corporation is a constituent corporation or the sale of all or substantially all of the assets of the corporation. If the certificate of incorporation contains such a provision, the procedures of this section, including those set forth in subsections (d) and (e) of this section, shall apply as nearly as is practicable.

(d) Appraisal rights shall be perfected as follows:

(1) If a proposed merger or consolidation for which appraisal rights are provided under this section is to be submitted for approval at a meeting of stockholders, the corporation, not less than 20 days prior to the meeting, shall notify each of its stockholders entitled to such appraisal rights that appraisal rights are available for any or all of the shares of the constituent corporations, and shall include in such notice a copy of this section. Each stockholder electing to demand the appraisal of his shares shall deliver to the

corporation, before the taking of the vote on the merger or consolidation, a written demand for appraisal of his shares. Such demand will be sufficient if it reasonably informs the corporation of the identity of the stockholder and that the stockholder intends thereby to demand the appraisal of his shares. A proxy or vote against the merger or consolidation shall not constitute such a demand. A stockholder electing to take such action must do so by a separate written demand as herein provided. Within 10 days after the effective date of such merger or consolidation, the surviving or resulting corporation shall notify each stockholder of each constituent corporation who has complied with this subsection and has not voted in favor of or consented to the merger or consolidation of the date that the merger or consolidation has become effective; or

(2) If the merger or consolidation was approved pursuant to §228 or 253 of this title, the surviving or resulting corporation, either before the effective date of the merger or consolidation or within 10 days thereafter, shall notify each of the stockholders entitled to appraisal rights of the effective date of the merger or consolidation and that appraisal rights are available for any or all of the shares of the constituent corporation, and shall include in such notice a copy of this section. The notice shall be sent by certified or registered mail, return receipt requested, addressed to the stockholder at his address as it appears on the records of the corporation. Any stockholder entitled to appraisal rights may, within 20 days after the date of mailing of the notice, demand in writing from the surviving or resulting corporation the appraisal of his shares. Such demand will be sufficient if it reasonably informs the corporation of the identity of the stockholder and that the stockholder intends to demand the appraisal of his shares.

(e) Within 120 days after the effective date of the merger or consolidation, the surviving or resulting corporation or any stockholder who has complied with subsections (a) and (d) hereof and who is otherwise entitled to appraisal rights, may file a petition in the Court of Chancery demanding a determination of the value of the stock of all such stockholders. Notwithstanding the foregoing, at any time within 60 days after the effective date of the merger or consolidation, any stockholder shall have the right to withdraw his demand for appraisal and to accept the terms offered upon the merger or consolidation. Within 120 days after the effective date of the merger or consolidation, any stockholder who has complied with the requirements of subsections (a) and (d) hereof, upon written request, shall be entitled to receive from the corporation surviving the merger or resulting from the consolidation a statement setting forth the aggregate number of shares not voted in favor of the merger or consolidation and with respect to which demands for appraisal have been received and the aggregate number of holders of such shares. Such written statement shall be mailed to the stockholder within 10 days after his written request for such a statement is received by the surviving or resulting corporation or within 10 days after expiration of the period for delivery of demands for appraisal under subsection (d) hereof, whichever is later.

(f) Upon the filing of any such petition by a stockholder, service of a copy thereof shall be made upon the surviving or resulting corporation, which shall within 20 days after such service file in the office of the Register in Chancery in which the petition was filed a duly verified list containing the names and addresses of all stockholders who have demanded payment for their shares and with whom agreements as to the value of their shares have not been reached by the surviving or resulting corporation. If the petition shall be filed by the surviving or resulting corporation, the petition shall be accompanied by such a duly verified list. The Register in Chancery, if so ordered by the Court, shall give notice of the time and place fixed for the hearing of such petition by registered or certified mail to the surviving or resulting corporation and to the stockholders shown on the list at the addresses therein stated. Such notice shall also be given by 1 or more publications at least 1 week before the day of the hearing, in a newspaper of general circulation published in the City of Wilmington, Delaware or such publication as the Court deems advisable. The forms of the notices by mail and by publication shall be approved by the Court, and the costs thereof shall be borne by the surviving or resulting corporation.

(g) At the hearing on such petition, the Court shall determine the stockholders who have complied with this section and who have become entitled to appraisal rights. The Court may require the stockholders who have demanded an appraisal for their shares and who hold stock represented by certificates to submit their certificates of stock to the Register in Chancery for notation thereon of the pendency of the appraisal proceedings; and if any stockholder fails to comply with such direction, the Court may dismiss the proceedings as to such stockholder.

(h) After determining the stockholders entitled to an appraisal, the Court shall appraise the shares, determining their fair value exclusive of any element of value arising from the accomplishment or expectation of the merger or consolidation, together with a fair rate of interest, if any, to be paid upon the amount determined to be the fair value. In determining such fair value, the Court shall take into account all relevant factors. In determining the fair rate of interest, the Court may consider all relevant factors, including the rate of interest which the surviving or resulting corporation would have had to pay to borrow money during the pendency of the proceeding. Upon application by the surviving or resulting corporation or by any stockholder entitled to participate in the appraisal proceeding, the Court may, in its discretion, permit discovery or other pretrial proceedings and may proceed to trial upon the appraisal prior to the final determination of the stockholder entitled to an appraisal. Any stockholder whose name appears on the list filed by the surviving or resulting corporation pursuant to subsection (f) of this section and who has submitted his certificates of stock to the Register in Chancery, if such is required, may participate fully in all proceedings until it is finally determined that he is not entitled to appraisal rights under this section.

(i) The Court shall direct the payment of the fair value of the shares, together with interest, if any, by the surviving or resulting corporation to the stockholders entitled thereto. Interest may be simple or compound, as the Court may direct. Payment shall be so made to each such stockholder, in the case of holders of uncertificated stock forthwith, and the case of holders of shares represented by certificates upon the surrender to the corporation of the certificates representing such stock. The Court's decree may be enforced as other decrees in the Court of Chancery may be enforced, whether such surviving or resulting corporation be a corporation of this State or of any state.

(j) The costs of the proceeding may be determined by the Court and taxed upon the parties as the Court deems equitable in the circumstances. Upon application of a stockholder, the Court may order all or a portion of the expenses incurred by any stockholder in connection with the appraisal proceeding, including, without limitation, reasonable attorney's fees and the fees and expenses of experts, to be charged pro rata against the value of all the shares entitled to an appraisal.

(k) From and after the effective date of the merger or consolidation, no stockholder who has demanded his appraisal rights as provided in subsection (d) of this section shall be entitled to vote such stock for any purpose or to receive payment of dividends or other distributions on the stock (except dividends or other distributions payable to stockholders of record at a date which is prior to the effective date of the merger or consolidation); provided, however, that if no petition for an appraisal shall be filed within the time provided in subsection (e) of this section, or if such stockholder shall deliver to the surviving or resulting corporation a written withdrawal of his demand for an appraisal and an acceptance of the merger or consolidation, either within 60 days after the effective date of the merger or consolidation as provided in subsection (e) of this section or thereafter with the written approval of the corporation, then the right of such stockholder to an appraisal shall cease. Notwithstanding the foregoing, no appraisal proceeding in the Court of Chancery shall be dismissed as to any stockholder without the approval of the Court, and such approval may be conditioned upon such terms as the Court deems just.

(l) The shares of the surviving or resulting corporation to which the shares of such objecting stockholders would have been converted had they assented to the merger or consolidation shall have the status of authorized and unissued shares of the surviving or resulting corporation.

A.7

New York Statute on Duty of Directors
New York Business Corporation Law §717

As a contrast to the Delaware antitakeover statute (Appendix A.5.2) we have provided two New York antitakeover laws here and in Appendix A.8. Section 717 gives directors broad discretion to consider long-term factors in deciding to turn down a takeover proposal.

717. Duty of directors

(a) A director shall perform his duties as a director, including his duties as a member of any committee of the board upon which he may serve, in good faith and with that degree of care which an ordinarily prudent person in a like position would use under similar circumstances. In performing his duties, a director shall be entitled to rely on information, opinions, reports or statements including financial statements and other financial data, in each case prepared or presented by:

(1) one or more officers or employees of the corporation or of any other corporation of which at least fifty percentum of the outstanding shares of stock entitling the holders thereof to vote for the election of directors is owned directly or indirectly by the corporation, whom the director believes to be reliable and competent in the matters presented,

(2) counsel, public accountants or other persons as to matters which the director believes to be within such person's professional or expert competence, or

(3) a committee of the board upon which he does not serve, duly designated in accordance with a provision of the certificate of incorporation or the by-laws, as to matters within its designated authority, which committee the director believes to merit confidence, so long as in so relying he shall be acting in good faith and with such degree of care, but he shall not be considered to be acting in good faith if he has knowledge concerning the matter in question that would cause such reliance to be unwarranted. A person who so performs his duties shall have no liability by reason of being or having been a director of the corporation.

(b) In taking action, including, without limitation, action which may involve or relate to a change or potential change in the control of the corporation, a director shall be entitled to consider, without limitation, (1) both the long-term and the short-term interests of the corporation and its shareholders and (2) the effects that the corporation's actions may have in the short-term or in the long-term upon any of the following:

(i) the prospects for potential growth, development, productivity and profitability of the corporation;

(ii) the corporation's current employees;

(iii) the corporation's retired employees and other beneficiaries receiving or entitled to receive retirement, welfare or similar benefits from or pursuant to any plan sponsored, or agreement entered into, by the corporation;

(iv) the corporation's customers and creditors; and

(v) the ability of the corporation to provide, as a going concern, goods, services, employment opportunities and employment benefits and otherwise to contribute to the communities in which it does business.

Nothing in this paragraph shall create any duties owed by any director to any person or entity to consider or afford any particular weight to any of the foregoing or abrogate any duty of the directors, either statutory or recognized by common law or court decisions.

For purposes of this paragraph, 'control' shall mean the possession, directly or indirectly, of the power to direct or cause the direction of the management and policies of the corporation, whether through the ownership of voting stock, by contract, or otherwise.

A.8

New York Statute Restricting Mergers
New York Business Corporation Law §912

Section 912 of the New York Corporation Law restricts mergers. It was the model for the milder compromise that Delaware enacted (Appendix A.5.2). New York also has a statute that legalizes flip-in poison pills, similar to the New Jersey statute reproduced in Appendix A.10.

912. Requirements relating to certain business combinations

(a) For the purposes of this section:

(1) 'Affiliate' means a person that directly, or indirectly through one or more intermediaries, controls, or is controlled by, or is under common control with, a specified person.

(2) 'Announcement date,' when used in reference to any business combination, means the date of the first public announcement of the final, definitive proposal for such business combination.

(3) 'Associate,' when used to indicate a relationship with any person, means (A) any corporation or organization of which such person is an officer or partner or is, directly or indirectly, the beneficial owner of ten percent or more of any class of voting stock, (B) any trust or other estate in which such person has a substantial beneficial interest or as to which such person serves as trustee or in a similar fiduciary capacity, and (C) any relative or spouse of such person, or any relative of such spouse, who has the same home as such person.

(4) 'Beneficial owner,' when used with respect to any stock, means a person:

(A) that, individually or with or through any of its affiliates or associates, beneficially owns such stock, directly or indirectly; or

(B) that, individually or with or through any of its affiliates or associates, has (i) the right to acquire such stock (whether such right is exercisable immediately or only after the passage of time), pursuant to any agreement, arrangement or understanding (whether or not in writing), or upon the exercise of conversion rights, exchange rights, warrants or options, or otherwise; provided, however, that a person shall not be deemed the beneficial owner of stock tendered pursuant to a tender or exchange offer made by such person or any of such person's affiliates or associates until such tendered stock is accepted for purchase or exchange; or (ii) the right to vote such stock pursuant to any agreement, arrangement or understanding (whether or not in writing); provided, however, that a person shall not be deemed the beneficial owner of any stock under this item if the agreement, arrangement or understanding to vote such stock (X) arises solely from a revocable proxy or consent given in response to a proxy or consent solicitation made in accordance with the applicable rules and regulations under the Exchange Act and (Y) is not then reportable on a Schedule 13D under the Exchange Act (or any comparable or successor report); or

(C) that has any agreement, arrangement or understanding (whether or not in writing), for the purpose of acquiring, holding, voting (except voting pursuant to a revocable proxy or consent as described in item (ii) of clause (B) of this subparagraph), or disposing of such stock with any other person that beneficially owns, or whose affiliates or associates beneficially own, directly or indirectly, such stock.

(5) 'Business combination,' when used in reference to any resident domestic corporation and any interested shareholder or such resident domestic corporation, means:

(A) any merger or consolidation of such resident domestic corporation or any subsidiary of such resident domestic corporation with (i) such interested shareholder or (ii) any other corporation (whether or not itself an interested shareholder of such resident domestic corporation) which is, or after such merger or consolidation would be, an affiliate or associate of such interested shareholder;

(B) any sale, lease, exchange, mortgage, pledge, transfer or other disposition (in one transaction or a series of transactions) to or with such interested shareholder or any affiliate or associate of such interested shareholder of assets of such resident domestic corporation or any subsidiary of such resident domestic corporation (i) having an aggregate market value equal to ten percent or more of the aggregate market value of all the assets, determined on a consolidated basis, of such resident domestic corporation, (ii) having an aggregate market value equal to ten percent or more of the aggregate market value of all the outstanding stock of such resident domestic corporation, or (iii) representing ten percent or more of the earning power or net income, determined on a consolidated basis, of such resident domestic corporation;

(C) the issuance or transfer by such resident domestic corporation or any subsidiary of such resident domestic corporation (in one transaction or a series of transactions) of any stock of such resident domestic corporation or any subsidiary of such resident domestic corporation which has an aggregate market value equal to five percent or more of the aggregate market value of all outstanding stock of such resident domestic corporation to such interested shareholder or any affiliate or associate of such interested shareholder except pursuant to the exercise of warrants or rights to purchase stock offered, or a dividend or distribution paid or made, pro rata to all shareholders of such resident domestic corporation;

(D) the adoption of any plan or proposal for the liquidation or dissolution of such resident domestic corporation proposed by, or pursuant to any agreement, arrangement or understanding (whether or not in writing) with, such interested shareholder or any affiliate or associate of such interested shareholder;

(E) any reclassification of securities (including, without limitation, any stock split, stock dividend, or other distribution of stock in respect of stock, or any reverse stock split), or recapitalization of such resident domestic corporation, or any merger or consolidation of such resident domestic corporation with any subsidiary of such resident domestic corporation, or any other transaction (whether or not with or into or otherwise involving such interested shareholder), proposed by, or pursuant to any agreement, arrangement or understanding (whether or not in writing) with, such interested shareholder or any affiliate or associate of such interested shareholder, which has the effect, directly or indirectly, of increasing the proportionate share of the outstanding shares of any class or series of voting stock or securities convertible into voting stock of such resident domestic corporation or any subsidiary of such resident domestic corporation which is directly or indirectly owned by such interested shareholder or any affiliate or associate of such interested shareholder, except as a result of immaterial changes due to fractional share adjustments; or

(F) any receipt by such interested shareholder or any affiliate or associate of such interested shareholder of the benefit, directly or indirectly (except proportionately as a shareholder of such resident domestic corporation) of any loans, advances, guarantees, pledges or other financial assistance or any tax credits or other tax advantages provided by or through such resident domestic corporation.

(6) 'Common stock' means any stock other than preferred stock.

(7) 'Consummation date,' with respect to any business combination, means the date of consummation of such business combination, or, in the case of a

business combination as to which a shareholder vote is taken, the later of the business day prior to the vote or twenty days prior to the date of consummation of such business combination.

(8) 'Control,' including the terms 'controlling,' 'controlled by' and 'under common control with,' means the possession, directly or indirectly, or the power to direct or cause the direction of the management and policies of a person, whether through the ownership of voting stock, by contract, or otherwise. A person's beneficial ownership of ten percent or more of a corporation's outstanding voting stock shall create a presumption that such person has control of such corporation. Notwithstanding the foregoing, a person shall not be deemed to have control of a corporation if such person holds voting stock, in good faith and not for the purpose of circumventing this section, as an agent, bank, broker, nominee, custodian or trustee for one or more beneficial owners who do not individually or as a group have control of such corporation.

(9) 'Exchange Act' means the Act of Congress known as the Securities Exchange Act of 1934, as the same has been or hereafter may be amended from time to time.

(10) 'Interested shareholder,' when used in reference to any resident domestic corporation, means any person (other than such resident domestic corporation or any subsidiary of such resident domestic corporation) that

(A) (i) is the beneficial owner, directly or indirectly, of twenty percent or more of the outstanding voting stock of such resident domestic corporation; or

(ii) is an affiliate or associate of such resident domestic corporation and at any time within the five-year period immediately prior to the date in question was the beneficial owner, directly or indirectly, of twenty percent or more of the then outstanding voting stock of such resident domestic corporation; provided that

(B) for the purpose of determining whether a person is an interested shareholder, the number of shares of voting stock of such resident domestic corporation deemed to be outstanding shall include shares deemed to be beneficially owned by the person through application of subparagraph four of this paragraph but shall not include any other unissued shares of voting stock of such resident domestic corporation which may be issuable pursuant to any agreement, arrangement or understanding, or upon exercise of conversion rights, warrants or options, or otherwise.

(11) 'Market value,' when used in reference to stock or property of any resident domestic corporation, means:

(A) in the case of stock, the highest closing sale price during the thirty-day period immediately preceding the date in question of a share of such stock on the composite tape for New York stock exchange-listed stocks, or, if such stock is not quoted on such composite tape or if such stock is not listed on such exchange, on the principal United States securities exchange registered under the Exchange Act on which such stock is listed, or, if such stock is not listed on any such exchange, the highest closing bid quotation with respect to a share of such stock during the thirty-day period preceding the date in question on the National Association of Securities Dealers, Inc. Automated Quotations System or any system then in use, or if no such quotations are available, the fair market value on the date in question of a share of such stock as determined by the board of directors of such resident domestic corporation in good faith; and

(B) in the case of property other than cash or stock, the fair market value of such property on the date in question as determined by the board of directors of such resident domestic corporation in good faith.

(12) 'Preferred stock' means any class or series of stock of a resident domestic corporation which under the by-laws or certificate of incorporation of such resident domestic corporation is entitled to receive payment of dividends prior to any payment of dividends on some other class or series of stock, or is entitled in the event of any voluntary liquidation, dissolution or winding up of the resident domestic corporation to receive payment or distribution of a preferential amount before any payments or distributions are received by some other class or series of stock.

(13) 'Resident domestic corporation' means an issuer of voting stock which:

(A) is organized under the laws of this state; and

(B) either (i) has its principal executive offices and significant business operations located in this state; or (ii) has, alone or in combination with one or more of its subsidiaries of which it owns at least eighty percent of the voting stock, at least two hundred fifty employees or twenty-five percent of the total number of all employees of itself and such subsidiaries employed primarily within the state; and

(C) has at least ten percent of its voting stock owned beneficially by residents of this state. For purposes of this section, the residence of a partnership, unincorporated association, trust or similar organization shall be the principal office of such organization.

No resident domestic corporation, which is organized under the laws of this state, shall cease to be a resident domestic corporation by reason of events occurring or actions taken while such resident domestic corporation is subject to the provisions of this section.

(14) 'Stock' means:

(A) any stock or similar security, any certificate of interest, any participation in any profit sharing agreement, any voting trust certificate, or any certificate of deposit for stock; and

(B) any security convertible, with or without consideration, into stock, or any warrant, call or other option or privilege of buying stock without being bound to do so, or any other security carrying any right to acquire, subscribe to or purchase stock.

(15) 'Stock acquisition date,' with respect to any person and any resident domestic corporation, means the date that such person first becomes an interested shareholder of such resident domestic corporation.

(16) 'Subsidiary' of any person means any other corporation of which a majority of the voting stock is owned, directly or indirectly, by such person.

(17) 'Voting stock' means shares of capital stock of a corporation entitled to vote generally in the election of directors.

(b) Notwithstanding anything to the contrary contained in this chapter (except the provisions of paragraph (d) of this section), no resident domestic corporation shall engage in any business combination with any interested shareholder of such resident domestic corporation for a period of five years following such interested shareholder's stock acquisition date unless such business combination or the purchase of stock made by such interested shareholder on such interested shareholder's stock acquisition date is approved by the board of directors of such resident domestic corporation prior to such interested shareholder's stock acquisition date. If a good faith proposal is made in writing to the board of directors of such resident domestic corporation regarding a business combination, the board of directors shall respond, in writing, within thirty days or such shorter period, if any, as may be required by the Exchange Act, setting forth its reasons for its decision regarding such proposal. If a good faith proposal to purchase stock is made in writing to the board of directors of such resident domestic corporation, the board of directors, unless it responds affirmatively in writing within thirty days or such shorter period, if any, as may be required by the Exchange Act, shall be deemed to have disapproved such stock purchase.

(c) Notwithstanding anything to the contrary contained in this chapter (except the provisions of paragraphs (b) and (d) of this section), no resident domestic corporation shall engage at any time in any business combination with any interested shareholder of such resident domestic corporation other than a business combination specified in any one of subparagraph (1), (2) or (3):

(1) A business combination approved by the board of directors of such resident domestic corporation prior to such interested shareholder's stock acquisition date, or where the purchase of stock made by such interested shareholder on such interested shareholder's stock acquisition date had been approved by the board of directors of such resident domestic corporation prior to such interested shareholder's stock acquisition date.

(2) A business combination approved by the affirmative vote of the holders of a majority of the outstanding voting stock not beneficially owned by such interested shareholder or any affiliate or associate of such interested shareholder at a meeting called for such purpose no earlier than five years after such interested shareholder's stock acquisition date.

(3) A business combination that meets all of the following conditions:

(A) The aggregate amount of the cash and the market value as of the consummation date of consideration other than cash to be received per share by holders of outstanding shares of common stock of such resident domestic corporation in such business combination is at least equal to the higher of the following:

(i) the highest per share price paid by such interested shareholder at a time when he was the beneficial owner, directly or indirectly, of five percent or more of the outstanding voting stock of such resident domestic corporation, for any shares of common stock of the same class or series acquired by it (X) within the five-year period immediately prior to the announcement date with respect to such business combination, or (Y) within the five-year period immediately prior to, or in, the transaction in which such interested shareholder became an interested shareholder, whichever is higher; plus, in either case, interest compounded annually from the earliest date on which such highest per share acquisition price was paid through the consummation date at the rate for one-year United States treasury obligations from time to time in effect; less the aggregate amount of any cash dividends paid, and the market value of any dividends paid other than in cash, per share of common stock since such earliest date, up to the amount of such interest; and

(ii) the market value per share of common stock on the announcement date with respect to such business combination or on such interested shareholder's stock acquisition date, whichever is higher; plus interest compounded annually from such date through the consummation date at the rate for one-year United States treasury obligations from time to time in effect; less the aggregate amount of any cash dividends paid, and the market value of any dividends paid other than in cash, per share of common stock since such date, up to the amount of such interest.

(B) The aggregate amount of the cash and the market value as of the consummation date of consideration other than cash to be received per share by holders of outstanding shares of any class or series of stock, other than common stock, of such resident domestic corporation is at least equal to the highest of the following (whether or not such interested shareholder has previously acquired any shares of such class or series of stock):

(i) the highest per share price paid by such interested shareholder at a time when he was the beneficial owner, directly or indirectly, of five percent or more of the outstanding voting stock of such resident domestic corporation, for any shares of such class or series of stock acquired by it (X) within the five-year period immediately prior to the announcement date with respect to such business combination, or (Y) within the five-year period immediately prior to, or in, the transaction in which such interested shareholder became an interested shareholder, whichever is higher; plus, in either case, interest compounded annually from the earliest date on which such highest per share acquisition price was paid through the consummation date at the rate for one-year United States treasury obligations from time to time in effect; less the aggregate amount of any cash dividends paid, and the market value of any dividends paid other than in cash, per share of such class or series of stock since such earliest date, up to the amount of such interest;

(ii) the highest preferential amount per share to which the holders of shares of such class or series of stock are entitled in the event of any voluntary liquidation, dissolution or winding up of such resident domestic corporation, plus the aggregate amount of any dividends declared or due as to which such holders are entitled prior to payment of dividends on some other class or series of stock (unless the aggregate amount of such dividends is included in such preferential amount); and

(iii) the market value per share of such class or series of stock on the announcement date with respect to such business combination or on such interested shareholder's stock acquisition date, whichever is higher; plus interest compounded annually from such date through the consummation date at the rate for one-year United States treasury obligations from time to time in effect; less the aggregate amount of any cash dividends paid, and the market value of any dividends paid other than in cash, per share of such class or series of stock since such date, up to the amount of such interest.

(C) The consideration to be received by holders of a particular class or series of outstanding stock (including common stock) of such resident domestic corporation in such business combination is in cash or in the same form as the interested shareholder has used to acquire the largest number of shares of such class or series of stock previously acquired by it, and such consideration shall be distributed promptly.

(D) The holders of all outstanding shares of stock of such resident domestic corporation not beneficially owned by such interested shareholder immediately prior to the consummation of such business combination are entitled to receive in such business combination cash or other consideration for such shares in compliance with clauses (A), (B) and (C) of this subparagraph.

(E) After such interested shareholder's stock acquisition date and prior to the consummation date with respect to such business combination, such interested shareholder has not become the beneficial owner of any additional shares of voting stock of such resident domestic corporation except:

(i) as part of the transaction which resulted in such interested shareholder becoming an interested shareholder;

(ii) by virtue of proportionate stock splits, stock dividends or other distributions of stock in respect of stock not constituting a business combination under clause (E) of subparagraph five of paragraph (a) of this section;

(iii) through a business combination meeting all of the conditions of paragraph (b) of this section and this paragraph; or

(iv) through purchase by such interested shareholder at any price which, if such price had been paid in an otherwise permissible business combination the announcement date and consummation date of which were the date of such purchase, would have satisfied the requirements of clauses (A), (B) and (C) of this subparagraph.

(d) The provisions of this section shall not apply:

(1) to any business combination of a resident domestic corporation that does not have a class of voting stock registered with the Securities and Exchange Commission pursuant to section twelve of the Exchange Act, unless the certificate of incorporation provides otherwise; or

(2) to any business combination of a resident domestic corporation whose certificate of incorporation has been amended to provide that such resident domestic corporation shall be subject to the provisions of this section, which did not have a class of voting stock registered with the Securities and Exchange Commission pursuant to section twelve of the Exchange Act on the effective date of such amendment, and which is a business combination with an interested shareholder whose stock acquisition date is prior to the effective date of such amendment; or

(3) to any business combination of a resident domestic corporation (i) the original certificate of incorporation of which contains a provision expressly electing not to be governed by this section, or (ii) which adopts an amendment to such resident domestic corporation's by-laws prior to March thirty-first,

nineteen hundred eighty-six, expressly electing not to be governed by this section, or (iii) which adopts an amendment to such resident domestic corporation's by-laws, approved by the affirmative vote of the holders, other than interested shareholders and their affiliates and associates, of a majority of the outstanding voting stock of such resident domestic corporation, excluding the voting stock of interested shareholders and their affiliates and associates, expressly electing not to be governed by this section, provided that such amendment to the by-laws shall not be effective until eighteen months after such vote of such resident domestic corporation's shareholders and shall not apply to any business combination of such resident domestic corporation with an interested shareholder whose stock acquisition date is on or prior to the effective date of such amendment; or

(4) to any business combination of a resident domestic corporation with an interested shareholder of such resident domestic corporation which became an interested shareholder inadvertently, if such interested shareholder (i) as soon as practicable, divests itself of a sufficient amount of the voting stock of such resident domestic corporation so that it no longer is the beneficial owner, directly or indirectly, of twenty percent or more of the outstanding voting stock of such resident domestic corporation, and (ii) would not at any time within the five-year period preceding the announcement date with respect to such business combination have been an interested shareholder but for such inadvertent acquisition.

(5) to any business combination with an interested shareholder who was the beneficial owner, directly or indirectly, of five percent or more of the outstanding voting stock of such resident domestic corporation on October thirtieth, nineteen hundred eighty-five, and remained so to such interested shareholder's stock acquisition date.

A.9

New Jersey Statute on Duty of Directors New Jersey Business Corporation Act §14A:6–1

> The two New Jersey antitakeover statutes reproduced below and in Appendix A.10 are close relatives of similar statutes in other states. This one, covering director duties, expands director discretion much more broadly than the similar New York statute reproduced in Appendix A.7. The second (Appendix A.10) is rather technical sounding but it legalizes the highly important discriminatory flip-in poison pill.

(1) The business and affairs of a corporation shall be managed by or under the direction of its board, except as in this act or in its certificate of incorporation otherwise provided. Directors shall be at least 18 years of age and need not be United States citizens or residents of this State or shareholders of the corporation unless the certificate of incorporation or by-laws so require. The certificate of incorporation or by-laws may prescribe other qualifications for directors.

(2) In discharging his duties to the corporation and in determining what he reasonably believes to be in the best interest of the corporation, a director may, in addition to considering the effects of any action on shareholders, consider any of the following: (a) the effects of the action on the corporation's employees, suppliers, creditors and customers; (b) the effects of the action on the community in which the corporation operates; and (c) the long-term as well as the short-term interests of the corporation and its shareholders, including the possibility that these interests may best be served by the continued independence of the corporation.

(3) If on the basis of the factors described in subsection (2) of this section, the board of directors determines that any proposal or offer to acquire the corporation is not in the best interest of the corporation, it may reject such proposal or offer. If the board of directors determines to reject any such proposal or offer, the board of directors shall have no obligation to facilitate, remove any barriers to, or refrain from impeding the proposal or offer.

A.10

New Jersey Statute Permitting Poison Pills
New Jersey Business Corporation Act
§14A:7-7

14A:7-7. Share rights and options.

(1) Subject to any provisions in respect thereof set forth in its certificate of incorporation in effect before the authorization and issuance of the rights or options, a corporation may create and issue, whether or not in connection with the issuance and sale of any of its shares or bonds, rights or options entitling the holders thereof to purchase from the corporation shares of any class or series for such consideration and upon such terms and conditions as may be fixed by the board. Such rights or options shall be evidenced in such manner as the board shall approve and, without limiting the generality of the foregoing, may be evidenced by warrants attached to or forming part of bond instruments or share certificates or existing independently thereof. The instruments evidencing such rights or options shall set forth or incorporate by reference the terms and conditions of their exercise, including the time or times, which may be limited or unlimited in duration, within which, and the price or prices at which such shares may be purchased from the corporation, and any limitations on the transferability of any such right or option. The rights or options may contain provisions which adjust the rights or options in the event of an acquisition of shares or a reorganization, merger, consolidation, sale of assets or other occurrence. The consideration for shares to be purchased upon the exercise of any such right or option shall comply with the requirements of sections 14A:7-4 and 14A:7-5. A good faith judgment of the board as to the adequacy of the consideration received for such rights or options is conclusive.

Notwithstanding N.J.S. 14A:7-1 and N.J.S. 14A:7-2 and any other provision of chapter 7 of Title 14A of the New Jersey Statutes, and unless otherwise provided in the certificate of incorporation in effect before the authorization and issuance of the rights or options, a corporation may before, on or after the effective date of this 1989 amendatory act, authorize and issue rights or options which include conditions that prevent the holder of a specified percentage of the outstanding shares of the corporation, including subsequent transferees of the holder, from exercising those rights or options or which invalidate any rights or options beneficially owned by the holder of a specified percentage of the outstanding shares of the corporation, including subsequent transferees of the holder.

A.11

List of State Antitakeover Statutes

MERGER MORATORIUM STATUTES

Arizona	ARIZ. REV. STAT. §§10–1221 to 10–1223
Connecticut	CONN. GEN. STAT. ANN. §§33–374d to 33–374f
Delaware	DEL. CORP. LAW §203
Georgia	GA. CODE ANN. §§14–2–1131, 14–2–1132
Idaho	IDAHO CODE §§30–1701 to 30–1710
Illinois	ILL. ANN. STAT. ch. 32, para. 11.75
Indiana	IND. CODE §§23–1–43–18 to 23–1–43–24
Kansas	1989 Kan. Sess. Laws S.B. 116 L. 89 (uncodified) (eff. 7–1–89)
Kentucky	KY. REV. STAT. ANN. §§271B.12–200 to 271B.12–230
Maine	ME. REV. STAT. ANN. tit. 13–A, §611–A
Maryland	MD. CORPS. & ASS'NS CODE ANN. §§3–601 to 3–603
Massachusetts	MASS. GEN. L. ch. 110F, §§1–4
Michigan	MICH. COMP. LAWS ANN. §450.1776 to 450.1784
Minnesota	MINN. STAT. ANN. §302A.673
Missouri	MO. ANN. STAT. §351.459
Nebraska	NEB. REV. STAT. §§21–2431 to 21–2453
New Jersey	N.J. STAT ANN. §§14A:10A–1 to 14A:10A–6
New York	N.Y. BUS. CORP. LAW §912
Ohio	OHIO REV. CODE ANN. §1704
Pennsylvania	15 PA. CONS. STAT. §§2551 to 2556
South Carolina	S.C. CODE ANN. §§35–2–201 to 35–2–226
Tennessee	TENN. CODE ANN. §§48–35–201 to 48–35–209, 48–35–401 to 48–35–406
Virginia	VA. CODE ANN. §§13.1–725 to 13.1–727.1
Washington	WASH. REV. CODE ANN. §23A.50.010 to 23A.50.901
Wisconsin	WIS. STAT. ANN. §180.726
Wyoming	WYO. STAT. §§17–18–101 to 17–18–104

EXPANDED CONSTITUENCY AND LONG-TERM INTEREST STATUTES

Arizona	ARIZ. REV. STAT. ANN. §10–1202
Connecticut	CONN. GEN. STAT. ANN. §33–313
Florida	FLA. STAT. ANN. §607.111(9)
Georgia	GA. CODE ANN. §14–2–202(b)(5)
Hawaii	HAW. REV. STAT. §415–35(b)
Idaho	IDAHO CODE §§30–1602, 30–1702
Illinois	ILL. ANN. STAT. ch. 32, para. 8.85
Indiana	IND. CODE ANN. §23–1–35–1
Iowa	IOWA CODE §493B.1108
Kentucky	KY. REV. STAT. ANN. §271B.12–210(4)
Louisiana	LA. REV. STAT. §12:92G
Maine	ME. REV. STAT. ANN. tit. 13–A, §716
Minnesota	MINN. STAT. ANN. §302A.251(5)
Missouri	MO. ANN. STAT. §351.347
Nebraska	NEB. REV. STAT. §21–2035
New Jersey	N.J. STAT. ANN. §§14A: 6–1, 14A: 6–14
New Mexico	N.M. STAT. ANN. §53–11–35D
New York	N.Y. BUS. CORP. LAW §717
Ohio	OHIO REV. CODE ANN. §§1701.59 to 1701.60
Oregon	OR. REV. STAT. §§ 60.357(5)
Pennsylvania	11 PA. CONS. STAT. §1721, 42 PA. CONS. STAT. §8363
Tennessee	TENN. CODE ANN. §§48–35–202, 48–35–204
Wisconsin	WIS. STAT. ANN. §180.305

CONTROL SHARE ACQUISITION STATUTES

Arizona	ARIZ. REV. STAT. ANN. §§10–1211 to 10–1217
Florida	FLA. STAT. ANN. §§607.109 to 607.110
Hawaii	HAW. REV. STAT. §§415–171 to 415–172
Idaho	IDAHO CODE §§30–1601 to 30–1614
Indiana	IND. CODE ANN. §§23–1–42–1 to 23–1–42–11
Kansas	KAN. STAT. ANN. §§17–1286 to 17–1298
Louisiana	LA. REV. STAT. §§12:135 to 12:140.2, 12:140.11 to 12:140.17
Maryland	MD. CORPS. & ASS'NS §§3–701 to 3–709
Massachusetts	MASS. GEN. L. ch. 110D, §§1–8, ch. 110E, §§1–7
Michigan	MICH. COMP. LAWS ANN. §§450.1790 to 450.1799

Minnesota	MINN. STAT. ANN. §302A.671
Missouri	MO. ANN. STAT. §351.407
Nebraska	NEB. REV. STAT. §21–2431 to 21–2453
Nevada	NEV. REV. STAT. ANN. §§78.378, 78.3793
North Carolina	N.C. GEN. STAT. §§55–90 to 55–98.1
Ohio	OHIO REV. CODE. ANN. §§1701.01, 1701.831
Oklahoma	OKLA. STAT. ANN. tit. 18, §§1145 to 1155
Oregon	1989 OR. LAWS Ch. 4, L'89, §§1–6
Pennsylvania	15 PA. CONS. STAT. §§2541 to 2548
South Carolina	S.C. CODE ANN. §§35–2–101 to 35–2–111
Tennessee	TENN. CODE ANN. §§48–35–301 to 48–35–312, 48–35–401 to 48–35–406
Utah	UTAH CODE ANN. §§61–6–1 to 61–6–12
Virginia	VA. CODE ANN. §13.1–728.1 to 13.1–728.9
Wisconsin	WISC. STAT. ANN. §180.25 (9)(a)

SUPERMAJORITY SHAREHOLDER VOTE AND FAIR-PRICE STATUTES

Arizona	ARIZ. REV. STAT. ANN. §10–1222
Connecticut	CONN. GEN. STAT. ANN. §§33–374a to 33–374c
Florida	FLA. STAT. ANN. §§607.108, 607.110
Georgia	GA. CODE ANN. §§14–2–232 to 14–2–235
Idaho	IDAHO CODE §§30–1701 to 30–1710
Illinois	ILL. ANN. STAT. ch. 32, para. 7.85
Kentucky	KY. REV. STAT. ANN. §§271B.12–200 to 271B.12–230, 271A.396.398
Louisiana	LA. REV. STAT. §§12:132 to 12:134
Maryland	MD. CORPS. & ASS'NS CODE ANN. §§3–601 to 3–603
Michigan	MICH. COMP. LAWS ANN. §§450.1775 to 450.1784
Mississippi	MISS. CODE ANN. §§79–25–1 to 79–25–9
New Jersey	N.J. STAT. ANN. §14A:10A–1 to 14A:10A–6
New York	N.Y. BUS. CORP. LAW §912
North Carolina	N.C. GEN. STAT. §§55–75 to 55–80
Pennsylvania	15 PA. CONS. STAT. §§2551 to 2556
South Carolina	S.C. CODE ANN. §35–2–219
Tennessee	TENN. CODE ANN. §48–35–206
Virginia	VA. CODE ANN. §§13.1–725 to 13.1–727
Washington	WASH. REV. CODE ANN. §23A.08.425
Wisconsin	WIS. STAT. ANN. §§180.725, 180.726

SPECIAL APPRAISAL RIGHTS STATUTES (PUT STATUTES)

Maine   ME. REV. STAT. ANN. tit. 13–A, §910
Pennsylvania   15 PA. CONS. STAT. §2546

HEIGHTENED DISCLOSURE STATUTES

Alaska   ALASKA STAT. §§45.57.010 to 45.57.120
Arkansas   ARK. STAT. ANN. §§23–43–101 to 23–43–117
Hawaii   HAW. REV. STAT. §§417E–1 to 417E–11
Indiana   IND. CODE ANN. §§23–2–3.1–0.5 to 23–2–3.1–11
Iowa   IOWA CODE ANN. §502.102, 502.211 to 502.218
Massachusetts   MASS. GEN. LAWS ANN. ch. 110C, §§1–13
Minnesota   MINN. STAT. ANN. §§80B.01 to 80B.13
Mississippi   MISS. CODE ANN. §§75–72–101 to 75–72–121
Missouri   MO. REV. STAT. §§409.500 to 409.566
Nebraska   NEB. REV. STAT. §§21–2418 to 21–2430, 21–2432
Nevada   NEV. REV. STAT. ANN. §§78.3765 to 78.3778
New Hampshire   N.H. REV. STAT. ANN. §§421–A:1 to 421–A:17
New Jersey   N.J. REV. STAT. ANN. §§49:5–1 to 49:5–19
New York   N.Y. BUS. CORP. LAW §§1600 to 1613
North Carolina N.C. GEN. STAT. §§78B–1 to 78B–11
Ohio   OHIO REV. CODE ANN. §1707.041
Oklahoma   OKLA. STAT. ANN. tit. 71, §§451 to 462
Pennsylvania   15 PA. CONS. STAT. §§71 to 85
South Dakota   S.D. CODIFIED LAWS ANN. §§47–32–1 to 47–32–48
Tennessee   TENN. CODE ANN. §§48–35–101 to 48–35–113
Wisconsin   WIS. STAT. ANN. §§552.01 to 552.07

PROFIT-RECOVERY STATUTES

Ohio   OHIO REV. CODE ANN. §1707.043
Pennsylvania   1990 PA. LAWS No. 1310 (adopted 1990)

MANDATORY CLASSIFIED BOARD STATUTE

Massachusetts   House Bill No. 5556 (adopted 1990)

A.12

Delaware Supreme Court Opinion in
Paramount Communications Inc. v. *Time Inc.*
(February 26, 1990)

The Delaware Supreme Court's opinion in the *Paramount–Time* case was handed down on February 26, 1990. When reading it, the main considerations to keep in mind are:

1. The delicate balance Delaware must maintain to retain its position as the leading state of incorporation for large U.S. companies. The conflicting interests being balanced are: the state's interest in placating managements of companies (because they initiate decisions on where companies will incorporate); institutional shareholders (because their dissatisfaction with Delaware law might provoke the long-dreaded Federal incorporation statute that would topple Delaware from its preeminent position in corporate law); and Delaware lawyers (because they flourish on takeover controversies in the Delaware courts).

2. The important role of ambiguity in maintaining this balance.

3. The enormous importance of court opinions and precedents in the U.S. legal system. The opinion is a good example of the way appellate courts deal with their own precedents and the precedents of lower courts in the same jurisdiction.

IN THE SUPREME COURT OF THE STATE OF DELAWARE

PARAMOUNT COMMUNI-
CATIONS, INC.
and KDS ACQUISITIONS
CORP.,

    Plaintiffs Below,
    Appellants,

v.

TIME INCORPORATED, T.W.
SUB, JAMES F. BERE, HENRY
C. GOODRICH, CLIFFORD J.
GRUM, MATINA S. HORNER,
DAVID T. KEARNS, GERALD
M. LEVIN, J. RICHARD
MUNRO, N.J. NICHOLAS, JR.,
DONALD S. PERKINS,
CLIFTON R. WHARTON,
MICHAEL D. FINKELSTEIN,
HENRY LUCE III, JASON D.
McMANUS, JOHN R. OPEL,
AND WARNER COM-
MUNICATIONS, INC.

    Defendants Below,
    Appellees.

No. 284, 1989

Court Below: Court of Chancery of
the State of Delaware in and for
New Castle County
C.A. No. 10866

LITERARY PARTNERS, L.P.,
CABLEVISION MEDIA PART-
NERS, L.P., AND A. JERROLD
PERENCHIO,

    Plaintiffs Below,
    Appellants,

v.

TIME INCORPORATED, TW
SUB INC., JAMES F. BERE,
MICHAEL D. DINGMAN,
EDWARD S. FINKELSTEIN,
MATINA S. HORNER, DAVID
T. KEARNS, GERALD M.
LEVIN, HENRY LUCE III,
JASON D. McMANUS, J.

No. 279, 1989

Court Below: Court of Chancery of
the State of Delaware in and for
New Castle County
C.A. Nos. 10866, 10670 and 10935

RICHARD MUNRO, N.J. NICH-
OLAS, JR., JOHN R. OPEL,
DONALD S. PERKINS, AND
WARNER COMMUNICA-
TIONS, INC.,

    Defendants Below,
    Appellees.

IN RE: TIME INCORPORATED
SHAREHOLDER LITIGATION

No. 283, 1989

Court Below: Court of Chancery of
the State of Delaware in and for
New Castle County
C.A. No. 10670

Submitted: July 24, 1989
Decided: July 24, 1989
Written Opinion: February 26, 1990

Before HORSEY, MOORE, and HOLLAND, Justices.

Upon appeal from the Court of Chancery. Affirmed.

HORSEY, Justice:

Paramount Communications, Inc. ('Paramount') and two other groups of plaintiffs[1] ('Shareholder Plaintiffs'), shareholders of Time Incorporated ('Time'), a Delaware corporation, separately filed suits in the Delaware Court of Chancery seeking a preliminary injunction to halt Time's tender offer for 51% of Warner Communication, Inc.'s ('Warner') outstanding shares at $70 cash per share. The court below consolidated the cases and, following the development of an extensive record, after discovery and an evidentiary hearing, denied plaintiffs' motion. In a 50-page unreported opinion and order entered July 14, 1989, the Chancellor refused to enjoin Time's consummation of its tender offer, concluding that the plaintiffs were unlikely to prevail on the merits. *In Re: Time Incorporated Shareholder Litigation*, Del. Ch., C.A. No. 10670, Allen, C. (July 14, 1989)

On the same day, plaintiffs filed in this Court an interlocutory appeal, which we accepted on an expedited basis. Pending the appeal, a stay of execution of Time's tender offer was entered for ten days, or until July 24, 1989, at 5:00 p.m. Following briefing and oral argument, on July 24 we

---

[1] Plaintiffs in these three consolidated appeals are: (i) Paramount Communications, Inc. and KDS Acquisition Corp. (collectively 'Paramount'); (ii) Literary Partners L.P., Cablevision Media Partners, L.P., and A. Jarrold Perenchio (collectively 'Literary Partners'), suing individually; and (iii) certain other shareholder plaintiffs, suing individually and as an uncertified class.

concluded that the decision below should be affirmed. We so held in a brief ruling from the bench and a separate Order entered on that date. The effect of our decision was to permit Time to proceed with its tender offer for Warner's outstanding shares. This is the written opinion articulating the reasons for our July 24 bench ruling.

The principal ground for reversal, asserted by all plaintiffs, is that Paramount's June 7, 1989 uninvited all-cash, all-shares, 'fully negotiable' (though conditional) tender offer for Time triggered duties under *Unocal Corp. v. Mesa Petroleum Co.*, Del. Supr., 493 A.2d 946 (1985), and that Time's board of directors, in responding to Paramount's offer, breached those duties. As a consequence, plaintiffs argue that in our review of the Time board's decision of June 16, 1989 to enter into a revised merger agreement with Warner, Time is not entitled to the benefit and protection of the business judgment rule.

Shareholder Plaintiffs also assert a claim based on *Revlon* v. *MacAndrews and Forbes Holdings, Inc.*, Del. Supr., 506 A.2d 173 (1986). They argue that the original Time–Warner merger agreement of March 4, 1989 resulted in a change of control which effectively put Time up for sale, thereby triggering *Revlon* duties. Those plaintiffs argue that Time's board breached its *Revlon* duties by failing, in the face of the change of control, to maximize shareholder value in the immediate term.

Applying our standard of review, we affirm the Chancellor's ultimate finding and conclusion under *Unocal*. We find that Paramount's tender offer was reasonably perceived by Time's board to pose a threat to Time and that the Time board's 'response' to that threat was, under the circumstances, reasonable and proportionate. Applying *Unocal*, we reject the argument that the only corporate threat posed by an all-shares, all-cash tender offer is the possibility of inadequate value.

We also find that Time's board did not by entering into its initial merger agreement with Warner come under a *Revlon* duty either to auction the company or to maximize short-term shareholder value, notwithstanding the unequal share exchange. Therefore, the Time board's original plan of merger with Warner was subject only to a business judgment rule analysis. *See Smith* v. *Van Gorkom*, Del. Supr., 488 A.2d 858, 873–74 (1985).[2]

---

[2] In the specific context of a proposed merger of domestic corporations, a director has a duty under 8 *Del. C.* §251(b), along with his fellow directors, to act in an informed and deliberate manner in determining whether to approve an agreement of merger before submitting the proposal to the stockholders. Certainly in the merger context, a director may not abdicate that duty by leaving to the shareholders alone the decision to approve or disapprove the agreement. *See Beard* v. *Elster*, Del. Supr., 160 A.2d 731, 737 (1960). Only an agreement of merger satisfying the requirements of 8 *Del. C.* §251(b) may be submitted to the shareholders under §251(c). *See generally Aronson* v. *Lewis*, Del. Supr., 493 A.2d 805, 811–13 (1984); *see also Pogostin* v. *Rice*, Del. Supr., 480 A.2d 619 (1984).

Smith v. *Van Gorkom*, Del. Supr., 488 A.2d 858, 873 (footnote omitted).

I

Time is a Delaware corporation with its principal offices in New York City. Time's traditional business is publication of magazines and books; however, Time also provides pay television programming through its Home Box Office, Inc. and Cinemax subsidiaries. In addition, Time owns and operates cable television franchises through its subsidiary, American Television and Communication Corporation. During the relevant time period, Time's board consisted of sixteen directors. Twelve of the directors were 'outside,' non-employee directors. Four of the directors were also officers of the company. The outside directors included: James F. Bere, chairman of the board and CEO of Borg-Warner Corporation (Time director since 1979); Clifford J. Grum, president and CEO of Temple-Inland, Inc. (Time director since 1980); Henry C. Goodwin, former chairman of Sonat, Inc. (Time director since 1978); Matina S. Horner, then president of Radcliffe College (Time director since 1975); David T. Kearns, chairman and CEO of Xerox Corporation (Time director since 1978); Donald S. Perkins, former chairman and CEO of Jewel Companies, Inc. (Time director since 1979); Michael D. Dingman, chairman and CEO of The Henley Group, Inc. (Time director since 1978); Edward S. Finkelstein, chairman and CEO of Macy's Inc. (Time director since 1984); John R. Opel, former chairman and CEO of IBM Corporation (Time director since 1984); Arthur Temple, chairman of Temple-Inland, Inc. (Time director since 1983); Clifton R. Wharton, Jr., chairman and CEO of The Henley Group, Inc. (Time director since 1978); and Henry R. Luce III, president of The Henry Luce Foundation, Inc. (Time director since 1967). Mr. Luce, the son of the founder of Time, individually and in a representative capacity controlled 4.2% of the outstanding Time stock. The inside officer directors were: J. Richard Munro, Time's chairman and CEO since 1980: N.J. Nicholas, Jr., president and chief operating officer of the company since 1986; Gerald M. Levin, vice chairman of the board; and Jason D. McManus, editor-in-chief of *Time* magazine and a board member since 1988.[3]

As early as 1983 and 1984, Time's executive board began considering expanding Time's operations into the entertainment industry. In 1987, Time established a special committee of executives to consider and propose corporate strategies for the 1990s. The consensus of the committee was that Time should move ahead in the area of ownership and creation of video programming. This expansion, as the Chancellor noted, was predicated upon

---

[3] Four directors, Arthur Temple, Henry C. Goodrich, Clifton R. Wharton, and Clifford J. Grum, have since resigned from Time's board. The Chancellor found, with the exception of Temple, their resignations to reflect more a willingness to step down than disagreement or dissension over the Time–Warner merger. Temple did not choose to continue to be associated with a corporation that was expanding into the entertainment field. Under the board of the combined Time–Warner corporation, the number of Time directors, as well as Warner directors, was limited to twelve each.

two considerations: first, Time's desire to have greater control, in terms of quality and price, over the film products delivered by way of its cable network and franchises; and second, Time's concern over the increasing globalization of the world economy. Some of Time's outside directors, especially Luce and Temple, had opposed this move as a threat to the editorial integrity and journalistic focus of Time.[4] Despite this concern, the board saw the advantages of a vertically integrated video enterprise to complement Time's existing HBO and cable networks would enable it to compete on a global basis.

In late spring of 1987, a meeting took place between Steve Ross, CEO of Warner Brothers, and Nicholas of Time. Ross and Nicholas discussed the possibility of a joint venture between the two companies through the creation of a jointly owned cable company. Time would contribute its cable system and HBO. Warner would contribute its cable system and provide access to Warner Brothers Studio. The resulting venture would be a larger, more efficient cable network, able to produce and distribute its own movies on a worldwide basis. Ultimately the parties abandoned this plan, determining that it was impractical for several reasons, chief among them being tax considerations.

On August 11, 1987, Gerald M. Levin, Time's vice chairman and chief strategist, wrote J. Richard Munro a confidential memorandum in which he strongly recommended a strategic consolidation with Warner. In June 1988, Nicholas and Munro sent to each outside director a copy of the 'comprehensive long-term planning document' prepared by the committee of Time executives that had been examining strategies for the 1990s. The memo included reference to and a description of Warner as a potential acquisition candidate.

Thereafter, Munro and Nicholas held meetings with Time's outside directors to discuss, generally, long-term strategies for Time and, specifically, a combination with Warner. Nearly a year later, Time's board reached the point of serious discussion of the 'nuts and bolts' of a consolidation with an entertainment company. On July 21, 1988, Time's board met, with all outside directors present. The meeting's purpose was to consider Time's expansion into the entertainment industry on a global scale. Management presented the board with a profile of various entertainment companies in addition to Warner, including Disney, 20th Century-Fox, Universal, and Paramount.

Without any definitive decision on choice of a company, the board approved in principle a strategic plan for Time's expansion. The board gave

---

[4] The primary concern of Time's outside directors was the preservation of the 'Time Culture.' They believed that Time had become recognized in this country as an institution built upon a foundation of journalistic integrity. Time's management made a studious effort to refrain from involvement in Time's editorial policy. Several of Time's outside directors feared that a merger with an entertainment company would divert Time's focus from news journalism and threaten the Time Culture.

management the 'go-ahead' to continue discussions with Warner concerning the possibility of a merger. With the exception of Temple and Luce, most of the outside directors agreed that a merger involving expansion into the entertainment field promised great growth opportunity for Time. Temple and Luce remained unenthusiastic about Time's entry into the entertainment field. *See* note 2.

The board's consensus was that a merger of Time and Warner was feasible, but only if: (1) a favorable stock-for-stock exchange could be negotiated; and (2) Time controlled the board of the resulting corporation and thereby preserved a management committed to Time's journalistic integrity. To accomplish these goals, the board stressed the importance of carefully defining in advance the corporate governance provisions that would control the resulting entity. Some board members expressed concern over whether such a business combination would place Time '*in play*.' The board discussed the wisdom of adopting further defensive measures to lessen such a possibility.[5]

Of a wide range of companies considered by Time's board as possible merger candidates, Warner Brothers, Paramount, Columbia, M.C.A., Fox, MGM, Disney, and Orion, the board, in July 1988, concluded that Warner was the superior candidate for a consolidation. Warner stood out on a number of counts. Warner had just acquired Lorimar and its film studios. Time–Warner could make movies and television shows for use on HBO. Warner had an international distribution system, which Time could use to sell films, videos, books and magazines. Warner was a giant in the music and recording business, an area into which Time wanted to expand. None of the other companies considered had the musical clout of Warner. Time and Warner's cable systems were compatible and could be easily integrated; none of the other companies considered presented such a compatible cable partner. Together, Time and Warner would control half of New York City's cable system; Warner had cable systems in Brooklyn and Queens; and Time controlled cable system in Manhattan and Queens. Warner's publishing company would integrate well with Time's established publishing company. Time sells hardcover books and magazines, and Warner sells softcover books and comics.[6] Time–Warner could sell all of these publications and Warner's videos by using Time's direct mailing network and Warner's international distribution system. Time's network could be used to promote and merchandise Warner's movies.

---

[5] Time had in place a panoply of defensive devices, including a staggered board, a 'poison pill' preferred stock rights plan triggered by an acquisition of 15% of the company, a fifty-day notice period for shareholder motions, and restrictions on shareholders' ability to call a meeting or act by consent.

[6] In contrast, Paramount's publishing endeavors were in the areas of professional volumes and text books. Time's board did not find Paramount's publishing as compatible as Warner's publishing efforts.

In August 1988, Levin, Nicholas, and Munro, acting on instructions from Time's board, continued to explore a business combination with Warner. By letter dated August 4, 1988, management informed the outside directors of proposed corporate governance provisions to be discussed with Warner. The provisions incorporated the recommendations of several of Time's outside directors.

From the outset, Time's board favored an all-cash or cash and securities acquisition of Warner as the basis for consolidation. Bruce Wasserstein, Time's financial advisor, also favored an outright purchase of Warner. However, Steve Ross, Warner's CEO, was adamant that a business combination was only practicable on stock-for-stock basis. Warner insisted on a stock swap in order to preserve its shareholders' equity in the resulting corporation. Time's officers, on the other hand, made it abundantly clear that Time would be the acquiring corporation and that Time would control the resulting board. Time refused to permit itself to be cast as the 'acquired' company.

Eventually Time acquiesced in Warner's insistence on a stock-for-stock deal, but talks broke down over corporate governance issues. Time wanted Ross' position as a co-CEO to be temporary and wanted Ross to retire in five years. Ross, however, refused to set a time for his retirement and viewed Time's proposal as indicating a lack of confidence in his leadership. Warner considered it vital that their executives and creative staff not perceive Warner as selling out to Time. Time's request of a guarantee that Time would dominate the CEO succession was objected to as inconsistent with the concept of a Time–Warner merger 'of equals.' Negotiations ended when the parties reached an impasse. Time's board refused to compromise on its position on corporate governance. Time, and particularly its outside directors, viewed the corporate governance provisions as critical for preserving the 'Time Culture' through a pro-Time management at the top. *See* note 4.

Throughout the fall of 1988 Time pursued its plan of expansion into the entertainment field; Time held informal discussions with several companies, including Paramount. Capital Cities/ABC approached Time to propose a merger. Talks terminated, however, when Capital Cities/ABC suggested that it was interested in purchasing Time or in controlling the resulting board. Time steadfastly maintained it was not placing itself up for sale.

Warner and Time resumed negotiations in January 1989. The catalyst for the resumption of talks was a private dinner between Steve Ross and Time outside director, Michael Dingman. Dingman was able to convince Ross that the transitional nature of the proposed co-CEO arangement did not reflect a lack of confidence in Ross. Ross agreed that this course was best for the company and a meeting between Ross and Munro resulted. Ross agreed to retire in five years and let Nicholas succeed him. Negotiations resumed and many of the details of the original stock-for-stock exchange agreement remained intact. In addition, Time's senior management agreed to long-term contracts.

Time insider directors Levin and Nicholas met with Warner's financial advisors to decide upon a stock exchange ratio. Time's board had recognized the potential need to pay a premium in the stock ratio in exchange for dictating the governing arrangement of the new Time–Warner. Levin and outside director Finkelstein were the primary proponents of paying a premium to protect the 'Time Culture.' The board discussed premium rates of 10%, 15% and 20%. Wasserstein also suggested paying a premium for Warner due to Warner's rapid growth rate. The market exchange ratio of Time stock for Warner stock was .38 in favor of Warner. Warner's financial advisors informed the board that any exchange rate over .400 was a fair deal and any exchange rate over .450 was 'one hell of a deal.' The parties ultimately agreed upon an exchange rate favoring Warner of .465%. On that basis, Warner stockholders would own slightly over 61%[7] of the common stock of Time–Warner.

On March 3, 1989, Time's board, with all but one director in attendance, met and unanimously approved the stock-for-stock merger with Warner. Warner's board likewise approved the merger. The agreement called for Warner to be merged into a wholly-owned Time subsidiary with Warner becoming the surviving corporation. The common stock of Warner would then be converted into common stock of Time at the agreed upon ratio. Thereafter, the name of Time would be changed to Time–Warner, Inc.

The rules of the New York Stock Exchange required that Time's issuance of shares to effectuate the merger be approved by a vote of Time's stockholders. The Delaware General Corporation Law required approval of the merger by a majority of the Warner stockholders. Delaware law did not require any vote by Time stockholders. The Chancellor concluded that the agreement was the product of 'an arm's-length negotiation between two parties seeking individual advantage through mutual action.'

The resulting company would have a 24-member board, with 12 members representing each corporation. The company would have co-CEOs, at first Ross and Munro, then Ross and Nicholas, and finally, after Ross' retirement, Nicholas alone. The board would create an editorial committee with a majority of members representing Time. A similar entertainment committee would be controlled by Warner board members. A two-thirds supermajority vote was required to alter CEO successions but an earlier proposal to have supermajority protection for the editorial committee was abandoned. Warner's board suggested raising the compensation levels for Time's senior

---

[7] As was noted in the briefs and at oral argument, this figure is somewhat misleading because it does not take into consideration the number of individuals who owned stock in both companies.

management under the new corporation. Warner's management, as with most entertainment executives, received higher salaries than comparable executives in news journalism. Time's board, however, rejected Warner's proposal to equalize the salaries of the two management teams.

At its March 3, 1989 meeting, Time's board adopted several defensive tactics. Time entered an automatic share exchange agreement with Warner. Time would receive 17,292,747 shares of Warner's outstanding common stock (9.4%) and Warner would receive 7,080,016 shares of Time's outstanding common stock (11.11). Either party could trigger the exchange. Time sought out and paid for 'confidence' letters from various banks with which they did business. In these letters, the banks promised not to finance any third-party attempt to acquire Time. Time argues these agreements served only to preserve the confidential relationship between itself and the banks. The Chancellor found these agreements to be inconsequential and futile attempts to 'dry up' money for a hostile takeover. Time also agreed to a 'no-shop' clause, preventing Time from considering any other consolidation proposal, thus relinquishing its power to consider other proposals, regardless of their merits. Time did so at Warner's insistence. Warner did not want to be left 'on the auction block' for an unfriendly suitor, if Time were to withdraw from the deal.

Time's board simultaneously established a special committee of outside directors, Finkelstein, Kearns, and Opel, to oversee the merger. The committee's assignment was to resolve any impediments that might arise in the course of working out the details of the merger and its consummation.

Time representatives lauded the lack of debt to the United States Senate and to the President of the United States. Public reaction to the announcement of the merger was positive. Time–Warner would be a media colossus with international scope. The board scheduled the stockholder vote for June 23; and a May 1 record date was set. On May 24, 1989, Time sent out extensive proxy statements to the stockholders regarding the approval vote on the merger. In the meantime, with the merger proceeding without impediment, the special committee had concluded, shortly after its creation, that it was not necessary either to retain independent consultants, legal or financial, or even to meet. Time's board was unanimously in favor of the proposed merger with Warner; and, by the end of May, the Time–Warner merger appeared to be an accomplished fact.

On June 7, 1989, these wishful assumptions were shattered by Paramount's surprising announcement of its all-cash offer to purchase all outstanding shares of Time for $175 per share. The following day, June 8, the trading price of Time's stock rose from $126 to $170 per share. Paramount's offer was said to be 'fully negotiable.'[8]

[8] Subsequently, it was established that Paramount's board had decided as early as March 1989

Time found Paramount's 'fully negotiable' offer to be in fact subject to at least three conditions. First, Time had to terminate its merger agreement and stock exchange agreement with Warner, and remove certain other of its defensive devices, including the redemption of Time's shareholder rights. Second, Paramount had to obtain the required cable franchise transfers from Time in a fashion acceptable to Paramount in its sole discretion. Finally, the offer depended upon a judicial determination that section 203 of the General Corporate Law of Delaware (The Delaware Anti-Takeover Statute) was inapplicable to any Time–Paramount merger. While Paramount's board had been privately advised that it could take months, perhaps over a year, to forge and consummate the deal, Paramount's board publicly proclaimed its ability to close the offer by July 5, 1989. Paramount executives later conceded that none of its directors believed that July 5th was a realistic date to close the transaction.

On June 8, 1989, Time formally responded to Paramount's offer. Time's chairman and CEO, J. Richard Munro, sent an aggressively worded letter to Paramount's CEO, Martin Davis. Munro's letter attacked Davis' personal integrity and called Paramount's offer 'smoke and mirrors.' Time's non-management directors were not shown the letter before it was sent. However, at a board meeting that same day, all members endorsed management's response as well as the letter's content.

Over the following eight days, Time's board met three times to discuss Paramount's $175 offer. The board viewed Paramount's offer as inadequate and concluded that its proposed merger with Warner was the better course of action. Therefore, the board declined to open any negotiations with Paramount and held steady its course toward a merger with Warner.

In June, Time's board of directors met several times. During the course of their June meetings, Time's outside directors met frequently without management, officers or directors being present. At the request of the outside directors, corporate counsel was present during the board meetings and, from time to time, the management directors were asked to leave the board sessions. During the course of these meetings, Time's financial advisors informed the board that, on an auction basis, Time's per share value was materially higher than Warner's $175 per share offer.[9] On this basis, the board concluded that Paramount's $175 offer was inadequate.

At these June meetings, certain Time directors expressed their concern that their stockholders would not comprehend the long-term benefits of the Warner merger. Large quantities of Time shares were held by institutional

---

to move to acquire Time. However, Paramount management intentionally delayed publicizing its proposal until Time had mailed to its stockholders its Time–Warner merger proposal along with the required proxy statements.

[9] Time's advisors estimated the value of Time in a control premium situation to be significantly higher than the value of Time in other than a sale situation.

investors. The board feared that even though there appeared to be wide support for the Warner transaction, Paramount's cash premium would be a tempting prospect to these investors. In mid-June, Time sought permission from the New York Stock Exchange to alter its rules and allow the Time–Warner merger to proceed without stockholder approval. Time did so at Warner's insistence. The New York Stock Exchange rejected Time's request on June 15; and on that day, the value of Time stock reached $182 per share.

The following day, June 16, Time's board met to take up Paramount's offer. The board's prevailing belief was that Paramount's bid presented a threat to Time's control of its own destiny and retention of the 'Time Culture.' Even after Time's financial advisors made another presentation of Paramount and its business attributes, Time's board maintained its position that a combination within Warner presented greater potential for Time. Warner presented Time with a much desired production capability and an established international marketing chain. Time's advisors presented the board with various options, including defensive measures. The board considered and rejected the idea of purchasing Paramount in a 'Pac Man' defense.[10] The board considered other defenses as well, including a recapitalization, the acquisition of another company, and a material change in the present capitalization structure or dividend policy. The board determined to retain its same advisors even in light of the changed circumstances. The board rescinded its agreement to pay its advisors a bonus based on the consummation of the Time–Warner merger and agreed to pay a flat fee for any advice the advisors rendered. Finally, Time's board formally rejected Paramount's offer.[11]

At the same meeting, Time's board decided to recast its consolidation with Warner into an outright cash and securities acquisition of Warner by Time; and Time so informed Warner. Time accordingly restructured its proposal to acquire Warner as follows: Time would make an immediate all-cash offer for 51% of Warner's outstanding stock at $70 per share. The remaining 49% would be purchased at some later date for a mixture of cash and securities worth $70 per share. To provide the funds required for its outright acquisition of Warner, Time would assume 7–10 billion dollars' worth of debt, thus eliminating one of the principal transaction-related benefits of the original merger agreement. Time also agreed to pay and amortize a $9 billion payment to Warner for the goodwill of the reputable and rapidly growing corporation.

Warner agreed but insisted on certain terms. Warner sought a control premium and guarantees that the governance provisions found in the original merger agreement would remain intact. Warner further sought agreements

---

[10] In a 'Pac Man' defense, Time would launch a tender offer for the stock of Paramount, thus consuming its rival. *Moran* v. *Household Intern., Inc.*, Del. Supr., 500 A.2d 1346, 1350 n.6 (1985).

[11] Meanwhile, Time had already begun erecting impediments to Paramount's offer. Time encouraged local cable franchises to sue Paramount to prevent it from easily obtaining the franchises.

that Time would not employ its poison pill against Warner and that, unless enjoined, Time would be legally bound to complete the transaction. Time's board agreed to these last measures only at the insistence of Warner. For its part, Time was assured of its ability to extend its efforts into production arenas and international markets, all the while maintaining the Time identity and culture. The Chancellor found the initial Time–Warner transaction to have been negotiated at arm's length and the restructured Time–Warner transaction to have resulted from Paramount's offer and its expected effect on a Time shareholder vote.

On June 23, 1989, Paramount raised its all-cash offer to buy Time's outstanding stock to $200 per share. Paramount still professed that all aspects of the offer were negotiable. Time's board met on June 26, 1989 and formally rejected Paramount's $200 per share second offer. The board reiterated its belief that, despite the $25 increase, the offer was still inadequate and that the Warner transaction offered a greater long-term value for the stockholders and, unlike Paramount, was not a threat to Time's survival and its 'culture.' Paramount then filed this action in the Court of Chancery.

II

The Shareholder Plaintiffs first assert a *Revlon* claim. They contend that the March 4 Time–Warner agreement effectively put Time up for sale, triggering *Revlon* duties, requiring Time's board to enhance short-term shareholder value and to treat all other interested acquirors on an equal basis. The Shareholder Plaintiffs base this argument on two facts: (i) the ultimate Time–Warner exchange ratio of .465 favoring Warner, resulting in Warner shareholders' receipt of 62% of the combined company; and (ii) the subjective intent of Time's directors as evidenced in their statements that the market might perceive the Time–Warner merger as putting Time up 'for sale' and their adoption of various defensive measures.

The Shareholder Plaintiffs further contend that Time's directors, in structuring the original merger transaction to be 'takeover-proof,' triggered *Revlon* duties by foreclosing their shareholders from any prospect of obtaining a control premium. In short, plaintiffs argue that Time's board's decision to merge with Warner opposed a fiduciary duty to maximize immediate share value and not erect unreasonable barriers to further bids. Therefore, they argue, the Chancellor erred in finding: that Paramount's bid for Time did not place Time 'for sale'; that Time's transaction with Warner did not result in any transfer of control; and that the combined Time–Warner was not so large as to preclude the possibility of the stockholders of Time–Warner receiving a future control premium.

Paramount asserts only a *Unocal* claim in which the Shareholder Plaintiffs join. Paramount contends that the Chancellor, in applying the first part of the *Unocal* test, erred in finding that Time's board had reasonable grounds to believe that Paramount posed both a legally cognizable threat to Time shareholders and a danger to Time's corporate policy and effectiveness. Paramount also contests the court's finding that Time's board made a reasonable and objective investigation of Paramount's offer so as to be informed before rejecting it. Paramount further claims that the court erred in applying *Unocal*'s second part in finding Time's response to be 'reasonable.' Paramount points primarily to the preclusive effect of the revised agreement which denied Time shareholders the opportunity both to vote on the agreement and to respond to Paramount's tender offer. Paramount argues that the underlying motivation of Time's board in adopting these defensive measures was management's desire to perpetuate itself in office.

The Court of Chancery posed the pivotal question presented by this case to be: Under what circumstances must a board of directors abandon an in-place plan of corporate development in order to provide its shareholders with the option to elect and realize an immediate control premium? As applied to this case, the question becomes: Did Time's board, having developed a strategic plan of global expansion to be launched through a business combination with Warner, come under a fiduciary duty to jettison its plan and put the corporation's future in the hands of its shareholders?

While we affirm the result reached by the Chancellor, we think it unwise to place undue emphasis upon long-term versus short-term corporate strategy. Two key predicates underpin our analysis. First, Delaware law imposes on a board of directors the duty to manage the business and affairs of the corporation. 8 *Del. C.* §141(a). This broad mandate includes a conferred authority to set a corporate course of action, including time frame, designed to enhance corporate profitability.[12] Thus, the question of 'long-term' versus 'short-term' values is largely irrelevant because directors, generally, are obliged to charter a course for a corporation which is in its best interests without regard to a fixed investment horizon. Second, absent a limited set of circumstances as defined under *Revlon*, a board of directors, while always required to act in an informed manner, is not under any *per se* duty to maximize shareholder value in the short term, even in the context of a takeover. In our view, the pivotal question presented by this case is: 'Did Time, by entering into the proposed merger with Warner, put itself up for sale?' A resolution of that issue through application of *Revlon* has a significant bearing upon the resolution of the derivative *Unocal* issue.

---

[12] In endorsing this finding, we tacitly accept the Chancellor's conclusion that it is not a breach of faith for directors to determine that the present stock market price of shares is not representative of true value or that there may indeed be several market values for any corporation's stock. We have so held in another context. *See van Gorkom*, 488 A.2d at 876.

A.

We first take up plaintiffs' principal *Revlon* argument, summarized above. In rejecting this argument, the Chancellor found the original Time–Warner merger agreement not to constitute a 'change of control' and concluded that the transaction did not trigger *Revlon* duties. The Chancellor's conclusion is premised on a finding that '[b]efore the merger agreement was signed, control of the corporation existed in a fluid aggregation of unaffiliated shareholders representing a voting majority – in other words, in the market.' The Chancellor's findings of fact are supported by the record and his conclusion is correct as a matter of law. However, we premise our rejection of plaintiffs' *Revlon* claim on broader grounds, namely, the absence of any substantial evidence to conclude that Time's board, in negotiating with Warner, made the dissolution or breakup of the corporate entity inevitable, as was the case in *Revlon*.

Under Delaware law there are, generally speaking and without excluding other possibilities, two circumstances which may implicate *Revlon* duties. The first, and clearer one, is when a corporation initiates an active bidding process seeking to sell itself or to effect a business reorganization involving a clear breakup of the company. *See, e.g., Mills Acquisition Co.* v. *Macmillan, Inc,* Del. Supr., 559 A.2d 1261 (1988). However, *Revlon* duties may also be triggered where, in response to a bidder's offer, a target abandons its long-term strategy and seeks an alternative transaction also involving the breakup of the company.[13] Thus, in *Revlon*, when the board responded to Pantry Pride's offer by contemplating a 'bust-up' sale of assets in a leveraged acquisition, we imposed upon the board a duty to maximize immediate shareholder value and an obligation to auction the company fairly. If, however, the board's reaction to a hostile tender offer is found to constitute only a defensive response and not an abandonment of the corporation's continued existence, *Revlon* duties are not triggered, though *Unocal* duties attach.[14] *See, e.g., Ivanhoe Partners* v. *Newmont Mining Corp.,* Del. Supr., 535 A.2d 1334, 1345 (1987).

The plaintiffs insist that even though the original Time–Warner agreement

---

[13] As we stated in *Revlon*, in both such cases, '[t]he duty of the board [has] changed from the preservation of ... [the] corporate entity to the maximization of the company's value at a sale for the stockholder's benefit ... [The board] no longer face[s] threats to corporate policy and effectiveness, or to the stockholders' interests, from a grossly inadequate bid.' *Revlon* v. *MacAndrews and Forbes Holdings, Inc.,* Del. Supr., 506 A.2d 173, 182 (1986).

[14] Within the auction process, any action taken by the board must be reasonably related to the threat posed or reasonable in relation to the advantage sought, *see Mills Acquisition Co.* v. *Macmillan, Inc.,* Del. Supr., 559 A.2d 1261, 1288 (1988). Thus, a *Unocal* analysis may be appropriate when a corporation is in a *Revlon* situation and *Revlon* duties may be triggered by a defensive action taken in response to a hostile offer. Since *Revlon*, we have stated that differing treatment of various bidders is not actionable when such action reasonably relates to achieving the best price available for the stockholders. *Macmillan,* 559 A.2d at 1286–87.

may not have worked 'an objective change of control,' the transaction made a 'sale' of Time inevitable. Plaintiffs rely on the subjective intent of Time's board of directors and principally upon certain board members' expressions of concern that the Warner transaction might be viewed as effectively putting Time up for sale. Plaintiffs argue that the use of a lock-up agreement, a no-shop clause, and so-called 'dry-up' agreements prevented shareholders from obtaining a control premium in the immediate future and thus violated *Revlon*.

We agree with the Chancellor that such evidence is entirely insufficient to invoke *Revlon* duties; and we decline to extend *Revlon*'s application to corporate transactions simply because they might be construed as putting a corporation either 'in play' or 'up for sale.' *See Citron* v. *Fairchild Camera*, Del. Supr., A.2d, No. 270, 1988 (Dec. 22, 1989), *Macmillan*, 559 A.2d at 1285 n.35. The adoption of structural safety devices alone does not trigger *Revlon*.[15] Rather, as the Chancellor stated, such devices are properly subject to a *Unocal* analysis.

Finally, we do not find in Time's recasting of its merger agreement with Warner from a share exchange to a share purchase a basis to conclude that Time had either abandoned its strategic plan or made a sale of Time inevitable.[16] The Chancellor found that although the merged Time–Warner company would be large (with a value approaching approximately $30 billion), recent takeover cases have proven that acquisition of the combined company might nonetheless be possible. *In Re: Time Incorporated Shareholder Litigation*, Del. Ch., C.A. No. 10670, Allen, C. (July 14, 1989), slip op. at 56. The legal consequence is that *Unocal* alone applies to determine whether the business judgment rule attaches to the revised agreement. Plaintiffs' analogy to *Macmillan* thus collapses and plaintiffs' reliance on *Macmillan* is misplaced.

B.

We turn now to plaintiffs' *Unocal* claim. We begin by noting, as did the Chancellor, that our decision does not require us to pass on the wisdom of

[15] Although the legality of the various safety devices adopted to protect the original agreement is not a central issue, there is substantial evidence to support each of the trial court's related conclusions. Thus, the court found that the concept of the Share Exchange Agreement predated any takeover threat by Paramount and had been adopted for a rational business purpose: to deter Time and Warner from being 'put in play' by their March 4 Agreement. The court further found that Time had adopted the 'no-shop' clause at Warner's insistence and for Warner's protection. Finally, although certain aspects of the 'dry-up' agreements were suspect on their face, we concur in the Chancellor's view that in this case they were inconsequential.

[16] We note that, although Time's advisors presented the board with such alternatives as an auction or sale to a third party bidder, the board rejected those responses, preferring to go forward with its pre-existing plan rather than adopt an alternative to Paramount's proposal.

the board's decision to enter into the original Time–Warner agreement. That is not a court's task. Our task is simply to review the record to determine whether there is sufficient evidence to support the Chancellor's conclusion that the initial Time–Warner agreement was the product of a proper exercise of business judgment. *Macmillan*, 559 A.2d at 1288.

We have purposely detailed the evidence of the Time board's deliberative approach, beginning in 1983–84, to expand itself. Time's decision in 1988 to combine with Warner was made only after what could be fairly characterized as an exhaustive appraisal of Time's future as a corporation. After concluding in 1983–84 that the corporation must expand to survive, and beyond journalism into entertainment, the board combed the field of available entertainment companies. By 1987 Time had focused upon Warner; by late July 1988 Time's board was convinced that Warner would provide the best 'fit' for Time to achieve its strategic objectives. The record attests to the zealousness of Time's executives, fully supported by their directors, in seeing to the preservation of Time's 'culture,' i.e., its perceived editorial integrity in journalism. We find ample evidence in the record to support the Chancellor's conclusion that the Time board's decision to expand the business of the company through its March 3 merger with Warner was entitled to the protection of the business judgment rule. *See Aronson* v. *Lewis*, Del. Supr., 473 A.2d 805, 812 (1984).

The Chancellor reached a different conclusion in addressing the Time–Warner transaction as revised three months later. He found that the revised agreement was defense-motivated and designed to avoid the potentially disruptive effect that Paramount's offer would have had on consummation of the proposed merger were it put to a shareholder vote. Thus, the court declined to apply the traditional business judgment rule to the revised transaction and instead analyzed the Time board's June 16 decision under *Unocal*. The court ruled that *Unocal* applied to all director actions taken, following receipt of Paramount's hostile tender offer, that were reasonably determined to be defensive. Clearly that was a correct ruling and no party disputes that ruling.

In *Unocal*, we held that before the business judgment rule is applied to a board's adoption of a defensive measure, the burden will lie with the board to prove (a) reasonable grounds for believing that a danger to corporate policy and effectiveness existed; and (b) that the defensive measure adopted was reasonable in relation to the threat posed. *Unocal*, 493 A.2d 946. Directors satisfy the first part of the *Unocal* test by demonstrating good faith and reasonable investigation. We have repeatedly stated that the refusal to entertain an offer may comport with a valid exercise of a board's business judgment. *See, e.g., Macmillan*, 559 A.2d at 1285 n.35; *Van Gorkom*, 488 A.2d at 881; *Pogostin* v. *Rice*, Del. Supr., 480 A.2d 619, 627 (1984).

Unocal involved a two-tier, highly coercive tender offer. In such a case, the threat is obvious: shareholders may be compelled to tender to avoid being treated adversely in the second stage of the transaction. *Accord Ivanhoe*, 535 at 1344. In subsequent cases, the Court of Chancery has suggested that an all-cash, all-shares offer, falling within a range of values that a shareholder might reasonably prefer, cannot constitute a legally recognized 'threat' to shareholder interests sufficient to withstand a *Unocal* analysis. *AC Acquisitions Corp.* v. *Anderson, Clayton & Co.*, Del. Ch., 519 A.2d 103 (1986); *see Grand Metropolitan, PLC* v. *Pillsbury Co.*, Del. Ch., C.A. No. 10319, Duffy, J. (Dec. 16, 1988); *City Capital Associates* v. *Interco, Inc.*, Del. Ch., 551 A.2d 787 (1988). In those cases, the Court of Chancery determined that whatever danger existed related only to the shareholders and only to price and not to the corporation.

From those decisions by our Court of Chancery, Paramount and the individual plaintiffs extrapolate a rule of law that an all-cash, all-shares offer with values reasonably in the range of acceptable price cannot pose any objective threat to a corporation or its shareholders. Thus, Paramount would have us hold that only if the value of Paramount's offer were determined to be clearly inferior to the value created by management's plan to merge with Warner could the offer be viewed – objectively – as a threat.

Implicit in the plaintiffs' argument is the view that a hostile tender offer can pose only two types of threats: the threat of coercion that results from a two-tier offer promising unequal treatment for nontendering shareholders; and the threat of inadequate value from an all-shares, all-cash offer at a price below what a target board in good faith deems to be the present value of its shares. *See, Interco*, 551 A.2d at 797; *see also BNS. Inc.* v. *Koppers*, D. Del., 683 F. Supp. 458 (1988). Since Paramount's offer was all-cash, the only conceivable 'threat,' plaintiffs argue, was inadequate value.[17] We disapprove of such a narrow and rigid construction of *Unocal*, for the reasons which follow.

Plaintiffs' position represents a fundamental misconception of our standard of review under *Unocal* principally because it would involve the court in substituting its judgment for what is a 'better' deal for that of a corporation's board of directors. To the extent that the Court of Chancery has recently

---

[17] Some commentators have suggested that the threats posed by hostile offers be categorized into not two but three types: '(i) *opportunity loss* ... [where] a hostile offer might deprive target shareholders of the opportunity to select a superior alternative offered by target management [or, we would add, offered by another bidder]; (ii) *structural coercion*, ... the risk that disparate treatment of non-tendering shareholders might distort shareholders' tender decisions; and ... (iii) *substantive coercion*,... the risk that shareholders will mistakenly accept an underpriced offer because they disbelieve management's representations of intrinsic value.' The recognition of substantive coercion, the authors suggest, would help guarantee that the *Unocal* standard becomes an effective intermediate standard of review. Gilson and Kraakman, *Delaware's Intermediate Standard for Defensive Tactics: Is There Substance to Proportionality Review?*, 44 The Business Lawyer, 247, 267 (1989).

done so in certain of its opinions, we hereby reject such approach as not in keeping with a proper *Unocal* analysis. *See, e.g., Interco,* 551 A.2d 787, and its progeny; *but see TW Services, Inc.* v. *SWT Acquisition Corp.,* Del. Ch., C.A. No. 10427, Allen, C. (March 2, 1989).

The usefulness of *Unocal* as an analytical tool is precisely its flexibility in the face of a variety of fact scenarios. *Unocal* is not intended as an abstract standard; neither is it a structured and mechanistic procedure of appraisal. Thus, we have said that directors may consider, when evaluating the threat posed by a takeover bid, the 'inadequacy of the price offered, nature and timing of the offer, questions of illegality, the impact on contingencies other than shareholders, the risk of nonconsummation and the quality of securities being offered in the exchange.' 493 A.2d at 955. The open-ended analysis mandated by *Unocal* is not intended to lead to a simple mathematical exercise: that is, of comparing the discounted value of Time–Warner's expected trading price at some future date with Paramount's offer and determining which is the higher. Indeed, in our view, precepts underlying the business judgment rule mitigate against a court's engaging in the process of attempting to appraise and evaluate the relative merits of a long-term versus a short-term investment goal for shareholders. To engage in such an exercise is a distortion of the *Unocal* process and, in particular, the application of the second part of *Unocal*'s test, discussed below.

In this case, the Time board reasonably determined that inadequate value was not the only legally cognizable threat that Paramount's all-cash, all-shares offer could present. Time's board concluded that Paramount's eleventh hour offer posed other threats. One concern was that Time shareholders might elect to tender into Paramount's cash offer in ignorance or a mistaken belief of the strategic benefit which a business combination with Warner might produce. Moreover, Time viewed the conditions attached to Paramount's offer as introducing a degree of uncertainty that skewed a comparative analysis. Further, the timing of Paramount's offer to follow issuance of Time's proxy notice was viewed as arguably designed to upset, if not confuse, the Time stockholders' vote. Given this record evidence, we cannot conclude that the Time board's decision of June 6 that Paramount's offer posed a threat to corporate policy and effectiveness was lacking in good faith or dominated by motives of either entrenchment or self-interest. Paramount also contends that the Time board had not duly investigated Paramount's offer. Therefore, Paramount argues, Time was unable to make an informed decision that the offer posed a threat to Time's corporate policy. Although the Chancellor did not address this issue directly, his findings of fact do detail Time's exploration of the available entertainment companies, including Paramount, before determining that Warner provided the best strategic 'fit.' In addition, the court found that Time's board rejected Paramount's offer because Paramount did not serve Time's objectives or meet Time's needs.

Thus, the record does, in our judgment, demonstrate that Time's board was adequately informed of the potential benefits of a transaction with Paramount. We agree with the Chancellor that the Time board's lengthy pre-June investigation of potential merger candidates, including Paramount, mooted any obligation on Time's part to halt its merger process with Warner to reconsider Paramount. Time's board was under no obligation to negotiate with Paramount. *Unocal*, 493 A.2d at 954–55; *see also Macmillan*, 559 A.2d at 1285 n.35. Time's failure to negotiate cannot be fairly found to have been uninformed. The evidence supporting this finding is materially enhanced by the fact that twelve of Time's sixteen board members were outside independent directors. *Unocal*, 493 A.2d at 955; *Moran v. Household Intern., Inc.*, Del. Supr., 500 A.2d 1346, 1356 (1985).

We turn to the second part of the *Unocal* analysis. The obvious requisite to determining the reasonableness of a defensive action is a clear identification of the nature of the threat. As the Chancellor correctly noted, this 'requires an evaluation of the importance of the corporate objective threatened; alternative methods of protecting that objective; impacts of the "defensive" action, and other relevant factors.' *In Re: Time Incorporated Shareholder Litigation*, Del. Ch., C.A. No. 10670, Allen, C. (July 14, 1989). It is not until both parts of the *Unocal* inquiry have been satisfied that the business judgment rule attaches to defensive actions of a board of directors. *Unocal*, 493 A.2d at 954.[18] As applied to the facts of this case, the question is whether the record evidence supports the Court of Chancery's conclusion that the restructuring of the Time–Warner transaction, including the adoption of several preclusive defensive measures, was a *reasonable response* in relation to a perceived threat.

Paramount argues that, assuming its tender offer posed a threat, Time's response was unreasonable in precluding Time's shareholders from accepting the tender offer or receiving a control premium in the immediately foreseeable future. Once again, the contention stems, we believe, from a fundamental misunderstanding of where the power of corporate governance lies. Delaware law confers the management of the corporate enterprise to the stockholders' duly elected board representatives. 8 *Del. C.* §141(a). The fiduciary duty to manage a corporate enterprise includes the selection of a time frame for achievement of corporate goals. That duty may not be delegated to the stockholders. *Van Gorkom*, 488 A.2d at 873. Directors are not obliged to abandon a deliberately conceived corporate plan for a short-term shareholder

---

[18] Some commentators have criticized *Unocal* by arguing that once the board's deliberative process has been analyzed and found not to be wanting in objectivity, good faith or deliberateness, the so-called 'enhanced' business judgment rule has been satisfied and no further inquiry is undertaken. *See generally* Johnson, Siegel, *Corporate Mergers: Redefining the Role of Target Directors*, 136 U.Pa.L.Rev. 315 (1987). We reject such views.

profit unless there is clearly no basis to sustain the corporate strategy. *See, e.g., Revlon,* 506 A.2d 173.

Although the Chancellor blurred somewhat the discrete analyses required under *Unocal,* he did conclude that Time's board reasonably perceived Paramount's offer to be a significant threat to the planned Time–Warner merger and that Time's response was not 'overly broad.' We have found that even in light of a valid threat, management actions that are coercive in nature or force upon shareholders a management-sponsored alternative to a hostile offer may be struck down as unreasonable and nonproportionate responses. *Macmillan,* 559 A.2d 1261; *AC Acquisitions Corp.,* 519 A.2d 103.

Here, on the record facts, the Chancellor found that Time's responsive action to Paramount's tender offer was not aimed at 'cramming down' on its shareholders a management-sponsored alternative, but rather had as its goal the carrying forward of a pre-existing transaction in an altered form.[19] Thus, the response was reasonably related to the threat. The Chancellor noted that the revised agreement and its accompanying safety devices did not preclude Paramount from making an offer for the combined Time–Warner company or from changing the conditions of its offer so as not to make the offer dependent upon the nullification of the Time–Warner agreement. Thus, the response was proportionate. We affirm the Chancellor's rulings as clearly supported by the record. Finally, we note that although Time was required, as a result of Paramount's hostile offer, to incur a heavy debt to finance its acquisition of Warner, that fact alone does not render the board's decision unreasonable so long as the directors could reasonably perceive the debt load not to be so injurious to the corporation as to jeopardize its well-being.

C.

Conclusion

Applying the test for grant or denial of preliminary injunctive relief, we find plaintiffs failed to establish a reasonable likelihood of ultimate success on the merits. Therefore, we affirm.

---

[19] The Chancellor cited *Shamrock Holdings, Inc.* v. *Polaroid Corp.,* Del. Ch., C.A. Nos. 10075 and 10079, Berger, V.C. (Jan. 6, 1989), as a closely analogous case. In that case, the Court of Chancery upheld, in the face of a takeover bid, the establishment of an employee stock ownership plan that had a significant antitakeover effect. The Court of Chancery upheld the board's action largely because the ESOP had been adopted *prior* to any contest for control and was reasonably determined to increase productivity and enhance profits. The ESOP did not appear to be primarily a device to affect or secure corporate control.

Table of Cases

This Table of Cases also functions as an index: the numbers following each citation show the page numbers on which the case is discussed.

Bibliography

Amihud, Yakov (ed.), *Leveraged Management Buyouts: Causes and Consequences* (Homewood, Ill.: Dow Jones–Irwin, 1989)

Arrow, Kenneth, *The Limits of Organization* (New York: Norton, 1974)

Auerbach, Alan J. (ed.), *Corporate Takeovers: Causes and Consequences* (Chicago, Ill.: University of Chicago Press, 1988)

Balotti, R. Franklin and Finkelstein, Jesse A., *The Delaware Law of Corporations and Business Organizations* (Clifton, NJ: Prentice-Hall, 2d edn, 1990)

Berle, Adolph and Means, Gardiner, *The Modern Corporation and Private Property* (New York, Macmillan, 1933)

Bhide, Amar, 'The Causes and Consequences of Hostile Takeovers,' 2 *Journal of Applied Corporate Finance* 36 (Summer 1989)

Black, Bernard S., 'Bidder Overpayment in Takeovers,' 41 *Stanford Law Review* 597 (1989)

Bradley, Michael, Desai, Anand, and Kim, E. Han, 'Synergistic Gains from Corporate Acquisitions and their Division between the Stockholders of Target and Acquiring Firms,' *Journal of Finance and Economics* (forthcoming)

Brealey, Richard and Myers, Stewart, *Principles of Corporate Finance* (New York: McGraw-Hill, 3d edn 1988)

Capatides, Michael G., *A Guide to the Capital Markets Activities of Banks and Bank Holding Companies* (New York: Bowne and Co. 1990)

Carleton, Dennis W. and Fischel, Daniel R., 'The Regulation of Insider Trading,' 53 *Standard Law Review* 857 (1983)

Cary, William L., 'Federalism and Corporate Law: Reflections Upon Delaware,' 83 *Yale Law Journal* 663 (1974)

Clark, Robert, *Corporate Law* (Boston, Mass.: Little, Brown, 1986)

Symposium, 'Contractual Freedom in Corporate Law,' 89 *Columbia Law Review* 1395–1774 (1989)

Davenport, Nicholas, 'Keynes in the City,' in Milo Keynes (ed.), *Essays on John Maynard Keynes* (New York: Cambridge University Press, 1975)

DeAngelo, Harry, DeAngelo, Linda and Rice, Edward M., 'Going Private: Minority Freezeouts and Stockholder Wealth,' 27 *Journal of Law and Economics* 367 (1984)

Dertouzos, Michael L., Lester, Richard K. and Solow, Robert M., *Made in America, Regaining the Productive Edge* (Cambridge, Mass.: MIT Press, 1989)

Dornbusch, R., Fisher, S. and Bossons, J. (eds), *Macroeconomics and Finance: Essays in Honor of Franco Modigliani* (Cambridge, Mass.: MIT Press, 1987)

Dresler, David A., Black, Lewis S. Jr. and Sparks, A. Gilchrist III, *Delaware Corporation Law and Practice* (New York: Matthew Bender, 1988, 1989)

Easterbrook, Frank H. and Fischel, Daniel R., 'Corporate Control Transactions,' 91 *Yale Law Journal* 698 (1982)

Easterbrook, Frank H. and Fischel, Daniel R., 'The Proper Role of a Target's Management in Responding to a Tender Offer,' 94 *Harvard Law Review* 1161 (1981)

Easterbrook, Frank H. and Jarrell, Gregg A., 'Do Targets Gain From Defeating Tender Offers?' 59 *New York University Law Review* 277 (1984)

Friedman, Milton, *Capitalism and Freedom* (Chicago, Ill.: University of Chicago Press, 1962)

Gilson, Ronald J., 'A Structural Approach to Corporations: The Case Against Defensive Tactics in Tender Offers,' 33 *Stanford Law Review* 819 (1981)

Gilson, Ronald J. and Kraakman, Reinier, 'Delaware's Intermediate Standard for Defensive Tactics: Proportionality Review,' 44 *Business Lawyer* 247 (1989)

Grossman, Sanford and Hart, Oliver, 'One Share/One Vote and the Market for Corporate Control,' 20 *Journal of Financial Economics* 175 (1988)

Grossman, Sanford and Hart, Oliver, 'Takeover Bids, the Free-Rider Problem, and the Theory of the Corporation,' *Bell Journal of Economics* 42 (Spring 1980)

Healy, Paul M.; Palepu, Krisha G.; and Ruback, Richard S., 'Does Corporate Performance Improve After Mergers?' (unpublished paper, April 1990)

Helman, Robert A. and Davis, Scott J., 'Merger and Acquisition Agreements in Competitive Bidding Situations: Rights and Obligations Created by Corporation and Contract Law,' 17 *Securities Regulation Law Journal* 3 (1989)

Herzel, Leo, Colling, Dale E., and Carlson, James B., 'Misunderstanding Lockups,' 14 *Securities Regulation Law Journal* 2 (1986)

Herzel, Leo and Harris, Daniel, 'Do We Need Insider Trading Laws?' 10 *Company Lawyer* 34 (1989)

Herzel, Leo and Katz, Leo, 'Insider Trading: Who Loses?' 165 *Lloyds Bank Review* (July 1987)

Herzel, Leo and Schmidt, John R., 'Shareholders Can Benefit from Sale of "Crown Jewels,"' VI *Legal Times* 21 (1983)

Herzel, Leo, Schmidt, John R. and Davis, Scott J., 'Why Corporate Directors Have a Right to Resist Tender Offers,' 61 *Chicago Bar Record* 152 (1979)

Herzel, Leo and Shepro, Richard W., 'An American Look at the Guinness Affair,' *Financial Times* (Feb. 12, 1987)

Herzel, Leo and Shepro, Richard W., 'Another Step Backwards for U.S. Takeovers,' *Financial Times* (June 8, 1989)

Herzel, Leo and Shepro, Richard W., 'Bondholder Suits in the U.S.,' *Financial Times* (Dec. 21, 1989)

Herzel, Leo and Shepro, Richard W., 'The Changing Fortunes of Takeover Defenses,' 15 *Securities Regulation Law Journal* 116 (1987)

Herzel, Leo and Shepro, Richard W., 'Controversial Disclosures,' 9 *Company Lawyer* 143 (July 1988)

Herzel, Leo and Shepro, Richard W., 'Danger Signals Raised by Expanded Disclosure,' *New York Law Journal* (Dec. 7, 1987)

Herzel, Leo and Shepro, Richard W., 'Delaware: No Hostility to Takeovers,' *Financial Times* (July 9, 1987)

Herzel, Leo and Shepro, Richard W., 'Delaware Supreme Court Boosts Powers of Takeover Target Boards,' *Financial Times* (March 22, 1990)

Herzel, Leo and Shepro, Richard W., 'Drexel Given a Push Before It Fell,' *Financial Times* (March 8, 1990)

Herzel, Leo and Shepro, Richard W., 'Lessons from Delaware,' *Financial Times* (April 7, 1988)

Herzel, Leo and Shepro, Richard W.,'The Limits of Indiana's Anti-takeover Legislation,' *Financial Times* (May 8, 1987)

Herzel, Leo and Shepro, Richard W., 'Negotiated Acquisitions: The Impact of Competition in the United States,' 44 *Business Lawyer* 301 (1989)

Herzel, Leo and Shepro, Richard W., 'Recapitalisation as an Alternative to Leveraged Buyout,' *Financial Times* (April 16, 1987)

Herzel, Leo and Shepro, Richard W., 'Room for More U.S. Insider Trading Legislation,' *Financial Times* (Dec. 10, 1987)

Herzel, Leo and Shepro, Richard W., 'Setback for US Takeover Defences,' *Financial Times* (Oct. 16, 1986)

Herzel, Leo and Shepro, Richard W., 'Setting the Boundaries for Disclosure,' 16 *Securities Regulation Law Journal* 179 (1988)

Herzel, Leo and Shepro, Richard W., 'Shareholders and Leverage,' *Financial Times* (January 5, 1989)

Herzel, Leo and Shepro, Richard W., 'Takeovers Hit by US State Laws,' *Financial Times* (London edition) (May 11, 1989)

Herzel, Leo and Shepro, Richard W., 'Telling the Truth about Mergers,' *Financial Times* (April 21, 1988)

Herzel, Leo and Shepro, Richard W., 'Time Beats Paramount in the Delaware Courts,' *Financial Times* (August 3, 1989)

Herzel, Leo and Shepro, Richard W., 'Ups and Downs of U.S. Takeover Defense,' 9 *Company Lawyer* 84 (May 1988)

Herzel, Leo and Shepro, Richard W., 'U.S. Court of Appeals rules SEC overstepped its authority,' *Financial Times* (June 28, 1990)

Herzel, Leo, Shepro, Richard W. and Katz, Leo, 'Next-to-last Word on Endangered Directors,' 65 *Harvard Business Review* 38 (1987)

Investor Responsibility Research Center Inc., Corporate Governance Service, Update to 1989 Background Report C (Washington, DC: Investor Responsibility Research Center Inc., 1989)

Jarrell, Gregg A., Brickley, James A. and Netter, Jeffry M., 'The Market for Corporate Control: The Empirical Evidence Since 1980,' 2 *Journal of Economic Perspectives* (Winter 1988)

Jarrell, Gregg A. and Poulsen, Annette B., 'The Returns to Acquiring Firms in Tender Offers: Evidence from Three Decades' (Study of the Office of Economic Analysis, SEC, working draft, June 1988)

Jensen, Michael C., 'Active Investors, LBOs, and the Privatization of Bankruptcy,' 2 *Journal of Applied Corporate Finance* 35 (Spring 1989)

Jensen, Michael C., 'The Agency Costs of Free Cash Flow: Corporate Finance and Takeovers,' 76 *American Economic Review* (May 1986)

Jensen, Michael C., 'Eclipse of the Public Corporation,' 67 *Harvard Business Review* 61 (Sept.–Oct. 1989)

Jensen, Michael C. (ed.), 'Symposium on the Market for Corporate Control: The Scientific Evidence,' 11 *Journal of Financial Economics* 5 (1983)

Jensen, Michael C., 'The Takeover Controversy: Analysis and Evidence,' IV *Midland Corporate Finance Journal* 6, 11 (1986).

Jensen, Michael C., 'Takeovers: Folklore and Science,' 62 *Harvard Business Review* 109 (Nov.–Dec. 1984)

Jensen, Michael C. and Ruback, Richard S., 'The Market for Corporate Control: The Scientific Evidence,' 11 *Journal of Financial Economics* 5 (1983)

Kaplan, Steven, 'Sources of Value in Management Buyouts,' *Journal of Financial Economics* (forthcoming)

Keynes, John Maynard, *The General Theory of Employment, Interest and Money* (New York: Harcourt, Brace, 1935)

Keynes, Milo (ed.), *Essays on John Maynard Keynes* (New York: Cambridge University Press, 1975)

King, Mervyn and Roell, Ailsa, 'The Regulation of Takeovers and the Stock Markets,' *National Westminster Bank Review* 2 (February 1988)

Kochan, Nick and Pym, Hugh, *The Guinness Affair: Anatomy of a Scandal* (London: Croom Helm, 1987)

Kraakman, Reinier, 'Taking Discounts Seriously: The Implications of "Discounted" Share Prices as an Acquisition Motive,' 88 *Columbia Law Review* 891 (1988)

Labor Department Opinion Letter on Tender Offers, Feb. 23, 1989, 16 *BNA Pension Reporter* 390 (March 6, 1989)

Lipton, Martin, 'Corporate Governance in the Age of Finance Corporatism,' 136 *University of Pennsylvania Law Review* 1 (1987)

Lorsch, Jay W. with MacIver, Elizabeth, *Pawns or Potentates: The Reality of America's Corporate Boards* (Boston, Mass.: Harvard Business School Press, 1989)

Loss, Louis, *Fundamentals of Securities Regulation* (Boston, Mass.: Little, Brown, 1988)

Loss, Louis and Seligman, Joel, *Securities Regulation* (Boston, Mass.: Little, Brown, 1989)

Lowenstein, Louis, *What's Wrong with Wall Street: Short-Term Gain and the Absentee Shareholder* (Reading, Mass.: Addison-Wesley, 1988)

Macey, Jonathan R. and Miller, Geoffrey P., 'Toward an Interest-Group Theory of Delaware Corporate Law,' 65 *Texas Law Review* 469 (1987)

Macey, Jonathan R. and Miller, Geoffrey P., 'Trans Union Reconsidered,' 98 *Yale Law Journal* 127 (1988)

Manne, Henry G., *Insider Trading and the Stock Market* (New York: Free Press, 1966)

Merton, Robert, 'On the State of the Efficient Market Hypothesis in Financial Economics,' in R. Dornbusch, S. Fisher and J. Bossons (eds), *Macroeconomics and Finance: Essays in Honor of Franco Modigliani* (Cambridge, Mass.: MIT Press, 1987)

Mintzberg, Henry, *The Structuring of Organizations* (Englewood Cliffs, NJ: Prentice-Hall, 1979)

Mitchell, Mark L. and Lehn, Kenneth, 'Do Bad Bidders Become Good Targets?' Study by the Office of Economic Analysis, Securities and Exchange Commission (1988)

The Complete Essays of Montaigne (Stanford, Cal.: Stanford University Press, Frame trans. 1965)

Morita, Akio and Ishihara, Shintaro, *The Japan that Can Say 'No': The New U.S.–Japan Relations Card* (typescript translation 1989)

O'Hara, Peg, Corporate Governance Service, *Poison Pills*, 1989 Background Report G (Washington, DC: Investor Responsibility Research Center Inc., 1989)

Posner, Richard A., *Economic Analysis of Law* (Boston, Mass.: Little, Brown, 3d edn 1986)

Raiffa, Howard, *The Art and Science of Negotiation* (Cambridge, Mass.: Belknap Press, 1985)

Rappaport, Alfred, 'The Staying Power of the Public Corporation,' 68 *Harvard Business Review* 96 (Jan.–Feb. 1990)

Ravenscraft, D. and Scherer, F., *Mergers, Sell-offs and Economic Efficiency* (Washington, DC: Brookings Institution, 1987)

Sametz, Arnold W., and Bicksler, James L. (eds), *The Battle for Corporate Control: Shareholder Rights, Stakeholder Interests and Managerial Responsibilities* (Chicago, Ill.: IICLE, 1990)

Schelling, Thomas C., *The Strategy of Conflict* (Cambridge, Mass.: Harvard University Press, 1960)

Schipper, Katherine and Thompson, Rex, 'Evidence on the Capitalized Value of Merger Activity for Acquiring Firms,' 11 *Journal of Financial Economics* 85 (1983)

Scott, Bruce R., 'Competitiveness: Self-Help for a Worsening Problem,' *Harvard Business Review* (July–August 1989)

Shepro, Richard W., 'Foreign Direct Investment in the United States: A Legal Analysis,' 4 *Wisconsin International Law Journal* 46 (1985)

Shepro, Richard W., and Colling, Dale E., 'Corporate Law Aspects of Restructuring,' in *Closely Held Corporations* (Chicago, Ill.: IICLE, 1985, revd edn 1990)

Shleifer, Andrei and Summers, Lawrence, 'Breach of Trust in Hostile Takeovers,' in Alan Auerbach (ed.), *Corporate Takeovers: Causes and Consequences* (Chicago, Ill.: University of Chicago Press, 1988)

Stein, Jeremy C., 'Efficient Capital Markets, Inefficient Firms: A Model of Myopic Corporate Behavior,' *Quarterly Journal of Economics* (November 1989)

Summers, Lawrence H., 'The Case for a Securities Transactions Excise Tax,' paper presented at the Salomon Brothers/Rutgers Conference on the Fiduciary Responsibilities of Institutional Investors, June 14–15, 1990

Tobin, James, 'On the Efficiency of the Financial System,' *Lloyds Bank Review* (July 1984)

Wayne, Leslie, 'How One Man's Ego Wrecked a Bank,' *New York Times* (March 4, 1990)

Weisman, Steven R., 'Japan, Weary of Barbs on Trade, Tells Americans Why they Trail,' *New York Times* (Nov. 20, 1989)

Williamson, Oliver E., *The Economics of Discretionary Behavior: Managerial Objectives in a Theory of the Firm* (Chicago, Ill.: Markham Pub. Co., 1967)

Williamson, Oliver E., *Markets and Hierarchies* (New York: Free Press, 1975)

Winter, Ralph K., 'The "Race for the Top" Revisited,' 89 *Columbia Law Review* 1526 (1989)

Glossary

This is a compendium of definitions of technical and legal terms used in discussions of takeovers in the U.S. We have tried to avoid unnecessary jargon. When technical or legal terms appear in the book for the first time they are defined in context in a commonsense way to avoid slowing the reader down. This list includes terms we have used as well as some we have not used explicitly, although we have used the ideas.

We have listed in SMALL CAPITALS terms in the definitions that are themselves the subject of Glossary entries.

agency The most important idea in the book, although we do not emphasize the word. The idea has a long history in ethics, law and economics. It covers the legal and moral obligations involved in acting for the benefit of another person or a group and applies to partners, directors and officers of corporations, employees, trustees, bankers, politicians, soldiers, among others. Agency problems are embedded in human nature. Sometimes they can be reduced, but never eliminated. *See* FIDUCIARY DUTY.

all-holders rule An SEC tender offer rule (Rule 14d–10(a)(2)) that requires all SHAREHOLDERS to receive the same offer. For situations where this is impossible there are some technical exceptions. The rule is reproduced in the Appendix, A.2.4.

antidilution provision Holders and issuers of securities, such as warrants, options or convertible debentures or PREFERRED STOCK, that depend for their value on the number of shares of common stock into which they can be converted, need protection against changes in the number of common shares, such as stock splits, reverse splits, unusual dividends, mergers and other transactions that could affect their interests unfairly. Antidilution provisions are designed to adjust the exchange ratio fairly for both sides. The formulas used can be detailed and complex or general and relatively simple.

antifraud rules A principal means of enforcing Federal and state securities laws in the United States. Rule 10b–5 under the Securities Exchange Act of 1934 is the most important Federal antifraud rule. It uses very broad language and prohibits fraudulent and manipulative acts in connection with buying or selling securities. The rule does not just cover what one would ordinarily think of as FRAUD. The meaning of the rule has evolved considerably since it was issued in 1942. It is the chief source of insider trading law. There are a number of similar laws and rules covering other parts of Federal securities law: for example, Rule 14a–9 deals with proxy solicitations and §14(e) of the 1934 Act with TENDER

OFFERS. Courts, the SEC and securities lawyers spend large amounts of time giving their views on what kinds of statements should be viewed as misleading and therefore illegal under antifraud rules. Rule 10b–5 and §14(e) are reproduced in the Appendix, A.1.2 and A.2.2. *See* CLASS ACTION, SHAREHOLDER LITIGATION.

antitakeover laws State statutes designed to inhibit takeovers. Usually the term does not include court-made law, or statutes that have this effect unintentionally. Examples and a list of state antitakeover laws are contained in the Appendix, A.5–A.11.

appraisal right A statutory right of SHAREHOLDERS to the fair value of their shares, in cash, as determined by a court. The right comes into play when a shareholder exercises a statutory right to DISSENT from certain extraordinary transactions such as a MERGER. It is supplemented by shareholder rights to sue for breach of FIDUCIARY DUTY. There are important substantive and procedural differences between appraisal and a suit for breach of fiduciary duty. In the latter, for example, it is possible to ask the court to have the transaction enjoined or set aside if completed (RESCISSION). PLAINTIFFS' LAWYERS can bring class actions for breach of fiduciary duty on behalf of all MINORITY SHAREHOLDERS. This is impossible in appraisal before shareholders have exercised their statutory rights to dissent. *See* GOING PRIVATE TRANSACTION, PUT, SQUEEZE-OUT MERGER.

arbitrager A professional speculator who buys and sells stock and other securities in the hope of making profits on takeovers. Arbitragers are a very important factor in the takeover market. If, for example, they do not buy heavily when an offer is announced, that means the offer is not being taken seriously. When the market price goes over the offering price, that means arbitragers are betting their money that the offering price is too low. Arbitragers depend on information. Their desperate search for information is closely related to the major insider trading scandals of the late 1980s. Usually the term emphasizes only short-term speculation, although sometimes arbitragers may hold stock for several years.

articles of incorporation *See* CHARTER.

auction In takeover usage any systematic effort to sell a company at the highest price obtainable. The auction may be conducted by the BOARD OF DIRECTORS or by a SPECIAL COMMITTEE advised by investment bankers and lawyers.

back end *See* TWO-STEP DEAL, FRONT-END LOADED.

bear-hug letter An unsolicited letter from a bidder to the BOARD OF DIRECTORS of a target making a proposal for a friendly takeover. Both the bidder and the target board understand that the point of the proposal is to put pressure on the target board to negotiate, since the existence of the proposal must be publicly disclosed by the target immediately. Once the disclosure is made the target is likely to be in play – that is, for sale to that bidder or someone else.

best efforts clause   A clause in an acquisition agreement that imposes a legal obligation on one or both of the parties to try hard to carry out the terms and intent of the agreement. It is a more complex idea than it appears. Implicit in it are other ideas such as GOOD FAITH and reasonableness. The point is to make it legally dangerous to try to avoid an agreement on a pretext. The limits of best efforts are not clear and some agreements define the limits more specifically.

blankcheck preferred stock   PREFERRED STOCK authorized by the SHAREHOLDERS with the terms left blank. Directors usually have the legal right to fill in the terms without further shareholder approval. In the 1960s, when blankcheck preferred stock came into general use, it was issued mainly to facilitate negotiated acquisitions and generally was freely authorized by shareholders. Now blankcheck preferred stock is considered an antitakeover device and for that reason is likely to encounter shareholder resistance. Furthermore, large shareholders are now much more skeptical about the value of making acquisitions. *See* BLOCKING PREFERRED STOCK, STANDSTILL AGREEMENT.

blocking preferred stock   The private sale of PREFERRED STOCK as a takeover defense. Common stock can be used but preferred stock is favored because the BOARD OF DIRECTORS can design the characteristics of the stock to fit the transaction without SHAREHOLDER approval. Once a general class of preferred stock has been authorized by shareholders, directors usually have the legal power to set the terms of each series, including conversion rights into common stock. *See* BLANKCHECK PREFERRED STOCK, STANDSTILL AGREEMENT, WHITE SQUIRE.

board of directors   Under state corporation statutes, the governing body of corporations. The board stands in an uneasy relationship between the CEO and SHAREHOLDERS. Directors are generally nominated by the board itself. They are elected by the shareholders, usually annually. Although generally the CEO runs the corporation, on most important matters the board is the ultimate authority. Even when a shareholder vote is required for certain extraordinary transactions such as MERGERS, the directors must initiate the action. Directors cannot act individually, but only as a board. *See* CLASSIFIED BOARD, INDEPENDENT DIRECTOR, PROXY CONTEST.

bondholder   Typically refers to the holder of any long-term debt of a corporation that is traded. Under state corporation law, directors owe a FIDUCIARY DUTY to SHAREHOLDERS. In contrast, the rights of bondholders and other creditors are based solely on their contract. The duty directors owe them is to respect the contract. In the case of bondholders, the contract is the indenture governing the bonds. Except in private placements issued to a few sophisticated holders, buyers of bonds have little opportunity to negotiate the terms of the indenture, which are set largely by the issuer and the underwriters working within the customs of the financial community and the pressures of financial markets. The terms of bonds are infinitely variable, ranging from unsecured bonds with almost no financial covenants (debentures) to bonds that are secured by a pledge of assets as collateral (mortgage bonds). If a company gets in financial trouble, files for bankruptcy protection or plans a RESTRUCTURING, mortgage bondholders have the most leverage. *See EX ANTE,* JUNK BONDS, SUBORDINATED DEBT.

break-up fee In a negotiated acquisition agreement a payment promised by the seller to the buyer if the buyer loses the deal to another bidder. Usually the buyer is concerned about losing out to higher bids, but sometimes it asks for more general protection against termination of the agreement. Break-up fees may be agreed to by the seller in exchange for a FIDUCIARY OUT in the acquisition agreement. They may also be offered (or asked for) as an inducement to a potential buyer to enter a bidding contest. The higher the fee in relation to the price, the more legally controversial it is. The usual range is 1–3% of the acquisition price. *See* TOPPING FEE.

bridge loan A short-term loan provided by an investment banking firm or commercial bank that is intended to be replaced quickly by permanent financing. Makers of bridge loans charge high fees but assume substantial risk when they lend in highly leveraged transactions. When the Allied and Federated department store chains, after being acquired by Campeau Corporation, filed for bankruptcy in 1990, their investment banker, First Boston, who had provided bridge loans was the largest creditor. *See* JUNK BONDS, SUBORDINATED DEBT.

business combination A general term used to cover the acquisition of one company by another or the consolidation of two companies, whatever the legal form – MERGER, acquisition of shares or assets, or other method. Sometimes the term is intended to convey that neither party is dominant, for example a combination of equals. Use of the term in ANTITAKEOVER LAWS and POISON PILLS, with a broad definition, makes it harder for bidders to find ways around the provisions. *See* MERGER, MERGER OF EQUALS.

business judgment rule A fundamental idea in corporation law, the term deals with the relationship between courts and directors of corporations. Where business questions are concerned courts will not second-guess business judgments of directors made in GOOD FAITH after reasonable investigation. In Delaware the rule is expressed as 'a presumption that in making a business decision the directors ... acted on an informed basis, in good faith and in the honest belief that the action taken was in the best interests of the company.' *Aronson* v. *Lewis,* 473 A.2d 805, 812 (Delaware Supreme Court 1984). The rule does not protect the decisions of directors if they are negligent or have a conflict of interest. *See* DUTY OF CARE, DUTY OF LOYALTY, ENTIRE FAIRNESS, *UNOCAL* RULE.

business purpose doctrine A requirement briefly (but no longer) used by Delaware courts. It restricted SQUEEZE-OUT MERGERS to those that served a legitimate business purpose; mergers designed solely to buy out the interests of the MINORITY SHAREHOLDERS were not considered such a purpose. The doctrine was overruled by the Delaware SUPREME COURT in 1983 in *Weinberger* v. *UOP, Inc.,* 457 A.2d 701.

by-laws Procedural rules for governing a corporation. Changes in a corporation's CHARTER must be proposed by the BOARD OF DIRECTORS and approved by a vote of the SHAREHOLDERS. Unlike the charter, by-laws can be enacted and changed by the board without any shareholder action. However, in some states such as Delaware the shareholders also can enact or change by-laws, without any action by the board of directors. Occasionally this power can be strategically important in a takeover fight.

CEO The Chief Executive Officer of a company. Generally the person who runs the company. The CEO is usually but not necessarily also the chairman of the board. The term CEO is more helpful in identifying function than a title like president (sometimes the president is number two). Often the term Chief Executive Officer is included in the legal job title in the company's CHARTER or BY-LAWS.

certificate of incorporation *See* CHARTER.

Chancery Court In Delaware, the specialized trial court where corporation law disputes are heard. Juries are not used. Appeals from the Chancery Court are heard by the Delaware SUPREME COURT.

charter The corporation's written constitution. Amendments must be initiated by the BOARD OF DIRECTORS and approved by a vote of the SHAREHOLDERS. The vote required depends on the state's corporation law and the terms of the charter itself. Also known (depending on the state) as articles of incorporation or certificate of incorporation.

class action A legal action filed on behalf of a class of persons, for example, all of the SHAREHOLDERS of a corporation who bought shares in the market after date A and before date B. In the illustration, the plaintiff's complaint might allege that during the time period A–B, the company had released misleadingly optimistic financial information and as a result the plaintiff and other members of the class bought shares and were damaged. Plaintiffs in this type of case are usually owners of only a relatively small number of shares and the defendants are the corporation and all or some of their officers and directors. The main economic interests in these cases are the PLAINTIFFS' LAWYERS' expectations of court-awarded fees for successful outcomes. Class actions cannot be settled without prior court approval after a hearing and notice to shareholders. Sometimes shareholders appear at the hearing to object to the settlement. *See* ANTI-FRAUD RULES, SHAREHOLDER LITIGATION, DERIVATIVE SUIT.

classified board A statutory method of avoiding the annual election of the entire BOARD OF DIRECTORS. Usually one-third of the board is elected every three years. Thus only one-third of the board comes up for election each year. Members of classified boards, unlike ordinary boards, usually cannot be removed before the end of their terms except for misbehavior such as fraud. A classified board is generally considered an antitakeover device affecting PROXY FIGHTS in particular.

closing The second of two milestones in an acquisition or other agreed transaction. The first is the signing of a definitive agreement, which contains conditions, such as the accuracy of representations and warranties, and SHAREHOLDER and government approvals. At the time of the closing these conditions must be satisfied or waived. The transaction is not actually accomplished until the closing when, for example, the companies are legally merged and stock or money is actually transferred. After that point the transaction is generally irrevocable. In theory, damages or RESCISSION are still possible but, in an acquisition of a public company, not practical for the acquirer. The money or shares paid have been scattered to the winds. So, for the acquirer, the closing generally is the point of no return.

coercive offer A TENDER OFFER that puts pressure on SHAREHOLDERS to tender, for example, by making a tender offer for less than all the shares at a very high price. Sometimes the term is used more generally to describe any tender offer. The argument is that a tender offer by its nature places shareholders in a PRISONER'S DILEMMA since they cannot cooperate to obtain the highest possible price.

commitment letter An agreement by a bank or other lender to provide funds for an acquisition. It has been customary for a bank to charge a substantial fee for providing a commitment letter (sometimes also even for considering providing a commitment letter) in addition to the fees and interest covering the loan itself. *See* HIGHLY CONFIDENT LETTER, LETTER OF INTENT, SUBORDINATED DEBT.

consent solicitation A contest for control of a company by soliciting agreement of a sufficient percentage of SHAREHOLDERS to take action without a formal meeting. In some states, such as New York, consent solicitation is impractical because shareholders may not take action without a meeting except by unanimous consent. Most states, such as Delaware, that allow consent also allow a corporation to provide in its CHARTER (which requires shareholder approval) that unanimous consent must be obtained. The insurgent group conducting the solicitation is usually proposing a resolution to remove the directors and replace them with a new slate. The percentage required is governed by state law. Consent solicitations are regulated by the SEC's proxy rules. The result is similar to a PROXY CONTEST but can be much quicker. Once the agreement of enough shareholders is obtained the consent is delivered to the incumbent board and the action is complete. If a shareholder owns a majority of the shares, it can replace all the directors immediately using the consent procedure unless there is a CLASSIFIED BOARD.

constituency laws A state ANTITAKEOVER LAW that allows directors facing a takeover bid to consider, in addition to shareholder interests, the interests of the company's employees, customers, suppliers and local communities. Directors have for a long time been permitted to consider other constituencies as an ordinary business judgment matter, but not as a takeover defense when all the SHAREHOLDERS are being given the choice of terminating their interest in the company by selling their shares. The Pennsylvania statute has been amended recently to allow the directors to give more weight to these other interests than to shareholders. Court reactions to this potentially powerful justification for takeover defense are largely untested although occasionally similar ideas have been expressed by courts in cases where there is no special statute.

debt security A security representing a corporation's promise to pay back borrowed money plus interest. Bonds and notes are examples of pure debt securities. *See* EQUITY SECURITY.

derivative suit A suit filed by a SHAREHOLDER on behalf of the corporation, alleging that the corporation's directors and officers (or even some other person) wrongfully damaged the corporation. An illustration is a suit attacking a SQUEEZE-OUT MERGER. The real defendants would be the parent corporation and all or some of the directors and officers of the corporation. (For procedural reasons, the corporation itself is named as a nominal defendant.) In a derivative suit, the plaintiff must allege that the corporation's directors are incapable of bringing the suit. In the illustration the reason is clear: the directors are defendants and have a conflict of interest. However, if some of the directors were not defendants, the board might be permitted to keep control of the case and to decide that it should not be continued. Like CLASS ACTIONS, plaintiffs in derivative suits usually own only a few shares and the real economic interests driving these cases are the PLAINTIFFS' LAWYERS' expectations of court-awarded fees. Court approval with a hearing and prior notice to shareholders is required for a settlement of a suit. *See* SHAREHOLDER LITIGATION.

directors *See* BOARD OF DIRECTORS.

directors' and officers' liability insurance (D&O insurance) An insurance policy that covers directors and officers for expenses, judgments and settlements arising out of lawsuits against them in their official capacities. The policy is usually divided into two parts. One insures directors and officers against all liabilities for which the company does not indemnify them. The other part calls for reimbursement of the company for all payments it makes to indemnify directors and officers. Many companies might prefer to buy insurance for the first part and self-insure for the other, but the two parts are usually only sold as a package. However, many policies allow the company to self-insure, for example, for the first one million dollars paid on a claim. *See* EXCULPATION OF DIRECTORS, INDEMNIFICATION OF DIRECTORS, PLAINTIFFS' LAWYERS, SHAREHOLDER LITIGATION.

discovery In litigation in the U.S., the legal right of parties to obtain facts relating to the litigation before trial. This right is very extensive. It includes out-of-court testimony under oath and papers from both parties and non-parties to the litigation. *See* SHAREHOLDER LITIGATION.

dissent Under state corporation statutes SHAREHOLDERS must dissent before they can seek appraisal. Dissent is manifested by not voting in favor of the proposal dissented from (if there is a right to vote) and by following exactly the notification and other procedures required by the statute. *See* APPRAISAL RIGHT, MINORITY SHAREHOLDERS, SHAREHOLDER LITIGATION, SQUEEZE-OUT MERGER.

drop dead provision A provision in an acquisition (or other) agreement specifying a date after which either party may terminate the agreement if the CLOSING has not occurred.

dry-up agreements Agreements entered into by a target (or a bidder) that attempt to cut a bidder (or competing bidders) off from credit or expert takeover assistance: for example, ENGAGEMENT LETTERS or other retention agreements entered into by a target that attempt to tie up large numbers of commercial banks, investment banks or law firms so that their services are unavailable to other parties. In the *Time–Paramount* litigation, the Delaware courts were critical of what they categorized as Time dry-up agreements designed to thwart Paramount.

dual class recapitalization In a dual class RECAPITALIZATION separate classes of common shares are given different voting rights. Dual class recapitalizations cannot be accomplished unless the CHARTER permits separate classes or there is a CHARTER amendment, which requires a SHAREHOLDER vote. They are usually not practical unless the company has a large shareholder who supports the proposal, generally a family that has controlled the company for a long time. For this reason it could never be a useful general antitakeover device. After 1988, SEC Rule 19c-4, the ONE-SHARE-ONE-VOTE rule, made most dual class recapitalizations after a company has public shareholders illegal, but in 1990 a U.S. Court of Appeals held that the rule was invalid because it was beyond the statutory powers of the SEC.

duty of care One part of a director's FIDUCIARY DUTY, the other being the DUTY OF LOYALTY. It is quite clear that directors violate their duty of care if they are negligent. However, the exact outlines of the duty and remedies are controlled by state law and the corporation's charter. *See* CLASS ACTION, DERIVATIVE SUIT, DIRECTORS' AND OFFICERS' LIABILITY INSURANCE, EXCULPATION OF DIRECTORS, INDEMNIFICATION OF DIRECTORS, SHAREHOLDER LITIGATION.

duty of loyalty The other part of a director's FIDUCIARY DUTY (in addition to the DUTY OF CARE). The Delaware courts have noted that a board's duty of loyalty runs strictly to SHAREHOLDERS, not, for example, to bidders or creditors of the company. Loyalty is a concept courts are at ease with and, therefore, usually very tough about. *See* CLASS ACTION, DERIVATIVE SUIT, DIRECTORS' AND OFFICERS' LIABILITY INSURANCE, SHAREHOLDER LITIGATION.

ERISA The short name for Employee Retirement Income Security Act. ERISA can be the cause of very large liabilities for underfunded pension plans. These liabilities are an important concern to potential bidders in evaluating takeovers. ERISA also regulates ESOPs, which can play an important defensive role in takeovers.

ESOP An abbreviation for employee stock ownership plan. ESOPs offer tax advantages. For example, contributions by employers are tax deductible. Leveraged ESOPs in particular can be used as an antitakeover device since employees generally are expected to support management in takeover controversies. The key assumption is that employees' jobs are more important to them than the value of their ESOP stock. ESOPs are regulated by ERISA. The main controversy about ESOPs under ERISA is the extent to which employees rather than plan fiduciaries (such as trustees and investment advisers) can determine how plan shares will be voted and whether they will be tendered. *See* RECAPITALIZATION.

efficient market theory An economic theory based on classical economics, mathematical probability (in a random walk) and the statistical testing of hypotheses. The commonsense heart of the theory is that investors cannot beat the market because stock prices fluctuate randomly (random walk). This part of the theory has been tested statistically many times and never been disproven. The explanation usually given is that almost all useful public information is already reflected in stock prices due to intense competition in the market for information (the classical economics element). This explanation leads to a more controversial variation of the theory that covers NON-PUBLIC INFORMATION as well and is very important in the rhetoric justifying takeovers: that stock market prices accurately reflect economic values. If everyone accepted this idea it could be argued that it is insincere for a target company BOARD OF DIRECTORS to say that the company under its present management is really worth more than its market value.

engagement letter The agreement between a bidder, target or SPECIAL COMMITTEE and an investment banking firm or other financial adviser for services in connection with a proposed acquisition, sale or takeover defense. Engagement letters usually cover the exact duties of the adviser, its fees and extensive indemnifications against legal liability and litigation expenses. The size of fees is usually tied quite closely to results. Courts are beginning to look closely at the incentives the fee arrangements provide from the standpoint of conflicts of interest when evaluating the actions of the BOARD OF DIRECTORS or a FAIRNESS OPINION provided by the adviser. Contingent fees, for example, are suspect.

entire fairness A rule applied by Delaware courts in judging BOARD OF DIRECTORS' decisions when there is a conflict of interest or badly flawed procedures. By contrast the BUSINESS JUDGMENT RULE is followed by courts when there is no conflict of interest. The UNOCAL RULE is an intermediate rule applied to decisions of target directors on takeover defenses.

equity security The only pure corporate equity security is common stock. It is a claim on the cash flow and assets of a corporation that is behind all other claims. In a liquidation the common SHAREHOLDERS receive whatever is left after everyone else has been paid. In contrast, no matter how well the company does, holders of DEBT SECURITIES such as bonds and notes have a right to receive only the money borrowed plus interest. Holders of common stock typically have voting rights; debt holders usually do not. Debt securities usually have a definite maturity date on which the debt must be paid; common stock usually is perpetual.

The distinction between debt and equity begins to blur with hybrid securities such as PREFERRED STOCK and convertible debentures (debt which the holder may convert into common stock). There are many securities with much more complicated combinations of equity and debt characteristics.

The holders of common stock are often referred to as the owners of the business but this is an oversimplification. Like the holders of debt and hybrid securities they too only have the rights granted to them by contract. In the case of common stock, however, the contract (the company's CHARTER and corporation law) can be changed fundamentally without unanimous consent. BOARDS OF DIRECTORS can be viewed as continuous arbitrators of this contract. In exchange for limited liability and the residual right to the corporation's cash flow and assets, the shareholders accept this highly flexible, changing contract, which was the subject of a good deal of our discussion in Chapters 2 and 5.

ex ante   Before the event. Economists' Latin used to emphasize the apparently obvious idea that it is important to recognize whether something happens before or after an agreement or other event. Nonetheless, this simple concept provides some very important, not so obvious, insights into legal and economic controversies. For example, it might appear on first thought that when BONDHOLDERS sue to stop a LEVERAGED BUYOUT or RECAPITALIZATION that would sharply reduce the value of their bonds they are expressing a grievance that should have a remedy. But this may be EX POST reasoning. The grievance may not look so good if we learn that, *ex ante*, the bondholders could have obtained protection by agreement against risks like this one by accepting a slightly lower rate of interest.

ex post   After the event. See the discussion in EX ANTE.

exculpation of directors   Allowed under a 1986 change in Delaware law (and now in many other states). In Delaware, with SHAREHOLDER approval, a corporation may adopt an amendment to its CHARTER eliminating or limiting the personal liability of directors to the corporation or its shareholders for money damages for violating their DUTY OF CARE to shareholders. Exculpation cannot cover breaches of the DUTY OF LOYALTY, nor does it prevent legal remedies other than damages, such as an injunction against a takeover defense. See Delaware General Corporation Law §102(b)(7). In some other states, exculpation is provided automatically by statute. *See* GOOD FAITH, DIRECTORS' AND OFFICERS' LIABILITY INSURANCE, SHAREHOLDER LITIGATION.

Exon–Florio Act   A Federal law enacted in 1988 that allows the President of the United States or his designee to block acquisitions by foreigners after a determination that the acquisition could be harmful to national defense. Notification requirements are an important part of this law.

externalities   Costs (or benefits) that are external to decisions made in the market. A name that helps to identify many difficult, important cooperation problems in law and economics. Environmental damage is an example of externalities – no one owns the air or the ocean so no one has an economic incentive to protect them; cooperation is usually difficult or impossible to achieve on a voluntary basis. Environmental laws attempt to set this right (very roughly) by imposing the costs of environmental damage on users. In takeovers, a controversial example would be a decline in corporate research and development caused by a widespread anticipation of takeovers. However, even without takeovers there are important externalities in R&D decisions since it is very difficult for the corporation undertaking the expense to be sure that it will capture most of the benefits. *See* FREE-RIDER PARADOX, PRISONER'S DILEMMA.

FTC   The FEDERAL TRADE COMMISSION.

fair dealing   *See* FIDUCIARY DUTY.

fair price provision   A CHARTER provision designed to protect MINORITY SHARE-HOLDERS in a SQUEEZE-OUT MERGER after a TENDER OFFER. In theory, this protection should have an antitakeover effect by making shareholders less eager to tender their shares. However, in fact, that does not appear to have happened. The likely reason is that shareholders (particularly ARBITRAGERS) place a very high value on getting their money quickly and do not place a high value on the prospects of being a minority shareholder, even with the added protection of these provisions and statutory APPRAISAL RIGHTS. Nonetheless, these provisions can cause bidders problems and must be carefully considered by them. Many states now have similar statutory provisions.

fairness opinion   A letter from an investment banking firm to a target BOARD OF DIRECTORS endorsing a takeover proposal as fair from a financial point of view. It is not entirely clear what the qualification 'from a financial point of view' excludes. Certainly legal and moral questions of fairness are excluded. In a SQUEEZE-OUT MERGER, for example, the bankers are only telling MINORITY SHARE-HOLDERS that the price is fair, not that it is fair that the law allows them to be squeezed out. This limitation probably does not provide the investment banker much legal protection if his work is sloppy. *See* ENGAGEMENT LETTER.

Federal court   Once they have jurisdiction, the Federal courts can decide issues of both state and Federal law. When a Federal statute is involved, such as the Federal securities or antitrust laws, the Federal courts have jurisdiction automatically. Appeals from a trial in a District Court are heard by one of the Courts of Appeals. The ultimate arbiter is the U.S. SUPREME COURT. However, it usually has complete discretion whether to hear a case. In fact, it hears only a tiny fraction of the cases submitted.

Federal preemption   A constitutional doctrine that Federal law is supreme in relation to state law on subjects where both the Federal Government and the states have the constitutional right to make laws and the laws conflict. The doctrine is very important in determining whether a state ANTITAKEOVER LAW is constitutional – that is, whether it interferes too much with Federal TENDER OFFER law. *See* WILLIAMS ACT.

Federal Trade Commission   One of the two Federal agencies that enforce the antitrust laws, partly through review of HART–SCOTT–RODINO FILINGS. The other is the Justice Department.

fiduciary duty   A key concept in the law of AGENCY, which imposes a highly general obligation of fair dealing on the agent. In corporation law, the main focus is on the fiduciary duty of BOARDS OF DIRECTORS and officers to the corporation and its SHAREHOLDERS.

fiduciary out   A provision in an acquisition agreement that permits the seller's BOARD OF DIRECTORS to deal with competing bidders. These provisions can be very broad and include a right to solicit other bids. Or they can be quite narrow, allowing, for example, consideration only of unsolicited bids where the board has been advised by a lawyer that it has a FIDUCIARY DUTY to consider the bid.

financial buyer   In acquisitions, someone who is buying a company for financial reasons, not to run the business over the long term. The financial reasons are of course the hope of making a profit, usually by reselling the company in parts or in stock flotations. Sponsors of LEVERAGED BUYOUTS of public companies generally fit this description.

flip-in   The most important characteristic of the most effective RIGHTS PLAN (POISON PILL) in use today. It gives SHAREHOLDERS the right to buy the company's shares at half price when someone becomes an 'INTERESTED SHAREHOLDER,' that is, crosses some stock ownership threshold such as 15 or 20%. The interested shareholder's rights are void. Other shareholders can (typically) use each of their rights to buy a number of shares equal to two times the exercise price (set in advance), divided by the current market price of the target company's stock. Usually, from the standpoint of a bidder, the flip-in right is a complete show stopper unless the bidder can convince a court that it should intervene. In the text we have tried to describe when courts intervene against poison pills under Delaware law. See Chapter 8 and Chapter 14 Section 2. However, since several important states (not Delaware) have recently legalized the device by statute, it is difficult to generalize about when a court will intervene. The name itself has no commonsense significance. It is part of history. *See* FLIP-OVER, RIGHTS PLAN.

flip-over   A provision in a POISON PILL that gives SHAREHOLDERS the right to buy the company's shares (or the shares of the surviving company after a MERGER) at half price. Unlike a FLIP-IN, a flip-over right does not become effective simply because an INTERESTED SHAREHOLDER buys some stock. Usually it becomes effective when (i) there is an interested shareholder and (ii) the company engages in certain transactions with the interested shareholder or an affiliate, such as a merger or a sale of all or a large part of its assets. Historically, the flip-over poison pill was devised several years before the more powerful flip-in. At that time the essential discrimination against the interested shareholder that the flip-in entails was widely considered illegal. Now the two are generally combined, although under most circumstances the flip-in provision of the pill dominates any potential bidder's attention.

foothold   The shares of a target acquired secretly by a bidder before news of the possibility of a bid reaches the market. For a time foothold positions were considered a very important hedge for bidders against losing out to higher bids. However, in the U.S., foothold positions in large targets have become much less important. SEC rules require a public filing within 10 days after acquiring 5% of the target's outstanding shares. More important, the HART–SCOTT–RODINO provisions of the antitrust laws require a filing when a bidder reaches $15 million or, if less, 15% of the target's outstanding shares. This $15 million limitation, now very hard to avoid legally, usually makes foothold accumulations of little practical value in large transactions. Other considerations such as a concern about loss of secrecy and tact (a hope for a friendly deal) often persuade a bidder that such a small foothold is not worthwhile. *See* 13D.

14D–1   When written with an upper-case 'D', a detailed SEC schedule specifying information that must be included by bidders in TENDER OFFER circulars and related filings with the SEC. With a lower-case 'd', a detailed SEC rule governing tender offers. Both are issued under Section 14(d) of the Securities Exchange Act of 1934. Rule 14d and Section 14(d) are included in the Appendix.

fraud   A term in securities law that covers a range of illegal actions far greater than its ordinary meaning might suggest. *See* ANTIFRAUD RULES.

free-rider paradox   Sometimes benefits and costs cannot be allocated accurately or at all to users by the markets or otherwise. A free rider tries to take advantage of this situation. The paradox is that if everyone tries to free ride no one can and everyone is worse off. An important example is the natural environment. Most industrial users of the natural environment are free riders. Everyone collectively is worse off but no one individually finds it worthwhile to stop. In takeovers, an important recent example is the basic research part of corporate research and development. It is impossible to limit the benefits from basic research to the corporation who pays the bill. Therefore, there will be a strong temptation for companies to free ride. Competition in the product and takeover markets should increase this temptation. In the text we also discuss the disagreement as to whether target SHAREHOLDERS are tempted to free ride on the presumed superior insights of bidders by holding back on tendering their shares. Free riding is closely related to the PRISONER'S DILEMMA. Both deal with situations where cooperation would be a solution but is hard to achieve without legal intervention. *See* APPRAISAL RIGHT, DISSENT, EXTERNALITIES, LEVERAGED BUYOUT, SQUEEZE-OUT MERGER.

friendly transaction   A NEGOTIATED TRANSACTION.

front end   *See* FRONT-END LOADED, TWO-STEP DEAL.

front-end loaded   Said of a TENDER OFFER for a TWO-STEP DEAL in which the consideration offered for shares in the tender offer (the front end) exceeds that which will be paid in the subsequent SQUEEZE-OUT MERGER (the back end). The idea is to encourage or coerce tendering by SHAREHOLDERS who will not want to be relegated to the back end. Now quite rare in the U.S. The compensation of advisers is also usually front-end loaded: they are paid long before the consequences of their advice unfold. This, of course, encourages bias.

going private transaction   A single SHAREHOLDER or a small group of investors acquiring all the shares of a public company. Two of the most important examples are the elimination of MINORITY SHAREHOLDERS in public companies by the majority shareholder in a SQUEEZE-OUT MERGER and LEVERAGED BUYOUTS of public companies. Usually in these cases, the shareholders have the right to DISSENT and have their shares appraised. They may also have the right to sue for breach of FIDUCIARY DUTY. The SEC has special disclosure rules (contained in Rule 13e–3) for these transactions, which are therefore often called 13e–3 transactions. *See* APPRAISAL RIGHT.

golden handcuffs   A lucrative executive employment agreement designed to bind the executive to the company by providing significant contingent compensation that would be lost if he or she left the company prematurely.

golden handshake   A lucrative severance package for an executive designed to avoid contention and bad publicity after a firing.

golden parachute   An employment contract for an executive that gives (often lucrative) benefits if there is a change in control of the company (single trigger) or if there is a change in control and the executive's employment is terminated (double trigger). Complex tax rules apply as the result of a misguided attempt to discourage the practice. Golden parachutes are usually not a takeover defense because they do not cost the buyer enough to be a significant economic deterrent. In fact, they may be an important factor in helping to mitigate managers' natural inclination to resist a HOSTILE BID.

good faith   A standard courts often use in looking at the behavior of BOARDS OF DIRECTORS and managements in takeover cases. There is no esoteric meaning here. The question is, did they believe in what they did and said or were they just faking and trying to fool SHAREHOLDERS and courts with empty rhetoric?

greenmail   A target company's purchase of its own shares at a premium price to fend off a would-be acquirer of the company. Greenmail payments are highly controversial and have declined sharply in the U.S. recently.

grey knight   A second bidder in a hostile takeover about whom management of the target has misgivings -- the grey knight may outbid the first bidder but it may not be clear whether being acquired by the grey knight would be preferable. *See* WHITE KNIGHT.

HLT *See* HIGHLY LEVERAGED TRANSACTION.

Hart–Scott–Rodino filing The antitrust notice filing under the Hart–Scott–Rodino Antitrust Improvements Act of 1976. Filing of extensive information is required for most acquisitions of either 15% or $15 million of a target company's stock. However, filing is not required for up to 10% with no dollar limit if the purchase is for investment only. After the filing the buyer must wait while the Justice Department and Federal Trade Commission decide whether to oppose the acquisition. For TENDER OFFERS the waiting period is 15 days plus another 10 days if additional information is requested; for other types of acquisitions the waiting periods are 30 days plus another 20 days. When additional information is requested the 10- and 20-day additional waiting periods do not begin to run until the government determines that the information provided is complete. In most acquisitions of companies worth more than $300 million the need for this filing is the most important limitation on the bidder's ability to accumulate shares in advance of a takeover bid. *See* FOOTHOLD, 13D.

highly confident letter A letter from an investment bank or commercial bank to a bidder stating that it is highly confident (or some similar formulation) that funds can be raised for an acquisition, usually through JUNK BONDS, SUBORDINATED DEBT, secured bank borrowings or BRIDGE LOANS. Many takeover bids are started on the basis of a highly confident letter rather than a firm COMMITMENT LETTER.

highly leveraged transaction Since late 1989 a set of bank regulatory policies has restricted bank lending in 'highly leveraged transactions.' It is commonly believed that these regulatory policies have been an important factor in reducing the number of LBO transactions and other HLTs in the U.S. *See* Interagency Definition by the Federal Reserve Board, Comptroller of the Currency and FDIC (October 1989) and related Interagency Interpretive Guidelines (Feb. 1990).

hold-separate order An order of a court or administrative agency requiring an acquirer to hold a newly acquired business separate from its other businesses while a legal claim (usually antitrust) is being decided. Sometimes there is no order, only an agreement with a governmental agency. Hold-separate orders are a compromise that allows acquisitions to go ahead. If the case is ultimately decided against the defendant it will be simpler to dispose of the asset than if full integration with the other businesses had taken place. However, the compromise is not always acceptable since neither buyer nor seller may be willing to assume the risk of having to sell the assets at an unknown later date. *See* RESCISSION.

hostile bid An effort to gain control of a target company that has not been agreed to by the target's management and board, usually through a TENDER OFFER or an unsolicited proposal to the board. Sometimes called an unnegotiated or UNSOLICITED BID. *See* NEGOTIATED TRANSACTION.

indemnification of directors State corporation laws permit corporations to indemnify directors against some liabilities and expenses of litigation. In some instances the law requires indemnification, for example, when the director has been successful in his legal defense. However, judgments for damages (and settlements of claims) under some of the Federal securities laws probably are not indemnifiable although as a practical matter they are probably insurable. *See* DIRECTORS' AND OFFICERS' LIABILITY INSURANCE.

independent director A director of a corporation who is not an officer of the corporation and has no personal stake in the transaction under consideration. Independent directors now make up a majority on most boards of large corporations because of legal and market pressures. *See* SPECIAL COMMITTEE.

insider information NON-PUBLIC INFORMATION about a company in the hands of insiders such as directors, officers and employees of the company. The term generally also includes non-public information that has been passed on by insiders to relatives or other favored persons. In the U.S., there is no general legal prohibition against trading by insiders. However, it is illegal under the Federal securities laws for insiders to trade using material inside information before it has been publicly disclosed. The same prohibition applies to people (tipees) who have received the information from insiders. It is also a violation of Federal insider trading laws for anyone to use material non-public information that is obtained unlawfully (e.g., by breach of trust or stealing) for trading in securities. In the case of TENDER OFFER information there is an even more restrictive rule (14e–3, reproduced in the Appendix, A.2.5) which dispenses with the condition that the information was obtained unlawfully. However, the SEC's statutory power to issue this rule was questioned in a recent U.S. Court of Appeals decision. *U.S.* v. *Chestman*, Fed. Sec. L. Rep. ¶ 95,214 (CCH) (2d Cir. 1990). Materiality of the information can be understood best from a commonsense standpoint. If the information is the reason for the trading, it is highly likely to be considered material by the SEC and the courts. Trading by true insiders appears not to have been an important factor in the insider trading scandals of the 1980s in the U.S. although illegal trading using non-public information was. SEC ANTIFRAUD RULE 10b–5 (reproduced in the Appendix, A.1.2), as interpreted in SEC rulings and court decisions, is the main source of most U.S. insider trading law. Insider trading is a crime and subject to civil damages and penalties. *See* FRAUD, SHORT-SWING TRADING.

institutional investor A large professional investor that invests money it holds as a fiduciary in stocks, bonds and other securities. Important examples are pension funds, insurance companies and mutual funds. Institutional investors play a large, controversial role in the takeover market as SHAREHOLDERS and BONDHOLDERS in targets and as lenders to and investors in bidders. In theory their long-term interests should transcend their interests in short-run profits from the sale of target shares in takeovers. However, for legal and practical reasons, institutions appear unable to cooperate with one another effectively as shareholders. *See* PRISONER'S DILEMMA.

interested shareholder   A term that turns up in state ANTITAKEOVER LAWS, antitakeover CHARTER provisions (FAIR PRICE PROVISION and SUPERMAJORITY PROVISION) and POISON PILLS. When a SHAREHOLDER passes a threshold percentage of the outstanding voting shares it becomes an interested shareholder and subject to the restrictions imposed by the statute, charter provision or poison pill. A range from 10% to 30% includes most of the percentages used. *See* FLIP-IN.

junior lender   *See* SUBORDINATED DEBT.

junk bonds   Bonds and other debt securities that pay high rates of interest to compensate for high risk. Their widespread acceptance by INSTITUTIONAL INVESTORS was an important innovation in the U.S. takeover market during the 1980s. In the last half of 1989 junk bonds suddenly became much more difficult to sell. The prospects for the junk bond market are not clear.

LBO   A LEVERAGED BUYOUT.

letter of intent   A very general letter outlining a transaction and signed before the detailed, definitive agreement is ready. It may or may not be legally binding, depending on its terms and the conduct of the parties. It serves as the preliminary milestone in some acquisitions but is not common in acquisitions of public companies, mainly because it tips the parties' plans to possible competing bidders before the parties are ready. *See* CLOSING.

level playing field   A fair set of rules applicable to all players. In takeover usage the term usually refers to rules established by sellers to deal with bidders. Unless there are complications caused by representations, promises or conflicts of interest, it is not clear why a seller owes a level playing field obligation to bidders.

leveraged buyout (LBO)   The acquisition of a corporation or division where a very high percentage of the purchase price is obtained by borrowing. If the management of the target company has a large participation it is also called a management buyout (MBO). A likely leveraged buyout range of prices has become a standard against which other bids are measured. *See* FAIRNESS OPINION.

lockup   An option on some of a takeover target's important assets (occasionally stock) given by the target to a favored buyer. The purpose is to discourage competing bids. Sometimes a lockup is used by a target board to obtain a last very high bid. Lockups are considered highly controversial and legally risky.

market sweep   *See* STREET SWEEP.

MBO   A management buyout. A LEVERAGED BUYOUT in which management has a large participation. The term is just beginning to be common in the United States; it is more common in Britain.

merger A statutory combination of two corporations. In the merger one of the companies becomes a part of the other and disappears as a legal entity. The surviving corporation is left with all of the assets and liabilities of the other, whose SHAREHOLDERS usually receive cash or securities of the survivor or its parent in exchange for their stock. Mergers are a form of corporate action and require a BOARD OF DIRECTORS' recommendation and shareholder approval. TENDER OFFERS on the other hand can be made directly to shareholders. This is an extremely important distinction and is the reason for many of the takeover and antitakeover practices in the U.S. *See* SHORT-FORM MERGER, SQUEEZE-OUT MERGER, TWO-STEP DEAL.

merger of equals A MERGER which (regardless of the legal form or which company legally survives) is intended as a combination of two businesses rather than an acquisition of one by another. Little or no premium is paid for the shares of either. Generally, both CEOs retain important positions and the new BOARD OF DIRECTORS is made up of representatives of both companies. Mergers of equals have been considered very risky by managements because they expose both companies to competing bids. The Time–Warner merger described in the text barely survived the competing bid by Paramount but had to radically change the form of the transaction and the price to do it.

mezzanine financing *See* SUBORDINATED DEBT.

minority shareholders When a single SHAREHOLDER or organized group of shareholders has a majority of the voting power, the remaining shareholders are minority shareholders. Rights of the minority versus the majority provide many of the most controversial issues in corporation law in the U.S. *See* APPRAISAL RIGHT, DISSENT, GOING PRIVATE TRANSACTION, SQUEEZE-OUT MERGER.

NASDAQ The automated (computer) quotation system of the National Association of Securities Dealers, which oversees the over-the-counter market. In practice, NASDAQ serves as a securities exchange without a trading floor for securities not listed on stock exchanges. Before NASDAQ, prices for over-the-counter securities were only available by telephone and by printed sheets that quickly became stale. The development of NASDAQ has meant that there is no longer a great benefit from the standpoint of liquidity to being listed on a stock exchange. However, there still appear to be important reputation benefits from stock exchange listing, particularly on the New York Stock Exchange.

negotiated transaction An acquisition or other transaction between companies in which both sides are willing participants. Because of state ANTITAKEOVER LAWS and target takeover defenses, such as POISON PILLS, most successful HOSTILE BIDS are in the end negotiated because there is no other practical choice for the bidder or the target.

no-action letter A form of written advice given by the staff of the SEC to lawyers. It is given in response to a request letter and is limited to the facts of a particular proposed undertaking. Generally, the advice concerns an ambiguity or apparently illogical result under the SEC laws or rules. If the request is granted, the staff says that, based upon the facts described, *it* (the staff) would not recommend that the Commission take any action against the conduct described. In theory, grant of a no-action letter does not foreclose private lawsuits or even prevent some action by the Commission itself. However, in practice the letter generally would be given great weight by a court.

non-public information   Information about public companies that is not generally available to the trading public. All INSIDER INFORMATION is non-public but not all non-public information is insider information. The term non-public information includes information obtained by conventional securities research, by breach of trust and by stealing. Generally in the U.S. it is legal to trade on non-public information that has not been obtained illegally. However, even this apparently innocuous statement may not be true where the trading is on material TENDER OFFER information and the trader knows or has reason to know that the information came from the offeror, target or anyone closely connected with any of them, such as a conventional insider, investment banker or lawyer (SEC Rule 14e-3). In that case, it is illegal to use material non-public information for trading. Recently the statutory authority of the SEC to issue this rule was questioned in *U.S.* v. *Chestman*, Fed. Sec. L. Rep. ¶ 95,214 (CCH) (2d Cir. 1990). Although most of the recent insider trading scandals associated with takeovers have not involved true insiders, non-public information obtained by breach of trust or stealing has been an important element in them. *See* ANTIFRAUD RULES, FRAUD and Rule 14e-3 in the Appendix, A.2.5.

no-shop provision   A provision in an acquisition agreement that prohibits the seller from searching for a better offer before the acquisition is completed or the agreement is terminated. However, the seller may not be prohibited from negotiating with an unsolicited bidder. The subject is complicated by disagreements over the FIDUCIARY DUTIES of target directors in this situation. But the trend in negotiations now appears to be to acknowledge that generally target directors must for legal or practical reasons be allowed to at least consider unsolicited bids.

one-share-one-vote   A rule that all common shares in a company must have equal voting power. The SEC's Rule 19c-4 on the subject was overturned by a court in 1990.

parachute   *See* GOLDEN PARACHUTE, SILVER PARACHUTE, TIN PARACHUTE.

plaintiffs' lawyer   A lawyer who engages in SHAREHOLDER LITIGATION against corporations on behalf of plaintiff shareholders. Generally the plaintiffs are small shareholders who have no important stakes in the outcomes of the cases. The real economic interest in these cases is held by the lawyers, who are awarded fees by the court based on results achieved and hours worked. *See* APPRAISAL RIGHT, CLASS ACTION, DERIVATIVE SUIT.

poison pill   A shareholder RIGHTS PLAN used as a defense against takeovers. The term is also used more broadly to cover any device that has an antitakeover effect, particularly if it is initiated by a target BOARD OF DIRECTORS without shareholder approval. *See* FLIP-IN, FLIP-OVER.

pooling-of-interests accounting   A method of accounting for MERGERS and other BUSINESS COMBINATIONS that adds together the financial statements of the combining companies, eliminating the need to show good will in the financial statements of the acquiring company. Although the rules for its use are complex, the main element is that the SHAREHOLDERS of the combining companies must receive or retain mainly common stock. *See* PURCHASE ACCOUNTING.

preferred stock   An early type of hybrid security, still in common use, that has some characteristics of both an EQUITY SECURITY and a DEBT SECURITY. It usually has a fixed dividend that must be paid before common stock dividends and, in liquidation, a claim that comes before common stock but after debt claims. Preferred stock is usually callable by the issuer after a certain time in accordance with a contract schedule of prices. It may have general voting rights or may have a vote only in special situations. As with all hybrid securities the characteristics of preferred stock may be varied to meet different circumstances.

prisoner's dilemma   A mathematician's puzzle used to analyze strategic problems such as takeovers where cooperation is important. The following matrix shows the puzzle in short form:

		Second Prisoner	
		C	–C
First Prisoner	C	10, 10	0, 20
	–C	20, 0	1, 1

Confession = C   Refusal to confess = –C

The numbers in the matrix represent prison sentences in years. The optimum result for both prisoners who have been arrested for the same crime is (–C, –C) in the fourth quadrant. They cooperate with each other, refuse to confess, and each receives a one-year sentence. However, if the first prisoner can exploit the second, the optimum result for him is (C, –C) in the second quadrant. He escapes without any sentence while the second prisoner receives a 20-year sentence. Conversely the second prisoner gets an optimum result in the third quadrant (–C, C). The dilemma is that if each prisoner tries to exploit the other, they end up in the first quadrant (C, C). Each receives a 10-year term. In TENDER OFFERS, SHAREHOLDERS of target companies are placed in a prisoner's dilemma. Tendering immediately can be equated with confessing. The dilemma is moderated by the tender offer rules which slow down the tender offer process and, acting as a substitute for cooperation, encourage competing bids. Defensive actions of

BOARDS OF DIRECTORS provide a cooperative solution. In fact, it is a perfect solution unless we suspect the board of conflict of interest. FREE RIDING is a result of a failure to find a cooperative solution and is important in takeovers. In voting, for example, most shareholders free ride by voting with management or not voting. They act on the assumption that better informed large shareholders will save the day if something is really wrong. In the prisoner's dilemma example, one could say that each prisoner is attempting to free ride on the gullibility of the other. See also our discussion in Chapter 2 Section 1.

proxy contest or proxy fight A contest for control of a company by soliciting SHAREHOLDER votes for the election of slates of directors. Usually the incumbent slate has a very big advantage unless the insurgents control a large block of stock: 20% or more. The process is regulated by the SEC's proxy regulations and state corporation law. *See* FREE-RIDER PARADOX, PRISONER'S DILEMMA.

purchase accounting Usually the only alternative to POOLING-OF-INTERESTS ACCOUNTING. In purchase accounting the financial statements of the acquiring company must include a good will account for the difference between the price paid for the acquisition and the fair market value of the individual assets (other than good will) of the company that is acquired. In the U.S. good will must be amortized in equal annual installments over 40 years or less and is not deductible for Federal income taxes.

put A right to sell a security or other asset at a specified or formula price. Some POISON PILLS and ANTITAKEOVER LAWS contain features allowing shareholders to put their shares to the company of the bidder if there is a takeover attempt. *See* APPRAISAL RIGHT, FAIR PRICE PROVISION.

recapitalization A change in the capital structure of a company. In the last few years recapitalizations in the U.S. usually have been associated with takeover defense or the restructuring of highly leveraged acquisitions. When used as a takeover defense, their main characteristic is a sharp substitution of debt for equity. Cash generated by the increase in debt is paid to the SHAREHOLDERS as a special dividend or by repurchasing shares in a SELF-TENDER or in the market. In some recapitalizations the percentage of equity held by public shareholders is unchanged but in some the percentage is reduced in favor of management, an ESOP or an outside group that provides financing and advice. The most important distinction between a recapitalization and a LEVERAGED BUYOUT is that public shareholders retain some of the equity in a recapitalization. One disadvantage of recapitalizations compared with LBOs is that they sometimes leave the company with a negative net worth on its balance sheet. An antitakeover effect is obtained by increasing the market value of the company. Cash paid out to the shareholders plus the market value of the remaining equity has a greater market value than the original equity. Why this happens is not obvious. It appears that shareholders prefer to have the cash in hand or maybe they like to have their managements heavily burdened by debt rather than flush with cash. In restructurings of highly leveraged acquisitions publicly held debt is usually acquired at a discount from face value using the proceeds of new equity and borrowing. *See* DUAL CLASS RECAPITALIZATION, RESTRUCTURING.

receiver Someone a court appoints to run a corporation in extraordinary circumstances when ordinary corporate government breaks down. In bankruptcy in the U.S., the receiver is called a trustee. When a company is being reorganized under the bankruptcy laws, the management generally stays in charge subject to close supervision by the bankruptcy court and committees representing creditors and shareholders. This combination has many of the characteristics of a receiver.

reincorporation The process of moving a corporation's place of incorporation from one state to another. This is accomplished by a merger into a shell corporation incorporated in the new state and requires SHAREHOLDER approval. Recently, it has become difficult for corporations to reincorporate in other states for antitakeover reasons because of opposition from INSTITUTIONAL INVESTOR shareholders.

rescission The undoing of a contract or transaction to restore the status quo. A common statutory remedy for FRAUD and similar legal violations in the sale of securities. However, it is rarely available after acquisitions of public companies. Once the CLOSING has occurred it is not practical to get money back from public SHAREHOLDERS and undo the integration of businesses. Compare HOLD-SEPARATE ORDER.

restructuring A very general term covering many kinds of reorganization of a business, such as a RECAPITALIZATION, a sale of a number of businesses or a reorganization of the chain of command.

rights plan A POISON PILL containing a FLIP-IN or a FLIP-OVER. Also called share purchase rights plan or shareholder rights plan.

SEC The U.S. Securities and Exchange Commission. The Commissioners establish rules under the Federal securities laws and act as an administrative tribunal. The SEC staff reviews and comments on securities law filings, provides informal advice to lawyers and issues NO-ACTION LETTERS when the securities laws are ambiguous or appear to require an illogical result under the circumstances. The SEC can also bring civil suits in the courts and participate with the Department of Justice in the prosecution of criminal cases to enforce the Federal securities laws.

secured lender In theory a lender (usually a bank) with a claim on specific assets in case its loan is not paid. However, under U.S. bankruptcy law the theory does not always work. Nonetheless, a secured lender will have a high priority claim in the bankruptcy proceeding.

self-dealing Having an interest in both sides of a transaction. A director of a corporation may be involved in a transaction with a company he owns or manages; managers may try to sell a public company to themselves in a LEVERAGED BUYOUT; or the owner of a majority of the shares of a corporation may want to merge it with another corporation it owns. All of these transactions raise conflict of interest concerns. However, the phrase does not necessarily connote illegal or immoral conduct. Some self-dealing transactions can be perfectly fair to all parties. Generally special procedures have to be followed to assure that self-dealing transactions are legal. State corporation statutes, court decisions and POISON PILLS all provide restrictions on self-dealing transactions.

self-tender   A TENDER OFFER by a company for its own shares. These are subject to special SEC rules.

senior lender   A lender (usually a bank) with the highest (non-exclusive) priority claim on a borrower. Sometimes senior lenders have an exclusive claim on specific assets, in which case they are SECURED LENDERS. However, quite often senior lenders are unsecured by assets of the borrower. In that case the loan agreement would usually prohibit giving security to any other creditor unless the senior lender receives proportional security. *See* SUBORDINATED DEBT.

share purchase rights plan   *See* RIGHTS PLAN.

shareholder   Following the usage in the Federal securities laws we have used the term shareholder to refer to the holders of common (and, depending on the context, preferred) stock of a corporation. Under Delaware law the term is STOCKHOLDER. *See* EQUITY SECURITY, PREFERRED STOCK.

shareholder litigation   The most important types of shareholder litigation are CLASS ACTIONS and DERIVATIVE SUITS. Generally the plaintiff is a small shareholder who does not have an important economic interest in the case. Occasionally, large shareholders bring their own suits but that is not mainstream shareholder litigation. Special characteristics of shareholder litigation are:

1 PLAINTIFFS' LAWYERS have the main economic interest in these cases. Naturally, their goal is to earn the largest possible fee.

2 To prevent collusive settlements between plaintiffs' lawyers and defendants, these cases cannot be settled without notice to shareholders and a court hearing.

3 Plaintiffs' lawyers' fees in these cases are set after a hearing by the court in which the case was tried. Fees are based on a difficult-to-fathom combination of the result achieved in the case and the number of hours worked.

In the U.S., shareholder litigation plays an important role in the enforcement of the Federal securities laws and director and officer fiduciary obligations under state corporation law. In these cases important public policy issues often are resolved in the context of the private disputes. Shareholder litigation appears to be far more effective as a discouragement to wrongdoing than as a method for compensating shareholders who have been damaged. The use of hours worked as a standard for the award of fees has turned out to be a bad choice because it discourages early settlement. Originally the standard was adopted because it appeared more moral. Some lawyers and judges objected to the very large fees awarded to plaintiffs' lawyers when they achieved large recoveries. They thought it made the profession look like freeloaders. On the other hand the hourly standard has all the disadvantages of cost-plus contracting. It encourages waste. The Delaware courts have never adopted the hourly standard.

shareholder rights plan   *See* RIGHTS PLAN.

short-form merger   A special kind of parent–subsidiary merger. Generally, mergers require a SHAREHOLDER vote but in most states if one company is the parent of the other and owns a very large percentage of its shares (in Delaware, at least 90%) it may eliminate the minority in a squeeze-out with only the approval of the parent's BOARD OF DIRECTORS. However, dissenters are still entitled to APPRAISAL RIGHTS and directors owe the same FIDUCIARY DUTY to the MINORITY SHAREHOLDERS with regard to fairness of price and procedure. *See* DISSENT.

short-swing trading   As defined in §16 of the Securities Exchange Act of 1934, a purchase and sale or a sale and purchase of an EQUITY SECURITY within a six-month period by an insider. Under §16(b) of that Act, if an insider engages in short-swing trading, the profits belong to the company. There are no criminal sanctions. The statute is enforced quite effectively by PLAINTIFFS' LAWYERS in SHAREHOLDER LITIGATION. Insiders are required by §16(a) of the Act to file monthly reports of trades of an equity security. This makes the statute easy to enforce. An insider is defined in the statute as a director, officer or 10% shareholder of the company. Section 16(b) is the only true insider trading rule in the U.S. since it applies to all insider short-swing trading without regard to whether INSIDER INFORMATION is used. *See* FRAUD, NON-PUBLIC INFORMATION.

silver parachute   A parachute for an executive that is not quite generous enough to be called golden. *See* GOLDEN PARACHUTE.

special committee   An ad-hoc committee of a BOARD OF DIRECTORS made up only of disinterested, INDEPENDENT DIRECTORS, to which an important board responsibility is referred when some members of the full board have a conflict of interest, such as being bidders for the company in an MBO .

squeeze-out merger   A merger designed to eliminate minority interests in a company. The common stock owned by the MINORITY SHAREHOLDERS is converted into cash or occasionally stock or DEBT SECURITIES of the parent company. Squeeze-outs can be accomplished in most states for the sole purpose of elim-inating the minority. No other reason need be given. State law requires fair treatment of the minority and, in many circumstances, grants them APPRAISAL RIGHTS. Shareholders also have the right to sue for breach of FIDUCIARY DUTY when they are complaining about something more than the price, for example, unfairness in the procedures used to determine the price or inadequacy of the disclosures. See BUSINESS PURPOSE DOCTRINE, DISSENT, GOING PRIVATE TRANS-ACTION, SHAREHOLDER LITIGATION, SHORT-FORM MERGER.

staggered board   A CLASSIFIED BOARD.

standstill agreement   An agreement not to buy additional shares or to solicit proxies for a period of years. These agreements are used frequently when a threatened takeover is settled short of takeover; when a large block of shares is sold privately by the issuer; and when a block of shares is purchased privately by the issuer. *See* BLOCKING PREFERRED STOCK, GREENMAIL.

stock appreciation right   A right used to compensate executives that resembles a stock option in value but gives no right to purchase stock and does not require payment for exercise. When the SAR is exercised the holder receives cash equal to the amount by which the price of the stock has increased over the price at the time the SAR was issued. In comparison to stock options, the employee benefits because no cash outlay is required for exercise. Holders generally can defer paying income tax until they actually receive the cash. From an employer standpoint, the main disadvantage is that after exercise the employee is no longer motivated by the equivalent of an equity interest.

stock parking   A concealment of the ownership of stock by holding it in someone else's name. This is illegal if it assists violations of disclosure requirements in the securities laws and the HART–SCOTT–RODINO statute. Some of the major 1980s Wall Street criminal prosecutions involved stock parking.

stockholder   *See* SHAREHOLDER.

street sweep   A substantial accumulation of shares of a takeover target, often in a matter of hours, through market purchases and privately negotiated transactions. The purchases are usually from ARBITRAGERS and institutions. Street sweeps generally are only possible after shares have been accumulated and held by arbitragers. If arbitragers have had enough time to assess the market it is easier to accomplish. The key legal issue is whether the street sweep is an illegal TENDER OFFER. This depends on the facts. An illegal tender offer can create big problems for the buyer.

subordinated debt   Money borrowed from a JUNIOR LENDER who has agreed that his claims will come behind those of SENIOR LENDERS. There are different types of subordination and subordination agreements can be very complex. Subordinated debt is very important in LBOs, where it is often called mezzanine financing.

Superfund   A commonly used name for a series of Federal environmental clean-up statutes enacted in the 1980s under the title, 'Comprehensive Environmental Response, Compensation and Liability Act,' often called CERCLA. The name Superfund comes from a Federal fund used for environmental clean-up that is derived from taxing the chemical, petroleum and other industries that generate hazardous substances. However, most clean-ups under Superfund must be paid for by the persons who created the problem. The law also gives the Federal Government a powerful financial tool in the form of high priority liens ('Super-liens') designed to compel enforcement. Superfund is important in takeovers because of the huge potential liabilities that may be hidden away in targets.

supermajority provision   A provision of a CHARTER requiring that a proposal obtain the support of more than a majority of the outstanding shares; for example, a requirement that there be 80% approval for MERGERS which, in Delaware, would otherwise only require a majority. Often supermajority provisions are an alternative or an addition to a FAIR PRICE PROVISION.

Supreme Court   A court of last resort, from which there can ordinarily be no further appeal. Depending on the context, either the U.S. Supreme Court or the highest court in a state. However, in some states the highest state court has a different name: Court of Appeals for New York, Supreme Judicial Court for Massachusetts; and in New York the trial court of general jurisdiction is called the Supreme Court.

takeover law   An ANTITAKEOVER LAW.

tender offer   A public bid for shares. Congress and the SEC have deliberately refrained from defining tender offer for fear that the innovative takeover market would find ways to circumvent a definition. Nevertheless all tender offers must comply with the WILLIAMS ACT, for example, by being held open for 20 business days and offering all SHAREHOLDERS an equal chance to participate. *See* FRONT-END LOADED, STREET SWEEP, TWO-STEP DEAL.

13D   Schedule 13D is the form prescribed under Rule 13d by the SEC for reporting purchases of more than 5% of an issuer's shares. It must be filed within ten days after the threshold is passed. During this ten-day period additional shares can be accumulated unless there is some other legal prohibition such as the HART-SCOTT-RODINO rules. *See* FOOTHOLD.

tin parachute   Valuable but not necessarily lavish parachute contracts extended to a wide range of employees, not just to senior executives. For example, in early 1990 Eastman Kodak Co. adopted a plan that would give all its 80,000 U.S. employees severance pay, health and life insurance benefits and assistance in finding new jobs if they were fired after a takeover. Some state laws now require the payment of similar termination benefits. Compare GOLDEN PARACHUTE.

topping fee   A type of BREAK-UP FEE paid to the acquirer in a friendly acquisition of a public company. Its purpose is to give the buyer some recompense in case it loses out to another bidder offering a higher price. The fee is a percentage of the amount by which the successful bidder's purchase price exceeds the price that is being topped. *See* FIDUCIARY OUT.

two-step deal   A negotiated or hostile acquisition done in two stages – a TENDER OFFER in which the bidder buys enough stock to obtain control, followed by a

SQUEEZE-OUT MERGER in which it obtains the remaining shares. The purpose is speed. Under U.S. legal rules cash tender offers can be completed much faster than MERGERS. If SHAREHOLDERS receive less in the merger (back end) than in the tender offer (front end) the acquisition proposal is said to be FRONT-END LOADED. Front-end loaded acquisitions are no longer common in the U.S. because of shareholder and judicial resistance. *See* COERCIVE OFFER.

two-tier offer A proposal for a TWO-STEP DEAL.

Unocal **rule** A modification of the BUSINESS JUDGMENT RULE used by courts in Delaware for evaluating takeover defenses. It requires that a response by the target's BOARD OF DIRECTORS be reasonable in relation to the threat to corporate policies posed by the bidder. The rule was announced by the Delaware SUPREME COURT in the case of *Unocal Corp.* v. *Mesa Petroleum Co.*, 493 A.2d 946 (Delaware Supreme Court 1985), in which the court approved a discriminatory defensive SELF-TENDER by Unocal to all its shareholders except Mesa. The rule makes it easier for courts to explain their decisions but is so general that it is of limited value in making predictions of what courts will do. See Chapter 2.

unsolicited bid Usually, a HOSTILE BID.

white knight A friendly bidder who volunteers or is solicited by a target as an alternative to a pending or anticipated HOSTILE BID.

white squire Someone who purchases a large position in the stock (usually PREFERRED STOCK) of a company as a takeover defense for the company. Generally the purchase is made directly from the company. A WHITE KNIGHT, on the other hand, seeks to buy the company. There is a risk that white squire arrangements will wind up less amicably than the target management and board may have expected when they negotiated the purchase. *See* BLOCKING PREFERRED STOCK.

Williams Act Sections 13d and 14 of the Securities Exchange Act of 1934 reproduced in the Appendix, A.2.1 and A.2.2. These contain the Federal statutes governing disclosures of accumulations of shares and TENDER OFFERS. The SEC has authority to prescribe rules to carry out the intent of these laws. See Appendix, A.2.3 to A.2.5. Occasionally an SEC rule expands the laws' coverage and is struck down by a court. The legal authority of the SEC to issue its ONE-SHARE-ONE-VOTE Rule 19c–4 recently was successfully attacked in the U.S. Court of Appeals in Washington, DC. See Chapter 9 Section 2. The decision suggests that the SEC rule against discriminatory tender offers, Rule 14d–10 (Appendix, A.2.4) may also be vulnerable.

winner's curse It helps to begin with a simple historical example, bids for oil and gas drilling rights. Ideally, oil companies who bid should have approximately the same information, technology and uses for the oil and gas. In that case, the arithmetic mean of the bids should be the best estimate of the real value of the rights. Not always correct, but correct on the average if the same procedure were repeated many times. It would appear then that a winning bid much over the mean must be over-optimistic and bring with it the winner's curse, a tendency to overpay. But we should also expect that oil companies would become familiar with this problem and adjust their bids to avoid the winner's curse. However, these bidders for oil and gas drilling rights may not all have the same information nor the same uses for the reserves. There are similar problems in takeover bidding, and similar problems in trying to adjust bids. Except for FINANCIAL BUYERS, takeover bidders usually do not have much repeated experience with takeover bids. Their advisers, such as investment bankers, do. But they may have a bias to be over-optimistic since they are usually paid much more when bids are successful, which they are more likely to be if the bid is high. Financial buyers, who usually do have extensive experience with takeover bidding, may have their own bias toward over-optimism when they receive large front-end fees for completing acquisitions. For these reasons, the winner's curse may provide a valuable insight into why bidders appear, in many cases, to be overpaying for acquisitions. See Chapter 11.

Subject Index

global economic empire, and public–private cooperation saw completion of the modern dream of the Channel Tunnel between England and France. On the other hand, however, privateer shipping was a 'feeble and corrupt system' where leading officials promoted partnership ventures with a 'motive of plunder', and the fragile financial position of the Channel Tunnel has now left citizens, governments and private investors all with huge uncertainties and losses. Arguments over efficiency, service quality and accountability in the two sectors have certainly been 'well rehearsed'[6] over centuries.

Governments always play language-games. To a large degree it is the very nature of political communication. What we choose to emphasize, how this is characterized and the word-pictures we present to others in our discussions all amount to a language-choice. Those supporting PPPs tend to emphasize the positive parts of past government–business interactions and characterize today's PPPs as simply an extension of historical economic development. For example, legal contracts are labelled 'partnerships' rather than 'commercial deals', and privatized finance is labelled a 'partnership arrangement' rather than a 'mega-credit card' to which governments sign up. On the other hand, those critical of today's PPPs emphasize the negative parts of past government–business interactions and call for corruption failures, for example, not to be repeated. Language-games are clearly applied every day to the PPP phenomenon. And in the land of claims and counter-claims during public policy debates, such language-games do indeed matter.[7]

Of equal importance is the governance perspective, that is, viewing PPPs as 'an organizational and financial arrangement'. This includes, for example, institutional marriages, such as the definition of Van Ham and Koppenjan (2001), or contractual arrangements tying institutions together and legally sharing risks and returns (Osborne, 2001; Grimsey and Lewis, 2004).[8]

Conceptually, there are five different families of possible partnerships (Hodge and Greve, 2007):

1. Institutional cooperation for joint production and risk sharing (such as the Netherlands Port Authority)
2. Long-term infrastructure contracts (LTICs), which emphasize tight specification of outputs in long-term legal contracts (as exemplified in UK Private Finance Initiative (PFI) projects)
3. Public policy networks (in which loose stakeholder relationships are emphasized)
4. Civil society and community development
5. Urban renewal and downtown economic development (and where, in

the USA, a portfolio of local economic development and urban re-growth measures is pursued).

These five PPP families[9] cover an array of governance types and are clearly more than just the PFI experience of the UK or the urban renewal practices of the USA. Indeed, they cover many potential institutional arrangements as well as numerous contract arrangements, including 'alliance' forms of contract.[10]

Defining LTIC-type PPPs
This handbook aims to provide a guide to a range of readers: expert practitioners; interested lay readers; academics across several fields; and students of government–business relationships. As well as providing guidance on the intellectual underpinnings of today's PPPs, their rationale(s) and their logistics, this project also aims to make progress in assessing the merits of PPPs. Such an evaluation is a large undertaking and, as with any public policy arena, it is also a sensitive one. If we were to mount an evaluation of our experience to date with LTIC-type PPPs as one strand of the above-mentioned PPP families, there would be many pitfalls to watch out for. A necessary foundation, though, would be questions of definition. What exactly are LTIC-type PPPs? Which perspectives might be most helpful in considering the worth of this phenomenon? Which institutional options seem to perform best? And what evaluation approaches might be most useful here?

The single family of LTIC-type PPPs is itself a large group. Campbell (2001, p. 1), for instance, suggested that an LTIC-type 'PPP project generally involves the design, construction, financing and maintenance (and in some cases operation) of public infrastructure or a public facility by the private sector under a long term contract'. But there are many different possible PPP definitions across different public–private mixes, and previous books on PPPs over the past decade have covered a multitude of these.[11] We will not repeat them all here.[12] It is sufficient to acknowledge that LTICs cover a wide range of possibilities. Conceptually, there is a continuum of options ranging from a public emphasis at one extreme to a private emphasis at the other.[13] These arrangements include, for example, the O&M (operations and maintenance) contract, BOOT (build, own, operate, transfer), BTO (build, transfer, operate), WAA (wrap-around addition), and DBFO (design, build, finance, operate), along with a host of other acronyms. In fact, there are many possible combinations of activities such as design, finance, operate, maintain, own, transfer, lease, develop and buy (Zarco-Jasso, 2005). LTIC-type PPPs clearly represent many contractual types depending on the degree

to which different activities are undertaken by the public or private sectors.[14]

It is important to understand that the contractual types being adopted under the PPP banner also depend on the policy and ideological persuasions of governments signing PPPs. For example, a major strength of PPPs appears to be that a wide range of infrastructure services can be specified in detail and bundled together as one big package for the winning consortium to deliver. This idea, which has evolved since the 1980s, has often enabled governments to 'crash' through policy inertia and policy disinterest, and allow policy arenas such as major new toll roads, school or hospital renewal and maintenance programmes, to get clearer approval as high political priorities. In other words, using bundled arrangements as a governance tool to attract policy approval has demonstrated real political merit. But under PFI-type policies such as those of the UK or copied elsewhere (such as Partnerships Victoria, in Australia), this bundling idea itself has been glued together with the assumption that private finance must somehow be the basis for such deals.[15] Missing from such practice has been the explicit recognition that PPPs may be as much a statement of government policy and a builder of symbolic relationships with the financial sector as they are a logistical or technical delivery mechanism for infrastructure projects.

There is certainly a huge amount of money at stake in today's PPPs. Blanc-Brude et al. (2007), for instance, report that for LTIC-type PPPs alone, the past 15 years in Europe has seen more than 1000 contracts at a capital value of almost €200 billion. IFSL Research (2008) also report more recent data showing that over the seven-year period 2001–07, PPPs have mainly been of macroeconomic and systemic importance in the UK (with 57.1 per cent of project expenditure), Spain (at 5.6 per cent), Italy (at 4.8 per cent) and Ireland (at 4.0 per cent), with a total of 694 projects throughout Europe involving deals of €73 821 million. Moreover, they are now also apparently spreading from traditional sectors such as transport, health and education into other fields including information technology, waste management and water.[16] In terms of professional experience and capability, the UK remains the intellectual leader.[17]

Multiple stakeholders and PPP cross-disciplinarity

The PPP discourse and evaluation space is filled with many different interest groups. Advocates include consultants, merchant bankers, legal firms and construction companies. Those involved directly in the financial transactions, not surprisingly, often speak highly of them. One such project leader explained to one of the authors of this chapter that because these new PPP arrangements enabled $1 billion to be spent on infrastructure in

the coming year compared to only $130 million in the previous 12-month period, the new arrangements were therefore some eight times better than the old! Governments, too, have also been among the most ardent advocates, through Ministers and their compliant Treasury and Finance Departments.[18] But PPPs have never been smooth waters to sail in, if we learn anything from history. High expectations about the formation of PPPs have often resulted in inadequate methods of interaction between public sector and private organizations (Koppenjan, 2005). Numerous faults can occur in these relationships, and critics have appeared across disciplines and across traditional ideological borders.

One implication is that a modern review of PPPs must be undertaken by those who clearly do not have conflicting interests – possibly taking a percentage of revenue from transactions as they pass through. Advocating governments face a conflict of interest as their own policy priorities and preferences are subject to assessment. Consulting businesses claim to provide balanced evaluations of PPP policy options through their professional reports, while simultaneously and openly discussing 'deal-flow' because of its importance to their core revenues. PricewaterhouseCoopers (2005), for example, see PPPs as sophisticated best practice and as 'delivering the PPP promise' . . . through 'connected thinking', while Ernst & Young (2007) view PPPs as having 'provided value to the Government and public sector'. But acknowledging conflicts of interest and governing them successfully is no small matter. Global consulting groups are now both influential and powerful. A few years ago, the global consulting sector employed some 463 000 employees across 123 countries, with revenues estimated at a total of $170 billion per annum.[19] These days, global consulting revenues are probably closer to around US$192 billion. And while governments use consultants as much as the other way around, the conflicts of interest between traditional business owners and those of governments have now become more blurred and more difficult to discern. As a consequence, such conflicts in policy arenas such as PPPs have also now become more difficult to avoid. In any event, powerful PPP lobby groups clearly exist.

What is also clear from the discussion thus far is that the PPP phenomenon is not limited to a particular discipline. In terms of the LTIC arena, for instance, legal contracts certainly form the basis of the agreements between parties. But both the manner in which government decisions to enter such contracts are made as well as the content of such contracts are clearly not simply legal matters. They are social and inherently political matters of public importance. Similarly, complex financing, costing and pricing matters are not limited to the interests of finance or accounting, but are also matters for public debate and scrutiny. Commercial arrangements

entered into for three or four decades will affect future generations and may limit their ability to make other decisions. These issues are not simply matters for consulting firms, construction engineering companies and corporate lawyers, but are inherently matters of governance and citizen expectations. The point here is that a wide range of disciplines is relevant to any examination of PPPs. It is little surprise, then, that this book is, as a consequence, multidisciplinary in nature.

All this is especially important as PPPs threaten to evolve in new directions. The global economy will get back on its feet and economic growth will remain an important policy priority for most world governments. But communities will struggle to rebuild trust in global markets. Recent experience has revealed the negative results of widespread systematic trading in complex financial deals with little real knowledge of the riskiness of these deals. Lucrative profits went to some cunning players and company executives. Trust was taken for granted, and losses were passed along the line to those less well informed. None the less, rebuilding global financial trust will no doubt occur in time, and the desire for trusted 'partnerships' between governments and business is likely to continue. Throughout history, governments in nearly every country have had a fundamental role in development of the nation state, including its physical, social and legal infrastructure.[20] Recently, most major governments have indicated a willingness to invest in new infrastructure in order to stimulate their economies. PPPs will inevitably continue to be promoted as having much potential to demonstrate government–business cooperation. However, the traditional role of government is also likely to be rediscovered over the coming years as market instabilities continue. Also, partnerships are likely to reappear in new guises and take new directions and forms, such as alliance contracts.

What will be constant, however, will be the need for careful examination of the PPP phenomenon and the common ground between public and private actors, whatever the exact government–business relationship. As Lindblom (1959) said, in any Western liberal economy, real power will continue to be held by the government and the business sector. So, in a sense, the desire for ongoing relationships between business and government is no real surprise. But citizens will also continue to remain sensibly sceptical of overblown policy promises from elected representatives. The global spread of privatization policies saw huge differences between the multiple lofty political promises of efficiency, lower prices and improved market choices, and the reality that there have been as many lessons in retrospect as there have been obvious success stories. And in any event, such success stories were usually delivered only when governments focused their efforts on regulating carefully and strongly to ensure that the new businesses did

not take undue advantage of citizens. Gains to citizens did not appear of their own volition through any inherent superior private sector performance (Hodge, 2000). Other fields too, remind us of similarly overblown promises. Genetically modified crops, according to former US president George Bush Jr and biotech companies, were going to 'end world hunger', and the information and communication revolution was going to put the world on the 'information superhighway' (Rayner, 2004). In reality, world hunger has continued under the weight of the international political economy, underpinned by personal indifference and selfishness. Likewise, the global 'digital divide' and the need to protect youngsters from a net full of pornography is now as much the topic of conversation as the promised gift of a superhighway. Policy promises involving public and private ideologies are often much more optimistic than the new reality.

Evaluating PPPs
A key task of this handbook will be to evaluate our PPP experience to date. But this is no easy task, as evaluation usually means many things to many people. For a start, evaluations can vary in strength, from personal impressions and 'back-of-the-envelope' assessments at one extreme, to more systematic and comprehensive studies using statistical principles and control methods at the other. They can also be undertaken for quite different reasons, such as the narrow perspective of improving PPP delivery processes and organizational learning, through to the broader perspective of assessing public policies themselves. Of course PPPs also have a wide range of objectives, ranging from the desire to remove infrastructure projects off government balance sheets to arguments around better value for money (VfM) and delivering superior on-time and on-budget performance. Several other objectives have also been proposed by various governments. A huge range of evaluation approaches is possible for any one particular objective. We shall return to this central issue in Chapter 5 of this handbook as we contemplate paths towards more evidence-based partnership policies. For the moment, however, setting out some primary dimensions that might underpin any evaluation of PPPs would seem sensible.

Policy alternatives can be evaluated using multi-goal analysis (Weimer and Vining, 2004). Weimer and Vining suggest four broad goals for government: allocative efficiency; equity (distribution); government budget impact; and politics. Focusing on the assessment of activities involving the public and private sectors, Hodge (2000) alternatively proposes evaluation using political, economic/financial and social goals.[21] Adopting these three broad dimensions, we could evaluate a PPP according to its impact of each goal for each of the three classic sectors: government, the business sector and the community.[22] This is illustrated in Table 1.1.

Table 1.1   Conceptual framework for evaluating PPPs

Goals	Stakeholders		
	A Government	B Business	C Citizens/ community
1. Political/ governance	+ / −	+ / −	+ / −
2. Economic/ financial	+ / −	+ / −	+ / −
3. Social	+ / −	+ / −	+ / −

This table shows, for example, that if a PPP were to be assessed against a government financial objective, such as the need to deliver an infrastructure project with no cost to its budget, then this assessment would occur in cell 2A. If we also wanted to consider the financial impact of this project (whether positive or negative) on stakeholders in the business sector and on consumers, we would need to examine cells 2B and 2C respectively as well. If we wanted a full multi-goal analysis, we would have to consider all cells.

It would be possible, of course, to make finer distinctions within each stakeholder group in order to study distributional implications in more detail. For example, government might be broken down into local or national, business might be broken down into PPP contractors or other businesses, and citizens could be subdivided into users or non-users.

Having said this, it is important to acknowledge that both PPP projects themselves as well as the PPP project delivery mechanism ought to be subject to evaluation. This handbook will focus primarily on reviewing PPPs as an infrastructure delivery mechanism, however, rather than assessing actual infrastructure projects themselves.

Structure of the book
In the context of these observations, this book seeks to provide an international perspective that makes a new contribution to our knowledge of PPPs. Whether we view them as an engineering tool, as a governance mechanism or as a public policy phenomenon, all cry out for clearer thinking and wiser evaluation of our experience to date.

Also, we should have an eye to the future in terms of crucial agenda items for this phenomenon. A renewed PPP research agenda might encapsulate a wide range of continuing sociopolitical as well as technical issues. Nine research domains seem apposite:

1. The merit/worth of LTIC PPPs
2. The circumstances when they may give highest VfM and innovation
3. The circumstances when they may act as a better governance tool
4. How we can in future better regulate PPPs in the public interest
5. The role and findings of auditors general to date
6. Why their promotion 'succeeds' in some jurisdictions but not in others
7. What is the nature and consequence of the global PPP industry?
8. What is the place of PPPs in the context of development?
9. What is the next chapter for PPPs and the implications of this?

By way of structure, this book proceeds by following four themes: underpinning intellectual PPP foundations; a range of lenses central to each of the disciplines; our international empirical experience to date; and future issues. The first theme, beginning with this introductory chapter, covers historical views of PPPs, in terms of both observations that might be made of partnerships through time and the more recent intellectual foundations of the movement. It also traverses the terrain of language and the multiple grammars of the phenomenon, as well as noting several challenges facing any serious evaluation of PPPs.

The second theme is the disciplines, looking specifically into traditional arenas including politics, economics, engineering, law and accounting. Also included, however, are the newer interest arenas of risk management and governance.

The third theme articulates international empirical experience and has a global reach. It begins with the UK, but also travels to the EU, North America, Asia Pacific and Scandinavia. To provide larger global overviews, we also add the experience of the World Bank and the United Nations.

Crucial issues for the future of the PPP phenomenon are covered by the fourth theme. Here, we analyse the global PPP industry and recent trends towards alliance contracts. Recognizing that the future of PPPs depends on evaluations made of their success or failure, three perspectives of PPP performance are also added, covering both developed and transition economies.

Finally a synthesis of lessons to date is made and some conclusions are articulated.

Conclusions

Today's PPP phenomenon represents many different public–private arrangements having long historical pedigrees and crossing several professional disciplines. Our debates over LTIC-type PPPs, though, have

thus far been closer to policy language-game-playing than evidence-based learning and synthesis. Evaluating the degree to which LTIC-type PPPs meet our expectations, however, is not an easy task, and demands a more sober and informed approach than taken to date. Multiple disciplines are involved in PPPs, each with their own emphasis on what is most important. There are also multiple stakeholders and many conflicts of interest buried within evaluation questions.

LTIC-type PPPs will continue to promise advantages to governments and those groups that are part of the PPP industry. And in the face of new market instabilities and our continuing search for economic growth in increasingly uncertain times, PPPs will continue to be put forward as an appropriate method for the delivery of public infrastructure projects and programmes. This handbook seeks not only to articulate the wide range of PPP types and approaches now possible, but also to assess the relative effectiveness of these options and clearly articulate the evidence on which assessments are based. It also seeks to identify new directions that our enquiries ought to be pursuing. The real opportunity here is to re-evaluate our own policy positions on PPPs, rearticulate shared knowledge and insights, and reassess common priorities on where we should turn next in our PPP research and practice. All these challenges offer an exciting international frontier in learning.

Notes

1. See for example Hodge (2006).
2. These colourful labels have been taken first from Grimsey and Lewis (2004), and second, from the film *Enron* (Jigsaw Productions, 2005). The second label does not imply illegal activity of businesses engaging in PPPs, of course, but does imply the need to think more carefully about the size of financial rewards, the existence and power of personal and corporate incentives, and the need to be vigilant regarding the price paid and the veracity of arrangements for risks to be 'managed' by others signing up to PPP contract deals. It also expresses strongly the need for far more intelligent regulatory scrutiny in place of blind trust in the re-engineered products sold within modern, and as we now know, imperfect, financial markets.
3. See Hodge (2006). Referring to the work of Parliamentary Committees in Australia, he notes that of the 76 recommendations to improve PPPs, two-thirds of these dealt directly with the three issues of private finance, complexity, and governance and accountability.
4. See Linder (1999).
5. To some scholars, the word 'cooperative' is misplaced here. Even the word 'partnership' should always be in quotation marks, as, to them, it is close to an oxymoron. Such commentators regard the term 'public–private partnership' as a clever marketing ploy by the private sector and government contracting organizations, both of which do very well in terms of strong profits and high salaries. In other words, PPP to these scholars should be more accurately defined as 'mutually beneficial' arrangements as distinct from 'cooperative'.
6. See McIntosh et al. (1997).
7. Previous work from Hodge and Greve (2007) referred, for instance, to the amusing situation in which the same PPP phenomenon was framed in two opposite ways for local

political gain. In the case of Victoria, Australia, the PFI-type PPPs are argued to have nothing to do with privatization and are vigorously separated from this policy. In the UK, however, the Treasury sees the two as inherently connected and speaks of PPPs as directly equivalent to privatization (HM Treasury, 2003).

8.   The degree to which PPP is fundamentally seen as being tied together on the basis of either being a joint institution or else through a formal legal contract continues to be a strong thread throughout PPP debates. Differing expectations exist in each of these cases in matters of control, funding, ownership and institutional relationship. Each also implies a different degree of joint-ness and separability.

9.   See also Weihe (2005) for her meta-view outlining five alternative PPP 'approaches', namely, local regeneration, policy, infrastructure, governance and development.

10. Most 'alliance' forms of contract include unanimous decision-making protocols, no recourse to the courts for dispute resolution and equal sharing of cost overruns or underruns (Davies, 2008).

11. See, for example, Allan (1989), Savas (2000), Berg et al. (2002), Grimsey and Lewis (2004) or OECD (2008) here.

12. In the EU, the Commission terms infrastructure PPPs 'institutionalized PPPs', but the term is still not legally defined in community law. Instead, the definition of a PPP continues to be interpreted in the light of community law on public procurement and concessions. For more information on PPPs in the EU, visit ec.europa.eu/internal_market/publicprocurement/ppp_en.htm.

13. OECD (2008, p. 20), for instance, also places PPPs somewhere in the middle of the continuum between purely public and purely private. The five points along this continuum in order of increasing private-ness were complete government production and delivery, traditional public procurement, PPPs, concessions and, lastly, privatization. Alternatively, Grimsey and Lewis (2004, p. 54) nominate some 21 alternative public–private business models in between either fully public provision or outright privatization, Savas (2000, p. 241) nominates ten models, and OECD (2008, p. 22) nominates 14 options.

14. Indeed, when thinking simply about the dimensions of PPP control, funding and ownership, some eight combinations of public–private mix are possible (Zarco-Jasso, 2005). These eight combinations are the result of two possible domains (public or private) for each of the three dimensions (control, funding and ownership) making a total of $2 \times 2 \times 2 = 8$.

15. Technically, this is purely a policy preference of government. Governments could, if they chose, publicly finance consortia projects through raising bonds, for example, or consider various hybrid financing options going back to the work of Heald (2003). The range of options available here, however, would need to be articulated by sympathetic observers, and away from conflicting interests.

16. IFSL (2008) lists the sector expenditure shares for UK PFI/PPPs (over the period 1987–2006) as being transport (28.4 per cent), health (23.2 per cent), education (15.5 per cent), accommodation (10.7 per cent), defence (10.1 per cent), telecommunications and information technology (4.5 per cent), waste management and water (4.2 per cent), local government (1.5 per cent) and other projects (1.9 per cent).

17. Interestingly, on the basis of expenditure as a proportion of GDP, PwC (2005, p. 37) suggests that Portugal spends more than double that of the UK. Another basis of ranking might be expenditure per head of population. In this case, Australia appears to lead the pack on the basis of OECD (2008) figures for PPP outlays, spending 6 per cent more than the UK and over double that of Portugal.

18. In some instances, after years of reforms introduced under the banner of 'new public management', such public servants are also on contracts, with an obvious incentive to deliver what the Minister wants in terms of his short-term policy preferences rather than advise what is in the public's long-term interest. Little wonder, perhaps, that those asking questions of PPPs have been characterized as 'critics' and as getting in the way of business.

19. See Hodge and Bowman (2006, p. 102). They presented the 2004/05 revenues of the 'Big Four' global consulting companies (Deloitte, Ernst & Young, KPMG and PwC as totalling US$71.1 billion). And assuming that the big four firms account for 45 per cent of the global market (*Consulting Times*, 2004), and that revenues have been increasing at say 4 per cent per year since then, the estimate for global consulting revenues for 2009/10 would be around US$192 billion.
20. Perhaps the outlier here was the USA, which facilitated desired development directions more through private sector incentives. This view, however, is also contestable, in that there are clearly disparities between the often-heard rhetoric of private sector entrepreneurship and small government, and the reality of a large US government that has historically provided strong subsidies to a range of military, industrial and developmental activities.
21. We could also add environmental goals to this list.
22. In effect, therefore, this framework also evaluates alternatives in terms of equity (i.e. the distribution of impacts).

References

Allan, J.R. (1989), *Public-Private Partnerships*, Institute for Public Policy, Working Paper Series, Yale University.

Berg, S., M. Pollitt and M. Tsuji (eds) (2002), *Private Initiatives in Infrastructure: Priorities, Incentives and Performance*, Cheltenham, UK and Northampton, MA, USA: Edward Elgar.

Blanc-Brude, F., H. Goldsmith and T. Valila (2007), *Public-Private Partnerships in Europe: An Update*, Economic and Financial Report 2007/03, European Investment Bank, p. 24.

Campbell, G. (2001), 'Public Private Partnerships – A Developing Market?', Melbourne, unpublished.

Consulting Times (2004), accessed at www.consulting times.com.

Davies, J. (2008), 'Alliance contracts and public sector governance', PhD thesis, Griffith University, August, unpublished.

Ernst & Young (2007), *The Road Ahead: Future of PPP in Australian Road Infrastructure*, Ernst & Young Australia.

Grimsey, D. and M. Lewis (2004), *Public–Private Partnerships: The Worldwide Revolution in Infrastructure Provision and Project Finance*, Cheltenham, UK and Northampton, MA, USA: Edward Elgar.

Heald, David (2003), 'Value for money tests and accounting treatment in PFI schemes', *Accounting, Auditing and Accountability Journal*, **16** (3), 342–71.

HM Treasury (2003), *PFI: Meeting the Investment Challenge*, London: The Stationery Office.

Hodge, G.A. (2000), *Privatisation: An International Review of Performance*, Boulder, CO: Perseus Books/Westview Press.

Hodge, G.A. (2006), 'Public-private partnerships and legitimacy', *University of New South Wales Law Journal*, Forum, **29** (3), 318–27.

Hodge, G.A. and D.M. Bowman (2006), 'The consultocracy: the business of reforming government', in Graeme Hodge (ed.), *Privatization and Market Development: Global Movements in Public Policy Ideas*, Cheltenham, UK and Northampton, MA, USA: Edward Elgar, pp. 97–126.

Hodge, G.A. and C. Greve (2007), 'Public-private partnerships: an international performance review', *Public Administration Review*, **67** (3), 545–58.

IFSL Research (2008), *PPPs in the UK & PPP in Europe 2008*, International Financial Services, London, 4 March, 'PPPs in partnership with City of London and UK Trade and Investment', www.ifsl.org.uk/research, accessed 13 January 2009.

Jigsaw Productions (2005), *Enron: The Smartest Guys in the Room*, public release feature film.

Koppenjan, J.F.M. (2005), 'The formation of public–private partnerships. Lessons from

nine transport infrastructure projects in the Netherlands', *Public Administration*, **83** (1), 135–57.

Lindblom, C.E. (1959), 'The science of muddling through', *Public Administration Review*, **19**, (Spring), 79–88.

Linder, S. (1999), 'Coming to terms with the public–private partnership: a grammar of multiple meanings', *The American Behavioural Scientist*, **43** (1), 35–51.

McIntosh, K., J. Shauness and R. Wettenhall (1997), *Contracting Out in Australia: An Indicative History*, Canberra: Centre for Research in Public Sector Management, University of Canberra.

OECD (2008), *Public-Private Partnerships: In Pursuit of Risk Sharing and Value for Money*, Paris: OECD.

Osborne, S. (ed.) (2001), *Public–Private Partnerships: Theory and Practice in International Perspective*, New York: Routledge.

Parker, D. (2004), 'The UK's privatisation experiment: the passage of time permits a sober assessment', CESifo Working Paper 1126, Cranfield University.

PricewaterhouseCoopers (2005), *Delivering the PPP Promise. A Review of PPP Issues and Activities*, available online at www.pwc.com/, viewed 26 November 2008.

Rayner, S. (2004), 'The novelty trap: why does institutional learning about new technologies seem so difficult?', *Industry and Higher Education*, **18** (6), 349–56.

Savas, E.S. (2000), *Privatization and Public–Private Partnerships*, New York: Chatham House Publishers and Seven Bridges Press.

Van Ham, H. and J. Koppenjan (2001), 'Building public–private partnerships: assessing and managing risks in port development', *Public Management Review*, **4** (1), 593–616.

Weihe, G. (2005), 'Public-Private Partnerships: Addressing a Nebulous Concept', Working Paper no. 16, Denmark: International Centre for Business and Politics, Copenhagen Business School.

Weimer, D. and A. Vining (2004), *Policy Analysis: Concepts and Practice*, 4th edn, Upper Saddle River, NJ: Prentice Hall.

Wettenhall, R. (2003), 'The rhetoric and reality of public-private partnerships', *Public Organisation Review: A Global Journal*, **3**, 77–107.

Wettenhall, R. (2005), 'The public–private interface: surveying the history', in Graeme Hodge and Carsten Greve (eds), *The Challenge of Public–Private Partnerships: Learning from International Experience*, Cheltenham, UK and Northampton, MA, USA: Edward Elgar.

Zarco-Jasso, H. (2005), 'Public–private partnerships: a multidimensional model for contracting', *International Journal of Public Policy*, **1** (1–2), 22–40.

2 Mixes and partnerships through time
Roger Wettenhall

Introduction: a rich history of public–private mixing

Aims of the chapter

A major purpose of this chapter is to point to the long history of public–private mixing in the world's governance arrangements. Within that context, the chapter explores the emergence of 'public–private partnership' ('PPP' or 'P3') as a term and a concept of great symbolic value in modern governance, arguing that the massive 'chatter' about it now being experienced leads to ambivalence and misleading language.[1] It suggests that two main agendas of discussion have developed, the one relating particularly to infrastructure-type projects and the other extending much more broadly to a wide range of mixing arrangements. Given that many treatments of the modern period focus primarily on the first, the chapter turns to consider a number of other arenas in which mixing has taken place over the centuries, and in many cases is still taking place. The three arenas encompass the intersectoral pooling effects of the global economy, developments in domestic and international security services, and movement relating to mixed public–private enterprises.

This chapter asserts that, while public–private mixing has existed since the beginnings of organized government, the private component of governance retreated as nation states became stronger in the 1700s and 1800s and centralized the performance of many public functions within their own establishments. But it has flourished again in the recent period, as the evolution of governance systems has required governments to develop new roles as they share significant power and influence with market institutions and civil society. In this context, it is important that we learn more about what has worked and what hasn't from our past experience with mixes of all kinds, and more good research into mixes and partnerships is needed in order to articulate the lessons from this experience.

Prelude: the 1980s back to the 1780s

At a Cities' Congress on Roads to Recovery hosted by Cleveland (Ohio) State University in 1984, many people spoke eulogistically of the great contribution said to be made to urban renewal in US cities by public and private sectors in collaboration, constituting a 'new era of public–private

partnerships' (Holland, 1984). More than a few critics complained, seemingly with good reason, that, while many decaying downtown areas had been thus rescued and beautified as administrative and cultural centres, nothing had been done to help the displaced urban poor. But there was general acceptance that the PPP represented a substantial and original new governance technique. Norman Krumholz, Director of Cleveland State University's Neighborhood Development Center, provided the coat-hanger for this chapter when he objected:

> None of this is new. Public–private partnerships are as old as the republic. Alexander Hamilton [recommended direct government] grants to business . . . Since Hamilton's day, government has provided business with subsidies on water, rail, and highway transportation; favorable tariff and trade policies; funds for research and development; tax abatements and low interest loans; and in times not-so-recently-gone-by, with the U.S. Marines to protect foreign investments. Today, giant corporations, like Lockheed, the Pennsylvania Railroad, and Chrysler, can be sure the public will bail them out if they fall on hard times. To say that public–private partnerships are a new idea in contemporary America is to overlook this rich history. (Krumholz, 1984, p. 182; see also Porter and Sweet, 1984, p. 216)

It has been interesting, in the context of the Great Financial Crisis of 2008–09, to consider to what extent such 'corporate welfare' (Bartlett and Steele, 1998) still operates. It certainly did in the General Motors case – but that is not the main purpose of this chapter. More significantly here, Krumholz does us the great service of indicating the ubiquity, versatility and longevity of such public–private mixing. My argument with him is simply that he was too USA-centred – why place the beginning with Hamilton's young US republic?

Donald Kettl suggested another defining moment in his early 1990s study of the myriad of contracts between US government bodies and private profit-oriented organizations:

> Every major policy initiative launched by the federal government since World War II – including medicare and medicaid, environmental cleanup and restoration, anti-poverty programs and job training, interstate highways and sewerage treatment plants – has been managed through public-private partnerships. (Kettl, 1993, p. 66)

Why just the USA, and why not before the 1780s?
When Farazmand (2001, p. 176) pointed out that the practices of contracting out, partnership building and marketization went back to 'the Persian World-State Achaemenid Empire', he was anticipating Krumholz and Kettl by around 2500 years. These practices were equally common in pharaonic Egypt, Imperial China and Rome, both imperial and republican, and they

carried over to the developing European states. In Geneva in 1628, a publicly owned 'chamber' was established to purchase, store and distribute corn, and it prospered for nearly two centuries through complex relations with individual suppliers, investors and merchants (Blanc, 1940).

My earlier survey of the history of PPPs (Wettenhall, 2005) identified a number of 'theatres' of economic and social activity in which such mixing could be observed over many centuries, though they were not watertight theatres and activity within one quite often connected with activity within another. States and their governments thus joined in various ways with private organizations and private individuals in systems of:

- privateer shipping;
- mercenary armies;
- trade, commerce and colonial expansion;
- treasury and public finance;
- collaboration in agriculture, health and education;
- infrastructure provision;
- organizing hallmark events; and
- public and mixed enterprises.

In public enterprise, as with the Geneva Corn Chamber, there was always mixing, as states bought and sold services and facilities through massive contracting, operated many services themselves and so interacted with countless millions of 'customers', and became involved in a myriad of commercial-style financial transactions. Sometimes the actual ownership of an enterprise was shared, producing a different kind of partnership arrangement, one that has great contemporary significance and will be further considered below.

In that earlier survey, I drew from work on the evolution of nation-state systems to suggest that the very clear distinction between public and private realms that had emerged in Western polities by the opening of the twentieth century was a mark of the maturing of their state-governance systems, and that such clarity has rarely been present in other times and in other circumstances. This was consistent with Charles Tilly's important observation that 'differentiation of the instruments of government from other sorts of organization and monopolization of the means of coercion' were vital ingredients in the formation of modern states in Western Europe. Tilly (1975) saw this process flowing after 1500, with control of a well-defined, continuous territory and being relatively centralized as other main ingredients of developing nationhood. What was gradually being displaced was a miscellany of ill-sorted traditional authorities, including feudal chiefs, with varying claims on the allegiance of parts of

the population. Private entrepreneurs discharging what would today be regarded as public functions were certainly among them (Tilly, 1975, pp. 24–7, 40; also Tilly, 1990).

In the earlier exercise I suggested that all the blurrings between public and private that were observable as the twentieth century passed into the twenty-first century indicated a retreat from the centralized and controlling state whose rise Tilly had been charting (Wettenhall, 2005, p. 23), and I believe that proposition is firmly supported by the additional evidence advanced in this chapter. The state must now work with market forces to an extent unthinkable in the earlier period.[2]

Mixing is central to modern governance thinking
Late twentieth- and early twenty-first-century thinking about 'governance' is related. Although the idea of governance has spawned many 'stories' (Jose, 2007), one highly influential position is that the governing/managing of states, economies and societies is now a process shared by three main sectors – the state, the market and civil society – all intimately associated though an intricate 'network' of connections (Rhodes, 1997; Goldsmith and Eggers, 2004). Some have proposed that there could even be governance without government, but the Great Financial Crisis of 2008–09 has shown that there would be a complete collapse without the existence of a strong state able to intervene at critical points. It is clear now that, for the foreseeable future, all three components of this governance equation will contribute in major ways to governing, and that there will be massive interconnectedness. The days when the forces of nationalization could seek to render to the state a monopoly of the means of production, distribution and exchange are long gone, as are the days when the forces of privatization could seek to deny to the state any but the most minimal functions.

For Salamon, who has developed the notion of 'third-party government' as a way of describing the 'new governance paradigm' that has resulted, the old 'public vs. private' has been replaced by 'public + private'. In the process, direct government 'tools' have been, if not supplanted, certainly heavily supplemented by a mass of indirect ones like social regulation, contracting, loan guarantees, grants, tax expenditures, fees and charges, vouchers and government-sponsored rather than government-owned enterprises (Salamon, 1989, 2002).

Students of the old government-owned enterprises noted that so-called privatizing action frequently resulted, not in clear-cut transfers from the public sector to the private, but rather to mixes of the sort to which Salamon was drawing attention. Privatizing governments retained influential 'golden' or 'kiwi' shares in some of the enterprises they were disposing, or sold part but not all of the shareholding in those enterprises. Often

they established strong regulatory regimes to monitor divested enterprises. Sometimes they let management contracts with private firms for enterprises they continued to own. And so on: the connections were many and diverse (Thynne, 1995; Ghuman and Wettenhall, 2001).

Organizational effects

Hybrids of many kinds
A major organizational consequence of all this is that there will be many hybrid bodies populating the ever-increasing fringe areas between the three governance sectors. Thus those concerned with public sector management observe large numbers of non-departmental but still public bodies with varying degrees of autonomy, sometimes called authorities, agencies or quangos, but sometimes also with representatives of businesses, NGOs or particular communities appointed to their governing boards. Those concerned mostly with NGOs observe numerous links between them and the state and market sectors. Sometimes, as already noted, the mixing is such that two or more sectors share actual ownership of the involved organizations.

And sometimes, of course, the mixing is of a different kind, involving varying distributions of planning/designing, financing, constructing, operating and monitoring responsibilities. There is a spectrum here. At one end is the simple division of functions long known as contracting out, where a public body decides not to do something itself but to pay another party to perform the function under a contract agreement. At the other is the more complex and now frequently encountered arrangement whereby the private involvement is more extensive and may run to financing a project for a public authority and operating it for a period of years, retaining earnings to recover capital and operating expenses and provide a return on investment. Ultimately the facility so created will return to the state after the project has matured.

Arrangements of this sort are widely considered to be PPPs (sometimes expressed as 'P3s'). As I have argued elsewhere (Wettenhall, 2007, 2008a), however, they often do not produce partnerships in the precise sense of that word. They are certainly 'public–private mixes', but the degree of collaboration may fall short of real partnership. This is why the matter of definition is so important.[3] Some of the other kinds of mixes alluded to briefly in the above paragraphs may provide better examples of partnership conditions in operation. In my view, it would be better to use 'mix' as the general descriptor for all these sorts of arrangements, and reserve 'partnership' for cases where there is real evidence that an actual partnership exists.

Defining what constitutes a 'real partnership' is not easy, and it is a problem that is sure to be addressed in other chapters in this book. As one sensible review put it:

> A minimal definition . . . would require the involvement of at least two agents or agencies with at least some common interests or interdependencies, and would also . . . require a relationship between them that involves a degree of trust, equality or reciprocity (in contrast to a simple sub/superordinate command or a straightforward market-style contract). (Powell and Glendinning, 2002, p. 3)

This will be the minimal position taken in this chapter. Clearly many of today's so-called PPPs do not qualify.

That we do not do use 'mix' as suggested above means that 'PPP' is used in a multiplicity of confusing and inconsistent ways. To say that there is a 'rich variety of PPPs' (English and Skillern, 2005, p. 17) puts a rosy gloss on what is really a pretty indefensible intellectual position. Both in practice and in reporting and analysis the field had become conceptually messy. Launching a 2006 symposium, the guest editors declared 'partnership' to be 'over-used and under-specified as a word and a policy response' (Laffin and Liddle, 2006). Leading Danish researcher Weihe (2006) described the PPP concept as 'nebulous', 'contested' and 'ill-defined'.

Efforts to classify, and origins of the PPP term
This sort of messiness leads to efforts to sort and classify. One such effort has sought to identify the various senses in which the term PPP is used (Linder, 1999); others have attempted to sort according to areas of application described as 'approaches' (Weihe, 2006, p. 4) or 'families' (Hodge, 2007, p. 3). Multiple categories have resulted. Yet other exercises have wrestled with the organizational and financial character of the so-called PPP. Thus, and importantly, in taking a broad compass Hodge and Greve (2005, p. 6) propose a division of the field into 'tight' and 'loose' arrangements based on the nature of the contract relationship.

Broadly summarized, in the 'tight' group the contracts are designed to connect participants on a horizontal sharing basis, whereas in the 'loose' group they will establish a vertical principal–agent relationship between a public purchaser and a private provider. In somewhat similar vein, others distinguish between organizational cooperation and contract (or concession) projects (Klijn and Teisman, 2005, p. 98), alliance-model and concession-model arrangements (van der Wel, 2004, p. 10; Koppenjan, 2005, pp. 137–8), institutionalized and purely contractual partnerships (CoEC, 2004, p. 9), and symmetrical and asymmetrical partnerships (Friend, 2006, pp. 264–5). Anticipating what is to come below, Flinders (2005) sorts the UK range into 'public interest companies' and the purely

contractual Private Finance Initiative (PFI) arrangements. For others, however, there is an Anglo-Saxon/British-versus-the-rest flavour in all this, with much stronger NPM (New Public Management) influence in the former and more emphasis on establishing trust between the partners on a network basis in the latter (English and Skillern, 2005; Hammerschmid and Meyer, 2006, p. 1).

There can be no question therefore that we are dealing with a complex field of governance experience, and it should not cause surprise that serious problems arise in understanding and reporting on it. To begin with, there is that fairly common tendency to deny history. Then, while many of us do acknowledge that there is some of it, in our reporting and analysis we do that in a couple of early paragraphs and then get taken up with the excitement and symbolism of the dominant 'new' applications – this to such an extent that previous applications mostly sink into obscurity. Any possibility of learning from them then disappears.

This chapter has noted that public–private mixing has been known from the world's earliest civilizations through to later middle-age Europe, and that it was also a significant instrument for urban redevelopment in the USA of the 1970s and 1980s. My sleuthing has revealed a substantial policy debate and a substantial literature in and around those US urban redevelopment schemes, with the term 'public–private partnership' seemingly first consciously developed in this context as a collective descriptor for this sort of activity. The publishing history of the relevant books and reports indicates that the practice, the scholarly interest and the terminology quickly spread to Europe. Now the advantages and disadvantages were widely canvassed. There were many claims to success, but also it was not long before complaints began to emerge that public value was losing out to private interest in the deals being fashioned.[4]

More or less separately, an international network on 'public and private sector partnerships' emerged in the early 1990s, with important innovatory work undertaken by Luiz Montanheiro at Sheffield-Hallam University in the UK. But its influence has waned, in part because it failed to take up seriously some of the conceptual and classificatory issues that now seem so important in this field.[5]

The infrastructure agenda

Private financing
The story is now taken up by other developments in the UK in the 1990s. In 1992 John Major's Conservative government introduced a scheme of private financing – known as the Private Finance Initiative or PFI – as a way of updating the country's social and economic infrastructure within

the context of strict public expenditure controls. The essential idea was that a private company or consortium would design, finance, build and operate a motorway, bridge, tunnel, school, hospital or prison subject to public specifications, recovering its costs and gaining its rewards over a period of time, after which the facility would revert to the state.[6] It is important to note that PFI was not initially conceived of as a partnership. At first Labour opposed it, seeing it as 'the thin edge of the wedge of privatization'. In 1994, however, Labour reversed its position, and its support for PFI was confirmed, to the comfort of a now enthusiastic private sector, when Blair won the 1997 general election (Ruane, 2002, pp. 200–202).

But Blair and his government wanted to put their own stamp on it. As *The Economist* put it (EIU, 2002, p. 2), they adopted a new label, 'the friendlier-sounding Public–Private Partnerships (PPP)', to play down the Conservative origins. But it was a reconceptualizing as well as a renaming, involving a new commitment to joint intersectoral action as a way of transforming the role of government. So, in what became 'an ideological project' (Ruane, 2002, p. 201; and see Hall et al., 2003, p. 2), PFI was transformed into PPP. With some carry-over from the older urban development usage, the PPP label had begun to appear in some official documents from 1996, and after the Blair conversion it was pushed aggressively (Broadbent and Laughlin, 1999, pp. 98, 101). The symbolism was immense; politicians, bureaucrats and commentators around the world took note, as did the big consulting firms and international grant- and loan-giving bodies. Soon many countries were adopting the PFI approach and calling the multitude of projects that followed in its wake PPPs. The UK Treasury could now boast:

> There is huge international interest in the UK's approach to developing partnerships between the public and the private sectors. It is an area of public policy where the UK leads the world. (HM Treasury, 2000, p. 9)

As I have remarked elsewhere (Wettenhall, 2008a, pp. 120–21), British imperialism was not dead. Although the empire was disappearing, Attlee's Britain had been seen as a world leader in mid-twentieth-century nationalization and Thatcher's Britain as a world leader in late twentieth-century privatization. Now Blair's Britain was seen – by itself and others – as a world leader in PPPs (Ghobadian et al., 2004, p. 2).

The consequence of Blair's semantic switch

The consequence of Blair's semantic switch is that the infrastructure field is now widely seen as the central area of PPP operation, with PFI-style schemes dominating discussion about PPPs. In much public discourse today, they are *the only* PPPs – notwithstanding that much serious analysis

shows that many of them do not function like partnerships at all. As noted, many contributions to the literature begin with recognition that the field is broad and diverse (as well as by no means new), but they advance quickly to commentary or analysis that focuses largely or even solely on the PFI-style schemes and basically neglects all the others. This is particularly true of the mass of writings that come from accounting, economics and law schools, fascinated by the contracting, accounting and risk issues involved.

It is as though there are two agendas, the broad one acknowledging that there are many types of mixes, some of which may be genuine part-nerships, and the narrow one focusing on PFI/infrastructure and, on any dispassionate view, leading away from the generally accepted sense of partnership. To a greater or lesser extent, we are all guilty, acknowl-edging the first but then losing sight of it in our fascination with the immediacy, conceptual compactness and excitement of the infrastructure field. We thus retreat from a concern with the questions the broader field invokes about the health and happiness of the myriad of relationships at the public–private interface, always existing and always challenging our capacity to understand.

When Carsten Greve (2006, pp. 68–9) speaks of the 'ambiguity of the concept' of PPP, he is covering much the same ground. For him, 'PPPs are still seen both as PFI-like financial arrangements and a broader organiza-tional mode of connecting people, resources and objectives from various actors'. But most of the 'players of the game', taking advantage of the 'policy window' created by Blair's conversion and forming an influential 'PPP epistemic community' (ibid., pp. 69–71), see the PFIs as the only PPPs and, by implication, the broader field gets lost.

But there are other infrastructure approaches!
In the context of a review of world experience with public–private mixes and partnerships, it needs to be added that the so-frequent matching of 'infrastructure' with PFI-style schemes that results can itself be highly misleading. For as long as the world has been concerned with infra-structure – roads, bridges, tunnels, ports, schools and all the rest – the public–private interface has been in evidence. Governments could fund and build themselves, fund and then contract out the building to private firms, or find other ways of inducing private involvement.

A nice reminder is furnished by the comparison drawn by travel-ling British statesman Sir Charles Dilke between then-dominant late nineteenth-century North American and Australian styles:

In the United States and Canada companies are brought into existence by enormous prospective gifts of land in return for the performance of certain

operations, and most of the various Pacific railroads were made rapidly on this plan. The companies were bribed to make them . . . The Australians have more logically, and there is reason to think somewhat more economically, decided to keep public works mainly in the hands of colonial Governments. (Dilke, 1890, pp. 195–6)

Another version of the public–private infrastructure mix is to be found in the so-called concession model, in common use in France since the nineteenth century. The essential feature is that public authorities retain ownership of a facility or service but grant concessions or leases under which private contractors carry the cost of operation and maintenance, collect the resulting revenues, and retain the surpluses as profit. Extended to many countries, this system has figured prominently in water supply systems and to a more limited extent in highway construction and maintenance and public transport services (Adam Smith Institute, 2002; Bovaird, 2004, pp. 231–3).

Since my own recent research indicates that the bulk of current discussion is now absorbed in the narrower infrastructure agenda, in what follows I focus mostly on the other agenda as a counterweight. I thus consider several broad areas of public–private mixing that are studied as parts of other areas of inquiry but not so far seriously as part of the PPP inquiry enterprise. My hope is that they may be brought into the mainstream of that enterprise and so provide a broader and more satisfactory perspective than that which exists at the present time.

The broader agenda

The argument restated
Taking the broader view demonstrates the huge scope of public–private mixing through the ages. And surveyed over several major arenas of such mixing, the relevant history connects closely with Tilly's thesis about modern nation-state formation in that it shows a retreat of such mixing as the instruments of government consolidated during the 1600s, 1700s and 1800s, to be followed by an avalanche of fresh mixing as the forces of globalization have indelibly changed the foundations of the nation-state system. It is too early to judge the governance impact of the world economic meltdown of 2008 and 2009, but it seems likely that there will be no weakening of the tripartite governance universe of state, market and civil society in which mixing flourishes. The state is not necessarily weakened, but it has to confront the reality that it no longer has the monopoly of governance power that it enjoyed for a century or more.

Arena 1: the global economy

The public–private interface is a reality in a great many areas of economic and social activity, both now and in the past, involving a mass of intersectoral mixing and partnering. A useful way to consider all the interactions comes from the notion of extending elementary ideas about organizing to networks of organizations contributing together, in one way or another, to the achievement of common purposes. So often some of the organizations involved in these networks will be public, and some private, and they may be associated through mechanisms of coordination or collaboration. Coordination is likely to produce principal–agent-type relationships; collaboration is more likely to lead to partnering arrangements. Thynne (2008, pp. 331–4) examines these mechanisms in the particular context of coping with climate change.[7]

We have long considered foreign relations to be a preserve of state action. In the globalizing period of the later twentieth and early twenty-first centuries, however, there have been two significant shifts making that premise increasingly untenable. First, individual states have frequently found themselves unable unilaterally to fix large policy problems that have emerged, so that international effort is required in the search for solutions. And that leads into the second shift: it now so often happens that even the collective effort of states is insufficient, and many private actors have 'taken on authoritative roles and functions in the international system'. A general analysis of this development instances 'private market institutions engaged in the setting of international standards', 'human rights and environmental non-governmental organizations', 'transnational religious movements', even 'mafias and mercenary armies' (Hall and Biersteker, 2002, p. 4).

It is easy to cite other instances. Private production organizations at all levels – individual firms, and national and often international industry associations – are heavily involved with governments in negotiating trade agreements. International public bodies such as the World Bank and the IMF join with donor national governments in contracting with vast numbers of private firms and individuals in advancing the world's development aid programmes. Big transnational private corporations invest in the developmental programmes of many states, buy out state enterprises and run others remaining in state ownership under management contracts with governments. Privately owned international credit-rating agencies are chased by governments for their goodwill accreditations. And state-generated regulators no longer have a monopoly of business regulation: thus, operating in the area of international standards, the private International Organization for Standardization imposes its ISO requirements on millions of transactions by public and private agencies alike within and across jurisdictions (Lipschutz and Fogel, 2002; Scott, 2003).

The versatility of the process of public–private mixing is indicated pretty clearly by such examples taken from the working of the global economy. But is this all comparatively new? There are connections here with the above-noted Tilly thesis (1975, p. 40) that nation states grew with 'differentiation of the instruments of government from other sorts of organization and monopolization of the means of coercion'. In Treasury organization, for example, effective state control of the public financial system came only with the mostly nineteenth-century introduction of annual parliamentary appropriations, consolidated revenue funds and a central independent but public audit system. As Naomi Caiden (1989, pp. 53–5) has described it, 'pre-budgetary financial administration' was much less state-centred: it drew heavily on the services of private bankers, tax collectors and so on.

At the international level, the earlier dependence on non-state actors was heavy, with the church playing a prominent role. Contracted tax collectors are recorded in the Bible. Around the time of the Wars of the Crusades, medieval orders like the Knights Templars and Knights Hospitallers were sponsored by various European kings and formalized by orders of the Catholic Church and the then Christian states of the Levant. They performed military duty in support of the Crusader enterprise, but were soon innovating in agricultural development and in the provision of financial services for monarchs and states throughout Europe. The Hospitallers (or the Order of St John) underwent the ultimate transformation to publicness by governing Malta as a sovereign state from 1530 to 1798 (Pirotta, 1996, pp. 24–39; Wettenhall, 2001).

So there was plenty of private effort in support of state regimes in the past. Public consolidation came with the formation of self-conscious nation states, and there was a noticeable reduction in private involvement for a couple of centuries. In the recent period of the globalizing economy, however, the wheel has been turning. The nation states are being forced to develop new roles in the context of globalizing pressures and the restructuring of governance systems to accommodate the market and civil society as sharers of effective political and economic power. In the process there has been resurgent private activity. For the public–private interface, public–private mixing is again the order of the day – it has demonstrated not only ubiquity and versatility but also, despite a period of some slackening, very clear longevity.

There is significant overlap with the security industry, which provides perhaps the most dramatic illustration of developments in the public–private interface over the last couple of centuries.

Name Index

Printed and bound by CPI Group (UK) Ltd, Croydon, CR0 4YY

16/04/2025

1465882|-0003